Russian Baptists and
Spiritual Revolution,
1905–1929

Indiana-Michigan Series in Russian and East European Studies

Alexander Rabinowitch

and

William G. Rosenberg,

general editors

Russian Baptists and Spiritual Revolution, 1905–1929

Heather J. Coleman

INDIANA UNIVERSITY PRESS

BLOOMINGTON AND INDIANAPOLIS

This book is a publication of

Indiana University Press
601 North Morton Street
Bloomington, IN 47404-3797 USA

http://iupress.indiana.edu

Telephone orders	800-842-6796
Fax orders	812-855-7931
Orders by e-mail	iuporder@indiana.edu

The paper used in this publication meets the minimum requirements
of American National Standard for Information Sciences—Permanence
of Paper for Printed Library Materials, ANSI Z39.48-1984.

Manufactured in the United States of America

Library of Congress Cataloging-in-Publication Data

Coleman, Heather J., date-
    Russian Baptists and spiritual revolution, 1905-1929 / Heather J.
Coleman.
        p. cm.—(Indiana-Michigan series in Russian and East European
studies.)
Includes bibliographical references and index.
ISBN 0-253-34572-3 (hardcover : alk. paper)
    1. Baptists—Russia—History—20th century.   2. Russia—Church
history—20th century.   3. Baptists—Soviet Union—History.
4. Soviet Union—Church history.   I. Title.   II. Series.
BX6310.R8C65   2005
286'.0947'09041—dc22

                                                2004021140

1 2 3 4 5   10 09 08 07 06 05

To my parents,
John and Margaret Coleman

CONTENTS

ACKNOWLEDGMENTS

It is a great pleasure at last to recognize the many people who have played a part in the completion of this project.

I am particularly grateful to Diane Koenker, for her sound advice and exacting standards, but also her warm friendship and sense of humor. Mark Steinberg has also been a great source of close readings, helpful suggestions, and infectious enthusiasm. Through his wonderful courses in Russian imperial history and many discussions, Andrew Verner played an important role in making me the historian I am today. As members of my thesis committee, Keith Hitchins and Paul Valliere provided stimulating criticisms and suggestions. I am happy to thank the professors at Queen's who first interested me in Russia and in history for their continuing friendship: Christine Johanson, Bob Malcolmson, Anna Matzov, Doris Macknight, and the late George Rawlyk.

I thank the staffs of the many archives, libraries, and institutes where I have worked. In Russia, these included the State Museum of the History of Religion, the Russian State Historical Archive, the Central State Archive of the City of St. Petersburg, the Russian Centre for the Preservation and Study of Documents of Modern History, the State Archive of the Russian Federation, the Russian State Archive of the Economy, the Russian State Archive of Photographic Documents, and the Manuscript Division of the Russian State Library. Special thanks to Irina Viktorovna Tarasova and Irina Poltavskaia for their advice. I thank S. I. Potolov and his research group at the Institute of Russian History of the Russian Academy of Sciences in St. Petersburg for providing an academic home in Russia. V. Iu. Cherniaev in particular was a great source of advice and a good friend. In the United States, I worked at the Southern Baptist Historical Library and Archives in Nashville and the Billy Graham Center at Wheaton College. It was a great pleasure to work with the marvelous collections of the Slavic Library at the University of Illinois and with its excellent staff, especially Bob Burger, Helen Sullivan, Terri Tickle, Julia Gauchman, and Angela Cannon. Kevin Murphy and Sascha Goluboff found and delivered some great material that I had missed at the State Archive of the Russian Federation.

For many wonderful discussions, the reading of countless drafts, and constant encouragement as I wrote the dissertation from which this book emerged, I am especially grateful to Tom Trice. Thanks also to my fellow sektant Nick Breyfogle, and to Peter Brock, for his interest in a young scholar. As I began the process of turning a dissertation into a book, Paul Werth, Jeff Sahadeo, Diane Koenker, and John Coleman offered helpful and critical readings. I thank my two "anonymous" readers with Indiana University Press, Christine Worobec and Nadieszda Kizenko, for their perceptive comments. I have done my best to follow their advice. All remaining flaws are my own. For their help in identifying and preparing illustrations for the book, I am grateful to Sharyl Corrado and Christine Varga-Harris. Thanks also to Dave Brown, at the Image Centre at the University of Calgary, for his help. I thank Janet Rabinowitch and her staff at Indiana University Press, especially Jane Lyle and Rebecca Tolen, for shepherding me through the publishing process, and my copy editor, Rita Bernhard, for her careful advice.

Many people have provided friendship and encouragement. During my time in Champaign-Urbana (and since), I enjoyed a wonderful circle of friends, including Petra Alince and Jeff Sahadeo, Tom Trice, Sascha Goluboff, Mary Stuart, Elise Moentmann, Joseph Alfred, Chris Cosner, Peter Fletcher, Jane Hedges, Judy Krajnak, Kathy Mapes, Mickey Moran, Andrew Nolan, Glenn Penny, Laura Phillips, Dan Peris, Paula Rieder, Steve Shoemaker, Randi Storch, Caroline Waldron, Julia Walsh, and Sally West. In Russia, Irina Kuptsova, Valerii Klokov and Galina Khartulari, the late Nina Konstantinovna and Nikolai Aleksandrovich Mizonovy, Oksana and Vadim Aristovy, Tania Rogovskaia (now Scratchley), Iuliia Lintsbakh, Maiia Varshavskaia, and Oleg Moseev all welcomed me. Svetlana Inikova rescued me from a bad case of early-dissertation anxiety and has remained a valued friend and colleague. I am deeply grateful to Lena and Sasha Kalmykovy, for their help, moral support, and for hosting me during a research trip to St. Petersburg in November–December 2001. In Calgary, I am grateful to my many friends at the University of Calgary, especially Jewel Spangler, Doug Peers, Betsy Jameson, Maggie Osler, Martin Staum, Holger Herwig, Tim Travers, Sarah Carter, Susan Graham, Pascale Sicotte, Catalina Vizcarra and Rich Sicotte, Bart Beaty and Rebecca Sullivan, Hendrik Kraay and Judith Clark, David Winter, Malek Khouri, Annette Timm and Scott Anderson, Ken MacMillan and Luna Ng, Nick Žekulin, Bohdan Harasymiw, and my two department chairs—and friends—in History, John Ferris and David Marshall. Others who made life in Calgary so pleasant include Julia Carter, Jill Carfra, Meredith McKague, Marla Orenstein, Daniel Lenfest-Jameson, Kirill Kalmykov, Chris and Rudi Kincel, Steve and Nancy Hallford, Olga Tanailova and Roman and Nikita Vakulin, and Tania, Roma, and Katia Murashko. Whether in Calgary or L'viv, I thank my Ukrainian "mama," Lusiia Yeremeyeva. As I move to the University of Alberta, in Edmonton, I thank colleagues there who have already contributed so much to my professional development: David Marples, Serhii Plokhy, Oleh Ilnytzkyj, Natalia Pylypiuk, and John-Paul Himka.

I am deeply grateful to my parents, John and Margaret Coleman, and to my sister Jennie and my brother Rob, for their unending love, support, encouragement, enthusiasm, sympathy, and for kidding me out of it when I couldn't see the forest for the trees. My aunt, Barbara Scobie, provided a home away from home when I was a graduate student. My cousins, Chuck Coleman and the late Mary Garson, were a great source of encouragement and fun. Thanks especially to Chuck for many helpful suggestions on how to spice up a manuscript! My husband François Bégin "joined" this project as I was wrapping it up, but he has made all the difference.

Many divisions of the University of Illinois provided financial support, including the Department of History, the Russian and East European Center, and the Graduate College. The Social Sciences and Humanities Research Council of Canada awarded me a doctoral fellowship that made possible an extended research trip to Russia in 1995–96. At the University of Calgary, the Faculty of Social Sciences and the University Research Grants Committee provided funding for two additional visits to Russia as I was revising the manuscript.

Finally, I thank the *Russian Review* for permission to reprint portions of an earlier version of chapter 3, which appeared as "Becoming a Russian Baptist: Conversion Narratives and Social Experience," *Russian Review* 61, no. 1 (January 2002): 94–112.

Russian Baptists and
Spiritual Revolution,
1905–1929

Introduction

Spiritual Revolutions and Soul Wars

In the late 1980s and early 1990s, a religious revival accompanied the collapse of the Soviet Union. As the old socialist ideals lost their luster, Soviet citizens, young and old, flocked to churches, synagogues, and mosques in search of new ways to understand their individual journeys on this earth, but also looking for alternative models of community and identity to replace Soviet ones. Meanwhile, foreign missionaries of every stripe flooded into the country, some seeking to assist coreligionists, others to launch their particular teaching on the newly open and spiritually hungry Russian religious market. Millions of people lined up to be baptized into the traditional church of the Russian people, the Orthodox Church, but an important minority found their place in evangelical Protestant denominations, among the Roman Catholics or within the myriad small groups that popped up in these years. For some members of the public, the variety of public religious activity reflected a beneficial new freedom. Others felt uncomfortable with religious competition and, often, with intense proselytization that seemed brash and disrespectful toward Russian national traditions. Newspapers reported huge numbers of adherents to various new religious movements or, as they were often termed, "totalitarian sects." Street kiosks flogged brochures such as "The Baptists as the Most Harmful Sect." And Orthodox leaders sought government protection against Protestant and Roman Catholic missionaries who

1

were allegedly wrongfully invading the "canonical territory of the Russian Orthodox Church."[1] Very quickly, then, this sudden religious pluralism, and especially the fact of numerous conversions to what were perceived as Western faiths, became a matter of public debate. What was the relationship between Orthodoxy and Russianness? Should the religious marketplace be wide open or did Orthodoxy constitute the only legitimate spiritual choice for citizens living in this traditionally Orthodox region? Were foreign religious teachings bringing with them values inimical to Russian society? What role, if any, should the state play in religious life? And, more generally, to what extent should the state regulate the public sphere?

Russians have asked these very questions before. Just as they did in the 1990s, Russians in the late nineteenth and early twentieth centuries lived in a time of wrenching change, when the meaning of Russianness, the correct relationship between the Russian state and its society, and the suitability of Western models of development for their country all came up for debate. Religious life felt the influence of the social, political, and intellectual turmoil unleashed by the emancipation of the serfs in 1861. In the sixty years thereafter the experiences of rapid industrialization, social change, and political revolution raised questions about religion and its place in private lives, public discourses, and state structures. This period saw the relationship between priest and parishioner shaken up by social change and by the publication and wide distribution of the Bible in Russian, the rise of popular dissident religious movements, and a growing fascination among intellectuals with the nature of the "peasant soul." For some, this investigation was driven by the conviction that only a spiritual revolution could resolve the political and cultural crises of their time and bring about a liberated Russia. Others advocated a return to the church as the protector of traditional moral ideals. This religious ferment sparked lively discussion about freedom of conscience, about the relationship between Orthodoxy and Russianness, and about the political implications of individuals' religious choices.[2] These debates only intensified after 1905, when Emperor Nicholas II signed an edict on religious toleration, which ended the earlier prohibition on Orthodox converting to other Christian faiths and permitted formerly persecuted groups to hold prayer meetings legally. From that year until 1929, when the Soviet government abolished the right to preach religious ideas and, for all intents and purposes, prohibited religious associational life, dissident religious groups emerged as highly visible and controversial players on the national cultural and political scene.

This study explores this time of profound religious searching, possibility, and change through the prism of the Baptists, the fastest growing of these non-Orthodox Christian movements among Russians. The Baptists appeared in the Russian Empire in the late 1850s, first within the German-speaking communities scattered across the western and southern peripheries of the empire. By the late 1860s some of their Russian and Ukrainian neighbors began to seek baptism into the new faith. Through word of mouth, itinerant evangelists, migrant laborers' travel between city and countryside, and the sponsorship of a few well-to-do believers, a movement developed by the early twentieth century, reaching from tiny villages to the big cities. Most of the converts were peasants, who crowded into one another's earthen-floored cottages to worship. Workers, artisans, and petty traders, many of them recent arrivals in the city, made up a substantial and growing component of the movement. They, too, met in their basement apartments or in warehouses to pray. At these simple services the believers read Scripture, sang hymns, and preached to one another. Male or female, with some education or none, they spoke of their spiritual experience and of the revelations they had received from the Bible. After their meetings became legal in 1905, separate prayer houses did not appear immediately but greater organization did. During the first decades of the twentieth century the Baptists developed a vibrant associational life, with programs for children, youth, and women, a lively press, and national organizations linking these scattered communities into a broader denominational family.

Contemporary observers from all across the political spectrum regarded the Baptists' presence and activities as emblematic of the penetration of Western ideas beyond the educated elite, the challenge of the emergence of a culture outside the boundaries of the society promoted by the state and its church, and the increasingly articulate demand of lower-class people for a voice and a role in shaping that culture. But it is more than the interest of commentators in state, church, and educated society that makes the Baptists a significant topic for the study of changing ideas of the individual and community in Russian society as a whole. The Baptists were at once insiders and outsiders in Russian society, for they were Russians who had chosen what was perceived as a non-Russian path. Yet their strong conversionist drive ensured that they would remain engaged with the society around them.[3] As a movement, they regarded themselves as modern, and they claimed to have answers to the challenges of modern life. In their drive to communicate this message, they ran up against state and church institutions and attracted public attention, thereby leaving a thick trail of archival documents and press commentary. And the Baptists' own beliefs also make them a rich subject for study: because of the value the Baptist faith places on individual spiritual experience and witness, the Russian Baptists have left us many records of their personal religious lives. Through them we glimpse ordinary people trying to make sense, by religious means, of a time of political, social, economic, national, and religious upheaval. And so, because of their relationship to wider Russian society, the way in which they were perceived, and the nature of their own beliefs, the Baptists serve as an especially fruitful case study for exploring fundamental issues in modern Russian history, including the emergence of new social and personal identities, the creation of a public sphere and civic culture, debates over the notion and nature of citizenship,

and the way in which religious ideas and ideas about religion were implicated in the modernization process.

The Baptists' experiences provide a window into the formation and con-
testation of new social identities in the revolutionary era. This is related to
the broader process of reordering the relationship between individual and
community in early-twentieth-century Russia. Like other Russians of this
time, Baptists lived in a society where the circumstances of one's birth largely
determined one's official social identity. The state, and to a large extent most
of its subjects, shared the view that membership in the village community,
in the Orthodox communion, and in the various estate [*soslovie*] categories
by which the imperial state organized its population was set at birth. But it
was also a society where such forces as education, industrialization, modern
communications, and labor migration were causing "social relationships, values, and structures [to be] battered and reconstructed."[4] By analyzing Baptists' daily encounters with their wider community and with state institutions,
we glimpse the negotiation of national, class, religious, and political identities in this period. After all, when communities respond to the presence of
dissidents in their midst, they reveal their own values, their legal perceptions,
and their ideas about identity and community boundaries.[5] These encounters generated public discourse about legitimate beliefs and behavior in imperial and Soviet society, discourse that, in turn, shaped the experiences of
the evangelicals. Most studies of identity formation in Russia have focused
on how, through social and work relationships, many Russians came to understand themselves in terms of class categories.[6] But this work has also revealed how contingent people's identities can be, for different aspects of
people's identity are dominant at different times. Certainly changing social
identities played a part in the evangelical movement, where (mostly) lower-
class Russians conceived a community in which they could express themselves
as individuals and find respect and opportunities for self-development and
leadership. But the Baptists drew fundamentally different conclusions from
similar circumstances. Although scholars are very familiar with the revolutionary narrative of self-transformation, an examination of Baptists' personal
narratives reveals how religious conversion offered itself as another means
for navigating the same problems of social inequality, of order and disorder,
of modernization and Westernization, and of national and social identity in
this rapidly changing society. I examine how these new religious identities
emerged from individuals' personal experiences and were then articulated
by the ritual re-telling of conversion stories and by forming organizations
that reflected and promoted their members' new sense of self.

Russian Baptists' spiritual choices forced them, whether they liked it or
not, onto the front line of experimentation with the possibility for cultural
and political pluralism in Russia. In the last fifteen years historians of late
imperial Russia have drawn attention to the emergence of a public sphere
populated by autonomous social, professional, cultural, and other voluntary

4

associations through which people expressed "intermediate identities between the family and the state."[7] Such civic activism has generally been regarded as a crucial building block for civil society, in which ordered, non-clandestine, collective activity generates public opinion, defends public interests from state interference, and constitutes the basis for democratic politics.[8] These historians have focused on how new associations based on class identities played a crucial role in shaping an emerging civic culture.[9] But the case of the Baptists, a group that defined itself in cultural rather than class terms, offers a new way of approaching the problem of the emergence of a public sphere and the prospects for a civil society in late imperial and early Soviet Russia. After all, other affiliations, be they religious, ethnic, or gender, could also play a role in organizing public identities and transforming attitudes about power in a society.[10] Both before and after the revolution a wide range of observers of varying political persuasions regarded as modern the Baptist church model of a voluntary association of adult believers who chose their own leaders, gave voice to all members, and organized an array of social and educational programs among themselves. Governments both before and after the 1917 Revolution labeled the Baptists "dangerous" precisely because of their organizational energies and active associational life. They thus became a catalyst for discussion about the potential for pluralism in Russian and Soviet culture and society. And they have remained so, at least for some historians of the Soviet period who have pointed to their vibrant organizations as evidence of the relative pluralism of social life in the 1920s.[11] More important, the Baptists' religious needs for freedom of conscience, to be able to meet and organize without restrictions, and for an unregulated religious marketplace in which to promote their ideas forced them to challenge official institutions and assumptions about society. Baptists tried constantly to promote these values in their encounters with governments and with their fellow citizens. And, although the imperial and Soviet states continued to attempt to curb their missionary zeal and active associational life, they simply behaved as though these freedoms were theirs, thereby expanding the boundaries of public life.

As they did so, the Baptists promoted a vision of a Russia where one could be at once Russian and non-Orthodox and, later, both Baptist and socialist. Indeed, their experiences highlight the continuing problem, across the revolutionary divide of 1917, of the nature of citizenship and the criteria for inclusion in the Russian body politic. Whether it was the Russifying strategy of the late imperial state or the proletarianizing one of its Soviet successor, Russian states tried to mold a particular citizenry rather than a universal one.[12] At the same time they assumed that estate, religious, or class origins were fundamentally immutable. But, as Gauri Viswanathan points out, "by undoing the concept of fixed, unalterable identities, conversion unsettles the boundaries by which selfhood, citizenship, nationhood, and community are defined, exposing these as permeable borders."[13] As a result of personal religious choices, Baptists ran up against these boundaries and challenged the notion that there was only one way to be a good subject of imperial Russia or a citizen of Soviet Russia. And it was not just state projects that they unsettled. Steve Smith has suggested that "the intense class struggles of 1917 [were], in part, struggles to define the meaning of the nation." In other words, they were about whom the state would represent, whose values and interests counted.[14] Although this process was given freest rein during that revolutionary year, the question of the criteria for legitimate membership in village, professional, political, and national communities persisted throughout the early twentieth century.

Finally, a study of the Baptists demonstrates the importance of religion and of debates over spiritual values in modernizing Russian society. If the battles about class were, in part, struggles to define the nation, they were also struggles over the moral direction of that nation. Across the revolutionary period, the solution to Russia's problems was widely understood through the language of salvation. And a multiplicity of groups competed for converts to their path to salvation. Baptists explicitly contrasted their vision of spiritual revolution to the morality of class war proffered by the revolutionary parties of their day.[15] In so doing, they joined thousands of other Russians who found their moral communities among religious groups, some within Orthodoxy, others on its edges or in the many growing sectarian movements of the time.[16]

Popular religious life in modern Russia was until lately a little-studied topic. Traditionally studies of religion have dwelt on the history of the Orthodox Church as an institution and the problem of the relationship between the church and the state.[17] However, the recent coincidence of a broader historiographical turn toward the study of issues of identity, culture, and language in European history, and vastly improved archival access to religious materials, has spurred a surge of research into religion as it was practiced and into Orthodoxy's symbolic and social status in nineteenth- and early-twentieth-century Russia.[18] The approach taken here draws on recent work on the history of popular religion and culture in Europe and contributes to the ongoing reconsideration of the relationship between religious belief and modernity. In the past, scholars of popular religious movements in Europe in the nineteenth and twentieth centuries tended to regard religion as a force of social control or a consolation in the face of oppression. Newer studies no longer automatically treat religious movements as antimodern protests, and seek, rather, to explain the persistence and evolution of religious devotion in the modern age. They focus on exploring how religious worldviews both shaped and were influenced by social and economic change and how popular religion served as an instrument of cultural power.[19] Looked at in this way, the Baptists' experiences provide new insights into questions about the relationship between church and state by examining the fundamental link between religious affiliation and the way the imperial state viewed its subjects, by illuminating the response of the Orthodox Church to religious dissidence and its search for a renewed association with both state and society, and by providing comparisons with the better-known relationship between Orthodoxy and the Soviet state. But this approach also reveals a culture of religious searching, where religious ideas, new and old, were being tested, adopted, and discarded in the face of new personal and national conditions. In Russia, as elsewhere in Europe, the process of secularization was experienced as one of intense religious competition, as religion became ever more clearly a personal choice rather than a birthright.[20]

Certainly the Baptists, a denomination centered in the United States and Britain, entered this competition with enthusiasm. The founding of the Baptist World Alliance (BWA) in 1905 launched a period of international organization and centralization aimed at global expansion. From the start the Alliance had great ambitions for the evangelization of Europe, and Russia in particular. Indeed, at the BWA's second congress in Philadelphia in 1911 the Russian delegation was accorded unique attention. The president of the British Baptist Union, Rev. J. H. Shakespeare, introduced each Russian representative individually, declaring that, "when Russia becomes the most Baptist country of the world, outside America, it will mark a turning point in the history of Europe."[21] Nevertheless, there has been little research on this European drive in the first half of the twentieth century. The Baptists' expansion on the European continent coincided with and contributed to the challenging of the position of state churches, the questioning of the role of religion in state and private lives, and the tension over the relationship between religion and identity that characterized the modernizing process. The Russian Baptists' story illuminates key themes in Baptist and broader evangelical historiography, including the diffusion of Anglo-American evangelicalism to the rest of the world, the cultural tensions associated with this process, and the significant role Baptists have played throughout their history in pushing for religious liberty.[22]

There is virtually no published scholarly work on the Russian Baptists in English.[23] Past studies fall into two categories. First, in the 1960s and 1970s Soviet scholars, led by A. I. Klibanov, gathered abundant data regarding the socioeconomic context in which the movement arose and the activities of evangelicals. Much of this work assumed that religion was merely politics in disguise, and suffered from the ideological imperative to treat evangelicalism as a bourgeois movement and to uncover class struggle within its ranks.[24] The second group includes three dissertations written in the United States and Canada, also in the 1960s and 1970s. These dissertations assembled valuable information, based primarily on published materials available in the West, to examine, respectively, the relationship between Russian evangelicals and the state, the causes of the rise of the movement, and the way in which, in the early Soviet period, evangelicals took refuge from a traumatic time in an enthusiastic religious form.[25] Nevertheless, these works are very much confessional histories, which tend to compartmentalize the Baptists rather than exploring them in relation to their milieu—and to the broader questions of Russian political, cultural, and social history. The same could be said for several thoroughly researched works produced by Russian and Ukrainian evangelicals since the collapse of communism.[26]

This study makes use of a wide variety of sources, including previously inaccessible archival materials of the imperial and Soviet governments and of the Baptists themselves, and an array of printed sources. Of particular importance is the archive of the State Museum of the History of Religion in St. Petersburg, which preserves the files of the Union of Russian Baptists for the years of this study, the papers of several major Baptist leaders, and the personal collections of ethnographers and activists interested in religious sectarianism in Russia.[27] The Russian State Historical Archive (RGIA) holds the records of the Department of Spiritual Affairs of the imperial government's Ministry of Internal Affairs and of the Holy Synod of the Orthodox Church. Surveyed at the State Archive of the Russian Federation (GARF) were prerevolutionary secret police files, records of Soviet-era government institutions that supervised religious life, and the papers of the League of the Godless. Finally, the former Central Party Archive, the Russian State Archive of Social-Political History (RGASPI), holds records of the secret Antireligious Commission of the Central Committee, the Agitation and Propaganda Department, and the personal papers of Emelian Iaroslavskii, the head of the League of the Godless. In addition to these archival materials I draw on printed sources ranging from the evangelicals' own journals and books to those of the Orthodox missionaries and Soviet antireligious activists who sought to combat them, the works of intellectuals who defended them, and the newspapers where the significance of the Baptist movement was debated. By combining "personal" and internal records with the archives of government and party institutions, this study explores the dynamic between the religious experience of its subjects and the wider political and cultural implications of this experience.

Finally, a few words on terminology. During the period of this study, between 1905 and 1929, the Russian Baptists were divided into two streams, the Baptists and the Evangelical Christians. Two other forms of Western evangelical Protestant Christianity also made strides in these years, the Pentecostals and the Seventh-Day Adventists, and Baptist and Evangelical Christian leaders exerted considerable energies to combat their inroads. However, it was the Baptists and Evangelical Christians who, together, were the fastest growing non-Orthodox denominations and the object of particular governmental and public attention. Both belonged to the Baptist World Alliance, and they shared the Baptist emphases on the Bible as the only source of doctrine, on the autonomous local congregation as the fundamental organizational unit, and on witness of individual religious experience through believers' baptism and evangelism. Because of the mutually acknowledged kinship of these groups, I treat them as two branches of a larger Russian Baptist movement.

8

As a shorthand in describing the joint activity of believers, or where specific affiliation to one or the other branch of the movement is unclear, I use the term "evangelical." "Evangelical" here conveys its Anglo-American sense of "movements which not only adhere to traditional Protestant principles but in addition emphasize personal religious conversion, a disciplined Christian life, evangelism, and revivalism," rather than the continental European use of the term to designate mainline Protestant denominations such as the Lutheran and Reformed churches.[28] Where the term applies specifically to the Evangelical Christian branch of the movement, it is capitalized.

Lastly I should note that, although there existed sizable German- and Latvian-speaking Baptist communities in Russia and the Soviet Union, this is the story of Russian, Ukrainian, and Belarusian Baptists—in other words, of those who were considered "Russian" by the imperial government. The years of my study coincide with the flowering of Ukrainian national consciousness. In the 1920s, both because the Baptists began to collect ethnic statistics of representatives to their national conferences and because a Ukrainian Baptist Union emerged, the fact that a disproportionate number of the "Russian" Baptists were actually Ukrainians became clearer. The first Ukrainian-language hymn book was published in 1925, the magazine *Baptist Ukrainy* [Baptist of Ukraine] published a large section of Ukrainian-language articles, and the All-Ukrainian Congress of 1928 called on ministers to develop their preaching skills in Ukrainian.[29] Belarusians, by contrast, remained largely invisible. The question of whether *shtundism,* the popular term for evangelicalism among Ukrainians, could be seen as an expression of Ukrainian peasants' rejection of the Russian church interested Ukrainian nationalist observers throughout this period. The evidence suggests that national frustrations did not play an important role in drawing converts to shtundism. Indeed, the great Ukrainian historian, Mikhailo Hrushevs'kyĭ, concluded with disappointment that, if anything, the evangelical movement had a "non-national" character and that, when shtundism had encountered Baptist organizing, this structure came in the Russian language. Certainly, in practice, groups seem to have mixed Russian-language prayers and songs with preaching and singing in Ukrainian.[30] Throughout the book I often treat all these groups as "Russian Baptists." This does not suggest that I am unaware of ethnic differences between them. Rather, this reflects the fact that government and society—and to a great extent the believers themselves—seem to have considered them as such, even into the 1920s.

Like everyone else in Russia, the Baptists used the Julian calendar before February 1918. All dates in this book are in the Old Style (thirteen days behind the Western calendar by the early twentieth century) through January 1918, and in the New Style thereafter. In the 1920s, the Baptists continued to celebrate religious holidays at the same times as their Orthodox brethren did, according to the Julian calendar.

Part I

Organizing for the Russian Reformation

1

The Damned Shtundist

The Russian Evangelical Movement to 1905

Boom, ye church thunders!
Flash forth ye curses of the Councils!
Crush with eternal anathemas
The outcast race of Stundists![1]

In the final days of the reign of Alexander III, on 3 September 1894, the Minister of Internal Affairs, Petr Durnovo, wrote to Russia's provincial governors advising them that the Committee of Ministers had declared the *shtundist* sect to be especially harmful and that its meetings were henceforth prohibited. According to Durnovo, reports indicated that the shtundists rejected church rituals and sacraments, did not recognize any authority, refused military service and oath taking, and preached socialist principles. In sum, "their teaching undermine[d] the fundamental bases of the Orthodox faith and Russian national character [*narodnost'*]." The shtundists, he concluded, were "one of the most dangerous and harmful sects for the church and the state."[2]

This circular launched a decade of widespread, systematic persecution of the various evangelical religious groups that had emerged in the Russian Empire over the past twenty-five years. Hundreds of people who called themselves Baptists or Gospel Christians or Christians of Evangelical Faith were brought to trial for participation in alleged shtundist meetings. The circular is significant for another reason as well: the description of shtundism that it provided would shape debate about the Russian evangelical movement for the next thirty-five years. Questions about evangelicals' attitudes toward the state, pacifism, and socialism, as well as the notion that they threatened Russian national identity and values, would be continually raised.

Religious communities of Russians and Ukrainians that would later identify themselves as Baptists first arose in unrelated strains in three widely separated regions of the Russian Empire in the 1860s and 1870s. The history of the first decades of the evangelical movement is the story of groups in Transcaucasia, Ukraine, and St. Petersburg gradually finding one another, acknowledging their spiritual kinship, and, by the early 1880s, seeking paths to joint activity.[3] This process of mutual discovery and preliminary organizing was also one of denominational self-definition. The combined force of non-Russian models of evangelicalism, the pronouncements of outside observers, and the responses of the state and its established Orthodox Church continually pushed these communities to clarify who they were and what they believed, transforming them from informal sectarian groups into Baptists.

From its emergence in England in the seventeenth century to its later flowering in the United States, the Baptist faith is usually considered a product of the English-speaking world. But in Russia, from the very start, it would be associated with Germans. The first subjects of the Russian Empire to be baptized, in 1858 in the Russian Polish city of Adamow, were ethnic Germans. And they had encountered Baptist ideas through the missionary work of German Baptists from East Prussia.[4] The Baptist movement at that time was relatively new to the European continent. Already well established in Britain and the United States, it was brought to Hamburg in the 1830s by Johann Oncken, a German who had been raised, educated, and converted in England. In its first years the "new English religion," as it was popularly dubbed, was subject to fierce persecution by German governments. From the mid 1850s, these attacks declined somewhat, and, with some English and American financial assistance, the German Baptists began to take their campaign for the souls of Europe abroad. Taking advantage of the large number of German speakers living scattered across Eastern Europe, they focused their attentions there.[5]

The message these missionaries brought with them proclaimed that, through a personal encounter with Jesus Christ and the resulting submission of one's will to the work of the Holy Spirit, the believer could attain certain salvation from sin.[6] The outward sign of this regeneration was believer's baptism by full immersion. The Baptists also taught that the Bible was the inspired Word of God and that it should be the only guide in all matters of faith and life. Several other ideas arose from these basic principles. Most important was that of the "gathered church": the congregation is made up of those who have had a personal conversion experience. Through believer's baptism and continuous discipline, the community seeks to maintain this regenerate membership. By virtue of his or her conversion, each member of the community has the authority and the responsibility to preach the Gospel and to participate actively in church affairs. Each local church enjoys full autonomy, even if it cooperates with others in the propagation of the faith. Finally, the Baptists have historically stressed the need for absolute freedom of conscience and the separation of church and state. Theirs is an individualistic creed, emphasizing the individual's own spiritual experience as the basis for a democratically organized church.[7]

In the Russian Empire, the movement spread quickly from the first congregation in Poland through the German communities in the Baltic, Ukrainian, and Volga provinces, among the Latvians and Estonians, and, eventually, to the Slavic peoples of the Empire. Groups of Germans influenced by pietistic and Baptist ideas soon were shaking up their own religious communities with hour-long meetings of Bible reading, prayer, and song. As Baptist ideas filtered into officially approved Lutheran, Reformed, and Mennonite communities, breakaway congregations of converts formed. Those who broke with the first two traditions called themselves Baptists, but former Mennonites became known as Mennonite Brethren. Although they retained several Mennonite practices, they embraced the central tenets of the Baptist faith.[8] These German-speaking converts would play a crucial role in spreading that faith to their Orthodox neighbors, both through personal evangelism and by providing a model for religious seekers.

The first Russians to call themselves Baptists lived in Transcaucasia, in what is today the capital of Georgia, Tbilisi (then Tiflis). In August 1867, the first Russian convert, Nikita Voronin, was baptized in the Kura River near Tiflis by Martin Kalweit, a German Baptist from the Baltic provinces who had settled recently in Tiflis. Voronin had been a member of the Molokan sect, an indigenous Russian sect with Quaker-like beliefs. By the late 1860s, a growing number of Molokans had begun to have doubts about the Molokan teaching that baptism and other sacraments were to be understood in a purely spiritual sense and to suggest that the physical ritual of water baptism was, in fact, essential to salvation.[9] After intensive study of the Bible, Voronin had experienced conversion and had become convinced of the need for the sacraments of water baptism and communion, but he did not know where to find a congregation that shared his views. Eventually Voronin met Kalweit, the leader of a tiny group of German Baptists in Tiflis. Lengthy discussion with Kalweit convinced Voronin that he had at last found a like-minded community, and he asked Kalweit to baptize him.[10] Within a few years Voronin, in turn, inducted several other Russian converts and formed the first Russian Baptist congregation, in Tiflis. In 1871, two young Molokans who were to be great pioneers of the Russian Baptist movement, Vasilii Vasil'evich Ivanov and Vasilii Gur'evich Pavlov, joined the small group. For the next few decades, Ivanov and Pavlov would preach the Baptist faith in the Molokan villages of Transcaucasia and across southern Russia and the Volga region.

Around the same time, in southern Ukraine, a new religious movement known as *shtundizm* was appearing among Orthodox peasants. Local Ukrainian or Russian peasants who worked for the German colonists who had settled in this region from the time of Catherine the Great began to attend revivalistic religious meetings occurring in their employers' communities. When they turned to organizing such Bible hours among their own people, the Slavic faithful were soon nicknamed *shtundisty*, after the German word for hour, *Stunde*.[11]

The shtundists did not start out to separate from the Orthodox Church. Rather, their own spiritual quests and the definitions and actions of outsiders eventually worked together to make them an independent sect. Contact with German Protestants forced early shtundists to ask themselves new questions about the path to salvation. The negative reaction of local Orthodox priests to their interest in the Germans' beliefs also contributed to their gradual rejection of Orthodoxy.[12] Although the German colonists were eager to answer questions about their faith and welcomed the local Slavic peasantry to their meetings, they held back from actually baptizing these new converts, fearing punishment for the illegal act of converting the Orthodox away from the official church. However, on 11 June 1869, Efim Tsymbal, a peasant from the Ukrainian village of Karlovka, in Kherson Province, persuaded the Mennonite Brethren preacher Abraham Unger to baptize him along with thirty converts in the nearby German colony of Staryi Dantsig. He thus became the first South Russian shtundist formally to join the Baptist faith. The act of re-baptism constituted the final break with Orthodoxy for Tsymbal. Some shtundists refused the rituals and structure of the Baptist faith, but many would follow Tsymbal's lead. Tsymbal soon traveled to the settlement of Liubomirka (also in Kherson Province) where he baptized a future leading shtundist, Ivan Grigor'evich Riaboshapka. In turn, Riaboshapka baptized the shtundist pioneer Mikhailo Ratushnyi, along with forty-eight of his followers from Odessa *uezd**, in 1871.[13] By then the movement had spread beyond Kherson Province to Kiev Province and throughout south Russia, thanks in large part to peasants' seasonal labor migration.[14]

Meanwhile, Protestant ideas were also making themselves felt in distant St. Petersburg, and in a very different social milieu. The movement in the north originated with what Edmund Heier described as a "drawing room revival." This revival began in 1874, when the Russian noblewoman Elizaveta I. Chertkova invited the well-known English preacher Granville A. W. Waldegrave, Lord Radstock, to lead evangelistic meetings in the salons of the capital. Radstock was a member of the Plymouth Brethren, a Calvinistic offshoot of the low Anglican church. He had converted Chertkova by his ardent preaching when she was on a trip abroad. Radstock was a huge hit in that season of 1874 and during his return visits in 1875 and 1878. Several leading members of St. Petersburg high society were converted, and the phenomenon of Radstockism was widely discussed in the press and in literature.

---

*An *uezd* is a local district.

Those who opened their palaces to Radstock and were converted included Count Modest M. Korf, Count Aleksei P. Bobrinskii, Princess Vera Lieven, her sister Princess Natalia Gagarina, and Colonel Vasilii A. Pashkov.[15]

Pashkov soon emerged as the leading light of this movement and guided it toward a philanthropic and social program. He and his noble followers took their message of the need for personal religious conversion and the development of the inner spiritual life through prayer and Bible reading to the peasants on their estates in the provinces of northern and central Russia. There they formed literacy circles and initiated classes to teach various skills. For the poor of St. Petersburg, they established tea rooms, a shelter for homeless children, work projects for the unemployed, a campaign against alcoholism, and hospital and prison visiting programs. In 1876, Korf founded the "Society for the Encouragement of Spiritual and Ethical Reading," which published a wide variety of religious books and brochures, as well as *Russkii rabochii* [Russian worker], a weekly newspaper aimed at a popular audience. And the new religious ideas filtered back to the villages of migrant workers who encountered them in the capital.

The movement soon became known as Pashkovism. The Pashkovite leaders originally envisaged a renewal of Orthodoxy rather than the founding of a new denomination. They did not preach a formalized creed, instead leaving their worker and peasant followers to elaborate their own interpretations of Scripture. Eventually, however, as a result of the directions this popular thinking took, Korf's own conversion to the Baptist faith while in Switzerland in 1879, and persecution as shtundists, the Pashkovite movement moved closer to the shtundists and Baptists, adopting many of their worship patterns and doctrines.[16]

Baptists, shtundists, and Pashkovites gradually became aware of one another through newspaper reports, travel, and the distribution of Pashkovite publications. By 1884, informal connections took formal shape. Two conferences brought together groups that shared evangelicalism's Bible-based and conversion-driven tenets to discuss common interests and begin to give structure to the movement. The first took place in St. Petersburg. At Pashkov's invitation, seventy delegates representing groups of shtundists, Pashkovites, Baptists (German and Russian), Mennonite Brethren, and an evangelical stream of Molokanism traveled to the capital in early April, where they met in the palaces of various Pashkovite sponsors. Halfway through the conference, however, the police arrested all the Russian delegates, imprisoned them overnight, and sent them back to their home provinces. Soon thereafter the "Society for the Encouragement of Spiritual and Ethical Reading" was closed down, and all Pashkovite meetings were prohibited. When Pashkov and Korf formally refused to agree not to preach, hold meetings, or meet with other evangelical sectarians, they were expelled from Russia.[17]

Soon after their return home from St. Petersburg that spring of 1884 Russian Baptists from the south held a conference of their own. This gathering, described in the protocol as a meeting of "believing baptized Christians or so-called Baptists," brought together representatives from Kherson, Kiev, Eka-terinoslav, and Taurida provinces.[18] The Caucasian and Transcaucasian Baptists were unable to attend but sent letters outlining their views on the issues to be discussed. The agenda dealt primarily with the tasks of agreeing on doctrinal and behavioral standards that would unify these disparate groups and establishing a network of missionaries. The centrality of mission is reflected in the fact that the permanent body formed to administer the "union treasury" was described as the "missionary committee." Because it set up the first permanent organization among Slavic Baptists and made binding decisions about doctrine, this conference is considered to be the founding gathering of the Union of Russian Baptists.[19]

The meeting took place in southern Ukraine, in the Molokan village of Novo-Vasil'evka, Taurida Province, on 30 April and 1 May 1884. The thirty-three official delegates included prominent shtundists such as Ratushnyi and Riaboshapka, converts from Molokanism such as Fedor Prokhorovich Balikhin (destined to become a very effective missionary), the ethnic German Ivan V. Kargel' representing the Pashkovites, and six envoys from the Mennonite Brethren church in the neighboring Molochna Mennonite colony.

The gathering concentrated on organizing missionary work among Russians, by Russians. At this stage Germans seem to have played a crucial role in providing advice on organization and doctrine, although their views were not necessarily adopted. Johann Wieler of Molochna chaired the meeting. Most of the discussion of money in the minutes dealt with fund-raising among Russian members, and all the missionaries appointed were Russians or Ukrainians. When the conference came to elect a permanent missionary committee, however, although all the regional representatives on the committee were Slavs, Wieler and I. F. Isaak, both members of the Mennonite Brethren, became president and treasurer, respectively. The participants also formally thanked the German congregations for their financial aid and noted that the itinerant preaching of V. G. Pavlov of Tiflis was funded by the German-American Missionary Committee, which sponsored Baptist missions from Germany.[20]

Over the next twenty years the Russian Baptists held ten other conferences. By 1887, when Dei I. Mazaev was elected union president, German speakers had become increasingly scarce at union meetings.[21] Although some interaction naturally remained, the German-speaking Baptists and the Russian Baptists developed into two very separate organizations by 1890. This process was aided not simply by cultural differences but also by the contrast between the German Baptists' legal status and the persecution increasingly suffered by the Slavs. For, as the Russian Baptists' influence spread, they drew the attention of church and state authorities, who regarded them as a serious threat to the status quo.

Of course, religious dissent was not unknown in Russia before the tumultuous 1860s unleashed a new wave of sectarian groups such as the evangelicals. For two hundred years the Russian state had battled a variety of nonconformist groups. The most important of these was the Old Believers. The Old Believers broke away from the official Orthodox Church in the 1660s amid a fierce conflict over corrections to church rituals and service books, and over the interference of the state in religious matters. Estimates range widely, but by the late imperial period they numbered in the millions. During the eighteenth century other sectarian groups also left the official church. The most significant included followers of the ecstatic "Christ-Faith" or *khristovshchina* (better known to outsiders as *khlystovshchina* or flagellantism), and the Quaker-like groups of Dukhobors and Molokans, which arose in Tambov Province in central Russia but were largely exiled to Transcaucasia in the 1830s. And, of course, in addition to dealing with these "Russian" sects, the ever expanding, multinational Russian Empire had long had to deal with the incorporation of non-Orthodox religious groups and to regularize their legal position.[22]

The result was a strict legal hierarchy of religious groups in the imperial Russian state. At the top stood the Russian Orthodox Church, which was effectively the established church. By 1900, it ministered to approximately 70 percent of the empire's population. As for the various religious minorities, Russian legal practice drew a sharp distinction between Russians and non-Russians in awarding religious rights. Subjects of the empire who belonged to the various non-Russian ethnic groups and had been born into faiths other than Orthodoxy were generally allowed to build houses of worship and hold services, on the condition that they made no attempt to spread their faith beyond their ethnic group. Thus, for example, in the 1860s the Germans of the empire enjoyed the right to worship as Lutherans or Roman Catholics or Mennonites. By contrast, all people considered to be of Russian nationality (Russians, Ukrainians, and Belarusians) were assumed to belong to the Orthodox Church. Only the Orthodox Church was permitted to proselytize, and it was a crime for an Orthodox person to convert to a different faith.[23] "Russians" who adhered to Old Belief or the various sects suffered a precarious existence. The law treated Orthodoxy as a marker of Russian nationality and as a hereditary characteristic. Thus the law regarded anyone whose ancestors had left the Orthodox Church as a schismatic from Orthodoxy, even if one had been raised in a sect from birth.

In the context of the Great Reforms of the 1860s, a special committee was formed in 1864 to address the legal position of these various "schismatics from Orthodoxy." Based on its recommendations, new laws were promulgated in 1874 and 1883. These laws standardized regulations on the administration of Old Believers and sectarians, and moved them out of the realm of secret government circulars. The law of 19 April 1874 allowed "schismatics" (generally understood as Old Believers but not other sectarians) to register their births, deaths, and marriages legally. Then, on 3 May 1883, a new law permitted most sectarians and Old Believers to hold services in private or in special prayer houses, to carry internal passports, and to occupy public positions. Public manifestation of non-Orthodox religious practice remained prohibited. These measures, although they were frequently ignored by local officials, resulted in some improvement in the condition of Old Believers, in particular.[24] By contrast, the Russian Baptists, who were perceived not merely as schismatics but as having adopted a "foreign" faith, presented a special challenge to this official structure.

Questions arose about which laws applied to the Russian evangelicals. A particular issue was the Governing Senate's decree of 12 September 1879, which regulated the "spiritual affairs of Baptists." Promulgated in response to the rise of the Baptist faith among Germans, this law allowed Baptists, "based on article 44 of the basic laws," to confess their faith and perform rituals without restrictions, and to hold services in buildings which the government approved for that purpose. Baptist leaders were to be approved by provincial governors, and foreign preachers were to be required to swear an oath of allegiance for the duration of their stay in Russia. Local civil authorities were charged with registering the Baptists' vital statistics.[25] Although there was no explicit mention of the nationality of these Baptists, the reference to article 44, which accorded non-Russians the right to worship according to their traditional faiths, signaled that the decree was not directed at formerly Orthodox people. Nevertheless, some local authorities in the Caucasus, in Transcaucasia, and in Ekaterinoslav Province initially made the mistake of registering congregations of formerly Molokan or Orthodox Baptists under the provisions of the 1879 law. This practice was soon reversed, but it led to considerable confusion.[26]

The government's answer to the dilemma of Russians claiming to be Baptists was to strengthen the legal distinction between Russians and non-Russians in awarding religious rights. Indeed, it is clear that in the period between the rise of the movement in the 1860s and the Decree on Religious Toleration of April 1905, when it became legal to leave the Orthodox Church, each successive decree or circular sought to strengthen the distinction between the rights of ethnic Russians and those of their non-Russian fellow subjects. This strategy became particularly pronounced after the assassination of Alexander II in 1881. His heir, Alexander III, and his advisers, alarmed by the apparent social disorder and political dissent unleashed by Alexander II's Great Reforms, aimed to bolster national cohesion through expanded police powers and coercive Russification, which included increased promotion of Orthodoxy by the state and its church.[27]

The spread and development of Russian and Ukrainian evangelical groups in the 1880s, concern about their increasing tendency to call themselves "Baptists," and an atmosphere of tightened police restrictions combined to draw hostile responses from local civil and religious authorities, as well as from the Holy Synod of the Orthodox Church in St. Petersburg. From

April 1880 until October 1905 the powerful conservative statesman and ideo-
logue of Alexander III's regime, Konstantin P. Pobedonostsev, served as Over
Procurator of this committee of bishops. He also sat on the Council of Ministers, essentially as "minister for the church." Pobedonostsev sought to restrict and destroy the power of minority religious groups, both by trying to
win dissidents back to Orthodoxy through missionary work and by clearly
defining the rights of Old Believers and sectarians (hence the May 1883 decree) so that they could be denied any rights not specifically granted them.

From his personal observations of the Pashkovite movement in the capital and reports from the provinces, Pobedonostsev became convinced that
the evangelicals represented a serious threat to the integrity of the empire.
He launched a campaign against the movement both through the church
on the ground and at the highest levels of the government. Within a month
of his appointment in 1880 to head the Synod, Pobedonostsev delivered a
detailed memorandum to the tsar regarding the dangers of the Pashkovite
movement and urging that Lord Radstock be forbidden to enter Russia and
that further meetings be banned. Famously declaring that, "there can be no
Russian Baptists," he worked to forbid the translation of foreign Baptist materials into Russian and to organize the clergy to fight the movement through
special conferences, the first of which was held in Kiev in 1884.[28]

A special mission against Old Belief and sectarianism was formed within
the Orthodox Church and held national congresses in 1887, 1891, and 1897.
These missionaries, often specially designated priests but also, increasingly,
lay professionals, led religious educational sessions designed to strengthen
Orthodox practice and participated in public debates with sectarians. They
also published and distributed anti-sectarian pamphlets and other literature.[29] Some of these publications were rather incendiary in character. For
example, in Khar'kov diocese the church hierarchy distributed a brochure
in schools titled "The Damned Shtundist." This nine-verse poem, apparently
sung as a hymn, spoke of the "outcast race of shtundists" and warned that,

> The simple-hearted but peep in
> To the lair of the perfidious beast,
> By detraction, slander, and cajolery
> They are entrapped by the damned Stundist.[30]

Finally, the missionaries took seriously their political role as protectors of the
national faith. They cooperated with the police by reporting incidents of
illegal propaganda of non-Orthodox teachings. At their 1891 congress in
Moscow, they called for a range of legal measures to be taken against religious dissidents and for several sects, including the shtundists, Molokans, Ju-
daizers, and Khlysty, to be declared "most harmful" and thus denied the rights
outlined in the 1883 law on Old Believers and sectarians.[31]

Pobedonostsev, in his anti-sectarian endeavor, cooperated with local government officials who, often citing their religious counterparts as sources,

complained to the Ministry of Internal Affairs that evangelicalism was threatening not merely the spiritual order of the Russian Empire but its civil stability and territorial integrity as well. For example, in 1885 the government's chief representative in the Caucasus connected Orthodoxy to the health of the empire: "The popular masses infected with shtundism are being trained as enemies of Russia and accomplices of Protestant Germany, which so obviously is preparing not the tearing away, but the simple falling away from Russia to Germany of our Western and even Southern districts, populated by Germans and by Germanized people."[32] Similarly, in a letter to the Minister of Internal Affairs in July 1893, the general governor of Kiev, Podol'sk, and Volynia warned that seized "shtundist" correspondence showed that the dissidents challenged the Orthodox character of the Russian state: they allegedly held out hope that the state would defend them against the Orthodox Church.[33]

Furthermore, from the early days of the appearance of the shtundists accusations about their alleged communist and pacifist beliefs circulated among Russian officials. For example, in February 1868 the Kherson Provincial Administration commissioned a report about the new sect. Among other accusations it claimed that the shtundists taught that "Christ suffered for the whole human race and thus his love for all people is equal; if love is equal for all, then it should be that all of the affairs of this world should be." Such ideas purportedly attracted peasants who could not live on the small land allotment they had received after Emancipation and dreamed of receiving more in a general redistribution of all land. "Communism," the report concluded, "is the magnet that brings new followers to [shtundism] and retains the old."[34] This became one of the standard accusations against the sectarians. It is not clear to what extent such aspirations existed or were realized; certainly numerous reports by local priests suggested that shtundists aspired to a more equal and free social and political structure in Russia, if not to communism.[35]

The campaign against the new religion centered on the problem of prayer meetings, which were seen as the principal means of spreading the faith and the political ideas associated with it. The general governor of Kiev emphasized this, for instance, in his influential 1893 letter.[36] The difficulty from the point of view of church and civil authorities was that the 1883 law had made it legal for religious sectarians to meet, so long as their teachings were not considered "dangerous" by the state. This dilemma was solved decisively in July 1894, when the Committee of Ministers declared the sect of shtundists to be "most dangerous" and prohibited its meetings. This followed and confirmed a Synod resolution to that effect, based on the recommendations of the 1891 missionary congress. A circular to provincial governors of 12 September 1894, which implemented the decision, accused the shtundists of rejecting Orthodoxy and state authority, of preaching socialist ideas, and of threatening Russian national identity. The problem of the interrelation of religious identity, national character, and political reliability was thus, at last, made explicit.

An atmosphere of uneven harassment of evangelical sectarians now gave way to widespread, systematic persecution. Punishment was meted out not simply for converting others but for mere participation in shtundist meetings. The decade after 1894 saw hundreds of people tried on this charge. In late 1894 and early 1895 many leaders were convicted and either imprisoned or exiled: Nikita Voronin, the first baptized convert from Tiflis, was exiled to Vologda under police surveillance for four years; Ivan Riaboshapka was sent from Kherson Province to Erevan for five years; and Vasilii Ivanov, already a tireless itinerant missionary, was sent in irons into exile for five years in the city of Slutsk. Many believers tried to escape persecution by migrating to Siberia or Central Asia. Others fled abroad. Vasilii Pavlov, after being released from exile in Orenburg in 1895, went to Tulcea, Romania, and Ivan Prokhanov, a young preacher from St. Petersburg, left for Stockholm, then Hamburg, then Paris, and finally Britain in early 1895.[37]

Difficulties at these trials soon arose over defining what constituted a shtundist. The defendants usually declared themselves to be not shtundists, but Baptists or Gospel Christians or Christians of Evangelical Faith. Moreover, they would insist that they did not meet the 1894 circular's criteria for a shtundist, such as the rejection of all authority and of all sacraments. In many instances the defendants would refer to the Baptist statement of principles: "We believe that the authorities are established by God," and "we consider ourselves obliged to give unconditional obedience to their laws, if these laws do not restrict the free performance of the requirements of our Christian faith." By contrast, the experts summoned to determine whether the defendants were shtundists were usually members of the church's anti-sectarian mission who denied the very existence of Baptists of Russian ethnicity and insisted they were shtundists. Some distressed observers alleged that these specialists often used the very definition of the shtunda presented in the 1894 circular as "proof" of the especially harmful character of those whom they identified as shtundists.[38]

In 1900, two very similar circulars from the Ministries of Justice and Internal Affairs endorsed the view of these religious experts. According to the Ministry of Justice version, "followers of the Russian sect of shtunda . . . have begun insistently to call themselves Baptists"; yet the Baptist faith "is recognized by our law only for the followers of the German Protestant sect." This circular also included three new criteria for defining a religious meeting as a shtundist one: use of any of a list of hymn books, all of which were either Baptist or Baptist favorites; reading and interpretation of the Bible by any member of the assembly "in the spirit of the false teachings of the sect"; and improvised prayer, performed while kneeling and without using the sign of the cross.[39] The distinction between Russian shtundists and German Baptists was now completely explicit.

The persecution—and legal prosecution—of religious dissidents drew many opponents of the autocracy to their cause. From the 1860s populists and liberals, and later Marxists, had looked to the Old Believers and sectarians as representatives of a truer form of Russian culture and as potential audiences for their revolutionary ideas. Writing in 1881, the prominent populist student of religious dissent, Aleksei S. Prugavin, contended that, among religious dissidents, "purely religious ideas and aspirations are intermingled in the most striking way with issues and aspirations of a purely day-to-day, social mold and character, such that very often it is virtually impossible to determine where the first end and the second begin."[40] On the ground, revolutionaries began to encounter sectarians in their visits to "the people" in the villages and among the workers in the cities, and tried to explore their potential as allies in the transformation of Russian society.[41] By the turn of the century Vladimir D. Bonch-Bruevich, a Social Democrat, and Prince Dmitrii A. Khilkov, a Socialist Revolutionary and follower of Tolstoy, were both actively promoting revolutionary agitation among religious dissenters.

As a young revolutionary in the 1890s, Bonch-Bruevich had developed an interest in religious sectarians and engaged in both ethnographic study and active assistance to them (he accompanied a group of Dukhobors as they traveled to exile in Canada in 1899). Throughout 1902 he published a series of articles in the Bolshevik journal Zhizn' [Life], suggesting that sectarian groups were a product of changing rural conditions in Russia and that revolutionaries needed to engage with them. The issue was placed on the agenda of the Second Congress of the Russian Social Democratic Workers' Party in the summer of 1903. Although this congress is best remembered for the split between the Bolshevik and Menshevik factions of the party, it passed the following resolution in support of Bonch-Bruevich's plan: "Taking into account that, in many of its incarnations, the sectarian movement in Russia is one of the democratic streams directed against the existing order of things, the Second Congress draws the attention of all members of the party to work among sectarians with the goal of enlisting them in social democracy." Consequently Bonch-Bruevich founded a short-lived monthly journal aimed at religious sectarians, Razsviet [The dawn], published in Geneva and smuggled into the Russian Empire.[42] From January to the autumn of 1904, Razsviet combined social democratic political appeals with reports by and about sectarians, as well as articles dealing with the workers' movement in Russia and Europe, strikes and uprisings, and various antireligious themes.

Thus, by the early twentieth century, the legal tribulations of the so-called shtundists had become a subject of discussion in the press and had attracted the sympathy of many leftist and liberal commentators. Even within the church a few brave voices raised questions about the wisdom of legal restrictions on freedom of conscience.[43] This discussion took place against a background of rising public disorder and political pressure on the government. An increasingly vigorous workers' strike movement, agrarian unrest, pressure from the newly formed liberal Union of Liberation, and complaints even from supporters of the regime about many governors' blatant disregard for law eventually persuaded Nicholas II and his government that some discussion of political change was in order. The emancipation of the Church and the emancipation of religious dissenters were the two prongs of a policy of religious reform conceived in 1904 by Sergei Witte, the chairman of the Committee of Ministers, and supported by the first hierarch of the Synod, St. Petersburg Metropolitan Antonii Vadkovskii. Witte's fundamental goal was the maintenance of the autocracy, and he had concluded that the repression of religious minorities was creating disorder rather than shoring up the state; moreover, he believed that religious minorities' support, especially that of the Old Believers, could be won over through the extension of religious freedom. However, he believed that if repression were to be lifted, the Church would also need to be unshackled from the dictates of the state bureaucracy in order to face its new competitors successfully. A manifesto in February 1903 exhorted government officials to be steadfast in observing the laws on the books, including those dealing with non-Orthodox subjects. Then, in December 1904, an edict that called for a review of the emergency regulations that had allowed governors vast administrative leeway since 1881, relaxation of censorship, and improvements in local government also proposed a revision of laws concerning religious minorities.[44]

The result was a decree on religious toleration, signed by Nicholas II on Easter day, 17 April 1905. By then, what would be a year-long revolution was building steam and the government sought to arrest it by making small concessions to the restless population. The new decree lifted the prohibition on leaving the Orthodox Church and promised "schismatics" freedom to build prayer houses and hold services there or in private homes. Although Orthodoxy remained the established church of the Russian Empire and preserved a monopoly on proselytizing, this law allowed the many people who were registered as Orthodox but actually practiced another faith to legalize their religious choice. The accompanying instructions by the Committee of Ministers formally lifted the 1894 prohibition on shtundist meetings.[45] Just a month earlier Nicholas had also promised that, "at a favorable time," he would convene a Sobor [Council] of the Orthodox Church to discuss a variety of issues, including the relationship of the Church to the Russian state.[46] His manifesto of 17 October 1905, which established a national legislature based on virtually universal male suffrage and proclaimed freedom of the person, conscience, speech, and assembly, transformed the Russian civic landscape and seemed to promise a new era of opportunity for Russian Baptists.

Indeed, Russian evangelicals responded with joy. The 1905 Revolution launched a period of rapid expansion for the Baptists, both numerically and organizationally. And this expansion provoked debate, whether it took place around the stove in a peasant hut or at the top levels of government in St. Petersburg. Many of the issues in this debate, however, had already been set up by 1894. These included the place of non-Orthodox subjects in an Orthodox state, the relationship between Russian nationality and Orthodoxy, and the social and political implications of religious choices. And now, in the years after the October Manifesto, the expanding evangelical movement also raised questions about the emergence of civil society in the constitutional era and the possibility for—and desirability of—pluralism in Russia.

2

The Era of "Open Storm"

Baptist Organization and Community after 1905

In early 1911, the veteran missionary and pastor of the Baku congregation, Vasilii V. Ivanov, looked back on six years of rapid growth since the declaration of religious toleration. "Armed with the truth of God," he wrote in an article in the magazine *Baptist*, the Baptists "boldly enter into the unequal battle with errors of all sorts and expand their spiritual territory with great success. . . . Since 1905 an era has begun in the history of the Baptists that can be called the era of open storm."[1]

Certainly the many civil rights victories of the 1905 Revolution transformed the status of the fledgling Baptist movement in Russia and opened up new vistas for its expansion and development. A government survey of religious sectarianism found that between the Edict of Religious Toleration of April 1905 and 1 January 1912, the Russian Baptists had added 21,140 people to their ranks, approximately one-third of their total membership of 66,788. The same study listed 29,988 people for the other branch of the movement, the Evangelical Christians, with approximately the same proportion (9,175) of new adherents having joined since 1905.[2] Considerable institutional expansion had accompanied this numerical growth. In the brief period since 1905 hundreds of congregations had been formed. The Union of Russian Evangelical Christians-Baptists and, after its establishment in 1909, the rival All-Russian Union of Evangelical Christians, held public national

27

and regional congresses annually. Both unions could boast a sizable network of missionaries. Between them, they also published various journals and a weekly newspaper, as well as a steady stream of pamphlets, hymn books, and other confessional literature. Their representatives had traveled to several international Baptist conventions abroad, and, in 1911, the Evangelical Christian leader Ivan S. Prokhanov had been elected a vice president of the Baptist World Alliance. Contemplating these accomplishments, Baptist leaders boldly proclaimed the coming of a new religious age, indeed an imminent Russian reformation.[3]

Organizational ability emerged as the hallmark of the evangelical movement as it expanded after 1905. Using techniques unfamiliar to the Orthodox and other official churches, the Baptists developed their congregational life, expanded missionary activity by Russians among Russians, and worked to create regional and nationwide organizations to further Baptist goals and unity in the period between 1905 and the onset of war in 1914. Religious dissidence was not new to Russia, but observers—from clergy and bureaucrats to members of the intelligentsia and the press and even curiosity seekers who came to their meetings—all agreed that the dissidence of the Baptists and Evangelical Christians differed from earlier models precisely in its extensive organization and missionary drive.

These features were the necessary by-product of Baptist teachings about faith and church organization. The Russian believers shared with other Baptists a conception of the church as a covenant of converted adults and were thus compelled to pay close attention to the nurturing of current members and the enlistment of new ones. This conversionist drive lay at the basis of local congregations and permeated all the organizations that linked them. As they formed associations based on voluntarist and democratic principles, Russian evangelicals modeled a very different type of society from that envisioned by the imperial state.

The evangelicals' organizational success both reflected the increasing pluralism of Russian society in the wake of the October Manifesto and challenged Russia's rulers to further expand the boundaries of the emerging public sphere. Nicholas II's 1905 decree on religious toleration had cracked open the door of religious choice in Russia: although it was still illegal to convert others, Russians could now leave the Orthodox Church according to their consciences. Peter Berger argues that pluralism implies a competitive, or market, situation. Using the techniques of revivalists in England and the United States where religious ideas already competed freely, Russian evangelicals simply ignored legal injunctions against proselytization and joined the clamor of voices proposing alternative models for Russian souls, society, and state in the period between revolutions.[4]

In comparison with the countries of Western Europe or North America, voluntary organizations and other forms of independent civic life were relatively undeveloped among the subjects of the Russian Empire. Although historians in recent years have trained their eyes on the nascent forms of middle-class organization and civic activism in the late imperial period, little is known about similar efforts among the lower classes. What work there is on this theme focuses on the urban working class and how it became politicized on the basis of an emerging class consciousness.[5] In the early years of the twentieth century the Baptists offered Russians new forms of intellectually and organizationally democratic community life, rooted in religious rather than political conversion. They provide an unusual example of a socially mixed, albeit mostly lower-class, group of people making use of greater freedom of organization and of the press—and also of the new railway system—to form an organization linking the country and the city.

LEGAL CHANGE AND BAPTIST RESPONSES

When religious toleration was declared in 1905, communities of Russian Baptists had existed in some places for more than thirty years. Although their illegal status had, in most cases, prevented them from acquiring such trappings as permanent prayer houses and stationery, in some places these groups were quite well developed and ready to emerge openly as recognizable organizations in 1905. Examples included those in the cities of Odessa, Tiflis, Baku, Kiev, St. Petersburg, and Rostov-on-Don, and the longstanding groups in such towns or villages as Liubomirka (Kherson Province), Astrakhanka (Taurida Province), Peski (Voronezh Province), and Balashov (Saratov Province).[6]

More often, however, believers were members of simple groups that gathered for worship when they could without formal, or at least formally ordained, leadership. Many of these groups were very small, some consisting of only a couple of households, and were isolated from one another. In these cases, the task after 1905 was to develop as a congregation and become integrated into the wider Baptist community.

By 1905, the Baptists had been loosely organized into a Russian Baptist Union for twenty years. The union was basically an organizational committee headed, and generously financed, by its president, Dei Ivanovich Mazaev, the scion of a well-to-do family of Molokan sheep farmers from the Kuban district who had converted in 1884 and headed the union since late 1887.[7] Although illegality and persecution had made any outward institutional development impossible, the union was not an insignificant entity. Almost every year, especially after the turn of the century when repression abated somewhat, representatives of Baptist congregations would gather to report on the affairs of their communities, to organize their missionary activity in the Russian Empire, and to resolve questions of church doctrine and polity. A union treasury paid two or three full-time and several more part-time missionaries.[8]

There was therefore some basis for Baptist activity on the eve of the declaration of religious toleration. In the days after April 17 evangelicals organized prayer meetings around the country to celebrate the new freedom. Mazaev also set straight to work, inviting 150 people to Rostov-on-Don, beginning on May 15, to celebrate the legal change and discuss new directions for the Baptist community.[9] In their enthusiasm to gather to rejoice and plot strategy in 1905, the Baptists resembled many other groups of religious dissidents, such as the Molokans and the Old Believers. In contrast to these counterparts, the Baptists would use their freedom to focus not just on internal development of their movement but especially on mission. This drive would push them to demand even more rights than the April 17 manifesto awarded.[10]

Despite Mazaev's efforts, during 1906 St. Petersburg emerged as the organizational center of the evangelical movement. Its focus was the first legal evangelical journal, *Khristianin* [The Christian], edited by Ivan S. Prokhanov, a prominent member of the St. Petersburg evangelical community. This extraordinary personality, born in 1869 into a Molokan merchant family in Vladikavkaz, would play an important role first in unifying and then dividing Russian evangelicals. When Prokhanov was a boy his father converted to the Baptist faith and thereafter suffered persecution for his proselytizing enthusiasm. Prokhanov arrived in St. Petersburg in the late 1880s to train as an engineer and there encountered the Pashkovite movement. A charismatic speaker and organizer, as well as a gifted writer, the young student threw himself into organizing the capital's evangelicals along Baptist lines and played a leading role in the underground journal *Besieda* [Discussion]. Increasingly at risk of arrest for his activities, Prokhanov fled Russia in 1895 and traveled through Europe to England, where he spent a year at the Baptist College in Bristol, learning some of the revivalist techniques he would later introduce in Russia. He returned home in 1898, and, after a brief stint as an instructor at the Riga Polytechnical Institute, he settled into a job at the Westinghouse Electric Company in the capital, a position he would hold into the Soviet period. In his spare time he would work prodigiously for the evangelical movement, publishing journals, composing scores of hymns, and serving as president of the St. Petersburg Evangelical Christian congregation.[11]

Prokhanov's journal, *Khristianin,* was born in the heady days of late 1905. A pilot issue was circulated in November of that year, and from January 1906 the journal was published monthly and distributed across the Russian Empire.[12] Beginning in March 1906 a complimentary supplement, *Bratskii listok* [Brotherly pamphlet], accompanied each issue. *Khristianin* and *Bratskii listok* explicitly sought to create and unify a broad coalition of evangelically minded Russians, not only Baptists and Evangelical Christians but also the evangelical Molokans, led by Zinovii Danilovich Zakharov, who, although they practiced infant baptism, shared very similar beliefs and called themselves Christians of Evangelical Faith. *Khristianin* offered its readers a variety of devotional articles, including religious stories and poetry, readers' reports of their conversions, articles about Baptists abroad, reprinted sermons by Russian leaders, translations of foreign Baptists' writings, and new hymns composed by Prokhanov. *Bratskii listok,* by contrast, focused on the day-to-day lives of believers and on building community among them. It published letters and reports of local activities submitted by believers, informed readers of legislation affecting them, recounted incidents of persecution, and reprinted letters of complaint submitted to government authorities, as well as reporting on congresses of believers. In this way *Khristianin* served not merely as a journal but as the coordinating body of an embryonic evangelical alliance. Apparently with considerable success, Prokhanov used the journal to organize congregations into participating in events such as special weeks of prayer, and the office of the journal became a collection point for donations to support evangelical activity across the country.

The immediate and enthusiastic response of Baptists and other evangelicals to *Khristianin* reveals a great thirst for community. As one reader, I.F.I. from the village of Bozhedarovka, Ekaterinoslav Province, reported feeling as he opened his first issue of the magazine in early 1906: "May *Khristianin* allow the children of God to come to know one another better and better, and to rally to the general cause across the whole expanse of Russia, that the power of darkness be broken and that the people might truly make themselves free from sin to the glory of the Lord Jesus Christ and the blossoming of our dear Russia."[13] Other readers wrote of how *Khristianin* had broken the isolation of small congregations in remote parts of the countryside. For example, Brother Evdokimov belonged to a community of five households on the steppe in the Don region. In a letter to *Bratskii listok,* he wrote, "I give thanks to my Lord for you, that He put in your heart the idea of publishing a journal in the strength and spirit of Christ. I have been living for thirteen years in Christ already, but could not feel myself so close to my heavenly fatherland as now upon reading 'Khr. [*sic*]'" He went on to report how the journal had inspired an atmosphere of revival at his group's meetings.[14] *Khristianin* clearly provided a welcome resource for small congregations of lay people searching for spiritual guidance: one reader reported that a recent meeting of his congregation had centered on readings from two recent issues.[15]

Many readers also wrote in to describe their congregations and to ask that a preacher visit them. For example, Iustin Kondrat'evich Savchenko of the village of Kobyzhcha, in Chernigov Province, 83 versts*from Kiev, wrote to say that his church was made up of twenty-two members and several regular attendees and that they were in great need of preachers. He asked the editor to print their request in the hope that a traveling evangelist might visit them.[16] These pleas were shown to be effective a few months later, when the Kobyzhcha church wrote to thank two preachers for calling on them.[17] In-

---

*A verst [*versta*] is a measure of distance equivalent to 3,500 feet, or approximately 1 kilometer.

deed, at a meeting organized by the St. Petersburg youth circle at the end of 1906, the visiting preachers Nikolai Odintsov, Vasilii Stepanov, and G. A. Boichenko looked back on a year of "introducing and setting up spiritual order in the internal lives of young churches, circles, and organizations" and recounted "the marvelous works of spiritual awakening in the middle and southern parts of Russia."[18]

The journal also helped readers cope with revolutionary times, by offering spiritual enlightenment as a solution to disorder and hatred. The week of prayer for Russia, organized in early 1906, was but one example. In a rather tortuously phrased letter written in early 1907, a reader from Baku Province described how *Khristianin* had allowed him to "solve many perplexing issues of Holy Scripture, as well as issues of human life":

> Living through such a grave time (revolts, strikes, crop failure, and so on) I have often pondered and asked myself the question, what is the need of our "brothers"? . . . And then again your *Khristianin* appeared as the key to this agonizing question. . . . May the Lord make all brothers become like in the times of the apostles, "and there were no needy among them."[19]

In the pages of *Bratskii listok,* the Russian evangelicals also discussed their evolving legal situation. In this respect, the key player was Ivan Petrovich Kushnerov. Kushnerov was a member of the Kiev congregation who served as a legal advocate for the Baptists during the persecution of the 1890s, by writing petitions and defending them at trials. From the very first issue of *Bratskii listok,* Kushnerov regularly reported on believers' legal difficulties and wrote detailed articles informing his readers of their rights and the laws that applied to them.[20]

Although the edict on religious toleration and the October Manifesto dramatically changed the conditions in which Russian Baptists lived and worshiped, the revolutionary settlement of 1905 nevertheless reserved important arenas of religious activity for the Orthodox Church alone. Most important among these was the right to preach and make converts publicly. Chapter 90 of the Criminal Code still punished, by imprisonment or arrest, anyone caught publicly soliciting the conversion of Orthodox people to another confession.[21] Russians were free to leave the Orthodox church, but it remained a crime to convert others to one's new faith. For the Baptists, inspired by Johann Oncken's slogan, "Every Baptist a Missionary," this restriction seemed incompatible with the freedom of conscience enunciated in the October Manifesto. Indeed, the goal of converting others drove all evangelical organizational efforts.

Although laws against becoming a Baptist and organizing prayer meetings had been overturned, the new legal situation remained unclear. A report by Kushnerov in early 1907 outlined the issues. In some places local officials refused to drop cases against believers who had been accused of converting the Orthodox before April 1905, allegedly in anticipation of a new criminal code that would clarify their status. Kushnerov knew of several incidents when believers complained to their governor that village authorities had broken up evangelical meetings but nothing was done to help them. Believers also faced problems when they refused to pay local levies for the support of the parish Orthodox church. Likewise, jurisdictional disputes over the use of village cemeteries had become a frequent problem. Finally, evangelicals still suffered from the fact that, before 1905, the state had not recognized their existence, and thus their marriages were unrecorded and their children considered illegitimate.[22]

The burning legal issue for Russian Baptists in 1906–7 was the decree of 17 October 1906, which regulated the formation of Old Believer and sectarian congregations. In exchange for registering its pastors and the congregation's vital statistics with the government, each community would receive the legal right to build churches, elect its own clerical and lay leaders, and levy tithes on its members.[23] Soon after the law was promulgated, Prokhanov acknowledged in a detailed article in *Bratskii listok* that its provisions constituted a "big step forward in comparison with the condition of Old Believers and sectarians two years ago." Nevertheless, he pointed out, many changes were still needed, since the law was more suited to the Old Believers' form of organization than that of evangelical sectarians, with their itinerant preachers and their communities formed through conversion rather than birth. Indeed, before the October 1906 decree was promulgated, both the Evangelical Christians in St. Petersburg and the Baptist Union had drawn up petitions to the Council of Ministers objecting to the prohibition on proselytization and to the notion that spiritual leaders would have to be approved by the government.[24]

In January 1907, a congress gathered in St. Petersburg to formulate a united response from evangelical groups to the law on registering congregations. Seventy representatives from at least seventeen provinces and including a delegation of the evangelical Molokans declared shared principles of freedom of propaganda and freedom from government meddling in the internal affairs of the congregation.[25]

Khristianin had played an important role in mobilizing congregations to discuss the October 1906 law and in suggesting what its problems were. In preparation for the congress, congregational meetings or regional conferences discussed the legal situation and drew up demands for change. Resistance to the law's requirement that all presbyters be approved by the state and be forced to perform the governmental task of keeping registers of vital statistics for their congregations was universal. Representatives of four village congregations near Novouzensk in Samara Province declared that, "the Gospel tells us to serve the Lord in full freedom; therefore, we want no governmental approval, which could only lay on us, sons of freedom, a heavy and undesirable yoke of slavery."[26] Similarly delegates at a local congress in Kiev expressed a widely accepted view when they objected to the requirement that congregations define their geographic area of activity on the grounds that a congregation's reach was "the whole world."[27] In these ways believers rejected all government efforts to regulate their activities and make faith a static marker of social and ethnic identity.

After a week of sessions, supplemented by festive prayer meetings every evening at various points around the capital, the delegates composed a detailed petition to the Ministry of Internal Affairs that proposed an alternative version of the law of 17 October 1906. Point by point the petition exchanged the government's static conception of a community based on birth, local by definition, and subject to governmental approval for a dynamic conception of a community of converted—and converting—believers with no geographical or social boundaries to its activity. Whereas the 1906 law guaranteed sectarians the right of "free confession of their faith and the performance of religious rituals according to the rules of their faiths," the evangelicals suggested a radical rephrasing of the first half of this formula to "free confession of their faith and the spreading of its teaching by means of personal conversation, preaching, and the printed word."[28] The 17 October 1906 law had been passed by an emergency provision after the First Duma was disbanded in July 1906 and before the Second was convened. According to the October Manifesto, this law should technically have lasted only until the elected representatives were able to approve a replacement. In fact, the October 1906 regulations would remain the only general law on religious dissidents up to 1917. Although the evangelicals' proposal for a radical transformation of the spirit of the 1906 edict attracted the attention and concern of Orthodox leaders, it languished in government files.

ORGANIZING FOR THE RUSSIAN REFORMATION

Once they had protested the failure of the 1905 Revolution to give them the full freedom they sought, the evangelicals proceeded to behave as though those freedoms were theirs. Through their speeches, their writings, and, most of all, their actions, the evangelicals asserted the right of proselytization as a moral and organizational principle.

The Baptist and Evangelical Christian denominations were organized along congregational lines. The congregation [*obshchina*] constituted the basic unit from which all other structures emerged. Each congregation was a self-governing community of converted and baptized adult believers who elected leaders from their midst. These communities could then join with others into the loose alliance of the Russian Baptist Union or, after its foundation in 1909, the Union of Evangelical Christians. These bodies aimed to unite believers doctrinally, represent them publicly, coordinate joint activities, and thereby strengthen their collective identity as part of a movement for religious change. On the day-to-day level, a network of missionaries, some commissioned by individual congregations and others representing

34

Baptists in Liubomirka, Kherson Province, bir
Ivan Riaboshapka, 1909.
Baptist Ukrainy, 1927.

one or the other of the national unions, worked to make new converts and
support the faithful, and also to create and strengthen this denominational
unity.

There was great variety in the size and sophistication of local communities. In a secret report in 1916 the Kaluga governor said that the largest congregation of Baptists in his province was the one in the village of Ukolitsi.
Many of the 144 members had converted around the turn of the century,
most likely as a result of contact with evangelists sponsored by the Pashkovite,
Princess Natalia Gagarina, from her nearby estate. Owing to the efforts of
an Orthodox church missionary, conversions had dropped off until 1905,
when believers could formally switch to the Baptists. Since that time this community of peasants had specially built a prayer house where they gathered
on Sundays and other holidays. Spiritual leaders, chosen from among the
peasant members, included a presbyter, a teacher, and two deacons. The affairs of the church were run by a council of members.[29]

The typical structure of a fairly large congregation was the following: the
presbyter was the main leader and performed baptismal, communion, mar-
riage, and funereal rites; teachers (also known as preachers or evangelists)

35

were called to preach and to preserve theological orthodoxy; and deacons assisted the presbyters and teachers in organizing services. In larger congregations a church council took charge of the day-to-day financial and organizational work of the community.[30] Most decisions, ranging from the approval of new members or exclusion of misbehaving ones to organizing spiritual education or charity work, were made by a majority vote of members (baptized male and female adults) of the congregation. Although it was rare, women could theoretically hold any congregational position save that of presbyter and teacher.[31]

In the Baptist branch of the movement, the presbyters, teachers, and deacons would usually have been ordained by a laying-on-of-hands service conducted by a group of visiting presbyters from other congregations.[32] Although the ordained were thereby set apart as leaders in their communities, Baptist doctrine insisted on their spiritual equality with ordinary members. Moreover, they constituted, almost without exception, a nonprofessional clergy, serving in their spare time and without formal theological education.

Of course, as a result of isolation or because they were newly established, many groups were very small and informal. For example, in 1906 L. N. Gorch wrote to *Bratskii listok* from Stavropol' to say how much he hoped that a preacher would visit his group of fifteen members. They were all workers, he wrote, "little familiar with the pen. But the thirst to know truth is great among them all." The believers met at one another's homes after nine or ten in the evening, since this was the only free time they had.[33] Similarly, in 1910, in the Cossack village of Otradnaia, Kuban region, about thirty Baptists gathered in members' houses every Sunday to pray. Since they did not have a formal spiritual leader, the literate members, in turn, took it upon themselves to read and explain scripture. One member, Sidor Il'ich Reshetov, a longtime Baptist, seems to have baptized several of his fellow members. A Baptist missionary, I. V. Babenkov, who visited periodically, reported performing baptisms or confirming the previously baptized by a laying-on-of-hands ceremony.[34]

Other groups might have been lacking proper prayer houses but were nonetheless reasonably formally organized. According to information collected by the Orel provincial government in 1908, in the factory town of Bezhitsa, near Briansk, there were fifty-two Baptists of both sexes. They were led by Daniil M. Timoshenko, a metal worker in the iron foundry of the Briansk plant and a longtime Baptist presbyter. Sixteen times each month, one of their members, Fedoseev, hosted meetings at his home. By 1907 they had organized a Sunday school for their children.[35]

The prayer meeting was the central activity of a congregation. Although the degree of formality and the quality of the preaching and singing varied depending on the size and sophistication of the congregation, the basic pattern of Baptist services resembled that in the village of Skrybyshei, Kiev Province, described in 1909 by a seventeen-year-old member named Ivan

Bilenko: "We gather at the prayer house and sing psalms until all have arrived and then many extol the teaching of Christ from the Gospels and of the holy ["pro——"; illegible] of the Bible; at the end of the preaching by the word and teaching of Christ, we pray on our knees. We end with a psalm and a prayer and the meeting disperses." The prayers, he wrote, "are done as the spirit calls."[36]

Observers of large urban congregations reported similarly informal services, with active lay participation. They generally seem to have held two kinds of meetings: "invitational" meetings aimed at a general audience that was called to turn to Christ, and other gatherings for members only.[37] Some meetings might also be specially aimed at women or youth. Most congregations, whether urban or rural, met several times each week.

Many descriptions of meetings in St. Petersburg, for example, show that in any one week in the capital there was a great diversity of form and social composition of evangelical meetings, ranging from intimate gatherings in a worker's lodgings or in the home of Princess Lieven to large services in rented public halls. The official of the Ministry of Internal Affairs who specialized in Baptists, Semen Bondar', attended a series of such meetings in December 1909. On a Monday night, for example, 130 people, mostly workers, gathered at the Nobel House, a large public hall in the working-class Vyborg district. About 35 of these people seemed to have just come in off the street and a few of them had to be escorted out after laughing loudly and misbehaving. The Evangelical Christian presbyter, Savelii A. Alekseev, a shoemaker by trade, and the congregation's missionary, Vasilii I. Dolgopolov, preached, inviting people to turn to God.

The following Sunday Bondar' began his day with a service at the principal meeting place of the Baptist congregation, the auditorium of the Tenishev school. Attended by "up to 480 people," half of whom were described as "public from the intelligentsia," the meeting lasted until 1:00 P.M. and featured sermons by the Baptist pastor, the British-trained Latvian Vilgel'm Fetler, and the visiting director of a missionary school in London. Then, from 3:00 to 4:00, Bondar' sampled a Sunday school lesson in a run-down hall on Staro-Petergofskii Prospect. He described how a female teacher read from the Bible and explained the story to the seventy children present. The children then knelt and prayed "Pashkovite-style" before singing hymns.

Bondar' also gained entry to more intimate meetings. For example, he attended a gathering of sixteen people, workers and their children, in a small laborer's apartment. Two workers preached. First, an old man read and explained a chapter from the Bible, repeating over and over that, "we accepted this not from academies or seminaries, but from the Lord himself." Then a young male worker told the story of his conversion.[38]

There are no exact figures for assessing who filled the seats at evangelical meetings, but in the capital and elsewhere it appears to have been a socially mixed group, with lower-class people predominating. Descriptions of social composition in police, government, and newspaper sources feature many factory and railway workers, small traders, shop assistants, artisans, low-ranking soldiers, and peasants, with a smattering of university students and other educated people. There were certainly prosperous members who were able to contribute large sums to the movement, such as converts from the rich Molokan sheep-farming families of Mamontovs and Mazaevs. In St. Petersburg, both the Baptist and Evangelical Christian camps continued to enjoy the financial and moral support of several members of high society who had converted under the influence of Pashkov, as well as the use of their palatial homes for meetings. However, this seems to have been unique to the capital. Reports do not comment on the exact social makeup of peasant congregations, except for the occasional observation that peasants tended to become more prosperous upon joining.[39]

More socially elevated or educated believers were overrepresented in positions of leadership. Dei Mazaev, the longtime head of the Russian Baptist Union, was a rich sheep farmer; Vasilii Pavlov, president of the Baptists from 1909, was the son of a Tiflis merchant who had enough money to send Vasilii to study with Oncken in Germany for a year, while Prokhanov, also a merchant's son, became a mechanical engineer. All three were former Molokans, another common characteristic of the first generation of evangelical leaders.

Most pastors, by contrast, emerged from decidedly humble origins. The shoemaker, Alekseev, served as presbyter of the St. Petersburg Evangelical Christians. During World War I, the capital's Baptists selected as their leader Semen Abramovich Khokhlov, a young peasant worker from Moscow province employed at the Lessner machine works. In Kiev one group of Evangelical Christians chose Sidor I. Sudorov, a tailor, to minister to them, and the other chose the shoemaker I. F. Shcheritsa. A police report described Vasilii P. Stepanov, of the town of Peski, Voronezh Province, as a "self-educated peasant." Indeed, the governor of Kiev Province, which was home to ten thousand Baptists, commented in a 1912 report that the evangelicals were successful precisely because their propagandists were of the same class as those "most suited to accepting" their faith: "in the large and small villages—peasants, and in the towns and cities petty artisans, janitors, cab drivers and such."[40]

Anecdotal evidence suggests that there were roughly equal numbers of men and women in evangelical congregations. In some places, especially in Ukraine, men and women sat on different sides of the room during prayer meetings.[41] Women frequently signed petitions to the government on behalf of their congregations, a few women attended national congresses of Baptists or Evangelical Christians as delegates of their communities, and outsiders commented on the activities of traveling female missionaries. Some women began to form separate groups devoted to Bible study, mission, and charitable work and to organize special women's prayer meetings. Debates in the evangelical press reveal some disagreement within evangelical ranks about whether women should preach. This was based both on suggestions that preaching women might neglect their domestic responsibilities and disputes over the correct interpretation of St. Paul's words on the subject. There was clearly considerable local variation, but it would appear that, in most cases, women voted in congregational meetings and took their turn preaching at services.[42] On the whole, however, despite their considerable numbers and an ideology of spiritual equality, women were much less visible in the leadership of the evangelical community than were men.

Both outside commentators and Baptists themselves pointed to two important features of congregational life that appealed to believers: the participatory nature of evangelical services and the opportunities for associational life and personal development for people of different ages, educational levels, and interests rarely available elsewhere. In 1906 one St. Petersburg journalist contended that this was the reason the "Pashkovites" had become "one of the most stylish [sects] in the capital."[43]

Evangelical religion provided an interesting spectacle to the casual observer. For one thing, the physical appearance of Baptist places of worship, as well as their forms of liturgy and music, were greatly at odds with the surrounding Orthodox culture. In the Western style, Baptist congregations sat on benches or knelt during services rather than standing as in the Orthodox church. Without the icons that adorn an Orthodox sanctuary, their halls seemed plain and businesslike. Also contrary to Orthodox practice, singing was often accompanied by instrumental music. Free-form prayer was the feature of the services most frequently commented upon by outsiders. In contrast to the set liturgy of the state church, Baptist ministers composed their own prayers, and the services reserved time for members, male and female, to pray freely out loud. A St. Petersburg reporter, describing the prayers at a public meeting of Baptists, was clearly jarred by them: "Common prayer, to which the preacher called the 'brothers' and 'sisters,' had an extraordinarily strange character," he wrote, "and in many ways recalled the noise in the markets, hardly worthy of the name prayer. But the sectarians like this fragmentary, often incoherent and monotonous 'outpouring from the Soul,' continually adding to it with the word 'Amen.'"[44] Adherents confirmed the appeal of spontaneous prayer. For example, Bondar' reported that a worker who preached at an Evangelical Christian meeting in St. Petersburg in 1909 had dwelt on the theme of how believers ought to "pray not with memorized and prepared prayers but on the example of Christ, freely."[45]

This kind of religious practice enacted a new, voluntarist, participatory concept of community based on individual conversion and social and spiritual equality. As John Walsh has suggested in his study of Methodist and Evangelical societies in eighteenth-century England, liturgies have social implications: leaders of the Church of England were deeply troubled by precisely the extempore prayer that these societies favored over the set forms of the Anglican service. These set forms, not unlike Orthodox liturgical practices, "were deeply symbolic of the Tory social ideal of a static, hierarchical, orderly community governed by prescription." Extempore prayer thus represented a transformative intrusion of religious individualism into the community's worship.[46] The prayer meeting modeled the new community of spiritual equals.

If the liturgy represented the notion of the church as a covenant of freely acting adults, so, too, did the congregational structure. Various organizations sought to reproduce a community that relied on conversion for its growth by preparing believers' children to experience conversion and by training its members to convert others.

Thus attention to youth was particularly important. Although the Pashkovites in St. Petersburg had already begun to work among students before 1905, youth groups were otherwise a great novelty and one of the major Baptist organizational initiatives after the declaration of religious toleration. Groups could be either self-initiated or the product of a pastor's efforts.[47] From about 1908 they became increasingly common, playing an important role in urban as well as rural congregational life. Teenagers and young adults met for their own services, held Bible studies, founded libraries and literary circles, organized Sunday schools for the younger children, performed charitable and evangelical work, and assisted one another financially. In fact, in Khar'kov, the lucky girls had the privilege of sewing underwear at cut rates for the male members of the group as part of their contribution to "mutual aid"! On the model of English evangelicals, they also organized "evenings of Christian Love," programs of religious singing and inspirational speeches, followed by tea and other refreshments that became a popular form of celebration and mission among the evangelicals. Young women as well as young men preached and gave recitations at these festivals.[48] The groups thus combined spiritual development with socializing. Leaders reported that such ventures promoted conversions among both Baptists' children and young Orthodox attracted to these groups.[49] Ironically the youth groups' liveliness can be deduced from the repeatedly expressed concerns of older leaders about how to rein in their enthusiasm and keep them under congregational control.[50]

In some places young women organized separate groups. One very active example was the young women's circle of the St. Petersburg Evangelical Christians. At first, members had trouble finding a meeting time, since many of them were in service and worked until 8:00 or 9:00 each evening, while nannies and parlormaids often had only a few hours of free time each month. In its first three years, nevertheless, membership grew to about fifty members. In addition to organizing prayer meetings and working in the Sunday school, members made and sold needlework to support the congregation's mission and to fund their own work with poor children.[51]

In April 1908, a small congress of twenty Baptists and Evangelical Christians met in Moscow to discuss youth groups as a new organizational form. Inspired by the model of youth groups abroad, which had their own evangelists, libraries, and programs of work, these delegates resolved to promote this idea widely.[52] The following year the Evangelical Christians founded an "Evangelical Union of Christian Youth" and established a journal, *Molodoi vinogradnik* [Young vineyard], which existed for several years.[53] Between 1911 and 1916 the Baptists also published a journal called *Drug molodezhi* [Friend of youth]. Both Evangelical Christians and Baptists supported special youth missionaries, such as the very popular young woman from Samara, Tereziia Kirsh, who traveled around starting new groups and providing support to those already in existence.[54]

Women and youth served actively in the emerging Sunday school system as well. In early 1910 the Ministry of Internal Affairs knew of at least ten addresses where children's meetings were held each week in St. Petersburg and noted their popularity with non-Baptist parents as well as with believers.[55] This was not merely a phenomenon of the capital. In 1909, in the Voronezh province town of Peski, for example, 110 girls and 90 boys attended the Baptists' Sunday school, guided by 8 male and 12 female teachers. These children's meetings, according to the pastor, had fostered conversions among the older youth, which, in turn, "led to an awakening in the church and among nonbelievers in our settlement."[56]

The Baptists also engaged in various forms of mutual aid and charitable work. Church and state observers frequently commented on these features as a source of appeal.[57] Some assistance was rather informal, such as selling one another land at reduced prices or providing shelter and food for a widow and her children.[58] Through *Bratskii listok* and other magazines, believers supported one another financially, as well as spiritually, in times of need. Money was collected for victims of fires, to help in the building of prayer houses, and for the missionaries' pension fund. Baptists were particularly proud of the asylum for orphans and elderly Baptists from across the national fellowship that they established in the town of Balashov, Saratov Province, in 1913.[59]

Mission formed the core of the Baptist outlook and was the driving force behind efforts at organization. The Baptists took seriously Jesus's commandment to "Go forth therefore and make all nations my disciples." These words from Matthew 28 graced the front page of their journal, *Baptist*, and made mission the trust of each individual member. As the Tambov governor wrote in a detailed report on missionary activity in his area, "Without distinction of sex, age, intellectual development, position in the congregation, and other criteria—every Baptist without fail strives for the propaganda of his religious teaching. Even semiliterate and completely illiterate members use all their efforts for the seduction [*soblazn*] of the Orthodox."[60] Certainly reports of missionary activity filled the pages of Baptist and Evangelical Christian magazines and peppered believers' private correspondence.

The evangelicals excelled at bringing their message to the places where people gathered and at speaking their language. Their services were in Russian, as opposed to the Church Slavonic of the Orthodox liturgy, and their hymns easily understood.[61] Believers handed out leaflets in the streets. They

41

made gramophone records of sermons and music. In the capital the Baptists' street mission ventured down to Nevskii Prospect at night, successfully drawing prostitutes and others to a midnight service, while missionaries along the Black Sea coast preached among workers in the dockyards. As an Orthodox guide to combating religious sectarianism declared: "They have penetrated where we are not and where we never are. So, they propagandize in factories, in plants, on the railway, on steamships, in the fleet, in mines, in pits, even in taverns, in public places and so on and so on."[62] These missionaries certainly made extensive use of the improved possibilities for mobility offered by the railroad and steamship. And trains not only supplied a means of transportation but also sites for proselytizing activity.[63]

If mission was the fuel that drove the evangelical movement, the missionary network served as a web to bind it together. The missionaries planted new churches, supported fledgling groups, performed rituals, resolved disputes, and provided legal advice. In all these ways they lent the authority of a broader movement to the initiatives of local congregations.

A small number of missionaries worked full-time, funded by the Baptist or Evangelical Christian unions or by various local groups of congregations. A good example of this type of missionary is Baptist Mikhail Fedorovich Iashchenko, a former painter living in the port city of Agapa, on the Black Sea coast. During 1907–8 he made five trips away from home, covering 5,704 versts by rail, 292 by wagon, and 2,145 by sea. He preached more than two hundred sermons in that time. Most of Iashchenko's work was in the Cossack regions of southern Russia and along the Black Sea coast, but he also traveled to Baku, Tiflis, and Batum in the Transcaucasus region.[64]

Individual congregations also worked to spread their faith throughout their local districts and beyond. This was accomplished by regular members, through personal contacts, by evangelists commissioned by their communities, and by many pastors who devoted one or more months each year to itinerant preaching. Among the most active of these was Fedor P. Balikhin, the presbyter of the large village of Astrakhanka, near Berdichev and the Sea of Azov coast. Balikhin had been born there into a family of poor Molokan peasants in 1854, and his education had been limited to two winters at the local *zemstvo* school. At the age of twenty-five, on a trip to Khar'kov, he had encountered a Bible Society book distributor who had challenged his Molokan convictions with new evangelical views. The further influence of visits from Baptist preachers such as Nikita Voronin and Vasilii Pavlov to Astrakhanka eventually led him to take water baptism in 1882. From that time on he spent part of each year traveling across Russia as a preacher for the Baptist Union. By 1908 he reported having visited thirty-five provinces.[65]

In the first two years after 1905 Balikhin brought a choir and the Baptist message to twenty-nine special meetings in small towns and larger cities across the south of the empire. Benefiting from the legal uncertainties of the revolutionary era and the apparent leniency of the governor of Taurida

Province, Balikhin was able to gain permission to hold large meetings in city theaters, in clubs, or in temperance society halls. He would advertise these events widely by means of posters and fliers. A curious public filled the seats. At a series of meetings in Berdiansk in 1907 he distributed 250 free copies of the New Testament as well as 72 pounds of brochures and tracts, which his congregation purchased.[66]

Balikhin also attended to the task of planting new churches and developing those already in existence. With this goal in mind, he ordained many new presbyters in the first years after 1905. In an example of the formation of new churches, he reported that he had held five meetings in the town of Bol'shoi Tokmak in Taurida Province in the spring of 1907 at the home of a believer, Petr Petrovich Perk. Many of those who attended had never been present at such a meeting before and, according to Balikhin, "turned out to be unaccustomed either to listening or to sitting." At the beginning of the first session Balikhin briefly explained the goal of Baptist meetings and their character. He then gave sermons about the love of God and the sacrifice of Christ, outlining the Baptist understanding of repentance and salvation. These were the first such meetings in the town, wrote Balikhin, and he felt as though he had penetrated a "deep forest."[67]

Another role for the evangelist was to fight division in the ranks of believers. In many cases this took the form of reinforcing the faith of congregations beset by competing influences. For example, in Alupka, near Yalta on the Crimean coast, the Baptist Union's missionary, Iashchenko, found himself combating the influence of a rival sect, the Seventh-Day Adventists, and of revolutionaries "who cause powerful harm to the local church." Complementing such efforts was the work of evangelists in mediating congregational disputes. Iashchenko recounted his trip to Kiev, where, although without success, he had attempted to reconcile two factions that had appeared in the church and were disputing whether to register the congregation in accordance with the law of 17 October 1906.[68]

The missionary network also provided advice on dealing with the legal intricacies associated with formally leaving the Orthodox Church, registering prayer meetings and congregations, or securing permission for prayer houses. The files of the Ministry of Internal Affairs contain reports from areas as diverse as Kursk Province in European Russia to the Terek district in the extreme south to Siberia, where applications for leaving the Orthodox Church were submitted on preprinted form letters. According to an investigation by the governor of Smolensk, the Baptist legal activist Kushnerov prepared such forms to assist local activists in aiding new members to formalize their conversions legally.[69]

Contact with a missionary often precipitated an atmosphere of religious revival in local congregations. For example, V. Novikov wrote to *Bratskii listok* to describe what happened during the five-day visit of Aleksei Vasil'evich Borisov in January 1907. During one meeting, as the congregation prepared to sing, "suddenly one semiliterate and ill-informed young brother stood up and with great fervor said to the meeting that sinners should repent because the voice of the Lord will not always call and so on[;] and at that moment the Lord aroused many souls and the grace of God touched the most cold and hardened of hearts and smashed them like a hammer; the whole gathering prayed with strong wailing, out of turn, tears of repentance and joy poured like a stream and up until the present time lively and blessed meetings are taking place."[70] By joining local groups at important moments in their congregational lives, bringing inspiration and sacraments to isolated communities, combating competing influences, and working to preserve unity in local groups, missionaries such as Iashchenko, Balikhin, and Borisov strove to create and reinforce a sense of common purpose among believers scattered across the great distances of Russia.

At the same time evangelists found themselves balancing the need to provide cohesion and common practices to local communities, the denomination's stress on congregational autonomy, and the inexperience of local leaders seeking guidance. This can be seen in a set of instructions drawn up in 1907 for Baptist missionaries. They were required to "do exclusively the work of evangelism; they may baptize, celebrate the Lord's Supper, and perform marriages only with the agreement of the local presbyter or, in his absence, of the congregation; in the interest of preserving unity and peace they should refrain from criticism of the decisions and practices existing in each particular location, not interfering at all in the internal affairs of the congregation."[71]

The overwhelming commitment to spreading the faith also underpinned attempts to unify evangelical congregations into some sort of national organization. Certainly this constituted a major theme of discussion at the 1907 St. Petersburg joint congress.[72] Ironically, however, 1907 saw the beginning of what would be a permanent split between the Russian Baptist Union and the followers of Prokhanov. By 1909 two separate unions, the Union of Russian Evangelical Christians-Baptists and the All-Russian Union of Evangelical Christians sought to coordinate this network of congregations and missionaries.

Baptists have historically recognized the value of forming denominational associations, but their individualistic spiritual and organizational tenets have also made them prickly about compromise.[73] As William Henry Brackney writes, "Baptists are a denominational family with a common heritage but at the same time they have done everything imaginable to atomize their respective identities."[74] Similarly Paul Steeves points out that Russian Baptists displayed a "marked reluctance to submit to the hierarchy of a nation-wide structure and a propensity to divide among themselves."[75]

The fact that agreeing on a name for the movement constituted one of the main obstacles to unification demonstrates the tenaciously congregational outlook of believers. Among converts, a fierce debate emerged in the early twentieth century over the use of the term "Baptist." When communities first formed they called themselves by a variety of names: Christians baptized in faith, Gospel Christians, the society of friends of God, Christians of evangelical faith, the society of converts to the new Russian brotherhood, or Baptists.[76] As these groups began to reach out to one another and form associations, the issue of a standardized name arose. The Baptist Union had long acknowledged variations in how its members designated themselves; in an effort to address the problem it had even adopted the name "Union of Russian Evangelical Christians-Baptists" in 1903. Many believers, however, remained unconvinced. At the first congress of the Union after the 1905 Revolution, held in Rostov-on-Don in May 1906, one of the delegates asked whether all members were required to call themselves "Baptist." He explained that there were many believers who were eager to form a union of all Russian Baptists but regarded the term "Baptist" itself as "nonbiblical and non-Russian."[77] After all, the term bore no relation to the Russian word for baptism, *kreshchenie.*

Questions of hierarchy and authority also played a part in dividing the Baptists and the Evangelical Christians theologically: although the groups basically shared common principles, the Baptists held to a stricter view of membership and ordination than did the Evangelical Christians. The latter generally placed less emphasis on doctrinal exclusiveness and had a looser approach to church formation, eschewing the need for ordination and advocating an open communion.[78]

Probably the most important factor contributing to the organizational split between the Baptists and Evangelical Christians was Prokhanov's ambition to dominate the movement. From the turn of the century on, he increasingly strove to differentiate the northern branch of the movement from the Baptists, insisting on the name "Evangelical Christians" and promoting himself as the visionary leader destined to lead all Russian Protestants.[79] In 1906 he tried to found a "Russian Evangelical Union" that would bring together various groups on the model of the international Evangelical Alliance. Although he solicited some interest among Pashkovites and various evangelical groups in the capital, the Baptists were divided in their response. The Union was approved by the Ministry of Internal Affairs in 1908 and held one meeting in early 1909, but, despite the loudly expressed anxieties of the Orthodox Church, it never came to much.[80]

Already existing divisions were solidified in September 1909, when Prokhanov convened a congress in St. Petersburg that laid the groundwork for a separate Evangelical Christian union, officially declared at a further congress over the New Year, 1910–11. Competition between the two streams of the movement—but also efforts to unify them—would henceforth divert a portion of their energies.

Both the Baptist and Evangelical Christian unions were basically loose coordinating bodies that met most years in congresses and between times worked through correspondence, missionaries, and magazines. Their main financial activity remained the support of missionary work. The Baptist

Union, for example, commissioned between thirteen and twenty-nine missionaries each year to spend from two to eight months in the mission field away from home.[81] These unions also represented Russian evangelicals in the emerging international Baptist arena. In 1905, a Baptist World Alliance was founded with the goal of creating and expressing a "Baptist world consciousness."[82] Russian delegations, made up of both Baptists and Evangelical Christians, attended its inaugural congress in London in 1905, as well as the 1908 European Baptist Congress in Berlin and the 1911 Baptist World Alliance Congress in Philadelphia, where Prokhanov was elected one of ten Alliance vice presidents.[83]

These unions were technically illegal. The law made no provision for the formation of associations of congregations, but believers were undeterred in their drive to unify for the purposes of mission. And, fundamentally, all this missionary activity and many aspects of congregational life rejected the limited interpretation of the rights of religious dissidents embodied in the 17 October 1906 law. The very idea of the itinerant preacher repudiated the notion of a fixed congregation with a spiritual leader tied exclusively to it. Local communities strove to register their area of influence as broadly as possible. The government, by contrast, tried unsuccessfully to prevent pastors such as Balikhin from describing themselves with titles such as "presbyter of the Russian Baptists" instead of using narrow, geographic designations.[84]

Through their ecclesiastical organization, their liturgical practices, their missionary network, and their associational life, the evangelicals behaved as though they lived in an individualistic, pluralistic polity. And these Baptist activities generated public curiosity and responded to needs not met elsewhere in the community. As chapter 4 will show, whether they approved or disapproved of the Baptists' activities, outsiders of sharply contrasting political persuasions were all agreed on two issues: that evangelical organizational techniques were modern, and that the expansion of the evangelicals was symptomatic of an emerging civil society in Russia. But first we turn to the personal narratives of the new converts who filled Baptist pews in order to glimpse how they understood their religious choices in a time of rapid social and political change.

3

A Community of Converts

Conversion Narratives and Social Experience

As the Russian Baptist movement expanded in the early twentieth century, its members were constantly telling one another stories. Preaching by ordinary believers and witnessing to personal conversion experiences played an important part in prayer meetings. Whether in public or private settings, converts sought to interpret and share with fellow believers and with society at large a vision of their religious life and social experience. These stories were not just part of an oral tradition. They permeated Baptists' personal papers and the poetry, hymns, stories, articles, and letters to the editor of the Russian evangelical press. Above all, they were features of a major literary art form of the Russian Baptists, the conversion narrative. In 1928 the journal *Baptist Ukrainy* even published instructions on how to write a conversion account.[1] This chapter examines the collective story that Russian Baptists developed for their movement, using more than one hundred personal narratives published in books and journals between 1906 and 1928 or written by Bible school applicants in the mid-1920s.[2] These accounts demonstrate the importance of the spiritual in the elaboration of new conceptions of the individual and community in an era of revolutions. In the stories of their faith journeys, Russian Baptists chronicled their coming to awareness as individuals, but they also asserted the importance of new kinds of communities to sustain these individuals in a turbulent age.

The very process of social and political modernization in Russia transformed the religious playing field. It raised questions about the place of the Orthodox religion in the Russian state and in Russian identity, and, more generally, about the relevance of faith in the modern age. Imperial Russia had long proclaimed itself Holy, and indivisibly Orthodox, but social and political change were giving voice to groups like the Baptists that challenged that self-image. This was a period of rapid economic and social transformation, of war and revolution. Well before the Bolshevik Revolution launched its drive to build a socialist society, the traditional isolation of the village was broken down through rapid expansion of the railway system and intensive state-driven industrialization, creating links to a Russia-wide market. Rising literacy, mass circulation newspapers, and widespread labor migration similarly altered traditional social patterns. These experiences made Russians of diverse walks of life into seekers, looking for ways to draw cultural sense out of the surrounding disorder and dislocation, and to carve out a place for themselves in the new society. Historians are familiar with the many workers who drew revolutionary conclusions from this tumultuous context.[3] Other possible new identities competed with the revolutionary model, however. Most accounts of the emergence and fostering of revolutionary consciousness tend to dismiss Orthodoxy as a tool of the imperial regime, of little relevance to the evolution of workers' identities. New research, however, is showing that a genuine spiritual quest animated Russian popular culture throughout the revolutionary period.[4] The secularizing process that made religion an individual choice, rather than a birthright, actually helped to unleash these spiritual forces.[5] Russian Baptists' conversion narratives constitute some of the best sources for examining the role of religion in the evolution of new identities in revolutionary Russia.

The Baptists' preoccupation with stories of their conversions is not surprising. Professing an adult personal conversion is the prerequisite for baptism by full immersion and membership in the church.[6] Moreover, as the evangelical movement grew rapidly, it experienced many new conversions and sought to encourage more. Through their conversion narratives, believers set out a model path for becoming a Russian Baptist and presented the Baptist faith as a legitimate spiritual choice for Russians. The Baptist faith was widely perceived as "foreign," but converts rejected this view, portraying evangelical conversion as a natural outgrowth of broader Russian popular aspirations and, indeed, as the solution to the ignorance, hatred, hierarchy, and spiritual emptiness that they believed plagued Russian society as a whole. Thus Russian Baptists used the stories of their own spiritual development to challenge others to see the world in their terms and to assert a religious solution to the problems of their times.

The great majority of Baptists, including those who told their conversion stories, were peasants, artisans, and industrial workers. Like other worker autobiographers, these lower-class Russians sought new means to express their deepening self-awareness as individuals.[7] In writing about their conversions, Russian Baptists asserted the significance of their individual spiritual experience and painted a picture of a social, intellectual, and spiritual community that could satisfy the popular spiritual aspirations and longings in Russian society. This was an egalitarian community that valued simplicity, mutual aid, and self-education, but one based on religious rather than class consciousness.

This chapter focuses on how the Baptists interpreted the social context of their conversions and related it to their religious experience. The events recounted in their conversion stories were selected and shaped to show a deeper meaning below the surface facts. Like all spiritual autobiographies, they aimed at holding the loyalty of the faithful while winning new converts to the cause. They can be said, as recent work on the use of stories and memoirs as historical sources suggests, not only to record but also to construct experiences. For the Russian Baptists, as for other communities, autobiographies, testimonies, and conversion discourses prove to be profoundly social, a means of relating one's personal experience to the larger social and cultural community.[8] The very process of recounting their conversions made ordinary laypeople into preachers. As they told of their spiritual rebirths, they both asserted their membership in the new community and invited prospective converts to reexamine their own lives and to join the community's collective narrative.

The archetypal Russian Baptist conversion narrative was that of Vasilii V. Skaldin, a missionary of the Russian Baptist Union who was serving in the town of Lozovaia, Ekaterinoslav Province, in 1914, when his account was published in the Baptist weekly magazine *Slovo istiny* [Word of truth]. As a professional missionary, he had no doubt perfected his story's dramatic effect. Certainly his article, titled "From Ignorance to Truth," opens with the didactic declaration: "The goal of describing my conversion—may the Lord give strength to this story—is for His glory and for the conversion of many spirits like me."[9] Nevertheless his tale illuminates important themes that recur in many other accounts, both published and unpublished: an ordinary person making his way in a changing world, the contest between political and religious answers to social problems, the search for salvation in Russian popular religion, the theological solution to these problems that the Baptist faith offered, the cultural conflict within oneself and in relation to others brought on by leaving the Orthodox Church, and the emergence of a Russian evangelical community.

Skaldin opened his own tale with a picture of how Orthodox ritual was embedded in peasant life and contrasted this with the temptations of the city, where he had gone to seek work. Born in 1873 to a family of poor peasants in the village of Almazovo, Orel Province, Skaldin left the village as a young man for work in the Iuzovka mines. His family and friends rose early to see him off to the "other side": as Skaldin stood with a sack containing his trousers, bast shoes, and several pounds of rye rusks, his parents, bearing the family's icons, gave him their blessing. This pious send-off did not have the desired effect. According to Skaldin, "all that I acquired in two years [at the mine] was not money, but only full knowledge of evil and debauchery." After a successful period of military service, during which he rose to noncommissioned officer, Skaldin married, but he soon left his wife in the village and went to Odessa for work. When all his money was stolen upon his arrival there, he fell into dissolute living and thoughts of suicide.

It was during this traumatic period for Skaldin that his "conscience awoke and [he] began to search for God with [his] whole heart." He began to reread the prayer books he had received during military service. After finding work as a policeman, he moved into a police barracks, where he drew the admiration of some and the mockery of others for his daily Bible reading and his assiduous care of the barracks' icon corner. He prayed so ardently before the iconostasis of the Panteleimon monastery that one day a monk shooed him away, accusing him of showing off.[10] Like many others who eventually became Baptists, a rediscovery of his Orthodox roots preceded Skaldin's final conversion. This process of gradual awakening was a popular theme in the conversion narratives.

Skaldin's account shared with others a strong sense that personal displacement brought the possibility not only of troubling disorder but also of new spiritual discoveries. Movement from one's place of origin, whether for military service, education, or employment, or through the vagaries of a period of war and revolution, echoed the spiritual journeys recounted in Russian Baptists' life stories.[11] One young man who converted in Siberia in 1920, after his family had fled famine in Moscow, recalled later that, "God sent us to Siberia, like Moses into the desert, so that we could meet God. Living in Moscow, we never would have had this encounter with Him."[12]

Although the conversion stories were shaped by the goal of turning their readers toward the Baptist salvation, they do reflect the social realities of the day. Government and church officials observed that peasants who moved back and forth to the cities for work played an essential role in disseminating new religious beliefs. The governor of Tambov Province, for example, attributed the spread of Baptist ideas in his jurisdiction in large part to this cause. In a 1912 letter to the Department of Spiritual Affairs of the Ministry of Internal Affairs, he wrote: "The Orthodox peasant heads for wage labor to the Caucasus, to the Don Region, to Petersburg, Moscow and other cities, lives in the sectarian milieu for a year or two and returns home a baptized Baptist, to the temptation of his relatives and fellow villagers."[13] In the 1920s the displacements, hunger, and disorder associated with war and revolution joined labor migration and military service in framing Baptists' conversions. Local reports in the journals *Baptist*, *Khristianin*, and *Baptist Ukrainy* of this later period frequently alluded to the role of converted soldiers returning from the front in organizing Baptist communities in their home towns.[14]

Like Skaldin, most writers described a period when the sinfulness of the world became very apparent to them, whether it was through their own experience of pleasure-seeking vice or through exposure to the ways of a disorderly and troubled society. Ivan Nikonorovich Ivanov, a Bible school applicant, left his village for Moscow at the age of fifteen to serve an apprenticeship in the foundry of a mechanical plant. Until the age of twenty he was "modest in all ways," led a quiet life, attended church regularly, and performed the Orthodox rituals meticulously. But then he "tasted the vice of drunkenness," and, he wrote, "soon I had a gloomy and bleak life, the worldly life seemed somehow inexplicable and until 1919 I don't want to describe any more the condition I was in."[15] Likewise Nikolai Ivanovich Ziubanov, an applicant to the Bible Courses for local activists run by the evangelicals in Leningrad in 1924, began work in the mines after finishing primary school at the age of thirteen. His earlier concern for his soul faded as "the bad fellowship of my comrades corrupted my good morals and I sank to sinning, vices: deception, card playing, disrespect for elders, foul language and even disbelief."[16]

Those on the path to conversion sought escape not just from a life of dissolution but also from worldly disorder and from public morality and human relations that did not conform to their ideals. When Skaldin first began to search for God, after his flirtation with a life of drink and revelry, he found himself tormented by the way in which he had enjoyed exercising power over his subordinates during his military service. Iosif Ivanovich Vol'skii, a machinist from Minsk, was wracked by guilt over turning his father in to the political police after the revolution.[17] Boris Alekseevich Borovkov wrote that he had been "witness to great events (civil war, famine in the Volga) and all this convinced me that the word of God is being realized, and the people without Christ and His love will perish."[18] In some cases the Bible provided ammunition for social criticism. A cab driver with whom Skaldin discussed his spiritual quest rattled Skaldin's reverence for authority by pointing out the biblical passage in Matthew 23:13, where Jesus said, "Alas, alas for you, lawyers and Pharisees, hypocrites that you are! You shut the door of the kingdom of Heaven in men's faces; you do not enter yourselves, and when others are entering, you stop them."[19]

The Baptists' stories were not simply about the inability of simple individuals by themselves to withstand the temptations and pressures of the urban-industrial environment. They also took aim at perceived flaws in the mainstream religious culture. The classic pattern of the conversion stories, of which Skaldin's is a model, implies that the traditional religion could not keep pace with developments in society. Orthodoxy was rooted in the highly ritualized cultural practices of the village. To the converts, it could not provide a sustainable defense against the pressures, temptations, and outright debauchery of cities and mining towns. According to their conversion stories, the solutions to these new evils proved not to lie in returning to the religion of their youths but in awakening to a new, evangelical religion encountered in the cities themselves. Yet at the same time that their stories criticize Orthodoxy, they also reveal the vitality of popular religious practices. They point to the importance, only recently being explored by historians, of religious attitudes in shaping lower-class Russians' search for meaning in late imperial and early Soviet Russia.

The great majority of writers recalled actively religious Orthodox childhoods. Foma Nikolaevich Konovalov, for example, wrote of growing up in the early years of the twentieth century in a village in Tula Province. His parents were religious and regularly attended church in the nearby village. Konovalov was the priest's star pupil, and by the age of ten he had been put in charge of teaching catechism to the younger children.[20] An Orenburg Cossack affectionately described the religious atmosphere of his childhood in a 1906 magazine account as follows:

> My grandfather and father were very religious people in the Orthodox sense. They attended church all the time; my father went to matins and mass before the ringing of the bells; at home, he had Holy Scripture and the lives of saints. On holidays after the liturgy all the old men and women came to his house and he read them these books. He himself did not like the bad life, took in wanderers, the poor, visited the sick, clothed the naked, gave alms, and prayed to God.

Such nostalgia, or at least acceptance of the genuineness of Orthodox spiritual experience, was unusual. Extensive description of Orthodox popular piety was not.[21]

Of course, not every conversion story contained the usual element of a personal evolution from Orthodoxy to evangelicalism. Not all converts came from families that provided Orthodox models for conducting one's life. For some, religious training was either absent or perfunctory.[22] Other Baptists conceded that their parents' faith had been genuine but portrayed it as based on ignorance and the ritualistic performance of religious duties. A convert with the suggestive pseudonym of "Saul" wrote in *Baptist Ukrainy* that, although he was born into an Orthodox family and learned the standard prayers, "my parents told me little about God, because they knew little themselves."[23]

Some conversion narratives left the misleading impression that Orthodoxy had not figured in the author's past. Nikolai Ziubanov, in his Bible school application, opened his conversion narrative by asserting that, "before conversion, I lived as do all people of this world, without religious convictions." Yet, on a separate piece of paper labeled "Biography," Ziubanov recounted being raised by a father who was an "enthusiastic performer of the rituals of the Orthodox Church" and reader of religious books. As a child, he recalled, he had learned all the Orthodox rituals and voraciously read "anything that came into my hands, including religious [literature], which had a deep effect on me." Indeed, one religious pamphlet had reduced him to tears over his sinful state and aroused the longing to enter a monastery.[24] Although Ziubanov downplayed his youthful piety to the point of denial in telling of his conversion to the Baptist faith, it is clear that the values of his childhood prepared the ground for his later religious searching. A comparison of Ziubanov's two accounts also illustrates what Lewis R. Rambo terms the "biographical reconstruction" implicit in the process of religious conversion and religious testimonials. Baptist autobiographers like Ziubanov drew from their experience the elements that conformed with major themes in other conversion stories they had heard and that best fit the inspirational message they were delivering.[25] Just as debauchery may have amounted to a couple of weeks of teenaged naughtiness, so a life "without God" may have actually involved considerable religious training.

Many converts with Orthodox roots, such as Skaldin, described their attempts to resolve by Orthodox means the spiritual questions that troubled them. Just as Skaldin's first idea, after his "conscience awoke," was to reread his prayer books and appoint himself guardian of the police barracks' iconostasis, so others turned to the writings, clergy, and spiritual practices among which they had been raised for guidance. One convert from the Amur region resolved to memorize the entire book of psalms; another became assiduous in fulfilling all fasts and rituals; and yet another was "moved by religious feelings after which I had to leave my house and take the form of a religious wanderer [*strannik*]."[26] Ultimately the future Baptists were disappointed by Orthodoxy, accusing it of tolerating debauchery and, more important, of being unable to assure its followers of salvation.

Apart from making their point about the inadequacies of Orthodoxy, these stories vividly convey how much the Russian popular culture of the day was imbued by religious searching. In reading aloud devotional literature and debating religious ideas, Skaldin and his friends in the police barracks were taking part in a popular pastime. It was in such discussions that some future converts remembered their first exposure to Baptist ideas. They recalled hanging around as children while their parents participated in religious gatherings or debated matters of the spirit with a shtundist passing through town. For example, the Orenburg Cossack who so proudly remembered his father's piety was first exposed to Baptist ideas when his father invited a man from another village, about whom it was said that "he believes in the Gospel in some kind of special way," to discuss religious questions.[27]

The long Orthodox tradition of monasticism and asceticism also played a central role in converts' accounts of their attempts to find religious answers by Orthodox means. Although many evangelical autobiographers such as Skaldin had merely sought a source of spiritual solace in Orthodoxy, a few went so far as to join a monastery.[28] The peasant Savva Kalenivich Lishchishin of Podol'sk Province recounted his spiritual autobiography to a Baptist in Kiev, who in turn reported the story in the pages of *Baptist* in 1910. Until the age of twenty-nine, Lishchishin had given little thought to questions of salvation. In 1906, however, he reported, "[the Lord] strongly disturbed my heart, and I began to think seriously about the condition of my soul, and therefore I decided to seek salvation at any price." He began zealously to read "books on saints and the ascetics of the caves; I read about their life in monasteries, about fasts, vigils, prayers." Through this reading he developed "a passion and desire . . . to travel and reverence the holy sites." He set off first for the famous Monastery of the Caves in Kiev, where he was distressed to find that the life of the monks did not live up to the ideals of his books; after similar experiences at two other monasteries, he concluded that in Orthodox monasteries "there was no living participation for the soul or the word of God acting in the soul." His quest took him to St. Petersburg to the charismatic spiritual leader Father John of Kronshtadt, and eventually to a renunciation of Orthodox practice in favor of the Baptist faith.[29]

Through reading groups, discussions, and visits to monasteries, future Russian Baptists participated in a vital popular culture of religious inquiry in early twentieth-century Russia. Brenda Meehan has observed that the late imperial period witnessed a "contemplative revival," stimulated on the popular level by the widespread distribution of lives of saints and other devotional literature.[30] Similarly Vera Shevzov has suggested that, in Vologda Province, "the striving of the rural faithful for spiritual guidance [was] a characteristic trait of mainstream Orthodoxy," and rural believers were ready to devote much of their free time to listening to instructive religious reading. Moreover, she contends, the message put forth by the most popular religious literature, such as lives of saints and brochures on spiritual issues, and implied in the approach of the study groups, was one that emphasized a personal path to faith and salvation rather than one mediated by the church.[31]

Both Baptist autobiographers and analysts of Russian popular culture of the time noted this widespread yearning for personal salvation. In a 1913 essay on the spiritual quests of Russian sectarians published in *Missionerskoe obozrienie* [Missionary review], the journal of the Orthodox internal mission, Georgii Chaikin argued that this striving was rooted in the condition of the Russian populace. "In the complete absence of any freedom and originality in civic and public life, our simple people naturally tried to make up for it with originality in its spiritual life, independence in the area of thoughts and feelings," he wrote. Protestant ideas were successful, he insisted, only because they were "a direct answer to really existing spiritual needs of the people." Indeed, he concluded, many converts to religious sectarianism had previously been models of Orthodox piety.[32] The accounts of the Baptist autobiographers implicitly argue that the Russian Baptist movement grew out of a culture of active religious inquiry and idealism, whereas the lifestyle of the Orthodox clergy and their inability to give seekers assurances of salvation were bound to disappoint.

The Baptist autobiographers recognized that religion was not the only po-

Baptists at home, early twentieth century.
From Iasevich-Borodaevskaia, Bor'ba za vieru, 1912.

tential source of solutions to the predicaments of individual Russians and their society. Several authors advanced the notion that revolution and religion were both understandable responses to their own and their country's need for salvation.[33] Skaldin recounted how, at his police post by the gates of Odessa's Aleksandrovskii Park, he was exposed to many new ideas. Some passers-by tried to interest him in politics, others in their religious views. Notwithstanding his newfound piety, Skaldin reported that, "I became fascinated by the spirit of revolution, became its fervent supporter and zealous propagandist." Skaldin quite explicitly connected his religious and political explorations: the Bible, with its condemnation of lawyers and pharisees, first led him to question the structures of authority he had taken for granted. Revolutionary literature explained the origins of injustice in social and power relations and offered class hatred as a solution; by contrast, his account implies, the Baptists answered the problem of class and social divisions through love and a community of spiritual equals.[34]

In a similar vein "Saul," before he was converted to the Baptist religion, had wrestled with the question of whether personal and collective salvation would come from revolution or religious revival. Fighting with the Reds in the civil war, he had believed that Russia could only be saved through a rejection of God. "I wanted," he wrote, "for all humanity and especially Russian people to reject God as quickly as possible. Burning with this desire, I always and everywhere preached godlessness."[35] One young woman, Irina Sergeevna Gavrisheva, joined the Ukrainian Socialist Revolutionaries when revolution came in 1917 but soon left because "the narrow national movement of the Ukrainian SRs [Socialist Revolutionaries] did not satisfy the needs of my spirit." She then spent the civil war years as a Bolshevik before finally resolving her spiritual quest among the Baptists.[36] Similarly Orthodox Church commentators also saw a connection between popular religious experimentation and political experimentation. As the annual report for 1911 of the St. Petersburg diocese stated, "The Russian people, after having lived through the revolutionary disturbances, disillusioned with human efforts to create a better life, having lost faith in the sincerity of human actions, in recent years increasingly seeks paths to God for its salvation. And, at that minute, sectarian preachers say to them . . . 'you're already forgiven.'"[37]

Russian Baptists' conversion stories usually drive home the point that, in the end, neither the religious traditions of their youths nor revolutionary politics could offer them the assurance of salvation that they craved. Instead, Baptist autobiographers emphasize the role of ordinary believers in shaping the thinking of potential converts and in guiding them toward achieving salvation. In so doing they paint a picture of an egalitarian, self-educating movement of working people.

In Skaldin's case, for example, the crucial actor was a simple pie seller. One day, as Skaldin stood at his post covertly reading a banned book, the pie seller engaged him in conversation, asking whether he was a Christian. Skaldin was initially insulted, replying: "And who do you think I am, a Tatar or something? . . . Do you want me to show you my cross?" But then the pie seller asked him whether he had been saved. Finding himself uncertain of the answer, Skaldin listened with interest to the simple trader's theological explanations and accepted his invitation to attend a Baptist prayer meeting. At a little house in the slums on the outskirts of Odessa, Skaldin found the believers' gathering friendly but strange, for it was so unlike the Orthodox religious practice to which he was accustomed. After the meeting Skaldin returned to the barracks, shaken by a profound awareness of his spiritual inadequacy. He wanted to pray to God to forgive him, but he did not know how. "It seemed to me," he wrote, "that everyone was following me and they had all guessed that I was already a traitor to the traditions and beliefs of our fathers."

After an extended period of spiritual anguish, Skaldin finally realized that the salvation he sought would come only from his own decision to repent and turn to God. One Sunday, at a Baptist meeting, he sat in trepidation, awaiting the time of prayer. He had prepared an elaborate prayer of repentance by heart, but when the time came, he cried out with simple words: "Oh, Lord! I am a great sinner, forgive me! Brothers, pray for me!" They prayed with him, and "the prayers were from the spirit, with faith." Finally, the group rose, and "brothers and sisters sang with tears in their eyes" a hymn of joy.[38]

Skaldin thus floundered in his religious quest until he learned from the humble pie seller the Baptist teaching that a person could know whether he had been saved, that one could be assured of forgiveness merely through repentance and turning to Christ.

Similarly the young man who had tried to memorize the entire Psalter in an attempt to find salvation later met an elderly woman who, he wrote, "told me more or less the following: 'I have proof and know that I am saved and a child of God.'" The author recalled being horrified at these words, "which in my view only an apostle could have pronounced, and not a simple old lady." At first he did not want to believe, saying that she was suffering from false pride, that a person cannot know that he is saved. For a long time he continued to believe that he could save himself through his own good actions. But the woman, using evidence from the Bible and from her own experience, eventually showed him that without faith there was no salvation.[39]

In another case a recent seminary graduate named V. I. Sinitsin abandoned Orthodoxy after hearing a Baptist metal worker [*slesar'*] preach. The worker was still covered in the soot of the railway yards and he spoke simply, relying on the Bible. Concluded Sinitsin, "My theological education did not give me anything in the sense of practical intimacy with God, but the sermon of a metal worker and the prayer of a believing soul brought me to the source leading to eternal life."[40] The message of these Baptist narratives was that it was ordinary laypeople, from elderly women to workers or peddlers, who played the role of mediators of salvation.[41]

These autobiographies also assert the significance of Baptist theological teachings in the ordinary person's spiritual quest. Salvation could not be found through the Orthodox traditions of their youth, that is, through the performance of rituals and good works and acceptance of the mediating role of the Church. Of course, Orthodoxy also emphasized personal repentance, but for the converts, what mattered most was the Baptist teaching that the individual could know that he or she was saved through a conversion experience of repentance and turning to God. This emphasis on Baptist conversionist theology occurs also in the narratives of converts from faiths other than Orthodoxy. Some described their previous religious affiliation as purely nominal, but others, whether raised Roman Catholic, Armenian-Gregorian, Jewish, or Molokan, had sought God through the rites they were taught as children but could find release from the torture of sinfulness only through Baptist teachings.[42]

As one peasant wrote in *Khristianin,* "I prayed a lot about [eternal salvation] to the Lord and asked Him to reveal this truth to me. I worried for a long time about my sins, I wanted to overcome them by my own powers, not revealing them to the Lord, however my efforts were unsuccessful." Although he knew that he should give himself to the Lord, he did not understand how. He was disillusioned with the behavior of people, like himself, who called themselves Christians. Only later did he find out "that the reason was disbelief, for it says clearly that disbelief is sin." Finally, he understood that pious actions were not enough and that his "powerlessness, [his] sinful state, [arose] from disbelief." This led to a renunciation of Orthodox methods: "My anguish and sadness were unbearable. . . . This torment continued until I renounced, not in words but in deeds, my previous faith, from its false hopes, long, memorized prayers and all that dead letter that had been instilled in me from childhood." But it was difficult to step out of this culture, he wrote: "I could not go beyond the limits of memorized prayers and express my need to the Lord in my own words. . . . I did not know how I should pray, but the Lord himself released my heart and I began to pray for the first time with a grief-stricken heart and a meek soul." And just as Skaldin recalled the joy of being released from sin—and from the constrictions of memorized prayer—so this peasant remembered how he "forgot about [himself] and all that was around [him] and poured out with [his] lips the fullness of [his] heart." "This is the miraculous path," he concluded, "by which the Lord revealed to me eternal salvation through heart-felt prayer with faith."[43] Most Russian Baptists' search for salvation did not begin with a rejection of their Orthodox tradition, but the Baptist conversion experience both enabled and forced them to transcend it.

Although the Baptists emerged amid a climate of religious striving and experimentation throughout Russian society, the cultural and social implications of conversion were great. Converts paid a stiff earthly price for their spiritual salvation as they faced questions about their Russian identity and rejection by family and friends. Skaldin's autobiography is particularly evocative on this count. At every stage of his period of religious transformation, he was plagued by anxieties about the relationship between his Orthodoxy and his status in the community as a Russian: his initial response to the Baptist pie seller's challenging question, "Are you a Christian?" was to equate Orthodox Christianity with Russian identity; his first Baptist meeting seemed odd, for unlike at an Orthodox service, there was little for the eyes; and as he made his first, hesitant steps toward the Baptists, he felt that everyone could tell that he was about to betray the traditions of his forefathers. Conversion itself was a moment of spiritual desperation and joyful redemption, where culture no longer mattered. "Leaving the meeting, I saw all of nature as if renewed," he recalled, and he shared his joy with everyone he met. But soon thereafter the countercultural implications of his religious choice became manifest, as he confronted the fear and anger of workplace and family. In the barracks people were afraid of touching his bed, and in the village his wife's family was horrified. His parents-in-law forbade their adolescent son to speak to him. His wife cried, fearing that he had killed his soul, and turned to traditional rituals to expel Satan from him. Finally, her father threw him out of the family, declaring that Skaldin had "put [him] to shame."[44]

Skaldin was very aware of how crossing oneself, venerating icons, wearing crosses, and other aspects of Orthodox piety were inextricably bound up with the culture of Russian daily life. Although evangelicals often complained that these rituals were meaningless, they consecrated daily life and human relations for much of the population around them. Just as Skaldin's fellow villagers feared that he had brought an evil spirit among them, so other converts reported village women following a Baptist around the village, marking his or her path with signs of the cross. People were warned that after only one encounter with a sectarian, they would stop crossing themselves.[45] Families were horrified when new Baptists removed the crosses of their Orthodox baptism from around their necks.[46] As Christine Worobec explains, "peasants understood the meaning of the Orthodox cross correctly as not only a signifier of the faith, but also as a talisman against demons. According to a manual for priests, making the sign of the cross protected a person from evil spirits."[47] Especially traumatic was the Baptists' refusal to venerate icons. After all, icons in the Orthodox tradition are a crucial vehicle of grace, reverenced as a means of connecting to the divine. Each person had a personal icon, received at baptism, which accompanied him or her through the rites of passage and finally to the grave.[48] Rejection of icons was seen by the society at large as the principal criterion for determining whether someone was a shtundist. For example, when Skaldin visited his wife's family in the village, her father declared: "I told you that he had fallen in with the shtundists and see, it's true that he is already a shtundist, see how he already doesn't smoke, doesn't drink, doesn't cross himself—and do you bow to icons?" When Skaldin acknowledged that he no longer venerated icons, his father-in-law triumphantly declared, "Now, see what he's become!"[49] Someone like Skaldin was a jarring presence in a religious and cultural system where the home was sanctified by the presence of icons and where nationality was denoted by religious affiliation.

Community rejection often followed family discord in Baptists' autobiographies. For example, a peasant from Kiev Province, Semen I. Vzbul'skii, recalled how "the whole village community [*obshchestvo*] rose up against me, even my brother implored the commune to deport me."[50] Even after the 1917 Revolution set about dismantling the old orthodoxies, the theme of family and community ostracism of Baptists continued. One applicant to Bible school in the mid-1920s recalled how his father, who had himself earlier flirted with religious experimentation and the Baptists, was upset and disapproving when his son converted. Other students had been expelled from the family home.[51] Local reports in the evangelical press repeatedly described village beatings of Baptists and attempts at their expulsion.[52] The painful feeling of being alone, cut loose from the ties that previously bound converts to the traditional community, was real but ambivalent. A sense of separation and martyrdom also emphasized the significance and authenticity of the individual's spiritual commitment. And, ironically, it reinforced the need for new kinds of community.

Most Baptist writers contrasted the rejection of the outside world with the support and inspiration that membership in the Baptist church afforded. After his wife's parents threw him out, Skaldin remained true to his new convictions and eventually persuaded his wife to return with him to Odessa, where they were warmly welcomed into the community of believers. The Baptists housed them, helped them find work, and supported them amid the religious persecution of coworkers and officials.[53]

The experience of being rejected by one's earthly family emphasized the importance of the community of Baptist believers. It led the Russian Baptists to picture themselves, in their life stories, as the true heirs to the faith of the early church. A middle-aged medical attendant observed this charismatic sense of community during her first encounter with the Baptists, at a weekday meeting in the Serpukhov district of Moscow in 1923: "My first impression was this: that this was a higher school of morality," and she thought "it was in just such simplicity and sincerity that the pupils of Jesus gathered after his ascension. . . . Everything that they said seemed somehow to apply to me alone and [I knew] that there was no more return to Orthodoxy for me."[54] Similarly Vsevolod I. Petrov described the evangelicals' meeting as a place "where one recognizes the simplicity of early Christianity."[55] References to the early church were part of a discourse of simplicity, persecution, and community that would become useful in the early Soviet era for advancing a vision of the Baptists as the Bolsheviks' fellow victims of tsarism and as a communally driven, progressive movement of popular thought compatible with the new Soviet society. Attention to this aspect of their past was very noticeable in the many Baptist history-writing projects of the 1920s. But long before the revolution, the Russian Baptists seem to have drawn inspiration from the parallel between themselves and the persecuted, but ultimately successful, early church.[56]

Both before and after the revolution, church and government observers who tried to understand the attraction of the evangelical movement stressed the appeal of the evangelicals' respectable way of life and the possibilities for personal development offered by their communities.[57] As Mikhail G. Zabrovskii wrote of his first encounter with the Baptists, as a Young Communist League member in Melitopol' in 1925, "before my eyes it immediately appeared that this was a special people."[58] Certainly many converts remembered first being drawn to the Baptists because of their clean living and simple sincerity. Skaldin initially persuaded himself that he was not good enough for the believers he had met. Similarly Efim Krashtan, after a childhood of smoking, swearing, and petty theft, first began to attend Baptist meetings as a teenager, after he left his village for an apprenticeship in the city of Elisavetgrad. He remembers being "surprised by their behavior" and working hard to "battle all my sinful habits."[59]

Another source of appeal was the movement's simplicity of doctrine and worship, and its accessibility to ordinary people. Baptist autobiographers stressed the importance of the priesthood of ordinary believers and under-lined its attractiveness. Converts in St. Petersburg told visiting priests that they liked "the reading of the gospel in Russian [rather than in Church Slavonic] and the freedom of preaching"; Grigorii Rudenko commented that he especially liked the Bible reading at Evangelical Christian meetings be-cause it reminded him of his childhood when his father and uncle would read scripture aloud.[60]

The evangelical community helped people to gain a sense of control over their own lives, both in terms of self-discipline and in terms of understand-ing their place in the world. In these ways evangelicals shared an esteem for "culture," sobriety, and a striving for personal development that politically "conscious" workers, too, wrote about and sought to promote.[61] Like those workers, they explicitly linked "respectable" lifestyles with enlightenment and empowerment.[62] The confidence engendered by the conviction that one was saved could interact with an assertion of lower-class independence and au-thority. An author writing in *Slovo istiny* in early 1914 proudly emphasized the social inversion brought on by conversion. Playing on the shared root of the Russian words for laypeople [*miriane*] and worldly [*mirskoi*], he asserted that, "There was a time when we, Russians, now brothers and sisters in Christ, bore that unattractive name 'layperson.' It suited us at that time, because our way of life clearly confirmed that we were worldly people." But once they saw the light of God, their world was transformed: "We started to read the Gospel to others, and immediately heard the threatening call from the watch-tower of the world: 'hey, you, doormen, female cooks, shoemakers, ignorant peasants, who allowed you to read and preach the Gospel, you, from what I can see, are not clerics, but laypeople, and therefore you do not have the right to preach."[63] In this way the author contrasted the hierarchical struc-tures of "the world"—and of Orthodoxy—with the egalitarianism of life in Christ.

Although themes of clean living and authority were important, converts stressed the religious appeal of the Baptist movement above all: it was through the Baptists that they had resolved their anxieties about salvation.[64] Attempts to find the means to live the right kind of life by their own powers had proved futile without God's help. The ideal community was meaningless—in fact, it could not exist—without the shared experience of conversion. Telling and retelling members' paths to conversion reinforced the basis of that community, while inviting new members in.

References to the first Christians and emphasis on the social virtues of the new faith served as a means of arguing for that faith's legitimacy, in terms of both traditional Russian values and new directions in society. Evoking sim-plicity and martyrdom appealed to a society alienated from the state and impressed by suffering. With their themes of clean living, social and rhetor-ical simplicity, and the right of all to preach, the Baptists constructed an im-age of their faith as a natural outgrowth of Russian popular aspirations and a legitimate means of satisfying these needs. They shared the widespread thirst for change in Russian society but rejected a purely political solution. While those on the conversion path may have flirted with political revolution, as Baptists they came to realize that only spiritual salvation could provide the basis for the egalitarian society they sought. The new community offered self-education, the chance for every member to speak about and interpret spiritual experience, and, most important, the assurance of salvation through repentance and turning to God. And according to Russian Baptists' autobiographies, this was what ordinary Russians sought; the true faith community capable of fulfilling their spiritual aspirations was a Baptist one.

This challenging spiritual and social community served to draw some potential members while repelling others. It has been argued that "strict churches" are strong precisely because they provide people with structure, making "demands for complete loyalty, unwavering belief, and rigid adherence to a distinctive lifestyle."[65] Although this source of attraction can clearly be observed in Russian Baptist spiritual memoirs, strictness also had the effect of limiting possible expansion. Moreover, the Baptists' certainty that they had the only correct path to salvation, and the cultural dislocation and family rejection that accompanied conversion, likely help to explain why the Baptists never moved beyond sectarian status.

With the exception of the many published in the Baptist youth magazine *Drug molodezhi* [Friend of youth], conversion narratives written by women seem to have been relatively rare. This may reflect their lower level of literacy and the fact that some congregations discouraged women's preaching. Perhaps also for these reasons, women applied in small numbers to the Bible schools whose application files are such a rich source of personal narratives. That said, one young applicant specifically mentioned being attracted to the Baptists out of curiosity about female preaching![66] Female converts' narratives that do exist share much in common with those of men, including earlier Orthodox piety and a search for salvation, as well as themes of displacement and social persecution. However, the experience of labor migration, so common in male accounts, is rare. One young Orthodox nanny's religious questioning was initially prompted by her employer's Molokan father; she subsequently led him to the Baptists' assurance of salvation in an account that rejoiced at the egalitarianism of true faith.[67] The women who took up their pens were more likely to have some secondary education than did their male counterparts—for example, several autobiographers were female teachers whose displacement and spiritual crises were related to education and employment.[68] Like these teachers, the women were generally single, whether young or widowed.

Baptist spiritual narratives between 1905 and 1928 recorded one facet of the process of rapid social and cultural change in this period, illuminating ordinary people's search for answers to the questions posed by these experiences. Their authors viewed the conversions they described as unique and divine interventions in a person's life. They would not have regarded them in any way as "stereotypical" or rooted in social factors.[69] Yet their chronicles demonstrate the power of religious ideas and experiences in shaping new notions of the individual and of community that were developing in early-twentieth-century Russia.

Baptist conversion narratives document concretely one aspect of the breaking down of the notion of a universal church based on territorial and cultural premises and the concurrent rise of a voluntaristic model of churches and of society as self-selected communities. These unusual sources for exploring popular religion in late imperial and early Soviet Russia are a product of the Baptist vision of the church as a voluntary community of converted adult believers. This concept differed sharply from the universal, hereditary, and geographic understanding of membership espoused by the Orthodox Church, as the established religion in late imperial Russia. Although other forms of spiritual narrative such as lives of saints and accounts of miraculous healing were widely read by ordinary Russians, Orthodox devotional literature generally did not feature spiritual autobiographies by the laity.[70] In part, this was because of the near identity of Orthodoxy with Russianness in this period: conversion by definition requires an acceptance of change and of difference, and thus a relative sense of individual independence or autonomy.[71] But theological understanding also shaped religious narrative. Hagiographies, healing narratives, and even private letters to John of Kronstadt emphasized the importance of spiritual guides in soliciting God's favor, whereas Baptists portrayed a more personal, unmediated relationship with the divine. Moreover, the Baptists' idea of religious membership as voluntary and inspired placed value on the spiritual experiences of ordinary people and gave them the confidence to speak and write about their lives and conversions.[72]

As Russian Baptists wrote their personal narratives in the early decades of the twentieth century, they joined a broader trend toward autobiographical writing that flourished from the 1860s. For the lower classes, this became particularly prevalent in the 1920s when Soviet citizens were frequently called upon to tell the stories of their lives in applications for work, higher education, or party or union membership. Moreover, projects to collect the memoirs of working-class people also generated many such narratives. Evangelical spiritual narratives appear little affected by these parallel accounts focused on proving class credentials or, literally, conversion to the Bolshevik faith.[73] Indeed, there is strikingly little change in either the form or the content of conversion narratives after the Bolshevik Revolution.

Russian Baptist autobiographers were, with few exceptions, people of humble origins with little education, but, along with the more politically active workers of their day, they experienced what Mark Steinberg describes as "heightened feelings of self-awareness and self-worth" that led them to demand respect and to seek out new communities that were based on, and thus legitimated, these new individual identities. The experience of conversion made the individual life significant precisely "because it manifested universal patterns of experience."[74] These narratives painted compelling pictures of individuals finding the means for self-expression and growth within a new kind of community, one based on a religious rather than a secular and humanitarian ideal. They were the product of a group that wished to be both in the world and not of this world, to be part of Russian culture but also to transcend it.

In the meantime, however, they had to live in Russian society. And the rejection Russian Baptists faced from their families and local communities paralleled a broader challenge of asserting political and ethnic legitimacy on the national stage. Despite a significantly improved legal situation and greatly expanded membership and organizational structure, the evangelical movement was still perceived as "dangerous" to the values and structures of official Russian society.

Part II

The Most Dangerous Sect

4

The Baptist Challenge

Although the official classification of the shtundists as a "most dangerous sect" lapsed with the declaration of religious toleration of 1905, the notion of danger nevertheless continued to pervade discussions in government and church circles of the rapid rise of the Baptists. The Baptists' vibrant activity seemed to threaten not just the national identity of the Russian state but also the very conception of society and power that imperial institutions embodied. Baptist associational life in particular attracted widespread attention. The 1905 Revolution had forced into the open the question of the relationship between the institutions of the autocracy and the Russian population. To both their opponents within the church and state, and their champions among the intelligentsia, discussions of the Baptist phenomenon provided a means for debating the emergence of civil society and its challenges to the traditional order. While liberals and the Left may have applauded these developments, for officials in the Ministry of the Interior the Baptist movement represented a facet of the problem of the rights and roles of the citizen in the state. At the same time, as the Orthodox Church wrestled with redefining the position of the laity in the church polity, the Baptists' participatory model also loomed large.

The Baptist organizing "storm" that Vasilii Ivanov described after 1905 took place against a backdrop of rising government hostility, a resurgence of the Orthodox anti-sectarian mission, and popular violence. The Baptists disrupted traditional social, religious, and political relationships. The responses of the state, the state church, ordinary villagers, and members of educated society to the Baptists' activities reveal the complicated process of making sense of the ideas enunciated in 1905. By 1908 and 1909 the missionary and organizational work of those first revolutionary years was beginning to coalesce as new congregations were formed, the evangelical press expanded, and communities founded youth groups, Sunday schools, and other institutions. This efflorescence coincided with the onset of a period of political retrenchment for the Russian autocracy, after the radical Second Duma was dissolved and a more restrictive electoral law introduced on 3 June 1907. Almost immediately, for example, the government launched a rather successful campaign to destroy the trade unions—an ominous development for other public organizations.[1] However, the Octobrist leadership in the conservative Third Duma was officially committed to enacting the freedom of religion proclaimed in the October Manifesto of 1905, and so the issue of the rights of religious minorities remained open to debate, at least until the defeat of the Duma's legislative proposals in late 1909 and 1910. This was also a period of restored confidence and strident conservatism for the national church: on the ground, 1908 saw the first coordinated steps to respond to the religious challenges unleashed in 1905; meanwhile, in the corridors of power in St. Petersburg, the voice of the Holy Synod in defense of the traditional prerogatives of the Orthodox faith reasserted its influence.

Opinion makers on the Left and the Right entered the fray to debate the significance of Baptist successes and struggles as markers in the evolving political and cultural situation. This contest of perceptions was colored by the concrete background of popular violence against evangelicals in the villages. For in the village, too, the converts were perceived as dangerous—to traditional family, social, religious, and political relationships. The disorder arising from Baptists' experiments in forging new kinds of religious communities helped to keep on the national agenda questions about the basic instincts of "the Russian people," about the suitability to Russians of the pluralist social model implied in the promises of 1905, and the general political and social implications of religious change.

GOVERNMENT POLICIES AND PERCEPTIONS

Several government agencies had dealings with religious sectarians. Primary responsibility lay with the Ministry of Internal Affairs. Initially, this was the dominion of its Department of General Affairs. In 1909, the affairs of sectarians and Old Believers were transferred to the ministry's Department of Spiritual Affairs of Foreign Confessions.[2] Also involved with sectarian issues were the Department of Police (another division of the Ministry of Internal Affairs) and, for appeals of the decisions of local courts, the Ministry of Justice and the Senate. The Holy Synod straddled the spheres of government and religious interests. Finally, the Duma, and especially its Committee on Religious Affairs, discussed and altered the bills regarding religious dissidents that were presented to the Duma by the Ministry of Internal Affairs.

In its relations with religious sectarians, the Ministry of Internal Affairs juggled functions of protection and control. On the one hand, the ministry was responsible for enforcing adherence to the principles enunciated in the Edict on Religious Tolerance and codified in the law of 17 October 1906 on Old Believer and sectarian communities. On the other hand, the ministry remained primarily interested in its traditional tasks of maintaining public order while closely monitoring public opinion and activity. Thus its officials often found themselves defending sectarians from arbitrary local officials or popular violence. Between 1905 and 1917, however, the "control" side of the ministry's mission became progressively more pronounced. This was the result of a constellation of factors, including the failure to get approval of its proposed legislation on religious minorities, anxiety arising from the rapid expansion of dissident activity, rising political reaction, and, eventually, the hysteria of wartime.

The law of 17 October 1906 was passed as emergency legislation after the dissolution of the First Duma in July 1906. According to Article 87 of the 1906 Fundamental Laws of the Russian Empire, the government was required to reintroduce such laws to the legislature within two months of its resumption. On 28 February 1907, the ministry submitted a bill identical to the law of 17 October 1906 to the Second Duma for approval. The issues it raised were discussed by the Duma's "Committee on Freedom of Conscience" during the brief life of that legislature, but no new law was passed.[3] Later that year, at one of the first sessions of the Third Duma, Prime Minister and Minister of the Interior Petr A. Stolypin tried again. Declaring that, "our task is to adapt Orthodoxy to the attractive theory of freedom of faith within the limits of our Russian Orthodox state," he introduced a series of bills intended to realize the principles enunciated in the Decree on Religious Toleration and the October Manifesto. These included proposals on the right to change one's faith, on the relations of the state to individual religions, on allowing non-Orthodox Christians and non-Christians to hold services and to build houses of worship, on non-Orthodox religious societies, and on removing restrictions on the civil rights of non-Orthodox subjects. With these measures the Ministry of Internal Affairs still sought to control all forms of religious life and to preserve the predominance of the Orthodox Church, but, as Alfred Levin points out, within these limits it was faithful to a conservative interpretation of the principles of 1905.[4]

As the Duma's committees on Old Believers, the Orthodox Church, and religious affairs set to work on these proposals, major issues of contention emerged. In particular, deputies were divided over whether the October Manifesto conferred on all religious groups the right to preach and make con-

69

verts, thus superceding the 17 April Toleration Decree. They also clashed over the problem of defining the boundary between the rights of the individual and those of the Orthodox Church as the established faith. These questions applied to all religious dissidents but were especially important for the evangelicals. Clearly government officials and deputies alike had been taken by surprise by the activism of the Baptists and Evangelical Christians in the newly liberalized atmosphere after 1905. Internal government correspondence suggests that the law of 17 October 1906 was written with the Old Believers, Molokans and Dukhobors in mind, all of them older, better established groups, less given to proselytism than the evangelicals. Only later did the implications of the Baptists' missionary energies become apparent.[5] And those energies seemed to threaten the Russian state in diverse ways. Over the years the theme of danger came to riddle tsarist officials' analyses of the evangelical movement. They came to perceive four major areas of concern in Baptist and Evangelical Christian activity: their foreign links, their enmity toward Orthodoxy, how their meetings and other activities affected public order, and the political implications of their teachings.

As the Third Duma, its committees, and eventually the State Council discussed and ultimately rejected the law projects on changing religion and on Old Believer communities between 1908 and 1910, the legal position of the Baptists and other sectarians remained ambiguous. On the last day of 1908, for example, Ivan Kushnerov wrote a survey of the legal troubles of evangelicals in the past year. He reported many trials for blasphemy or for conversion of the Orthodox, fines for holding prayer meetings, expulsions of Baptists from their place of residence, imprisonment for spreading shtundism, as well as the closing down of meetings and the rejection of applications for legal registration.[6] At its congress the following year, the Union of Russian Baptists decided to lodge a formal complaint with the chairman of the Council of Ministers over restrictions to their civil rights. Although the Baptists blamed the central government for not fully implementing the law of 17 October 1906, they charged that the main irritant remained officials at the provincial and local levels who refused to grant them their rights.[7]

Initially the strategy of appealing to St. Petersburg seems to have worked. The use of the ministry as a court of appeal for the unfair actions of local officials was a constant theme in evangelical journals. This may have been intended, in part, to demonstrate loyalty and a willingness to work within the system, but it was repeatedly backed up by concrete examples of problems solved and general clarifications to the law issued.[8] For example, Interior Ministry circulars in 1908 reiterated that local officials were to take no more than one month to clear applications of people leaving the Orthodox Church and confirmed that women were eligible to sign a congregation's petition for registration. In 1909 the ministry informed local officials that sectarians were not required to register formally as congregations in order to hold prayer meetings and that, although sectarians were required to notify the local authorities of the place and time of their meetings, they did not need to do so on each occasion for regular meetings. Another order declared that one did not have to be a member of a local congregation in order to preach and perform rites.[9]

However, such "administrative" measures did not provide a reliable set of guidelines for the relationship between the state and groups such as the Baptists. As the government became increasingly frustrated by its failure to pass laws on religious dissidence through the Duma and State Council, the policies of that same Ministry of Internal Affairs shifted toward a greater effort to control and limit the public expression of sectarian ideas and practice. In fact, many of these measures responded directly to activities that were associated with the Baptists. For example, Ministry of Internal Affairs circulars forbade sectarian congregations from distributing invitations, postcards, leaflets, or posters to nonmembers, or invoking the law of 4 March 1906 (permitting the establishment of political parties and trade unions) in order to organize public lectures on religious themes. A circular outlining the correct procedures for changing from Orthodoxy to a new religion specifically addressed the issue of how to treat applications that took the form of a prepared document with blanks filled in, a Baptist practice much commented on. On 30 December 1909 the ministry ruled that the open-air baptism of the Baptists was a religious procession requiring special permission from the ministry on each occasion.[10]

Two important measures in 1910 dealing with sectarian congresses and the organization of prayer meetings sought directly to contain the proselytizing fervor of sectarian groups. The regulations of 14 April on sectarian congresses demanded that delegates from no fewer than twelve registered congregations apply to the Ministry of Internal Affairs in advance for permission to hold a congress. Only people of legal age might attend, and foreigners were not allowed to act as organizers or leaders, or to vote. The Ministry was to approve the program and the list of participants in advance, and to appoint a representative to attend all sessions. No congregation could hold more than one business and one spiritual congress each year, and not simultaneously.

In his letter accompanying these new rules, Minister of Internal Affairs Stolypin argued that, because of the lack of guidelines on sectarian congresses, "not a few abnormalities" had emerged. These conferences were not simple gatherings of believers but instead were large meetings organized across the country by the same group of activists. Without actually changing the approved program, Stolypin charged, these leaders gave short shrift to business items on the agenda and turned the meetings into a "public lesson of catechism," open to all. Congresses, he alleged, were often organized by foreigners who either lived in Russia or traveled there especially for such events. In Stolypin's view, this aspect was particularly troubling in Russia, where state and religious life were so intertwined.[11]

In October of the same year another circular brought even more serious restrictions to the daily lives of sectarian groups. A new set of rules for the organization of sectarian prayer meetings sought tightly to restrict access exclusively to adult members of each local community and to intensify police surveillance at meetings. Meetings and services in places other than approved prayer houses were allowed but would require special application to the local governor in each instance. Nonlocal people could perform rites or preach only with the special permission of local authorities; if they were foreign subjects, they were to seek such permission from the Ministry of Internal Affairs. The rules forbade meetings not fully devoted to prayer (for example, discussions) as well as children's meetings and gatherings of youth circles that had not been approved by the government. A representative of the local police was to attend every meeting and close it down if it turned out to be a business meeting or to involve either criticism of the Orthodox Church or calls to leave Orthodoxy. Moreover, all open-air services, religious processions (excluding ordinary funerals), or children's meetings required permission from the minister himself.[12]

The circulars of 1910 launched a concerted government campaign against sectarian propaganda, especially that of the Baptists. Part of this campaign was a drive to learn more about such activity. Beginning in 1909 the Ministry of Internal Affairs repeatedly sought information from its provincial representatives, and its Department of Spiritual Affairs closely studied the activities of local St. Petersburg groups—almost exclusively evangelical ones.[13] In 1912, the minister Nikolai Makarov wrote to provincial governors that, despite efforts to curtail public displays of sectarianism, the survey had revealed that "the most energetic sects—the Baptists and Adventists—are not only not stopping, but with every year are ever more broadly developing their exceptional infringement of the religious convictions of individuals who do not belong to them." Makarov asked that the rules of 4 October 1910 be strictly enforced and that governors send in their opinions as to whether those rules met the government's goal of protecting the Orthodox Church.[14]

What did the Ministry of Internal Affairs fear in this proselytizing? Certainly one concern was the significance of foreign links—and the nature of ideas filtering into Russia from abroad. The government did not know how to assess the loyalty of a Russian who had forsaken the faith associated with Russian nationality and the Russian state.[15] But the broader issue the Baptists raised was that of the relationship of citizens to the state—as political and religious actors. In this respect the files of the Department of Police and the Department of Spiritual Affairs reveal the ministry struggling to resolve a question that continues to tantalize historians: What is the relationship between religious protest and political protest, and is the former merely the pursuit of the latter by other means?

Government investigations into Baptist practices and propaganda methods concluded that these ran counter to the principles of the Russian state. First, the Baptist custom of itinerant preaching challenged the established structure of religious life in Russia. With the exception of the Old Believers and sects, religious groups in Russia had traditionally shared two features: organization on the basis of territorially defined parishes, and legitimation based on state recognition and regulation of the confessional group's life. Although the state had a special—and especially intertwined—relationship with the established Orthodox Church, it also exerted considerable control over other legal denominations. This was a static notion of religion, fitted to what Ernst Troeltsch termed the "church type" of religiosity: religious identity was perceived as an inherited and inclusive characteristic. Every person in the Russian Empire was supposed to have been born into one of the approved faiths and, through it, all his or her civil rites of passage were solemnized and recorded, thus tying the religious denominations into the service of the state. The Baptists in late imperial Russia, by contrast, conformed to Troeltsch's model of the sect as a covenant community of adult converts, striving for self-perfection. Fired by their own conversion to achieve that of others, the formal territorial and legal structures of the parish seemed unimportant.[16] Thus, as government concern over the practice of itinerant preaching deepened, the idea that the Baptists simply ignored the entire established religious system in Russia was repeatedly expressed. A 1911 Department of Spiritual Affairs document that described Baptist proselytizing methods declared, for example, that the Baptists "quite often do not take into account the actual position of Orthodoxy in Russia."[17] Similarly the Minister of Internal Affairs, Nikolai Maklakov, writing in 1913 to Vladimir Kokovtsov, chairman of the Council of Ministers, maintained that the Baptists sought a "privileged position, such as none of the approved faiths of the empire enjoys." Whereas the others restricted their activities to particular parishes, sectarian preachers "consider so-called 'evangelistic' activity their chief purpose [and] are not linked at all with any parish organizations run by them and consider themselves free preachers not only among any group of sectarians but even in places with an exclusively Orthodox population." This approach, he declared, "contradicts the fundamental principle, applicable to all faiths in the empire, of the parish."[18] In this regard the Russian state was confronting issues that its English counterpart had faced from the seventeenth century. As Deryck W. Lovegrove points out, a new emphasis on religious voluntarism beyond the Anglican Church at that time raised similar issues regarding the extent of the English state's power over the consciences of its subjects and about whether the basis of its authority was prescriptive or derivative.[19] In other words, the question arose of whether religious or political authority were implicit in jurisdictional boundaries or whether they derived from contracts based on individual conviction and voluntary affiliation. The evangelicals' form of religion was dynamic and difficult to control. And the state had always been concerned about Baptist and Evangelical Christian statements of faith which declared that they would obey laws insofar as they did not restrict their religious expression.[20]

In addition to this concern about the challenge Baptist activity presented to the general principles of Russian religious life, government officials worried about the kind of attitudes toward popular intellectual and political power that Baptist communities fostered. As Semen Bondar' concluded in his widely distributed booklet, "The Current State of the Russian Baptist Movement," written for the Department of Spiritual Affairs in 1911, "The strength of the Baptist faith is its congregational [obshchinnoe] organization. Members of Baptist communities are themselves the initiators of affairs; they freely and easily gather and deliberate; at meetings every thought is heard out, no matter to whom it belongs."[21] The legitimacy of popular authority was a hotly debated topic after the dissolution of the Second Duma, and the democratic practices of the Baptists aroused anxious comment. The Department of Spiritual Affairs closely monitored press reports on sectarianism and investigated all cases that involved social confrontation or that were tinged with politics. One such article reported that, when a visiting Baptist preacher spoke at a meeting in Saratov, he was challenged by the policeman in attendance for not having official permission to preach. The speaker allegedly turned to the assembled congregation and asked, "Brothers, do you permit me?" The crowd shouted "yes," and the speaker turned to the official and said, "I don't need anything more, and I don't recognize your authority."[22] In another case the director of state security in Moscow expressed a mixture of derision and anxiety about the Baptists' belief that the voice of God spoke through their elections.[23]

Bureaucrats voiced concern about the political implications of the habits of community-based decision making that ordinary Russians acquired through participation in the Baptist movement. In fact, in his description of the proceedings of the Russian Baptist Union's national congress in Moscow in 1911, a state security agent observed that, "the Baptist movement is a serious school of public activism [obshchestvennoi shkoloi]":

> In the congregation every member has a decisive vote, takes part in the discussion of all economic and legal questions of the life of the community, and this imparts to even the completely uncultured Baptists certain social skills. This jumped to my eyes at the congress, where simple peasants very sensibly discussed the more complicated issues in the organization of congregations and of the whole union. In general, there is every basis to suggest that the Baptist movement is not only a serious religious force but a no less serious social one as well.[24]

This image of Baptist religion as a "civic school" was later taken up in the evolving report of basic information on Baptists produced by the Department of Police and in Department of Spiritual Affairs memoranda.[25]

Within a few years what at first had been uncertainty about the political implications of Baptist activity began to look like confirmed fact. At the Department of Spiritual Affairs, letters from provincial governors warning of the social disorder and political threat brought on by the Baptists in their areas poured in, and several special investigations revealed alarming evidence of organizational and propagandistic vitality.[26] Moreover, after a governor reported that a Baptist had told him that upon converting he had promised not to bear arms, the Department of Spiritual Affairs issued a secret circular in November 1911 asking governors to monitor Baptists closely for pacifism.[27] Then, in 1913, in response to a warning from the Khar'kov governor that the Baptists were intensifying their propaganda among low-ranking soldiers and were expressing antimilitary and antistate views, the ministry's Department of Police took action. On July 31, at the order of the Minister of Internal Affairs, secret letters were sent to the Department of Spiritual Affairs, the Over Procurator of the Holy Synod, and to all heads of provincial Gendarme (political police) organizations asking them to answer a question: "Do the religious teachings of the Baptists and other sects in the places under your surveillance include revolutionary or social-democratic slogans, and is there anything in their activity that could present a threat to the state and social peace?" They were also asked whether ordinary police surveillance should be augmented by the systematic infiltration of these groups.[28]

Ironically the fifty-five Gendarme chiefs who responded over the next few months did not see much of a threat in the Baptists. Only seventeen thought that agents should be placed in Baptist groups, while twenty-three disagreed and fifteen gave no opinion on the matter. The majority also had seen no antistate behavior on the part of local evangelicals. In many cases even officials from regions where there were sizable Baptist populations did not think infiltration was necessary—including the head of the Khar'kov Gendarme administration who tersely replied, contradicting his governor, that they were not a threat. The Department of Spiritual Affairs reported that its own research into the issue of antimilitarism in late 1911 suggested that "antimilitaristic teachings, social-democratic and revolutionary currents have not achieved such a solid position in the religious understandings of Russian sects that one could consider these negative phenomena to be tightly connected with religious doctrines." Rather, they were more likely the result of political propaganda among sectarians. Nevertheless, he wrote, the Baptist sect "deserve[d] special attention because of its large numbers [and] capacity for growth, and also in view of the presence in its membership in Russia of a significant number of former anarchist and socialist converts."[29] The director also warned at length of the Baptists' close foreign connections.

This theme of potential for radicalism rather than an observed pattern of political activism permeated the reports of regional political police chiefs between 1910 and 1913. As the head of the Gendarme administration in Poltava Province wrote, "everyone inclined toward protest goes into sectarianism."

Similarly the Kherson provincial director contended that, although no evidence of revolutionary slogans had been found in Baptist teachings, "the fact of sympathy of this sect for the revolutionary movement is not to be doubted, since with [the revolutionary movement's] success the Baptists envision receiving full freedom of action in the spreading of their teaching and for unchecked organizational activity." Likewise his colleague in Voronezh Province asserted that, "with the spread of the Baptist faith among the people, suitable material for revolution is being prepared."[30]

By the time the results of the survey were disseminated in a secret circular to Gendarme directors on 7 March 1915 the onset of world war had brought a new urgency to the questions it had asked about the relationship between religious and political radicalism. Wartime bred heightened official and public paranoia about foreign influence, making the Baptists easy targets. It also made perceptions about antimilitarism more acute and lent heightened significance to the scattered examples of conscientious objection reported among religious dissenters. What had once been a suspicion of potential unreliability now became a governmental conviction. The secret circular made clear these perceptions, stating, "there is no doubt that there exists a close link between the destructive aspirations of the revolutionaries and the wavering of the foundations of the ruling church in Russia, the Orthodox Church, since these and other efforts in the end result are directed toward one goal—the overthrow of the existing structure of the Empire." The circular drew particular attention to the Baptists' alleged teaching "against the use of weapons even in war" and warned that, therefore, "in the conditions currently being experienced in Russia, Baptism [sic] is one of the most dangerous sectarian teachings." Surveillance of all sectarians, but especially of Baptists, was to be intensified.[31]

Thus, although the process may have begun and ended with assertions of the danger presented by Baptists, throughout the period between 1905 and 1914 we see a more complex process of the Russian state trying to work out the meaning of the changes initiated by the 1905 Revolution. Management of the sectarian issue by the Ministry of Internal Affairs fits into the broader pattern of a retreat from the openings of 1905 but must also be understood as responding to a wider context of unexpected evangelical organizational vitality, pressure from the Orthodox Church to control religious dissent, and concern about popular violence against evangelicals.

THE ORTHODOX CHURCH
AND EVANGELICAL COMPETITION

The political revolution that swept Russia in 1905 had rejected the powerlessness of the tsar's subjects in Russian state life. It also challenged the Orthodox Church to reconsider its relationship with the state and the position of the laity within the Orthodox polity. The activities of the newly lib-

erated religious dissidents loomed large in this discussion. Baptist evangelization energies and methods, in particular, served both to spur change and
to expose deep tensions within the state church.

The Church as a whole experienced the upheavals of 1905 with a mixture of excitement and dismay. On the one hand, in March 1905 Nicholas
II promised that, at "a favorable time," he would convene a long-hoped-for
Sobor (council) of the Church to discuss spiritual and administrative issues,
including the relationship of the Church to the Russian state.[32] The prospect
of the first council of the entire Church since 1666–67 excited a flurry of
discussion about how a newly independent Church would be governed.[33] On
the other hand, the 1905 Revolution ended the monopoly the Orthodox
Church had on Russian souls by allowing individuals to leave the Church for
another Christian faith and by promising freedom of conscience. This
prompted deep anxiety about the future position of Orthodoxy in Russia
and the Church's ability to preserve the exclusive right of proselytization that
it still enjoyed. As the complicated consequences of the revolution unfolded,
and especially as prospects dimmed in 1906 and 1907 for the summoning
of the Sobor, many voices in Church circles complained that, whereas religious dissidents had been granted new privileges, "the [C]hurch had been
abandoned by the politicians after having been constrained to serve as the
mainstay of autocracy."[34] The Church tended to take the view that the spiritual aspect of national life was its purview and that the government was il-
legitimately interfering in its sphere.

Especially aggrieved by the new rights of religious dissidents were the members of the anti-sectarian mission of the Orthodox Church. Whereas missionaries' earlier efforts to prevent disgruntled Orthodox believers from
abandoning the Church had been backed up by the sanctions of secular law,
now the apostates could point to imperial decrees permitting them to do
just that. Feelings of betrayal and discouragement were widespread. As religious sectarians now felt able to refuse to engage missionaries in debate, and
social upheaval spread through the countryside and the cities, the author
of the annual report of the Kherson diocese for 1905 wrote that these "un-
propitious circumstances for mission inspired in the spirit of many missionaries painful doubts regarding the further existence of the mission; some
missionaries were close to disillusionment with their service."[35] Indeed, looking back on the first three years after 1905, Vasilii M. Skvortsov, the leader
of the internal missionary movement and founder of its official journal, *Missionerskoe obozrienie* [Missionary review], recalled that the mission had found
itself "adrift without a rudder" [*bez rulia i vietril*].[36]

The internal mission was the arm of the Church most particularly concerned with the laity's religious experience. Between the revolutions of 1905
and 1917 the mission's publications increasingly became the place to discuss the Church's relationship to its parishioners. The missionaries would
find themselves preoccupied by many new challenges, ranging from the

evangelical movement to the apostasy of forcibly converted Orthodox who returned in droves to Catholicism or Islam after 1905 to the competition of godless socialism. When it came to discussing methods of pastoral work among Russians, however, the Baptists unquestionably took center stage.

Missionerskoe obozrienie responded to the April 17 edict in a shocked and defensive tone. Not so subtly, the author of a commentary on the new law warned that the tender-hearted tsar's gift of religious tolerance could threaten the integrity of the Russian Empire and its autocratic system of government: "We will hope, we will pray and believe, that the enemies of the Orthodox Church will be disarmed by the example of love that the Most Orthodox, Most Autocratic Tsar has shown them . . . , and that henceforth they will renounce their designs to [C]atholicize the west of Russia, Germanize her south through the shtunda, [I]slamize and [B]uddhize [*sic*] her east, and pervert her north and center with Old Belief."[37] In other words, although they respected the wishes of their tsar, the missionaries should steel themselves for the challenges ahead.

In the pages of *Missionerskoe obozrienie*, anti-sectarian missionaries surveyed with unconcealed anxiety the first public steps of Russia's Old Believer and sectarian communities in conditions of religious toleration. Because of their proselytizing drive, the Baptists loomed large as the primary new threat. Aleksandr Platonov, Georgian diocesan missionary and the journal's senior editor, worried that "*We are on the eve of the broad expansion of the Baptist faith.*" Describing them as a "colossal force," he contended that the Russian Baptists deserved particular attention, since they had "a splendid, strictly consistent organization, large capital, a large book-publishing business, excellent preachers and orators, a huge galaxy of missionaries who are disciplined and devoted to their cause . . . [and] direc[t] their efforts at swallowing up many tens of thousands of Molokans and at engendering at all costs a new great schism in the Orthodox Church." In his view it was this organizational sophistication that made Baptists a far more difficult target for missionary work than the "naive rationalism" of the Molokans. To meet this challenge, not just the missionaries but the whole Orthodox Church would have to put its house in order.[38]

All concurred that the conditions of Russia's new age would require an intensification of missionary work. More difficult was agreeing on the implications for the mission's methods of work. The archbishop of Kherson Diocese, Dimitrii Koval'nitskii, made this very point to a regional conference of missionaries in Odessa in September 1905, the first such conference after the proclamation of religious toleration. "'Freedom of conscience,'" he declared, "creates a new condition for the mission, sets it new tasks. Henceforth, the means of missionary activity must alter to a considerable extent."[39] The mission had long seen its chief purpose as protecting Orthodoxy from sectarian "infection" (a favorite metaphor) and training priests to do the same. Its methods had traditionally had a strong coercive element, using the power of the police to compel sectarians to participate in public debates, for example.[40] Now missionaries complained that they were forced to stand by at sectarian meetings, unable to raise their voices to protest against blasphemy and religious errors for fear of being arrested for disturbing the peace.[41] Although the Orthodox Church still retained a substantial arsenal of legal supports—from its monopoly on conversion to anti-blasphemy laws—the changes in the relationship between society and state set in motion by the revolution also raised the question of whether the missionaries should even make use of such weapons.

By 1908, as revolutionary hopes faded and after a couple of years of observing the upsurge of sectarian activity, the mission began to find its feet. A series of congresses, both local and national, met to debate the implications of the new rights for sectarians and to devise strategies to meet the unprecedented competition. In St. Petersburg, for instance, a series of conferences on pastoral issues raised by the activities of local sectarians were held throughout 1908 and 1909. Similar meetings took place in the dioceses of Nizhnii Novgorod and Kiev. Most important, the Fourth All-Russian Missionary Congress, held in Kiev in July 1908, attracted more than five hundred delegates, including the three Orthodox metropolitans, for a broad discussion of new directions in the relationship between the Church and the laity.[42]

The discussion at these congresses, especially at the national one in Kiev, revolved around the tension between pastoral and police methods in dealing with religious dissidents. Underlying this debate were disagreements about the role of the laity, as well as the place of Orthodoxy in Russian social and state life. The years after 1908 found the Church taking an increasingly defensive political stance. Its leaders argued that, by giving privileges to the enemies of the Orthodox Church, the state was interfering in the religious sphere that the Church considered its own. At the same time the experience of competition with sectarian activity led even missionaries who had long supported a more police-based method of dealing with dissent, and who had resisted the involvement of "amateurs" in mission work, to advocate a new model of mission as a broad-based movement of the laity. As the annual report of the Over Procurator of the Holy Synod for 1908–9 explained, Church and mission leaders began to realize that, until 1908, the mission had remained "one-sided," with all its work in the hands of specialized missionaries, no participation at the parish level, and very little collaboration from parish priests who had little training in this area.[43] In other words, they realized that, in post-1905 Russia, mission was too important to be left to the missionaries alone.

Missionaries explicitly invoked the Baptist approach of active associational life and community-based proselytizing as both the spur to reform and as the model for a new, popular Orthodox missionary movement. Throughout Church circles, the Baptists were widely viewed as particularly dangerous precisely because of these features. As the annual report of the Over Procurator of the Synod for 1910 stated, "the most numerous and organized sects are the rationalistic ones and in particular the shtundo-Baptists. The latter distinguish themselves by their inclination for propaganda of their teaching among Orthodox-Russian people, and therefore they are also the most dangerous for the Orthodox Church."[44] Moreover, Church statistics continued to show that the Orthodox Church was making far fewer converts from the sects than it was losing to these faiths, and confirmed the contention that the Baptists were the most popular and fastest growing sect among formerly Orthodox people. The Synod did not publish such figures for 1905–6, but, between 1907 and 1909, 5,420 people formally left the Orthodox Church for the "shtundobaptists" or the Pashkovites; in the three years thereafter 8,678 took that step. In 1914 a new category of "Evangelical Christians" was added to the statistical tables. This category probably took in both followers of Prokhanov and many Tolstoyans, who also sometimes used this name. Figures for 1914 show 3,768 Orthodox becoming Baptists, 11 becoming Pashkovites, and 1,164 becoming Evangelical Christians, for a total of 4,943 apostates or 83.5 percent of converts to all sects in that year. Those joining the state church from these categories numbered only 1,265.[45]

The connection between Orthodox efforts at pastoral reform and the challenge of the evangelical movement in Russia had roots in the period before 1905. For example, the rise of the Pashkovite movement in St. Petersburg spurred an association of priests interested in the revitalization of parish life to form the Society for the Propagation of Religious and Moral Enlightenment in the Spirit of the Orthodox Church in 1881.[46] As the Orthodox Church and its missionary wing struggled with how to elicit—but also channel—greater lay activism after 1905, the evangelical model again loomed large. As Mikhail Kal'nev, the prominent diocesan missionary from Odessa, declared in a programmatic statement of this new view in 1910,

> the sectarians, *from whom we could learn a lot regarding the organization of mission,* have excellently understood all the great importance and necessity of popular [*narodnoi*] mission; almost everywhere, even in the remote khutors [small villages of Ukraine and south Russia], they have organized Sunday missionary discussions for the people, child and youth meetings during which they study Holy Scripture and methods of discussion with the Orthodox, go over the objections and arguments of our missionaries and the apologetic anti-sectarian literature, and familiarize themselves with sectarian literature.[47]

Similarly, when a group of St. Petersburg priests founded a journal to promote the renewal of parish life in 1911, they freely acknowledged the challenge of sectarianism as a motivation for their work.[48] Authors in *Missionerskoe obozrienie* also evinced a strong interest in Baptist methods, scouring evangelical journals and conference materials for insight.[49]

More often than not, Orthodox missionaries traced the evangelicals' success specifically to their achievements in organizing community life. Writing in the Mogilev diocesan magazine in 1910, one such missionary made the point that the most worrying aspect of Baptist activity was the spontaneous missionary drive the Baptists managed to animate. "Rank-and-file sectarians—men and women—are in this field," he warned, and each

> strives in one way or another to take part in the work of God. One opens a small shop and stops every passer-by, discussing faith and reading the Gospel. . . . Another organizes open-air meetings around his house in the summer with preaching and reading of the Gospel. A third goes around to private houses of the Orthodox and persistently offers his services to read the word of God. During peasants' fieldwork, sectarians at every convenient opportunity try to read out to the Orthodox those places in Holy Scripture which they direct toward the refutation of the Orthodox Church.[50]

Even the 1910 report of the Synod Over Procurator uncharacteristically devoted four full pages to outlining the most effective Baptist methods for drawing in the Orthodox, including discussions with friends and acquaintances, which it termed "the most powerful means of propaganda."[51] The lesson was clear: it was by being where people were and making mission the work of each believer that the Baptists reaped their harvest of souls.

In response, the Orthodox Church set out quite explicitly to fight fire with fire by copying these methods. In 1908, the Synod formed a missionary committee to direct a general campaign against religious dissent. The committee's deliberations led to two important steps in the planning of mission. The first was the decision to call the Fourth All-Russian Missionary Congress in Kiev mentioned earlier; second, the committee drew up a set of rules for internal mission that was approved by the Synod in late May 1908.[52]

These rules, in the words of the Chief Procurator's annual report, were designed to put the task of internal mission into the hands of ordinary Orthodox parishioners. Mission was to be the collective work of parish councils, groups of enthusiasts [*revnitelia*] of Orthodoxy, missionary brotherhoods, and other parish-based institutions. Under the "main leadership of the local priest," these groups were to strive to put parish life on a morally sound basis by promoting clean living and establishing popular reading rooms, religious choirs, and material aid to the poor while keeping their pastor informed of any appearance of false teaching in the area. The priest would conduct Bible study with members and teach them how to counsel those who had fallen into error. In addition to directing this lay activity, the parish priest was to concentrate on making the liturgy more relevant to the ordinary parishioner through education and congregational singing, and by having literate parishioners serve as readers. Completing this pyramid of missionary activity was the diocesan mission. Each diocese was to establish a missionary council and employ a diocesan missionary to lead a team of district missionaries. These men were to travel to problem areas in the diocese and assist local clergy in their missionary work. Similarly the Synod's recommendations for combating Baptist inroads, based on the resolutions of the Kiev missionary congress and published in 1909, explicitly sought to match evangelicals' congregational vitality with rival Orthodox institutions. These proposals borrowed Baptist forms, but they remained suspicious of the opportunities for popular spontaneity implied in their content. The Synod aimed to keep the clergy firmly in charge of congregational activism.[53]

In 1914 Aleksandr Vvedenskii, an Odessa missionary priest, wrote a wide-ranging guide to missionary work with sectarians that summarized the lessons of recent years and argued strenuously for the new, lay-based approach to mission. Once again, rivalry with the evangelicals was the guiding theme. Throughout the book Vvedenskii looked for the sources of Baptist appeal and recommended Orthodox ways to neutralize them. In fact, an entire chapter, titled "Worthy of Imitation," used only Baptist examples. He drew special attention to the power of the Baptist practice of "witnessing" publicly about individual spiritual experience. "It would not hurt us," he wrote, "as a counterweight to Baptist propaganda . . . to introduce among ourselves a similar kind of meeting at which those who have turned from the path of sin and ruin and have definitively become disillusioned with sectarianism might share their feelings, their religious experience with their brothers in faith and through this they might strengthen them in the faith." Yet, despite the admiration of Baptist techniques which he implied here and throughout his book, Vvedenskii sought at several points in his work to show that his pastoral model had native roots in pre-Petrine Russian life. In this way he joined a long tradition of interest in, but anxiety about, the use of foreign models to reform the Orthodox Church.[54]

Vvedenskii proposed a popularly based Orthodox mission and yet also sought to keep lay activism firmly reined in, both doctrinally and organizationally. He approvingly quoted an article on fighting the Baptists on the parish level in which the author warned of the dangers of inadequately supervised lay activity: "Some enthusiasts from among the simple people, invited by the priest to participate in the parish mission, *fall into self-importance,* begin to regard themselves as church teachers."[55] Indeed, Orthodox missionaries often suggested that converts to the sects had formerly been enthusiastic Orthodox whose spiritual explorations had not received adequate attention and guidance from their local priests.[56] Nevertheless, Vvedenskii argued, although this was a definite risk, the potential benefits of popular mission far outweighed such hazards.

The call for the formation of lay missionary societies and for more lay involvement in mission in general did not go unheeded. The year after the Synod endorsed such groups, the Over Procurator's report revealed that circles had been opened, sometimes in large numbers, in the Don, Kherson, Podol'sk, Orel, and Pskov dioceses. Parish priests had generally taken the initiative in founding these societies. In the Omsk area, groups of peasant enthusiasts, both men and women, met regularly with their priest to hear him preach and to read anti-sectarian tracts together. Kal'nev reported that when he founded a circle of enthusiasts of Orthodoxy in Odessa many Orthodox who had been attending sectarian meetings eagerly joined, as did several former sectarians. According to Kal'nev, they openly acknowledged the appeal of a group where they could "not only study the truths of the faith, but also have the opportunity to 'unburden their hearts' in a society of believing people."[57] Similarly, in the parishes of St. Petersburg, popular missionary courses mobilized ordinary people, especially women, in defense of the church.[58] Other experiments in expanding opportunities for lay education and participation included the Kherson-Odessa Diocesan House, a sort of religious community center opened in Odessa in January 1910. The house provided space for children's groups, meetings of enthusiasts of Orthodoxy, lectures, and special events including ceremonies to welcome former sectarians back into the fold.[59]

At the same time the confrontational tradition of the Orthodox mission did not simply die out. In practice, missionaries around the country continued to advocate public debates with sectarians, to train members of the new missionary circles and the older Orthodox brotherhoods to stand up in sectarian meetings and object whenever Orthodox doctrine was violated, and to report illegal activities to the police. For example, although Kal'nev, the Kherson diocesan missionary, called for a lay-based mission, this did not preclude his own use of confrontation and police power. In 1915, Kal'nev continued in the long tradition of Orthodox missionary participation in trials of sectarians by acting as expert in the blasphemy trial of Odessa's Baptist pastor, Vasilii Pavlov, who had published a translation of a brochure by the famous English Baptist Charles H. Spurgeon criticizing the practice of baptizing children.[60] In Elisavetgrad (also in Kal'nev's diocese) groups of local Orthodox enthusiasts regularly attended Baptist meetings, interrupting the proceedings to question the sectarians on issues of ritual and dogma.[61] In some cities these groups became closely associated with local chapters of the radical right-wing Union of Russian People, which joined the enthusiasts of Orthodoxy in pestering local and central government authorities to repress the Baptists as blasphemers.[62]

The clergy were very suspicious of the Ministry of Internal Affairs as the source of legislation protecting religious dissenters and frequently complained that it did not adequately defend the interests of Orthodoxy as the established religion.[63] Despite these fears, the Church was actually quite successful in keeping before the government the idea that the loss of Orthodox faith was "nationally" and thus politically (patriotically) suspect. Representatives of the Church hierarchy played an important role in the government's management of religious dissent. Provincial governors, the central government's main source of knowledge on these matters, tended to rely heavily on information and opinions supplied by the local bishop and his staff of missionaries.[64] In St. Petersburg the Holy Synod, or at least its Over Procurator, not only drew the government's attention to issues relating to sectarians but was also formally consulted regarding policy decisions. Moreover, because the Synod was represented at the Council of Ministers, whose approval was necessary for any Duma law to pass, the Church had a formal position at the center of power.[65] The Department of Police also directed to the Synod secret information it thought might be of interest.[66] And the civil authorities solicited the Synod's cooperation and offered their assistance. Nevertheless the Ministry of Internal Affairs did resist proposals from the Synod asking for more control regarding religious dissent and for a binding policy of regular consultation with diocesan authorities on the grounds that, while consultation was desirable, ultimately the civil authorities could not be subject to the religious ones.[67]

Thus the Baptists' presence and activities came to symbolize for Orthodox churchmen the many uncertainties unleashed by 1905. Anxieties about the relationship between clergy and laity, about defining a Russian pastoral tradition, and about the place of Orthodoxy in the mission of the Russian state predated the revolution, but these issues took on new significance as the state launched its constitutional experiment in 1905–6. The Baptists' expansion demonstrated the Church's lack of control over the laity and served as a spur for seeking new forms of pastoral work. But it also seemed to show that the state had abandoned the Orthodox masses of the villages to the depredation of heretics and had handcuffed the church in its efforts to defend its flock. It is worthwhile to examine these encounters between Baptists and Orthodox in the village and the varying meanings that were attributed to the resulting conflict.

CONFRONTATION IN THE VILLAGE
AND ITS POLITICAL SIGNIFICANCE

Despite increasing government pressure and the efforts of Orthodox anti-sectarian missionaries, the Baptist fellowship continued to grow quickly between 1910 and the outbreak of the war. The many reports of crowds flocking to Baptist meetings, especially in the cities, reveal that, beyond the relatively small core of full-fledged members, there was considerable public interest in, or at least curiosity about, evangelicals' message and practices. Nevertheless, for many other people, Baptist activity clearly threatened traditional Russian and Ukrainian cultural and religious norms. Village culture, in particular, was imbued with these norms. Whereas the government considered the Baptists a menace to the structure of Russian state life and the Church regarded them as a threat to its relationship with the laity, their fellow villagers often saw the Baptists as a disruption to the rhythm of village life and lashed out at them in anger. Indeed, the theme of violence pervaded accounts of rural Baptist life between 1905 and 1917, and into the 1920s.

In the late imperial period both Baptists and their opponents constructed narratives of violence that would further their respective collective goals by appealing to the sensibilities of various elites. This violence helps to explain both the government's efforts to protect sectarians and why officials developed an association between Baptist activity and social disorder.

In a petition to the Department of Spiritual Affairs submitted in June 1910 a group of Baptist peasants from Ekaterinoslav Province complained that, when they had voiced an objection to the local peasant authorities that their Orthodox neighbors were disrupting their meetings and beating them up, they were told, "we will beat you up so long as there are only a few of you!" "Where on earth is the freedom of confession and conscience that our Ruler gave if even the authorities do not pay attention to it?" these petitioners asked.[68] What had been decreed in distant St. Petersburg was not necessarily played out in day-to-day relationships. Long before the Baptists could operate legally, they had been victims of popular violence, often performed with the connivance of local officials. The gruesome torture to which evangelical converts were allegedly subjected by their fellow villagers was a topic of outrage among their defenders before 1905.[69] But now, as the Ekaterinoslav peasants pointed out, although their meetings were legal, the persecution had not stopped. Leaving the Church and performing non-Orthodox rites in an Orthodox milieu aroused enmity within the family, interfered with the administration of the village, and ruptured the ritual unity of village life.

Orthodox families were understandably troubled when one of their number abandoned the ancestral religion. Many such families would appeal to the local priest or Orthodox missionary for help in bringing a Baptist back into the Orthodox fold.[70] There are numerous reports, in government archives and in both the Baptist and secular press, of friction arising from new Baptists' refusal to perform the everyday rituals of Orthodox life, such as venerating icons and crossing themselves. Families objected to converts giving away, selling, or even burning their icons.[71] They were also offended by the Baptists' explanations of their actions. Manifold complaints from all over the country suggest that, whatever words the Baptists actually used, Orthodox listeners heard blasphemous disrespect for their most sacred objects. Villagers from all over Russia told police and priests that Baptists had described their icons as "planks."[72] Nor did the Baptists' condemnation of the veneration of icons as idol worshiping endear them to the surrounding Orthodox community.

The practice of adult baptism also presented a direct challenge to Orthodox teachings and to notions of family and community. Scholars of the radical Protestant tradition have pointed out that social separation and conflict is implied in the very practice of baptizing (and especially re-baptizing) only adult believers. As John Bossy argues with regard to the Anabaptists in the Reformation, "believers' baptism was a doctrine of division, and not just in the eyes of princely bureaucrats and unity-haunted municipalities; it provoked a growl from the average soul in defense of his conviction that through their baptism he and his children were living in Christianity."[73] Likewise, in his study of Baptist history, William Henry Brackney contends that a covenant of consenting adults "represented an absolute break" with the established church because it "bypass[ed] tradition altogether and ma[de] a compact with God Himself."[74]

Conflict over ritual life and faith could spread beyond the walls of the family hut to become the basis for village action. For example, in 1911 the missionary Vasilii Skaldin reported that the village assembly had gathered and decided to expel those who had joined his Baptist congregation in a southern Ukrainian settlement. When the Baptists arrived at their prayer house that Sunday, they found it surrounded by a mob of armed peasants. Skaldin asked what they wanted and they replied, "[We would like for you] not to meet here and not to corrupt our families." To the Baptists' pleas that they had the will of the tsar and the permission of the governor to practice their faith came the uncompromising voice of popular justice: "We don't recognize anything, we have our law and we passed a verdict to expel you and we don't want to know anything more."[75] Just as Natalie Zemon Davis has shown that religious rioters during the Reformation regarded their violence as legitimate defense of true doctrine that the government had failed to uphold, so the villagers sought to restore the traditional boundaries of their community by rooting out heresy.[76] In fact, in numerous cases, Orthodox villagers explicitly justified their actions by asserting that the law of the village had primacy over what was decreed in St. Petersburg or by defining their local problem of religious dissidence as a broader issue of social and political reliability in order to gain acceptance of their plea from central government officials.[77]

Communities that took action against their Baptist members seem to have had two basic complaints: first, that their evangelizing was intolerable, and, second, that their presence interfered with the running of the village. As the minutes of one village assembly that decided to expel its Baptists in 1907 declared, "[The Baptists] boldly appear everywhere, in the streets and in homes, with their propaganda and, in trying to make converts to their teaching, do not stop at any public sacrilege, any effrontery and even blasphemy against the Orthodox Church, holy icons, rituals, sacraments; their impertinence and the importunity with which at every instance, upon every meeting with Orthodox people, they try to spread their teaching has of late become intolerable."[78] But also, as was stated in one village's appeal to the governor to exile a group of new converts, they "undermine[d] the social structure of the life of our settlement."[79] Religious dissidence wreaked havoc on a village system in which administration of the religious aspects of life was closely woven into secular village administration. Although the village and parish communities were administratively and juridically distinct, it was the village assembly that voted to set a compulsory "donation" from all villagers toward the construction and maintenance of the local church.[80] Now the Baptists were refusing to participate in what their neighbors regarded as an inseparable part of village life, the church.

Villagers often objected to the public performance of non-Orthodox rituals in what had once been the exclusively Orthodox space of the village. The Baptist practice of celebrating open-air baptisms of adults in a nearby river could provoke reactions ranging from relatively benign interest to violent confrontation.[81] Funerals, in particular, ignited conflict.[82] Certainly funerals brought together issues of religious legitimacy and questions relating to the allocation of space and resources in the village. In one 1911 incident, in the Cossack town of Batalpashinskaia in the Kuban region, a crowd tried to prevent the burial of a local Baptist leader. According to a Department of Police report, when the Baptist funeral procession arrived at the cemetery, the crowd began to shout, "We don't need apostates . . . get out of here." The local Ataman intervened to calm things down, ordering that a section of the cemetery be set aside for the Baptists, but the crowd made it impossible for the Baptists to dig a hole by standing by and throwing the earth back in as they worked, all the while shouting, "we won't allow him to be buried on our land at any cost." Finally, the Baptists gave up and took the body twenty versts away to the estate of a prosperous Baptist family, the Mamontovs, for burial. According to the police, they were accompanied all the way by Orthodox villagers who whistled and beat on empty buckets.[83] This incident reveals many typical features of accounts of violence that reached the authorities in the capital, including accusations of blasphemy, crowds interested in and offended by Baptist ritual in the streets of their community, and protection of community land from sacrilege.

The files of the Ministry of Internal Affairs and of the Holy Synod were full of complaints from both Baptists and their fellow Orthodox villagers. As one government official wrote, in a 1911 report to Prime Minister Petr A. Stolypin, "in almost all settlements where the Orthodox form the majority, numerous complaints have been heard from the Baptists about oppression and persecution by their fellow villagers. In tears they told [me] about their cheerless existence, finding themselves under constant fear of being beaten, not daring to leave the house, to light a fire in the hut, without the risk of attack or outrage."[84] At the same time provincial authorities and officials in the Ministry of Internal Affairs in St Petersburg were also besieged by pleas from individuals complaining about persecution of Orthodox family members by relatives who had left the Church and appeals from village assemblies for the exile of religious dissidents from their midst. In Stavropol' Province, for example, the village assembly of Spasskoe was willing to pay for the removal of its Baptists "as seducers and sowers of their errors among us Orthodox, and as detractors and blasphemers of the Orthodox faith and its sacred things."[85]

Orthodox Church authorities, government officials, the sectarian press, and secular observers of all political persuasions concurred that there existed a problem of violence against religious dissidents in the villages. However, agreeing on what that violence signified was another story. Some viewed it as evidence that the Orthodoxy of the peasantry needed protection; others thought it represented the pernicious influence of Orthodox priests on the people; and still others saw it as a sign that the village was too backward to accept notions of freedom of conscience.

Charges that the Orthodox clergy were the instigators of incidents of popular persecution and violence were a frequent refrain in Baptist accounts of community conflict.[86] Confrontations reported in petitions and in the press were often alleged to have followed a sermon criticizing the Baptists.[87] For example, Baptists in the village of Gurovtsy, Kiev Province, bitterly complained that the village priest was responsible for stirring up enmity toward them in his sermons and claimed that he had sparked a beating of Baptists by hitting a man named Iatsyk in the chest and shouting, "get out of here, shtundist!"[88] There were also allegations that priests stood by as villagers pummeled religious dissidents.[89]

It is difficult to ascertain fully what role Orthodox priests and missionaries actually played in fomenting anxiety about the presence of religious dissidents. Priests may have acknowledged the presence of tensions, but they generally denied any involvement in—and often the very existence of—acts of brutality.[90] Certainly, just as it is unclear what Baptists actually said that offended their Orthodox interlocutors, it is not always apparent that a priest actually suggested attacks on sectarians in a sermon or simply conveyed a message regarding Baptist theological errors. After all, Orthodox parish priests had a pastoral responsibility to warn their flocks about, and protect them against, what the Church perceived to be heresy. Indeed, a diocesan investigation of the case in the Kiev diocese village of Gurovtsy praised the priest as an energetic young pastor who had brought new life to a previously demoralized Orthodox parish. Like many other parish priests, especially after 1905, he had devoted great energy to countering Baptist inroads in his congregation by organizing public debates with the sectarians in the parish school building as well as special missionary evenings.[91] Moreover, many families appreciated the work of priests and missionaries, trusting them to perform this role when they were faced with the apostasy of a son or daughter.[92]

What is clear is that Baptist allegations that their popular mistreatment originated with the clergy struck a chord with many members of the liberal and leftist intelligentsia. For one thing, as Stephen P. Frank has observed, the urban press was intrigued by incidents of village violence as examples of a retrograde and alien culture.[93] Furthermore, such incidents reinforced these observers' tendency to regard the clergy as intellectually and politically backward representatives of state power in the village. The Baptists were aware of both these inclinations and exploited them to their advantage by personally informing writers interested in the cause of religious freedom of their troubles and by widely publicizing such incidents in their own press, which often served as the source for later articles and investigations in the secular press.[94] Reports of altercations were so common that there can be no doubt that real conflict did occur, even if details are often clouded. But these accounts also helped to create a common evangelical identity as an unfairly persecuted people, which drew strength from the example of the first Christians.[95]

Several observers commented on the particular frequency and severity of attacks on evangelicals compared to other religious dissidents. Writing in 1908 and 1909, two prominent commentators on religious dissent, Sergei Mel'gunov and Aleksei Prugavin, each made a direct connection between an alleged resurgence of popular attacks on Baptists and the change in the political fortunes of the liberation movement after 1907. As Mel'gunov warned in 1908, "Reaction is growing, and, along with it, reports about the persecution of sectarians are becoming more frequent."[96] Prugavin connected this phenomenon with the revival of the old demons of village life: "Attacks on Baptists and shtundists and incidents of fierce beating of them are becoming more and more common. In the majority of cases, these attacks take place, as they did in the past, with the favorable assistance, and sometimes even with the participation of representatives of village authority, the police, and even the clergy; the initiative not infrequently belongs to the latter."[97]

Such accusations against priests and police were necessary, in part, to retain the liberal and populist faith in the democratic potential of the people. In an example of such idealization, an article in the liberal newspaper, *Riech'*, reported an incident of a crowd mocking local Baptists as they attempted to perform an open-air baptism; the author concluded that someone must have incited the "picture of a full pogrom" which ensued, for,

> our simple people usually relates very tolerantly to all non-Christian and non-Orthodox people. The sight of people praying, regardless of how strange the form of prayer, never arouses even simple mockery in the Russian person, not to mention enmity and violence. How indeed the celebrated "placidity" of the Russian peasant had to be turned upside down in order to lead him to such a pogrom! And they are leading them.[98]

Perhaps in some cases ignorant villagers did succumb to the intolerant instigation of representatives of church or state. More likely, such incidents provide evidence that both peasant communities and the evangelicals those communities rejected could use the perceptions of various elites to further their collective goals. Just as the evangelicals made sure that liberal and left-wing observers heard of their plight and spared no time in blaming the priests whom their supporters would expect to act in an intolerant and brutal manner, so some village assemblies, such as the community that wanted to expel its Baptists as "dangerous both for us Cossacks and for the whole State," were not averse to appealing to the beliefs of government and right-wing observers about the Russian peasant's devotion to defending Orthodoxy or the relationship between Orthodoxy and political reliability. And such arguments were taken up in the missionary and right-wing press. For example, a 1909 article in the Moscow newspaper *Vieche,* under the ironic title "Fruits of 'Freedom of Conscience,'" described how the Baptists had so "tried the tolerance" of the population of a particular village that villagers felt forced to break the windows in the dissidents' prayer house—an action that initiated a violent fight.[99] Thus such accounts of violence served as grist for the mills of intellectuals' debates about the nature of the Russian soul, the suitability of Western European models of religious tolerance to the Russian milieu, and the political implications of religious change.

These frequent reports of violence arising from religious dissidence produced a dilemma for the policy makers in St. Petersburg, who actively followed press reports about sectarians and regularly investigated incidents of violence. On the one hand, the rhetoric and practice of violence helps to explain the association between Baptist activity and social disorder that developed in officials' minds; on the other hand, because the government was concerned above all with keeping order, the authorities in St. Petersburg often found themselves in the position of defenders of religious dissidents against the actions of their Orthodox neighbors.[100]

Between 1910 and the outbreak of World War I the Russian Baptists came to symbolize the challenges of changing popular mentalities and competing visions of the polity to various groups in government, church, and society. Discussions surrounding the Baptists animated many of the key contests after 1905, from questions about the reshaping of traditional institutions to those concerning the nature of citizenship to those regarding the suitability of democratic politics to the Russian national character. Whether in the village or in the broader national community, through their actions, but also simply by their presence, the Baptists disrupted traditional social, religious, and political relationships. Both their opponents and their supporters were convinced of this. Diverse voices in Russian society labeled the Baptists as heretics, as dangerous revolutionaries, as pacifists, as democrats, or as martyrs. One thing they all agreed on was that the Baptists represented a new, participatory social model that challenged imperial institutions to rethink their relationship with the Russian population after the 1905 Revolution.

The evangelicals were often brash in their dogged pursuit of converts, even as church and state strengthened measures to combat their influence. They caused social upheaval and forced government response. In these ways they reflected a broader pattern in the emergence of modern notions of the tolerant—or completely secular—state. In many Western countries where today the ideas of religious tolerance or the separation of church and state are taken for granted, such principles did not appear as a matter of ideology per se but rather emerged through a process of negotiation, as states and local communities tried to work out a way to cope with dissent in their midst. William G. McLoughlin has written of how, in colonial New England, the challenge of early Baptists to traditional beliefs and customs invited "violent reactions from both respectable and disreputable members of the community." He and other historians of early America chart a "process of expansion of liberty" rather than a straightforward "victory" of the idea of separation of church and state.[101] Similarly, in early-twentieth-century Russia, the case of the Baptists illuminates the halting beginnings of this process of negotiating change in the relationship of the late imperial state to the individual beliefs of its subjects.

After 1910 evangelical leaders became increasingly pessimistic about the prospects for such change, but still the process continued. For the most part the Baptist campaign was not explicitly political. Above all, converts sought the ability to practice their religion and make new converts. To do so, however, required a new kind of state and society, and so, unwittingly, as a result of personal spiritual choices, the Baptists found themselves on the front line of this process of ideological and institutional change in Russia. An important aspect of this new kind of state would be the removal of Orthodoxy as a crucial criterion for full membership.

5

Russian Baptists
and the "German Faith"

"Remain Russian and Orthodox, beware the German *shtunda*!" With this concluding sentence, a 1912 pamphlet sought to warn readers away from converting to the Baptist faith and drive home the alien and dangerous character of evangelical Protestantism for the Russian soul.[1] Such attitudes were not merely the stuff of popular pamphlets. In fact, they shaped government policy. In his annual report for 1910 the Governor-General of the Steppe (an area covering parts of present-day western Siberia and Kazakhstan) devoted considerable attention to the spread of Baptist religion among Russian settlers in this area. The Governor-General regarded these conversions as a danger to state interests, arguing that "so long as the Russian *muzhik* [peasant] has not lost his Orthodoxy, Russia will be strong and powerful, but with its loss, that dangerous cosmopolitanism, which the enemies of our motherland so energetically sow, will take root." Tsar Nicholas II was certainly moved by this analysis: in the report's margins, he scribbled, "one is gripped by horror upon reading the chapter of the report on sectarianism" and "we need to battle this dangerous evil fully armed." The Minister of Internal Affairs then commissioned a major report on the situation which concluded that, indeed, by rejecting Orthodoxy, that "essential expression of Russian national identity," the Baptist convert "gradually becomes alienated from all that is Russian." Even the accent of the Baptist convert allegedly took on a German quality![2]

The conversion of Russians to the Baptist faith radically challenged fundamental assumptions about the relationship between the Orthodox Church and the state and between Orthodoxy and Russian nationality. For church, state, and probably most Russians, to be Russian was to be Orthodox. Until 1905 government policy on Russian evangelicalism was animated by the famous 1881 statement of the powerful Over Procurator of the Holy Synod, Konstantin Pobedonostsev: "There are and must be no Russian Baptists."[3] However, with the Decree on Religious Toleration of that revolutionary year, the state implicitly acknowledged that the Russian Baptists and other religious minorities were a fact of Russian life. But whether they had a legitimate place in Russian society remained an open question. It was not simply in the villages that converts faced ostracism. Their opponents in church and state used notions of authentic national identity to brand them with cultural and political illegitimacy. The evangelicals countered by adopting the imagery and language of Russian national myth and Russia's messianic mission to assert their rightful place in the Russian body politic and to advance a vision of a reformed Russian state, where Orthodoxy would no longer be the criterion for Russian nationality. The Russian Baptists' attempts to make their faith Russian and to promote a vision of a Russian Reformation provide an illuminating example of the popular acceptance and reformulation of Western ideas that was taking place in all areas of the rapidly changing late imperial Russian society. They also reveal how the very idea of Russianness was an ambiguous and hotly contested one in this period.

MAKING THEIR FAITH RUSSIAN:
EVANGELICALS DEFINE THEIR MOVEMENT

From the inception of the Russian evangelical movement one of the central questions its members had to address was that of national allegiances and the cultural legitimacy of their spiritual choices. Not only outside pressures but also ideas about Russianness and religious practice among the believers themselves posed this problem acutely. As the denomination formed in the late nineteenth century, evangelicals struggled to deal with their common heritage of foreign ideas and people. This conversation was strongly shaped by the climate of opinion in which it occurred: discussion of the Baptist challenge quickly became a vehicle for a variety of voices in Russian society to address the significance of increasing penetration of Western ideas in Russia. Each of the contending sides in this broader public debate believed that Russian nationality had certain essential and immutable characteristics that could be identified and described. The controversy centered on defining what these immutable features actually were.

The problem of how early tutelage by non-Russians affected the character of Russian evangelicalism as it developed into a movement was debated both within the Baptist community and by outside observers. The English model, brought by Lord Radstock or filtered through Russian nobles who had been abroad, dominated in St. Petersburg. The Evangelical Christian leader, Ivan Prokhanov, and the Baptist pastor in St. Petersburg, Vil'gel'm Fetler, had both studied at Baptist colleges in England before 1905.[4] The English model also penetrated the country through the British and Foreign Bible Society, which had a large network to distribute Synod-printed Bibles in Russia, and whose agents often (illegally) provided future Baptists with their first exposure to Protestant ideas.[5] In most of the empire, by contrast, the German example, by way of the Russian Germans, provided the most immediate model in form and content for organizing scattered groups of believers into a budding denomination. Early leaders from south Russia also traveled to Johann Oncken's mission school in Hamburg and looked to his many publications for guidance. However, the Slavs quickly began to organize and lead themselves. By the early years of the twentieth century, when the Russian organization had clearly established itself as separate from the German-speaking branch, Hamburg remained a center of inspiration but was no longer the metropolis for Russia's Baptists. With the founding of the British- and American-dominated Baptist World Alliance in 1905, Britain and the United States became competing sources of ideas, moral support, and, on occasion, money.

German influence remained a particularly sensitive issue, however. As Walter Laqueur points out, Germans had long been the principal foreign element within European Russia, and Slavophilism and Russian nationalism emerged in part out of resentment of their strong influence.[6] Such animosity animated one of the most widely read works on the Russian Baptist movement, by Bishop Aleksii Dorodnitsyn, a former missionary in Kherson and Ekaterinoslav dioceses. In discussing the founding conference of the Russian Baptist Union in 1884, he mocked the preamble to the minutes which stated that it was "the first independent conference of Russian baptized brothers in our beloved fatherland Russia," warning that,

> this sect, which has cast its net so broadly over the south of Russia, represents a great force that is inimical not only to the Orthodox Church, but also to the state structure of Russia—a force all the more dangerous, because its activity is directed by the experienced hands of the German leaders [*vozhakov*] of the shtunda-neobaptists, who do not miss the most insignificant opportunity to be of use in service to the never-to-be-forgotten *Faterland* at the expense of the "beloved fatherland," Russia.

Thus, in his view, "our south-Russian *shtunda* is the work of German inspiration."[7] Converts to the Baptist faith were dupes of the national enemies of the Russian Empire.

In fact, although Russian Baptists constantly engaged foreign ideas and models, these were not accepted without challenge, and indeed much soul searching. Despite their strong conviction that truth knew no human borders, the question of national character continually vexed the Russian Baptists. As they sought to name their movement, find music and liturgies to celebrate their faith, and establish a network of congregations, Russian evangelicals repeatedly confronted the problem of establishing a native Russian version of an imported Baptist faith. In so doing they defined themselves in opposition to the Russian Orthodox Church but also in dialogue with the most immediately available model, that of the German Baptists within the Russian Empire.

As the debate over the use of the term "Baptist" shows, the very naming of the groups of Russians that came to believe in the adult baptism of believers, in the priesthood of every believer, and in a congregational form of church organization was a process fraught with strategic significance. For both supporters and critics of the movement, at issue was the degree to which a name conveyed a Western affinity and whether this Western affinity was desirable.

Conflict over what to call themselves constituted not merely an internal issue among converts. It was also about controlling the public perception of the movement. For this reason they rejected the term "shtundist." The believers do not seem to have called themselves "shtundists," and throughout their history they made strenuous efforts to reject the term.[8] Not only did it have a foreign ring, but it had been used to persecute the Russian Baptists in the Pobedonostsev era. The word remained charged with political and cultural illegitimacy. Indeed, long after 1905 Orthodox anti-sectarian missionaries continued to signal the danger of some revivalistic religious movements among the Slavs by affixing the prefix "shtundo-" to the names of the various groups.[9]

The chief alternative to the name "Baptists" proposed by Russian believers came to be *evangel'skie khristiane*. Although I follow the practice of previous English-language studies of the evangelical movement in Russia that have translated the name *evangel'skie khristiane* as "Evangelical Christians," this does not convey important messages implied in the selection of the word *evangel'skie* over *evangelicheskie*.[10] The term *evangel'skie* is more properly translated as "gospel" and it reflects the aim of some Russian believers to emphasize that the source of authority for them was the Bible alone, and not also the "holy tradition" of the Orthodox Church. Moreover, the term differentiated the Russian evangelicals from the German Lutherans in Russia, to whom the term *evangelicheskie* had previously been exclusively applied and whose principles of faith were rather different. When opponents of the Gospel Christians used the term *evangelicheskie*, they colored them with a culturally foreign hue.[11]

Yet an editorial in the first issue of *Baptist* pleaded that it would be a shame if "we [were] forced for the sake of some one or more hundred uneasy and feeble of our brothers to break the link and destroy our unity with ten million foreign Baptists who make up with us one body and one soul."[12]

Whether they called themselves Evangelical Christians or Baptists, the problem of reconciling the craving for spiritual and organizational autonomy that underlay the movement with the drive to organize and expand according to foreign models loomed large. Russian evangelicals expressed pride in belonging to an international communion and tended to be quite candid about the part that non-Russians had played in the evolution of their church. They insisted, however, that this role was primarily catalytic. Foreigners or Russian Germans had provided language and forms that systematized already existing ideas and aspirations. Nevertheless the memoirs and personal correspondence of early leaders reveal the practical and intellectual difficulties of reconciling borrowed structures with popular native aspirations. For example, the influential Baptist missionary and later pastor of Baku, Vasilii Ivanov, described the tension between Russians and Germans over liturgical practices in his unpublished recollections of the early days of the Tiflis congregation. Although the faith was the same, he explained, "the nation and habits were different." "The Russian Baptists," he elaborated, "wanted to hold to many Molokan practices in the service, such as singing psalms in the Molokan way, and performing bows during singing and prayers and so on." The Germans, by contrast, "wanted to toss out everything Russian and Molokan from the service and set up everything in the German manner."[13] The former Molokans were not the only new Baptists who initially combined aspects of their previous traditions in their services: the first converts in the Odessa area started out by singing Orthodox prayers and songs, and retained many Orthodox tunes even after they had begun either to compose their own hymns or to borrow words and melodies from German hymns.[14]

The issue was not simply one of Germans against Russians, however. The Russians themselves were divided over which path to take. For example, disagreements about strategy often surfaced in the memoirs and lifelong correspondence of two founders of the Russian Baptist movement, both members of that first Tiflis congregation, Vasilii Ivanov and Vasilii Pavlov. Ivanov tended to resist organizational strictures on religious expression, stressing the wisdom of the popular spiritual drive that had given birth to the movement. Pavlov, by contrast, emerged as the Russian missionary of German ideas and organizational methods.

Ivanov was the progeny of an old Molokan family from the village of Novo-Ivanovka, Elisavetpol Province. After his baptism in 1871 Ivanov traveled widely across Transcaucasia, preaching the new faith in Molokan communities. Between 1880 and 1895, as an official missionary of the nascent Baptist Union (and with its not always reliable financial support), Ivanov worked tirelessly to spread Baptist ideas to the northern Caucasus, along the Volga, in Ukraine, and into the central provinces of Russia. Although the government ignored his earlier work among Molokan populations, once these Orthodox areas became Ivanov's target he began to suffer arrest and restrictions on his movement. From 1895 to 1900, he and his family were exiled to Kalisz Province in Russian Poland. Thereafter he served as presbyter of the Baku congregation until 1917 and continued to work as a missionary for part of each year.[15] Pavlov also converted in 1871. He soon showed himself to be a gifted preacher with a quick mind and a talent for languages, and in 1875 he attended Oncken's seminary in Hamburg. After having been ordained a missionary by Oncken in 1876, Pavlov returned to Russia an enthusiastic preacher not merely of Baptist religious ideas but also of the German Baptist organizational and liturgical model. Armed with this knowledge, he played a crucial role in setting up a network of congregations and creating some unity of belief and practice. As with Ivanov, Pavlov's activity drew the negative attention of the authorities: between 1887 and 1891, and again from 1891 to 1895, Pavlov was exiled to Orenburg under close police surveillance. There, weakened by hunger, his wife and four of his five children died of cholera in 1892. In 1895 Pavlov fled to Tulcea, Romania, at the invitation of the local Russian-German Baptist congregation and remained there until 1900. After 1905 Pavlov would serve as presbyter of the Odessa congregation from 1907 to 1914, be elected president of the Baptist Union in 1909, and edit the journal *Baptist* in 1910–11.[16]

The organizational development that Pavlov spearheaded in the 1880s and 1890s was not achieved without some strain. In their correspondence, Ivanov and Pavlov continued to work out the tension between the appeal of borrowing from the obviously successful German model and honoring the indigenous aspirations that had given rise to their movement. Ivanov returned many times to the problem of finding a distinctively Russian path. For example, he repeatedly expressed anxiety about Pavlov's dedication to standardizing the movement by translating German "Protestant" statements of faith, such as the Hamburg confession of the German Baptists.[17] In an 1899 letter to Union president Mazaev, Ivanov wrote passionately that he had concluded that Russian leaders should not follow the path laid out by non-Russian Baptists. All forms of Western Christianity, in his view, seemed to be driven by materialist goals. In fact, he suggested, "our Russian brotherhood has nothing to learn from scholars, and therefore we have to take a different direction in our spiritual life in order that we not fall into lifelessness, as other Christians have. That we might have less formality and more spiritual life."[18] And yet this Russian lack of formality also troubled him. In a letter the following year, Ivanov wrote of his mixed feelings upon observing the lives of German Baptists in Poland. He had found orderliness in their congregations but had also found what seemed to him to be "cold formality." Nevertheless, he confessed, he was discouraged by the Russian believers' inability to achieve the formal organization of the Germans. Instead of practical advice, the Russians were interested in borrowing from the Germans only "all that gratifies bodily feeling, bare phrases such as 'My sins are forgiven.'"[19] In this way Ivanov expressed a broader conflict between admiration of German organization and the conviction that free, unstructured religious expression was more in the nature of the Russian soul. His writings evoke the considerable ambivalence about the "Western" model in a movement accused of being "Western."

A fine example of the challenge of meshing the local with the borrowed in Russian Baptist culture—and also of the opportunities provided by 1905—can be found in the history of Baptist music in Russia. The need for hymns and the search for suitable tunes had been a theme since the early days of the movement. For a long time local practice seems to have combined Orthodox or Molokan favorites with borrowed Western spiritual music. Moreover, just as the Russian Baptists adopted the Western habit of sitting in church, they also introduced instrumental music into their services, including balalaika, guitar, or violin ensembles and, in a few affluent congregations, pump organs. One prominent missionary expert on the Baptists contended that, although the shtundists originally sang Orthodox hymns at their meetings, their switch to a popular collection of translated religious verse, titled *An Offering to Orthodox Christians,* marked the first step in their decisive separation not only from the faith but also from the liturgy of the Orthodox Church. Then, in 1902, the emerging Evangelical Christian leader, Prokhanov, was able to slip past the censor a collection of 570 spiritual songs, with music, described as "collected verse of some Russian writers," known as *Gusli* [Psaltery]. Composed, in fact, mostly of translations of foreign verse, it nevertheless became the most popular hymnal among all branches of the evangelical movement for decades.[20]

Russian Baptists and Evangelical Christians continued to grope for a distinctively Russian evangelical style of music. In the memoirs he wrote for an American audience many years later, Prokhanov summarized the problem at hand. "When the freedom came," he wrote, "I used it for printing my hymns according to my inspiration and general ideas. While highly appreciating the translation of Western hymns, I thought that the Russian Evangelical Christianity should produce hymns according to the character of the Russian people and their tastes." Although he had contributed some of his own verse to *Gusli,* he became especially active in this area after 1905, when he began to write a hymn each month and publish it in his widely read journal, *Khristianin.*

In his autobiography Prokhanov praised the beauty of Russian church and secular music, but he argued that its style was inappropriate to the ideas of evangelical Christianity. The Orthodox faith, he asserted, was inherently pessimistic. "But the music of the Evangelical Christian movement could not be mournful like the popular music, nor sad like the music of the Greek Orthodox Church," he wrote. "Our music must be of such a character as to contain the joy of the Gospel, a joy overwhelming and overcoming the sadness of former Russian music." For this reason he enlisted an evangelical student at the St. Petersburg Conservatory, K. P. Inkis (a Latvian, ironically!), to compose new melodies in the Russian style for most of his hymns and to assist him in selecting foreign tunes for the remainder. By the time of the writing of these memoirs in 1933, Prokhanov claimed to have composed 624 hymns and translated an additional 413.[21]

The problem Prokhanov described was highlighted at the Baptists' national congress in St. Petersburg in 1910, when a heated debate broke out about the contents of a proposed hymn book. One representative complained that Protestant melodies did not satisfy him in comparison with the singing he heard in Orthodox or Catholic churches. Others disagreed, saying that the tone of the music suited them fine or pointing out that Orthodox missionaries attributed sectarians' success precisely to their music. Elena Beklemisheva, representing Stavropol' Province, suggested that, in compiling the new hymnal, the Baptists ought to transcribe the tunes composed and sung by local congregations in Kiev and Khar'kov provinces. Delegates eventually elected a commission of choir directors and presbyters to begin work on the volume.[22] Although, in the end, the Baptists do not seem to have published their own new hymnal before 1917, the collection and dissemination of local musical compositions would be an important project for both branches of the evangelical movement before and especially after the 1917 Revolution.[23]

Of course, charges of "cosmopolitanism" against the Russian evangelicals were not entirely unfounded. The experiences of interaction with Germans and of persecution for their faith refined Russian Baptists' sense of themselves as Russians. But, as William James had argued, in the new convert, "religious ideas, previously peripheral in his consciousness, now take a central place, and . . . religious aims form the habitual center of his energy."[24] Certainly the conviction of having found the true faith made Russian evangelicals into internationalists, more concerned with spiritual than ethnic kinship. The evangelical press celebrated multiethnicity with accounts of joint meetings of Latvian, Estonian, and Russian congregations in St. Petersburg, or of Russian and German and Jewish Baptists in Odessa.[25] Several people of non-Slavic origin threw in their lot with the Russians. Among these was the German Ivan V. Kargel', a member of the first Tiflis congregation and later the leading theological thinker of the Russian movement.[26] The pastor of the St. Petersburg flock, Vil'gel'm Fetler, was a Latvian who initially ministered to both Latvians and Russians in the capital.

The foreign aspect of their faith, from the movement's inception, was therefore a subject of both pride and anxiety for Russia's Baptists. In 1908, Ivanov wrote in *Baptist* that, "the question of where a faith comes from has no significance in and of itself and believers do not dwell on it . . . it is interesting only from a scholarly point of view." Yet, in the same article, he acknowledged that Russian Baptists were affected by the wider society's preoccupation with this issue, when he observed that, "the assertion of Orthodox spiritual writers that the Baptist faith was brought here by the Germans has at its basis the one goal of blackening sectarians in the eyes of the Orthodox masses . . . and it is well known that our simple people to this day react with hostility to anything '*German*.'"[27] From the village to the church to the government department, the Baptists were surrounded by people who cared deeply about ethnicity and who questioned the suitability of their spiritual choices.

BAPTIST SPIRITUALITY AND THE RUSSIAN SOUL

From the first appearance of the Russian Baptists, Orthodox anti-sectarian missionaries had been primarily responsible for setting the terms of public discussion about this new religious phenomenon. Both in its own self-image and through its place in the state structure, the Russian Orthodox Church was the main official guardian of culture and promoter of Russian identity. As a result, questions about the nature of Russian religious identity and the Russian soul, and about the challenge of new influences, infused Orthodox writers' discussions of the problem of religious sectarianism. The conversion of people whom the church saw as its own—Russians, Belarusians, and Ukrainians (described collectively in the sources as Russians)—to a Western form of Christianity posed in stark terms the question that was troubling Russian society in all aspects of its life, that of the place of Western values in Russia. Especially after 1905 Orthodox churchmen were acutely aware that they were living in a revolutionary era, one that a professor of Orthodox missions described as "a time of reevaluation of all values, when so often white appears black, and black—white."[28] In such a time they needed to steer a straight course to preserve both the Orthodox faith and what they perceived to be true Russian values and identity. In this spirit, the annual report of the Over Procurator of the Holy Synod for 1905–7 looked back nostalgically to a simpler, holier time and bemoaned the pernicious effect of new ideas: "Holy Russia knew no sectarianism. . . . Sectarianism is a product of Western European culture, a bridge to unbelief. And in this respect it is inimical not only to Orthodoxy but to the genuine nature of the Russian person."[29] Many contemporary commentators, whether they represented the Church, the state, the liberal and leftist intelligentsia, or the evangelicals themselves, shared this view that religious dissidence was a product of Russia's changing times. The suitability of this path for the Russian soul, by contrast, was deeply disputed.

A wide spectrum of both Orthodox and secular commentators asserted that the Russian evangelical movement was, in some way, an expression of what they called "rationalist" ideas. They disagreed, however, over the place of such ideas in Russian culture. Although members of the liberal and leftist intelligentsia tended to follow the famous Populist student of sectarianism, A. S. Prugavin, in asserting that "teachings of an ethical-rationalist character are not at all alien to the spirit of the Russian people," most Slavophile or Orthodox Church–based writers classified rationalist ideas as inherently Western and incompatible with Russian spirituality.[30] As was explained in the opening paragraph of a guide on sectarians for parish clergy: "A dry, rational approach to faith is not characteristic of the Russian people. . . . Therefore, although some rationalist ideas have been expressed in the Russian Church almost from the first days of its existence, they were not of Russian origin but rather were brought in from outside."[31]

Church studies and seminary textbooks on religious sectarianism generally classified Russian sectarian groups as either "mystical" or "rationalistic" in their teachings. According to this scheme, the mystical sects, such as the *khlysty* and the *skoptsy*, taught the direct link of a person to God through the experience of the Holy Spirit and the possibility of unification of humans with God. This led to their tendency to find Christs, prophets, and mothers of God among their members. These groups were said to appeal to "people of uncontrollable feeling." By contrast, the rationalistic sects approached the divine through the power of the mind and an individual reading of the Bible. "Rejecting the authority of the church," explained one popular textbook, "they govern themselves only by reason and therefore, naturally, allow freethinking" in their interpretation of scripture.[32] Although this textbook and others were quick to note that both elements were found in most sects, this was the standard framework for understanding religious dissent.[33]

According to Orthodox authors, both the mystical and the rationalist sects resulted from deviations in the normal spiritual development of the Russian people. A guide for village priests contended that "rationalist sectarianism brings into the religious worldview of the Russian people a completely new element that contradicts its previous faith and therefore aims at [that people's] destruction."[34] Vladimir N. Terletskii, an instructor at the Poltava seminary, explained in his textbook that a tension between the principles of body and mind underlay all religious sectarianism. In the West, the Roman Catholic Church exaggerated the first aspect of human nature, while the Protestant churches were too given over to the latter. The Orthodox Church alone, he asserted, maintained the perfect balance between the two.[35] The Baptists had succumbed to a foreign deviation from the true Christian faith that was preserved in the Russian Orthodox Church. Only Orthodoxy could save the Russian people.

Liberal and populist observers who disagreed with the church on just about everything were nevertheless equally likely to find rationalistic ideas at the core of the Baptist movement. Although most did trace the source of these ideas in Russia to Western influences, such authors argued that Russians had enthusiastically embraced them because they suited certain innate Russian qualities. One well-known study asserted that two major characteristics of the Slavic peasantry had made it fertile ground for the evolution of rationalist ideas. First, rationalism suited the spirit and character of the "free-communal Slavic life;" second, it naturally appealed to ordinary Russians in their practical efforts to improve their lives.[36] Similarly a St. Petersburg writer, reporting on the 1909 Baptist Congress in St. Petersburg, wrote that, despite its German roots, "the Baptist faith found sympathy for itself in the Russian soil, in the spiritual needs and psychology of the Russian person. The majority of Baptists at present . . . are native Russian people. The ponderous quality of the Great Russian character, apparently, fits well with the Baptist faith."[37]

Whereas church writers portrayed the emergence of rational sectarianism as a deviation from Russian nature, liberals and populists saw it as a natural development fitting into their ideas about the nature of historical development in general. The views of Varvara Iasevich-Borodaevskaia, a prominent specialist on sectarianism and a follower of Lev Tolstoy's religious teachings, are a good example. She argued that, in the turbulent atmosphere of post-emancipation Russia and with the widespread distribution of the Bible in the Russian vernacular to the peasantry after 1862, it was not surprising that, as it had in the West, access to the Bible had led to Protestant movements. In her view, "sectarianism with a rationalist orientation appeared as a completely natural stage of development of popular belief."[38] This perception that Russian religious life was bound to follow universal historical laws shared with the West similarly underlay the famous historian and liberal politician Pavel N. Miliukov's discussion of the place of sectarianism in Russian culture. In his view, the general law of all religious development was a "gradual spiritualization of religion, the gradual transformation of the religion of the ritual to the religion of the spirit." He connected the Baptist movement to a long tradition of what he termed "spiritual" Christianity (including the Molokans and Dukhobors) in the Russian popular milieu, arising from ideas that had penetrated Russia following the Reformation in the West.[39] Another liberal, Sergei Mel'gunov, similarly averred that rationalist sectarianism was "the product of progressing popular thought, the first level of its development and attempt at [laying] a philosophical basis to questions of faith."[40]

There were practical political and organizational reasons for both the missionaries and the intelligentsia to be interested in this question of the origins of rationalist sectarianism and its compatibility with Russian popular culture. For Orthodox students of the Baptist movement, the answer to the question about whether the movement expressed indigenous or imported ideas would shape anti-sectarian missionary strategy. In the first instance, the focus of missionary work would be on educating the popular spirit away from a deviation in its natural development. By contrast, if rationalism could be traced to external influences, missionaries would concentrate on eliminating the "organically unrelated" forces that had artificially created the conditions leading to this spiritual aberration.[41] The missionaries' overwhelming preference for the argument for "external" causes reflected their conception of the Russian soul as essentially Orthodox. As a result, they tended to focus on exposing the errors of Protestant theology in presentations to the faithful and in debates with sectarians rather than on reforming parish life in response to legitimate aspirations expressed through popular dissidence.

Members of the intelligentsia, searching for evidence of the revolutionary potential of the Russian people, were fond of drawing political conclusions from their observations of sectarian religious life. Indeed, describing his impressions of the Baptist Congress in St. Petersburg in 1909, one observer commented that, "looking at the thickset, bearded figures of the Baptist delegates, listening to their well-considered, staid, and weighty speech, unwittingly imagining them in the deputies' seats in the Taurida palace, you would not say that anyone could compel these people of strong conviction to 'dance to his tune.'"[42] Vladimir Bonch-Bruevich, the Bolshevik student of Russian religious sectarianism, argued in 1910 that "the Baptists, politically very moderate people, all the same always felt and understood the obsolescence of the previous order." It was the demands of their faith, he asserted, that made this so:

> For their "faith," freedom of the word was necessary, since they wanted to preach their faith; and freedom of conscience, since they wanted to confess openly that in which they believed; and freedom of assembly, since they needed to gather to perform the established rituals of worship and gather others for preaching; and freedom of the press, since they needed to publish books for their own use and also for propaganda. What they needed was a *constitution.*[43]

Thus there was a perception of a reasoned approach to faith among the Baptists and a recognition that the demands of such a faith led inherently to a civic order different from that of autocratic Russia.

Orthodox writers shared this view that leaving the church challenged the political status quo, but they drew rather different conclusions. The very idea of Russians becoming Baptists, they believed, threatened the Russian character of the state. One anti-sectarian textbook presented a typical explanation of the connection between Orthodoxy and the survival of Russia as follows:

> Since the Orthodox faith is the main basis of the national self-consciousness of the Russian people, with the destruction of the former comes an unavoidable danger to the latter. History clearly bears witness to the fact that the Russian person who has betrayed the Orthodox faith breaks his internal, spiritual link with the Russian people and becomes a cosmopolitan (our liberal intelligentsia), or even assimilates to a different nationality (polonized West-Russian noble names, resulting from switching to Catholicism). In this way, rationalist sectarianism proves to be extraordinarily dangerous not only from the point of view of the Orthodox Church but also for the state.[44]

From the inception of an organized anti-sectarian missionary movement in the late 1880s, its leaders had emphasized these alleged political implications of religious dissidence as a means of drawing state attention and material support to their cause. The anti-shtundist law of 1894, for example, represented a victory in this effort to define the problems the Church faced as state interests.[45]

As we saw in the opening paragraphs of this chapter, important state officials accepted the Church's argument that Orthodoxy was intimately tied to political reliability. Indeed, the notion of a "spiritual link" between state and people was elaborated in state documents, where Orthodoxy became the crucial criterion for assessing a person's allegiances. For example, in his preamble to new regulations on sectarian congresses published on 14 April 1910, the Minister of Internal Affairs, Petr Stolypin, outlined the reasoning behind restrictions on the participation of foreigners. "With the tight unity that exists in Russia between state and religious life," he wrote, "regardless of religious teaching, the active interference of foreigners, who have no spiritual link with Russia, in the religious life of Russian subjects, and even more their leadership of religious affairs, from the general-state perspective is obviously completely unacceptable."[46] Moreover, the government was acutely convinced that the Baptist religious teaching was incompatible with the political and religious principles of the Russian state and inappropriate to the Russian subject. As the draft of a confidential 1911 letter by the director of the Department of Spiritual Affairs suggested, "The Baptist movement, brought here from the West, carried with it also such approaches and forms for expressing its vital activity [zhiznedeiatel'nosti], which, arising on the basis of rationalism and in the conditions of Western European freedom of conscience, aim not so much at satisfying the prayer and religious needs of members of the Baptist sect, as at the most successful evangelization of the Russian Orthodox population in the Baptist spirit."[47] The document went on to say that, as a result of this intellectual genealogy, the movement gave no heed to any laws that restricted its proselytizing drive. Freedom of conscience was a Western European concept, alien to Russian values. The Baptists' very presence in Russia represented the infiltration of this idea into Russian public life at a time when the Russian government was becoming increasingly ambivalent about its flirtation with the Western liberal model since 1905.

FLAG-WAVING BAPTISTS

In an atmosphere that tied Orthodoxy to political and cultural reliability, the Russian Baptists were careful to affirm their patriotism in many ways. The legacy of the 1894 anti-shtundist law's definition of a shtundist as one who rejected all authority made believers eager to affirm their respect for established government in order to assert their legitimacy as faithful citizens of Russia. Even before legalization of the movement, police reports repeatedly noted that the portrait of the tsar was displayed at the front of the room during prayer meetings.[48] Such displays of patriotism only increased after 1905. Congresses often opened with the singing of the national anthem or prayers for the monarch. Although evidence indicates that there was some resistance among the Baptists to the endorsement of tsarist power, formal messages were sent to the tsar thanking him for declaring freedom of conscience.[49] The strategic aspect of this monarchism was particularly evident in a large poster published by the Baptists in 1911: all the laws and government circulars dealing with the rights of non-Orthodox Christians to hold prayer meetings were reprinted around a large photograph of the tsar captioned with the opening words of "God Save the Tsar." Another such example was a 1913 appeal to the government in which the St. Petersburg Baptist pastor Fetler suggested that, in honor of the tricentennial of the Romanov dynasty, the emperor grant further religious liberties and add "Tolerant" to the list of his titles.[50]

Just as Fetler sought to place his group's support for religious pluralism at the very core of monarchic power by presuming to change the tsar's title, so other Baptists adopted the language, imagery, and forms of Russian national history and culture to assert their vision of a new kind of Russia with freedom of conscience for all. This vision combined love of country and admiration for the achievements of the Western Reformation in a messianic Russian blend. After 1905, evangelicals enthusiastically availed themselves of the new opportunities for freer expression with a call to their fellow Russians to join them in bringing about the Russian Reformation.

The sense of being the vanguard of a new stage in Russian religious history was very important to the Baptists. In the first issue of the magazine *Baptist* an editorial article explained why, of all the many faiths that existed abroad, Russians were turning to the Baptists. "It is fully natural," wrote the author, "for if we were now, as once our Russian Prince Vladimir did, to send our ambassadors to seek out the 'true faith,' we are certain that our ambassadors would settle on neither the Catholics, nor on the Lutherans, nor on any other Gospel congregation, but would settle on the Baptists alone."[51] With this allusion to the famous legend of the "testing of the faiths" that led to the adoption of Orthodox Christianity as the state religion of the Eastern Slavs in 988, the editor of the new journal implied that Russia was embarking on a new religious age.

Vladimir was not the only icon of Russian national myth to be pressed into the service of the Russian Reformation. The Baptists enthusiastically appropriated the very concept of Holy Russia to their vision. For example, in his autobiography, the preacher Fedor P. Balikhin wrote of returning to "the motherland, to holy Russia," after attending a Baptist conference abroad.[52] Indeed, the first detailed exposition of their history and goals, written (and published) by the evangelicals themselves in a January 1905 appeal for legalization, made the Reformation of Holy Russia a driving theme. The petition explicitly brought together the ideas of Russian popular longings and Protestant religious answers. The authors argued that, "if the Russian people in their sincere search for religion come to essentially Protestant views," to accuse them of want of patriotism would be the same as to accuse the Westernizers and Slavophiles of non-Russian character for basing their work on the ideas of the German philosophers. Indeed, they compared themselves explicitly to the Slavophiles, who had used these ideas to defend and promote the cultural particularity of their own people. Combining the language of Western Reformation with that of Russian national myth, they insisted that their aim was that "their dear Russia become truly Holy Russia."[53] In this way the Baptists invoked the Christian history and essence of Russia in order to lay claim to Russia's future for themselves.

In the last years of the empire notions of patriotism and religious renewal along the lines of the Western Reformation were intimately intertwined in the minds of the Baptists. A leading article in Prokhanov's weekly newspaper, *Utrenniaia zviezda* [Morning star], recorded signs of a growing movement for national religious transformation under the headline, "The Reformation Moves Ahead!"[54] References to the Baptists' spiritual mission for Russia abounded in their hymns and poetry. For example, at the opening of the Baptist prayer house in St. Petersburg in 1911, a special hymn declared: "We will save Russia by the Crucified Christ."[55] Similarly a poem in *Baptist* announced: "Our Rus', our native land, has begun to arise and its heart has begun to open to the Gospel of Christ."[56]

Evangelicals also attempted to place the Russian Baptists in a broader tradition of Slavic Reformation through references to the sixteenth-century Hussite movement in Bohemia. For example, in a 1915 appeal to the government for an end to wartime persecution Prokhanov pointed out that the beliefs of the Russian evangelicals, especially regarding communion and the baptism of adult converts, conformed to those of the Hussites rather than to the practices of Luther. Thus, he concluded, "it is clear, that Evangelical Christians in Russia did nothing less than realize the Gospel principles for which Slavic Christians, named the Bohemian Brothers, suffered before the Reformation."[57] Now Russian believers would spread their own Slavic reformation.[58]

Among the many examples of appropriation of national symbols by the Baptists, the singing of their own, non-Orthodox version of the national anthem, "God Save the Tsar," caused the greatest uproar in the right-wing press and considerable consternation among government officials. When, at their national congress in St. Petersburg in September 1910, the Baptists changed a line from "rule to the terror of our enemies, Orthodox Tsar" to "rule to the terror of sin, our glorious Tsar," a Ministry of Internal Affairs official in attendance stood up and ordered that the singing cease. He was ignored. After the meeting a public exchange took place between the official and Fetler, the St. Petersburg pastor, in which the official declared that the government could not tolerate a situation whereby "in Russia each person composes his own national anthem for himself."[59] But regardless of what the government was prepared to tolerate, this is precisely what the Baptists continued to do.

Thus, in their attempts to make their faith Russian and to promote a vision of a Russian Reformation, the Russian Baptists waded into the dangerous waters of debates about the nature of Russian identity and the popular acceptance of Western ideas in the rapidly changing late-imperial Russian society. This concern about Russianness infused their relationships with the state, the national church, the press and their fellow villagers. It also formed a central preoccupation in their conversion narratives. But the very definitions of what constituted "Western" or "Russian" identities and values were being contested in these years. The Baptists provided an important example for a variety of groups interested in these problems; each seized on different aspects of what Russianness might mean in their evaluations of the Baptists.

Baptists' patriotic assertions were continually judged insincere by their enemies. Certainly Baptists must have donned the cloak of patriotism partly in an effort to shield themselves from government suspicions and get on with the more important business of the salvation of souls. This was the analysis of the Minister of Internal Affairs, Nikolai Maklakov, in a 1913 letter to Vladimir Kokovtsov of the State Council. In that letter, Maklakov stated that a recent investigation by his department had revealed that "an insistence on monarchism and nationalism are a standard method of this sect," but that, in fact, they systematically ignored laws regulating their communities, and "their attempt at denationalizing their societies by isolating them from all that is Russian radically contradicts the above-mentioned principles proclaimed by the Baptists."[60] Maklakov was quite right in one sense: in practice the evangelicals simply behaved as though they had the freedom of proselytization which they were legally denied between 1905 and 1917. But the Baptists, like most of the population in these years, kept coming back to the state with appeals and petitions as a way of solving problems. Although it might be too much to suggest a kind of naive monarchism at work, some observers in the late nineteenth century reported a tendency among new believers to replace the icons in their huts with pictures of the tsar and a belief that his government would protect them from the persecutions of the Orthodox Church.[61]

Even if many formal displays of monarchism after 1905 had a strong practical motivation, the prevalence of images of Holy Russia in Baptist hymns, poetry, and other writings may reflect broader popular conceptions of the nature of the Russian land itself. If the image of Holy Russia was indeed, as Michael Cherniavsky has argued, "the myth of the peasant masses attempting to express their collective personality against the overpowering image of the centralized State through the only common and obvious quality they possessed—their faith," then it can be suggested that there was a deeply held tendency in Russian popular culture to see Russia as an essentially religious concept and the country's mission in the world and the problems it faced as fundamentally religious. If this was so, then popular religiosity was intimately tied up with the whole notion of Russia. The evangelicals' pretensions to transform their country through religious reformation may seem less like a cynical borrowing of language and imagery than an expression of a deeper popular tradition.[62]

After 1905, the Russian state confronted an array of groups that, metaphorically, wanted to compose their own national anthem. As a variety of social and cultural groups found their public voices, Russian national identity became a contested concept as never before. The conversion of Russians to Western-style Christianity challenged fundamental assumptions about the relationship between Orthodoxy and Russian nationality. The Baptists repeatedly sought to separate not only the concepts of Russian nationality and Orthodoxy but also the Russian state from the Russian church in order to allow themselves to claim a legitimate place in the new Russia. For its part, the government saw this separation of Orthodoxy from the state as a major danger of the Baptist movement. Before the first Russian revolution, this problem could be treated as a criminal one, with the state defining the criteria for Russian identity, but after the promulgation of religious toleration, state and state church were challenged to compete in a cultural debate over the nature of the Russian soul and of the identity of the Russian nation. This process parallels that in countries such as England or Germany where the gradual removal of legal disabilities for religious dissenters in the nineteenth century forced a reassessment of what had once been, for example, "an unquestioned equation of Englishness with mainstream Anglicanism." Wherever they occurred, debates about religious liberties were also debates about modern citizenship and nationality.[63] The Baptist experience shows how new notions of national identity could be a strategic means for redefining the Russian body politic. As the Baptists borrowed the images and forms of Russian national mythology to assert their legitimate place in Russian national life, they were also advancing a vision of a radically reformed Russian state where Orthodoxy would no longer be the criterion for nationality.

6

Dashed Hopes

1910–1917

The intensification of government, church, and social pressure on Russian Baptists coincided with, and was fueled by, continued activism and increasing visibility of evangelical groups in the center of power in St. Petersburg. Although somewhat chastened by the 1910 regulations on congresses and prayer meetings, the Baptists' seemingly irrepressible missionary spirit continued to promote expansion and institutional development in the years before World War I. When war against the Central Powers came in 1914, the Baptists at last saw a chance to prove their patriotic allegiances by contributing to the war effort. However, the chauvinistic upsurge of the first months of the war soon dashed their hopes of integration into the community of full-fledged Russian subjects. In the broader context of a rejection of all things German, accusations of Baptist "Germanism" rang out ever more loudly and the devastating effect of arrests, exile of leaders, and closure of prayer halls after the outbreak of war sharply curtailed evangelical activity. Thus the crisis of war encouraged the government to act on earlier suspicions about Baptists' national allegiances, dangerous organizational ability, and alleged pacifism. Like many other Russians by 1917, no matter what they had believed before the war, the Baptists would give up on the idea of reaching an accommodation with the imperial government.

The period between 1910 and 1914 saw continued institutional development of the movement. The evangelical press expanded, as *Baptist* and *Khristianin* were joined, in 1910, by Ivan Prokhanov's new weekly newspaper addressing religious and political life, *Utrenniaia zviezda* [Morning star]. Other journals aimed at a national audience also appeared: in St. Petersburg *Gost'* [Guest] began publication in 1910, edited by Vil'gel'm Fetler; a youth-oriented Baptist journal, *Drug molodezhi* [Friend of youth], was published in Balashov from 1911 to 1916; and between mid-1913 and late 1914 Baptists in Odessa produced the weekly *Slovo istiny* [Word of truth]. In 1908 Prokhanov, together with a group of Mennonite Brethren, founded an evangelical publishing house that issued a steady stream of tracts and books. Soon thereafter they opened a bookstore in St. Petersburg. The following year Fetler organized his own competing publishing house that distributed between 90 and 180 titles annually.[1]

Russian evangelicals also took the first steps in establishing some sort of Biblical training in their own language. In the first years after the 1905 Revolution the St. Petersburg Evangelical Christians ran informal six-week training courses for preachers, attended by both Evangelical Christians and Baptists from across the empire. A few young Baptists also continued to attend the German Baptist seminary in Łodz, Russian Poland, until it was closed down in 1911. In 1912, the All-Russian Union of Evangelical Christians received government permission to establish a two-year Bible course in St. Petersburg. Nineteen young men came to the capital in February 1913 to begin their studies in scripture, exegesis, dogma, homiletics, comparative religions, philosophy, ethics, the history of Christianity, and church music.[2]

The Russian evangelical movement became increasingly visible to the central government and the broader public in these years. Between 1909 and January 1912 the Evangelical Christians held three congresses in the capital. Meanwhile, the Union of Russian Baptists, whose activities had traditionally been centered in the southern reaches of the empire, convened a national congress in St. Petersburg in 1910 and in Moscow in 1911. These conventions allowed the Baptist message to be heard and commented upon by the public, the national press, and government officials.

On Christmas day, 1911, the proud dedication of a splendid Baptist house of worship in St. Petersburg also contributed to this growing visibility. Leading Russian Baptists, along with representatives of the capital's Evangelical Christian and non-Russian Baptist congregations and several foreign guests, gathered for the festive opening of the new Dom Evangeliia [House of the Gospel] on Vasil'evskii Island. After a four-year fund-raising campaign throughout the empire and among Baptists abroad, the largest evangelical prayer house in Russia, with seating for two thousand people and lodging for visitors, opened its doors.[3]

Also in these years, more than ever before, the Russian Baptists enjoyed the support and attention of their foreign brethren. In particular, Baptists from the English-speaking world, both directly through their activities and via the translation of their tracts and hymns, replaced the Germans as a source of inspiration and assistance. This foreign interest was both a blessing and a curse, for although it brought money to finance projects such as Dom Evangeliia and the moral protection of visibility abroad, it also aroused resentment and suspicions about Baptist loyalties.

By 1911 the Baptist World Alliance, founded in 1905, had developed into a force to be reckoned with. Its British and American leaders took a particular interest in developing and supporting Baptist communities on the European continent. In 1908, for example, they organized a European Baptist conference in Berlin, attended by hundreds of delegates, including several Russians.[4] Baptist World Alliance leaders also sought to defend the rights of Baptists around the world. In Russia, for instance, at the time of the opening of the House of the Gospel, Dr. Robert Stuart MacArthur, the president of the Alliance, appealed personally to the chairman of the Council of Ministers, Vladimir N. Kokovtsov, for permission to allow himself and all foreigners to speak at the ceremony and also for permission to establish a theological college in the capital.[5] However, a later attempt by MacArthur to intercede before the central government on behalf of persecuted Baptists in mid-1914 would be sternly rebuked as foreign interference.[6]

At the Russian Baptist Union's 1910 congress in St. Petersburg, a letter from John Howard Shakespeare, the secretary of the Baptist World Alliance, was read aloud. It announced that the Alliance would hold a Second International Congress in Philadelphia in June 1911 and that it would contribute £20 for each delegate toward the expenses of between forty and fifty delegates from the Russian Empire. Shakespeare requested that two-thirds of the delegates be of Russian ethnicity and also expressed a particular interest in seeing those "who have suffered persecution or exile in the name of Christ."[7]

In the end, despite difficulty in obtaining departure visas, twenty-four Russians attended the congress, including Prokhanov of the Evangelical Christians and most of the leading Baptists. In Philadelphia the Russians were feted as heroes and martyrs of the international Baptist cause. The opening remarks of the congress chairman dwelt at length on the Russian situation. Later, when Shakespeare introduced the Russian delegation, he declared that the story of how he had brought the Russians to the United States "would read like a romance." He then introduced each individual Russian delegate, with a brief sketch of his or her work for the faith, the only national delegation so honored. Finally, the Russians' attendance at the congress was crowned by Prokhanov's election as one of the Alliance's ten vice presidents, a position he would hold until 1928.

Alarmed, the Russian ambassador in Washington notified St. Petersburg that, from reading the American press, one might think that the Russian Baptists were the center of the congress.[8] Certainly the Russian cause clearly inspired the delegates and received heavy press coverage, including a lengthy front-page article in the *Philadelphia Inquirer*.[9] In fact, more than forty-five

Members of the Russian delegation to the Second Congress of the Baptist World Alliance, Philadelphia, 1911. Fifth from right, second row, seated, is Vasilii V. Ivanov. Next to him, sixth from right, is Vasilii G. Pavlov. Same row, third from left, is Fedor P. Balikhin.
From Baptist World Alliance. Second Congress. Record of Proceedings, 1911.

years later, a major Baptist encyclopedia wrote, in one of only two sentences devoted to the 1911 congress, that "notable . . . was the presence of a large Russian delegation and the spontaneous raising of more than $30,000 to establish a Baptist seminary in Russia."[10]

The congress drew press attention back in Russia, as well as the concern of the central government. The government was not only offended by the way the Baptist World Alliance had turned the Russian Baptists into martyrs; it was also anxious about American and British Baptist leaders' expression of radical, "social gospel" politics at the congress. Government studies worriedly cited statements by the Alliance's outgoing president, John Clifford, about the Baptists' fight for freedom, equality, and brotherhood—and against war. They also fretted about theologian Walter Rauschenbusch's speech, "The Church and the Social Crisis," in which he described the Baptists as the descendants of the most radical party of the English Reformation and in which he envisioned a program of broad social reform based on the teachings of Jesus.[11]

The events of the Philadelphia congress bore serious implications for the subsequent attitude of the government toward the Baptists. A few months later, on the eve of the Russian Baptist Union's planned national convention in Moscow in late September 1911, the director of the Ministry of Internal Affairs, S. Kryzhanovskii, told the chairman of the Council of Ministers, Kokovtsev, that, in view of what had gone on at the Philadelphia congress, he attached "great significance to this Russian congress." He had thus decided to order the director of the Department of Spiritual Affairs personally to attend its sessions.[12]

The events of the Moscow congress were emblematic of the achievements and difficulties of the Baptists by 1911 in terms of the topics discussed, the behavior of the Baptists, and the reactions of outsiders. Between September 25 and October 1, eighty-two delegates, the overwhelming majority of whom were described in the official report to the Minister of Internal Affairs as belonging to the "lower classes," and thirty-five guests with consultative votes crowded together in the Moscow congregation's prayer hall. The topics of discussion resembled those of previous congresses: problems with persecution, extensive planning for mission, the Baptist press, the administration of the Union, relations with the Evangelical Christians, and efforts to develop Baptist charitable and educational institutions. As always, the Baptists' vision was grandiose: delegates discussed plans for a large prayer house and seminary, to be built in Moscow with the aid of foreign donations.[13]

The national congress was also the scene of typical examples of both the Russian Baptists' patriotic strategies and their defiant proselytism. In their opening sessions, delegates composed a telegram to the emperor expressing their devotion and stood to honor the recently assassinated prime minister Stolypin. As a Moscow secret police agent wrote in his report, the congress "draws attention to itself by the demonstrative emphasis of its patriotism and nationalist aspirations."[14] At the same time these seemingly patriotic Baptists also used the congress for a large, public, and thus illegal presentation of their beliefs. Complaining that there was not enough room in the Baptist prayer house for both their members and the visitors to attend the prayer meetings scheduled to take place each evening of the conference, the Baptists were able to secure the permission of the Moscow City governor to hold their services in the auditorium of that symbolic locus of modern, public, secular culture, the Polytechnical Museum. These prayer meetings provoked a row that had serious implications for the future of Russian Baptists.

It was not only the government that expressed interest and anxiety over the summoning of this congress in Moscow. Indeed, the delegates gathered amid a flurry of objections in the right-wing press against allowing dangerous displays of anti-Orthodox and anti-Russian ideas in this center of Russian national culture.[15] Inspired by Moscow Metropolitan Vladimir Bogoiavlenskii and the prominent activist Archpriest Ioann Vostorgov, both ardent supporters of the reactionary Union of Russian People and advocates of a militant approach to religious dissidence, the local Orthodox missionary organizations mobilized to defend Moscow's religious terrain. Several Orthodox missionaries joined the crowd of thirteen hundred that packed the museum auditorium to hear the Baptists preach. Meanwhile, in the next room, Vostorgov gave an alternative program of anti-sectarian lectures, which also attracted a sizable audience, including many young "enthusiasts of Orthodoxy."

The first evening passed without incident, although the young Orthodox took it upon themselves to taunt the Baptists as they dispersed at the end of the meeting. On September 26, however, Vostorgov's followers began to heckle the Baptist preachers, and when the meeting ended the Orthodox missionary Varzhanskii demanded that the Orthodox be allowed to present a rebuttal. The police, who were on hand for fear of an incident, escorted him out and confiscated the anti-sectarian leaflets that his allies were handing out at the exit, on the grounds that they did not have legal permission to do so. Among them was a priest, Krupenin, a former Baptist who was known for his fierce anti-sectarian attitudes. Krupenin refused to relinquish his leaflets and eventually was arrested. In response to the distressing sight of a priest being dragged to the police station, the Moscow City governor shortened the congress from eleven to ten days and forbade any further Baptist meetings at the Polytechnical Museum.

The prayer meetings then moved to the Baptists' prayer hall, but tension did not dissipate. During services, small groups of Orthodox teenagers repeatedly burst into the room, shouting, "Help! There's a fight!" [*Karaul, b'iut*] and then ran away. One evening, the priest Krupenin returned, with a group of young "enthusiasts," to break up the prayer meeting by loudly singing Orthodox hymns and cursing the Baptists.[16] One result of these confrontations was to intensify the debate in the press between the assertively Orthodox elements of the right-wing press and the liberal press, which came increasingly to see the Baptist experience as the crucial test case for the fate of freedom of conscience in Russia. The other was to ensure that no congress of the Russian Baptist Union would again be permitted before 1917.[17]

Certainly the period after 1910 brought new difficulties alongside further missionary successes. Just as the Baptists were forbidden to hold national congresses after 1911, so the Evangelical Christians' conference over the New Year in 1912 would be their last until after the revolution. Evangelical journals occasionally found themselves shut down or fined by the authorities, and, in 1913, *Baptist* did not publish a single issue because of official restrictions.[18] In many places the 1910 regulations on sectarian meetings curtailed separate gatherings for children and youth or resulted in the closing of services and even prayer houses.[19] Complaints poured in to the evangelical leaders almost as soon as the regulations were distributed, and on 9 December 1910, a delegation consisting of P. V. Kamenskii, the chairman of the Duma's Religious Affairs Committee, Duma member and evangelical Molokan leader Zinovii Zakharov, and senior leaders of the Baptist and Evangelical Christian unions met with the head of the Department of Spiritual Affairs to seek clarification of major points of the circular.[20] This was but the first of several protests to high officials in St. Petersburg that the evangelicals would undertake after 1910.[21]

The Baptists' legal troubles were also the subject of several inquiries launched by liberal and leftist groups in the Duma after 1910. Following publication of the new rules regulating sectarian prayer meetings in October 1910, the liberal Kadets (Constitutional Democrats) made a formal protest, arguing that the law violated the principles of the Decree on Toleration. Then, in 1913, a group of fifty centrist and leftist deputies led by the Social Democrats complained that local authorities were routinely violating religious sectarians' right to meet. In their request for an inquiry, they cited fourteen examples of such persecution, ten involving Baptists and Evangelical Christians. An investigation found all the allegations to be true, but formal complaints about the behavior of local authorities do not appear to have had much effect.[22]

The evangelicals' experience was symptomatic of a broader restriction of civic freedoms that took place after the heady days of 1905–7. When war broke out in the summer of 1914, Russia was in a state of internal tension and disorder. Sharp social cleavages divided the country, alienating the mass of the population from the institutions of the empire, as well as educated society from the lower classes. Yet, in the early days of the war, the nation rallied to the national cause. Huge crowds gathered before the Winter Palace in St. Petersburg to greet the tsar's declaration of war. Workers called off the strikes that had been crippling industry. The Duma voted its support for the war and then agreed to its own prorogation for the duration of the hostilities.[23]

From their embattled position the Baptists shared the widely expressed hope that the crisis of war would erase previous differences and at last draw Russians together to the common cause of defending their country. "From the first cries of military battle our brother sectarians shuddered along with the whole Russian people," wrote Vasilii Ivanov in *Baptist*, and "difference in faith ceased to separate the great Russian family from us."[24] Likewise, in the capital, Fetler continued his strategy of demonstrative patriotism. As war brewed in July 1914 Fetler and a group of church members joined the crowds demonstrating outside the Winter Palace. Then, on September 1, Petersburg and Moscow Baptists issued an appeal to their fellow believers around the country to pray for the emperor and his family, and for God's blessing on Russia during the war. They supplied a form letter, through which local congregations could express their loyal sentiments, to be signed and returned to the St. Petersburg congregation for delivery to the tsar. Prokhanov likewise led his flock in statements of loyalty; according to A. I. Klibanov, 130 Evangelical Christian congregations sent their regards to Nicholas II.[25] Without necessarily suggesting that these statements were insincere, such expressions of patriotic fervor were no doubt also intended to shield evangelicals from nagging questions about their loyalties.

Clearly evangelical leaders hoped that the war would open the way for national political renewal. Soon after the outbreak of hostilities, the leading article in Prokhanov's *Utrenniaia zviezda* marveled at the unity of political and national groups in the Duma in response to the war, and argued that the conflict "should strengthen the idea of popular representation here in

Russia."[26] Similarly, in *Baptist,* Ivanov expressed the wish that the war would at last reunite the fissured Russian polity and secure the Russian Baptists their rightful place in the broader society:

> We were always faithful sons of Great Russia, faithful subjects of our rulers and good workers for the good of society and state. Our sorrow, however, consists in the fact that, until now, we have been artificially separated from our native Russian family, suffered persecution that restricted our rights. . . . We hope that the war, which now has shaken Europe and has touched Russia with its bloody hand, will pass over our motherland not as a devastating hurricane but as a refreshing storm, after which will come peace and calm and freedom for the spiritual prospering of our fatherland.[27]

Other previously marginalized groups also voiced such hopes. For example, in the autumn of 1914 Old Believer bishop Mikhail similarly called for an end to national divisions on the basis of religion.[28]

It is impossible to say exactly how many young Baptists served in the Russian army during World War I. Anecdotal evidence suggests, however, that they generally went to war in numbers similar to their Orthodox neighbors. As Semen Khokhlov, who took over the leadership of the St. Peterburg Baptists during the war, wrote in a May 1916 appeal to the government, "A significant portion of our members of the male sex are in military service and bear all obligations identically to the Orthodox."[29] In September 1914, and again in September 1916, first one editor and then another of *Drug molodezhi* went off to war.[30] *Utrenniaia zviezda* regularly published letters from believers who had volunteered to serve and reported on those who died.

Baptists in various cities and towns around the empire also worked actively on the home front. Both the Baptist and Evangelical Christian communities in St. Petersburg opened infirmaries for wounded soldiers. To support this cause, they founded a joint "Good Samaritan" fund which raised 14,978 rubles in the first four months of the war. In the village of Astrakhanka, Taurida Province, Fedor Balikhin's Baptist congregation sponsored thirty-two wounded soldiers.[31] In late 1914 a detailed report in *Baptist,* illustrated with photographs, described how the women of the Balashov Baptist Church had set up sewing machines in the prayer house to make towels, nightshirts, underwear, and bedding for soldiers. Meanwhile, in Baku, women gathered in the prayer house every evening to sew for the infirmaries, singing hymns as they worked. The report's author, Ivanov, rejoiced that the war had, in this way, given everyone the chance to show devotion to Russia through actions as well as words. He concluded on a tone of optimism, writing, "Thank God it has become obvious to all that the apparent discord in peacetime between the Orthodox and sectarians has disappeared completely now in this difficult time and all have become one friendly Russian family."[32] Ironically Ivanov's hopes would soon be dashed: even as he wrote, congregations were being closed, their leaders exiled, and sectarian journals suspended. This would be the last issue of *Baptist* until it reappeared, in drastically changed circumstances, in 1925.

In late 1915, Prokhanov composed a detailed report to the government in which he quoted at length from the personal letters he had been receiving from believers, describing their experiences since the onset of the war. Dementii Sopil'niak, an Evangelical Christian in the city of Gaisin, Podol'sk Province, had given evidence of some potential for social reconciliation in the face of the threat of an outside enemy, reporting that, when war was declared, he had gathered with other evangelicals and some Orthodox to discuss the war and to pray together for tsar and country. But a sense of disappointment dominated the letters addressed to the Evangelical Christian leader. For example, Prokhanov quoted a believer from Perm, E. P. Sokolov, who recounted an incident of police harassment and the disillusioning conclusions he had drawn from it. Sokolov and a coreligionist had been drinking tea and singing hymns from *Gusli*, when suddenly the police burst in, seized their Bible and hymn book, and wrote them a citation for an illegal meeting. Wrote Sokolov:

> As I returned home, I thought: "Why are they treating us like this?" I remembered the emperor's manifesto of 20 July 1914, in which it says that, "in the terrible hour of trial, may all internal discord be forgotten," and so on. . . . Local authorities seem to circumvent these great words.[33]

The experiences of the early war days thus points to the considerable longing on the part of Baptists not merely to avoid persecution but to contribute to Russian society.

However, the general rhetorical atmosphere of wartime did not encourage inclusive politics just as it did not in the more pluralistic states allied with Russia. As Walter Laqueur has observed, the war unleashed an outpouring of speculation about "the Russian soul's deep, instinctive rejection of occidental Roman-German culture."[34] A popular image was that of the war as a spiritual struggle, a battle of ideas and principles and against secularization. Now that Russia was fighting Protestant Germany, neo-Slavophile thinkers such as Vasilii Rozanov, Semen L. Frank, Sergei Bulgakov, and Nikolai Berdiaev argued that the founders of Protestantism had been "reasoners, devoid of all feeling of holiness," who had therefore humanized and secularized religion, while Orthodoxy alone had remained faithful to true Christian principles.[35] In such an atmosphere the situation was bound to be awkward for Russia's Protestants. The many ethnic Germans of the empire, Protestant or not, suffered physical attacks on their property by crowds as well as legal difficulties with the government. In December 1915 a law, passed as emergency legislation under Article 87, expropriated the lands of German colonists in the empire.[36] As for Russian and Ukrainian converts to Protestantism, the accusations of "Germanism" that had been persistent but relatively free of concrete consequences before the war now appeared more serious.

For the Baptists were not alone in regarding the war as a potentially critical turning point for Russia. In particular, the war reinvigorated the religious authorities' sense of the need to protect Russia's Orthodoxy. A Synod decree of 5 August 1914 reminded diocesan missionaries that their contribution to the war effort would be to preserve devotion to the national faith among the soldiers of this multiethnic and multiconfessional empire.[37] Church leaders forcefully reasserted their arguments about the relationship between Orthodoxy and political reliability. As the Bishop of Kherson diocese wrote in his annual report for 1915, "The war was a touchstone for all rationalistic sects with their fascination with German Protestantism and poorly concealed antistate and antimilitaristic views."[38] That test, he declared, had made plain the treachery of the Baptists, Pashkovites, and Adventists who allegedly refused to pray for victory, who resisted Orthodox missionaries, and who displayed dangerous pacifism.[39]

Archpriest Ioann Vostorgov led the charge against the evangelicals' alleged treachery with a widely publicized speech titled "The Hostile Spiritual Vanguard—The German Faith," which he delivered in October 14 to the Moscow Missionary Brotherhood of the Resurrection of Christ. Vostorgov opened by asking whether Russian Baptists or Adventists would be able to generate a suitably high level of outrage against the cruelty and violence of the Germans. "Can they," he continued, "sincerely recognize and show that the Germans have turned out to be so cruel precisely because they, as Protestants, are only apparently Christians?" The answer, in his view, was a resounding no. These were "weak spirits that had . . . [fallen] out of spiritual unity with their people and accepted the faith, spirit, leanings, aspirations, the entire spiritual style of the enemy." He then went on to warn that their insidious influence on the Russian body politic had now been revealed by war:

> German sectarianism is . . . a spiritual German vanguard, and the Germans have made use of everything—violence and deception and betrayal of many Russian rulers and Russian open-heartedness and the credulity of the Russian government and the liberal direction of our Russian literature . . . — [they] used and are using decisively anything in order to plant this, their spiritual vanguard, strongly in Russia.[40]

Proof of this, claimed Vostorgov, could be gleaned from the fact that the Baptists did not pray specifically for a Russian victory but rather for an end to the war.

This speech was reprinted in full on the front page of the conservative, monarchist newspaper *Moskovskiia viedomosti* [Moscow record] and was later distributed in booklet form. The right-wing press widely and approvingly commented on it and reported the public polemical exchange it prompted between Vostorgov and a Baptist representative named Gedeonov.[41]

Vostorgov's warnings also drew the attention of the authorities in St. Petersburg. In a secret circular to provincial governors of 12 December 1914, the Minister of Internal Affairs, Nikolai Maklakov, noted that the right-wing press had recently published a flurry of articles on the subject of religious sectarians' susceptibility to "Germanism." Consequently the ministry thought it useful to pass on some basic facts about this topic. The circular asserted that "rationalist sectarianism, in the form of its major representatives, the Baptists, Evangelical Christians, and Adventists," used a full arsenal of propagandistic methods to implement their "carefully elaborated plan for the religious reformation of Russia." They were in close contact with foreign, particularly German, organizations, it warned, which assisted them in "creating artificial conditions for the spread of ideas of sectarianism among the Orthodox." In this way the sectarians abused the emperor's gift of freedom of confession. The minister concluded by asking that the already close surveillance of rationalist sectarians be increased and that the ministry be informed of all related cases.[42]

The theme of the Baptist threat resurfaced in August 1915, in the midst of Duma debates about forming a committee to address "German dominance" in all areas of Russian life. Among the many examples of the influence of people of German origin on the empire's industry, government, and society, several deputies pointed to the Baptist phenomenon as an alleged means of German cultural infiltration of the Russian population. Father Stanislavskii, a right-wing deputy and Orthodox priest from Khar'kov, even called for shtundist and Adventist meetings to be banned. A flurry of discussion focusing on the Baptists ensued. The Minister of Internal Affairs, Prince N. B. Shcherbatov, insisted that he was tolerant of all faiths but argued that there were "not a few unconscious weapons of the German government" among the Baptists.[43] Aleksandr Kerenskii of the Trudovik (Laborite) party and Pavel Miliukov, the head of the Kadet Party and historian of Russian culture, vehemently disputed this suggestion. In the end, the formation of a committee on German dominance was approved, and the question of whether evangelical activity should be banned during wartime was launched.

Already in the summer of 1913 there had been rumors in the press that the Baptists were to be declared an extremely harmful sect, thus depriving them of the rights given to sectarians in 1905. In late July Fetler, the St. Petersburg Baptist pastor, finally wrote to the Minister of Internal Affairs asking whether this were true. He received a negative reply, and the Baptists breathed a brief sigh of relief.[44] However, with the outbreak of the war, the theme of danger reasserted itself in government correspondence, and in March 1915 the secret police stepped up surveillance of all sectarians, with special attention to the Baptists.[45] In 1916, the Minister of Internal Affairs and the Minister of Justice exchanged letters about closing down the Union of Evangelical Christians and having that sect, and others similar to it, declared "most dangerous" to state interests. It was eventually decided that this move carried too much political risk, especially the risk of upsetting Russia's British ally.[46]

Similarly wartime breathed new life into long-standing concern among tsarist officials that the faith of the Baptists and Evangelical Christians might encourage pacifist tendencies. Yet there was nothing in the formal statement of faith of either branch of the movement to suggest that it opposed military service. On the contrary, both emphasized believers' responsibility to perform civic responsibilities, including military service, although it should be noted that the Evangelical Christian statement added the phrase "but we have relations with those who think otherwise on this question."[47] But because both groups also declared that they obeyed earthly laws only insofar as these did not contradict their religious beliefs, the tsarist government had long harbored suspicions about their willingness to serve and made a concerted effort to seek out the truth. Its prewar investigations consistently found that evangelical pacifism presented neither a widespread nor serious enough threat to warrant closing evangelical congregations.[48] At that point, the Department of Police and the Department of Spiritual Affairs renewed their attention to this potential threat.[49]

There was an element of truth to the charges against the Baptists. Certainly war presented the evangelicals with the dilemma of reconciling the values of their earthly community with those of their spiritual one. For many years evangelical leaders had been anxious and uncertain about the issue of pacifism. On the one hand, they were careful to assert their flock's loyalty to the Russian state and willingness to perform all civic duties. One young man who refused to serve in 1917 claimed that, although from the moment of his conversion he had understood that he could not kill a human being, he had gone off to war "fully trusting senior brothers . . . who proved from the Word of God, mostly the Old Testament, that we should go with a calm conscience and do 'all that the authorities order.'"[50] On the other hand, private communications reveal less certainty. For example, Vasilii Ivanov expressed antiwar, if not pacifist, ideas when he wrote in a 1900 letter to Vasilii Pavlov that, although each believer had to follow the dictates of his or her conscience, "he who goes to war by compulsion will be less guilty before God than he who of his own will holds a police or military position or performs the diabolical responsibility of the executioner or even [experiences] zeal in killing at war."[51] More important, a 1907 letter by the Tolstoyan Ivan M. Tregubov, which was seized by the secret police, indicates that he had the approval of the leaders of the St. Petersburg Evangelical Christians for an appeal he was mounting to extend to other sectarians the privilege of alternatives to military service available to the Mennonites.[52] Also revealing is a letter from one rank-and-file evangelical in a garrison in Siberia to a fellow believer in January 1912 in which he expressed confusion over the lack of clarity on where the movement stood on the issue of pacifism and his distress at the division it was causing in evangelical ranks.[53] Therefore, although there was nothing in the statements of faith to suggest a pacifist stance, these denominations, with their emphasis on personal interpretation of the Bible by individual believers, clearly did not enjoy unanimity on this issue.[54]

Unquestionably some evangelicals did refuse military service during World War I. A mid-1916 internal Department of Spiritual Affairs report on the Baptists indicated that of 600 convictions for refusing military service on religious grounds since the outbreak of war, approximately half involved Baptists and Evangelical Christians.[55] By 1 April 1917 the government had recorded 840 such cases, of which the largest two confessional categories besides "unlisted" (249 cases) were "Baptists/shtundists" (114 cases) and Evangelical Christians (256 cases). Molokans and Dukhobors, by contrast, had been convicted in only 22 cases.[56] These figures represent a drop in the bucket of the nearly fifteen million men who served during the war.[57] As a proportion of the Baptists and Evangelical Christians, they were also small but probably significant.

Accusations of propaganda among the soldiers were not unfounded either. *Utrenniaia zviezda* tried to mobilize congregations to send a copy of the Gospels to every soldier in the army.[58] An intercepted letter from the presbyter of the Omsk Baptists, Gavriil Mazaev, written in February 1915 to a coreligionist, reported extensive propaganda work among soldiers heading off to the front.[59] On a more personal level, the many reports of soldiers returning from World War I as converts suggest that enlisted men clearly engaged in the illegal act of sharing their faith with their comrades-at-arms.[60] Moreover, Fetler, now exiled from the Russian Empire, organized extensive missionary work among Russian prisoners of war in central Europe.[61]

These public accusations and government suspicions signaled a turn for the worse in Baptist fortunes. Already, on a cool September Sunday morning in 1914, the Odessa congregation of Russian Baptists had arrived at their prayer house to find the courtyard packed with people bearing flags, national ribbons, and a portrait of the tsar. A children's choir sang the great hymn "Heavenly King" and members of the local Orthodox brotherhood incited the crowd to protest against traitors who practiced the German faith in Russia.[62] On the night of December 6, nine preachers from the Evangelical Christian, Baptist and Adventist congregations in Odessa were arrested on the orders of the Commander of the Odessa Military District and General Governor, M. I. Ebelov, on the pretext that their preaching was dangerous in wartime conditions. In early 1915, he ordered all Baptist and Evangelical Christian congregations in Kherson, Bessarabia, and Taurida provinces closed and all major preachers from this important area for the movement exiled to Siberia.[63] January 1915 also saw the forced removal of Fetler from his position as Baptist pastor in the capital. Although he was threatened with exile to Siberia, he was able to have this commuted to permanent exile from the Russian Empire with no right to return.[64] In August of that same year, the

Supreme Commander of the army of the Northwest front ordered the closing of all evangelical congregations in Petrograd and Olonets provinces. Permission to hold meetings in those areas, on the condition that no enlisted soldiers attended, was later granted on and off, but the Baptists' House of the Gospel in the capital remained requisitioned for use as a militia barracks. To the believers' distress, the large electric sign reading "God is Love" was removed from the roof of the house, while, inside, tobacco smoke and swearing replaced the sound of prayers.[65] Evangelical presses virtually ground to a halt. The infirmaries that Baptists set up across the nation to care for wounded soldiers were subject to sharp restrictions or even closed down.[66]

Persecution also touched congregations far from the eyes of the central government. In some small villages Orthodox parishioners, worked up into a frenzy by anti-German propaganda, denounced their Baptist neighbors as traitors and sought to expel them from their midst. Yet, as one Ukrainian peasant, I. P. Kreshchenko of the village of Lebedin, Kiev Province, wrote: "If there had not been the war, we would not have known that there is a Germany."[67]

By 1916, both the Evangelical Christian and Baptist unions ceased meaningful activity. As early as June 1915 Vasilii Ivanov wrote to Vasilii Pavlov that the "[Baptist] Union has basically disappeared."[68] The Evangelical Christian leadership was less affected by exile and more dominated by one man, Prokhanov, so that union's council, at least, was better able to continue work during the war. In late 1916, however, its members were arrested on charges of antistate activity, and *Utrenniaia zviezda* folded.[69]

Once again the Baptists' tribulations drew the attention of liberal and leftist deputies in the Duma. In February 1916, Miliukov complained to the Duma about the closing and exile of evangelical congregations. The following June a group of leftist deputies petitioned the Duma to investigate the closing of the Omsk Baptist prayer house because of alleged pro-German propaganda. The legislature approved the request, and a detailed investigation by the Ministry of Internal Affairs ensued.[70] However, it was only after the revolution in 1917 that the congregation would gather in the Omsk prayer house to celebrate its reopening.[71]

The Baptists' experience during World War I demonstrated the failure of their pluralistic vision of a Russia where Orthodoxy would no longer be the measure of national belonging and political reliability. In the years before the outbreak of war the evangelical movement continued to grow, despite increased pressure from a suspicious society, an anxious government, and a threatened state church. With the onset of conflict, the evangelicals were dismayed to find renewed negative attention focused on them by state and Orthodox officials, as long-standing concerns about the political implications of Baptist religious beliefs again came to the fore. The war revealed the fundamental inability of the regime to handle diversity and to find a means of cooperating with public initiative. Throughout the period between the 1905

Revolution and the war the regime wavered between the competing autocratic and constitutional principles it simultaneously proclaimed. As the Russian war effort failed, so did the aspirations of the Baptists and other public groups for pushing the regime to rebuild itself as a pluralistic, tolerant state. Along with much of society, Evangelical Christians and Baptists would rejoice in the collapse of the autocracy in February 1917. Indeed, they would delight in the new condition of citizenship, advancing more directly than ever their Christian vision of citizenship in the new democratic republic. But soon the old question of the relationship between their religious and political views would again command attention.

Part III

A Spiritual Revolution

7

The Revolution of the Spirit

In the first weeks after the collapse of the tsarist regime in late February 1917, Moscow Baptist Evgeniia Ofrova took up her pen to describe the exciting vision of a world of engaged citizenship, of class reconciliation, and of liberty, equality, and fraternity in Christ that the revolution had unleashed:

> Like a crash of thunder, the nationwide news
> Has spread across great Rus'
> That powerful song of great freedom
> Has rung out like a war cry.
>
> The heartless hangman is dismissed forever,
> The age-old fetters have snapped . . .
> But the dawn of freedom will begin to burn,
> When people come to know the fundamentals,
>
> The fundamentals that Christ commanded us,
> That people should love one another . . .
> And then the peace question will be solved;
> Only if the commandment of the Lord is preserved.
>
> No longer will people stagnate in an iron grip
> The death penalty will disappear, like a legend;

Russia will no longer see the Jew in tears,
In the desecration of expulsion.

The rod will no longer whistle in policemen's hands
Casemates will no longer hide the innocent.
And the most simple will become dignitaries
If their genius is apparent.

"Bourgeois" and people [*narod*] will merge into one family,
The days of equality and brotherhood will come.
And now there will be no division of races,
And you won't buy a title with wealth.

People-brothers, citizens of great Rus'!
May Christ now govern all!
Rus', offer up a prayer of petition to Him,
May He Himself appoint the authorities.

Rus', declare him your leader and Sovereign,
May everything be placed under His command.
And under the power of Christ's great love
Our Rus' will blossom, it will not wither.[1]

Meanwhile, in distant Baku, the local Baptist pastor and veteran missionary, Vasilii V. Ivanov, expressed similar wonder and excitement at the civic upsurge around him in frequent letters to his son, Pavel, a lawyer then working for the city council in the Crimean city of Evpatoriia. After the dark days of wartime repression, his first thoughts, not surprisingly, were of possibilities for the Baptist movement. "No one knows what will happen next, but now all political prisoners will probably be freed, and our brother-sufferers will leave the prisons and return from exile and our gatherings will open!" he rejoiced on March 4. Two days later he reported that the Baptists had elected representatives to the newly formed Baku executive committee. In later letters Ivanov described the new revolutionary Baku: "Now there is a new world, now there are no different estates, but all are free citizens of the great Russian land. . . . All power has been given by God to the people." Ivanov was eagerly attending public lectures on literature, on humanity, on the purpose of life—and lectures where he listened to "such things about the tsar that are terrible to hear." The police had been dismissed, and, in the streets, "people of all kinds walk[ed] with red flags and [sang] revolutionary songs," and the Baptists preached openly. Ivanov urged his son to action, writing, on March 9, that "a wide door for civic activism is opening up for all citizens. . . . Now all the most unreliable have become the most reliable."[2]

For both Ofrova and Ivanov, the February Revolution was at once a political and a religious experience. Just as Ivanov echoed the biblical teaching that "the stone the builders rejected has become the capstone" in describing the reversal of social positions wrought by the revolution, so he used the Bible to interpret the revolutionary events. On March 17, he sent Pavel a postcard, which read: "The prophetic words have been fulfilled in all ways: Psalm 149: 4–9, read it." Psalm 149 paints a picture of social inversion, where God "crowns the humble with salvation" and allows them to "bind their kings with fetters."[3] It was God who had granted the new experience of citizenship and the collapse of old hierarchies. And God had not finished His work. As Ofrova pointed out in her poem, the revolution now opened up the possibility, indeed the necessity, for a further revolution, a revolution of the spirit whereby Jesus would solve Russia's problems of war, capital punishment, anti-Semitism, social inequality, class conflict, unjust imprisonment, and ethnic strife.

Since the time of Herzen, members of the Russian intelligentsia had discussed the power of religious ideas and imagery to stir the oppressed to political action. Among other questions, opponents of the autocracy debated the wisdom of using religion in the service of what were often atheistic ideologies. They were particularly interested in the revolutionary potential of religious dissidents. Like the government, they wondered whether sectarians' religious nonconformity expressed latent political rebellion. Before 1917 the Evangelical Christians and Baptists, like other religious sectarians, cautiously strove for a relatively apolitical stance. Their primary goal remained to ensure suitable conditions for practicing and preaching their faith. But in early 1917 they were swept up in the excitement of the revolution, and for the first time they openly expressed a politically engaged Christianity. As the first editorial of the revived Baptist journal *Slovo istiny* [Word of truth] declared: "In resuming the publication of the journal . . . we join our voice and the aspiration of our heart to the choir of builders of the new life."[4] From the very first days of the political revolution, the Baptists used the vocabulary of democratic and revolutionary politics to call for a complementary revolution of the spirit, arguing, as did Ofrova's poem, that true freedom would come only when the citizens of Russia turned to Christ.

Baptist leaders and local communities greeted the fall of the monarchy in the intertwined languages of democracy, revolution, and Christianity. The subsequent experience of that revolutionary year of 1917 forced the Baptists to grapple concretely with how these threads of religion and politics were bound up in their movement. In an increasingly charged political atmosphere, they agonized over the civic implications of their religious beliefs and the Christian's role in the affairs of this world.

Although previous studies have noted the Baptists' use of revolutionary language, they have not probed the prevalence of this language, developments in its meaning, and the role it played in shaping evangelical responses to the evolving political situation. It is clear that Baptist and Evangelical Christian leaders were, first and foremost, preoccupied in 1917 with exploiting the new missionary opportunities made possible by the revolution. As a result, what partisan statements they did make were in support of the Provisional Government, which they saw as best able to effect the orderly trans-

fer of power needed to ensure good conditions for their religious work.[5] In
this sense A. I. Klibanov was right in pointing to the evangelicals' commitment to preventing "the development of the bourgeois revolution into a socialist one." Klibanov regarded their frequent use of socialist language as
merely a "demagogic" ploy by the bourgeois leadership to "pervert" the political consciousness of lower-class believers and retain their allegiances.[6] But
this interpretation ignores the broader process whereby political views and
language were negotiated against a background of pressures from within the
movement and the evolution of the revolution in the streets in 1917. Just as
the meaning of the slogans of liberty, equality, and fraternity were debated
and transformed during the French Revolution, so ideas about citizenship,
democracy, and socialism were shaped, and in turn given meaning, by the
events of 1917. Russian Baptists struggled to define and defend these concepts as moral imperatives, arising from a Christian ideal of brotherly love.
And just as many of the protesters against the de-Christianization campaigns
of the French Revolution used revolutionary language, for they saw themselves not as counterrevolutionaries but as defenders of the very principles
the revolution had enunciated, so, along with Vasilii Ivanov, Russian evangelicals gave religious content to socialist language as they explored the meaning of Christian citizenship in this revolutionary period.[7]

Throughout 1917 local evangelical communities reported an explosion
of activity and a surge in conversions. But amid this energy there was also
anxiety: political ideas, religious ideals, and conflicting visions of the believer's role on this earth were up for agonizing debate in 1917. This chapter
opens with a review of the controversy over religious sectarians' revolutionary potential, the place of evangelicals in these arguments, and the evangelicals' political inclinations during the tsarist period. It then examines how
religious and revolutionary language were intertwined, as some Baptists
stepped forward onto the political stage in 1917. Finally, it explores the problems this politicized vision presented and how attitudes changed, as Baptists
came to experience the revolution no longer as a liberating Easter Day but
as something closer to the terror of the Day of Judgment.

DEBATES ABOUT
SECTARIANS' REVOLUTIONARY POTENTIAL

Both in Russia and the West the early twentieth century saw an intense
debate about the relationship between religion and politics, within both religious groups and political parties. From the German Karl Kautsky's explorations of the "proletarian" nature of early Christianity to the God-building
of Bolsheviks like Anatolii Lunacharskii in Russia, and among Christian socialists or proponents of the "social gospel," people of faith and politicians
pondered the place of Christianity in the modern world and the possibility
of a socialist Christianity.[8]

In Russia interest in the political implications of religious dissidence was long-standing and widespread among liberals, populists, and Marxists. Each saw in the communities of Old Believers or sectarians evidence that the Russian people was eminently suited to his or her enlightened plan for the political and social transformation of the empire. But not everyone believed that change would be achieved through violent revolution. From their exile in England, followers of Tolstoy's philosophy of Christian pacifist anarchism, such as Vladimir and Anna Chertkov and Ivan M. Tregubov, contested the assertion of the Social Democrat Vladimir Bonch-Bruevich or the Socialist Revolutionary Prince Dmitrii Khilkov that sectarians could be attracted to revolutionary politics.[9] Indeed, in an effort to prove this point, in 1902 they launched an extensive survey of religious sectarians, with the goal, as they wrote, of asking "the sectarians themselves whether or not what these educated people [were] saying and writing about them [was] true." The crucial, opening question on the survey form read: "Is it good or evil to revolt against oppressors, to rob and kill rulers?" F. M. Putintsev's study of sectarians' responses found that the vast majority rejected violence in favor of peaceful reform. Although one must treat the conclusions of this 1935 antireligious work with great care, the scattered Baptist and Evangelical Christian responses found in secret police files, in Bonch-Bruevich's papers, and in the Chertkovs' papers support Putintsev's interpretation.[10] The only exception was E. N. Ivanov, one of the pillars of the Evangelical Christian community in Khar'kov, who expressed great sympathy with revolutionaries in a letter to Tregubov, writing that "one way or another we all are striving for one goal, which is to establish the Kingdom of God on earth . . . the name is different but the goal is the same, the means of battle are different but the goal is the same."[11]

Although he had long cooperated with them in collecting and publishing sectarian manuscripts, Bonch-Bruevich refused to accept the Tolstoyans' arguments. Both he and the Tolstoyans were especially enthusiastic about the Dukhobors' potential as allies, but the question of whether the quickly growing sect of Baptists or shtundists had revolutionary potential also permeated Bonch-Bruevich's writings on religious sectarianism and the articles he published in his newsletter for sectarians, *Razsviet* [The dawn]. In fact, reports in *Razsviet* on Social Democratic organizers' personal experiences with sectarians dealt exclusively with shtundists. In a 1902 letter to Chertkov, Bonch-Bruevich argued that the Baptist confession of faith's declaration that Baptists would refuse to obey the government if it infringed on their religious beliefs was "not only disloyal, not [the behavior] of loyal subjects, *but frankly revolutionary*, because it openly declares that your ways do not suit us." Bonch-Bruevich basically regarded the Baptists as a petty-bourgeois movement whose supreme political goal was a constitutional order. But, as he argued in his report to the Second Party Congress in 1903, "until Russia is a constitutional [state] . . . the Baptists will be, despite their assurances of loyal subjecthood, an *oppositional* element in the country."[12] Thus, although Bonch-Bruevich never held out the same kind of hope for the Baptists displaying collectivist and revolutionary instincts as he did for other groups, he certainly included them among his potential allies against autocracy.

There is no question that the Baptists were politicized by their faith itself, as Bonch-Bruevich pointed out. From the late nineteenth century through the 1920s believers' various formal confessions of faith articulated a call for a political and social order that would not limit the expression of that which they valued most, their Christian beliefs. The experience of persecution sharpened the political awareness behind this demand. A survey of the contents of the underground Baptist journal, *Besieda*, for 1895–96 reveals that virtually all the articles dealt with politics, the courts, Orthodox missionaries, and the problem of persecution in general. The few excerpts of *Besieda* articles available reveal admiration of republican ideas or of the English political system.[13] As for cooperation with revolutionary groups, government files do not suggest any widespread oppositional activity on the part of rank-and-file evangelicals before 1905. Social Democrats active in the Kiev area between 1880 and 1905 did report some interaction with Baptists or shtundists, and suggested that their aspirations to self-perfection and study, albeit of the Bible, made them worthy targets of socialist agitation. These sectarians were usually not interested in overtly political causes, but some had, nevertheless, at one time participated in a joint study group with Social Democrats, and their community had aided strikers on numerous occasions.[14] Revolutionaries and evangelicals also encountered one another in exile and prison. In an effort to publicize persecution, Vasilii Pavlov supplied Bonch-Bruevich with large numbers of documents on the history of the movement in Russia from his place of exile in Tulcea, Romania, in the late 1890s.[15] At the same time he insisted that he did not share the revolutionary's political views. As he wrote in a letter to Chertkov, "I, as a Christian, am against all violent revolutions and stand for peaceful development of our fatherland and all humanity."[16] The evangelicals were thus definitely no strangers to various revolutionary groups and their ideas by 1905. However, the Socialist Revolutionary Khilkov was probably right when he suggested, in a 1905 pamphlet, that the Baptists and Pashkovites were more preoccupied with personal salvation and with avoiding the government's attention than with fomenting political revolution.[17]

During the revolution of 1905–7 and after, some evangelicals do seem to have been swept up in the increasing politicization of their society. Beginning in December 1905, for example, young Baku Baptists formed a circle that met twice each week to read and discuss issues of religion, philosophy, politics, and social life.[18] Around the same time Nikolai V. Odintsov of the Baptists and the Evangelical Christian Ivan Prokhanov apparently joined with Peter Friesen of the Mennonite Brethren in Sevastopol' to form a "Union of freedom, truth, and peaceableness" on a platform of rejecting all violence and calling for civil, economic, and religious progress. According to G. S. Lialina, this short-lived union cooperated with the local Kadets in the election campaign for the first Duma.[19] It appears that the Tiflis congregation of Baptists was divided over whether to take an active role in the revolutionary upheaval of October 1905.[20] And Odessa believers proudly reported praying for the liberation movement during 1906.[21]

Soviet researchers have accepted Bonch-Bruevich's basic view that the Baptists represented a democratic force of the rising bourgeoisie and have suggested that they were satisfied by the semi-constitutional era in Russian politics after 1905.[22] In reality, of course, the 1905 Revolution did not provide the conditions Russian evangelicals needed for the full flowering of their work. Certainly Baptist and Evangelical Christian leaders made a special effort to present a nonthreatening face to a suspicious autocracy between 1905 and 1917. Despite this reticence, however, a survey of their activities and writings reveals certain political tendencies that would be more fully expressed in the revolutionary period. Most significant among these were flirtation with socialist parties and ideas, resistance to class-based politics, a rejection of violence, and an ambivalence about the whole idea of engaging in the affairs of "this world." It is clear that the evangelical movement was in dialogue with the political atmosphere of its day, and with theories about sectarianism and political transformation abroad in their society.

Certainly there were numerous cases of people who had flirted with revolutionary ideas or even belonged to socialist parties and later joined the Baptists. It is difficult to gauge whether the 1908 expulsion of Daniil M. Timoshenko and his son, Mikhail, from Bezhitse, Orel Province, for illegal political activity was the result of their own initiatives or was connected to the fact that Mikhail's two brothers were deeply involved in the anarchist cause. Although this could be seen as the result of paranoia, there may also be some truth to the case; for example, a young applicant to Bible School in 1924, Foma N. Konovalov, explained that his father, a Baptist, had been imprisoned from 1913 until the amnesty of early 1917 "for an explicit political tendency which he mixed together with the idea of Christ."[23]

Although they were never dominant, collectivist ideas, often expressed in terms of the need to build the Kingdom of God on earth, had been circulating in the evangelical movement from its inception. Indeed, in 1870, one of the first communities of evangelicals, led by Ivan Riaboshapka, had applied (unsuccessfully) to the governor of New Russia for permission to found a collective farm of twenty households modeled on the early church. Later, in the mid-1890s, a group of evangelicals, including the future leader of the Evangelical Christians, Ivan Prokhanov, founded a Christian agricultural community in the Crimea, which they farmed collectively until their efforts were thwarted by the intensified persecution of shtundists. Furthermore, in a 1910 article on the building of the Kingdom of God, Vasilii Ivanov had recommended to believers to "unite and build public factories or workshops and work in them, each according to his abilities and occupations, distributing their fruits equally; or unite to work common land."[24] In each of these cases the communal drive was presented as a moral principle arising from spiritual conversion, rather than as a call to political engagement.

This anxiety about revolutionary or socialist ideas reflected a broader concern about the proper role of believers in worldly matters that continuously resonated in Baptists' private letters and public writings. Ivanov wrote to Pavlov in 1900 that "we should not get involved in discussion about governmental affairs, our task is to preach not war, not gallows and death, but love and peace and life!" "The believer does not have the power to change the existing order in the world," his letter concluded, "because every evil is removed by the force of a physical weapon, and the children of God do not have the right to take up such a weapon. They should combat evil only with the Godly weapon, with the sword of the Word of God."[25] Similarly, upon learning about the Social Democrats' appeals to sectarians, the Baptist missionary Fedor P. Balikhin wrote Tregubov that "the key of freedom is in the hands of Christ" and that anyone denying Christ and opposing authority was bound to fail.[26] The overwhelming focus of Baptist leaders' correspondence on matters of faith and community organizing to the virtual exclusion of politics would appear to have been not merely the result of anxiety about their letters being intercepted by censors—their many tales of proselytization were incriminating anyway—but mostly the product of concentrating on the more pressing task of evangelization.

Nevertheless, because these men were committed to establishing the conditions for unhindered evangelization, they could not merely ignore the secular world of politics. After 1905 the evangelical leadership was eager to preserve the movement's opportunities for expansion by discouraging overtly oppositional displays. Assertions of patriotism and loyalty to the tsar became standard fare at evangelical congresses, particularly as the political situation for religious dissidents became more tenuous after 1909. But the idea of the Kingdom of God on earth could also be used to challenge this strategy. For example, a manifesto addressed to the 1909 Baptist congress, signed "Sermiaga" and published by "a group of Socialist Revolutionaries," protested the plan formally to declare loyalty to the tsar. It warned that the Baptists were renouncing their past struggle against the power of this world by wanting "to be loyal subjects of the earthly Russian tsar, of this sworn enemy of Christianity," and that they risked being perceived as traitors to the people in the coming revolution.[27] Despite this warning, the resolution passed.

These assertions of loyalty were, of course, partly a response to accusations of national cultural betrayal and revolutionary sympathies. Indeed, both their friends and enemies drew parallels between the Baptists' meetings and the study circles of the workers' movement. And the evangelicals themselves contributed to this pervasive image of their movement as parallel to—or perhaps the inverse of—the revolutionary one. In their writings they frequently portrayed themselves as competing for the allegiances of the same kind of people as did revolutionaries, and the figure of the former revolutionary converted to evangelicalism appeared repeatedly.[28] The message of these allusions was always the same: that politics was a poor substitute for true faith. And if this were so with regard to the soul of the individual, it was also true for society as a whole. Evangelicals' call for a Russian Reformation was not only an effort to combine the dual Western and Russian inspirations of their movement but was also a response to the politics of revolution and to suggestions that the evangelicals espoused revolutionary ideas.

Baptist discussion of the Reformation presented two kinds of political messages. First, it was accompanied by undisguised admiration for the democratic, constitutional systems of Great Britain and the United States, which were presented as the glorious results of Protestant religious inspiration.[29] At the same time it was a shorthand for a different kind of revolution, not merely one of political systems but rather the complete transformation of Russia through religious conversion. Part of this vision was of a new, non-Orthodox polity based on the voluntaristic principles of the Baptist community. But the idea of reformation also implied an alternative to emerging trends in Russian politics. Just as they did in their private correspondence before 1905, the evangelical leaders called for a rejection of the political methods of "this world," based on class hatreds, and contrasted them with a Christian politics of love. For example, responding to news of the Social Democratic complaint in the Duma about persecution of sectarians in 1913, an editorial in Prokhanov's weekly, *Utrenniaia zviezda,* asserted that sectarians were grateful for all kind words but that the deputies' claim that they were a peasant movement was incorrect, as was any intimation that they supported revolutionary politics. On the contrary, the editorialist declared, playing on the similarity of the Russian words for "peasant" and "Christian":

> Sectarianism is not an estate, class movement; it is first of all a Christian and not a peasant [*khristianskoe a ne krest'ianskoe*] movement, although the majority in its ranks are peasants. . . . The ideal of sectarianism is the spiritual-moral rebirth of the country, the establishment of the Kingdom of God on earth. This ideal, which takes in all small human ideals, cannot be identified with any party program.

In his view, although individual believers might hold political views, religious sectarianism as a whole was not a political ideology. "Drawing sectarianism (as a whole) into political battle," he averred, "is a completely impossible task."[30] This editorial was clearly intended to ensure that the Social Democrats' advocacy would not taint the evangelical movement with the mark of revolution, but it also expressed a more widespread view among evangelical leaders that opposed class-based politics and contended that believers had a greater, alternative plan for the transformation of Russia.

The idea of the religious reformation had much in common with that of

revolutionary socialism. Both believed there was a relationship between national transformation and the changed consciousness of individuals.[31] Marx-
ist revolution and the evangelical vision of reformation also shared an apocalyptic vision of an "ideal, future, collective state of salvation in this world."[32]
At the same time, however, the notion of reformation countered the materialist ideas of the revolutionary movement by suggesting that social change
would follow from individual spiritual change, and not vice versa. In early
1908, for example, Vasilii Pavlov had written in *Baptist* that the law of love
"can solve all our social questions, and there is no other exodus from sharpened class and economic conflict."[33] A few years later he contrasted the
"method of Christianity" to the "method of scientific socialists" for the improvement of the social structure. Explicitly rejecting the path of violent revolution, he argued that "these scientific socialists and Socialist Revolutionaries forget that moral evil is the root of all social injustice." Rather, Pavlov
preached a vision of social peace based on Jesus's command to love one's
neighbors as oneself: "bosses should love the workers, as themselves, and the
workers, likewise—their employers," he wrote.[34] There was some variation in
conceptions of the politics of love—from Ivanov's social equality to Pavlov's
social peace—but all shared a rejection of politics as they were practiced.
Despite changed circumstances, this belief that "sin [was] the mother of the
social question" would continue to dominate evangelical social and political thinking during and after 1917.[35]

Two intertwined ideas thus animated the Russian evangelicals' limited previous political expression as they greeted the revolutions of 1917. First, they
tended to avoid political engagement in favor of religious activism, making
compromises with the existing order when this was necessary for continuing their spiritual activities. In addition, they advocated an alternative vision
of the social and political order, based on the model of the early Christians,
a reformation that would build the Kingdom of God on earth. Both these
ideas suggested that believers' preoccupations and methods did not belong
to the world as it presently existed. However, the idea of reformation also
embodied a plan to bring the whole Russian nation into the community of
converts and thereby solve that nation's many problems. Thus the evangelicals' disdain for worldly politics and values ought not to be equated with a
withdrawal from responsibility for shaping that world. In 1917, the politics
of the world would force itself onto the evangelical agenda, compelling believers to refine and contest these earlier values and tendencies.

TALKING REVOLUTION

In a few short days in late February and early March 1917 the tsarist regime
collapsed in the face of a massive general strike, the mutiny of the Petrograd
garrison, and the unwillingness of the major imperial institutions to support
the monarchy any longer. On March 2, Nicholas II abdicated on the unan-

imous advice of his commanders. Meanwhile, the leaders of the Duma set up a Provisional Government to carry out urgent reforms and to steer the country toward a Constituent Assembly that would decide on Russia's future constitution. Almost overnight, in Lenin's famous phrase, Russia became the "freest country in the world." The liberal Provisional Government immediately set out to overturn the former political and social order by declaring the equality of all citizens. Freedom of assembly, speech, press, and religion was proclaimed, an amnesty released political prisoners and exiles, and reform of the justice system, the abolition of capital punishment, and a new form of democratic local self-government were announced. But members of the Provisional Government knew that they were not really in full control of the country, for at the same time the Petrograd Soviet, a loosely organized council of workers' and soldiers' deputies, formed as a sort of watchdog co-government to defend the interests of the lower classes. Thus, from the very moment the monarchy fell, Russia found itself in a situation of "dual power." In fact, as Orlando Figes suggests, beyond the capital, authority would never really be even dual; rather it soon further splintered into a "multitude of local powers."[36] But in March 1917 no one seemed very worried about this state of affairs. Instead, people euphorically flooded the streets and crowded into meetings, calling one another "citizen," singing the *Marseillaise,* tearing down symbols of tsarist power, and proclaiming their liberty.[37]

The revolution found the evangelical movement in disarray, with many congregations closed, numerous leaders in exile, and their national organizations paralyzed. As news of the fall of the autocracy spread across the country, Baptists stepped forward to claim a public presence in Russia. Cases against arrested believers were dropped, and an estimated eight hundred exiled Baptists at once began the journey home from Siberia to celebrate their inclusion in a new democratic polity.[38] One believer, who had spent most of the war in either a penal battalion or in prison, wrote: "I cannot describe in words my condition, when I first read about the freedom. I wanted immediately to break open the seal from the doors of the prayer house."[39] In May 1917, one past president of the Baptist Union, Il'ia A. Goliaev, described to another, Dei Mazaev, how the revolution had prompted "a holy impulse for a Congress of the brothers" and a drive "toward Evangelization in our country."[40] Civic transformation and emancipation revitalized religious energies and propelled the evangelicals into the fray of those offering visions for the new Russia.

Religious and revolutionary ideas, language, and imagery were tightly intertwined in these early responses. In the first days of March 1917 believers across the country gathered for special prayer meetings of thanksgiving. Many composed telegrams to the Duma and, in some cases, to the Council of Workers' and Soldiers' Deputies, expressing joy at the fall of the autocracy and offering support to the new government. On March 3, for example, the Berdiansk Baptists wrote that "today we had the happiness of freely meeting again in a general assembly with our dear brothers who came from Siberia, exiles for truth, in the presence of a large concourse of people." They had offered up "impassioned prayers" for the Duma and the Council of Workers' and Soldiers' Deputies. "Long live the democratic republic!" the telegram concluded. In keeping with the long-standing idea of a Russian Reformation, most of these telegrams saw political and religious liberation as inextricably linked. As Goliaev wrote on behalf of the Balashov community to the chairman of the Duma and "Citizen of Free Russia," M. V. Rodzianko:

> I recall the memorable night in Petrograd on the eve of February 27 of this year 1917 and, comparing it with the night of struggle for freedom at Gethsemane, the congregation of Russian Baptists in Balashov with great gratitude expresses heartfelt sympathy to you and to your fellow fighters for popular freedom, calling for God's blessing on you and yours. May the further and holy work of consolidating the freedom of resurrected Russia toward the quickest setting up of free popular life and the protection of it not only from internal enemies but also from external mastery be with you.[41]

Just as Jesus had overcome fear in the Garden of Gethsemane on the eve of his crucifixion, so Russia had suffered the agonies of autocracy and, like Christ, had been resurrected in freedom. Now Baptists across the country offered themselves as active partners in building the new Russia.

Evangelicals also participated in the "sudden craze for political meetings" that swept the country.[42] In Moscow, at a series of large public rallies held over Easter week (in early April), the Baptists preached a Christian message in the language of the democratic revolution. Most of these meetings took place at "houses of the people" around the city and were attended by between three hundred and five hundred people. On April 3, the Baptists returned to the site of the controversial 1911 congress, the Polytechnical Museum, where one thousand people paid to hear lectures by Vasilii Pavlov on "The Separation of Church and State," by his son Pavel, the pastor of the Moscow Baptists, on "The Political Demands of the Baptists," and by Mikhail D. Timoshenko, Pavlov's former assistant in Odessa who had just returned from Siberian exile, on "The Principles of the Baptists." The proceeds raised were used to assist people who had suffered for their religious or political convictions.[43]

Just as their telegrams pledged evangelicals' energies to the construction of a new democratic Russia, so the believers proclaimed a new era of social engagement in other ways. The community in Berdichev, for instance, reportedly celebrated Pentecost by organizing a religious parade around the city, singing hymns and carrying banners that proclaimed, "Now we freely preach Christ crucified" and "Long live freedom!"[44] In Moscow, the Pavlovs and Timoshenko resurrected the journal *Slovo istiny,* which Timoshenko had edited in Odessa in 1913–14. Its opening editorial declared: "Our life of faith should manifest itself in relations with those around. Our Christianity should not be somehow abstract, ineffectual, but precisely—practical, realistic, definite, coordinated with the cause."[45] And, indeed, the new journal actively engaged the problems of the day, from socialism to pacifism, in addition to offering reports of local endeavors and devotional poetry and fiction. Similarly the Evangelical Christian branch of the movement also greeted the revolution as an opportunity for practical action. As stated in a letter from the council of the Evangelical Christian Union to a Baptist congress, hurriedly summoned in Vladikavkaz in April: "The dawn of freedom has been lit over Russia. The door to the great work of spiritual renovation of the country has opened before us." They, too, were planning a congress in May in Petrograd, in order to "reconstruct the whole activity of the union in accordance with the horizons that are newly open before us, in the sense of participation in the building of the state, but mostly in the sense of creating the church of Christ on earth."[46] For many evangelicals, this goal involved participating in secular politics. Just as Ivanov reported that the Baptists of Baku had elected a representative to the city's new executive committee, so other believers took part in the meetings, committees, and councils of the new democratic era.[47]

The Baptists were not alone in experiencing the February Revolution in religious terms. Recent research into the language and practices of the February Revolution is beginning to demonstrate how a religious vision of the revolution was also part of the broader national celebration. For example, many villages greeted the tsar's abdication with religious processions and prayers for the new government.[48] Numerous peasant communities, like the evangelicals, sent telegrams to the Provisional Government and the Petrograd Soviet in which they "described the old regime as sinful and corrupt, praised the revolutionary 'freedom fighters' as Christ-like saviors of the people, and projected their religious hopes and ideals onto the new government."[49]

The likening of the political revolution to the festival of the resurrection of Christ, Easter, was a striking feature of the response of a wide swath of the population to revolution. Just as the Balashov pastor had done in his telegram to the Duma, many others seized upon the idea of resurrection to describe and interpret Russia's revolutionary renewal.[50] Indeed, people in the streets are reported to have greeted one another with the traditional Easter blessing of "Christ is risen," sometimes even adapting it to "Russia has arisen!"[51] The Baptists in *Slovo istiny* likened Russia to Lazarus, whom Jesus brought back from the dead; meanwhile, Prokhanov and some of his Evangelical Christian supporters founded a new Christian democratic political party named "Resurrection" to make the views of religious dissidents heard in the cacophony of voices on the public stage.[52] That the actual feast of Easter took place a month after the revolution also contributed to the intermingling of these two experiences in people's experiences and memories. One young Evangelical Christian, Alexander Dobrinin, looked back with nostalgia on those days in his 1931 memoir:

> Twice in my life I experienced a height of enraptured joy that can never be forgotten. The first time was in 1908, when I was converted, and the second was in 1917, in that marvelous Easter season when Russia received her freedom. We were intoxicated with liberty, after the persecutions we had endured before, and especially during the last year of the war. It was as if we had lost our bonds.[53]

The experiences of Easter and of personal and national conversion were thus intertwined in Dobrinin's—as well as others'—understanding of the events of early 1917.

In addition to the image of resurrection, several other themes that were raised in those early Baptist telegrams to the new government continued to feature prominently in evangelical writing and preaching throughout 1917. Concepts of citizenship, of salvation, and of revolution, along with the slogan "liberty, equality, fraternity," were all marshaled in the service of a new variation on the Baptist aspiration to complete social transformation through religious reformation: the revolution of the spirit.

This theme of revolution dominated the speech of Pavel Pavlov, the Moscow Baptist pastor, at the Moscow Polytechnical Museum auditorium on April 3. "Christ was the most terrifying revolutionary," he declared dramatically, "for He carried out and is now carrying out the most terrifying revolution, the revolution of the spirit." Although nonviolent, this spiritual revolution had the power to topple earthly structures of authority and injustice. Contended Pavlov: "Christ had neither a weapon nor an army when He stood before the representative of the most powerful state in the world—Pilate—and nevertheless that realm soon began to sway and collapsed, when that revolution of the spirit, thirsting for the renewal of humanity, moaning under the Roman yoke, began to be accomplished." He went on to bemoan the fact that after nineteen hundred years of institutionalized religion, a widespread "falsification of Christianity" had repressed this emancipatory message. It was no wonder, therefore, that many of those fighting for popular liberation associated the Gospel with oppression and saw religion as an obstacle to progress. But the Baptists marched behind the banner of the early Christians. "Liberty, equality, fraternity—was inscribed on this banner," he asserted, "for they are the slogans proclaimed by Christ and some people now try in vain to realize them without Christ—this will not succeed."[54]

This idea that Christian faith was inextricably intertwined with both the formulation of the notion of revolution and with successfully carrying out political revolution became the mantra of the evangelical movement in 1917 and 1918. One widely distributed pamphlet argued, "The revolution of the spirit—that is what is now essential for us all in the wake of the state revolution." Each individual needed to work to abolish the paralysis brought on by the "autocracy of sin." The pamphlet's concluding sentence also evoked the language of socialist politics: "To him who is with us—give us your hand, Comrade!"[55] This notion appeared in sermons, lectures, articles, and pamphlet titles.[56] Prokhanov signaled its connection to the earlier idea of reformation in his speech to the Evangelical Christians' national congress in Petrograd in May, when he used the term to make the same point that Pavlov had implied in describing the revolution of the spirit: "After the revolution in Russia, a reformation must take place, or, more precisely, something greater— a religious illumination—a spiritual resurrection of the people. This is the great task laid on the followers of the Gospel, on Russian people of the Gospel faith."[57] And indeed, Prokhanov's young follower, Dobrinin, later recalled that this goal inspired the tremendous activism of the believers in 1917: "We tried to put evangelical substance into revolutionary forms," he wrote, "and we spoke eagerly about a revolution of the spirit, a revolution of bettering morals, regeneration through Christ."[58]

The Baptists' vision of a revolution of the spirit no doubt resonated with similar ideas abroad in their society. For one thing, some Orthodox priests preached the notion of a revolutionary Jesus.[59] As a speaker for the nominally Orthodox but evangelically inclined Christian Student movement, Vladimir Martsinkovskii traveled widely, preaching on themes such as "The Gospel and Freedom" and "Revolution of the Spirit."[60] Since the 1890s this had been an image for a group of intellectuals who mounted a significant challenge to the materialism and positivism of the revolutionary intelligentsia.[61] Later, figures as diverse as the Symbolist writer Andrei Bely, the literary group of Scythians, the Bolshevik poet Vladimir Mayakovsky, and the Proletkult activists who sought to create a new, proletarian culture after 1917 would embrace the notion that political revolution required a subsequent, finishing spiritual revolution.[62]

This religious pattern of interpretation reflects, in part, the use of traditional imagery and rituals to express new political experiences. More important, it brought together the venerable custom of viewing Russia itself as a religious concept and the long tradition of a religious idiom of revolution. The analogy between the resurrected Jesus and a resurrected Russia permeated even Bolshevik rhetoric in 1917 and 1918 and provided a model of revolutionary martyrdom.[63] The evangelicals would become alarmed as socialist revolution assumed the messianic mantle in the months after the February Revolution.

Evangelicals frequently connected the notion of spiritual revolution with two other themes: citizenship and socialism. First, they claimed the language of citizenship for their religious message. Prokhanov composed a new hymn in the early days of the revolution whose words, "We are called to freedom, brothers! . . . We are not slaves, we are citizens of the fatherland," summarized the theme of Christian duty to participate in shaping a new Russia. For the first time in his long correspondence with his son, Ivanov addressed the envelopes to "Citizen" P. V. Ivanov. When Vasilii Pavlov spoke at the Moscow Polytechnical Museum in early April he opened with the word, "CITIZENS!" and telegrams sent to the Duma by congregations across the country were full of the language of citizenship and the slogan "liberty, equality, fraternity." Several preachers reported organizing their sermons around this maxim.[64]

If, according to Baptists like Pavel Pavlov, "liberty, equality, fraternity" were the catchwords of the early church, believers also invoked the model of the apostolic church's communal experimentation to assert their own moral conception of socialism.[65] The socialism of the evangelicals was inseparable from religious conversion. For example, on October 15 the elder Ivanov traveled to Evpatoriia, where he preached at a prayer meeting of five hundred people held in that Crimean city's Pushkin auditorium. He chose as his text two passages from the Acts of the Apostles that describe how the first Christians lived communally. He recounted how, on the day of Pentecost, three thousand people had converted after a short sermon by the apostle Peter. "Under the influence of the Holy Spirit," he explained, "real liberty, equality, and fraternity appeared among them, and the social question was instantly solved."[66] Similarly, in his speech at the Moscow Polytechnical Museum on April 3, Pavel Pavlov had presented the Baptists and their church organization as a model for the new era in Russia, both for the "democratization of administration" and resolving class tensions. In Baptist congregations, Pavlov claimed, "the present class dissension is reconciled—the poor and the rich consider themselves brothers." This was achieved through the "revolution of the spirit." "The Baptists strive for socialism," he told his audience, "but not one based on seizure, built on the declaration of another's property to be one's own, . . . [O]ne needs to achieve such moral perfection so as not to consider anything earthly one's own."[67] In other words, it was not changed material conditions that would transform human existence; rather, changed people would naturally be driven to alter social conditions.

What this religious "socialism" meant in practice was unclear. Indeed, the evangelicals rapidly became embroiled in a debate about whether and how to act on the political stage in 1917. An important part of the debate revolved around defining the content of the terms "revolution," "citizenship," and "socialism" in relation to Christianity. These terms spread rapidly throughout Russian society in early 1917.[68] In fact, the famous Russian historian and Kadet leader Aleksandr Kizevetter wrote of a "fashion for socialism" sweeping through society. Not surprisingly, as Boris Kolonitskii points out, the term "socialism" took on many different and competing meanings in this atmosphere.[69] Rather than arguing, as Klibanov did, that evangelical use of the language of socialism was merely a cynical ploy, it is useful to see it as a signal marking Baptist aspirations to enter the "democratic" discussion about the future of Russia. Indeed, the universal problem in 1917 was precisely to define the kind of revolution Russia needed and for whom the revolution was being made. As the politics of class, a concept the movement's leadership had always rejected, came to dominate Russian life in the months between February and October, Russian evangelicals were forced to refine their vision of the revolution in relation to this development and perhaps grapple with the reality of class divisions in their own midst. The concrete political transformation of 1917 demanded tangible definitions and action.

POLITICS AS A PROBLEM IN 1917

The political energies ignited in early 1917 quickly spilled into church life. This was part of the broader politicization that engulfed all areas of Russian existence during that year of political uncertainty and social strife. *Slovo istiny*'s first editorial proclaimed a Christianity that was actively engaged in building the new Russia. At the same time, although Goliaev marveled at the activism spawned by the revolution in his letter of May 17 to Dei Mazaev, he also warned that the new freedom had created an unsettled mood among believers.[70] A few months later, upon visiting the long-established congregation in Novo-Vasil'evka, Taurida Province, Vasilii Ivanov was distressed to find a community absorbed by political rather than spiritual issues. The congregation, he wrote, "is in a pitiful state, in which the brothers have excessively given themselves over to the contemporary current, and are greatly enamored of social questions, which are the only thing they talk of on every encounter."[71] Ivanov, who had rejoiced at Baptist participation in Baku city politics in early March, had not resolved his long-held anxieties about the proper role of Baptists in this world. It is also significant that, at its May 1917 congress, the Union of Evangelical Christians, usually so pliant to its leader Prokhanov's will, resolved that it was undesirable to be distracted by politics and that Prokhanov's proposed Christian Democratic "Resurrection" Party would be regarded as a private initiative of particular members rather than as a Union organization.[72] The notion of a revolution of the spirit, or a Russian Reformation, blurred the lines between the sacred and the profane, and between religious and social thought; nevertheless, nagging doubt about participation in the profane world of politics troubled the evangelicals.[73]

Baptist leaders could proclaim the notion of Jesus as a revolutionary, but it was more difficult to influence how ordinary believers would interpret this notion in practice. The idea of Christ as a revolutionary certainly seems to have had some appeal among the faithful. As one soldier from the trenches wrote upon receiving copies of evangelical journals: "How many political books of various persuasions there were [here before this], but among them there was not one book talking about the great politics of Jesus Christ."[74] And a contributor to *Slovo istiny* marveled at the contemporary relevance of Jesus's teachings of social inversion with these words: "'He who is great, be like the subordinate, and the ruler—like a servant'—it is [the teaching of] perfectly free regimes, it is of the most leftist democratic republic, it is freedoms that are hardly achieved in the promises of the anarchists and Communists. Yes, in truth, where the Spirit of the Lord is, there is freedom!"[75] Some local communities clearly saw themselves as competing on the same field with political groups. A member of the Trapezond congregation proudly reported, for example, that their meeting place was "in the center of the city—in the same lively place where the clubs of the political parties are located."[76] But was Christianity its own party, or should believers live out Christ's teachings within secular political parties?

When evangelical leaders tried to give guidance to their fellow believers on political questions, they tended to focus on rights rather than on economic principles. For example, when Pavel Pavlov outlined the Baptists' political demands, the concrete ones were for civil rights and a liberal democratic political system, whereas what he meant by socialism was less clear. Socialism seemed to represent a moral vision of social peace and the absence of selfishness rather than any specific plan entailing equal division of wealth or public ownership of the means of production. Indeed, Pavlov asserted that Russian Baptists had nothing against their powerful and rich Western brethren, British Liberal Prime Minister David Lloyd-George and the industrialist John D. Rockefeller, so long as their power or riches were used for the common good.[77]

As noted, Prokhanov also sought to provide political guidance to his flock, by founding a Christian Democratic party named "Resurrection." A rather minor affair, the party did have representatives across the country and fielded at least one list of candidates, in Petrograd, in the elections for the Constituent Assembly that was to decide Russia's new political structure.[78] The party's platform endorsed civil reforms similar to Pavlov's but also addressed social and international issues. It promised a limited land reform including the "introduction on the principle of allotment, according to labor, of crown, monastic, and entailed-estate lands for the use of the people" with compensation determined by legislative bodies. The platform also included a wide range of proposed social legislation guaranteeing the right to strike, the eight-hour day, state pensions, and universal education. "Resurrection" demanded that Russia be transformed into a federal state, with "broad autonomy for individual regions of the country." On the international front, it called for the Russian state to direct all its activity toward the establishment of "an international arbitration court, worldwide disarmament, the removal of the possibility of war," and international peace. The Christian Democrats also hoped for the "unification of all states into one 'Worldwide Union of States'" that would regulate international life.[79]

These two sets of political proposals hint at the views of major evangelical leaders in the rush of excitement of the early revolutionary period, but it is probably unwise to draw too many conclusions from their content or by comparing them. For one thing, because Prokhanov was attempting to found a political party, he was called upon to state views on a wider range of topics than Pavlov had. Both these programs paralleled the Kadets' emphasis on civil liberties over social change. Certainly they shared the Kadets' underlying rejection of class-based politics and aspiration to social reconciliation. Klibanov emphasizes the similarities between the program "Resurrection" proposed and that of the liberal Kadet Party, right down to claiming that "Resurrection" endorsed the policy of continuing the "war to a victorious conclusion."[80] In fact, based on the only available copy of the platform, produced by the Kiev branch of the party, it would seem that "Resurrection" instead advocated an internationalist solution to the problem of the war, one the Kadets would have judged utopian.[81] It is worth remembering that the conditions set by the Petrograd Soviet in early March for its support of the Provisional Government were limited to similar political—rather than socioeconomic— demands.[82]

Divisions would develop throughout Russian society in the face of rising disorder and class conflict, forcing all groups to clarify their political stance. Already in the second issue of *Slovo istiny*, published in June, the editorial declared that the "exultation of victory" was over and Russians now faced the troubling question of what would come next. The death penalty, briefly abolished, had been reinstated, summary justice had returned to the countryside, and anarchy had "raised its head." A poem in the same issue lamented a "freedom that ha[d] devoured freedom," having been born in a time of bloodshed. However, the editorialist still proclaimed the hope that "each individual citizen" could be born again, and that Russia would soon embark on the path of "equality, fraternity, and liberty."[83]

Pavlov's oration on the political demands of the Baptists and the revolutionary nature of Christ's message had taken place the day before Vladimir I. Lenin delivered his famous April Theses, the call to the Bolsheviks to withdraw their support for the Provisional Government and move forward to establish the dictatorship of the proletariat. In the following weeks, as the Provisional Government first decided to remain in the war and then went on to launch an unsuccessful offensive, political divisions and social tensions became inflamed. By early July the coalition cabinet of the Provisional Government was collapsing over the question of Ukrainian independence, while workers, soldiers, and sailors took to the streets in stormy protest against the Provisional Government and the Soviet. Meanwhile, the economy was suffering from a dramatic drop in production, and from inflation, unemployment, disorder in the countryside, and lockouts in the factories.

Pavlov had used a revolutionary political vocabulary to frame his demands, but he rejected the class-based content that the slogan "liberty, equality, fraternity" was taking on as the revolution evolved. The vagueness of his political statement is symptomatic of a broader ambivalence about politics in the evangelical movement as a whole, which was foreshadowed in prerevolutionary discussion about whether it was appropriate to participate in the affairs and ways of human society. By early July an article in *Slovo istiny* was expressing doubt about the alleged benefits of civic organizations. The author wrote that although Russians were accustomed to thinking of such associations as the crucial step in the "unification of all humanity into one family," in fact "they lead humanity only to greater division [by separating people] into large, mutually opposed groups." He warned that any union that promised brotherhood and unity while at the same time devoting its energies to fighting competing organizations was, in fact, promoting hatred rather than brotherhood.[84] Indeed, throughout their discussions of politics, it is clear that, regardless of their other views, Baptists took seriously the term "fraternity" from the revolutionary triumvirate of liberty, equality, and fraternity, and saw it as a call for social peace rather than a rallying cry among competing camps.

Amid this sharpening social polarization, both the Evangelical Christian and Baptist camps of the movement struggled with the question of whether it was acceptable for Christians to belong to political parties. In July the editors of *Slovo istiny* launched a survey of Baptists' views on the subject. Readers were writing to the journal asking about the appropriate attitude for believers to adopt in relation to civic and political organizations. Rather than providing a direct answer themselves, the editors instead posed this question to their readers: "Can believers be members of the parties of Social Revolutionaries, Social Democrats, and other political organizations, and does this not contradict the spirit and teaching of the Word of God?"[85]

Why did the editors of *Slovo istiny* resort to this survey and why did they word it as they did? Their decision to consult the readership reflects a constellation of factors: the novelty of the problem of politics; the importance Baptist theology placed on the individual conscience; on congregational practice; a history of persecution; and probably also the editors' awareness that they were but self-appointed spokesmen for the movement. As for why they chose to single out only the two revolutionary groupings in posing their initial question, there are several possible hypotheses. Their decision could indicate that these were the perceived political choices available to rank-and-file Baptists writing in for advice. By contrast, the wording could imply that what was in question was participation in revolutionary parties rather than in political parties in general. However, the editors never mentioned any suitable alternatives in their presentation of the survey or their comments on its results, emphasizing instead the danger of worldly politics of any type. Moreover, despite disapproval of their methods, the editors of *Slovo istiny* seemed willing to have at least occasional dealings with leftist parties: not only did their press print some Bolshevik propaganda during 1917, but Vasilii Pavlov's diary indicates that the Moscow Baptists held some meetings at the Social Democrats' club.[86]

In their summary of the responses, apparently written soon after the Bolsheviks seized power in Petrograd in late October, the editors emphasized the alleged unanimity of the faithful. "From all the opinions we received, one answer emerges," they contended: "*the believer cannot and should not be a member of any form of political party.*"[87] Yet a review of the small sample of opinions printed reveals that, even though none of the respondents eagerly endorsed joining political parties, most took a far less uncompromising view. The most commonly shared theme was that Christians should maintain some separation from the ways of the world. At the same time many also revealed sympathy with the goals of socialism and hesitation about dictating to the conscience of others by unequivocally denying Christians the right to engage in politics.

In essence, respondents seemed to believe that politics posed a temptation requiring careful management. A participant named "A. F." perhaps best summed up the tension between individual conscience and the interests of collective spiritual mission that animated this discussion. He believed that life was too complex ever to use the word "never." Like others who shared his approach, A. F. emphasized that believers who did engage in politics should be careful not to lose themselves in the affairs of this world. As he concluded, "it is not a sin to be a member of the parties of Social Revolutionaries, Social Democrats, etc., but blessed, blessed is he who is not weighed down and completely serves his straightforward purpose."[88]

Most of the respondents suggested that an acceptable party's program should promote liberty, equality, and fraternity, generally conceived somewhat vaguely as values arising from Christian brotherly love. A few also judged platforms in terms of whether they approximated a similarly ethical ideal of socialism. This was particularly explicit in the response of G. Sergeev, who wrote that, "our sympathies are undoubtedly on the side of the most just of them (ideas), i.e., love, freedom, brotherhood, and equality, true equality, not on paper and in words, but in fact, equality in everything, and also brotherhood, true socialism. These ideas were given to us by our Leader [*Vozhd'*] Jesus Christ." The task of the believer was to show that Christ was "the key to opening the 'door' of the Kingdom of Liberty, Equality, and Fraternity, i.e., love, joy, and peace."[89] Another contributor questioned whether the revolutionaries could match Jesus's promises of freedom from sin and equality before God, and whether the brotherhood of revolutionaries, "brotherhood without love, *without a father*, imaginary brotherhood, is the same as our brotherhood in Christ?"[90]

The editors' summary suggested that most respondents sympathized with the goals of the socialist parties but could not support their methods for achieving them. Although many reiterated the idea that the slogans of fraternity and socialism were meaningless without God's love, only one answer took a dark view of socialism per se.[91] The inclination to set themselves apart from the values of the political world remained strong, but several writers asserted that Christians could not stand completely aloof from the issues of the day.[92] Ambivalence about politics was reflected in respondents' intermingling of political and religious ideas and in their struggle to understand the relationship between ends and means in public life.[93]

As this discussion took place, between July and November 1917, Russians experienced massive strikes, an attempted coup, and, eventually, the Bolshevik seizure of power in Petrograd. In response to the deterioration of the national situation, evangelical leaders began to speak out in favor of the Provisional Government that had realized the first revolution. At the Moscow State Conference, organized by Prime Minister Aleksandr Kerenskii in mid-August to rally public support for the Provisional Government, Prokhanov spoke as a representative of what he called "the new democratic religious Russia." Before 1917, he explained, there had been two liberation movements, one political, the other religious. The political stream had achieved its revolution, but its religious counterpart was still working for the spiritual transformation of Russia. In this spiritual revolution lay the answer to Russia's troubles and to the question posed by the State Conference: how to "save" Russia. Prokhanov's newspaper reported that the Evangelical Christian leader had tried to organize a unanimous declaration of support for the Provisional Government at the conference but without success—not surprisingly, given the deep chasm dividing the leftist and rightist delegates.[94] The editors of the Baptist *Slovo istiny* supported Prokhanov's efforts by reprinting his speech. They repeatedly wrote of how Russia stood at the "crossroads" or the "precipice." One editorial decried the fact that, "beautiful freedom has turned into abominable dissipation. Not one of the creative tasks brought forward by the revolution has been achieved. Class dissension is becoming more severe and the specter of popular civil strife and fratricide is hanging over us."[95] Here and elsewhere, the Baptists would seek to defend the revolution that had given them the freedom to preach and organize.[96] In so doing they rejected the Bolshevik view that further political revolution was in order: the February Revolution was foundation enough for the necessary revolution of the spirit.

And, as contributors to *Slovo istiny* asserted, without this revolution of the spirit, efforts to resolve the breakdown of political arrangements, such as the Moscow State Conference or the leftist Democratic Conference in September, were failing. One author commented on how Russians of all types—"old and young, Left and Right, workers and industrialists, peasants and nobles"—could agree on but one thing, that Russia needed to be saved. However, despite their use of such religious language, all had "forgotten Him, Who long ago pointed out the path of salvation."[97] Likewise A. Vodlinger complained that, "the Russian revolution has locked itself within the limits of materialism and intrigue [*politikanstva*], ignoring the higher demands of the spirit. . . . In it there is not the religious inspiration, the ecstasy of the Holy Spirit that inspire people to heroic triumphs and sacrifices of love . . . without a revolution of the spirit, all will remain wretched and destitute slaves, regardless of the freedoms and new forms of state structure."[98] Baptists thus countered

148

the materialist conceptions of the socialist parties by reiterating the view that
political and economic structures could not change consciousness, rather
the reverse.

OCTOBER REVOLUTION AND APOCALYPSE

Then, in late October, what *Slovo istiny* called the "fratricidal nightmare"
became reality with the Bolshevik seizure of power. Articles regarding the
October Revolution returned to the theme of the ideals of "liberty, equality, and fraternity" betrayed by the politics of class conflict. The patriarch of
the Baptist movement, Vasilii Pavlov, lamented that, "we wanted liberty, but
one party (the Bolsheviks), drawing the soldiers to their will, continues to
perpetrate violence and horrors no worse [*sic*] than were done under
Nicholas II. We wanted fraternity, but instead of fraternity [we have] fratricide! We expected equality, but instead of equality [we have] theft and ar-
son."[99] In contrast to the Baptist leaders' understanding of this slogan as a
recipe for class reconciliation, it was now decorating the banners of class warfare. Yet, as Orlando Figes has pointed out, "the language of 1789, once it
entered Russia in 1917, soon became translated into the language of class."
Moreover, he contends, "this was not just a question of semantics. It showed
that for the vast mass of the people the ideals of 'democracy' were expressed
in terms of a social revolution rather than in terms of political reform."[100]
Evangelical leaders' continued use of words like "socialism" and "fraternity"
to describe a condition of social peace and compromise quickly left them
out of step with a society rent asunder by social conflict.

In April, the younger Pavlov had argued that conversion had solved the
problem of class tensions within evangelical communities, but discussions
in *Slovo istiny* suggest that cracks in this unanimity were revealed as the revolution unfolded. Indeed, the journal's launching of its survey on political
participation may well have arisen out of concern over the emergence of divisions in the movement's ranks regarding the definition of these ideals and
the political implications of Christian beliefs. The tone of the editors' summary, with its emphasis on consensus among believers, may have been an effort to unify the faithful in the face of the divisive politics of the day and the
uncertainty prompted by the Bolshevik seizure of power.

Certainly two articles published in the first months of 1918 lend credence
to the idea that the Bolshevik Revolution had heightened political divisions.
One contributor, "Baptist," in what seems to be a "late entry" to the survey
on political participation, agreed that Baptists should not join political parties. He emphasized, however, that this was not because politics was "sinful"
but rather because believers were already "members of the Christian party."
Baptists had a responsibility to participate in civic organizations, but as Baptists, holding high Christ's banner. When it came to voting, "Baptist" declared,
class divisions among believers were bound to emerge. Some members sug-

gested that Baptists could belong to any party, so long as it did not bear the prefix "social," he reported. However, the author rejected this view. "Clearly," he contended, "they will not follow the socialists to the barricades, they will not take part in their affairs, but they will give them their votes in elections." Similarly, he argued, more "well-off brothers" would obviously never vote for such parties.[101] In this way "Baptist" laid bare the possibility—and, presumably, the existence—of social tensions within the Baptist movement. At the same time he preserved a sense of separation from the "world" of these tensions by insisting that Christianity itself was the party of all evangelicals.

Evidence of divisions arising from the Bolshevik victory surfaced more pointedly in an article by Vasilii Ivanov in the same issue of *Slovo istiny*. According to Ivanov, "many poor brothers want to receive the earth and all happiness from the hands of the socialists who do not recognize God, and with pride say: no one but we ourselves will create a new life in Russia!" He went on to give examples from his encounters with believers: "One said to me directly that he had long ago turned away from God," Ivanov reported, while "another openly declared that the 'revolutionary' Social Democrat knows neither compassion, nor God, nor other assumptions of the old world. He knows only one principle: expediency."[102] Thus it would appear that the challenge facing evangelical communities was no longer merely agreeing on the meaning of the terms of political and social revolution and their implications for believers' political activity but also actively defending the notion of the revolution of the spirit as a necessary prelude to social transformation.

After the Easter of revolution in early 1917, the Baptists had eagerly awaited the revolution of the spirit that would bring about the social reconciliation of Pentecost. But as the war effort failed, social tensions became inflamed, economic crisis and political paralysis deepened, and, especially after the Bolshevik seizure of power, it was increasingly the darker expectation of the day of judgment that excited their imaginations. In late 1917 and early 1918 apocalyptic visions began to appear in missionaries' reports in the Baptist press about attitudes among members. As E. Gerasimenko wrote, describing his travels along the Black Sea coast in autumn 1917, "On the basis of all that I heard and saw, it is a pleasure for me to confirm that many children of God, sensing the nearing of the great day of the appearance of our Lord Jesus Christ, do their best to free themselves from all that interferes with loving the Lord." He had also found many nonbelievers who were seeking God and converting to the Baptist faith.[103] Several contributors warned that believers should prepare themselves, as the last days were imminent. Stories and poems expressed apocalyptic themes.[104] Drafts of Ivanov's sermons from the spring of 1918 preserved among his papers reveal him trying to ascertain the signs of the last times, to understand teachings about victory over the Antichrist, and to describe the "thousand-year reign of Christ on earth."[105] In his early 1918 article describing the corrosive influence of the socialists' platform on Baptist communities, Ivanov went on to demonstrate in no uncertain terms that the Antichrist wore the leather jacket of a Red Guard. "The Social Democrat," he asserted, "he is John's vision of the beast in Revelations, coming out of the ground. . . . Now the devil has similarly led people to the high mountain and shown them all the universal kingdom and promised to give them power over all these kingdoms and their glory (Luke 4:5–7)."[106] Thus Ivanov, whose optimism had overflowed in early 1917 with ambition to build the Kingdom of God on earth, now interpreted the events of his day through the apocalyptic vision of the Book of Revelation.

Expectations of an apocalyptic solution to Russia's distress were widespread throughout Russian society, from peasant to worker to intellectual in the revolutionary period of 1917–18.[107] In fact, one contributor to *Slovo istiny* highlighted this fact, if only to reiterate the ubiquitous theme of the revolution's need for Christ. "Humanity," he wrote,

> as if instinctively, has a presentiment of the nearing of something catastrophic, takes measures toward staving off the approaching calamity. Unfortunately, the essence of that which approaches is hidden from the children of this world and, therefore, considering earthly prosperity to be the highest good, they try to protect and secure themselves in the worldly sense. Our Russian revolution was accomplished with this goal. With this same goal various groups and parties organize themselves. All these events in no uncertain terms tell all humanity and especially the Church of Christ of the proximity of the Second Coming.[108]

The evangelicals' concept of the revolution of the spirit had always had significant apocalyptic underpinnings: the revolution would usher in Christ's rule on earth. At the beginning of 1917 this was an optimistic vision: as in Ofrova's poem, which opened this chapter, the Baptists tended to emphasize the role of humans, through proselytization, in building a kingdom for Christ to rule. The aspiration and ability to build an ideal society would arise naturally out of conversion, and Christ would then return to rule a converted humanity. There was no discussion of a period of suffering and judgment before the realization of that kingdom—indeed, the evangelicals seemed to believe that they had come through such a period already. But by 1918 more emphasis was being placed on the idea that Christ himself would return after a period of judgment to build that kingdom. The revolution of the spirit had always been directed at creating a new life on earth, but it had also always been ambivalent about participating in the ways of this earth in its unconverted state. As the state of "this world" became less and less attractive, believers became more eager to witness its end.

However, regardless of one's view about the details of Christ's return to earth, the need to convert as many people as possible in anticipation of that great moment remained. At first, some believers appeared stunned and immobilized by the Bolshevik Revolution. Soon, however, the Baptists began explicitly to counter Bolshevik propaganda with their own. In late 1917 the editorial board of the Baptist journal *Drug molodezhi*, published in Balashov, decided to raise money and organize local groups to distribute free brochures on such spiritual themes as "news about salvation" and "revolution of the spirit." The editors of *Slovo istiny* approved, noting that in the face of political parties' print shops working "day and night," the evangelicals needed to "flood our country with the pure evangelical Word in order that every Russian citizen might be born again" for "our motherland must experience still another internal-spiritual revolution of the spirit."[109] In Samara, over the Christmas season, the Baptists held parades and large open-air meetings at which the "public was startled by the slogans on the banners, when they read in white letters on red banners the great words 'God is love'" and other Christian slogans.[110] On the eve of the gathering of the Constituent Assembly in early January, the Evangelical Christians convened a youth congress in Petrograd that again emphasized the need for spiritual transformation to complement political change.[111]

With the Bolshevik victory, believers also now faced in concrete terms the questions of political strategy and the compatibility of socialist and Christian visions with which they had struggled throughout 1917. *Slovo istiny* directly addressed this problem by running a series of articles on "Socialism and Christianity" in which the author, "Arvid," explored the relationship between the two concepts, the attitudes of Christians and socialists toward each other, and the correct path to building socialism. According to "Arvid," misunderstandings arose from the fact that, although there was only one socialism, there were many parties, each of which had seized on one small aspect of the broader concept. True socialism was the equalization of wealth in the interest of a more spiritual and humane life.[112] In fact, there was no conflict between true socialism and Christianity—indeed, Arvid pointed to "social democratic" ideas in the Old Testament—for they were one and the same. The question, as always, was the means for realizing this socialism:

> Socialism that rejects neither religion, nor the family, nor marriage, that is against violence, hatred, and malice, but that is for freedom, for equality, for brotherhood based on loving alliance—that socialism does not contradict Christianity, and true Christianity in turn does not contradict such socialism. But socialism created out of partisan narrowness, rejecting religion, marriage, family and other Christian sacred ideals, inflaming class hatred and calling for violence and vengeance—such socialism really is incompatible with Christianity.[113]

As "Arvid" concluded, "there can be no realization of socialism outside the kingdom of God."[114]

The evangelicals would continue to speak of an impending revolution of the spirit throughout the civil war that followed the revolution. They would also persevere in their efforts to transform life on earth through conversion, in anticipation of the Second Coming. The idea of a revolution of the spirit had provided a basis not only for asserting Baptist inclusion in the rush to national transformation of February 1917 but also for criticism of the revolution as it evolved during 1917. Throughout the 1920s this notion of common goals to be achieved by different means would appear again and again in Baptist and Evangelical Christian communications with the Soviet government and the increasingly necessary declarations of attitudes toward Soviet power. What had been a topic of discussion about tactics and ideals during 1917 would become the evangelicals' slogan as they sought to prove to Russia's new rulers that there was room for a Christian socialism in Bolshevik Russia.

8

Revolution and Opportunity

The first decade of Soviet power has frequently been portrayed as a golden age for Russian religious dissidents, and for evangelical groups in particular.[1] In his report to the Third Baptist World Congress in Stockholm in 1923 J. H. Rushbrooke, the Baptist Commissioner for Europe, rejoiced that "the most conspicuous fact of recent Baptist development in Europe is the amazing growth of the Russian work. . . . It is impossible even yet to obtain detailed and absolutely reliable statistics regarding the expansion of the Baptists; but many thousands of churches have come into being, and I regard an estimate of 1,000,000 members as probably well within the mark."[2] Observing religious developments in Russia from a left-wing, Western perspective, Julius F. Hecker similarly commented in 1927 that "Russia swarms with sects." In its haste to destroy the former state church, the Bolshevik regime had actually "created an unusually favorable situation for spiritual religion." In particular, he noted, "the Evangelical Movement in Russia is growing so rapidly as to become an important factor in the religious life of the country."[3]

During these years both the activities and the numerical growth of the Baptists and Evangelical Christians were certainly quite visible. For example, an article in *Baptist Ukrainy* reported on how, at the January 1928 celebration of his tenth anniversary as presbyter of the Baptist congregation in the Ukrainian city of Poltava, Roman D. Khomiak rejoiced at the community's

Хрічний Ювелей
1917р. Полтавської Громади Баптістів. 1927р.

Members of the Poltava congregation of Baptists during their tenth anniversary celebrations, 1927. They are photographed in front of the local Lutheran church, where they worshiped. *Baptist Ukrainy, 1928.*

growth from 15 to 190 members in a decade. In the wider Poltava region a further 60 churches had been formed in this period. This was the work, he emphasized, of male and female deacons and evangelists who, together with Khomiak and his wife, had devoted themselves to preaching the faith and planting new churches.[4] The Poltava flock met in the local Lutheran church, but these were also years when numerous congregations across the country joyously celebrated the opening of newly built prayer houses.[5] And, almost every summer, citizens of the Soviet capital could witness a mass baptism from the banks of the Moscow River.[6]

Like other Soviet citizens, the evangelicals experienced the period of revolution and the ensuing civil war from 1917 to 1921 as one of political upheaval, hunger, and violence. At the same time these years also launched a decade of great activity, expansion, and experimentation. Despite the Bolsheviks' attack on religious institutions, on the property of the Orthodox Church in particular and on religious beliefs in general, the early Soviet period also offered new opportunities for formerly dissident religious groups. Not only did the new constitution proclaim freedom of religious propaganda but the historical legacy of the tsarist government's persecution of religious dissidents, and their past interaction with the Bolsheviks, set sectarians apart from other religious denominations in the minds of Russia's new rulers. The Baptists and Evangelical Christians thus benefited from several favorable policies that the new government offered sectarian groups. These included, for example, the possibility of release from military service because of religious convictions and incentives to found agricultural communes. Baptists and Evangelical Christians responded enthusiastically to these opportunities, presenting themselves to the government as partners in the building of socialism. They also continued actively to proselytize, to develop local youth and women's groups, to hold local and national congresses, to publish journals, and to envision new forms of Christian community. The movement's apparent rapid expansion and activity have often been held up as evidence of the social space for autonomous associational life in early Soviet Russia and of the way in which the revolution unleashed popular enthusiasm for social experimentation beyond that sponsored by the ruling Bolshevik Party.[7]

In many ways this picture is correct. During the chaos of the civil war period, and the calmer years of reconstruction under the New Economic Policy (NEP) in the mid-1920s, the evangelicals joined countless groups interested in exploring the opportunities for artistic and social experimentation seemingly opened up by the revolution. The shared experience of religious conversion served as the basis for Baptists and Evangelical Christians to develop an entire subculture devoted to building Christ's kingdom on earth. Although it would be rash to describe Soviet society before the rise of Stalin as displaying the traits of a civil society, with a web of independent organizations legitimized by legal safeguards, its relative pluralism stands in stark contrast to the situation by 1930.[8]

However, these circumstances of Soviet society in the 1920s did not necessarily reflect the Bolsheviks' desire for it to be so but rather the fact that they could not yet manage to have it any other way.[9] Everyone listening to Khomiak's speech at the Poltava congregational celebration in 1928 would have known that their pastor had failed to mention his recent arrest for expressing antimilitarist views, or his exile to the distant Narym region after complaining, at the Baptist Union's national congress in late 1923, about the beating of imprisoned Baptists by Poltava prison administrators.[10] In general, the new revolutionary regime sent out mixed messages about religious practices: valuables were seized from churches, but Soviet institutions still closed for important Orthodox holidays; religious sectarians were urged to build model communes in the countryside, but these communes were then forbidden to join the national association of collective farms because of their religious character. These inconsistencies reflected, in part, disagreements among leading Bolsheviks about how to combat the persistence of religious influence in Soviet Russia—about whether religion would simply die out as socialist society modernized or whether more forceful measures were needed. But it is important to remember that neither camp cared for the chaotic, hybrid nature of NEP society. They agreed that the conversion of all Soviet citizens to Bolshevism was the party's ultimate goal. For this reason, groups like the Baptists, which ultimately competed with the Bolsheviks for converts, may have found considerable room to maneuver in the 1920s, but they never felt secure. Although this evangelical society could exist inside, and interact with, the Soviet one, the Bolshevik regime regarded this existence as a temporary, undesirable phenomenon.

This chapter addresses the positive side of this story—the privileges religious sectarians enjoyed and the flourishing of evangelical associational life. In this confusing and uncertain time, evangelical communities provided increasing numbers of people with a shared sense of meaning and belonging. They involved their members in a myriad of group activities built around three interrelated goals: personal and spiritual development, mutual aid, and, most important of all, the conversion of new members. All this took place against a background of constant harassment by local government officials, however. The next two chapters, dealing, respectively, with the question of pacifism in Baptist ranks and youth organizations, will reveal that the limits on the possibilities for creating a legitimate, Soviet, evangelical culture came not simply from overzealous or uninformed local Bolsheviks but instead from the Central Committee in Moscow.

THE ATTACK ON THE CHURCH:
OPPORTUNITIES FOR EVANGELICALS?

Russia's new rulers after October 1917 aimed to transform not only the economic and social structures of their country but to shape a new society of committed, activist builders of communism, liberated from otherworldly preoccupations such as religion. In the short term, this meant destroying the institutional power of religion in Soviet Russia; in the long term, the goal was to destroy religious belief. An important first step in this process came on 23 January 1918, when the Bolshevik regime decreed the separation of church and state, and of schools from the church. The decree prohibited religious organizations from owning property, having legal status, or providing religious education outside the family setting. Although formerly dissident religious groups were affected by these measures, the Orthodox faith, with its intimate involvement in primary education and its extensive land holdings, stood to lose the most from this new state of affairs. While the newly elected Patriarch Tikhon Belavin pronounced an anathema on all who engaged in bloody reprisals and theft, local communities of Orthodox believers rallied to defend themselves against the seizure of their parish churches, the confiscation of property from local monasteries, and the removal of parish registry books to civil offices. Evangelicals, with little wealth and even less power to lose, watched from the sidelines as the legal and financial position of the former state church was rapidly decimated. Some antireligious propaganda accompanied these actions, but, as a rule, in these early days the debunking of the religious beliefs of the populace generally took second place to the administrative attack on the Orthodox Church as an institution.[11]

In fact, the Bolsheviks had not focused much attention on religious questions before coming to power. To some extent, all assumed that religious faith would simply fade away with the victory of modern, materialist socialism. However, some party leaders, such as Leon Trotsky, thought that confrontational methods were necessary to speed this process along, whereas others, led by Vladimir Bonch-Bruevich, considered a gradual program of reeducation more promising. During the first years of Soviet power this disagreement over tactics, along with optimism about the "withering away" of religion under socialist conditions, the need to gain and preserve the allegiance of the still religious peasantry, and the obvious fact that the Bolsheviks' salient priority was to win the civil war, combined to make the religious policy of the Soviet state unsystematic and its implementation uneven. In fact, as Arto Luukkanen points out, throughout the entire first decade of Soviet power these policies were shaped mostly by political expediency rather than ideology. As a result, the tactics of those in favor of a moderate approach to religious belief often coexisted with sharply militant antireligious strategies.[12]

As far as former religious dissidents were concerned, the policy of the new Soviet government was one of "benevolent neutrality."[13] Bonch-Bruevich, who served as the administrator of the Council of People's Commissars and Lenin's right-hand man from 1917 to 1920, now saw a chance to prove his argument that sectarianism had been merely political protest against the tsarist regime cloaked in religious guise. During the civil war years and beyond, Bonch-Bruevich played an important role, both by arguing for legal concessions to the sectarians and by acting as an advocate for the many believers who appealed for his help in solving their legal problems at the local level. Under his influence, as we will see in greater detail in the next chapter, in January 1919 the Soviet government issued a decree providing for the release of sectarians from military service, if their convictions prevented them from taking up arms. This was followed in early October 1921 by a further appeal to sectarians and Old Believers to settle abandoned estates and farm them collectively.[14] And even party members who nursed no hopes about religious sectarians as potential allies were quite explicitly still willing to give them some leeway, as a measure against their shared enemy, the Russian Orthodox Church.[15]

This is not to say that sectarians were unaffected by the blanket restrictions that the Separation Decree laid on all believers. For example, Orthodox and non-Orthodox alike chafed under the prohibition on religious education for minors.[16] They also shared the difficulties associated with their organizations being denied legal status. Without such status, for example, it became increasingly difficult to rent or buy property or to give out letters of reference to members traveling on church business.[17] Furthermore, local officials often disregarded legal niceties if they stood in the way of their goals.

Thus congregations frequently appealed to the central government, in particular to Bonch-Bruevich, for help when their prayer houses were closed or their members arrested.[18] In the first decade of Soviet power Bonch-Bruevich and others usually looked into these pleas and often came to sectarians' defense. Overall, however, religious sectarians like the Baptists and Evangelical Christians escaped much of the harsh treatment meted out to the Orthodox, whether it was the closure of churches, the shooting of priests, or the violent seizure of church valuables.

And so, despite the restrictions and inconsistencies of the new era, former sectarian groups, including the Baptists and Evangelical Christians, took enthusiastic advantage of the anti-Orthodox bias in state policy and made full use of the freedom of religious and antireligious propaganda promised by the new Soviet Constitution of July 1918. Regardless of dire economic conditions and the onset of civil war, evangelicals' journals, letters, diaries, and memoirs describe the early Soviet period as one of rapid expansion and considerable public enthusiasm for their message. Many of the faithful continued to believe that they were living through the last days before the Second Coming of Christ. In anticipation of Jesus's imminent revolution of the spirit, they sought to expand their ranks through missionary work and to live out their renunciation of the ways of "this world" through conscientious resistance, the founding of communal Christian communities, and a drive to unify the Evangelical Christian and Baptist factions of the movement.

Permeating Baptist writings in 1918 was an awareness of the opportunities presented by this drastic loss of position of the Orthodox Church, as well as a sometimes unseemly joy in seeing the old rival brought down. "Who would have thought a few months ago that the ruling, satisfied, well-fed, somnolent Orthodox department would suddenly stand in the ranks of the persecuted and cry out about this to all of Rus'," gloated the first *Slovo istiny* editorial after the separation of church and state. Now the Baptists' longstanding demand that religious faith be made a private matter had been realized. Nevertheless the editors were uneasy about the Bolsheviks' means to that end. "If we cannot approve of the means of violence to which the current regime turns in many areas of the life of the country," the article declared, "all the same we think that if the interference of the authorities in church life is restricted *only* to establishing order in the material side of the Orthodox faith, then it is still early to shout about persecution." They also asserted, however, that the program of separation of church and state ought to be implemented on the "legal basis of a general resolution of popularly elected representatives."[19] Echoing the terms of the 1917 debate about the attitude of the Christian to revolutionary parties, the editors seemed torn between applauding the Bolsheviks' policies and criticizing their methods.

Despite their initial dismay at the Bolshevik Revolution, Baptist leaders displayed a willingness to make common cause with Russia's new rulers throughout 1918 and beyond. In addition to rejoicing in the separation of church and state, in the pages of *Slovo istiny* and in their letters to government and party officials they intensified their emphasis on the modest social origins of Baptists and their rejection of ecclesiastical ritual and hierarchy. By the summer of 1918 Baptist prayer meetings in Moscow were being advertised as "popular religious meetings." Perhaps more significant, *Slovo istiny* responded to the party's policy of attacking the economic power of the Orthodox church by seeking to differentiate true faith from the structures of powerful, worldly religion. The slogan "Faith is from God, religion is from people!" emblazoned the cover of one issue, which included an explicit attack on the Orthodox Church as a "Religion without Christ."[20] When the Bolsheviks took to opening the coffins of saints to reveal that, contrary to Orthodox belief, their relics had been corrupted, evangelicals enthusiastically approved this action as a campaign against superstition. In fact, delegates to the 1921 Baptist congress in Moscow took a field trip to the Museum of Public Health to see an exhibit on the subject.[21] And evangelical congregations were happy to make use of the former buildings of the Orthodox Church that the authorities assigned them for their meetings.[22]

In their letters to the government, but also at congresses and in their magazines, evangelicals in these early years often portrayed themselves as active partners in the building of socialism. In each case, however, they argued that it was their work for the revolution of the spirit that made them so. For example, in a letter of October 1918 to a department of the Moscow Soviet, Vasilii Pavlov noted that, "the Baptist teaching, which experienced the most brutal persecution under tsarism, also preaches international communism but without the use of violence, setting the moral rebirth of the individual as the first condition."[23] The Baptists and the Evangelical Christians also reasserted their claim to be reviving the principles of the first Christians. This was a useful image in view of the tendency of Bolshevik propagandists to contrast positively early Christianity with later churches perverted by riches and hierarchy.[24] In 1918 the Evangelical Christian leader Ivan Prokhanov published a brochure titled "Gospel Christianity and the Social Question," in which he proposed three different types of labor collectives modeled on early Christian communities.[25] That same year an editorial in *Baptist* described the simplicity and purity of early Christian communities, and asked, "Is it not time to bring about the spiritual revolution?"[26] And when Evangelical Christians and Baptists held a joint congress in Moscow in 1920 to discuss unification, Vasilii Pavlov wrote in his diary that the majority of delegates preferred "Union of First Christians" as the name for a new organization.[27]

The Baptists had long hoped for disestablishment of the state religion. For them this did not imply the secularization of society but rather the opening of a level playing field for religious competition for the hearts and minds of the Russian population. Only with the separation of church and state could their voluntaristic communities of converts grow and prosper. In early 1918 they thus rejoiced that the Bolsheviks had made religion "the private affair of every believer."[28] However, the Baptists gradually came to realize that there was to be no "private" spiritual life in the new Communist state. Between 1918 and 1920 the distinctions between "state" and "party" and the notions of "private" and "public" collapsed in Bolshevik thinking. The Bolsheviks' aspirations to establish the dictatorship of the proletariat and to fashion a "new Soviet man" carried in them the seeds for this fusion of the public and state spheres.[29] As the lines between the antireligious Bolshevik Party and the officially nonreligious Soviet state virtually disappeared in practice, so, too, did any notion that religion could be a private matter. The goal of the regime now became an effort to replace the worship of God with the exaltation of the socialist state.[30] The Bolsheviks sought to create not just a secular state but also an atheistic society. To do this they needed to effect a cultural revolution, to convert the populace to their own political message of salvation through radical self-transformation.[31] And although they did not yet have the power to transform their society forcibly, they did enjoy the propaganda advantage of a ruling party.

The demotion of the Orthodox Church and the official promotion of atheism naturally unsettled and sharpened general public attitudes, making the civil war period a time of great public interest in questions of religion. Whether evangelical, Orthodox, or Bolshevik, observers reported the tremendous popularity of lectures on religious themes, and especially of debates between religious figures and antireligious activists organized by the party in towns and villages across the land.[32] The Bolsheviks' antireligious message was trumpeted everywhere: icons disappeared from public buildings, banners declaring that "religion is the opiate of the people" or that "there is no God" adorned city streets, religious buildings were closed and reassigned to new purposes, while religious leaders were arrested, imprisoned, and, in numerous cases, shot.[33] No one could simply take religious affiliation for granted anymore. In early 1920 Petr A. Krasikov, the head of the department at the Commissariat of Justice, charged with implementing the separation of church and state, described the "passionate" and "enormous" interest in religious questions among the laboring population. In his view this phenomenon was not a sign of political reaction but rather evidence of a spiritual thirst which it was the regime's task to quench. Indeed, he opined, people were experiencing "a real need for the working out of a whole new worldview, suited to the great revolution which is taking place in the structure of society and the powerful upsurge of the working class and peasantry."[34]

Evangelicals were similarly convinced that the revolution was forcing a reconsideration of values and beliefs, but they hoped that they, rather than the Bolshevik Party, would reap the benefits. Certainly optimism about Baptist prospects abounded during the civil war years. Around the same time that Krasikov penned his observations, for example, the Evangelical Christians were holding large public meetings in the "Uran" Theater and at the

Shaniavskii University in Moscow, in conjunction with a national congress. A report in their journal appeared to relish the competitive atmosphere surrounding religious ideas, declaring that "the huge halls were overflowing with people. There were penitents, there were objectors, and in everything the Lord displayed His power."[35] Likewise a contributor to the Petrograd Baptist magazine, *Istochnik iz kamnia* [Spring from a stone], observed in late 1920 that, although the revolution had initially spawned a cooling of spiritual ardor, the "storm of revolution [had] blown past" and people were beginning to behold the glorious vision of Christ's invitation to all. In contrast to the party's message of salvation for the working classes alone, the Baptists' invitation was "not only [to] the chosen, specifically all who labor and are burdened, [but] to all without differentiation, without any privilege one before another."[36] Indeed, the evangelicals became rather hyperbolic about their conversion successes during the first years of Soviet power: at the 1921 annual meeting of the Baptists, the Siberian division of the Baptist Union alone claimed to have half a million members—and that one congregation had baptized three thousand people in one day![37]

Although this rate of growth may seem exaggerated, there is no question that the turbulent conditions of the civil war did contribute to spreading evangelical ideas and prompting many new conversions. The very movement of people brought on by the return of soldiers from World War I, the mobilization of recruits to the Red Army, and the flight of urban dwellers from the starving cities to the countryside opened up new fields for evangelization.[38] Already in early 1919 an émigré Russian Baptist journal in Philadelphia was commenting that returning soldiers were a "marvelous means of spreading the good news."[39] Certainly the figure of the soldier who had converted while in service returning home to found a congregation pervaded local reports in 1920s evangelical journals. For example, in the large village of Novo-Pavlovskoe in the Melitopol' area, several young men returned from military service bringing with them their new Baptist faith; by 1928 they had built a congregation of more than one hundred members, with a choir and its own prayer house.[40] As war ravaged their lives, religion, whether evangelical or Orthodox, helped some people to make sense of their existence.[41]

This growth appears to have continued throughout the first decade of Soviet rule. Once again, it is hard to say exactly how many new members joined, as widely varying estimates were bandied about. This clearly arose from competition between the two branches, as well as a desire to impress their significance upon both the Soviet government and Baptists abroad.[42] In 1926 alone, various official Baptist statements put the number at 400,000 members or one million members or 6,500 congregations with 500,000 members.[43] At the Ukrainian Baptists' congress in Khar'kov in 1925 a resolution declared that numerical expansion averaged 15 percent per year, although no concrete numbers were given.[44] Between 1922 and 1926 the Baptist Union attempted to collect detailed statistics from its member congregations including the date they were founded and the number of members, as well as information about youth groups, choirs, leadership, and so on.[45] In 1928–29 the Baptist camp revised its figures downward, informing both the Soviet government and the Baptist World Alliance that it numbered 200,000 actual adherents and an additional 800,000 family members and other regular attendees.[46] The Evangelical Christian branch also started to collect similar statistics in 1922 but does not appear ever to have made specific public statements about membership numbers.[47] However, at the Tenth Evangelical Christian Congress in December 1926 the union vice president Iakov I. Zhidkov did announce that the union represented approximately 2,500 congregations and were aware of a large number of unregistered groups.[48] Despite the lack of reliable statistics, it would be safe to say that the two denominations together at least tripled their membership level before World War I, when the tsarist government counted 114,652 Baptists and Evangelical Christians by January 1912.[49]

THE UNIONS AND THEIR ACTIVITIES

In addition to this rising membership, the first decade of Soviet power witnessed the substantial expansion of nationwide and regional Baptist and Evangelical Christian associations. Despite increasing interference and obstruction by the Soviet authorities, in the 1920s both groups developed more formal administrative centers in Moscow and Leningrad, respectively, and successfully labored to spread their message by holding congresses, distributing regular circular letters to congregations, publishing monthly journals, training local leaders in central Bible schools, and supporting a roster of itinerant missionaries. During the hungry years of the civil war and the famine in the Volga thereafter, they also coordinated relief shipments from groups in unaffected areas. Through these efforts the unions considerably enlarged their institutional presence.

After 1918, the administration of the Baptist Union was transformed from a committee with members scattered across the provinces to a permanent institution in the new Soviet capital. As we have seen, in 1917 a senior Baptist leader, Vasilii G. Pavlov, his son, Pavel V. Pavlov, and his former assistant, Mikhail D. Timoshenko, had resurrected the journal they had published in prewar Odessa, *Slovo istiny*, and founded a press and publishing house under the same name in Moscow. After the civil war ignited, the two younger men used the institutional base provided by *Slovo istiny* to defend and promote Baptist interests before the new government. Although they had merely been members of the union executive board elected in Vladikavkaz in 1917, by 1919 the Pavlovs and Timoshenko had declared Moscow the union's center and proceeded to call national congresses and to negotiate unity with the Evangelical Christians on behalf of the Baptists.[50] The organization occupied a building in central Moscow, administered a legally recognized cooperative publishing house, and employed several people. The Evangelical Christians similarly improved their administrative strength. Although their union had always been centered around Ivan S. Prokhanov and his congregation in St. Petersburg, in the first years of Soviet power they were able to establish a permanent office in central Petrograd (later Leningrad) which employed several full-time secretaries and organizers.[51]

During the civil war, when communications were disrupted and a general regionalization of the former Russian Empire took place, communities of believers in various areas also formed local associations that left their mark on both unions in the 1920s. Since 1907 the Baptist Union had spawned several regional subgroups, including branches in Siberia, the Caucasus, and the Far East. From 1918 this decentralization became more pronounced: when Siberia and the Far East were under the control of the Whites from 1918 to 1920, the regional organizations there were very active and, indeed, asserted their independence from the Russian Baptist Union. Likewise, in October 1918, Ukrainian Baptists met in Kiev to found a Ukrainian Baptist Union. Regional interests would continue to shape the Baptist Union into the 1920s. Although, together with an array of other local groups, the Siberian and Far East branches permanently returned to the fold of the All-Russian Union, the Khar'kov-based Ukrainian Union reasserted its independence in 1925, after a three-year experiment in unity. This would appear to have been a rather amicable decision, reflecting the different laws of the Ukrainian Republic and a heightened sense of Ukrainian identity in the context of the Bolsheviks' Ukrainization policies of the 1920s. In recognition of this fact, at its national congress in 1926, the Baptist Union formally adopted a federal structure.[52] By contrast, among the Evangelical Christians, there is less evidence of efforts to form independent regional associations. On the contrary, although the civil war period certainly saw many regional congresses in different parts of the country, the initiative for forming local organizations seems to have come from Petrograd.[53] These local committees and congresses existed throughout the 1920s, but they do not seem to have exerted much pressure on Prokhanov's central organization.

The apocalyptic moods of the revolutionary period had initially prompted evangelicals to renew efforts to unify their ranks. Indeed, the goal of joining forces into a single union constituted one of the most important topics of discussion at local and national congresses of both the Baptists and Evangelical Christians during the civil war period. Already in 1917, in many areas across the country, local amalgamated congregations had begun to heal the rifts among believers and to call on others to follow their lead.[54] During the course of 1919 the groundwork was set for talks on unifying the two unions, and in January 1920, huddled in their coats and subsisting on dried rusks and tea, representatives of both groups met in starving Petrograd to plan a joint congress to be held in Moscow in June. In one of the four sermons given at the opening of the meeting, a Baptist representative, Vasilii Georg'evich

Ivan S. Prokhanov (*center*) photographed with the Kiev District Council of
Evangelical Christians, June 1928.
From Prokhanoff, In the Cauldron of Russia, 1933.

Melis', declared: "At these sessions we should have one goal, to prepare ourselves and our unions to meet our God who is coming soon." Likewise, after
the meeting, the epistle sent out to all the congregations of Baptists and Evangelical Christians in Russia opened by emphasizing the apocalyptic religious
mood behind these efforts: "Among the indescribably hard conditions of life
and the clear signs of the imminent coming of Christ surrounding us, we
proclaim to you a great joy: the unity of the children of God, about which we
have all prayed for so long." And the letter closed with this warning: "The steps
of the coming Christ are already audible, the sound of God's trumpets reaches
us. In what condition will the Lord find us: uncoordinated or united?"[55]
Meanwhile, on the local level, neighboring congregations continued to amal-
gamate and regional congresses to declare the end of competition and the
beginning of cooperation.[56] The planned joint congress did take place in
June and an agreement creating one unified union was signed, but during
1921 these efforts broke down. Hopes for a second such meeting in Petrograd in June 1921 appear to have been unrealized.[57] Some informal collaboration continued—regarding Bible schools, for example—but overall, by
the mid-1920s, the two camps of Evangelical Christians and Baptists would
find themselves as far apart as ever. In fact, relations became quite nasty by
the December 1925 Plenum of the Baptist Union Council, when the Baptists formally severed relations with Prokhanov's union and appealed to the

Baptist World Alliance to remove Prokhanov as vice president on the grounds that he was trying to use this position to foment a schism in local Baptist congregations.[58]

The civil war period also saw Baptists and Evangelical Christians working with other groups of former religious dissenters to break down barriers and advance common interests. Together with the Mennonites, they transformed the Christian Soldiers' Circles they had organized during 1917 into a tent mission that traveled widely throughout southern Russia and Ukraine until 1923. In various areas, the Caucasus in particular, Baptists, Evangelical Christians, Mennonites, Molokans, and other groups held joint congresses.[59] Various sectarian leaders in Moscow met for ecumenical discussions in these years, and there was even, apparently, cooperation with some Orthodox priests.[60] Especially significant was active Baptist participation in the United Council of Religious Communities and Groups. Pavel V. Pavlov served as vice president of this organization that was formed on the initiative of Tolstoyan leaders in 1918. Its primary task involved helping believers to secure release from military service on the basis of their religious convictions, but the council also worked more generally to promote sectarian interests. The Baptists would remain active in this organization until about 1922.

Just as in prerevolutionary days, the primary purpose of both the Evangelical Christian and Baptist unions remained to facilitate missionary activity. This work took four main forms: the publication of journals, the support of missionaries in the field, the training of new activists, and the promotion of evangelization campaigns. Despite economic and political difficulties, both unions published official journals during most of the first decade of Soviet power. Until 1922 the Baptists continued to issue *Slovo istiny* from their own print shop in Moscow, and the Evangelical Christians sporadically published their *Utrenniaia zvezda*. After a hiatus in evangelical publishing in 1923, the Evangelical Christian organ, *Khristianin*, began to appear in January 1924. The competing *Baptist* resumed monthly publication a year later. By 1926 the Ukrainian Baptist Union also had its own monthly journal, *Baptist Ukrainy*. It was written primarily in Russian, but, reflecting the surge in Ukrainian national consciousness of the era, it also included regular sections filled with Ukrainian-language poetry, hymns, and local reports. These journals maintained a regular publication schedule until late 1928. In addition to offering a steady stream of inspirational articles, stories, and poems, these lively magazines played an organizational role by promoting campaigns such as the annual "week of prayer and evangelization," disseminating advice about preaching and music, and facilitating the exchange of ideas through local reports. This active publishing program stood in sharp contrast to the dearth of similar Orthodox publications in this period.[61]

As in prerevolutionary times, union-supported missionaries traveled around the country, making new converts and offering guidance to already existing congregations. Their work tended to focus on visiting local congresses or attending special celebrations in order to inspire local churches, as well as to promote uniformity of belief and practice, and the authority of the national organization.[62] Their visits could prompt great excitement and an atmosphere of revival. For example, in March 1927 the well-known preacher and hymn writer Vasilii Stepanov visited Baku. Believers came from far away to crowd into the local prayer house. On the second day twenty people came forward to declare their repentance and salvation. Each evening more and more people flocked to hear Stepanov speak. On the Sunday after his arrival, 51 people were baptized. The next day the revival continued at an evening festival of singing and recitations and prayer at which a further 25 people declared their desire to follow Christ. In all, during Stepanov's nine-day visit, 146 people converted.[63]

The number of such evangelists varied throughout this period, depending on the financial circumstances of the respective unions. At the October 1921 Baptist Congress P. V. Pavlov reported that the union had sponsored more than 30 missionaries, who had worked in 27 provinces, conducted 4,153 meetings, baptized 1,227 new believers, and traveled 73,726 versts in the process.[64] After a slump in numbers in 1923–24, in 1925, thirty-four full-time and six part-time missionaries worked on behalf of the Baptist Union.[65] The Evangelical Christian Union was more vague in its public pronouncements about the number of its evangelists: its national congress in 1920 chose 52 people to serve in this capacity, and the 1923 meeting announced the intention to expand mission work further. Prokhanov claims in his memoirs that the central union had up to 100 missionaries in 1928, but no precise figures are available.[66] Both the Baptists and Evangelical Christians also made their first systematic attempts to expand their missions to the non-Russian and non-Christian peoples of the Soviet Union. Each group appointed special missionaries to this task, whose exotic reports of life among the heathen became a frequent feature in the movement's magazines.[67]

The unions' missionaries were joined in their work by a larger army of evangelists supported by local congregations and regional associations. In fact, the Evangelical Christians' 1920 congress recommended that congregations acquire a map, study their areas, and systematically evangelize places that had not been hit! At the 1923 Baptist Congress, Pavel Pavlov estimated that there were approximately one thousand such local preachers.[68] Also working to further the Baptist cause were some twenty to fifty indigenous missionaries supported by the Russian Missionary Society, a London-based association with links to Vil'gel'm Fetler, the former Petrograd Baptist leader who had emigrated during the war.[69]

Efforts to increase theological training in Russia went hand in hand with the goal of expanding mission and developing the work of congregations.

During the early Soviet period continuous, full-time Bible schools were offered in Leningrad, and later in Moscow. Even after the collapse, in the civil war period, of negotiations for an amalgamation of the Evangelical Christian and Baptist camps, efforts to cooperate in the area of theological education persisted into the mid-1920s. Both groups organized small-scale training for preachers throughout the early 1920s, but plans for a jointly run Bible School in Petrograd were jettisoned just before the courses were set to open in the spring of 1924. From January 1925 until mid-1929 the Evangelical Christians conducted regular, year-long programs. Subjects included study of the Bible, the art of writing and preaching sermons, church history, Hebrew and Greek, and, notably, the required civics course of the Soviet curriculum, *politgramota* (political literacy).[70] Meanwhile, the Baptists began to organize their own competing courses. After a lengthy appeal process to various government agencies, final permission came in late 1927. From 1 December 1927 until the arrest of the school's director, Pavel Ivanov-Klyshnikov, in March 1929, forty-four male and six female students from all over the USSR gathered in Moscow to study under the guidance of leading members of the Baptist Union Council.[71] At the same time local churches and regional associations across the Russian and Ukrainian republics launched training programs for pastors and missionaries. For example, in 1921 the Odessa Evangelical Christian community opened residential courses for thirty students, and the Tver' provincial association of Evangelical Christians organized a three-month Bible study and choir-directing course.[72] As a result of these educational efforts, several hundred young believers of both denominations were trained for evangelism and community leadership.

Finally, evangelization campaigns became a major means of connecting the missionary goals of central denominational organizations with the daily lives of believers on the ground. Indeed, a report on the "month of evangelization" planned by the Baptists in April 1921 described it as a successful "test of the organizational work of the Baptist Union." Local groups recounted how they had organized special meetings at their prayer houses, in the streets, in neighboring villages, and in prisons and hospitals; in one village believers paraded through the streets singing and stopping to preach at every intersection.[73] This organizational work sometimes had a distinctly Soviet tone to it, complete with vanguardist and military metaphors. A letter from the Baptist leadership presented the 1921 campaign as "a battle, exposing superstition and false Christianity, which are a more terrible weapon of darkness than disbelief." Youth were to be the "avant-garde" of the crusade. To assist them, the leadership suggested a "battle song for the evangelization front" and offered a set of slogans, such as "Without rebirth of the individual, there can be no new life."[74] Over the years the language associated with these evangelization campaigns was gradually toned down, perhaps as its novelty wore off and as the denominational leaders became more cautious regarding the government.[75] Nevertheless, up to the late 1920s, these events continued to promote renewal and expansion within local communities, and strengthened believers' sense of unity in a greater cause.

EVANGELICAL ASSOCIATIONAL LIFE

Hand in hand with the greater development of the Baptist Union and the Union of Evangelical Christians, local communities in the first years of Soviet power also tended to increase their organizational complexity and lengthen their missionary reach. Leaders emphasized the importance of giving each member a specific task in the work of the congregation.[76] Youth and women's groups, choirs and musical ensembles, charity and missionary teams, as well as various festivals and other events, became common in these years. Although none of these forms was new, they became more widespread and more developed in the 1920s.

One novelty in the 1920s—an especially popular one—was the harvest festivals that many congregations organized each autumn, with the encouragement of the central denominational organizations. Congregations would spend many hours elaborately decorating their prayer halls with plants and fresh produce for these events, which combined spiritual edification with entertainment.[77] In a typical example, in late 1925, members of the Nikol'skaia congregation in the Caucasus and their guests from neighboring congregations filled their 500-capacity prayer house to overflowing for a harvest celebration. After the service, tables were hastily set up in the prayer house and 350 people enjoyed tea, while the choir sang and members spoke. A very successful collection was also taken up.[78] Such events took place in the cities as well as in the countryside, for they were celebrations not only of the gifts of the land but of the harvest of souls. For example, in Vladivostok in 1925 the harvest celebration coincided with the end of a four-month course designed, echoing official Soviet phraseology, to "liquidate illiteracy among members of the local congregation." At the meeting women, who a few months earlier had been unlettered, now read aloud to the assembly.[79] These festivals thus allowed congregations to display the spiritual, material, and educational benefits of conversion to the evangelical way. They no doubt also served to compete with traditional Orthodox harvest celebrations of Pokrov day and the Soviet Harvest Day, introduced in 1923 to coincide with them.[80]

The extensive development of musical ministry in the evangelical churches contributed significantly to congregational festivals like these. During the 1920s many churches founded choirs, balalaika groups, and other instrumental ensembles, which both participated in their services and provided a means to reach potential converts. For example, on warm summer evenings in the far eastern city of Blagoveshchensk, the Baptist congregation's spiritual orchestra would set up in the park adjacent to their prayer house and play hymns to members and other city dwellers out enjoying the evening.[81] *Baptist, Baptist Ukrainy,* and *Khristianin* published new hymns in most issues.

Prokhanov continued his prolific hymn writing, producing, among others, special collections for youth and for women.[82] Both denominations published several new hymn books, including a Ukrainian-language Baptist one in 1925. The Baptist Union, in particular, placed great emphasis on the development of musical skills. In 1920 it founded a special music department which promoted the training of choir directors, worked on the publication of a new hymn book, and disseminated advice on singing and conducting in the denominational press. The first month-long choir director course, held in Moscow in that year, trained twenty-two local representatives. Regional Baptist organizations avidly followed suit with similar courses.[83] For local congregations, musical activities and education were important for recruiting and involving members, especially the young.

Youth groups often played a leading role in organizing these special events and providing the entertainment. Such clubs seem to have been a subject of tension with local authorities, since the law prohibited religious education of minors. In several instances, in fact, congregations were closed or threatened with closure owing to the activities of their youth.[84] Nevertheless most communities organized programs for young people. Applicants to the central Bible courses generally reported active involvement in the youth groups of their home congregations. Several also mention having regional youth congresses and organizations.[85] These groups met regularly for Bible and other study; where it was tolerated by local authorities, they also conducted their own special services.[86] Evangelization constituted an important area of their work: some clubs had "street missions," others visited surrounding villages in groups, and some regional organizations designated official youth missionaries.[87] In the area around Moscow young people regularly visited taverns where they persuaded the owners to allow them to sing a hymn or to speak to the public.[88] Similarly, in the summer of 1927, young Evangelical Christians from the Cherepetskaia congregation in Kaluga Province traveled 300 versts on foot in a missionary campaign that covered three cities and ten towns.[89] For young believers, these groups clearly provided companionship, an environment for improving their knowledge and skills, and a place to discuss the issues of their day and how a person of faith should live in Soviet society. For example, Iurii Grachev recalled, in his memoirs of Samara in the late 1920s, discussions among the young about whether one could read secular literature, about the right attitude toward fashion, about drunkenness, about the cult of the poet Esenin, about conscientious objection, and about the dilemma of a young student teacher who was under pressure to renounce his Baptist faith.[90]

As they had before the revolution, congregations and their youth groups enjoyed "evenings of love," filled with music, poetry, "witnessing," and tea drinking, as a form of recreation and of proselytization.[91] Like the harvest festivals, these concerts also provided a setting for presenting an alternative vision to that of the atheistic Bolsheviks. One Communist observer reported,

Baptist string ensemble, Tarashcha, Kiev Province. Sign reads "Praise the Lord with strings." *Baptist Ukrainy, 1927.*

for example, that at a Baptist youth meeting in Leningrad there had been a skit in which a young Baptist woman and a female Komsomolite (member of the Young Communist League) met on the street and fell to discussing matters of faith; the Baptist, of course, completely outclassed the Komsomolite, who ended up following the Baptist to a prayer meeting.[92] Similarly an émigré magazine reported that at a big youth evening given by the Baptist youth group in Leningrad in May 1926 the theme of the holiday had been, "Is it true that there will soon be no Christians?" In this way Baptist young people responded directly and publicly to the challenge of irreligion.[93]

The numbers and activities of women's groups similarly expanded in the early Soviet period. Where once they had been a rarity, now local reports frequently involved accounts of women's activities, especially in urban congregations. In addition to holding Bible studies and special services for women, women's groups were particularly prominent in raising money for mission and in charitable work both among the believers and beyond their congregations. For example, Evangelical Christian women in Kiev organized a soup kitchen and in early 1926 were hard at work raising money for a larger stove for this purpose. Members of the handiwork section of the same group knit, sewed, and did laundry for the imprisoned and the homeless.[94] In many places women also worked on improving their skills so as to serve their congregations better. For example, teams practiced their preaching in order to engage in missionary work and lead women's services.[95] Indeed, a member of a Jewish Baptist congregation wrote that, "our brethren have the idea that women should not preach the Gospel, although I can frankly say that in our women's meeting we frequently hear sisters whose sermons are both deeper and more interesting than those of some men."[96]

It is clear that both this activism and the revolution's rhetoric of equality for women forced long simmering questions about the place of women in evangelical communities onto the agenda in both branches of the movement. There had always been considerable regional variation in women's participation in church affairs: some women served as missionaries, preaching far and wide, whereas others did not even speak in congregational meetings. Local reports often suggested that women's activism needed to be stimulated further, but what constituted appropriate activities remained a topic for debate.[97] In the early 1920s the Evangelical Christian journals *Utrenniaia zvezda* and *Khristianin* carried authoritative articles addressing the proper role of women in the church.[98] These sought to deal with the tension between spiritual equality and social difference among women and men. For example, Prokhanov responded directly to the language of women's emancipation when he wrote, in 1922, that "the latest events of political life have brought a significant amount of economic liberation in the life of women, which, however, cannot satisfy them, because it has laid upon them work that is not suited to the particularities of her [*sic*] nature." Because Christianity offered women full spiritual equality, he explained, only a spiritual transformation of Russia would truly liberate women. This equality would come with responsibilities suited to women's particular qualities, including charitable and missionary work, as well as raising the younger generation.[99]

Tension over the position of women was articulated more visibly in the Baptist wing of the movement. In March 1926 a small conference of the "Sisters' initiative group" met in Moscow to discuss work among women, to draft a sample charter for women's circles, and to resolve questions about the position of female believers. Participants drew up a series of statements about the role of Baptist women in the family and in the church. In an attempt to resolve uncertainty among believers on the question of equality, they declared that the only limit to women's spiritual equality with men was that they could not aspire to be presbyters.[100] They also asked the president of the Baptist Union, Il'ia A. Goliaev, to rule on a controversial question in local congregations: whether women should cover their heads to pray. Following his presentation, they decided that, although married women should wear scarves to pray or to preach (but not in other settings), spinsters and widows were free to go without.[101] But disagreements at this meeting lingered and spilled into the Baptist press. Soon after, one of these women, E. V. Iagubiants-Tarasova, an activist from the Nakhichevan congregation in the Don area, wrote an article in *Baptist* allegedly aimed, in general, at a broader environment where accusations were being levied against the Bible, and, in particular, about the Bible standing in the way of equal rights for women. She systematically examined key Bible verses used to support such views, and did so with fairly sophisticated arguments about the historical context of the ancient Israelites or with the claim that the broader spirit of Saint Paul's writings contradicted his famous injunction, in what she regarded as the specific case of the troubled Corinthian church, that women keep quiet. Her conclusion was that "it is not the Bible, but people, ignorant people, who have incorrectly interpreted places in the Holy Scriptures for their own benefit, in the name of their own interests." The following issue of *Baptist* featured a response by Goliaev, which implied that this, too, was very much an internal Baptist issue. He objected to the very practice of applying the worldly criterion of equality to the Bible, saying instead that believers needed simply to follow its eternal truths, specifically the eternal truth that the Bible set women below men to remind women of their original sin. As a sign of a husband's power over his wife, wrote Goliaev, a married woman ought to grow her hair and cover her head when praying, unlike some women, both believers and unbelievers, who seemed to think it was acceptable to wear stylish haircuts and forgo their scarves.[102]

The subject was dropped in the Baptist press, but clearly the correct place of women continued to be an issue for many Baptists. Although photographs of congregations, choirs, and youth groups in the Baptist press do not suggest any particular gender imbalance among believers, men clearly dominated church councils and the ranks of ordained deacons. Local congregations seem to have had different cultures. Thus Khomiak's Poltava congregation had several female deacons, whereas the Leningrad Baptists, despite their active women's group and apparent preponderance of female members, voted 43 to 42 in 1926 to go ahead with elections after the objection was raised that there were no women on the slate for the congregational council.[103] In 1928 one enthusiastic young woman, upon hearing that there would be Bible courses in Moscow, wrote: "My heart was overfilled with joy that women could go, too." In her part of Ukraine women did not preach, but she thirsted for more than reciting verse, telling stories, and witnessing to her faith through private conversations. One can well imagine how she must have felt when she received a letter saying that, because of the number of applications, course administrators were considering not admitting women that year.[104]

These various congregational activities built on prerevolutionary practices and ambitions. Certainly more congregations had women's and youth groups, developed choirs, and held harvest festivals and "evenings of love." This process seems to have been largely the result of the greater maturity of the movement and the liberation of missionary energies during the revolution. To a lesser extent, the new context of the young Soviet government's efforts to mobilize society through similar youth, women's, and other voluntary associations shaped such congregational activities. In the language of the two unions' organizing, one can certainly hear the influence of Bolshevik vanguardist imagery. And harvest festivals seem to have taken off around the time that the regime was trying to introduce them. On balance, however, although one could say that there was enough room in Soviet society for this kind of organizing, it was not specifically Bolshevik policy that made it possible or necessary. But the early Soviet period also saw the development of evangelical communes, economic cooperatives, and even plans to build an ideal Christian city in Siberia. In these economic and social experiments, evangelicals were definitely inspired by social idealism abroad in society at large and took advantage of new opportunities offered them by Soviet power. Through these ventures they explored concretely the possibility of the coexistence of a Christian socialism with the Bolshevik model.

ECONOMIC AND SOCIAL EXPERIMENTATION

The establishment of religious agricultural communes was the most prominent example of new possibilities offered to religious dissidents by the early Bolshevik regime. In October 1921, as Soviet Russia began the process of rebuilding its devastated economy after years of foreign and civil war, the Bolshevik government appealed to former religious dissidents to go out to the countryside and form "model" communal settlements on abandoned estates. A significant minority, from a wide range of groups, responded enthusiastically.[105] In fact, well before the appeal, Baptists, Evangelical Christians, and other former religious dissidents had spontaneously been establishing various types of collective farms. In this respect they were part of a broader pattern of interest in 1918 among poor peasants, workers, and artisans in founding communes and organizing their lives according to Communist principles.[106] Now Lenin had approved the formation of a "Commission on the Settlement of State Farms, Free Lands, and Former Estates by Sectarians and Old Believers," which formally sought to enlist religious dissidents as the regime's partners in the rebuilding of the countryside.[107]

The Gethsemane commune, founded in 1919, serves as a good example. In the midst of the civil war eleven Evangelical Christian worker and peasant families settled on an estate in Tver' Province; the buildings of the estate had partially collapsed and the land was exhausted. Their goal was to recreate the first community of Christians, where, according to the Book of Acts, everything was held in common. They immediately set about reconstructing and expanding the farm buildings, and refurbishing the land and livestock. In 1920, the believers built their own electrical station, to light their commune and the neighboring village. From the fruits of the fields and of several artisanal shops they had established on their property, commune members soon acquired several agricultural machines which they also shared with nearby peasants. At first the estate's fifty *desiatiny* of plowed land yielded 40 to 45 *pud* of grain per *desiatina**; by 1926 the farmers on the commune reported that the yield had risen to an average of 60 to 75 *pud* per *desiatina*, and up to 100 *pud* in a good year. Commune members lived together in two buildings and shared their meals in a common dining room. Clothing and footwear were acquired with the group's money and distributed to each according to his or her need. The commune was run by a council elected by all members aged eighteen and older. It operated on the basis of the standard Soviet charter for agricultural collectives, and in 1923 it took part in the All-Russian Agricultural Exhibition in Moscow.[108]

It is difficult to determine how many of these communes existed. According to a memo drawn up by a bureaucrat in the All-Union Agricultural Cooperative Union in April 1925 using figures supplied by sectarian groups, the Evangelical Christians counted approximately one hundred such collectives and Baptist communes numbered twenty. Based on other figures presented to the government by denominational organizations, these numbers seem plausible regarding the Baptists and vastly exaggerated for the Evangelical Christians: a list apparently submitted by the Evangelical Christians just after the bureaucratic tally was drawn up enumerated five communes, two collective farms, and nine agricultural artels (producers' cooperatives), in addition to fourteen urban cooperatives and artels.[109] Although these organizations were few and far between, and many were also rather short-lived, they served as important models of Christian socialism that generated substantial interest within the movement. For example, upon visiting the Gethsemane commune in December 1920, Prokhanov was inspired to write "Song of the First Christians," which celebrated how, "in brotherhood, in the community of property, in the Life of the first Christians is the model for the generations, a plan for contemporary life." It became part of an entire collection of his hymns based on this theme.[110]

In addition to these agricultural communes, groups of evangelical workers and artisans in urban and rural areas also formed agricultural, building, and artisanal artels and other types of cooperatives. Like the establishment of agricultural communes, this process began spontaneously. For example, in the summer of 1918 a group of Baptist "peasant grain farmers, blacksmiths, joiners, carpenters, cobblers" and others banded together to form the "Basan" labor artel in Enisei Province in Siberia, despite the hostility to such ventures of the anti-Bolshevik government of Admiral Kolchak then ruling that area. Living in sod barracks, twenty-three families constructed a flour mill and collectively owned workshops to build and repair agricultural equipment.[111] Similarly, in the cities, groups of workers founded artels en-

---

*A desiatina is a land measurement equivalent to 2.7 acres. A pud is a measure of weight equivalent to 16.38 kg or 36 lb.

gaged in such diverse activities as construction work, carpentry, shoe making, and baking. In Moscow the Baptists cooperatively ran six cafeterias until 1928. According to a participant's recollections, one of these restaurants was actually located in the main building of the All-Union Central Executive Committee, the Soviet government, and frequently catered to participants in sessions and congresses.[112]

The Brotherly Aid Credit Union crowned this network of Baptist cooperative enterprises. Organized in 1922 by Pavel Pavlov as part of the mission of the Baptist Union's central office in Moscow, Brotherly Aid promoted Baptist rural and urban cooperative ventures and soon opened branches across the country, including in Balashov, Omsk, Kursk, Khar'kov, Piatigorsk, Akmolinsk (Briansk Province), Peski (Tambov Province), and Prikumsk (Terek Province), by some accounts reaching fourteen branches.[113] It is worth noting that correspondence between Baptist leaders suggests that this organization was indeed active but was also controversial among believers. At least one local leader complained that Pavlov was too busy with the affairs of the cooperatives to focus on spiritual matters, and that local communities were dissatisfied with the credit union's work.[114]

In early 1922, the Council of the Union of Evangelical Christians wrote to the All-Union Central Executive Committee requesting permission to found a similar coordinating organization for its communes and other cooperatives. This organization, to be called the Accord Cooperative, would facilitate trade between Evangelical Christian enterprises, assist them in purchasing expensive equipment, and allow members to supply one another with food, an important challenge in the famine-stricken years of 1921 and 1922.[115] It is not clear, however, whether the organization received the legal recognition it sought.

Many of these economic initiatives must be seen as developments in a longer tradition of mutual financial aid within the evangelical community. Certainly these new ventures provided politically acceptable ways to improve the availability of goods and to provide employment for community members.[116] For example, when the young Sergei P. Fadiukhin arrived in Moscow from Siberia in 1922, his fellow believers found work for him in the Baptists' "Honest Toiler" construction artel.[117]

However, this practical element was balanced by a visionary component. Indeed, these cooperative ventures expressed the aspirations of some believers to transform daily life and mores along Christian lines and provided inspiration for further social experimentation. In January 1925, inspired by the joyous labor he had witnessed on a recent visit to the Gethsemane commune, Prokhanov called for the creation of a new, evangelical way of life. Reflecting both his training as an engineer and his religious values, the Evangelical Christian leader proclaimed a vision of a new society built on the principles of faith, collective labor, technology, hygiene, creativity, sober habits, and the striving for self-perfection. These principles were endorsed by the December 1926 congress of the Evangelical Christian Union in Leningrad.[118]

The following year, armed with a permit from the Commissariat of Agriculture, Prokhanov and another engineer led an expedition to the Altai region near Mongolia where, after enlisting the assistance of experts from Tomsk University, they proceeded to survey various potential sites for a grand evangelical ideal settlement, the City of the Sun or Evangel'sk (both terms were used). With local government representatives looking on, they planted three cedars and three maples to mark the chosen spot. Plans progressed after their return to Leningrad, and in the spring of 1928 the same team set off for the Bethany commune in Tver' Province to study in detail whether it might serve as a model for organizing the new Christian society.[119]

The City of the Sun was never built, for by 1927–28 the tide was turning against religious organizations, independent public initiatives, and dreamers whose visions could not be channeled to the party's cause. But the Evangel'sk proposal stands out as a prime example of the possibilities for exploring alternative models of social transformation in the early Soviet era. At this very time the Party press was full of projects to reconstruct not just the structure of everyday life (*byt*) but citizens' whole worldview along Communist lines. Visionary town planners were also imagining new kinds of cities that would express the collective spirit of a radically transformed humanity.[120] Here was Prokhanov, proposing to bring a Christian perspective to this utopian thinking—and receiving government assistance to do so!

During the 1920s evangelicals thus made use of comparatively good relations with the Soviet government to develop their communities, building on previous work and experimenting with the possibilities of the new socialist society. As their Orthodox counterparts suffered the seizure of church valuables during the famine of 1921–22, the government allowed Baptists and Evangelical Christians to organize their own shipments of relief and receive aid from their brethren abroad.[121] Moreover, around the same time, just as a fierce attack on the Orthodox Church was launched, the Bolshevik regime called on sectarians to work with it to rebuild the war-torn countryside. Baptists and Evangelical Christians took advantage of such invitations and of the official attack on the former state church. In both words and actions they sought to reassure the Bolshevik government that their Christian faith was compatible with the socialist society. Meanwhile, early Soviet society provided enough room for them to carry on an active public associational life and to draw new members throughout 1920s.

The new believers who flocked to evangelical congregations in the early Soviet period continued to be motivated, above all, by a search for salvation, for an escape from sin, and for meaning in the world. In their conversion narratives they continued to mention the support they received from their "brothers and sisters" in faith; particularly notable was that, in this period of displacement, people could usually happen upon a group of believers wher-

Groundbreaking for a new prayer house, May 1927, Peski, Tambov Province.
The sign reads "All for the House of Salvation."
Baptist Ukrainy, 1927.

ever they found themselves.[122] Their new congregations quickly drew them
into various activities where they met other believers, developed their skills,
and received moral support. Although converts of the 1920s were more apt
to mention the challenge of a godless culture, there was virtually no concern
about political circumstances in their personal writings. Instead, one gets the
sense of people simply moving on with their lives, suffering many of the same
problems of rejection by family and society, but fundamentally preoccupied
with spreading the news of the Gospel.

But the possibilities for development in the 1920s were accompanied
from the start by continual harassment. As an editorial in the London-based
Friend of Russia pointed out in mid-1923, despite what Rushbrooke told the
Baptist World Alliance about evangelical successes in Soviet Russia, *Friend of
Russia*'s contacts reported constant persecution.[123] It was not simply that the
Baptists and Evangelical Christians were trying to organize in a climate that
denied religious institutions legal recognition and forbade the teaching of
religious ideas to youth. Archival records confirm frequent arrests, the clos-
ing down of prayer meetings, and the seizure of halls.[124] Evidence of these
troubles appears even in evangelical magazines published in the Soviet
Union. For example, a report on Evangelical Christian women in Kiev in 1926

mentioned their work on behalf of jailed believers, and other articles alluded to difficulties with local authorities over the use of buildings for prayer meetings.[125] Frequent tactics in this respect included charging extremely high taxes on local groups, requiring permits for each meeting, or threatening closure if certain expensive repairs were not made.[126] There was still enough social autonomy in Soviet life to allow the evangelicals to mature as a movement, but, on balance, it would be hasty to suggest that these developments were thanks to the Bolshevik government rather than in spite of it. After all, similar kinds of religious activity, whether in the form of charitable organizations, theological education, artels, or simply attendance at services, also continued among the Orthodox in these years.[127]

In public, evangelical leaders usually attributed persecution to uninformed and over-zealous local officials. For example, Pavel Pavlov wrote in late 1921 that, of the sixty-seven incidents of persecution registered by the Baptist Union since the end of 1920, the "majority show that we cannot regard this as a systematic policy of the center."[128] This was basically true in 1921 but would not remain the case for long. For in the early 1920s high-level party and secret police officials in Moscow turned their attention to breaking evangelical organizations from inside.[129] And to do so, they would focus on what was, perhaps, the greatest of the privileges accorded religious sectarians by the young Soviet government: a 1919 law allowing them to seek release from military service. The whole idea of such special rights for religious sectarians had been, from the start, very controversial within the Bolshevik Party. The evangelicals' enthusiastic use of the privileges that this 1919 law afforded provoked concern in party circles but also dissension among the Baptists and Evangelical Christians. Thus this ostensible opportunity would soon come to look like a curse for the evangelical movement.

9

A Mixed Blessing

Sectarian Pacifism and Political Legitimacy

On 21 July 1923, a People's Court in Piatigorsk district in the northern Caucasus heard the appeal of a young Baptist, Iakov Loginov, for release from military service based on his Christian conviction that he could not participate in the spilling of blood. The court concluded that Loginov was sincere in his request and declared that he would be able to substitute service in a hospital for his military duty. The wording of the resolution warrants attention. It noted, first, that the witnesses in the case had shown that Loginov "leads his life according to the teaching of Jesus Christ, i.e., he helps his neighbor, as he can, does not smoke, drink or swear" and that he was acting sincerely. The court agreed to spare Loginov combat duty but concluded that he should serve in a military hospital, thereby "offer[ing] help to his neighbor." "This service cannot be against his religious teaching," wrote the judge, since Loginov could only cite the biblical injunction "do not kill" as the basis of his refusal, a commandment "by which every Christian abides, including those who do not refuse military service."[1]

This is just one of many examples of the rather incongruous situation of agents of the avowedly atheistic Soviet state being called upon to wade into the waters of Christian theology and moral conduct in order to enforce Soviet law. Since January 1919, a decree of the Council of People's Commissars granted alternative service, and sometimes even complete exemption from military service, to religious conscientious objectors. Although exact figures are unavailable, hundreds and perhaps thousands of young Baptists such as Loginov and other members of small religious groups benefited from this law.[2] This fact often serves as evidence of the exceptional favor accorded by the Bolsheviks to members of religious groups that had been persecuted before the revolution. But by the time Loginov stood before the court, pacifism had been transformed from an area of cooperation to the central site of conflict between the new Bolshevik state and religious sectarians. This chapter examines the relationship between Baptists and Bolsheviks embodied in the 1919 decree, and the process of negotiating its true meaning in the context of revolution, civil war, and postwar reconstruction. For both sides, the decree proved to be a mixed blessing, entered into out of a mixture of opportunistic and idealistic motives, and bringing consequences neither had bargained for. The Bolshevik state soon found itself embroiled in questions of personal conscience, while the Baptists discovered that the law was not a guarantee of room for alternative visions but rather a test of civic legitimacy in the new Russia. Indeed, by the mid-1920s, the forced renunciation of pacifism as a doctrine and practice became the prerequisite to the continued legal existence of Baptist and Evangelical Christian organizations.

BACKGROUND TO THE DECREE OF 4 JANUARY 1919

Although Bolshevik leaders had initially conceived of the Red Army as a voluntary force, by April 1918, with foreign troops landing in Vladivostok and the north and widespread evidence of domestic resistance, they were already concerned about whether an all-volunteer army could withstand this pressure. The Central Executive Committee of the new Soviet state thus decreed obligatory military training for all male workers and peasants between the ages of eighteen and forty. When civil war broke out in late May, the Bolsheviks turned to conscription. These moves were unpopular with a war-weary nation, and in the summer and fall of 1918 military tribunals were introduced which tried and executed hundreds of soldiers for treason, sabotage, desertion, and looting. However, desertion problems continued.[3] Yet, amid anxieties about how to engage the populace in enthusiastic defense of the revolution, the Bolsheviks announced comprehensive measures to release conscientious objectors from military service. And, paradoxically, the atheistic Soviet state extended this privilege only to those who claimed a religious basis for their pacifism.

The decree of the Council of People's Commissars of 4 January 1919 provided for alternative civilian service, and, in some cases, unconditional exemption from all forms of service, for religious conscientious objectors. Aside from laws on conscientious objection introduced in Britain in 1916, this decree was the most liberal the world had ever seen.[4] Even more remarkable, considering the Soviet state's attitude toward religion, it assigned a committee of representatives of religious sectarian groups a crucial role in administering its provisions. The decree entreated judges deciding cases of refusal to serve to solicit the opinion of experts from the United Council of Religious Communities and Groups "in each individual case."[5] Agents of this organization of representatives of the Tolstoyans, Baptists, Mennonites, Trezvenniki (a sect of abstainers), and Seventh-Day Adventists would be called upon to demonstrate that the religious faith in question forbade participation in military service and to attest to the sincerity of the applicant. At the height of the civil war, amid official attacks on religious life across the land, this decree thus created a partnership between a religious organization and the judicial organs of the Soviet state in the matter of release from military service. The entire burden of determining an applicant's integrity lay with the United Council.[6]

The 1919 decree had its origins in both the Bolsheviks' political strategy and in their past history of relations with religious dissidents. On one level the decree was aimed at needling the Orthodox Church, the Bolsheviks' real problem on the "religious front," by favoring its enemies.[7] At the same time the policy can be seen as part of a wider drive among important elements in the top party leadership to gain and preserve the allegiance of the peasantry, by limiting antireligious activity to attacks on Orthodox wealth and political influence rather than on the practice of the faithful.[8] But it also reflected the strain of Bolshevism that regarded religious sectarians as potential allies whose support could be easily won through a few concessions. In particular, Vladimir Bonch-Bruevich, now the administrator of the Council of People's Commissars, cooperated with religious sectarians in a creative use of their past sufferings, and occasional past interactions with the party, to press for such policies.[9] Finally, this measure fits a broader pattern in the uncertain early days of Soviet power of enacting symbolic legislation and of trying to prove Bolshevik moral superiority over the Whites. The government's lack of time, money, and will to develop its own apparatus to monitor the process of screening candidates probably accounts for the large role accorded the United Council.[10]

EVANGELICALS RESPOND

Although pacifism appeared to have only shallow roots in the evangelical movement, Baptists and Evangelical Christians were soon flocking to the courts to apply for release from service in the Red Army. Over the centuries some individual Baptists had concluded that their faith precluded participation in war, but as an international denomination they had never formally been pacifists.[11] Rather, they tended to teach that believers should "give unto Caesar that which is Caesar's" and focus on spiritual matters. Among Russian evangelicals there had always been a strain of pacifist thinking, and they made up approximately half of those who refused to bear arms on religious grounds during World War I.[12] In fact, stating that "this question worries many people," the editors of *Slovo istiny* [Word of truth] followed up their 1917 survey on participation in political parties with another on whether a Christian could bear arms. All the responses published, in the first half of 1918, insisted that believers were called to love their enemies and could have nothing to do with war.[13] This presaged the blossoming of evangelical pacifism during the civil war. The disillusioning experience of total war, broader peasant resentment of the civil war as a "war between brothers," an apocalyptic aspiration to reject the ways of the world, and the ascendancy of new leaders with pacifist views in the Baptist branch of the movement combined, after January 1919, with the legal means to refuse military service to bring about this change.[14]

If the goal of the January 1919 decree had been to secure the support of religious sectarians for Soviet power, it was certainly a success as far as the evangelicals were concerned. For both idealistic and opportunistic reasons, the Baptists and Evangelical Christians responded to the January 1919 decree with enthusiasm. The Baptist journal *Slovo istiny* ebulliently declared: "This remarkable step of the government is worthy of every praise and clearly shows that among the ranks of Soviet power there are people with a sensitive spirit and a clear mind who attentively take care not to cause violence on the conscience and religious feeling of those who cannot take part in military service."[15] The new decree seemed to offer the long-persecuted evangelicals a new legitimacy and the opportunity, as agents of the United Council of Religious Communities and Groups, to cooperate in the shaping and implementation of government policy. The leaders of both branches of the movement made an effort to widely publicize this new law. *Slovo istiny* sent out a free publication to all Baptist communities in Russia which, among other topics, offered a detailed description of the United Council, its activities, and the procedure for obtaining assistance in applying for release from military service. Similarly, at the Evangelical Christians' annual congress in October, delegates praised the new laws, emphasizing the importance of making sure that all congregations had copies of this decree and other laws on freedom of conscience.[16] After Ukraine came under Soviet control, believers there formed a Ukrainian Council of Congregations and Groups of Baptists and Evangelical Christians to defend freedom of conscience and facilitate release from military service.[17] The council of the Caucasus Union of Baptist Congregations even produced printed forms, one confirming that Baptist religious convictions precluded participation in warfare, the other for young men appealing for alternative service.[18]

Meanwhile, in Moscow, Baptist leaders Pavel Pavlov and Mikhail Timoshenko threw themselves into the work of the United Council, with Pavlov serving as vice president. This activism was replicated around the country. As Paul Steeves points out, most of the United Council's 117 local agents were Baptists.[19] Moreover, evidence from early 1921 reveals that Baptist congregations were responsible for more than two-thirds of financial contributions to the council's work.[20] If the Bolsheviks were willing to supply such a procedure for a mix of idealistic and opportunistic intentions, the evangelicals were willing to play their part based on a similar mix of motives.

The legislation thus opened the doors for pacifism to go from being the conviction of isolated individuals to a common phenomenon in the evangelical community. Indeed, in recalling the mood among believers at the time, the prominent Baptist leader Pavel V. Ivanov-Klyshnikov would later explain, "it was as if that decree legitimized the mood that had arisen and now gave a legal and easy means of freeing oneself from military service." Moreover, he contended, Baptists came to "look upon those who recognize military service with a weapon as traitors and apostates or, in the best case, as mistaken."[21]

Unfortunately no figures are available to judge how many young evangelicals took advantage of the new law, but anecdotal evidence suggests that refusal to bear arms, although not unanimous, was very common. Among the forty-six male applicants to the Baptists' Bible School between 1922 and 1925, fifteen had been released from service by the courts, although at least one had spent eighteen months in a labor battalion as a result (and reported that it had been an excellent opportunity for making converts!). Another simply wrote that he considered military service to be against Christ's teachings.[22] Obviously this was not a very representative sample, but it does suggest that the young people who were regarded by their congregations as future leaders were clearly disinclined to serve. Although often vague and incomplete, reports on this issue from provincial justice departments dating from late 1921 also describe the clear majority of Baptist or Evangelical Christian communities as opposed to military service but mostly positively disposed toward Soviet power.[23] And evangelical delegates at the Congress of Non-Church Religious Currents, organized by the United Council in June 1920, reported thousands of applicants for release from military service in their areas.[24]

All over the country Baptist and Evangelical Christian communities declared themselves to be opposed to the bearing of arms. The law stated that the United Council would have to testify that it was not just the individual believer's view but his denomination's teaching that explicitly forbade participation in warfare. It was therefore in the interest of religious groups to declare their rejection of war collectively. Many local declarations ensued, in part because of the congregationalist tradition of the evangelical churches, and also as a result of the breakdown of communications because of the war. It is important to note that this process had begun before the legal situation made it in any way advantageous: for example, in December 1920 a Kuban area regional congress reaffirmed its 1918 resolution against military service. But the practice became increasingly widespread.[25] In some areas Baptists joined with other sectarian groups to speak out against military service for their members: for instance, in September 1919 Baptists, Evangelical

Christians, Mennonites, and Molokans of the Orenburg and Turgai regions met for this purpose, and a congress of Baptists and Mennonites in the Samara area did the same the following week.[26]

This local process was completed by a resolution of the All-Russian Congress of Baptists in Moscow in May 1920. Discussion at the meeting revealed that a broad swathe of the delegates linked participation in political parties with involvement in military service—and rejected both activities outright. According to the resolution they approved, political party membership not only deflected believers' attention from their central task of building the Kingdom of God, but it also required individuals to take an inimical attitude toward other political parties, and frequently demanded acquiescence to violence. "Guided by his internal conviction and experience on the basis of the teaching of the Gospel," the resolution continued, "every Evangelical Christian-Baptist should consider it his Holy responsibility to openly refuse military service in all its forms, trying with all his heart to be a faithful follower of the One who teaches universal forgiveness and love." Although, ideally, believers would take up alternative duties in the purely civilian sphere, the congress left the question of what constituted suitable service to the conscience of individual members.[27] This statement echoed the anxieties Baptists had expressed in 1917 about participation in politics and their rejection of a morality of hatred, but it made it official teaching for the first time. The Evangelical Christians do not seem to have gone this far at their national congress. However, the leadership in Petrograd approvingly reported on the declarations of local conferences against military service and sought to distribute copies of the 4 January 1919 decree to each congregation.[28]

BOLSHEVIK RESPONSES

The Bolsheviks quickly became alarmed by what one 1920 report of the Military Revolutionary Tribunal described as an "epidemic" of refusals.[29] Soviet officials charged that the evangelicals were using the law of January 1919 as a recruiting device and that their members were flocking disproportionately to the courts, hoping to be absolved of service.[30] The Commissariat of Justice polled both the Central Commission to Fight Desertion and the Army and Navy Inspectorate in early 1920 about misuse of the conscientious objection law, but neither reported having sufficient evidence to give an opinion on the subject.[31] Nevertheless these accusations, regardless of how grounded they were in fact, had important consequences. Throughout 1919 the Red Army struggled with serious desertion problems and with the attempts of peasant communities to sabotage conscription by declaring their members "indispensable" or unable to serve on the grounds of their religious beliefs.[32] The enthusiastic response of religious sectarians, and of evangelicals in particular, to the law of 4 January 1919 rubbed salt in these wounds and soon led the government to rethink its strategy regarding religious pacifism.

Within high party and government circles that dealt with religious policy, privileges for religious sectarians had been controversial from the start. Fundamentally all religious activity was politically suspect to Bolshevik policy makers, whether they were inclined to believe that religion would die out naturally in the new socialist society or that its elimination would require forceful measures. Significantly Petr A. Krasikov, who headed the division of the Commissariat of Justice charged with implementing the exemption decree, belonged to the latter camp and had opposed the measure since its inception.

The intertwined problems of defining membership in the new socialist body politic and of defining an appropriate proletarian morality lay at the heart of the Bolsheviks' anxieties about sectarian pacifism. The issue brought together the question of the meaning of Soviet legislation on freedom of conscience and that of the relationship between military service and citizenship. The new Soviet state was not unique in this: with the widespread adoption of conscription in most European countries by the early twentieth century, service had become both a duty and a training ground of citizenship.[33] During the gestation period of the decree of 4 January 1919, some Bolshevik leaders such as Bonch-Bruevich and Emelian Iaroslavskii had argued that such a measure would strengthen the authority of Soviet power, whereas others vehemently protested the whole idea of making concessions to conscientious objectors. Krasikov, for instance, forcefully made the point to Lenin that, "he who does not wish to defend the land from the robbers of imperialism does not have a right to make use of [the land], he also cannot elect or be elected to Soviet institutions and enjoy the social services laws. There is even a question about whether or not this passive element should be exiled from the territory of the Soviet Republic as an antisocial element."[34] For Krasikov, to refuse to fight Soviet Russia's class enemy was to renounce one's rights as a citizen. Passivity could not be reconciled with the class-war morality of the new state.

Throughout 1919 the conflict intensified between Bonch-Bruevich, who was receiving a flood of complaints from religious sectarians about mistreatment, and the Commissariat of Justice, where Krasikov oversaw a rather lukewarm enforcement of the decree.[35] By 1920 complaints were emerging from various quarters that the Tolstoyans and Baptists who led the United Council were insincere, using pacifism and religion to mask anti-Soviet beliefs and activities. A press campaign began to question the motives of conscientious objectors and to discredit the Baptists as disloyal to the Soviet state and Soviet morality. Krasikov led the charge with a 1920 article in *Revoliutsiia i tserkov'* [Revolution and the church], the journal of the section of the Commissariat of Justice that oversaw the separation of church and state, provocatively titled, "Do They Know What They're Doing?" In it he reviewed the contents of *Slovo istiny*, asking whether the Baptists were willful or merely unconscious defenders of "agents of the Entente." The main thrust of the article centered on a contrast between proletarian morality and religious morality. How, Krasikov asked, could the Baptists "justify their agitation against the armed defense by workers and peasants of the life, land, [and] freedom of the socialist country from attack by the bandits of the world and their hired killers?" Moreover, he could not accept the Baptists' alleged concern for the individual souls of the Bolsheviks' opponents. Could their God really love these people? he asked.[36] Proletarian morality was a morality of collective, class salvation, and the salvation of the proletarian state was its highest calling.

Certainly interpreting what was meant by conscience and determining sincerity were central to the problems that Soviet power faced in implementing its own law on conscientious objection. What, for example, was a judge to do with someone like Mikhail Semenovich Nesterenko? Nesterenko acknowledged that he had indeed served in the tsarist army but had done so out of fear and against his conscience; now that Soviet power had supplied a law for people like him, he asked to be released from all forms of military service.[37] Or take the case of Evdokim Stepanovich Afanas'ev, another veteran of World War I, who had become a Baptist in 1918 and now refused to carry a weapon or even to serve in a noncombatant capacity in the Red Army?[38] Even more difficult to deal with were the young men who were already in the Red Army and now claimed to have experienced a conversion to both the Baptist faith and pacifism.[39]

Amid the chaos of civil war, local answers to these questions varied widely. In some areas applicants were shot en masse for desertion, whereas, in other places, release from all forms of service was quite routine.[40] In August 1920, and again in August 1921, Commissariat of Justice circulars tried to regulate local abuses, reaffirming each time that soldiers who had developed pacifist convictions while already in service remained eligible to apply for alternative service, on the condition that they remain at their posts until a judge had rendered a decision on their applications.[41] On December 14 of 1920 a new decree on religious conscientious objectors superseded the law of 4 January 1919. Although it did not change the basic principle of offering release from military service to those whose religious beliefs prohibited participation in war, it no longer mentioned the United Council in its paragraphs describing implementation procedures. Now local representatives of the faith of the particular applicant, preferably ones who knew the applicants well, would be called upon as expert witnesses.[42] The accompanying article in *Revoliutsiia i tserkov'* emphasized that the law aimed to eradicate the error of giving a monopoly on expertise to "an interested party," the United Council.[43]

Sincerity is always difficult to determine. That there is evidence that some Baptists refused military service under both the Whites and the Reds does not confirm the integrity of every applicant.[44] This was especially problematic for Soviet officials, who were not supposed to believe in the reality of religious convictions and were charged with deciding cases according to their "revolutionary conscience and revolutionary legal consciousness."[45] Indeed, one frustrated agent of the United Council wrote in April 1920 that, "to give out documents about religiosity cannot have any significance to a government that stands on an atheistic platform."[46] After all, the Bolsheviks sought to create not just a secular state but an atheistic society in the first years after the revolution. Ironically, with their 1919 decree, they waded into the area of conversion and conviction at a time when the pressures of war and their own revolutionary policy were forcing widespread reconsideration of values and beliefs.

Amid all this change the new Soviet leaders looked to what they regarded as the relatively static notion of class origins as the best predictor of political inclinations. Class status came to define a person's rights and responsibilities vis-à-vis the state. Ironically, however, as Sheila Fitzpatrick has noted, determining class affiliation turned out to be tricky for the Bolsheviks in the civil war atmosphere of exceptional social and physical mobility.[47] Despite all this mobility, the emphasis on class origins contained the seed of a process that was turning class into a legal, hereditary category very similar to the *soslovie* [estate] ranks of old.[48] As class was transformed from a dynamic to a static concept, a parallel process in religious policy increasingly denied the idea of religious change or conversion by asserting that religious affiliation was an innate personal characteristic. A series of circulars from the Commissariat of Justice sought to restrict the applicability of the law on sectarian pacifism by emphasizing that it pertained only to people raised within antimilitaristic faiths and, eventually, by explicitly enumerating the particular religious groups considered to meet that criterion. Thus a circular of 15 February 1922 began to deny the principle of conversion by entreating judges to examine the consistency of an applicant's behavior and religious beliefs since his childhood and the attitude of the faith in which he had been raised toward bearing arms.[49] More significant, on 5 November 1923, the Commissariat declared that applicants needed to belong to sects that had been formed under tsarism and had long rejected military service, declaring (not exactly correctly) those groups to have been limited to the Dukhobors, the Mennonites, the Molokans, and the Netovtsy (a priestless Old Believer group). Members of other sects might apply if they could show that they or their family had suffered under tsarism for refusing military service.[50] In the words of a joint complaint by a group of Moscow sectarians, this amounted to a "de facto abolition of the decree of 4 January 1919."[51] These moves to restrict the application of conscientious objector provisions were finally enshrined in the Law on Compulsory Military Service of 18 November 1925. That measure retained some arrangements for religious sectarians but only for "citizens who by birth and upbringing belong to families that belong to sects whose teaching now and before 1917 forbade military service."[52] The individual could not transcend the conditions into which he or she had been born; rather, a person's beliefs were treated as permanently fashioned by those conditions.

The phenomenon of religious pacifism made clear the extent to which citizenship in Soviet Russia was not automatic; instead, one had to prove one's eligibility for membership. In the 1918 Constitution, rights were awarded according to social and political criteria, with the main stipulation "for enjoying full civil rights [being] that a person engage in socially useful, productive work and not exploit hired labor, except under the most extraordinary circumstances." Thus private traders and people who employed hired labor joined entire categories of people such as former police agents, clergy, high-level officials, members of the former ruling house, and the insane, who, regardless of their current occupation, were completely disenfranchised. As Elise Kimerling has shown, "discrimination based upon social origin was built into legislation regulating virtually all areas of a person's public life."[53] The 1918 Constitution also made a clear connection between citizenship and soldiering. No longer, as in the first eight months of Soviet power, was armed service merely a right. Now it was declared to be the duty of every citizen. Those deprived of citizenship could not bear arms, but they were still required "to serve in rear formations in non-combat duty."[54] Along with the privileges of voting, serving in the armed forces, publishing, or receiving food rations, the proclaimed rights of freedom of conscience and of religious propaganda belonged only to citizens, defined as those who labored.[55] And yet there was a paradox even for this once subordinate and now privileged group: since their social origins allegedly dictated a natural affinity for the revolution, and religion was, by definition, counterrevolutionary, if a member of the laboring classes was a believer, it surely meant that he or she was the dupe of counterrevolutionary elements.

For these reasons, in practice the laws on religious conscientious objectors became tests of loyalty rather than liberties freely awarded. Anyone who needed to make use of the promised exemption was, by definition, a son of the non-exploiting classes. If his heart was in the right place, he would understand that to fight in the Red Army was to defend proletarian freedom. After 1921, as his own position at the center of power declined, Bonch-Bruevich gradually abandoned his sectarian allies and took to approvingly contrasting, for example, the Baptists' pernicious pacifism with the Novyi Izrail sect whose members, despite their declaration of May 1920 asking the Soviet government for release from military service, had allegedly continued to defend the nation in the Red Army.[56] The right was there for symbolic purposes, not to be actually invoked.

The legal changes after the civil war combined with a shift in antireligious policy to set the stage for a showdown between the evangelicals and the Soviet state over pacifism, political loyalty, and organizational legitimacy. Once the civil war was won, the party moved on to the task of building a socialist society under the auspices of the New Economic Policy, which proposed to rebuild the economy by allowing a partial return to market mechanisms. With this economic liberalization came a tightening of political control, however.

In the religious sphere the party found itself forced to confront the contin-uing strength of the Orthodox Church and other religious groups. On the one hand, from 1922 Bolshevik policy makers moved from an erratic pro-gram of undermining the Orthodox Church as an institution to more sys-tematic antireligious education designed to eradicate all forms of religious belief and practice. On the other hand, this new orientation in party pro-paganda was accompanied on the administrative level by rising intolerance of religious organizations. Despite more or less sporadic persecution, reli-gious associations had nevertheless managed to preserve their basic func-tions during the civil war. Now the Soviet government, by means of its secret police, became increasingly interested in preventing their formation and in meddling in their affairs.[57]

The famous 1922 campaign to seize church valuables for the alleged benefit of famine victims formed the centerpiece of the regime's attack on the Russian Orthodox Church. First, the Soviet government refused any Church-initiated efforts to aid the starving and instead forced the faithful to part with their valuables at gunpoint. Then, having provoked the Church into resistance, it inaugurated a series of highly publicized show trials of clergy for counterrevolution. Finally, the secret police worked to foment a schism within the church over the question of cooperation with the government.[58]

As part of this new focus on antireligious activity, in September 1922 the party's Central Committee formed a top-secret "Commission on the Im-plementation of the Separation of Church and State," otherwise known as the Antireligious Commission. Members included representatives from the security organs (now renamed the GPU), the Commissariat of Justice, the Agitation and Propaganda Department of the party, and prominent antire-ligious activists. At regular (usually monthly) meetings between 1922 and 1929 they reviewed an array of issues ranging from secret police strategy aimed at breaking apart the Orthodox Church to the size of print runs of religious journals to whether individual religious leaders would be allowed to travel abroad or if Mozart's Requiem could be performed on Soviet ter-ritory.[59] At the commission's first meetings, discussion focused on the work of fomenting division within Orthodox ranks. With regard to former reli-gious dissenters, the main subject in these early days was the activities of var-ious groups and their attitudes toward military service. Members also com-missioned the preparation of anti-sectarian brochures and approved the search of Baptist, Evangelical Christian, and Tolstoyan prayer houses and leaders' homes "with the goal of discovering counterrevolutionary materi-als which undoubtedly must be [there], based on their activities." On 12 June 1923 the commission approved "the proposal of the GPU to use Prokhanov to change the attitude of sectarians toward the Red Army." Two weeks later the commission decided to launch a press campaign to "compromise sec-tarians from the point of view of their anti-militarism," "to call on the GPU to strengthen work on the demoralization of sectarianism," and to raise before the highest body of the Soviet government, the All-Union Central Executive Committee, the issue of "abolishing the decree on freeing sectarians from the military, so that they cannot misuse this as they have so far."[60]

Why did the Bolshevik leadership identify the Evangelical Christian leader Ivan S. Prokhanov as the wedge for splitting apart the evangelicals—with an eye to the sectarians in general—using the pacifism issue? First of all, the reports of Evgenii A. Tuchkov, the chief of the security service's religious department who oversaw the whole affair, reveal the belief that the Baptists and Evangelical Christians were the fastest growing religious groups, in part because of their clever use of pacifism. Thus the department made it a priority to ensure that these groups recognized military service and lost their momentum.[61] On a practical level, Prokhanov's organization was more centralized than the Baptists' and, moreover, was centralized around his person. Thus he was far more of a lever than any one of the Baptist leaders. Indeed, Tuchkov made this very point in his final report.[62] Furthermore, Prokhanov had infuriated the authorities in September 1922 by issuing an appeal to all Christians in Russia and across the world, titled "Voice from the East." The appeal called on believers to follow the model of the Russian Evangelical Christians who had declared "their non-desire to take any part, direct or indirect, in military acts." Now they were extending their call for a reformation on their model to the whole world.[63]

The Petrograd authorities had allowed this epistle to be published, but the GPU was not pleased. In March 1923, the Antireligious Commission decided to exile Prokhanov abroad. This plan was apparently changed, however; the following month Tuchkov summoned him to Moscow and, after informing him that "Voice from the East" amounted to a counterrevolutionary act, imprisoned him in the GPU prison.[64] After three months of pressure and in a state of physical illness, Prokhanov finally agreed to sign a new letter that essentially contradicted the message of his original appeal. Co-signed by five other leaders, the new declaration explained that, naturally, the antimilitarism mentioned in "Voice from the East" was directed "only at those believers who live outside Soviet Russia and, because of their lack of consciousness, still defend to this day the interests of capital." Soviet power was unique because it was dedicated to building a proletarian world order in which wars would no longer be needed. Evangelical Christians thus felt called to be loyal citizens and willing participants in the Red Army.[65] Prokhanov was immediately released and allowed to travel to the congress of the Baptist World Alliance in Stockholm in July. In Tuchkov's triumphant words, "this represented the first shift by the sects away from an antimilitarist position."[66]

Meanwhile, the Baptist leaders had devised a plan to use the moral authority of the Baptist World Alliance to back up the Russian believers' pacifism, with mixed results. Upon arriving in Stockholm, they proposed that the congress endorse a resolution "declaring army service under all conditions unlawful for Christian men." Although the other delegations refused to do so, the congress still provided some useful international attention: a memorandum expressed respect for the practices of the Russians and declared that "members of the Congress are gratified to know that the Russian Soviet Government accepts alternative service from those who on conscientious and religious grounds are unable to serve in the army."[67] Both the Baptist and the Evangelical Christian factions of the movement had thus tried to make real the privilege of conscientious objection by taking these symbolic provisions at face value and, by publicizing the existence of the 1919 and 1920 decrees on the international stage, shame the Soviet government into honoring its commitment to religious pacifists.

When Prokhanov returned from Stockholm, the letter that he and his five acolytes had signed was published in the newspaper *Izvestiia*, arousing great dismay and surprise among his followers.[68] Soon thereafter, in early September 1923, after a hiatus of two years during which no congresses were permitted, three hundred Evangelical Christian delegates gathered in Petrograd for a national meeting. Tuchkov "ran" the congress, to use GPU terminology, employing informers to compel Prokhanov not to bow to pressure and renounce the letter, and establishing an atmosphere of terror by periodically whisking Prokhanov and others out of the meetings so that he might give them "advice" himself. After a bitter debate, the intimidated delegates voted to disavow "Voice from the East" and declare military service compulsory for members. The presbyter of the Moscow congregation, Fedor S. Savel'ev, who was one of the original signatories, now renounced the letter. Under his leadership an independent group formed that tried to mobilize the congregations against the resolution. Savel'ev soon found himself arrested and exiled to the concentration camp in the former monastery at Solovki.[69]

Tuchkov then turned his attention to the Baptists. In this respect he benefited from the fractious nature of the evangelical movement and exploited divisions between Evangelical Christians and Baptists, and within the Baptist wing itself. On the one hand, after having succumbed to pressure, Prokhanov's followers were eager to have the Baptists also renounce pacifism, for they were alarmed by the defection of many of their members to the Baptist camp. On the other hand, although Tuchkov found that he could not work from the top down with the Baptists, his strategy of sowing dissension in provincial congregations seems to have succeeded, in part because of longstanding resentment in some quarters over Pavlov and Timoshenko's unilateral takeover of the Baptist Union during the civil war years and also because of the genuine dissension over the practice of refusing military service.[70] After two years of denying the Baptists a national congress, the government now sanctioned such a gathering in Moscow in November 1923. Tuchkov reported that the mood was so tense that when one delegate defended what the Evangelical Christians had just done, all the others immediately jumped to the conclusion that he must be a secret agent of the GPU.

As the sessions unfolded, Pavlov and Timoshenko tried to avoid raising the question of pacifism, but as various delegates were arrested and those co-operating with the GPU pressed for a discussion of the military issue, the chairmen finally relented and a compromise resolution was passed.[71] The resolution combined a Christian anarchist vision of the polity with an asser-tion that, until all were converted, a state, with its implicit violence, could not be avoided. The congress declared that there was "no unanimity re-garding military service" among the Baptists; nevertheless "Baptists cannot escape from the sphere of state life which is permeated with violence." The shedding of blood was morally reprehensible, and so it was preferable for Baptists to perform public work or medical work within the military, although the resolution left the degree of participation in war to the individual con-science of believers.[72] In view of the pressure to which they were subjected, the pacifist Baptist leadership was thus remarkably successful in not fully bow-ing to Tuchkov's demands.

This partial victory was a pyrrhic one, however. Having been thwarted, Tuch-kov further intensified the pressure on the Baptists, arresting Timoshenko and other leaders. He seems also to have been able to exploit the feeling among some delegates that the results of the congress constituted evidence of the failed leadership of Pavlov and Timoshenko. In the face of such pres-sure, and on what Tuchkov described as his recommendation, Baptist lead-ers worked out a letter "to the whole Baptist brotherhood in the USSR," signed by the members of the Baptist Union Council and approved by N. Popov, a member of the Antireligious Commission.[73] Distributed on 1 February 1924, this message alleged that the congregations had unwisely sent delegates from the formerly privileged classes to the congress and that it was they who had expressed radical and incorrect views on the subject of military service and the state. The epistle went on to "clarify" that Baptists recognized all gov-ernments and considered themselves obliged to fulfill all state duties includ-ing military service.[74]

After this letter was issued, the leadership of the Baptist Union was re-configured and taken over by members of the older generation who had watched askance from the provinces as Pavlov and Timoshenko had pursued their pacifist policy. In December 1924, a plenum of the union's council de-cided to change from a collective form of leadership back to the prerevolu-tionary model of a president with assistants. The new president was Il'ia A. Goliaev, the presbyter of the prominent Balashov congregation in Saratov Province and a past-president of the prerevolutionary Baptist Union. His per-sonal papers reveal that he had been a strong opponent of Pavlov's and Tim-oshenko's leadership.[75] Meanwhile, Timoshenko and others deemed to be troublemakers were exiled to Turkestan, the Far East, or Solovki.[76]

The pacifist issue remained the source of sharp division in both the Evan-gelical Christian and the Baptist camps of the movement throughout the mid-1920s. Iu. S. Grachev, a teenager in Samara in the late 1920s, recalled knowing both people who were freed from service and others who were imprisoned for alleged insincerity. The question of pacifism, he remembered, "worried many, especially in the 1920s, and believing youth, both in Samara and in other cities, were almost unanimously ready to bear any military service, so long as it did not involve using a weapon."[77] The issue seems to have been kept alive by the fact that in many areas local judges continued to award release from military service to evangelicals, despite a succession of government circulars trying to reverse this practice. Anecdotal evidence indicates that, in some areas, some kind of alternative service remained quite standard. For example, one local report in 1927 made this assumption when it stated: "There are few congregations in Ukraine that have not parted this year with one or several of their young brothers who, having been freed from combatant service by the people's courts, have now been called to some works."[78] Indeed, despite the law seeming technically to exclude Baptists and Evangelical Christians from eligibility, a document in the military archives indicates that the labor battalion of conscientious objectors formed in Ukraine in 1928 included 185 Evangelical Christians and a comparable number of Baptists. The antireligious press made similar reports.[79] In other areas, arranging for alternative service was much more difficult. A secret police report for a district of Smolensk Province noted that, of the five members of the local Evangelical Christian community drafted into military service in 1926, only one "still refuse[d]." "Our punishment policy played a big role in this," the agent wrote: after a little time in jail, many agreed to serve rather than be imprisoned again.[80] Nevertheless the American journalist William Henry Chamberlin reported in 1929 that, on a visit to the Baptist Union headquarters in Moscow, he was told that "a considerable number of the younger members of the sect had conceived such an abhorrence for war that they were willing to endure any penalties rather than serve in the army." Certainly conditions in the labor battalions were very unpleasant, both physically and in terms of the psychological pressure to which recruits were subjected. And, while Chamberlin was there, he met a young Ukrainian who had just completed a prison term for conscientious objection.[81]

Signs of continuing tension over this issue dominated congresses held by both the Evangelical Christians and the Baptists in late 1926. For the Baptists, the need to make a formal declaration of loyalty to the Soviet state and willingness to make service in the Red Army compulsory for their members clearly dominated the agenda, since this had never been done formally at a congress. Grachev remembered that it was common knowledge that, at meetings preceding the 1926 congress, Baptist leaders had come to the conclusion, through prayerful discussions, that each person should decide whether to serve according to his conscience. When Tuchkov heard this, he summoned the delegates to his office and told them to "go, and pray again."[82] They apparently did, for delegates voted 221 to 9 in favor of the proposed resolution. Meanwhile, the continuing dissension on this matter among the

Evangelical Christians, who had already endorsed military service in 1923, required that their 1926 congress reaffirm earlier resolutions. In fact, at the Evangelical Christian gathering, seventy-six delegates, or more than 20 percent of those who would later vote on the resolution, crowded the podium to speak their mind on the issue. During the voting one-third of delegates either opposed the resolution or abstained.[83]

A series of local congresses followed the 1926 national congresses, attended by representatives from each denomination's central organization who pushed through resolutions declaring support for military service. Levels of local enthusiasm clearly varied.[84] A report on congresses held in various regions of Ukraine stated that all had passed an identical resolution approving the 1926 decision on the military issue and stressed that, contrary to some members' interpretation, the resolution made military service compulsory for all Baptists.[85] Confusion among believers was an obvious problem. For example, the leader of a small group of Baptists reported that, after the local congress where the protocol of the 1926 national congress was considered, members of his flock asked, "How is it that you used to say 'do not kill' and now one may, how is it that you will now preach Christ?"[86] On the applications to the Baptist Union's Bible School a new line was added, asking for the candidate's views on the 1926 congress resolution. Apparently several of the applicants missed the point that they should convey their unqualified support for participation in military service.[87] Following the 1926 congresses and the subsequent local meetings, there would be no further national evangelical gatherings until the 1960s. The Soviet state, having exacted the declarations of loyalty it needed, no longer felt any necessity to permit further public meetings.

The Bolsheviks' accommodation of religious antimilitarism offered the Russian evangelicals the opportunity not only to develop a new identity based on their religious interpretation of the experiences of war and revolution but also the chance to participate in the implementation of government policy in this area as expert witnesses. In the end, however, the law on religious conscientious objectors was meant only as a symbol of old bonds of victimhood dating from the period of tsarist oppression. The acknowledgment of some sort of shared past and social idealism were the stated goals; but the law also served as a test of these former potential allies. Thus, for both Baptists and Bolsheviks, the decree of 4 January 1919 proved to be a mixed blessing. Initially the Bolsheviks enjoyed the endorsement of religious sectarians such as the Baptists at home and praise from these groups' supporters abroad. When the evangelicals and other sectarians actually took the Bolsheviks up on their offer, however, the ideological and organizational implications were threatening to the Bolsheviks' aspirations for a monopoly in these areas. Ironically, once the civil war was over and the party focused its attention on building the socialist society, renunciation of pacifism became the key to holding congresses, reopening journals, organizing Bible courses, and carrying on

Members of the Baptist Union Plenum, 1928. Second row, second from left, seated, is Pavel V. Ivanov-Klyshnikov; same row, second from right, is Nikolai V. Odintsov. Third row, fourth from left, is Pavel V. Pavlov. Back row, second from left, is Mikhail D. Timoshenko.

Baptist Ukrainy, 1928.

the many other evangelical activities that have led to the perception of NEP as a golden age for Baptists, activities that had been suspended in the years of "negotiation" from 1922 to 1923.[88] The evangelicals did enjoy an active associational life in the mid- and late 1920s, but it was always against a background of internal distrust and division arising from the pacifism issue and the door it opened to interference from the GPU.

In this respect the Baptists and Evangelical Christians were treated not unlike the Orthodox or, for that matter, various other faiths. During these same years, in their bid to break up the former state church, the party and GPU actively sponsored the Renovationist movement, which sought to combine Orthodoxy and socialism. As Edward Roslof demonstrates, here again they struggled with the ideological dilemma of a Communist regime apparently supporting a religious group.[89] No one would deny that the scope of the Bolsheviks' "problem" was much greater with Orthodoxy because of its position as the traditional religion with a vast network of parishes and property holdings, and its hold over minds and customs. However, a lengthy report of the Antireligious Commission to the party Central Committee in September 1923 made it clear that this was merely the most intense and visible part of a continuum of policies designed to destroy all religious organizations as organizations. The Bolsheviks' strategy of seizing financial assets and then breaking up religious organizations from the inside carried over to other groups. For example, valuables of the Roman Catholic Church were seized and their leaders arrested and tried in 1922–23. Around the same time the secret police sponsored a similar renovationist movement to divide the Old Believers. Similar efforts were planned among Muslims, Buddhists, and Jews.[90] Because of the different organizational structure and comparative lack of material wealth of the sectarians, the attack on the Baptists and Evangelical Christians was simply less visible. Overall, however, this was part of a process of gradually squeezing out all religious organizations, which counted as some of the most important autonomous associations with national scope remaining in the Soviet Union. The challenge was not merely to neutralize religious leaders but also to combat the ideological and organizational challenge their denominations represented. Evangelical organizing would play a special role in shaping Bolshevik thinking about the mobilization of Soviet society and the creation of an activist, socialist public.

10

Parallel Lives?
Religious Activism and Godless Fears

We are not Baptists.
We are Communists.
The poison of gospel fables
Is alien and completely innocuous to us.

—Dem'ian Bednyi,
Izvestiia, 24 August 1927

In May 1930, students from the Antireligious Division of Leningrad State University traveled to the Stalingrad area to study the variety of religious life there. One of the professors leading the group asked the young camera man, An. Terskoi, to join him at an Evangelical Christian baptism in the Volga River one evening. When Terskoi expressed surprise that the new converts were three young workers from the Red October metallurgy plant, his professor countered that, actually, the Baptists and Evangelical Christians were the most successful of all sects in drawing youth to their movement. Their secret was the variety of their techniques, he explained:

> There is the Khristomol—the Union of Christian Youth . . . ; organizationally, it's something like our Komsomol. In general, the sectarians quite often copy our methods of work. They organize their own holidays in parallel with Soviet ones.

Having set up this analogy between evangelical youth groups and the Young Communist League (Komsomol), the professor regretfully concluded that the score that night would show three more members for the Bapsomol (as he now termed it), as the Komsomol stood idly by.[1]

Foreign observers at the time and later scholars have noted this same theme of parallelism between religious and Bolshevik organizations. For example, in his study of utopian experimentation in the Russian Revolution, Richard Stites describes how Communist commentators were at once fascinated and annoyed by sectarians' "conscious emulation of Bolshevik codes and rituals in order to compete with them." The Bolsheviks, anxious about the Baptists' impressive conversion record, in turn "urged their activists to emulate the methods of the sectarian groups." Thus the Baptists—and especially their Bapsomol—seem to provide a fascinating case of the syncretic blending of religious and revolutionary ideas and methods in the early Soviet period.[2] The historical record reveals a more complicated situation than mere mutual emulation, however.

The notion of parallels between religious and political radicalism was built into the relationship between evangelicals and Bolsheviks. Well into the 1920s, members of the Soviet leadership who advocated favorable policies for sectarians did so on the grounds that their communities offered valuable "models" of communal living and mutual aid from which the broader population could learn. Similarly, from early 1918, before any of these policies were announced, the Baptists and Evangelical Christians began continually to emphasize the compatibility of a religious vision, based on the communal practices of the early Christians, with the building of a socialist society.[3] As we have seen, believers acted on this idea, founding agricultural communes in the countryside and cooperatives in the cities, working out visions of a new, Christian way of life, and even laying the foundations for a utopian, collectivist City of the Sun, Evangel'sk.[4] Various renditions of a Christian version of the great revolutionary anthem, the "Internationale," even circulated among evangelical congregations.[5] But by the late 1920s it was precisely because of this alleged parallelism that a different, and now dominant, camp within the party singled out the evangelicals as the most threatening of religious forces.

The notion that the evangelical community represented a society parallel to, but ideologically incompatible with, the Soviet socialist one to which Communist leaders aspired came to dominate press coverage and party discussion of religious sectarianism in the mid- and late 1920s. This chapter examines how the idea of such parallels was worked out in party policy on social mobilization and cultural change in the 1920s, focusing on the youth groups and religious agricultural communes that so concerned the Bolshevik authorities. Although evangelicals did occasionally use Soviet-style acronyms such as Ispolkom [executive committee] to describe their own organizations in the 1920s, the terms "Bapsomol" and "Khristomol," perhaps the most commonly employed by Bolshevik writers in complaining about evangelical organizational energies, never appear in Baptist or Evangelical Christian materials.[6] Instead, the elaboration of the idea of the Bapsomol as the religious mirror image of the Komsomol, with a similar name, a similar constituency, and similar organizational methods, was emblematic of Communist anxieties about the broader problem of social mobilization and the formation of an activist, socialist society and culture in the years of the New

Economic Policy. For the party, the topics of social transformation and organizational success were intimately bound up with each other.[7] And by the mid-1920s religious organizations remained the most important legal, nationwide entities competing with Bolshevik efforts in these respects. Their existence became an emblem for party leaders of the limits of their control over society and their failure to rapidly transform social values and behavior. Active religious organizing thus challenged the Bolsheviks to explore and define the limits of social autonomy in the emerging socialist society. An examination of their evolving perceptions of, and policies toward, the Baptists illuminates the process of gradually squeezing out the social pluralism that so troubled them during NEP years.

COMPETITION IN THE MISSION FIELD: GOVERNMENT PERCEPTIONS AND POLICY

Ironically members of the Bolshevik party and various sectarian leaders cooperated in elaborating the notion of parallel religious and political societies in the early Soviet period. Starting immediately after the revolution, Russian religious sectarians of various persuasions began to promote the idea that their communities were compatible with the new socialist ethos. Some of their members who had emigrated to North and South America even proposed to return home to build the new society.[8] Working as a self-appointed representative of the sectarians, the Tolstoyan Ivan M. Tregubov, an employee of the Commissariat of Agriculture, strove to bring this potential to official attention and was given a rather sympathetic hearing in the party press. In July 1919, for example, he published an article in the leading party newspaper, *Pravda* [Truth], advocating cooperation between Bolsheviks and sectarians in building communism. An accompanying note from the newspaper's editorial board explained that, although it did not share Tregubov's views about the correct path to communism, it was "enthusiastically" printing this piece and calling for cooperation between party comrades and religious sectarians in "build[ing] a new life, do[ing] our shared precious work." Moreover, when another contributor objected to such joint activity, the editors again stepped in to say that to limit those who could build communism to people who advocated "scientific communism" was "not revolutionary policy, but the worst sort of revolutionary sectarianism."[9] Beginning in the Civil War period, therefore, the issue of collaboration with former religious dissidents was, for the Bolsheviks, a component of the broader political problem of work with the so-called non-party masses.

The idea that sectarian communities provided models of communist living became clearly enunciated early in the era of the New Economic Policy. It was first made explicit in a joint circular of 15 August 1921 of the Commissariats of Justice, Internal Affairs, Agriculture, and the Worker-Peasant Inspectorate on the separation of church and state. The circular declared that many religious sectarians had been persecuted before the revolution precisely because, in practice, they had "destroyed private property in their economic life," and that such groups were now "organically bringing themselves into Soviet construction as agricultural and industrial cells, regardless of the fact that their communist aspirations were clothed in religious form owing to historical conditions." Local soviets should ensure that these experiments "serve as a practical example of the feasibility and all-round advantageousness of communism for laborers."[10] A few months later, on 5 October 1921, the Commissariat of Agriculture appealed formally to sectarians and Old Believers to realize their aspirations for a communal way of life by settling abandoned estates and farming them by collective means.[11] Finally, at the Thirteenth Party Congress in May 1924, the principle of looking to sectarian organizational models became official party policy. The congress's resolutions on work in the countryside called for an "especially attentive attitude toward sectarians" who had suffered under tsarism, and affirmed that the party ought "to direct the considerable economic-cultural elements among sectarians into the stream of Soviet work."[12]

There was no unanimity within the Bolshevik leadership about religious policy in general, nor, in particular, about the idea of special measures for former dissidents from the Orthodox Church. Indeed, in the weeks preceding the Thirteenth Party Congress, divisions over religious policy were laid bare in a rancorous debate in *Pravda* over the proposed policy toward sectarians—and the accompanying call for an end to confrontational "administrative measures" such as church closings in favor of intensified antireligious education. This debate was intimately linked to the broader question of how the Bolsheviks would reach socialism and whether the New Economic Policy represented a temporary setback in the revolutionary course or the onset of a long and steady transition period in economics and culture.[13] For example, at the congress itself one of the opponents of the new religious policy, I. I. Skvortsov-Stepanov, argued forcefully that Bolsheviks could not be "vegetarians" and should not surrender to the "repentant moods" reflected in the proposed conciliatory policies.[14] This issue of whether the Bolshevik Party required revolutionary methods of work was to be resolved in favor of radical action in the late 1920s, with the launching of rapid industrialization, forced collectivization of agriculture, and cultural revolution, but in 1924 it was still open to very public debate.

Bolshevik policy on religious associations in general, and those of formerly dissident groups in particular, thus intersected with broader social and cultural policy issues. The problem of regulating religious organizations was connected to efforts to transform Russian popular culture into an atheistic, socialist, proletarian one. Bolsheviks proposed to create a new Soviet way of life and a new Soviet person that would embody these characteristics.[15] In other words, the new regime needed to make converts to the Bolshevik worldview. But it had already become clear to most revolutionaries that this would be no easy task. As the Commissar of Education, Anatolii Lunacharskii, pointed out in 1919, "One can make a political revolution in an hour, but it takes decades to make a social revolution, a revolution in morals, economics, and culture."[16]

During NEP the Soviet regime's main technique for achieving this transformation was to draw the populace voluntarily into state-sponsored institutions and organizations. In an effort to rekindle the relationship between the regime and the social groups that they saw as their natural allies, the workers and the peasants, the Bolsheviks sponsored membership drives to fill the ranks of the unions, of the Komsomol, and of the party, and launched a constellation of mass voluntary organizations to promote virtues such as literacy, sobriety, and atheism.[17]

This move to involve the population in public organizations was a response to the changed political and social circumstances of the early 1920s. A series of social changes in the working class after 1917 had forced the party to rethink what constituted a proletarian. Most important among these changes were the collapse of the social structure during the civil war and the high unemployment of the early NEP era, which made objective criteria of workplace experience difficult to apply; moreover, there had appeared the problem of classifying former workers who now held white-collar jobs as party cadres. Now that the Bolsheviks were firmly in power, they also faced the challenge of communicating the values of their revolution to the vast rural population. As a result, argues Sheila Fitzpatrick, the Bolsheviks "moved toward a concept of *formative proletarian experience* as a determinant of class position." Initially this included long factory experience before the revolution or service in the Red Army during the civil war. But as the prerevolutionary and revolutionary past dimmed, the Bolsheviks gradually "redefined the concept of proletarian consciousness into a notion of revolutionary and ultimately civic responsibility."[18] This was the context for the party's intensified interest in mass social organizations, especially after 1924. Participation in public and party organizations would be the means for inculcating Soviet socialist values.

This goal seemed particularly pressing amid the perceived pressures for embourgeoisement in NEP society. Indeed, as Elizabeth Wood points out, "in 1923 . . . the issue of everyday life [*byt*] for the first time took on a broad salience beyond the almost clichéd rhetoric of the initial years of the revolution."[19] The problem of creating a new society with socialist values in the face of a "retreat" to a mixed economy stumped the Bolsheviks. In Moshe Lewin's words, they struggled with a "cultural lag" arising from "the disparity between the party's ideology and aspirations and the frustrating reality of a petit bourgeois country."[20] Atheism was an important aspect of the desirable proletarian mentality, but a difficult one to purvey. From both an organizational and ideological point of view, religious groups presented a particularly insidious threat, for they represented the combined challenges of the persistence of traditional culture, the petty-bourgeois values of the family, and alternative forms of social organization.

Numerous party statements presented the Baptist faith as an ideology eminently suited to this difficult NEP era. Already in February 1922 a resolution of the Central Committee proposed that the social conditions of early Soviet Russia provided especially propitious material for "deviation to the Protestant-evangelical side." "In connection with the colossal social change that is going on," the resolution stated, "one can also expect among the masses (especially the peasant masses) a deviation in the direction of rationalization of their previously mystical religious world view and the use of this change by bourgeois elements." Thus, it concluded, "it is essential to explain that this deviation to the Protestant-evangelical side presents the danger of a new spiritual enslavement of the masses."[21] Commentators often contrasted the collapse of Orthodoxy in the early Soviet era with the ability of Baptists and Evangelical Christians to modernize their message and methods, and to give a voice to the petty bourgeois sentiments supposedly elicited by NEP. Evangelicals' allegedly rationalistic approach to the Bible and their championing of principles of individual activism were considered broadly compatible with processes taking place among the Russian populace—and affecting not just bourgeois and kulak elements but also members of the Bolsheviks' desired constituency of workers, peasants, and youth, who were suffering from hardships on the path to building socialism.[22] NEP, declared one local party official at a high-level meeting in Moscow in 1926, was the "nourishing broth of sectarianism."[23]

More important than the ideological challenge of evangelical religion, however, was its organizational dynamism. To a large extent, Bolshevik policy makers in the mid-1920s were preoccupied less by the content of Baptist teachings than by how believers went about organizing themselves and spreading their faith. In fact, change in religious policy paralleled the broader policy shift toward devising participatory means of fashioning new mentalities. The Thirteenth Party Congress in 1924 confirmed a marked change in the tactics of antireligious policy. In contrast to earlier violent confrontations with the Orthodox Church, Bolshevik policy makers now turned their attention to more systematic antireligious education directed at eradicating all forms of religious belief and practice. In addition to an active publishing program, the new antireligious effort also involved lectures, museums, the establishment of "godless" corners in factories and village reading huts, and, in 1925, the creation of a mass voluntary society, the League of the Godless.[24] Now that the party's goal was to convert the religious enemy, the antireligious and religious camps faced off as direct competitors in what the Baptists called the mission field.[25]

PARALLEL SOCIETY?

By the late 1920s much of Bolshevik concern about Baptist organizing, both in Moscow and in the context of local administration, centered on the opportunities these religious groups offered to adolescents and young adults. For the Bolsheviks and the evangelicals alike, recruiting the younger generation was obviously crucial to their continued viability. The Soviet government sought to transform the worldview of the young and inculcate Communist values such as hard work, collectivism, sobriety, atheism, and devotion to the workers' state.[26] Meanwhile, evangelicals continued to develop their own work among youth, for they, too, needed a constant supply of converts to fill their ranks. There is no question that one purpose of evangelical youth groups was to provide an alternative to Soviet youth organizations. Nevertheless, despite the repeated warnings of antireligious activists about a Bapsomol menace, it is hard to see in evangelical activity a concerted, national strategy to combat Bolshevism by emulating it.

In the first years of Soviet power, the Baptists and Evangelical Christians had formed special youth associations to channel local activism. However, they soon became associated in the official mind with pacifism and with a refusal to participate in party- and state-sponsored organizations and other forms of entertainment. Already in May 1921 the Cheka had arrested forty-two participants of the Sixth All-Russian Congress of Evangelical Christian Youth as deserters and counterrevolutionaries.[27] Although the Evangelical Christians' Union of Christian Youth was officially registered by the Petrograd provincial administration in January 1922, three months later that same body closed it down for allegedly "arousing religious fanaticism among the young generation of citizens."[28] Even worse, the "youth department" of the Baptist Union suffered a serious blow in early 1924 when the two people most involved in its work, Mikhail D. Timoshenko and Nikolai A. Levindanto, were exiled to Turkestan until June 1925. From exile, Levindanto and Timoshenko sent a letter to the Baptist Union asking it to distribute a circular they had prepared to all congregations with youth groups, suggesting that the Baptist Union appoint new youth leaders in their absence. Their assertion that their appeal was in response to "numerous requests regarding the work of the youth branch" suggests that the youth branch was an active organization at the time of their arrest.[29]

After this 1924 letter, no evangelical source again made specific mention of nationwide youth leagues in either branch of the movement. In fact, youth as a specific topic disappeared from the protocols of congresses. The last direct reference to organizing the young came at the Baptists' national congress in Moscow in late 1923 where Timoshenko spoke of success with youth groups "despite obstacles" but made no mention of a national organization; in their local reports at that same congress delegates revealed that youth were active across the country but were similarly mute regarding any wide-scale organization.[30] Reporting on youth activities became extremely fragmentary. The arrest of Timoshenko and Levindanto and widespread incidental evidence of the activism of local youth groups seem to suggest that this silence

Choirs and other members of the Leningrad Baptist community, November 1927.
Baptist Ukrainy, 1928.

was probably the result of press censorship and government refusal to approve topics related to youth on conference programs.[31] One way or another no large-scale organization modeled on the Komsomol coordinated these activities, be it a Bapsomol or Baptomol or Khristomol.

However, to many Bolsheviks, the continued visibility of individual religious youth groups implied that they were acceptable options for young workers and peasants. They worried that people might become confused and believe that they could combine religious and Soviet identities. In a March 1929 letter to the editor of *Bezbozhnik* [The godless] a member of a local godless cell wrote of having become a Bolshevik during World War I but later joining the Baptists, "whose teaching, because of my inexperience, seemed then to be identical to the program of the Bolsheviks."[32] During the mid-1920s anyone who got his or her hands on a copy of *Khristianin* could read about Ivan Prokhanov's son, Vsevolod, who graduated from Leningrad University in 1925 in social and economic sciences and taught *politgramota* [political literacy] at the Evangelical Christians' Bible School. After he was accidentally killed in July 1927, an obituary described him as a state employee who "dreamed of serving the Worker-Peasant power in developing the economic side of the USSR."[33] Such intertwining of what they regarded as incompatible identities made the Bolsheviks nervous.

They also feared that similar confusion was fostered by the regime's endorsement of sectarian economic and social experimentation. Certainly it was in this respect that there is most evidence of evangelicals interacting with Soviet models and trying to create their own parallel society. Although the official policy was that religious sectarians' communes would serve as models of socialist living in the countryside, the efforts of these sectarians to pursue their own vision of socialism soon got them into trouble with the authorities. The Bolsheviks had to confront the contradictions in their policy toward former religious dissidents—and in their general attitudes toward public activism, which sought to instill initiative [*samodeiatel'nost'*] among the population while avoiding the dreaded spontaneity [*stikhiinost'*] that might take public organizations in directions contrary to party objectives.

The activities of evangelical economic organizations, especially their efforts to promote trade among themselves, lent credence to Bolshevik accusations that the evangelicals were trying to set up a parallel society or a state within a state.[34] The same argument could be applied to their attempts, in coalition with seven other sectarian denominations, to form an All-Union Cooperative Fraternal Union of sectarian agricultural and credit unions, artels, collectives, and communes in May 1925. In their appeal to the authorities, after rehearsing the history of Soviet appeals to sectarians to participate in the building of socialism, they emphasized that their collectives owed their comparative success to the values fostered by their shared religious faith. Thus, in order to preserve and develop these advantages, the signatories to the appeal believed that these collectives required a "shared economic and financial center" and the right to restrict membership to fellow believers.[35] It was no doubt galling to the Bolsheviks to be reminded by a group of religious believers that no social revolution was possible without a spiritual revolution. Although the central council of the Spiritual Christians–Molokans apparently reported to its followers in June 1925 that this proposal had been well received, there is no evidence of its having been successful.[36] On the contrary, party concern about sectarians' economic activities seems to have intensified. In late 1925 and early 1926, the antireligious press published two articles defending the social and revolutionary role played by Russian sectarians, but each was preceded by a blistering response by the party's new specialist on sectarian matters, Fedor Putintsev.[37] Putintsev wrote: "We are not against sectarian communes, . . . but we are against their isolation in a special network on an all-union or even provincial level."[38]

To be sure, there is substantial evidence for Putintsev's contention that Baptists and Evangelical Christians were seeking, as were other religious groups, to put forward a religious, socialist alternative to Soviet organizations. For instance, in the very first issue of *Baptist* after it resumed publication in 1925 an article by Pavel Ivanov-Klyshnikov laid out in detail the idea that Baptist congregations were "natural collectives." Even before the revolution, Baptist communities had been "hidden labor collectives" built on mutual aid; now, "under more favorable government conditions," this aspect was being expanded. The success of these communities was proof that a group of people who united based on shared faith would automatically achieve better material conditions. His conclusion left no doubt about the Baptists' desire to be part of Soviet society, without adopting its values:

> We have before us an impetuous stream of new forms of social-economic life and an ever sharpening battle for survival. We inevitably should enter this stream. . . . However, we enter it as we are; that is to say, as well-composed ranks of chosen, reborn people, with half a century's experience with communal soldiering [*obshchinnoi spaiki*], with a special structure of collective life, which will be defined in its details in the future with faith in God, under the banner of Christ![39]

Nevertheless it is important to recognize the contradictory messages implicit in Bolshevik policy. Although it is true that the Thirteenth Party Congress had called for drawing sectarians' alleged cultural and economic skills into "the channel of *soviet* work," the implication in the pronouncements of 1921 had been that sectarians were invited to settle empty lands as self-contained communities.[40] The Commissariat of Agriculture also worked out sample charters, especially for sectarian communes and artels, suggesting that officials assumed these would be needed.[41] Contradictions in policy also prompted sectarian efforts to organize independent religious communal associations: although believers no doubt wished to preserve the confessional nature of their economic experiments, it is also true that their enterprises were formally excluded from membership in the official All-Russian Union of Agricultural Cooperatives, Sel'skosoiuz.[42] In fact, in August 1923 the Baptists' Brotherly Aid Credit Union tried and failed to gain admission to Sel'skosoiuz.[43] Thus the shadowy legal position of religiously based collectives encouraged the very separatism that official policy about channeling sectarians' skills into general work sought to destroy.

The continued existence, and worst of all the success, of religious communes similarly confronted Bolshevik policy makers with the contradictory nature of their policy and the dilemma presented by the notion of sectarian "models." Efforts to organize the countryside communally advanced only very slowly during the first ten years of Soviet power, and some local officials had to acknowledge that the only successful communes in their areas were religiously based. For example, in 1922 the Tver' provincial executive committee's cooperatives and collective farms branch wrote to the authorities in Novotorzhskii uezd supporting the application of a group of Evangelical Christians who wished to form a commune on the grounds that there were already several such Evangelical Christian communes in the province, all of which were "notable for model management."[44] In fact, in Vyshne-Volotskii uezd of the same province, groups of children from several different schools visited the large Evangelical Christian "Bethany" commune every year from

1924 to 1927. The small children's thank-you notes were full of enthusiasm for the pigs and other such exciting aspects of farm life. But a letter from one high school class revealed the dilemma for teachers in a Communist school system trying to explain these field trips to their pupils:

> The farm in our view looked ideal. What especially interested us was the collective work and collective consumption. On the side of production and consumption they approach the society discussed by scientific socialism. One must note that religious conviction serves as the unifying stimulus in their work. From our side, we support the further spread of such communes but not on the basis of religious convictions (although they, too, can lead to a bright future), but on the basis of the realization of the future tasks of socialist society.[45]

That the students were guided to view the commune they had visited in this basically positive light emphasizes the mixed attitudes toward these groups among the authorities. In fact, it appears that, from the first days of the revolution, there was confusion among Bolsheviks and sympathizers about the proper attitude toward former religious dissidents: sources hint that the Red Army was told to make clear its support to sectarians when it entered territories formerly held by the Whites; occasional Baptist and Bolshevik autobiographers both recount thinking that evangelical and revolutionary teaching were just two sides of one coin; and during the 1921 crackdown on violations of the party's rules against religious activity, local reports suggested a willingness among many party members to accept religion as broadly compatible with the revolution.[46] In 1926, when the League of the Godless wrote to its local organizations concerning the value of using "Harvest Day" celebrations for antireligious purposes, it felt it necessary to emphasize that this did not mean getting involved with sectarian harvest festivals.[47] Just as their leaders did in letters to the central authorities and in journals, so local evangelical leaders seem to have implied in their preaching that their organizations and faith were compatible with the new order. For example, in 1921 a report of the Tver' provincial Cheka claimed that "in the achievement of their goals, of widespread dissemination of their preached teaching, the evangelicals and Baptists were not hampered by any means. All the time and everywhere they tried to inspire the mass of the population and demonstrate that, allegedly, Soviet power was on their side."[48] Perhaps local officials, in Tver' Province, in particular, had been uncertain of how to act from the start. It certainly appears that authorities in the party were surprised and angry to learn that officials in the Commissariat of Agriculture had assisted Prokhanov in organizing his "City of the Sun" expedition to the Altai in 1927.[49] Ultimately, the party wanted Soviet citizens to choose its materialist, socialist path, not to attempt to combine various identities.

EVANGELICAL ORGANIZING AND THE PROBLEM
OF CULTURAL PLURALISM DURING NEP

The activism of evangelical organizations was particularly prominent among the justifications presented to party meetings for the transition in emphasis in antireligious work. Several party statements made it clear that it was not just the content of evangelicals' preaching but the actual form of their work that was judged counterrevolutionary. For example, a set of directives on dealing with sectarians issued by the Central Committee in February 1922 argued at length that religious youth organizations constituted fronts for counterrevolution, "which forbid their members not only to join any political parties but also to attend Soviet schools, lectures, movies, and theater, in other words, which forbid social and political activity . . . and cut them off from joining into all the cultural-educational life of the Republic."[50] By arguing that religious youth organizations were dangerous both as covers for counterrevolutionary activity and because they isolated young people from the new Soviet culture, this set of directives anticipated later arguments that the Baptists had created a parallel society to the general Soviet one. Meanwhile, the Antireligious Commission of the Central Committee repeatedly ordered the secret police to infiltrate the sects in order to sap their organizational energies; in late 1924 it specifically charged the OGPU (as the GPU had been renamed) with "taking measures toward the disbandment and impermissibility of sectarian religious youth circles."[51]

Despite the overwhelmingly Orthodox population, the Bolsheviks paid remarkable attention to the sectarians, particularly the Baptists and Evangelical Christians, in the articulation of antireligious policy. In fact, it was a central element in arguments about the form that would be adopted by the Bolsheviks' organizational answer to religion, the League of the Godless. Part of the move toward an educational approach to antireligious propaganda was the founding, in late 1922, of *Bezbozhnik*, an antireligious weekly aimed at a popular audience. In August 1924 its editor, Emelian Iaroslavskii, established a fan club known as the "Society of Friends of the Newspaper *Bezbozhnik*" (ODGB); the following April the club would be reorganized as the All-Union League of the Godless.[52]

On 15 December 1924, when the Antireligious Commission made its first formal report to the Central Committee's Organization Bureau (Orgbiuro), the problem of sectarian activity took center stage. The main point of the presentation, given by Iaroslavskii, was to receive the Central Committee's blessing for the further development of the new ODGB. The religious threat, as Iaroslavskii described it, came overwhelmingly from the evangelicals. He contrasted the inadequacy of the Agitation and Propaganda apparatus's antireligious propaganda with the organizational successes of the sectarians. As he explained, "regarding the sects I should say that they have worked out a whole array of extraordinarily interesting methods of work." In particular, he said ominously, "an extraordinarily serious battle for youth is going on. . . . There have been incidents of Komsomol cells going over wholesale to the sectarian organization." The sectarians were besting the Communists at their own game by borrowing Communist methods.[53]

In addition to approving the work of the ODGB, at this meeting the Central Committee decided to collect further information about the sectarian movement throughout the country. On 30 January 1925 it issued a secret circular ordering all regional party committees to make clandestine investigations and provide detailed reports about the activities and influence of religious sects in each district. As Iaroslavskii had done in his report to the Orgbiuro, so the circular emphasized the particular threat presented by sectarian organizational endeavors. Once again, among the forms of "dangerous antistate work" of which the sectarians were accused, pride of place went to propaganda among youth, the formation of youth circles, and illegally holding special youth prayer meetings.[54]

The idea that the sects, especially the Baptists and Evangelical Christians, were evolving a strategy of competition with the Communists through associations was further developed eighteen months later at a special meeting on antireligious questions for local party Agitation and Propaganda cadres, convened in Moscow in April 1926. Again, the sects dominated the discussion of the actual activity of religious organizations. Putintsev, the new party expert on sectarian issues, opened his keynote address by underlining the special status of religious organizations in Soviet society. "The only mass, non-proletarian, widespread, legal organizations in the [Soviet] Union are religious organizations," he declared. "And the most adaptable organizations, which accommodate themselves to the given time, are precisely sectarian organizations." He went on to explain that the Orthodox Church had compromised itself as a counterrevolutionary organization and had lost authority but that the sects, which were more "democratic," presented a far greater danger for they were developing into mass, non-proletarian movements. Particularly worrying, he noted, were evangelicals. "The mass sects and at the same time the growing sects are the Evangelicals and the Baptists. We will need to talk about the growth and the reasons for the spread of these two sects, because the Evangelicals and the Baptists are now the evil of the day," he declared.[55]

According to Putintsev, the very form of Baptist and Evangelical Christian work had been fundamentally important in promoting their expansion. And these forms had been directly copied from the party's structures, ranging from women's departments, children's circles, reading huts, and collective farms to agitation detachments [agit-otriadi]. And, in his view, the godless might be good at criticizing religion, but "from an economic perspective, from the angle of daily life, we cannot compete with sectarianism."[56] Various local representatives chimed in with reports of Baptist organizational prowess, the dangers of evangelical youth, choir, and women's groups, and the failures of Soviet alternatives. The delegate from Smolensk, for example, declared that sectarian groups were more appealing to peasants than the ODGB cells, whose members got drunk after their antireligious campaigns. Furthermore, he said, young women preferred sectarian singing groups to the Komsomol. His conclusion was that "sectarianism stands before us as our most important competitor for ideological influence over the peasantry."[57] By implication, the Bolsheviks had to think more about reorganizing daily life. Making their organizations part of people's lives was crucial to achieving this.

This 1926 conference approved a detailed set of theses that established the paradigm by which all Baptist and Evangelical Christian activity would be explained in the late 1920s: the idea of a parallel society. According to the delegates, in the early revolutionary years the sectarians' neutral position had encouraged them to develop "non-class" or "class-transcending" theories and organizations. The Evangelical Christians and the Baptists, in particular, had allegedly copied party techniques but with the goal of creating "an isolated sectarian society [*obshchestvennost'*]," immune from Bolshevik propaganda efforts.[58] In presenting this analysis during the conference, participants constantly employed Bolshevik acronyms such as *zhenotdel* (women's department) to underline the similarities between the Baptist and Bolshevik communities. And Putintsev described the people whom the evangelicals called *priblizhennymi* [people drawing near] as "in our way of speaking— candidates, sympathizers."[59]

In the next couple of years both the press campaign and repressive measures against sectarians and their organizations were intensified. The party and state worked out more direct measures against sectarian organizations, based on what had been learned at the agitprop antireligious conference.[60] On 22 August 1927, the All-Union Central Executive Committee issued a secret circular demanding that regional and local governments not accord any special privileges to sectarians relative to other organizations. This meant forbidding religious meetings and congresses from discussing any but narrowly religious issues and banning special children's, youth, or women's circles and other organizations.[61] Judging from the forceful complaints to the central authorities from various religious groups soon after this circular went out, it was apparently broadly enforced. For example, the Baptists' central council wrote to the Central Executive Committee of the USSR, declaring that "as if by a signal" a press campaign, arrests, closure of meetings, and other forms of repression had begun all over the country. The Evangelical Christian leaders presented similar complaints, and proceeded to "guess" that a secret order had been issued and to lay out its probable contents.[62]

By 1928 the alleged threat of a parallel evangelical society moved to the center of the political stage. At the Eighth Congress of the Young Communist League in May of that year, the prominent party leader Nikolai Bukharin declared that, in conjunction with a general intensification of class and in-

ternational conflict, the battle between the Communist Party and its enemies for the allegiance of Soviet youth was escalating. He pointed to religious organizations as the Komsomol's principal competitors. The party's
youth wing faced a "whole array of sectarian organizations," which, Bukharin
claimed, counted among their ranks "roughly as many [members] as the
Komsomol." "All these 'baptomols,' 'khristomols,' [and] 'unions of believing young people,'" he asserted, united "a large stratum of young workers
and peasants." Furthermore, their advocacy of a sober way of life appealed
to some of the better elements of this youthful population.[63]

Bukharin's warning that sectarian youth organizations could outpace the
Komsomol's growth precipitated a flood of journalistic comment on the
Baptist—and especially the Bapsomol—threat. "The Komsomol does not
see how the 'Bapsomol' is growing. The enemy is not dozing!" screamed one
headline the following summer.[64] *Komsomol'skaia pravda* warned in August
1928 that the Baptists were the "most harmful [*vrednaia*] and powerful sect
under present conditions"; meanwhile, Communist organizations were not
responding in kind, and the League of the Godless was "not yet a mass organization."[65] The language of parallels permeated discussion of the religious
enemy. For example, at the Moscow printers' conference in October 1928,
one delegate declared that, "in Moscow there are sects of evangelists—this
is already not a religion but a party."[66] As the anti-sectarian campaign intensified, numerous short books also appeared on the subject, all of them focused on associational life, especially that of Baptists and Evangelical Christians.[67] For example, a book titled *Religion in the Fight for Worker Youth* allotted
twenty-six pages to evangelicals' strategies and only three to those of the Orthodox Church.[68] With respect to the evangelicals, these works tended to focus on two main issues: how their organizational methods paralleled those
of the party, and how, in spite of these similarities in form, the morality that
these organizations fostered was contrary to the Bolshevik ethic of class war.
Their purpose, of course, was to criticize the Bolsheviks' own organizational
and propaganda methods and their failure to generate greater activism
among the so-called nonparty masses.

A primary concern was to explain how it was that the Baptists could appeal to working-class young people. The young Aleksandr Klibanov, the future dean of Soviet sectarian studies, wrote in his 1928 book on sectarians
that sectarians and the Komsomol were engaged in a fierce battle over the
large field of unaligned youth. "The Leninist Komsomol," he insisted, "is ex-
erting all its strength in order not to give a single member of its class family
over to the power of an alien and hostile ideology." Yet he grudgingly suggested that the evangelicals could be more responsive to the needs of young
workers. He described his experiences at evangelical meetings in the most
lyrical terms: the rooms were simple, bright, and clean, and there was a whole-
some, quiet, family atmosphere. "But set our meeting alongside this," he sug-

gested, "how about one somewhere in the countryside, with the dry, monotonous speech of the speaker, with noise and smoking! Tell me, where is it more appealing?" In his view, worker youth aspired to precisely the social atmosphere the Baptists created. This was why young workers made up a sizable proportion of the alleged 90 percent of youth in the Melitopol' region [okrug] who were "under the influence of the Bapsomol," or the 50 percent allegedly claimed by the Khristomol in Samara. The reasons, he averred, were clear:

> Worker youth aspire to culture at present. They demand a healthy, cultured, sober life. And in one way or another, they can find it among the sectarians.[69]

In this way he echoed Bukharin's warning that the sectarian youth groups appealed to the very people whom the Komsomol sought to enroll.

Similarly Bolshevik commentators also displayed great interest in the actual details of sectarian organization. Here again, the message was that Komsomol groups could benefit from similar attention to cultivating good leaders and to being flexible and imaginative in their methods of mass work. For example, in his book on religion and worker youth, I. Eliashevich used an elaborate diagram to sketch out the organizational structure of the Baptist congregation and its constellation of groups and committees. He also set down the weekly schedule of a Baptist community in Novgorod region [okrug] to show that "work among the sectarians is done according to a plan." This plan was sensitive to the interests of young members, whereas the work of the Komsomol and the youth sections of clubs was often performed "according to a template." Committed and effective leaders were specially chosen to attend to this work. In the words of one investigator of evangelicals in Voronezh Province: "Sectarian congregations assign special members of their councils to lead work among youth, something like our party members who are assigned to the Komsomol."[70] But in the spirit of individual activism, the evangelical youth did not leave all this work to their leaders; rather, they had understood that it was best to send out youth to attract and educate youth.[71]

One of the results of this clever use of Bolshevik methods was that evangelical sectarians were attracting in large numbers a group that continued to elude the mobilizing aspirations of the Bolsheviks: young women.[72] Handiwork circles, and especially choirs, seemed to appeal more to young women than the activities offered in clubs and at Komsomol meetings. A lead article in *Derevenskii bezbozhnik* [Rural godless] quoted a young female Baptist, Lidiia Plotnikova from the village of Peski in Tambov Province, as saying, "What do you have that's good in the Komsomol—they all smoke, act like hooligans, curse; you'll never attract young women."[73]

Some activists suggested that the Bolsheviks, in turn, might benefit from copying Baptist methods in this area. One Leningrad godless, who had attempted to organize musical evenings to counteract those run by sectarians, wrote to the journal *Antireligioznik* [Antireligious activist] in 1927 to argue that "religion enthusiastically dons the patterned clothing of art. By creating artistic forms of antireligious propaganda, we can strengthen our positions in the battle with religion."[74] In a later book he similarly maintained that, in areas where the Komsomol had intensively studied issues of cultural work, "the influence of religious organizations has begun to drop noticeably."[75]

Impressive though Baptist methods might be, Bolshevik activists argued that their ends were completely contrary to those of the Bolsheviks. The sectarians were separating their members from Soviet society both physically and morally. Declared Putintsev in a 1928 brochure: "Sectarian leaders [*vozhaki*] try with all their strength to protect their rising generation [*smena*] from the influence of the party and the Komsomol" by forbidding them to participate in secular culture.[76] Moreover, their preaching denied the reality of class differences and the morality of class warfare. As Putintsev explained, "Sectarian preaching about love of the enemy is most profitable for counterrevolution and most dangerous for the revolution." It led to dangerous pacifism and a refusal to participate in socialist construction.[77] The theme of proletarian conscience betrayed and recovered similarly permeated the public recantations of ex-evangelicals published in the newspapers. As one former Evangelical Christian longshoreman wrote, "My worker's conscience began to speak inside me and I understood that I had become entangled in the nets of enemies. . . . I am a proletarian—and an enemy of my working class, which builds its life by its own hands, rather than awaiting the 'heavenly paradise' that we promise them."[78] Despite his admiration for some sectarian methods, Klibanov, too, insisted that the Baptist spirit behind these methods was unsuitable for the era of cultural revolution. The fun at sectarian festivals was of a "very doubtful character," he wrote, for their "asceticism more than anything else is in contradiction to our age of lively, energetic construction to re-create society and reconstruct life on new Communist principles."[79]

Throughout this discussion, Communist writers repeatedly applied Bolshevik terminology to evangelicals and their activities. By applying their own specific language to the structures and activities of the evangelical sectarians, the Bolsheviks constructed a worthy enemy with which to rally—but also to browbeat—their own cultural forces. It is undoubtedly true that the Baptists and Evangelical Christians took an interest in Bolshevik ideas and methods of work. However, it is also clear that the history of Bolshevik fears of the Bapsomol has far more to do with internal party politics than with the real activity of the evangelicals. Although the Bapsomol and Khristomol, the alleged youth organizations of the Baptists and Evangelical Christians, respectively, were by far the most frequently cited examples of alleged religious emulation of Bolshevik language and methods, they were, in fact, not the only ones. Surely it is not possible that all religious groups were taking the same approach to the challenge of surviving in Soviet Russia, yet discussions of the Bapsomol and Khristomol sometimes also mention other groups such as an Evsomol, a Trezvomol, and even a Molomol, allegedly formed, respectively, by the Jews, the sect of Trezvenniki, and the Molokans. In some contexts, Khristomol was also applied to Orthodox initiatives.[80] These terms reveal more about Bolshevik strategy about sectarians—and perhaps of the self-absorption of a one-party system—than about real sectarian activities.

This campaign took place just as the party was trumpeting the onset of a Cultural Revolution in all areas of Soviet life in the spring of 1928. As is well known, the impetus for this revolution was frustration with the gradualist policies of the party on the "cultural front" under NEP and the failure to rapidly transform social life and create mentalities compatible with a new, socialist society.[81] Fearing the degeneration of the party's proletarian class ethic amid the perceived cultural backwardness of the 1920s, radical elements in the party launched campaigns for the education of proletarians and their promotion to leadership in the workplace, for a proletarian ethos in culture, and for the rapid transformation of the bases of daily life. As the tide turned against the gradualist approach to changing popular mentalities, the mass voluntary societies that had been devised with this goal in mind came under renewed scrutiny for their failure to deliver a reserve of committed, active cadres.[82] More generally, the widespread perception within the party that religious groups were using rural cooperatives and other "Soviet" organizations to their own ends raised real doubts about what Communists had assumed would be the transformative power of new institutions.[83]

In fact, these books on the sectarian threat, with their interest in improving organizational efforts in order to meet the challenge of religious associations, reflected the gradualist or "culturalist" view of antireligious work that was under fire in the era of the Cultural Revolution. Their attention to the way in which sectarian organizations were breeding grounds for counterrevolution, however, hinted at the new approach that was rising to take its place. In late 1927 and early 1928 a growing number of Komsomolites rejected their League's experiment with conciliatory policies on religion and forcefully reasserted the confrontational, blasphemous approach they had taken in the early Soviet era.[84] As Daniel Peris has shown, the onset of the Cultural Revolution saw the resurfacing of an earlier debate in antireligious circles between what he terms "culturalists" and "interventionists." Broadly speaking, this was a conflict between those who wanted to convert the religious enemy and those who sought to destroy that enemy.[85] During 1928 this tone of self-criticism and the focus on finding ways to compete for converts remained dominant. The debate about the Bapsomol, and about religious sectarianism in general, in the second half of the 1920s had focused on the chal-

Thirtieth anniversary celebrations of the Omsk and Leninsk congregations of Baptists, held in the Omsk prayer house during the November 7 holiday (marking the tenth anniversary of the Bolshevik Revolution), 1927.

Baptist Ukrainy, 1928.

lenge religious groups presented as the only legal, independent organizations in the country. Discussion of their success as communities of believers and as proselytizing associations was, to a large extent, directed toward solving concrete problems of social mobilization that the Bolsheviks were experiencing in their own efforts to transform Russia.

The winds were shifting toward confrontation, however. In January 1929 a secret circular of the party Central Committee warned that, with the stresses of socialist construction, religious organizations, especially sectarian ones, were enjoying a surge in popularity. "In places," it said, one could observe "the mass involvement of workers in sectarian organizations and, in particular, the formation of khristomol evangelical and Baptist circles, brotherhoods, sisterhoods, and so on." Noting that these religious groups were the "only legally active counterrevolutionary organizations having influence on the masses," the circular concluded by ordering that all laws regarding religious societies be stringently followed and by calling on all voluntary organizations to include antireligious activity in their educational work.[86] A few months later, however, the party decisively solved the problem of competing with its only remaining organized enemy: the regime out-lawed the associational life to which it aspired but also which it most feared. On 8 April 1929 a new law, "On Religious Associations," specifically deprived all religious groups of the right to form "special children's, youth, women's prayer or other meetings, as well as general Bible, literary, handiwork, la-bor, religious studies, and similar gatherings, groups, circles, departments, as well as to organize excursions and children's playgrounds, to open li-braries and reading rooms, to organize sanatoria and medical aid." It also forbade them to form "mutual-aid funds, cooperatives, production associ-ations," and any other economic activities not directly related to "satisfying religious needs." In short, the law eliminated all aspects of religious com-munity life except for the actual worship service.[87] In May, the constitution was amended to allow "freedom of religious confession" in place of the pre-vious guarantee of "freedom of religious propaganda." Only the right to antireligious propaganda remained.[88] As Arto Luukkanen points out, this sealed the shift in party policy from trying to achieve, with the help of the secret police, docile and loyal religious organizations to aiming at their com-plete elimination.[89]

These legal changes signaled the onset of a renewed campaign to destroy religious life in the Soviet Union once and for all. Officials sought to strip all religious organizations of their economic resources, to liquidate their parishes, and to deport their leaders to prison camps. These policies affected Orthodox and sectarian alike. Across the country evangelical leaders were arrested, many prayer houses were closed down, and choirs and other con-gregational groups were forbidden. For example, after collecting signatures in favor of such a move at a series of large antireligious meetings attended by union and Komsomol members, authorities in the Lower Volga town of Balashov seized the Baptist, Molokan, Seventh-Day Adventist, and Jewish meet-ing places in April 1929. Town officials claimed that they were forced to break leases with these groups because they were not maintaining the buildings, and because the space was "needed for expanding cultural work here." The Bap-tist prayer house became a cinema, the Molokan one a pioneer club, and the other two reverted to housing purposes.[90] Similarly, religious communes were disbanded. In the first months of 1929, for example, the very successful Evan-gelical Christian Bethany commune was forcibly handed over to a Commu-nist collective and renamed Budennyi after the civil war hero. People also lost their union membership, and presbyters, missionaries, and even ordinary members of congregational councils were deprived of their voting rights as "clergy." To lose one's voting rights was a disaster, for it meant ineligibility for union membership and thus almost certain unemployment—in conditions where access to food was increasingly tied to the workplace.[91]

An atmosphere of fear engulfed evangelical congregations. Iurii Grachev, then a teenaged Baptist in Samara, remembered how, despite some pessimism owing to problems with educational authorities and difficulty finding work, he and his friends also rallied around imprisoned members. Ignoring their elders' warnings to be careful, the young still met on Saturdays, prepared aid packages for those under arrest, and even stood outside the local jail and sang hymns.[92] Others also stood up to the government. In late July 1929, the council of the Far East branch of the Baptist Union sent an appeal to the Soviet government asking for the law of 8 April to be overturned.[93]

Both the Baptist and Evangelical Christian unions suffered as well. Already the directors of the Baptist Bible courses in Moscow, Ivanov-Klyshnikov and Pavel Datsko, did not appear on the morning of March 1, for they had been arrested overnight. The following week, the courses were disbanded and the students sent home.[94] Soon thereafter Ivanov-Klyshnikov was exiled to Kazakhstan for three years. Both *Baptist* and *Baptist Ukrainy* folded. As a result of the arrest of their leaders, all the regional Baptist unions collapsed. Because financial support for the federal union was collected through these local associations, by December 1929 the Baptist Union was forced to suspend its activity. In May 1930, the building where the union headquarters, the Bible courses, and housing for the union's employees were located was seized. Similarly, the Evangelical Christian Union in Leningrad was hit by arrests, and its journal, *Khristianin*, was closed. Its leader, Prokhanov, had not been allowed to return from a trip to the Baptist World Alliance Congress in Toronto in 1928. In early 1930, the union's national council formally ceased its work.[95]

A mystery remains about the Baptist response to this repression, and about the exchange of methods between religion and revolution in particular. In October 1929, the central council of the League of the (now) Militant Godless distributed a secret circular letter "to individual comrades." The letter purported to reprint an appeal from "the circle of active brothers and sisters of the Council of Baptist Congregations," a group previously unheard of. The circle called for spiritual fortitude in the face of the "great persecution" that Satan had unleashed on the children of God. More specifically it argued that Baptists needed to fight Bolsheviks with Bolshevik methods: "in order to beat the enemy," it stated, "we need to master his weapon, study his approaches, tactics, methodology. We, preachers of the Gospel in the conditions of the current moment, should occupy ourselves with serious and thorough study of the godless press and literature."[96] In militant language the group emphasized Jesus's proletarian origins and his Communist ideas and gave extensive guidance on how to engage the godless in debate over religious questions and emerge triumphant. The letter concluded by saying that the "theses" of the "methodological council" on the topics of Marxism and Christianity, religion and science, religion and class war, and religion and the peasantry were enclosed.

It is possible, of course, that a group of militants, speaking the language of strife, had emerged among the Baptists in the crisis of 1929. More likely, however, this letter was a hoax, designed to galvanize the ranks of the League of the Godless by proving the argument that Baptists were copying Bolshevik methods for counterrevolutionary purposes. Despite the use of religious imagery and forms of address ("brothers and sisters"), its militant, and often social-scientific ("methodological") tone and its format bear no resemblance to any other Baptist Union circular preserved in the union's archives. And although Iurii Grachev wrote in his memoirs that he was advised, as a young man in Samara, to read *Bezbozhnik*, he recalled this as a way of keeping up with news of the suffering of fellow believers rather than as a source of ideas.[97] Moreover, despite Godless officials in the Kuban area having been chastised by the League's central council in late October 1929 for distributing the letter widely to its activists rather than keeping it top secret, by late 1929 it was receiving extensive coverage in the League's newspaper, *Bezbozhnik*.[98] A 1931 book on sectarianism in the Ivanovo region also quoted the letter as the source of a Baptist strategy of copying Communist methods.[99]

Ironically, then, the antireligious activists of the Bolshevik regime focused their attention on the very same evidence of organizational prowess as had the Orthodox missionaries of the ancien régime. For both, evangelical activism provided a means of discussing the relationship between regime and people, the need to generate voluntary activism, and the question of acceptable limits of social autonomy. However, the conditions in which this organizing took place changed significantly. On the whole, contrary to Bolshevik assertions, evangelical communities were mostly building on prerevolutionary practices in the 1920s rather than specifically copying Communist ones. Baptist techniques clearly did not remain unaffected by Bolshevik organizing. But those new forms of organization that most resembled the Communist forms did so because the sectarians had been invited by the regime to do just that. What was really new was the big difference between the mobilizing Soviet regime and the more passive attitude of the tsars toward their subjects. As *The Friend of Russia* pointed out in 1924, this diverse approach meant that, whereas before 1917 the government had looked upon the Baptists as revolutionaries, Russia's new rulers saw them as counterrevolutionaries.[100]

Baptist and Evangelical Christian organizing did not receive much secular press attention until the mid-1920s. However, as the party began to try in earnest to spark public activism in support of the Bolshevik regime, the only legal competitors to the party's own mass organizations reared their heads. Through police pressure, arrests, and surveillance, the Soviet regime guaranteed that there would be no institutionally established nationwide religious youth leagues after the early 1920s and ensured that the Baptists' and Evangelical Christians' central unions would enforce military service and loyalty to Soviet power among their members. But in their anxiety about the implications of NEP for mass culture, they created a Bapsomol in the image of their own Komsomol as a means of discussing the relationship between party and people. Meanwhile, the evangelicals continued, with apparent success, to maintain youth and other organizations on the local level and to support a staff of evangelists to link them and to assist in forming new groups. When the Bolsheviks lost patience with the slow rate of social transformation, however, it was this associational life that became the target of their efforts to legislate an end to religious practice in Russia.

Afterword

The April 1929 law on religious associations sharply curtailed religious activity and began to push it underground. In the months after it was promulgated, more than one hundred local Baptist preachers and national leaders were arrested and many of them imprisoned or exiled. Congregations all over the Soviet Union lost their meeting places. For example, in Ukraine, where the Ukrainian Baptist Union alone had claimed approximately one thousand congregations with sixty thousand members in 1926, fewer than ten local churches still enjoyed official sanction in 1931.[1] The faithful resumed their pre-1905 practice of meeting in members' homes. Many ordinary believers found themselves in dire economic straits after being denied voting rights and trade union membership on the grounds that their preaching at meetings classified them as clergy.[2]

In the winter of 1929–30, both the Baptist Union and the Evangelical Christian Unions were forced to close their doors. A few months later a central Baptist council was reconstituted under the leadership of Nikolai V. Odintsov, the former president of the Federal Union of Baptists; at the insistence of the OGPU, two local missionaries, Ivan I. Bondarenko and Vasilii I. Kolesnikov, joined the new board. They would assist in Odintsov's arrest in 1933. Thereafter the elderly past president of the union, Il'ia A. Goliaev, took over the leadership of that small and ineffectual board until he left Moscow in early 1935, apparently fearing detention. The Baptist Union remained in the hands of the OGPU's men, Bondarenko and Kolesnikov. When they themselves were arrested in March 1935, the last remnant of the Baptist Union collapsed. Meanwhile, Ivan Prokhanov never returned to the USSR. His followers succeeded in resurrecting the Evangelical Christian Union in mid-1931. Although most of its member churches had closed, the committee survived throughout the 1930s.[3]

Like many other denominations, the Evangelical Christians and Baptists benefited from the easing of antireligious measures during World War II. In 1944, surviving leaders from both camps united to form an All-Union Council of Evangelical Christians-Baptists. In the 1960s and 1970s, the evangelicals would again play a significant role in challenging Soviet government-sponsored society and values. They did this through their daily existence but also in the context of the developing dissident movement. For example, the Council of Prisoners' Relatives, one of the first human rights groups in the USSR, was set up in 1964 by Baptist women whose husbands were incarcerated in labor camps.[4] Since the collapse of the Soviet Union in 1991, evangelical Christianity has flowered, although it once again faces problems of national and social definition that echo its members' experiences in the early twentieth century.[5]

Just as their descendants would discover in the Brezhnev era, so evangelicals in the first three decades of the twentieth century found that their private spiritual experiences forced them willy-nilly into a public challenge to the political and cultural structures of their society. New religious identities were partly the product of new social identities and the greater civic space that came with socioeconomic change in the late imperial and early Soviet periods. Evangelical ideas served at once to help believers to make sense of the cultural dislocations arising from rapid modernization and to articulate a place for themselves in the emerging society. As it did for other members of the lower and lower-middle classes, rapid change made these people increasingly self-aware and shook up traditional social patterns. When believers told one another and potential new converts about their spiritual experiences, they were advancing Baptist ideas about salvation as the answer to the problems of hierarchy, social and economic inequality, and cultural dislocation that Russian society faced.

The story of the Russian Baptists and Evangelical Christians between 1905 and 1929 illuminates the way in which groups that shared cultural rather than class identities could play an important role in the emergence of the public sphere. This process has traditionally been associated with the rise of bourgeois, class society; more recent work has begun to demonstrate that associational life among the lower classes also contributed to expanding civic space in Russia and elsewhere. Conversion to the Baptist faith served as motivation for demanding and living out an alternate vision of society to that sponsored by the Russian state. Evangelicals' experience of religious communities based on voluntary membership, democratic organization, and intellectual egalitarianism led them to envision a social and political space where people could live and make choices according to their individual convictions. Eager to spread their message, the Baptists and Evangelical Christians asserted the idea of a market in religious ideas through a network of itinerant missionaries and an active associational life. Evangelists took a religious message out of church buildings to the new sites of their society, from trains and steamships to the factory floor and the village bazaar.

Russian evangelicals pushed open the boundaries of the public sphere not merely through such activities but also by exciting public debate about the nature and legitimacy of their faith and practice. The political and social changes of the era raised an array of questions about the nature of Russian nationality, as well as the relationship between Orthodoxy and Russian identity and between Orthodoxy and the Russian state. When Russians accepted the Baptist faith, they became symbols of the penetration of Western ideas beyond the social elites of Russia. Similarly, from bureaucrat to priest, liberal *intelligent*, or revolutionary, outside observers agreed with the gendarme's evaluation that the Baptist movement was "a serious school of social activism." The Baptists came to symbolize the increasingly spirited attempts of lower-class Russians to lend their voices to the shaping of a new society. As educated society discussed the phenomenon of Russian evangelicalism, it was grappling with the problems of dissent, of order and disorder, of modernization and Westernization, and of national and social identity in their society.

The theme of competing visions of radical religion and radical politics runs through the evangelicals' lives. Outside observers puzzled over whether evangelical religion implied an affinity with revolutionary politics or, rather, flight from the turbulent political and socioeconomic change of their day—a "chiliasm of despair," to borrow E. P. Thompson's famous interpretation of Methodism in early industrial England.[6] Baptists and Evangelical Christians agonized over these questions themselves, especially in the excited atmosphere of 1917. In their conversion narratives and in their journals the Baptists and Evangelical Christians asserted that their spiritual solution provided the true answer to the problems revolutionaries aimed to resolve through political confrontation. Evangelicalism was not simply a refuge from modern life, nor was it political radicalism in religious guise. But it was also not a purely religious form of radicalism, untouched by and uninterested in the political questions of its day. Despite a fundamental ambivalence about politics as a worldly practice, persecution of their prized religious faith engaged believers' interest in plans to transform life on this earth. Through the notion of the revolution of the spirit, the evangelicals set out to compete with socialist politics by presenting a spiritual path to a shared utopia of social and economic egalitarianism. This concept would later serve as the basis for Baptist efforts to assert a place for alternative visions of socialism in the new Soviet state.

The first decade of Soviet power is often imagined as a golden age for religious dissidents. Certainly, despite the Bolsheviks' attack on religious institutions, especially on the property of the Orthodox Church, and on religious beliefs in general, the revolutionary period was also one of opportunity for some religious groups. Like other sectarians, the Baptists benefited from certain important government concessions, including the 1919 decree granting exemption from military service to religious conscientious objectors and the October 1921 appeal to Old Believers and sectarians to establish agricultural communes in the war-ravaged countryside. Baptists responded enthusiastically to these possibilities, emphasizing to the government their willingness to build a socialist society, albeit on their own Christian terms. At the same time they also applied their missionary prowess to making full use of the freedom of religious propaganda guaranteed in the Soviet constitution of 1918. Under Soviet power, both streams of the movement, the Baptists and the Evangelical Christians, experienced rapid numerical growth and tremendous institutional development. By all accounts, the ranks of evangelicals grew rapidly in the 1920s, reaching perhaps half a million. However, the Soviet government soon became very anxious about the vibrant associational life evangelicals offered in competition with the Bolsheviks' own state-sponsored public organizations. Ironically the parallels between religious and Bolshevik paths to socialism soon found new expression in a Bolshevik campaign against a dangerous, alternative society of evangelical organizations that were parallel to, but resisted integration into, the new socialist society.

The experience of individual evangelicals and their movement thus illuminates how popular religious ideas, and ideas about popular religion, were implicated in discussions about the nature of the Russian or Soviet bodies politic and the Russian or Soviet states. Through their very existence and the voluntarist principles of their communities, the Russian Baptists challenged the ascriptive quality of prerevolutionary Orthodoxy and the increasingly ascriptive culture of class in Soviet Russia. In their private and public lives, believers' personal religious experience forced them into daily testing of the limits of cultural and political pluralism in Russia.

GLOSSARY AND ABBREVIATIONS

desiatina	land measure equivalent to 2.7 acres
pud	measure of weight equivalent to 16.38 kg or 36 lb.
uezd	local district
versta	measure of distance equivalent to 3500 feet or approximately one kilometer
zemstvo	local elected administrative body
PSZ	*Polnoe sobranie zakonov Rossiiskoi Imperii*
RGASPI	Rossiisskii gosudarstvennyi arkhiv sotsial'no-politicheskoi istorii, Moscow
GARF	Gosudarstvennyi arkhiv Rossiiskoi federatsii, Moscow
RGAE	Rossiiskii gosudarstvennyi arkhiv ekonomiki, Moscow
OR RGB	Otdel rukopisei Rossiiskoi gosudarstvennoi biblioteki, Moscow
RGA KFD	Rossiiskii gosudarstvennyi arkhiv kino-foto dokumentov, Moscow
GMIR	Gosudarstvennyi muzei istorii religii, St. Petersburg
RGIA	Rossiiskii gosudarstvennyi istoricheskii arkhiv, St. Petersburg
TsGA g. SPb	Tsentral'nyi gosudarstvennyi arkhiv goroda Sankt-peterburga, St. Petersburg
DP/OO	Departament politsii, obshchii otdel (Department of Police, General Division)
WKP	working papers (of the Smolensk archive)
GPU	State Political Administration (political police) (later United State Political Administration)

Archival notation follows the accepted Russian form of abbreviation:

f.	*fond* (collection)
op.	*opis'* (inventory)
g.	*god* (year)
otd.	*otdelenie* (division)
st.	*stol* (department)
koll.	*kollektsiia* (collection)
k.	*korobka* (box)
t.	*tom* (volume)
vyp.	*vypusk* (installment)
ch.	*chast'* (part)
d.	*delo* (file)
l., ll.	*list, listy* (page, pages)
ob.	*oborot* (verso)

NOTES

INTRODUCTION

1. Marat S. Shterin and James T. Richardson, "Local Laws Restricting Religion in Russia," *Journal of Church and State* 40, no. 2 (spring 1998): 332–33. *Baptisty kak naibolee zlovrednaia sekta* (Moscow: Pod'bor'e russkogo na Afone Sviato-Panteleimonova monastyria v g. Moskve, 1995). See also Alexander Agadjanian, "Revising Pandora's Gifts," *Europe-Asia Studies* 53, no. 3 (2001): 473–88.

2. A. Iu. Polunov, *Pod vlast'iu ober-prokurora* (Moscow: "AIRO-XX," 1996), 72–73, 97. V. I. Iasevich-Borodaevskaia, *Bor'ba za vieru* (St. Petersburg: Gosudarstvennaia tipografiia, 1912), 19–20. Cathy A. Frierson, *Peasant Icons* (New York: Oxford University Press, 1993), 9; Bernice Glatzer Rosenthal and Martha Bohachevsky-Chomiak, eds., *A Revolution of the Spirit* (New York: Fordham University Press, 1990), vii.

3. For a similar situation in Mexico, see Kurt Bowen, *Evangelism and Apostasy* (Montreal and Kingston: McGill-Queen's University Press, 1996), 183, 191.

4. Stephen P. Frank and Mark D. Steinberg, eds., *Cultures in Flux* (Princeton, N.J.: Princeton University Press, 1994), 3. On the relationship between *sosloviia* and identity, see Gregory L. Freeze, "The Soslovie (Estate) Paradigm and Russian Social History," *American Historical Review* 91, no. 1 (1986): 11–36.

5. For example, Carla Gardina Pestana, *Quakers and Baptists in Colonial Massachusetts* (Cambridge: Cambridge University Press, 1991), 21.

6. For example, Edith W. Clowes, Samuel D. Kassow, and James L. West, eds., *Between Tsar and People* (Princeton, N.J.: Princeton University Press, 1991); Frank and Steinberg, *Cultures in Flux;* Leopold H. Haimson, "The Problem of Social Identities in Early Twentieth Century Russia," *Slavic Review* 47, no. 1 (spring 1988): 1–21; Victoria E. Bonnell, *Roots of Rebellion* (Berkeley: University of California Press, 1983); Mark D. Steinberg, *Moral Communities* (Berkeley: University of California Press, 1992).

7. Clowes, Kassow, and West, *Between Tsar and People,* 6. See also Joseph Bradley, "Subjects into Citizens," *American Historical Review* 107, no. 4 (October 2002): 1094–1123.

8. Nancy Bermeo and Philip Nord, eds., *Civil Society before Democracy* (Lanham, Md.: Rowman and Littlefield, 2000), xiii–xiv. Bermeo and Nord point out that, paradoxically, active civil society has not always translated into democratic political systems; see xvi, xxiii–xxvii.

9. See, for example, Clowes, Kassow, and West, *Between Tsar and People;* Haimson, "Problem of Social Identities."

10. For example, Craig Calhoun, ed., *Habermas and the Public Sphere* (Cambridge, Mass.: MIT Press, 1992); Willfried Spohn, "Religion and Working-Class Formation

in Imperial Germany, 1871–1914," in *Society, Culture, and the State in Germany, 1870–1930,* ed. Geoff Eley, 163–87 (Ann Arbor: University of Michigan Press, 1996),

11. Lewis H. Siegelbaum, *Soviet State and Society between Revolutions* (New York: Cambridge University Press, 1992), 4, 84, 136, 163, 165; Richard Stites, *Revolutionary Dreams* (New York: Oxford University Press, 1989), 121, 225.

12. On Russification, see Geoffrey A. Hosking, *Russia* (Cambridge, Mass.: Harvard University Press, 1997), 319, 367–68. On class and citizenship in early Soviet Russia, see Elise Kimerling, "Civil Rights and Social Policy in Soviet Russia, 1918–1936," *Russian Review* 41 (January 1982): 24–46.

13. Gauri Viswanathan, *Outside the Fold* (Princeton, N.J.: Princeton University Press, 1998), 16.

14. S. A. Smith, "Citizenship and the Russian Nation during World War I," *Slavic Review* 59, no. 2 (summer 2000): 325.

15. Stites, *Revolutionary Dreams,* 115–23; and Igal Halfin, *From Darkness to Light* (Pittsburgh: University of Pittsburgh Press, 2000).

16. For example, Nadieszda Kizenko, *A Prodigal Saint* (University Park: Pennsylvania State University Press, 2000); William Edgerton, trans. and ed., *Memoirs of Peasant Tolstoyans in Soviet Russia* (Bloomington: Indiana University Press, 1993); Mark D. Steinberg, "Workers on the Cross," *Russian Review* 53 (April 1994): 213–39; Kimberly Page Herrlinger, "Class, Piety, and Politics" (Ph.D. dissertation, University of California, Berkeley, 1996).

17. Prominent studies include John Shelton Curtiss, *Church and State in Russia* (New York: Columbia University Press, 1940); idem, *The Russian Church and the Soviet State, 1917–1950* (Boston: Little, Brown, 1953); Dimitry Pospielovsky, *The Russian Church under the Soviet Regime, 1917–1982* (Crestwood, N.Y.: St. Vladimir's Seminary Press, 1984); and Gregory Freeze, *The Parish Clergy in Nineteenth-Century Russia* (Princeton, N.J.: Princeton University Press, 1983), a social history of the institution of the Orthodox Church. The flood of recent Russian work on religion has, not surprisingly, dealt overwhelmingly with the problem of church-state relations; for example, Polunov, *Pod vlast'iu;* M. I. Odintsov, *Gosudarstvo i tserkov'* (Moscow: Znanie, 1991).

18. For example, Chris J. Chulos, "Peasant Religion in Post-Emancipation Russia" (Ph.D. dissertation, University of Chicago, 1994); Laura Engelstein, *Castration and the Heavenly Kingdom* (Ithaca, N.Y.: Cornell University Press, 1999); Gregory Freeze, "Counter-reformation in Russian Orthodoxy," *Slavic Review* 54 (summer 1995): 305–39; idem, "Subversive Piety," *Journal of Modern History* 68 (June 1996): 308–50; Kizenko, *A Prodigal Saint;* Roy R. Robson, *Old Believers in Modern Russia* (DeKalb: Northern Illinois University Press, 1995); Edward E. Roslof, *Red Priests* (Bloomington: Indiana University Press, 2002); Vera Shevzov, "Popular Orthodoxy in Late Imperial Rural Russia" (Ph.D. dissertation, Yale University, 1994); Christine D. Worobec, *Possessed* (DeKalb: Northern Illinois University Press, 2001); Glennys Young, *Power and the Sacred in Revolutionary Russia* (University Park: Pennsylvania State University Press, 1997).

19. Natalie Zemon Davis, "From 'Popular Religion' to Religious Cultures," in *Reformation Europe,* ed. Steven Ozment, 321–41 (St. Louis: Center for Reformation Research, 1982); idem, "Some Tasks and Themes in the Study of Popular Religion," in *The Pursuit of Holiness in Late Medieval and Renaissance Religion,* ed. Charles Trinkaus, with Heiko A. Oberman, 307–36 (Leiden: Brill, 1974); and Lynn Hunt, ed., *The New Cultural History* (Berkeley: University of California Press, 1989). This historiography

is discussed in Caroline Ford, "Religion and Popular Culture in Modern Europe," *Journal of Modern History* 65 (March 1993): 152–75. On popular movements and the nature of power, see James C. Scott, *Domination and the Arts of Resistance* (New Haven: Yale University Press, 1990). See also the definition of culture in Frank and Steinberg, *Cultures in Flux,* 7.

20. Hugh McLeod, *Secularisation in Western Europe, 1848–1914* (New York: St. Martin's, 2000), 28.

21. *Baptist World Alliance. Second Congress* (Philadelphia, 1911), 235.

22. William Henry Brackney, *The Baptists* (New York: Greenwood, 1988); Peder A. Eidberg, "Baptist Developments in the Nordic Countries during the Twentieth Century," *Baptist History and Heritage* (winter–spring 2001): 136–52; Sebastien Fath, "Another Way of Being a Christian in France," *Baptist History and Heritage* (winter–spring 2001): 153–73; idem, "L'Etat face aux enjeux 'autorité-pouvoir' chez les baptistes," *Social Compass* 48, no. 1 (2001): 51–61; F. Townley Lord, *Baptist World Fellowship* (Nashville: Broadman, 1955); Robert G. Torbet, *A History of the Baptists,* 3rd ed. (Valley Forge: Judson, 1963); William L. Wagner, *New Move Forward in Europe* (South Pasadena, Calif.: William Carey Library, 1978). Surveys written at the time remain important sources: Rev. Chas. T. Byford, *Peasants and Prophets,* 2nd ed. (London: Kingsgate, 1912); and J. H. Rushbrooke, *Some Chapters of European Baptist History* (London: Kingsgate, 1929).

23. The exceptions are Edmund Heier, *Religious Schism in the Russian Aristocracy* (The Hague: Martinus Nijhoff, 1970); and Walter Sawatsky, *Soviet Evangelicals since World War II* (Kitchener, Ont.: Herald Press, 1981). Neither deals with the period under examination here. See also a popular account, based primarily on secondary sources: Michael Rowe, *Russian Resurrection* (London: Marshall Pickering, 1994).

24. A. I. Klibanov, *Istoriia religioznogo sektantstva v Rossii* (Moscow: Izdatel'stvo "Nauka," 1965); idem, *Religioznoe sektantstvo i sovremennost'* (Moscow: Izdatel'stvo "Nauka," 1969); Z. V. Kalinicheva, *Sotsial'naia sushchnost' baptizma* (Leningrad: Izdatel'stvo "Nauka," 1972); G. S. Lialina, *Baptizm: illiuzii i real'nost'* (Moscow: Izdatel'stvo politicheskoi literatury, 1977); L. N. Mitrokhin, *Baptizm,* 2nd ed. (Moscow: Izdatel'stvo politicheskoi literatury, 1974). More recent is a fine candidate's dissertation: Vasilii Viktorovich Sarychev, "Sotsial'no-ekonomicheskie i politicheskie aspekty rasprostraneniia baptizma v Rossii" (Candidate dissertation, Gor'kii, 1989).

25. Andrew Quarles Blane, "The Relations between the Russian Protestant Sects and the State, 1900–1921" (Ph.D. dissertation, Duke University, 1964); Samuel John Nesdoly, "Evangelical Sectarianism in Russia" (Ph.D. dissertation, Queen's University, 1971); and Paul D. Steeves, "The Russian Baptist Union" (Ph.D. dissertation, University of Kansas, 1976). Steeves also provides a useful analysis of the ways in which the beliefs and practices of Russian Baptists paralleled or deviated from those of their co-religionists in England, Germany, and the United States.

26. S. V. Sannikov, *Istoriia baptizma,* Vyp. 1 (Odessa: OBS "Bogomyslie," 1996); S. N. Savinskii, *Istoriia evangel'skikh khristian-baptistov Ukrainy, Rossii, Belorusii (1867–1917)* (St. Petersburg: Bibliia dlia vsekh, 1999).

27. The Baptist collection includes the archives of the Baptist Union and the historical materials that Pavel V. Ivanov-Klyshnikov had been collecting, which were seized when he was arrested in March 1929: Georgii Vins, *Tropoiu vernosti,* 2nd ed. (St. Petersburg: Bibliia dlia vsekh, 1997), 185.

28. Albert W. Wardin Jr., *Evangelical Sectarianism in the Russian Empire and the USSR*

(Lanham, Md.: American Theological Library Association and Scarecrow Press, 1995), xxiii. On the general problem among Baptists everywhere of defining what unites this often fractious denominational family, see Brackney, *The Baptists*, xiii–xxi.

29. 5-i Vseukrainskii S"ezd Khristian Baptistov," *Baptist Ukrainy*, no. 7 (1928): 34.

30. Mikhailo Hrushevs'kyĭ, *Z istoriĭ relihă̆noĭ dumky na Ukraĭni* (Winnipeg: Ukrainian Evangelical Alliance of North America, 1962). On language use, see "Vopros o malorusskom nariechii v otnoshenii k shtundizmu," *Kievskiia eparkhial'nyia viedomosti*, no. 4 (28 January 1881): 1–4.

1. THE DAMNED SHTUNDIST

1. *Prokliatyi shtundist* (Khar'kov: Tipografiia gubernskago pravleniia, 1889). Found in RGIA, f. 1574, op. 2, d. 126, ll. 88–89. Translation from E. B. Lanin, "The Tsar Persecutor," *Contemporary Review* 61 (January 1892): 15; quoted in Lawrence Klippenstein, "Religion and Dissent in the Era of Reform: The Russian Stundobaptists, 1858–1884" (M.A. thesis, University of Minnesota, 1971), 118–19.

2. V. I. Iasevich-Borodaevskaia, *Bor'ba za vieru* (St. Petersburg: Gosudarstvennaia tipografiia, 1912), 560.

3. This overview of the early years of the movement relies on Andrew Blane, "Protestant Sects in Late Imperial Russia," in *The Religious World of Russian Culture*, vol. 2, ed. Andrew Blane (The Hague: Mouton, 1975), 2:267–86; A. I. Klibanov, *Istoriia religioznogo sektantstva v Rossii* (Moscow: Izdatel'stvo "Nauka," 1965), 187–254; V. P., "Pravda o baptistakh," *Baptist*, no. 42 (12 October 1911): 331–33; no. 43 (19 October 1911): 337–38.

4. Albert W. Wardin Jr., "Baptists (German) in Russia and USSR," in *Modern Encyclopedia of Religion in Russia and the Soviet Union*, ed. Paul D. Steeves, Vol. 3 (Gulf Breeze, Fla.: Academic International Press, 1991), 192–93. See also William L. Wagner, *New Move Forward in Europe* (South Pasadena, Calif.: William Casey Library, 1978), 7, 107–9.

5. J. H. Rushbrooke, *The Baptist Movement in the Continent of Europe*, 2nd ed. (London: Carey, 1923), 35–36; Wagner, *New Move Forward*, 15–17, 30–31.

6. Paul D. Steeves, "The Russian Baptist Union, 1917–1935" (Ph.D. dissertation, University of Kansas, 1976), 331–32.

7. William Henry Brackney, *The Baptists* (New York: Greenwood, 1988), xiii–55; Robert G. Torbet, *A History of the Baptists*, 3rd ed. (Valley Forge: Judson, 1963), 17–32, 61; Steeves, "Russian Baptist," 448.

8. Wagner, *New Move Forward*, 197.

9. See V. V. Ivanov's detailed description of the religious atmosphere among Transcaucasian Molokans in the mid-nineteenth century: GMIR, koll. 1, op. 8, d. 516, ll. 1–100b.

10. V. P., "Pravda o baptistakh," *Baptist*, no. 43 (19 October 1911): 337.

11. Blane, "Protestant Sects," 270–71.

12. A. Rozhdestvenskii, *Iuzhno-russkii shtundizm* (St. Petersburg: Tipografiia Departamenta Udelov, 1889), chap. 2.

13. V. P., "Pravda o baptistakh," *Baptist* no. 42 (12 October 1911): 332.

14. A. Voronov, "Shtundizm," *Russkii viestnik* 170 (March 1884): 15–16. Rozhdestvenskii, *Iuzhno-russkii*, 75–78, 174–76.

15. Edmund Heier, *Religious Schism in the Russian Aristocracy* (The Hague: Mari-

nus Nijhoff, 1970), viii, 57–105. Among prominent writers who attended these salons were N. Leskov, F. Dostoevsky, and L. Tolstoy. Leskov wrote a famous study of the movement: Nikolai Leskov, *Schism in High Society*, ed. and trans. James Muckle (Nottingham: Bramcote, 1995).

16. Blane, "Protestant Sects," 276; Heier, *Religious Schism*, 107–24, 145–46; Klibanov, *Istoriia religioznogo sektantstva*, 246; Dmitrii Skvortsov, *Pashkovtsy v tverskoi eparkhii* (Tver': Tipografiia gubernskago pravleniia, 1893), 3, 10, 37.

17. Blane, "Protestant Sects," 279; *Istoriia evangel'skikh khristian-baptistov v SSSR* (Moscow: Izdanie Vsesoiuznogo Soveta Evangel'skikh Khristian-Baptistov, 1989), 98–102; for V. G. Pavlov's memoirs, see Vladimir Bonch-Bruevich, ed., *Materialy k istorii i izucheniiu russkago sektantstva i raskola*, Vyp. 1 (St. Petersburg: Tipografiia B. M. Vol'fa, 1908), 4–5.

18. See the conference protocol in Aleksii (Dorodnitsyn), *Materialy dlia istorii religiozno-ratsionalisticheskago dvizheniia na iugie Rossii* (Kazan': Tsentral'naia tipografiia, 1908), 569–84. Many years later V. G. Pavlov reported that the original protocol was lost but that he had "held it in [his] hands" and could thus attest to the accuracy of the version in Dorodnitsyn's collection (GMIR, koll. 1, op. 8, d. 32, folder 3, l. 1).

19. Ibid., 569. There had been two previous conferences of Germans at which Russians were in attendance, but this was the first Russian-focused meeting.

20. Ibid., 573–75, 584. Wagner, *New Move Forward*, 30.

21. *Istoriia evangel'skikh khristian-baptistov v SSSR*, 128–30. There was no conference between 1891 and 1898, the years of the sharpest persecution of shtundists.

22. Eugene Clay, "The Theological Origins of the Christ-Faith [Khristovshchina]," *Russian History* 15 (1988): 21–22; Nicholas B. Breyfogle, "Heretics and Colonizers" (Ph.D. dissertation, University of Pennsylvania, 1998); Robert P. Geraci and Michael Khodarkovsky, *Of Religion and Empire* (Ithaca, N.Y.: Cornell University Press, 2001).

23. Peter Waldron, "Religious Toleration in Late Imperial Russia," in *Civil Rights in Imperial Russia*, ed. Olga Crisp and Linda Edmondson, 103–5 (Oxford: Clarendon, 1989). See also Geraci and Khodarkovsky, *Of Religion and Empire*, 5, 335–39.

24. Iasevich-Borodaevskaia, *Bor'ba za vieru*, 31–32; Peter Waldron, "Religious Reform after 1905," *Oxford Slavonic Papers*, New series 20 (1987): 114.

25. See text in Vladimir Bonch-Bruevich, ed., *Presliedovanie baptistov evangelicheskoi sekty* (Christchurch: Izdanie "Svobodnago slova," 1902), 68–69.

26. RGIA, f. 1284, op. 221 (1885), d. 74, ll. 3–7.

27. For an excellent survey of the evolution of legislation regarding religious sectarians, used by Witte and the members of the Committee of Ministers in preparing the decree of 17 April 1905, see Iasevich-Borodaevskaia, *Bor'ba za vieru*, 1–108. More generally, see Theodore R. Weeks, *Nation and State in Late Imperial Russia* (DeKalb: Northern Illinois University Press, 1996).

28. Robert F. Byrnes, *Pobedonostsev* (Bloomington: Indiana University Press, 1968), 179–83.

29. J. Eugene Clay, "Orthodox Missionaries and 'Orthodox Heretics' in Russia, 1886–1917," in Geraci and Khodarkovsky, *Of Religion and Empire*, 38–69.

30. Translation quoted in Klippenstein, "Religion and Dissent," 118–19. See also "Zapiski D. A. Khilkova," *Svobodnoe slovo*, no. 1 (1898): 120; and S. Mel'gunov, *Tserkov' i gosudarstvo v Rossii*, Vyp. 2 (Moscow: Izdanie tovarishchestva I. D. Sytina, 1909), 151.

31. The conference minutes were published as an appendix to V. M. Skvortsov,

Dieianiia 3-go Vserossiiskago Missionerskago S"iezda (Kiev: Tipografiia I. I. Chokolova, 1898), 335–50.

32. RGIA, f. 1284, op. 221 (1885), d. 74, ll. 110b.–12.

33. RGIA, f. 821, op. 5, d. 1014, ll. 18–180b.

34. RGIA, f. 821, op. 5, d. 985.

35. Rozhdestvenskii, *Iuzhno-russkii,* 206–08.

36. RGIA, f. 821, op. 5, d. 1014, ll. 18–180b.

37. *Istoriia evangel'skikh khristian-baptistov v SSSR,* 119–21.

38. Bonch-Bruevich, *Presliedovanie,* v–vi, 70–77. See also Iasevich-Borodaevskaia, *Bor'ba za vieru,* 37–108; A. M. Bobrishchev-Pushkin, *Sud i raskol'niki-sektanty* (St. Petersburg: Senatskaia tipografiia, 1902), 139–50, 160; and S. Mel'gunov, "Shtundisty ili baptisty?" *Russkaia mysl'* 24, no. 11 (November 1903): 159–66.

39. Ministry of Justice circular #10677 of 3 April 1900. The similar Ministry of Internal Affairs circular was dated 17 May 1900 (Bonch-Bruevich, *Presliedovanie,* xxv–xxvii).

40. A. S. Prugavin, *Raskol i sektantstvo v russkoi narodnoi zhizni* (Moscow: Tipografiia tovarishchestva I. D. Sytina, 1905), 9. On this debate, see G. P. Camfield, "The Pavlovtsy of Khar'kov Province, 1886–1905," *Slavonic and East European Review* 68, no. 4 (October 1990): esp. 711–12; and Alexander Etkind, "Whirling with the Other: Russian Populism and Religious Sects," *Russian Review* 62, no. 4 (October 2003): 565–88.

41. See the accounts by Social Democrats who encountered shtundists in Kiev: B. Pravdin, "Otnoshenie 'shtundizma' k sotsial'demokratii," *Razsviet,* no. 2 (February 1904): 43–46; Nik. Nilov, "K voprosu o revoliutsionnoi rabotie sredi sektantov. Pis'mo pervoe," *Razsviet,* no. 3 (March 1904): 72–74; P. Raevskii, "Vstriechi i riechi. (Iz vpechatlienii i nabliudenii sotsial'demokrata)," *Razsviet,* no. 4 (April 1904): 110–11; idem, "Sluchainyia vstriechi (Iz nabliudenii sotsial'demokrata)," *Razsviet,* no. 5 (May 1904): 135–36. See also Iu. P. Vylegzhanin, "O rabote sotsial-demokratov sredi religioznykh sektantov (1903–1904 gg.)," *Nauchnye trudy po istorii KPSS,* Vyp. 123 (Kiev: Vishcha shkola, 1983), 55.

42. A. I. Klibanov, "V. D. Bonch-Bruevich i problemy religiozno-obshchestvennykh dvizhenii v Rossii," in Vladimir Bonch-Bruevich, *Izbrannye sochineniia,* Vol. 1, *O religii, religioznom sektantstve i tserkvi* (Moscow: Izdatel'stvo Akademii Nauk SSSR, 1959), 7–21; Institut Marksizma-leninizma pri TsK KPSS, *Vtoroi s"ezd RSDRP. Iiul'–avgust 1903 goda. Protokoly* (Moscow: Gosudarstvennoe izdatel'stvo politicheskoi literatury, 1959), 400–401, 429. See also Glennys J. Young, "Bonch-Bruevich, Vladimir Dmitrievich (1873–1955)," in *Modern Encyclopedia of Religion in Russia and the Soviet Union,* ed. Paul D. Steeves, Vol. 3 (Gulf Breeze, Fla.: Academic International Press, 1991), 149–56.

43. Bobrishchev-Pushkin, *Sud i raskol'niki-sektanty,* 106–14. See also M. I. Odintsov, *Gosudarstvo i tserkov' v Rossii* (Moscow: Rossiiskaia akademiia upravleniia, 1994), 6.

44. James W. Cunningham, *A Vanquished Hope* (Crestwood, N.Y.: St. Vladimir's Seminary Press, 1981), 79–80, 94, 126, 294; John Sheldon Curtiss, *Church and State in Russia* (New York: Columbia University Press, 1940), 227; Waldron, "Religious Toleration in Late Imperial Russia," 109–12; Abraham Ascher, *The Revolution of 1905* (Stanford: Stanford University Press, 1988), chap. 1, 71–72; Hans Rogger, *Russia in the Age of Modernization and Revolution* (London: Longman, 1983), 54–55, 159.

45. PSZ, Sobranie tretie, tom 25. otd. 1, nos. 26125 and 26126.

46. *Tserkovnyia viedomosti,* 2 April 1905, official part, 99.

2. THE ERA OF "OPEN STORM"

1. V. V. Ivanov, "Polozhenie baptistov," *Baptist*, no. 9 (23 February 1911): 69. Note the anxious discussion of this statement in a 1911 government report: RGIA, f. 821, op. 133, d. 289, l. 35.

2. See the booklet "Statisticheskiia sviedieniia o sektantakh (K 1 Ianvaria 1912 g.)," published by the Department of Spiritual Affairs of the Ministry of Internal Affairs: RGIA, f. 1278, op. 5, d. 605, ll. 10–21. The study also reported 47,864 Baptist converts from non-Orthodox faiths (basically, the German Baptists). While it would be unwise to accept these figures as exact, they are similar to estimates made by the Baptists themselves in this period. On the difficulty of interpreting what figures exist, see A. I. Klibanov, *Istoriia religioznogo sektantstva v Rossii* (Moscow: Izdatel'stvo "Nauka," 1965), 224–25, 274–80. Insight into the process of collecting these statistics can be gleaned from RGIA, f. 821, op. 10, d. 263. Russian Baptists at the Second Congress of the Baptist World Alliance in 1911 estimated their numbers at 50,000; see Andrew Blane, "Protestant Sects in Late Imperial Russia," in *The Religious World of Russian Culture: Russia and Orthodoxy*, vol. 2, ed. Andrew Blane, 268–303 (The Hague: Mouton, 1975), 294. The Baptists attempted to collect their own statistics, with limited success, in 1909–10; see V. A. Fetler, *Statistika russkikh evangel'skikh khristian baptistov za 1910 god* (St. Petersburg: Tipografiia poleznoi literatury, 1911). At that time the Baptist Union counted 420 congregations, but only 146 seem to have returned forms sent out by Fetler.

3. On the reformation theme, see A. Ivanov, *Otchet o sobranie* (Novgorod, 1910), 6.

4. Peter L. Berger, *The Sacred Canopy* (New York: Doubleday, 1967). See also Alan D. Gilbert, *Religion and Society in Industrial England* (London: Longman, 1976), 8; David Zaret, "Religion, Science, and Printing in the Public Spheres in Seventeenth-Century England," in *Habermas and the Public Sphere*, ed. Craig Calhoun (Cambridge, Mass.: MIT Press, 1992), 212–35.

5. See Edith W. Clowes, Samuel D. Kassow, and James L. West, eds., *Between Tsar and People* (Princeton, N.J.: Princeton University Press, 1991); Joseph Bradley, "Subjects into Citizens," *American Historical Review* 107, no. 4 (October 2002): 1094–1123; Adele Lindenmeyer, *Poverty Is Not a Vice* (Princeton, N.J.: Princeton University Press, 1996); Victoria E. Bonnell, *Roots of Rebellion* (Berkeley: University of California Press, 1983); Mark D. Steinberg, *Moral Communities* (Berkeley: University of California Press, 1992).

6. *Istoriia evangel'skikh khristian-baptistov v SSSR* (Moscow: Izdanie Vsesoiuznogo Soveta Evangel'skikh Khristian-Baptistov, 1989), 482–83; GMIR, koll. 1, op. 1, d. 84, folder 6, l. 11.

7. GMIR, koll. 1, op. 8, d. 68, ll. 2–3.

8. Protocols are found in GMIR, koll. 1, op. 8, d. 32, folders 5–9.

9. RGIA, f. 1284, op. 222, d. 78, l. 6; *Istoriia evangel'skikh khristian-baptistov v SSSR*, 141–42; *Missionerskoe obozrienie*, pt. 2, no. 10 (July 1905): 291–95. I have been unable to locate a protocol of this meeting. Mazaev also published a souvenir book of photographs of forty-one leading Baptists in honor of the new religious freedom: *12 Dekabria 1904 g. Na pamiat' o svobodie v religioznykh ubiezhdeniiakh. 15 Maia 1905g* (Rostov-on-Don, 1905).

10. RGIA, f. 1574, op. 2, d. 131, ll. 1–20b.; Klibanov, *Istoriia religioznogo sektantstva*, 72, 172–73; Roy R. Robson, *Old Believers in Modern Russia* (DeKalb: Northern Illinois

University Press, 1995), 29. S. P. Mel'gunov, *Iz istorii religiozno-obshchestvennykh dvizhenii v Rossii XIX v.* (Moscow: Zadruga, 1919), 21–30.

11. I. S. Prokhanoff, *In the Cauldron of Russia 1869–1933* (New York: All-Russian Evangelical Christian Union, 1933).

12. Ibid., 137–38.

13. *Bratskii listok* (March 1906): 12.

14. Ibid. (September 1906): 4.

15. Ibid. (February 1907): 4.

16. Ibid. (October 1906): 8.

17. Ibid. (February 1907): 33. Individual congregations and even the individual believer mattered a lot. Every donor to *Khristianin*'s mission fund, even one who sent in 5 kopecks, was named in the journal. For example, see "Pozhertvovaniia v fondy," *Bratskii listok* (October 1906), 16–20.

18. I. S., "Vecheria Khristianskoi liubvi v iunosheskom kruzhkie," *Bratskii listok* (December 1906): 3.

19. Ibid. (May 1907): 7.

20. GMIR, koll. 1, op. 8, d. 14. When asked his occupation in a 1902 questionnaire, Kushnerov, a member of the urban lower middle-class estate (*meshchanin*) of the city of Kiev, wrote that he manufactured boot trees (RGIA, f. 1022, op. 1, d. 14, l. 31; GMIR, f. 14, op. 3, d. 1870); one source suggests he had legal training (*Istoriia evangel'skikh khristian-baptistov v SSSR,* 482). The Baptist Union provided him with limited financial assistance, but later he got in trouble with the Union for leaving his family in penury while he worked on his legal cases (GMIR, koll. 1, op. 8, d. 68, folder 1, ll. 6, 10, 15; koll. 1, op. 8, d. 32, folder 10, l. 2.

21. Aleksandr Vvedenskii, *Dieistvuiushchiia zakonopolozheniia kasatel'no staroobriadtsev i sektantov* (Odessa: Tipografiia Odesskikh Novostei, 1912), 88.

22. "Ot br. Kushnerova," *Bratskii listok* (February 1907): 35–36. On 22 February 1907 the government recognized sectarian and Old Believer marriages (Vvedenskii, *Dieistvuiushchiia,* 44). The law of 1883 allowed registration of Old Believers' births and marriages but only of those who had been registered as Old Believers from birth. See John Sheldon Curtiss, *Church and State in Russia* (New York: Columbia University Press, 1940), 140, 149–50.

23. See PSZ, 1909, sobranie 3, t. XXVI, no. 28424. See also Robson, *Old Believers,* 116.

24. I.S.P., "Vysochaishii Ukaz 17-go oktiabria 1906 g.," *Bratskii listok* (December 1906): 12, 16–22.

25. The evangelical Molokans withdrew from the final petition because they could not agree with the Baptist/Evangelical Christian view that only adults could be baptized and only these baptized adults could be considered church members (GMIR, koll. 1, op. 8, d. 32, folder 11, ll. 9–90b.).

26. GMIR, koll.1, op. 8, d. 32, folder 11, ll. 3–30b.

27. GMIR, koll. 1, op. 8, d. 33, folder 1, ll. 2–50b.

28. Vvedenskii, *Dieistvuiushchiia,* 33, 176; the entire petition is reprinted on pages 176–92.

29. RGIA, f. 821, op. 133, d. 198, l. 79.

30. For a detailed study of the Baptist congregation, see Episkop Aleksii, *Vnutrenniaia organizatsiia obshchin iuzhno-russkikh neobaptistov* (Kazan': Tsentral'naia tipografiia, 1908), 10–13. See also *Otchet obshchago sobraniia chlenov SPB obshchiny evangel'skikh khristian, sostoiavshagosia 15-go avgusta 1908 goda* (n.p., n.d.).

31. V. P., "Pravda o baptistakh," *Baptist* no. 46 (9 November 1911): 361.

32. Note that the Evangelical Christian branch of the movement generally did not regard ordination and the laying on of hands as necessary. The overall structure of congregations was similar, however. Andrew Quarles Blane, "The Relations between the Russian Protestant Sects and the State, 1900–1921" (Ph.D. dissertation, Duke University, 1964), 65.

33. *Bratskii listok* (October 1906): 9.

34. RGIA, f. 821, op. 133, d. 194, l. 59; *Baptist* (19 May 1910): 107.

35. RGIA, f. 1284, op. 185, d. 83 (1908), l. 52; *Bratskii listok* (May 1907): 14. On Timoshenko, see "Konchina D. M. Timoshenko," *Slovo istiny*, no. 27 (February 1914): 323.

36. GMIR, f. 2, op. 16, d. 187, ll. 1–8.

37. RGIA, f. 821, op. 150, d. 449, ll. 2–20b.; f. 821, op. 133, d. 194, ll. 97–98ob.

38. RGIA, f. 821, op. 133, d. 164, ll. 1–6.

39. See, for example, secret police assessments for various areas of the empire in 1913: GARF, f. 102 (DP/OO), op. 1913, d. 85, ll. 6, 15, 380b., 78, 104, 126ob., 128, 1470b., 176, 1790b., 191, 193, 197, 2340b., 248, 2770b., 292, 294ob. Soviet-era analyses concurred: GARF, f. 5407, op. 1, d. 12, ll. 26–27; f. 5407, op. 1, d. 18, l. 9; f. 5407, op. 1, d. 20, l. 46; RTsKhIDNI, f. 89, op. 4, d. 119, l. 9; f. 89, op. 4, d. 119, l. 2; f. 17, op. 60, d. 461, ll. 5–7; f. 12, op. 50, d. 792, ll. 88–89.

40. RGIA, f. 821, op. 133, d. 331, l. 53; GARF, f. 102 (DP/OO), op. 1914, d. 85, ll. 51–510b.; GARF, f. 102 (DP/OO), op. 1913, d. 85, l. 292; RGIA, f. 821, op. 133, d. 194, l. 2490b.

41. V. I. Iasevich-Borodaevskaia, *Bor'ba za vieru* (St. Petersburg: Gosudarstvennaia tipografiia, 1912), 291; RGIA, op. 133, d. 164, l. 3; op. 150, d. 452, l. 2; GARF, f. 102 (DP/OO) (1911) d. 85, l. 11.

42. See, for example, *Baptist* no. 12 (December 1908): 4; RGIA, f. 821, op. 133, d. 194, l. 98; Evangelistka, "Dolzhny li zhenshchiny prorochestvovat'?" *Drug molodezhi*, no. 9 (September 1912): 100–102; and the discussion in *Utrenniaia zvizda* in 1915.

43. N. Tal'nikov, "Sektanty v Peterburgie," *Peterburgskii listok*, 23 February 1906, 2.

44. Sobranie sektantov-baptistov," *Peterburgskii listok*, 2 February 1909. Clipping found in RGIA, f. 821, op. 5, d. 1046, l. 95.

45. RGIA, f. 821, op. 133, d. 164, l. 90b.

46. John Walsh, "Religious Societies: Methodist and Evangelical 1738–1800," in *Voluntary Religion*, ed. W. J. Sheils and Diana Wood (Oxford: Basil Blackwell, 1986), 285.

47. For the case of the Baku youth's philosophical study group in 1905 in the first instance, see *Bratskii listok* (March 1906): 5; for successful efforts to promote activity among youth in Balashov, see *Bratskii listok* (July 1906): 4; (December 1906): 5.

48. RGIA, f. 821, op. 133, d. 168, esp. ll. 16, 38; Aleksandr Kondrashev, "Soobshchenie s khutorov: Fadina i Viechnago Samar. gub.," *Drug molodezhi*, no. 5 (August 1911): 11; S. Petrov, "Vecheria liubvi i vstriecha Novago Goda iunosheskago kruzhka v Blagovieshchenskie na Amurie," *Drug molodezhi*, no. 3 (March 1912): 34–35.

49. *Bratskii listok* (December 1906): 5. See also *Pervyi Vserossiiskii S"iezd Kruzhkov baptistskoi molodezhi, iunoshei i dievits* (Rostov-on-Don: Tipografiia tovarishchestva Pavlova i Slavgorodskago, 1909).

50. This was discussed at the 1911 Baptist Union Congress: RGIA, f. 821, op. 150, d. 452, l. 28.

51. Kratkii Obzor dieiatel'nosti S.P.B.D.K.E.Kh. za tri goda ego sushchestvo-vaniia," *Bratskii listok,* no. 7 (July 1910): 10–12.

52. Timo, "O pervom s"iezdie iunoshei i dievits v g. Moskvie," *Baptist* (October 1908): 12.

53. RGIA, f. 821, op. 133, d. 168, l. 1.

54. Nasha blagoviestnitsa," *Drug molodezhi,* no. 11–12 (December 1911): 23–24.

55. RGIA, f. 821, op. 133, d. 168, l. 24.

56. *Pervyi Vserossiiskii S"iezd,* 41–44.

57. See, for example, RGIA, f. 796, op. 442, d. 2407, l. 118; GARF, f. 102 (DP/OO) (1913), d. 85, l. 220.

58. RGIA, f. 821, op. 133, d. 200, l. 20b.

59. See, for example, "Pozhertvovaniia dlia pogoriel'tsev," *Bratskii listok* (October 1906): 20; "Obrashchenie k dobrym serdtsam" and "Otchet o pozhertvovaniiakh," *Baptist* (December 1908): 38; and "Otchet blagotvoritel'nago zavedeniia obshchiny baptistov v g. Balashove, Sarat. Gub. za 1913-i god," *Drug molodezhi,* no. 1 (January 1914): 11.

60. RGIA, f. 821 op. 133 d. 194, l. 215.

61. *Missionerskoe obozrienie* (January 1905): 508–11; RGIA, f. 796, op. 442, d. 2598, l. 81; RGIA, f. 821, op. 133, d. 195, l. 314; RGIA, f. 821, op. 133, d. 288, ll. 22–23.

62. Nochnoe sobranie v S.-Peterburgie," *Baptist* no. 15 (7 April 1910): 118. RGIA, f. 821, op. 133, d. 249; A. Vvedenskii, *Bor'ba s sektantstvom* (Odessa: Tipografiia Eparkhial'nogo doma, 1914), 50.

63. Examples of encounters on trains include K. Borozdin, *Russkoe religioznoe razno-myslie,* 2nd ed. (St. Petersburg: Izdanie "Prometei," 1907): 164–72; G. M., "Poiezd No. 6," *Baptist* no. 7 (April 1912): 5–8.

64. *Otchet baptistskago missionerskago obshchestva za 1907–1908 god. God pervyi* (Odessa: Tipografiia Aktsionernago Iuzhno-Russkago Obshchestva Pechatnago Diela, 1909), 11.

65. Fedor Prokhorovich Balikhin, *Kratkaia avtobiografiia* (Rostov-on-Don: Tipo-grafiia F. Pavlova, 1908), 3–6.

66. F. Balikhin, "Vody v pustynie," *Baptist,* no. 3 (September 1907): 14–16.

67. F. P. Balikhin, "Organizatsiia tserkvei," *Baptist* (March 1908): 17–18; idem, "Vody v pustynie," 13–14.

68. *Otchet baptistskago missionerskago obshchestva,* 7–11.

69. RGIA, f. 821 op. 133, d. 289, l. 47; d. 288, l. 9; d. 82, ll. 1, 53.

70. *Bratskii listok* (May 1907): 7.

71. GMIR, koll. 1, op. 8, d. 33, folder 3, l. 2.

72. *Bratskii listok* (February 1907): 21.

73. Robert G. Torbet, *A History of the Baptists,* 3rd ed. (Valley Forge, N.Y.: Judson, 1963), 31.

74. William Henry Brackney, *The Baptists* (New York: Greenwood, 1988), xix.

75. Paul Steeves, "The Russian Baptist Union, 1917–1935" (Ph.D. dissertation, University of Kansas, 1976), 60.

76. A. Rozhdestvenskii, *Iuzhno-russkii shtundizm* (St. Petersburg, Tipografiia De-partamenta Udielov, 1889), 2.

77. GMIR, koll. 1, op. 8, d. 32, folder 10, l. 3. It took both believers and the government quite a while to consistently spell "Baptist" properly, and not as "babtisty."

78. Blane, "The Relations," 65.

79. Prokhanoff, *In the Cauldron of Russia;* Steeves, "The Russian Baptist Union, 1917–1935," 46–47.

80. *Istoriia evangel'skikh khristian-baptistov v SSSR,* 151–52; RGIA, f. 821, op. 133, d. 310; f. 797, op. 77 (2 otd., 3 stol) d. 578, ll. 21–320b.

81. GMIR, koll. 1, op. 8, d. 32, folder 10 (1906 congress), l. 10b., folder 18 (1911 congress), ll. 1–4; S. Bondar', *Sovremennoe sostoianie russkago baptizma* (St. Petersburg: M.V.D. Departament Dukhovnykh Diel, 1911), 48; *Otchet baptistskago missionerskago obshchestva,* 3.

82. Torbet, *A History,* 168.

83. F. Townley Lord, *Baptist World Fellowship* (Nashville: Broadman, 1955), 1–29.

84. RGIA, f. 1284, op. 185, d. 49 (1907), l. 36.

3. A COMMUNITY OF CONVERTS

1. "Kak Vy uverovali vo Khrista?" *Baptist Ukrainy,* no. 2 (1928): 55.

2. Applications to Bible school can be found in GMIR, koll. 1, op. 8, d. 35, folder 11, ll. 1–204; GMIR, Koll. 1, op. 8, d. 371, ll. 500–680; GMIR, koll. 1, op. 8, dd. 311, 312. The journals surveyed include *Baptist, Slovo istiny, Khristianin, Drug molodezhi,* and *Baptist Ukrainy.*

3. See, for example, Stephen P. Frank and Mark D. Steinberg, eds., *Cultures in Flux* (Princeton, N.J.: Princeton University Press, 1994); Reginald E. Zelnik, "Russian Bebels: An Introduction to the Memoirs of the Russian Workers Semen Kanatchikov and Matvei Fisher," *Russian Review* 35, no. 3 (July 1976): 249–89; no. 4 (October 1976): 417–47. On social changes, see Jeffrey Burds, *Peasant Dreams and Market Politics* (Pittsburgh: University of Pittsburgh Press, 1998).

4. See, for example, Nadieszda Kizenko, *A Prodigal Saint* (University Park: Pennsylvania State University Press, 2000); Vera Shevzov, "Popular Orthodoxy in Late Imperial Rural Russia" (Ph.D. dissertation, Yale University, 1994); Mark Steinberg, "Workers on the Cross: Religious Imagination in the Writings of Russian Workers, 1910–1924," *Russian Review* 53 (April 1994): 213–39; and Reginald E. Zelnik, "'To the Unaccustomed Eye': Religion and Irreligion in the Experience of St. Petersburg Workers in the 1870s," in *Christianity and the Eastern Slavs,* vol. 2, ed. Robert P. Hughes and Irina Paperno, 49–73 (Berkeley: University of California Press, 1994).

5. Hugh McLeod, introduction to *European Religion in the Age of Great Cities, 1830–1930,* ed. Hugh McLeod, 23–24 (London: Routledge, 1995).

6. William Henry Brackney, *The Baptists* (New York: Greenwood, 1988), xvii, 71; Susan F. Harding, "Convicted by the Holy Spirit: The Rhetoric of Fundamental Baptist Conversion," *American Ethnologist* 4 (February 1987): 167.

7. Mark D. Steinberg, "Worker-Authors and the Cult of the Person," in idem, *Cultures in Flux,* 169–70. I follow the practice of this collection in using the term "lower-class" to describe the majority of Russian Baptist autobiographers, since urban and rural identities seem to have been nebulous for a large proportion of them.

8. Peter A. Dorsey, *Sacred Estrangement* (University Park: Pennsylvania State University Press, 1993), 8; see also Mary Jo Maynes, *Taking the Hard Road* (Chapel Hill: University of North Carolina Press, 1995), 4–5, 190; Sara Maza, "Stories in History," *American Historical Review* 101, no. 5 (December 1996): 1500; and Lewis R. Rambo, *Understanding Religious Conversion* (New Haven: Yale University Press, 1993), 7, 137–38, 158.

9. Vasilii Skaldin, "Ot neviezhestva k istinie," *Slovo istiny,* no. 31 (March 1914): 365–66; no. 32 (April 1914): 361–62; no. 33–34 (April 1914): 397–98; no. 36 (May 1914): 420–21; no. 37 (May 1914): 432–33. Skaldin went on to work as a Baptist missionary, pastor, and, by the 1920s, national activist. His conversion narrative gives no dates, but these can be gleaned from personal information forms he filled out as a delegate to the 1923 and 1926 national Baptist congresses in Moscow. He listed his date of birth as 1873, his ethnicity as Russian, and the date of his conversion as 1902. He also confirmed that he had only primary education, although his excellent handwriting suggests further self-education and that he was capable of writing this account himself (GMIR, koll. 1, op. 8, d. 35, folder 11, l. 192 and d. 371, l. 613).

10. Skaldin, "Ot neviezhestva k istinie," 365–66, 381–83.

11. Among many examples, see GMIR, f. 2, op. 16, d. 155, l. 17; f. 2, op. 16, d. 190, ll. 1–3; F.F.O., "Moe pokaianie i obrashchenie," GMIR, koll. 1, op. 8, d. 311, ll. 115, 24–28, 40–44, 57–70, 74–78; *Khristianin* 1 (June 1906): 59–60; and A. Ovchinnikov, "Ot t'my k svetu," *Khristianin,* no. 5 (1924): 65–66. See also, the collection of conversion stories, N. I. Makarevskii, *Sbornik obrashchenii na evangel'skii put' zhizni* (St. Petersburg: Tipografiia Andersona i Loitsianskago, [1914]), 3–20, 36–42.

12. S. P. Fadiukhin, *Vospominaniia o perezhitom* (St. Petersburg: Bibliia dlia vsekh, 1993), 64. On the vulnerability of migrant peasants' beliefs see Zelnik, "'To the Unaccustomed Eye,'" 54.

13. RGIA, f. 821, op. 133, d. 194, ll. 216ob.–17; see also l. 40.

14. See, for example, G. Burunov, "Svidetel'stvo ob obrashchenii," *Khristianin,* no. 5 (1925): 55; GMIR, koll. 1, op. 8, d. 311, ll. 19–20; koll. 1, op. 8, d. 319, folders for Borovkov, Zabrovskii.

15. GMIR, koll. 1, op. 8, d. 311, l. 76.

16. GMIR, koll. 1, op. 8, d. 311, l. 70.

17. GMIR, koll. 1, op. 8, d. 312, l. 31.

18. GMIR, koll. 1, op. 8, d. 319, k. 1, file on Borovkov. See also GMIR, koll. 1, op. 8, d. 319, file on Zabrovskii; GMIR, koll. 1, op. 8, d. 320, l. 107; and Burunov, "Svidetel'stvo ob obrashchenii."

19. Skaldin, "Ot neviezhestva k istinie," 366.

20. GMIR, Koll. 1, op. 8, d. 311, l. 16.

21. O. P. K-v, "Moe obrashchenie ko Khristu," *Khristianin,* no. 8 (August 1906): 40. Other happy Orthodox childhoods are described in GMIR, koll. 1, op. 8, d. 311, ll. 16, 86, 93–93ob., 131; N. Kupriianov, "Uspokoennyi gospodom posle mytarstv i skitanii," *Baptist* (July 1927): 41; E. O. Kulish, "Na puti istiny," *Baptist Ukrainy* (November 1928): 24.

22. Makarevskii, *Sbornik obrashchenii,* 4–6, 27–28; GMIR, koll. 1, op. 8, d. 311, ll. 310ob., 35, 43, 105.

23. Savl, "Za Khristom," *Baptist Ukrainy* no. 6 (1927): 30–31. In the Acts of the Apostles, Saul, the persecutor of the Christians, underwent a conversion experience on the road to Damascus and became Paul, the great apostle of the early church.

24. GMIR, koll. 1, op. 8, d. 311, ll. 69–70. This portrayal of past religious life as insignificant was not limited to converts from Orthodoxy; see the former Molokan who reported that he was "like a pagan" (Stepan Efimov Suriapin, "Moe obrashchenie," *Baptist,* no. 8 [October 1908]: 18).

25. Rambo, *Understanding Religious Conversion,* 137–38.

26. S.V.N., [untitled], *Khristianin* (October 1906): 41; GMIR, koll. 1, op. 8, d. 311, ll. 1310b., 19.

27. O. P. K-v, "Moe obrashchenie ko Khristu," 40; GMIR, koll. 1, op. 8, d. 311, ll. 16, 43.

28. Among many examples are GMIR, koll. 1, op. 8, d. 311, ll. 70, 770b., 129; and "Pis'mo A. I. Romanenko," *Baptist*, no. 5 (November 1907): 21.

29. I. P. K-v, "Zhizn' i obrashchenie k Gospodu Savvy Lishchishina," *Baptist*, no. 16 (14 April 1910): 124. Other monastic experiences include GMIR, f. 2, op. 16, d. 190, ll. 1–2; letter to the editor in *Baptist* (October 1908): 22; *Khristianin*, no. 11 (1925): 55; *Khristianin*, no. 5 (1926): 17; and *Baptist Ukrainy*, no. 7 (1927): 41. On Father John, see Kizenko, *A Prodigal Saint*.

30. Brenda Meehan, "Popular Piety, Local Initiative, and the Founding of Women's Religious Communities in Russia, 1764–1907," in *Seeking God*, ed. Stephen K. Batalden (DeKalb: Northern Illinois University Press, 1993), 85, 88.

31. Shevzov, "Popular Orthodoxy," 692; see also 607, 658, 674, 701–2.

32. Georgii Chaikin, "Sovremennyia iskaniia v russkom sektantstvie (Opyt sektantskoi ideologii)," *Missionerskoe obozrienie* 18 (May 1913): 35, 38; (November 1913): 395–96. Note that virtually every example of "sectarianism" in this five-part article involved Baptists and Evangelical Christians.

33. F. N. Konovalov recalled that his father, who converted to the Baptists in the 1910s, spent time in prison "for an overt political tendency that he combined with Christ's ideas" (GMIR, koll. 1, op. 8, d. 311, l. 160b.). Other cases of former revolutionary activity include *Gost'*, no. 5 (1911): 78; "Pis'mo br. A. S. Makarenko iz g. Odessy," *Bratskii listok*, no. 6 (June 1910): 3; GMIR, koll. 1, op. 8, d. 339, l. 29.

34. Skaldin, "Ot neviezhestva k istinie," 361–62.

35. Savl, "Za Khristom," 31–32.

36. GMIR, koll. 1, op. 8, d. 319, k. 1, Gavrisheva I. S.

37. RGIA, f. 796, op. 442, d. 2473, l. 15300b.

38. Skaldin, "Ot neviezhestva k istinie," 397.

39. S.N.V., [untitled], *Khristianin* (October 1906): 41.

40. V. I. Sinitsin, "Moe obrashchenie," *Baptist*, no. 2 (February 1925): 22.

41. See also I. Iaitskikh, "Moe obrashchenie ko Khristu," *Khristianin* (March 1906): 64–65; GMIR, koll. 1, op. 8, d. 311, ll. 310b., 34, and 80. This is a crucial theological difference from another marvelous source of religious narrative, letters to John of Kronstadt: Kizenko, *A Prodigal Saint*, chap. 4.

42. Examples include Mariia Kurilenok, "Kak ia prishla k soznatel'noi vere v Boga," *Khristianin*, no. 3 (1924): 22–24; I.O.E., "U odra umiraiushchago," *Baptist*, no. 2 (1908): 25–27; GMIR, koll. 1, op. 8, d. 311, ll. 153–55; A.M. V. and A.S.A., *Obrashchenie na istinnyi put' i vospominaniia baptista G.I.M.* (Omsk: Pravlenie Sibirskago Otdela Soiuza Baptistov, 1919), 6–34. The understanding of conversion as a specific event similarly shaped American Baptist narratives. See Susan Juster, *Disorderly Women* (Ithaca, N.Y.: Cornell University Press, 1994), 4–5, 47–49; and Carla Gardina Pestana, *Quakers and Baptists in Colonial Massachusetts* (Cambridge: Cambridge University Press, 1991), 65, 120. On the importance of theology distinguishing Russian Baptist narratives, see Nicholas B. Breyfogle, "Heretics and Colonizers" (Ph.D. dissertation, University of Pennsylvania, 1998), 22.

43. Krest'ianin S. Ia. O., "Kak ia byl spasen Khristom," *Khristianin* (February 1906): 49–50.

44. Skaldin, "Ot neviezhestva k istinie," 408–9, 420–21; on temporary release from culture, see Harding, "Convicted by the Holy Spirit," 167.

45. See, for example, I. Semenov, "S rodnykh polei (Iz pis'ma)," *Khristianin*, no. 4 (1924): 54.

46. I.P.K-v, "Zhizn' i obrashchenie k Gospodu Savvy Lishchishina," *Baptist*, no. 4 (14 April 1910): 125.

47. Christine Worobec, *Possessed* (DeKalb: Northern Illinois University Press, 2001), 70.

48. Pierre Pascal, *The Religion of the Russian People*, trans. Rowan Williams (London: Mowbrays, 1976), 16–18.

49. Skaldin, "Ot neviezhestva k istinie," 421.

50. GMIR, f. 13, op. 1, d. 202, l. 13. He was not deported. This was fairly common, however. For example, see GMIR, f. 2, op. 16, d. 155.

51. GMIR, koll. 1, op. 8, d. 311, l. 430b., 1050b. See also F.F.G., "Moe obrashchenie," *Khristianin* (September 1906): 41; "Soobshcheniia s mest," *Baptist Ukrainy*, no. 9 (1928): 44–45.

52. See, for example, *Khristianin*, no. 8 (1927): 59–60; *Baptist Ukrainy*, no. 9 (1928): 44–45.

53. Skaldin, "Ot neviezhestva k istinie," 432–33. See also Fadiukhin, *Vospominaniia*, 78–85.

54. GMIR, koll. 1, op. 8, d. 311, ll. 128–1280b.; see also ll. 19–20, 28.

55. "Obrashchenie Vsevoloda Iv. Petrova, opisannoe im samim," *Drug molodezhi*, no. 6 (1914): 66.

56. See, for example, *Baptist*, no. 11 (November 1908): 23; Timo, "Znamenie vremeni," *Slovo istiny*, no. 38 (May 1914): 438. On history writing, see *Baptist Ukrainy*, no. 6 (1928): 44; and *Khristianin*, no. 3 (1927): 64.

57. RGIA, f. 821 op. 133, d. 177, l. 232; d. 288, l. 220b.; f. 796, op. 442, d. 2473, ll. 1510b.–52; RTsKhIDNI, f. 17, op. 60, d. 792, ll. 112–14.

58. GMIR, koll. 1, op. 8, d. 319, k. 1, Zabrovskii, l. 60b.

59. GMIR, koll. 1, op. 8, d. 311, l. 28.

60. RGIA, f. 796, op. 442, d. 2473, ll. 152–1520b.

61. Steinberg, "Worker-Authors," 179.

62. Mark Steinberg, *Moral Communities* (Berkeley: University of California Press, 1992), 243–44.

63. A. Pultstov, "Miriane," *Slovo istiny*, no. 22 (January 1914): 261.

64. Interviews in the St. Petersburg diocese in 1911 found that the "dominating motive" in switching to sectarianism was the "certainty of one's salvation" (RGIA, f. 796, op. 442, d. 2473, l. 151).

65. Laurence R. Iannaccone, "Why Strict Churches Are Strong," *American Journal of Sociology* 99, no. 5 (March 1994): 1181.

66. M. Kudlaeva, "Razskaz o svoem obrashchenii," *Drug molodezhi*, no. 7 (July 1912): 76; GMIR, koll. 1, op. 8, d. 320, l. 2050b.

67. Damar' II, "Spasli drug druga," *Drug molodezhi*, no. 3 (Mar 1912): 33.

68. Minaeva, "Razskaz o svoem obrashchenii," *Drug molodezhi*, no. 8 (August 1913): 91–94; no. 9–10 (September 1913): 103–5; A. M-na, "Iz pisem," *Drug molodezhi*, no. 3 (March 1914): 34.

69. Ralph Gibson makes this point in his study of the life paths of French nuns ("Female Religious Orders in Nineteenth-Century France," in *Catholicism in Britain*

and France since 1789, ed. Frank Tallett and Nicholas Atkin [London: Hambledon, 1996], 106).

70. The classic characterization of the "church" and "sect" types of religious organizations is found in Ernst Troeltsch, *The Social Teaching of the Christian Churches,* vol. 1, trans. Olive Wyon (Chicago: University of Chicago Press, 1981), 331–41. On reading trends, see Jeffrey Brooks, *When Russia Learned to Read* (Princeton, N.J.: Princeton University Press, 1985), 22–27. An example of tales of healing in the Orthodox press includes: "Chudesa po molitvam k Sviatiteliu Feodosiiu Uglitskomu," *Pribavlenie k Chernigovskim eparkhial'nym izvestiiam* 36, no. 3 (1 February 1896): 91–127. I thank Christine Worobec for drawing my attention to this and other such accounts.

71. David Martin, *Tongues of Fire* (Oxford: Blackwell, 1990), 186. See also Judith Pellmann, "A Different Road to God: The Protestant Experience of Conversion in the Sixteenth Century," in *Conversion to Modernities,* ed. Peter Van der Veer (New York: Routledge, 1996), 52–57; and David Vincent, *Bread, Knowledge, and Freedom* (London: Europa, 1981), 16.

72. See "Chudesa po molitvam"; Kizenko, *A Prodigal Saint,* chap. 4.

73. Igal Halfin, "From Darkness to Light: Student Communist Autobiography during NEP, " *Jahrbücher für Geschichte Osteuropas* 45, no. 2 (1997): 210–36; Sheila Fitzpatrick, "Lives under Fire: Autobiographical Narratives and their Challenges in Stalin's Russia," in *De Russie et d'ailleurs,* ed. Martine Godet (Paris: Institut d'études slaves, 1995), 225–26.

74. Steinberg, "Worker-Authors," 170.

4. THE BAPTIST CHALLENGE

1. Geoffrey A. Hosking, *The Russian Constitutional Experiment* (Cambridge: Cambridge University Press, 1973), 41–45; Victoria E. Bonnell, *Roots of Rebellion* (Berkeley: University of California Press, 1983), 303–4, 319.

2. RGIA, f. 821, op. 10, d. 73.

3. Alfred Levin, "Toward the End of the Old Regime: The State, Church, and Duma," in *Religion and Modernization in the Soviet Union,* ed. Dennis J. Dunn (Boulder, Colo.: Westview, 1977), 38. The committee's deliberations are found in RGIA, f. 1278, op. 1, d. 806 (2 sozyv).

4. Levin, "Toward the End of the Old Regime," 30, 26.

5. RGIA, f. 821, op. 10, d. 602, ll. 40b., 77; f. 821, op. 133, d. 196, ll. 187–88.

6. *Bratskii listok* (March 1909): 5–10.

7. RGIA, f. 821, op. 133, d. 177, l. 3020b.

8. See, for example, "Vazhnoe ministerskoe raz"iasnenie," *Baptist,* no. 11 (November 1908): 39; "Brat'ia! Pomogaite osushchestvleniiu religioznoi svobody," *Bratskii listok* (July 1909): 13; "Ministerstvo Vnutrennykh Del i vieroispoviednyi vopros," *Baptist,* no. 15 (1910): 116.

9. Circulars of 18 March 1908, 29 October 1908, 10 December 1909, 23 December 1909. RGIA, f. 821, op. 133, d. 1.

10. Andrew Quarles Blane, "The Relations between the Russian Protestant Sects and the State, 1900–1921" (Ph.D. dissertation, Duke University, 1964), 74–77.

11. RGIA, f. 821, op. 133, d. 1, ll. 64–640b. A circular of 12 July 1910 clarified that these rules applied only to sectarian groups, not Old Believers. See l. 70. Note

that this accusation of foreign domination at congresses is completely unfounded, as far as the Baptists and Evangelical Christians were concerned.

12. RGIA, f. 821, op. 133, d. 1, ll. 71–730b.

13. RGIA, f. 821, op. 133, d. 1, ll. 57 (12 January 1909), 59 (9 October 1909), 85 (17 April 1912), 97 (24 July 1912); d. 196, l. 207 (April 1911). For St. Petersburg, see RGIA, f. 821, op. 133, dd. 164, 177, ll. 125–33, 229–320b.

14. RGIA, f. 821, op. 133, d. 1, ll. 92–93. Circular of 14 May 1912. The Department's large file on open-air sectarian meetings between 1910 and 1914 included one Adventist case; all the rest were public baptisms by evangelicals (RGIA, f. 821, op. 133, d. 254).

15. Vera Shevzov similarly comments that the only interest government officials had in peasant Orthodoxy was as a gauge of political loyalty ("Popular Orthodoxy in Late Imperial Rural Russia" [PhD. dissertation, Yale University, 1994],19).

16. Ernst Troeltsch, *The Social Teaching of the Christian Churches,* trans. Olive Wyon, 2 vols. (Chicago: University of Chicago Press, 1981), 2:331. On the confessional system of the Russian Empire, see M. M. Persits, *Otdelenie tserkvi ot gosudarstva i shkoly ot tserkvi v SSSR* (Moscow: Izdatel'stvo Akademii Nauk SSSR, 1958), 15–26.

17. RGIA, f. 821 op. 133, d. 196, ll. 2070b.–208.

18. RGIA, f. 821, op. 133, d. 196, ll. 1880b., 1900b.

19. Deryck W. Lovegrove, *Established Church, Sectarian People* (Cambridge: Cambridge University Press, 1988), 5.

20. See, for example, RGIA, f. 821, op. 133, d. 289, l. 41.

21. S. D. Bondar', *Sovremennoe sostoianie russkago baptizma* (St. Petersburg: M.V.D. Departament Dukhovnykh Diel, 1911), 65.

22. RGIA, f. 821, op. 133, d. 195, l. 212. Clipping from *Volga,* 2 June 1915.

23. GARF, f. 102 (DP/OO), op. 1913, d. 85, l. 243.

24. GARF, f. 102 (DP/OO), op. 1911, d. 85, l. 15.

25. See, for example, GARF, f. 102 (DP/OO), op. 1913, d. 85, l. 94; RGIA, f. 821, op. 133, d. 289, l. 28.

26. RGIA, f. 821, op. 133, dd. 200, 288, 289.

27. RGIA, f. 821, op. 133, d. 1, ll. 83–830b.

28. GARF, f. 102 (DP/OO), op. 1913, d. 85, ll. 28–280b., 32.

29. GARF, f. 102 (DP/OO), op. 1913, d. 85, ll. 136, 233–380b.

30. GARF, f. 102 (DP/OO), op. 1913, d. 85, ll. 1000b., 221, 292.

31. GARF, f. 102 (DP/OO), op. 1914, d. 85, ll. 25–260b.

32. See *Tserkovnyia viedomosti,* 2 April 1905, official part, 99.

33. James W. Cunningham, *A Vanquished Hope* (Crestwood, N.Y.: St. Vladimir's Seminary Press, 1981).

34. Ibid., 94. See also Peter Waldron, "Religious Toleration in Late Imperial Russia," in *Civil Rights in Imperial Russia,* ed. Olga Crisp and Linda Edmondson (Oxford: Clarendon, 1989), 109–12; and V. Skvortsov, "So skrizhalei serdtsa," *Missionerskoe obozrienie* (December 1906): 576.

35. RGIA, f. 796, op. 442, d. 2127, l. 1300b.

36. V. Skvortsov, "Nedavnee-proshloe i nastoiashchee pravoslavnoi missii: Skazano na otkrytii pervago sibirskago obshche-missionerskago s"iezda," *Missionerskoe obozrienie* (October 1910): 1735.

37. S. L., "Missionerstvo i raskolosektantstvo," *Missionerskoe obozrienie,* no. 7 (May 1905): 1197–1202.

38. A. Platonov, "Molokanstvo, baptizm i nasha velikaia tserkovnaia nuzhda (Po povodu pervago vserossiiskago s"iezda molokan)," *Missionerskoe obozrienie*, no. 13 (September 1905): 493.

39. Arkhiepiskop Dimitrii Koval'nitskii, "Sovremennyia zadachi vnutrennei missii," *Missionerskoe obozrienie* (January 1906): 1–5.

40. See, for example, Vladimir Bonch-Bruevich, ed., *Presliedovanie baptistov evangelicheskoi sekty* (Christchurch: Svobodnoe slovo, 1902), xii–xxv, 46–50.

41. See, for example, Pravoslavnyi balashovets, "Sektantskii molitvennyi dom v Balashovie i baptistskiia propoviedi (Iz nashego korrespondenta)," *Missionerskoe obozrienie* (October 1910): 1691.

42. This regeneration was noted in the secular press; see, for example, V. Nil'skii, "Samodietel'nost' dukhovenstva," *Russkoe slovo*, 5 July 1908, 1. On the Kiev congress, see Heather J. Coleman, "Definitions of Heresy: The Fourth Missionary Congress and the Problem of Cultural Power in Russia after 1905," *Jahrbücher für Geschichte Osteuropas*, 52, no. 1 (2004): 70–91. On similar congresses in Kazan' and Irkutsk in 1910, see Skvortsov, "Nedavnee-proshloe i nastoiashchee pravoslavnoi missii," 1735; and F. M. McCarthy, "The Kazan Missionary Congress," *Cahiers du monde russe et soviétique* 14, no. 3 (1973): 308–32.

43. *Vsepoddannieishii Otchet Ober-Prokurora Sviatieishago Sinoda po viedomstvu Pravoslavnago Ispoviedaniia za 1908–1909 gody* (St. Petersburg: Sinodal'naia tipografiia, 1911), 168. For a review of this debate, see D. I. Bogoliubov, *Religiozno-Obshchestvennyia techeniia v sovremennoi russkoi zhizni* (St. Petersburg: Tipografiia I. V. Leont'eva, 1909), 3–4, 241–88.

44. *Vsepoddannieishii Otchet Ober-Prokurora Sviatieishago Sinoda po viedomstvu Pravoslavnago ispoviedaniia za 1910 god* (St. Petersburg: Sinodal'naia tipografiia, 1913), 169. See also "V niedrakh sektantstva," *Missionerskoe obozrienie* (April 1911): 933, 936.

45. Figures from the appendixes of *Vsepoddannieishii . . . za 1905–1907 gody*, 72–73; *Vsepoddannieishii . . . za 1908–9*, 83, 86; *Vsepoddannieishii . . . za 1910*, 48–52; *Vsepoddannieishii . . . za 1911–12*, 68–71; and *Vsepoddannieishii . . . za 1914 god*, 34–41. Note that these figures are for those who formally left the Orthodox Church; some converts clearly did not go through this procedure, while others belonged to other denominations such as the Molokans before becoming Baptists.

46. Simon Mark Dixon, "Church, State, and Society in Late Imperial Russia" (Ph.D. dissertation, University of London, 1993), 299; and RGIA, f. 796, op. 442, d. 2290, l. 127.

47. M. Kal'nev, "Chto dielat'? Sovremennyia, novyia zadachi pravoslavnoi vnutrennei missii," *Missionerskoe obozrienie* (October 1910): 1594 (emphasis added). Note that this article dealt entirely with "shtundists," the term Kal'nev used for Baptists and Evangelical Christians. It was reprinted as a booklet that became standard reading. See A. Vvedenskii, *Bor'ba s sektantstvom* (Odessa: Tipografiia Eparkhial'nogo doma, 1914), 8–10.

48. *Prikhodskii sviashchennik* 1, no. 43–45 (November 1911): 1–2.

49. See, for example, M. Kal'nev, "Pochemu pravoslavnyie otpadaiut v sektantstvo?" *Missionerskoe obozrienie* 7–8 (July–August 1906): 62–73; V. A. Cherkesov, "Iz periodicheskoi sektantskoi pechati," *Missionerskoe obozrienie* (November 1908): 1530–34.

50. Reprinted in "V niedrakh sektantstva," *Missionerskoe obozrienie* (April 1911): 934–35.

51. *Vsepoddannieishii Otchet . . . 1910 god,* 170–71.

52. *Vsepoddaneishii Otchet . . . 1908–1909 gody,* 167–77.

53. Synod decisions of 20–26 May 1908, no. 3443: *Tserkovnyia viedomosti,* no. 22 (1908) (official part); and of 15 April–4 May 1909, no. 3130: *Tserkovnyia viedomosti,* no. 23 (6 June 1909): 235–36.

54. Vvedenskii, *Bor'ba s sektantstvom,* 200, 143, 188. Although this book made reference to nineteen different groups, 70 percent of examples were "Baptist" or "shtundist." On the search for an authentically Russian Orthodox style of preaching and pastoral work, see Dixon, "Church, State, and Society in Late Imperial Russia," 83–136.

55. Vvedenskii, *Bor'ba s sektantstvom,* 14. Quoting Prot. I. Troitskii, "Osobennaia zlovrednost' shtundo-baptizma i niekotoryia miery prikhodskoi bor'by s etoi sektoi," *Rukovodstvo dlia sel'skikh pastyrei,* no. 17 (1912): 512–17.

56. See, for example, Kal'nev, "Chto dielat'?" 1596–98.

57. *Vsepoddannieishii Otchet . . . za 1910 god,* 186; Vvedenskii, *Bor'ba s sektantstvom,* 8–10; Kal'nev, "Chto dielat'?" 1598.

58. RGIA, f. 796, op. 442, d. 2290, ll. 243–44.

59. RGIA, f. 796, op. 190, d. 354, ll. 12, 19–44.

60. GMIR, f. 2, op. 16, d. 157, ll. 1–8.

61. RGIA, f. 821, op. 133, d. 194, ll. 322–23. For similar activity in Moscow, see GMIR, koll. 1, op. 8, d. 69, l. 332.

62. For example, RGIA, f. 796, op. 190, d. 354, l. 46; f. 821, op. 133, d. 177, l. 23. In 1909 the Synod reviewed the Union of Russian People's repeated appeals to that body for the repeal of the Decree on Toleration of 17 April 1905 and rejected them outright. See "Pravye o svobodie soviesti," *Russkoe slovo,* 14 February 1909, 5; "Zasiedanie Sinoda," *Russkoe slovo,* 18 February 1909, 3.

63. RGIA, f. 821, op. 133, d. 288, l. 25.

64. For example, RGIA, f. 1285, op. 185 (1907), d. 49, ll. 33, 36–37; GARF, f. 102 (DP/OO), op. 1913, d. 85, ll. 111, 124–25, 148, 159.

65. The Over Procurator of the Holy Synod may not always have accurately represented the views of the clerical members of the Synod, and his position was seen as the prime example of the government's meddling in church affairs. Nonetheless, the bishops remained his key source of information and views regarding the religious situation, and he was the spokesman for at least one view of the Church's position within the state.

66. RGIA, f. 796, op. 190 (3 st. 4 otd.) d. 354, ll. 1–2.

67. RGIA, f. 796, op. 191 (6 otd., 3 st.), d. 259, ll. 4–33.

68. RGIA, f. 821, op. 133, d. 194, l. 42.

69. See, for example, K. K. Arsen'ev, *Svoboda soviesti i vieroterpimost'* (Saint Petersburg: "Obshchestvennaia Pol'za," 1905), 199–201; S. P. Mel'gunov, "Shtundisty ili baptisty? (Po povodu presliedovaniia sektantov po 29 st. Ust. o nak.)," *Russkaia mysl'* 24, no. 11 (November 1903): 159–66.

70. For example, GMIR, f. 2, op. 16, d. 155, l. 18; and *Baptist,* no. 18 (23 March 1911): 102. On the families' denunciation of religious dissidents, see also Jeffrey Burds, "A Culture of Denunciation," in *Accusatory Practices,* ed. Sheila Fitzpatrick and Robert Gellately (Chicago: University of Chicago Press, 1997), 54.

71. For example, RGIA, f. 821, op. 133, d. 310, l. 1750b.; and RGIA, f. 821, op. 133, d. 301, l. 38.

72. GMIR, koll. 1, op. 8, d. 13, ll. 1, 40b., 29.

73. John Bossy, *Christianity in the West, 1400–1700* (Oxford: Oxford University Press, 1985), 110.

74. William Henry Brackney, *The Baptists* (New York: Greenwood, 1988), 3

75. *Baptist*, no. 10 (2 March 1911): 77. On the strong link between peasant perceptions of morality and legality, see Cathy Frierson, "Crime and Punishment in the Russian Village," *Slavic Review* 46, no. 1 (spring 1987): 57.

76. Natalie Zemon Davis, *Society and Culture in Early Modern France* (Stanford: Stanford University Press, 1975), 160–65.

77. For example, RGIA, f. 821, op. 133, d. 301, ll. 49–50; and GMIR, f. 2, op. 16, d. 155, ll. 12–14. In both these cases, the governor refused to endorse the decision of the village assembly to expel their Baptists. But in some instances, even after 1905, certain petitions were approved (GMIR, f. 2, op. 16, d. 155, ll. 17–18).

78. GMIR, f. 2, op. 16, d. 155, ll. 12–14.

79. GMIR, f. 2, op. 16, d. 155, l. 3.

80. Shevzov, "Popular Orthodoxy in Late Imperial Rural Russia," 274–75, 72.

81. Peaceful accounts include *Baptist*, no. 10 (1911): 79; no. 4 (October 1907): 15; on confrontations, see RGIA, f. 821, op. 133, d. 254, ll. 59, 74–75.

82. RGIA, f. 821, op. 133, d. 194, ll. 150b.–16.

83. RGIA, f. 821, op. 133, d. 301, ll. 38–39. This is a particularly well documented case; although it is impossible to know all the details of such incidents, there at least seems to be general agreement about the basic chain of events. See ll. 38–39, 49–50, 52, 53, 55, 77, 78–81.

84. RGIA, f. 182, op. 133, d. 289, l. 490b.

85. GMIR, f. 2, op. 16, d. 155, l.13. For an accusation of persecution by Baptist converts, see RGIA, f. 821, op. 133, d. 195, l. 750b.

86. See, for example, *Bratskii listok*, no. 3 (1906): 8; and *Baptist*, no. 10 (2 March 1911): 77.

87. For example, RGIA, f. 821, op. 133, d. 254, l. 18; "Vypiska iz diela no. 147," *Utrenniaia zviezda*, 19 October 1912, in RGIA, f. 821, op. 133, d. 301, l. 221.

88. RGIA, f. 797, op. 80 (2 otd., 3 st.), d. 390, l. 30b., 110b.

89. RGIA, f. 1284, op. 185 (1907), d. 39, ll. 151–1520b.; f. 1284, op. 185 (1908), d. 72, l. 40.

90. For example, RGIA, f. 1284, op. 185 (1907), d. 39, ll. 151–1520b.

91. For the activities of other parish priests, see Vasilii Luzanov, "Kakimi sredstvami mozhet raspolagat' prikhodskii pastyr' v bor'be s shtundo-baptizmom? (Iz zapisok pastyria-missionera)," *Missionerskoe obozrienie*, no. 10 (October 1906): 438–42.

92. For example, M. D. Tkachenko, "Manusinsk, Enis. g.," *Baptist*, no. 18 (23 March 1911): 102; GMIR, f. 2, op. 16, d. 155, l. 18.

93. Stephen P. Frank, "Popular Justice, Community, and Culture among the Russian Peasantry, 1870–1900," *Russian Review* 46 (1987): 257, 264. There are innumerable press accounts of popular beatings of Baptists; see, for example, Vladimir Bonch-Bruevich, "Presliedovanie baptistov v Rossii," *Viestnik Evropy* 45, no. 6 (June 1910): 160–83; "Izbienie evangelistov," *Riech'*, 23 April 1908; "Presliedovanie Odesskikh sektantov," *Novaia Rus'*, 21 May 1909; "Napadenie na sektantov," *Riech'*, 18 January 1911; "Gonenie na sektantov," *Birzhevyia viedomosti*, 2 June 1913.

94. V. G. Pavlov was a major source of information and primary documents on Baptist life and persecution for the most prolific researcher of Russian religious sec-

tarianism, the Bolshevik V. D. Bonch-Bruevich. In 1910, as editor of *Baptist* in Odessa, he wrote that, "as editor, our fellow believers send much information to me which is inconvenient to print. If you want I can send you such information for collection" (GMIR, f. 2, op. 16, d. 62, l. 27). Among many newspaper articles that list the Baptist press as their source are I. M. Tregubov, "V zashchitu gonimykh sektantov," *Rus'*, 21 July 1907; and Christianus, "Pod znakom svobody soviesty," *Riech'*, 2 July 1911.

95. See, for example, "Goneniia nashego vremeni," *Bratskii listok* (May 1909): 2–18; D.I.M., "S nashego polia," *Baptist*, no. 11 (November 1908): 23; S. Bielousov, "Vpechatlieniia ot s"iezda," *Baptist*, no. 44 (27 October 1910): 347–48.

96. S. Mel'gunov, *Tserkov' i gosudarstvo v Rossii. V perekhodnoe vremia.* Vol. 2 (Moscow: Izdanie tovarishchestvo I. D. Sytina, 1909), 107.

97. A. Prugavin, "Raskol i biurokratiia," *Viestnik Evropy* 44, no. 11 (November 1909): 174–75.

98. Christianus, "Pod znakom svobody soviesty," *Riech'*, 2 July 1911, found in RGIA, f. 821, op. 133, d. 254, l. 71.

99. See, for example, A. Vvedenskii, "Gosudarstvo i tserkov' v otnoshenii k sektantam," *Golos tserkvi* 3, no. 3 (March 1914): 205–11; no. 5 (May 1914): 162–63. See also Burds, "A Culture of Denunciation," 53.

100. For example, RGIA, f. 821, op. 133, d. 194; f. 1284, op. 185, d. 49, l. 60; f. 1284, op. 185 (1908), d. 83, l. 78; *Baptist*, no. 15 (1910): 116; *Bratskii listok*, no. 9 (1909): 10.

101. William G. McLoughlin, *Soul Liberty* (Hanover: University Press of New England, 1991), ix–x, 197, 200. See also Carla Gardina Pestana, *Quakers and Baptists in Colonial Massachusetts* (Cambridge: Cambridge University Press, 1991), 120.

5. RUSSIAN BAPTISTS AND THE "GERMAN FAITH"

1. N. Griniakin, *Beregis' shtundy!* (St. Petersburg: Tipografiia "Kolokol," 1912), 8.

2. RGIA, f. 821, op. 133, d. 289, ll. 5, 8, 38.

3. Robert F. Byrnes, *Pobedonostsev* (Bloomington: Indiana University Press, 1968), 182.

4. I. S. Prokhanoff, *In the Cauldron of Russia, 1869–1933* (New York: All-Russian Evangelical Christian Union, 1933), 97–100; RGIA, f. 821, op. 133, d. 298, l. 353.

5. Stephen K. Batalden, "Colportage and the Distribution of Holy Scripture in Late Imperial Russia," in *Christianity and the Eastern Slavs*, Vol. 2, *Russian Culture in Modern Times*, ed. Robert P. Hughes and Irina Paperno (Berkeley: University of California Press, 1994), 86–87.

6. Walter Laqueur, *Russia and Germany* (New Brunswick, N.J.: Transaction, 1990), 51.

7. Aleksii (Dorodnitsyn), *Iuzhno-russkii neobaptizm* (Stavropol'-Kavkazskii: Tipolitografiia T. M. Timofeeva, 1903), 180–81. The quotation from the 1884 conference minutes is found in Episkop Aleksii, *Materialy dlia istorii religiozno-ratsionalisticheskago dvizheniia na iugie Rossii* (Kazan': Tsentral'naia tipografiia, 1908), 569.

8. A. Rozhdestvenskii, *Iuzhno-russkii shtundizm* (St. Petersburg: Tipografiia Departamenta Udielov, 1889), 2; Andrew Blane, "Protestant Sects in Late Imperial Russia," in *The Religious World of Russian Culture*, Vol. 2, *Essays in Honor of Georges Florovsky*, ed. Andrew Blane (The Hague: Mouton, 1975), 277.

9. For example, M. A. Kal'nev, ed., *Russkie sektanty, ikh uchenie, kul't i sposoby propagandy* (Odessa: Tipografiia E. I. Fesenko, 1911), 35–46.

10. J. H. Rushbrooke, *The Baptist Movement in the Continent of Europe*, 2nd ed. (London: Carey, 1923), 137.

11. I. S. Prokhanov, *Presliedovaniia evangel'skikh i srodnykh im khristian v Rossii vo vremia voiny* (Petrograd, 1915), 20.

12. Nazvanie 'Baptisty,'" *Baptist*, no. 1 (June 1907): 3.

13. GMIR, koll. 1, op. 8, d. 516, l. 240b.

14. Rozhdestvenskii, *Iuzhno-russkii shtundizm*, 244–47.

15. GMIR, koll. 1, op. 8, d. 470, ll. 1–24; d. 516, ll. 16–37.

16. Vladimir Bonch-Bruevich, ed., *Materialy k istorii i izucheniiu russkogo sketantstva* (St. Petersburg: Tipografiia V. M. Vol'fa, 1908), 1–21; *Istoriia evangel'skikh khristian-baptistov* (Moscow: Izdanie Vsesoiuznogo Soveta Evangel'skikh Khristian-Baptistov, 1989), 540–41.

17. GMIR, koll. 1, op. 8, folder 1, l. 34; V. P., "Pravda o baptistakh," *Baptist*, no. 46 (9 November 1911): 362.

18. GMIR, koll. 1, op. 8, folder of letters to D. I. Mazaev, l. 26.

19. GMIR, koll. 1, op. 8, folder 1, l. 287.

20. M. A. Kal'nev, *Istoriia sektantskikh molitvennykh piesnopienii i razbor ikh soderzhaniia*, 3rd ed. (Odessa, 1911), 28–29, 7, 24–27.

21. Prokhanoff, *In the Cauldron of Russia*, 143–44, 148. These hymns are still in current use. An older Baptist woman told me in 1995 that, "as I go about my day, I sing the songs of Prokhanov."

22. *Bratskii listok* (October 1910): 12–13.

23. A.I.K., "Evangel'skaia pesn'," *Utrenniaia zvezda*, no. 3–5 (1922): 15–16; "K vykhodu Ukrainskogo sbornika pesen 'Arfa,'" *Baptist*, no. 3 (1925): 15–16.

24. William James, *The Varieties of Religious Experience* (New York: Image, 1978), 203.

25. *Baptist*, no. 7 (July 1908): 30; V. V. Ivanov, "'Ne dremlet i ne spit khraniashchii Izrailia," *Baptist*, no. 12 (December 1908): 21.

26. According to V. V. Ivanov, Kargel' shared the Russian view about the "coldness" of the German Baptists (GMIR, koll. 1, op. 8, d. 69, folder of letters to N. V. Odintsov, l. 1); Kargel' ended up in the Evangelical Christian camp: Paul D. Steeves ("The Russian Baptist Union, 1917–1935" [Ph.D. dissertation, University of Kansas, 1976], 44–46).

27. V. V. Ivanov, "Kniga episkopa Aleksiia," *Baptist*, no. 9 (September 1908): 24.

28. Kal'nev, *Russkie sektanty*, 1.

29. *Vsepodannieishii otchet ober-prokurora sv. Sinoda po viedomstvu Pravoslavnago ispoviedaniia za 1905–1907 gody* (St. Petersburg: Sinodal'naia tipografiia, 1910), 159–60.

30. A. S. Prugavin, *Raskol i sektantstvo v russkoi narodnoi zhizni* (Moscow: Tipografiia T-va I. D. Sytina, 1905), 83. See also Christopher Read, *Religion, Revolution, and the Russian Intelligentsia* (London: Macmillan, 1979), 98–105.

31. N. Gumilevskii, *Kratkaia istoriia i oblichenie novykh ratsionalisticheskikh sekt* (Kiev, 1910), 1.

32. Sergei Margaritov, *Istoriia russkikh misticheskikh i ratsionalisticheskikh sekt*, 3rd ed. (Simferopol': Tavricheskaia gubernskaia tipografiia, 1910), 1.

33. T. I. Butkevich, *Obzor russkikh sekt i ikh tolkov* (Khar'kov: Tipografiia gubernskago pravelniia, 1910), 12–14.

34. Gumilevskii, *Kratkaia istoriia i oblichenie*, 4.

35. V. N. Terletskii, *Ocherki, izsliedovaniia i stat'i po sektantstvu*, vyp. 1, 2nd ed. (Poltava: Elektricheskaia tipografiia G. I. Markevicha, 1913), 25.

36. E. R., "Russkie ratsionalisty," *Viestnik Evropy*, no. 7 (1881): 279, 295–96.

37. N. Ognev, "Russkii baptizm i evangel'skoe khristianstvo," *Nizhegorodskii listok*, 21 October 1911 (clipping found in GMIR, f. 2, op. 26, d. 47, l. 280b.).

38. V. I. Iasevich-Borodaevskaia, *Bor'ba za vieru* (St. Petersburg: Gosudarstvennaia tipografiia, 1912), 19–20.

39. P. Miliukov, *Ocherki po istorii russkoi kul'tury, Chast' vtoraia*, 4th ed. (St. Petersburg: Izdanie redaktsii zhurnala "Mira Bozhii," 1905), 96, 99, 143. For a conservative critique of the idea that Russia must inevitably replicate the Western path, see N. M. Sokolov, *Ob ideiakh i idealakh russkoi intelligentsii* (St. Petersburg: M. M. Stasiulevich, 1904). See also Read, *Religion, Revolution, and the Russian Intelligentsia*, 97–106.

40. S. Mel'gunov, *Tserkov' i gosudarstvo v Rossii* (Moscow: Izdanie T-va I. D. Sytina, 1907), 75.

41. Aleksii (Dorodnitsyn), *Iuzhno-russkii Neobaptizm*, 117–18.

42. Ognev, "Russkii baptizm i evangel'skoe khristianstvo." The Taurida palace was the seat of the Duma.

43. Vladimir Bonch-Bruevich, "Presliedovanie baptistov v Rossii," *Viestnik Evropy* 45, no. 6 (June 1910): 181–82.

44. Gumilevskii, *Kratkaia istoriia i oblichenie*, 4.

45. Redaktsiia, "Nashe dielo i ego zadachi," *Missionerskoe obozrienie*, no. 1 (January 1896): viii; "Missionerstvo, sekty i raskol (Khronika)," *Missionerskoe obozrienie*, no. 1 (January 1896): 57–74; and Vl. A. Maevskii, *Vnutrenniaia missiia i ee osnovopolozhnik* (Buenos Aires, 1954), 19, 59, 165.

46. RGIA, f. 821, op. 133, d. 1, ll. 64–64ob.; also, l. 75.

47. RGIA, f. 821, op. 133, d. 196, l. 207ob.

48. Kal'nev, *Istoriia sektantskikh molitvennykh piesnopienii*, 29; RGIA, f. 1022, op. 1, d. 14, l. 64; f. 821, op. 133, d. 177, l. 125.

49. RGIA, f. 821, op. 133, d. 177, ll. 225ob., 320. For tension over this, see GMIR, koll. 1, op. 8, d. 32, ll. 1–6.

50. RGIA, f. 821, op. 133, d. 253, l. 13; d. 196, l. 186.

51. "Nazvanie 'Baptisty,'" *Baptist*, no. 1 (June 1907): 3.

52. Fedor Prokhorovich Balikhin, *Kratkaia avtobiografiia* (Rostov-on-Don: Tipografiia F. Pavlova, 1908), 7.

53. Ivan Petrovich Kushnerov, Vasilii Ivanovich Dolgopolov, and Vasilii Nikolaevich Ivanov, *Kratkaia zapiska* (St. Petersburg, 1905), 13, 15.

54. "Reformatsiia idet!" *Utrenniaia zvezda*, 2 April 1910, 1.

55. RGIA, f. 821, op. 133, d. 257, l. 7ob. See also *Bratskii listok*, no. 6 (June 1908): 8.

56. "Nasha Rus'," *Baptist*, no. 7–8 (1914): 23. It is interesting to note the continued popularity of this theme in Baptist hymns and poetry of the late twentieth century; see Georgi Vins, *Testament from Prison*, ed. Michael Bourdeaux, trans. Jane Ellis (Elgin, Ill.: David C. Cook, 1975), 63, 96, 256.

57. Prokhanov, *Presliedovanie*, 22. On the theme of the Czech reformation, see also Kushnerov, Dolgopolov, and Ivanov, *Kratkaia zapiska*, 7; I. S. Prokhanov, "Ian Gus i Petr Khel'chitskii, kak uchiteli dukhovnoi zhizni," *Khristianin*, no. 5 (1924): 6–21.

58. For example, V. V. Ivanov wrote to V. G. Pavlov upon returning from the World

Baptist Alliance Congress in Philadelphia in 1911. Ivanov was thrilled at having seen "the Kingdom of God in action" and stated that it had given him hope for the future in Russia. He continued to "believe that the Lord will send us our Martin Luther" (GMIR, koll.1, op. 8 d. 69, l. 429).

59. RGIA, f. 821, op. 133, d. 263, ll. 17–18. For the words of the anthem, see N. A. Soboleva and V. A. Artamonov, *Simvoly Rossii* (Moscow: "Panorama," 1993), 169.

60. RGIA, f. 821, op. 133, d. 196, ll. 195–195ob.

61. Daniel Field, *Rebels in the Name of the Tsar* (Boston: Unwin Hyman, 1989); Samuel John Nesdoly, "Evangelical Sectarianism in Russia" (Ph.D. dissertation, Queen's University, Kingston, 1971), 346–47; RGIA, f. 821, op. 5, d. 1014, ll. 17ob.–18ob.

62. Michael Cherniavsky, *Tsar and People* (New Haven: Yale University Press, 1961), 227.

63. Gauri Viswanathan, "Religious Conversion and the Politics of Dissent," in *Conversion to Modernities*, ed. Peter Van der Veer (New York: Routledge, 1996), 89. See also Hugh McLeod, *Secularisation in Western Europe, 1848–1914* (New York: St. Martin's, 2000), 216–17.

6. DASHED HOPES

1. *Istoriia evangel'skikh khristian-baptistov v SSSR* (Moscow: Izdanie Vsesoiuznogo Soveta Evangel'skikh Khristian-Baptistov, 1989), 139; I. S. Prokhanoff, *In the Cauldron of Russia* (New York: All-Russian Evangelical Christian Union, 1933), 148–49.

2. Prokhanoff, *In the Cauldron of Russia*, 168–69.

3. RGIA, f. 821, op. 133, d. 257; V. A. Fetler, "Molitvennyi dom baptistov v S. Peterburge," *Baptist*, no. 1 (January 1908): 26; Paul Steeves, "The Russian Baptist Union, 1917–1935" (Ph.D. dissertation, University of Kansas, 1976), 66.

4. F. Townley Lord, *Baptist World Fellowship* (Nashville: Broadman, 1955), 15–17.

5. RGIA, f. 821, op. 133, d. 257, l. 13; d. 298, l. 190.

6. RGIA, f. 821, op. 133, d. 301, l. 363.

7. S. D. Bondar', *Sovremennoe sostoianie russkogo baptizma* (St. Petersburg: M.V.D. Departament Dukhovnykh Diel, 1911), 33, 58. Bondar' personally attended the congress (RGIA. f. 821, op. 133, d. 263, l. 18).

8. RGIA, f. 821, op. 133, d. 263, l. 39.

9. *Baptist World Alliance. Second Congress. Record of Proceedings.* Philadelphia, 19–25 June 1911, 3, 235–38. The *Philadelphia Inquirer* article of 16 June 1911 is found in RGIA, f. 821, op. 133, d. 298, ll. 95–96.

10. Louie Devotie Newton, "Baptist World Alliance," *Encyclopedia of Southern Baptists*, Vol. 1 (Nashville: Broadman, 1958), 150.

11. RGIA, f. 821, op. 133, d. 289, ll. 41–42. These speeches were reprinted in the Baptist press.

12. RGIA, f. 821, op. 133, d. 263, l. 50. The department sent two officials, Kologrivov and Bondar'. The title "Director of the Ministry of Internal Affairs" appears to have been a temporary designation in the weeks after the assassination of Petr Stolypin and before the appointment of his successor as minister, A. A. Makarov.

13. The detailed report of the proceedings presented to the Minister of Internal Affairs are in RGIA, f. 821, op. 150, d. 342, ll. 1–29. For the Union board's report, see GMIR, koll. 1, op. 8, d. 32, folder 18, ll. 1–7.

14. GARF, f. 102 (DP/OO), op. 1911, d. 85, ll. 2-20b.

15. I. A., "Revoliutsionnaia tsitadel' ili podlinnyi 'baptizm,'" *Kolokol*, 2 September 1911; "Sektanty baptisty i 'svoboda soviesti'," *Kolokol*, 24 September 1911; *Moskovskiia viedomosti*, 21 September 1911, 28 September 1909.

16. This account is based on that made to the Minister of Internal Affairs (RGIA, f. 821, op. 150, d. 452, ll. 30-37). It generally conforms with the reports of other ministry and secret police officials (RGIA, f. 821, op. 133, d. 263, ll. 79-86, 108-1090b). The Moscow City governor was severely reprimanded for allowing these meetings to take place: first, because the Ministry of Internal Affairs had allowed the Baptists only a "business" congress and the law of 14 April 1910 did not allow simultaneous spiritual and business congresses; second, for allowing the humiliation of a priest and not defending Orthodoxy; and, finally, for allowing the Baptists to use the "spacious and universally accessible hall of the Polytechnical Museum, which is popular among the population of Moscow" (RGIA, f. 821, op. 133, d. 263, ll. 93-96).

17. Failed requests and government memos harkening back to the 1911 congress as justification for denying a congress are held in RGIA, f. 821, op. 133, d. 263, ll. 188, 190-900b., 245, 247, 251, 253, 259, 269, 288. On the Right, see "Razgrom baptizma v Moskvie," *Kolokol*, 1 October 1911; and P. Ukhtubuzhskii, "Baptistskii soblazn," *Zemshchina*, 12 October 1911. For liberals and populists, see "Religioznyia stesneniia," *Riech'*, 18 October 1911; and D. Filosofov, "Missionery i baptisty," *Riech'*, 1 October 1911.

18. See, for example, RGIA, f. 796, op. 442, d. 2619, l. 30; V. Stepanov, "Ot Redaktora," *Drug molodezhi*, no. 9-10 (September 1913): 112; "Ot redaktsii," *Baptist*, no. 1-4 (January-February 1914): 1.

19. RGIA, f. 821, op. 133, d. 194, l. 98 (Moscow); "Izviestiia s nashego polia," *Baptist*, no. 9 (23 February 1911): 71; "Besiedy 'Baptista,'" *Baptist*, no. 14 (30 March 1911): 108. See also the strict regulations agreed to for the St. Petersburg Evangelical Christian Sunday School in early 1911 (RGIA, f. 821, op. 133, d. 249, l. 33).

20. Avtoritetnoe raz"iasnenie tsirkuliara i pravil 4-go oktiabria 1910 g.," *Baptist*, no. 52 (22 December 1910): 413.

21. "Deputatsiia baptistov u predsedatelia soveta ministrov," *Riech'*, 12 March 1913, 3; and "Deputatsiia baptistov u ministra vnutrennykh diel," *Riech'*, 17 March 1913, 3. See also V. A. Fetler, *Pokornieishee khodataistvo* (St. Petersburg, 1913); and RGIA, f. 821, op. 133, d. 1, ll. 102-1020b.; f. 821, op. 133, d. 298, ll. 330, 332, 428.

22. See the report, and the recommendation of the Duma's Committee on Inquiries that it be followed up by the Ministry of Internal Affairs, in *Prilozheniia k stenograficheskim otchetam gosudarstvennoi dumy. Chetvertyi sozyv. Sessia vtoraia. 1913-1914 gg. vyp. 5.* (St. Petersburg, 1914), no. 447; "Zapros o presliedovaniiakh sektantov," *Utrenniaia zviezda*, 10 May 1913, 1-3. See also John Shelton Curtiss, *Church and State in Russia* (New York: Columbia University Press, 1940), 332.

23. Leopold Haimson, "The Problem of Social Stability in Urban Russia, 1905-1917," *Slavic Review* 23 (1964): 619-42; 24 (1965): 1-22; Hans Rogger, "Russia in 1914," *Journal of Contemporary History* 1, no. 4 (October 1966): 95-120; Geoffrey Hosking, *Russia: People and Empire* (Cambridge, Mass.: Harvard University Press, 1997), 449.

24. V.V.I., "Na pomoshch' ranenym voinam," *Baptist*, no. 15-16 (August 1914): 18.

25. Klibanov, *Istoriia religioznogo sektantstva*, 272. Note that in 1923 the Baptists would maintain that these were Fetler's personal initiatives, opposed by the movement at large (GMIR, koll. 1, op. 8, d. 35, folder 8, l. 40b). They were proving their allegiance to a rather different political system by that date.

26. Voina i narodnoe predstavitel'stvo," *Utrenniaia zvezda*, 8 August 1914, 1.

27. V.V.I., "Na pomoshch' ranenym voinam," 18.

28. Episkop Mikhail, "Staroobriadchestvo i voina," *Birzhevyia viedomosti*, 5 December 1914, 2–3.

29. RGB OR, f. 435, k. 96, d. 20, l. 5.

30. "Ot redaktsii," *Drug molodezhi*, no. 1 (January 1915): 2; A. Goliaev, "V poslienii raz," *Drug molodezhi*, no. 9–10 (September–October 1916): 90.

31. RGIA, f. 821, op. 133, d. 195, l. 182. *Istoriia evangel'skikh khristian-baptistov v SSSR*, 163.

32. "Na nuzhdy voiny. Rabota Balashovskikh baptistov," *Baptist*, no. 21–24 (1914): 5–6.

33. I. S. Prokhanov, *Presledovaniia evangel'skikh i srodnykh im khristian v Rossii vo vremia voiny* (Petrograd, 1915), 5.

34. Walter Laqueur, *Russia and Germany* (New Brunswick, N.J.: Transaction, 1990), 49.

35. Ben Hellman, "Kogda vremia slavianofil'stvovalo. Russkie filosofy i pervaia mirovaia voina," in *Problemy istorii russkoi literatury nachala XX veka* (Helsinki: Department of Slavonic Languages, University of Helsinki, 1989), 215–18. Of course, Russia was also allied with Protestant Great Britain.

36. N. S. Andreeva, "Pribaltiiskie nemtsy i pervaia mirovaia voina," in *Problemy sotsial'no-ekonomicheskoi i politicheskoi istorii Rossii XIX–XX vekov*, ed. A. N. Tsamutali et al. (St. Petersburg: Izdatel'stvo "Aleteiia," 1999), 465.

37. RGIA, f. 796, op. 442, d. 2680, l. 370b.

38. RGIA, f. 796, op. 442, d. 2743, l. 360b.

39. RGIA, f. 796, op. 442, d. 2743, l. 38.

40. Protoierei I. Vostorgov, *Vrazheskii dukhovnyi avangard* (Moscow: "Russkaia pechatnia," 1914), 1–3.

41. Protoierei I. Vostorgov, "Eshche o 'niemetskoi vierie.' Otviet g. Fetleru," *Moskovskiia viedomosti*, 29 November 1914, 1; 30 November 1914, 2; L. Pasynkov, "Kashchei," *Birzhevyia viedomosti*, 3 December 1914, 5. Note that the "answer to Mr. Fetler" was in response to an article in Fetler's magazine that was authored by a Gedeonov, not Fetler.

42. RGIA, f. 821, op. 133, d. 1, ll. 116–17.

43. See the debates of the Duma of 3 August 1914, reprinted in *Novoe vremia*, 4 August 1914, 3.

44. RGIA. f. 821, op. 133, d. 195, ll. 143–45.

45. GARF. f. 102 (DP/OO), op. 1914, d. 85, ll. 25–260b.

46. RGIA. f. 821, op. 133, d. 310, l. 272; d. 198, ll. 74, 78.

47. *Istoriia evangel'skikh khristian-baptistov v SSSR*, 176; RGIA, f. 821, op. 133, d. 198, l. 67.

48. RGIA, f. 821, op. 133, d. 1, l. 83; GARF, f. 102 (DP/OO), op. 1913, d. 85, ll. 380b.–39, 2370b.–2380b. Indeed, the Gendarme director of the city of Kronshtadt, with its important naval base, reported that there were no problems in his area

in this respect and opined that such accusations were merely Church fabrications (l. 128).

49. RGIA, f. 821, op. 133, d. 198, ll. 10, 68, 95; GARF, f. 102 (DP/OO), op. 1915), d. 132.

50. G. Sergieev, "Khristianstvo i voennaia sluzhba (Otviet na ankety)," *Slovo istiny*, no. 7–8 (1918): 72.

51. GMIR, koll. 1, op. 8, d. 69, folder 1, l. 72.

52. GARF, f. 102 (DP/OO), op. 1907, d. 16, l. 68. A 1915 article in *Missionerskoe obozrienie* charged that in 1908 Prokhanov had appealed to the State Council for Evangelical Christians to be allowed to perform alternate service. However, that this was never mentioned in government analyses suggests that this may have been an accusation made in the heat of war (Kal'nev, "Sostoianie sektantstva," 549–50).

53. GARF, f. 102 (DP/OO), op. 1912, d. 85, l. 2.

54. Of course, these statements of faith were not written in an atmosphere of freedom of conscience but rather were modeled on those of the similarly embattled Baptists of the German Empire.

55. RGIA, f. 821, op. 133, d. 196, l. 300b. Examples of refusals to serve based on personal conviction include GMIR, f. 13, op. 1, d. 202, ll. 43–44; RGIA, f. 821, op. 133, d. 195, l. 226; d. 198, ll. 10, 68; and GARF, f. 102 (DP/OO), op. 1912, d. 85, l. 2.

56. RGIA, f. 821, op. 133, d. 23, l. 113. Similarly, among cases still awaiting decisions on 1 April 1917, of 241 cases, 113 were Baptists or Evangelical Christians and 100 were "unknown" (ll. 124ob.–125). For a list of conscientious objectors drawn up after the war, see GARF, f. 130, op. 3, d. 217, ll. 47–135.

57. Hans Rogger, *Russia in the Age of Modernization and Revolution* (London: Longman, 1983), 257.

58. *Utrenniaia zviezda*, 15 August 1914, 1.

59. RGIA, f. 821, op. 10, d. 595, l. 20.

60. See, for example, *Drug*, no. 2 (February 1919): 15.

61. William Fetler (Basil Malof), *The Marvellous Results of Work among Russian War Prisoners and the Greatest Missionary Challenge of the Christian Era*, 2nd ed. (Chicago: Russian Missionary Society, n. d.).

62. M. D. Timoshenko, *V Narymskii krai* (Moscow: Slovo istiny, 1917), 11–12.

63. Background on this decision and the extensive role of the local bishops in pushing for these closures can be found in RGIA, f. 797, op. 84 (2 otd., 3 st.), d. 614; and V. P., "General Ebielov v roli gonitelia baptistov i drugikh sektantov pri starom rezhimie," *Slovo istiny*, no. 11 (October 1917): 158–60. On closures, imprisonment, and exile, see RGIA, f. 821, op. 133, d. 23, ll. 90–900b., 95–101; and Prokhanov, *Presliedovaniia*, 7–10. RGIA, f. 821, op. 133, d. 23,

64. *Istoriia evangel'skikh khristian-baptistov v SSSR*, 163–64.

65. Iz proshlago i nastoiashchago Rossii," *Drug*, no. 4 (April 1919): 32; RGIA, f. 821, op. 133, d. 331; d. 332; OR RGB, f. 435, k. 96, d. 20.

66. RGIA, f. 821, op. 133, d. 23, ll. 95–101; "Kak byvshee provitel'stvo zabotilos' o ranenykh," *Slovo istiny*, no. 2–3 (June 1917): 45.

67. Prokhanov, *Presliedovaniia*, 30.

68. GMIR, koll. 1, op. 8, d. 69, l. 501.

69. *Otchet 4-go Vserossiiskago S"iezda Evangel'skikh Khristian* (Petrograd: "Raduga," 1917), 1–2. The journal *Gost'*, published by the Petrograd Baptists, did appear in January 1917.

70. Curtiss, *Church and State*, 386. The investigation materials are found in RGIA, f. 821, op. 10, d. 595; op. 133, d. 196, ll. 20–37.

71. "Na Bozhiei nivie," *Slovo istiny*, no. 13–14 (November 1917): 196.

7. THE REVOLUTION OF THE SPIRIT

1. E. Ofrova, "Svoboda tol'ko vo Khriste," *Slovo istiny*, no. 2–3 (June 1917): 40.

2. GMIR, koll. 1, op. 8, d. 69, ll. 197–200.

3. GMIR, koll. 1, op. 8, d. 69, l. 204. Pavel V. Ivanov (who later called himself Ivanov-Klyshnikov, in memory of his persecuted Molokan ancestors who had hidden under the common surname Ivanov) appears to have become president of Evpatoriia's Committee for Social Safety in March 1917 (GMIR, koll. 1, op. 8, d. 69, l. 2050b.).

4. "K Momentu," *Slovo istiny*, no. 1 (May 1917): 2.

5. Fuller access to these materials bears out conclusions along these lines reached by earlier Western scholars on the basis of quotations in Soviet works; see Andrew Quarles Blane, "The Relations between the Russian Protestant Sects and the State, 1900–1921" (Ph.D. dissertation, Duke University, 1964), 130–57; Paul D. Steeves, "The Russian Baptist Union, 1917–1935" (Ph.D. dissertation, University of Kansas, 1976), 486–87, 495–505.

6. A. I. Klibanov, *Istoriia religioznogo sektantstva v Rossii* (Moscow: Izdatel'stvo "Nauka," 1965), 277–85. See also Z. V. Kalinicheva, *Sotsial'naia sushchnost' baptizma* (Leningrad: Izdatel'stvo "Nauka," 1972), 22–39; and G. S. Lialina, "Liberal'no-burzhuaznoe techenie v baptizme (1905–1917 gg.)," *Voprosy nauchnogo ateizma*, vyp. 1 (Moscow: Izdatel'stvo "Mysl'," 1966), 312–40.

7. Suzanne Desan, *Reclaiming the Sacred* (Ithaca, N.Y.: Cornell University Press, 1990). See also Roger N. Lancaster, *Thanks to God and the Revolution* (New York: Columbia University Press, 1988).

8. Christopher Read, *Religion, Revolution, and the Russian Intelligentsia, 1900–1912* (London: Macmillan, 1979), 57–81, esp. 77; Edward E. Roslof, *Red Priests* (Bloomington: Indiana University Press, 2002), 1–18; Jay Bergman, "The Image of Jesus in the Russian Revolutionary Movement," *International Review of Social History* 35 (1990): 220–48. See also Paul T. Phillips, *A Kingdom of God on Earth* (University Park: Pennsylvania State University Press, 1996); Franco Rizzi, "Socialist Propaganda in the Italian Countryside," in *Disciplines of Faith*, ed. Jim Obelkevich, Lyndal Roper, and Raphael Samuel (London: Routledge and Kegan Paul, 1987), 467–76; M. M. Sheinman, *Khristianskii sotsializm* (Moscow: Izdatel'stvo "Nauka," 1969), 69–125; Paul Misner, *Social Catholicism in Europe* (New York: Crossroad, 1991).

9. OR RGB, f. 369, k. 352, d. 23, ll. 1–40b.; Vladimir D. Bonch-Bruevich, *Izbrannye sochineniia*, Vol. 1, *O religii, religioznom sektantstve i tserkvi* (Moscow: Izdatel'stvo Akademii Nauk SSSR, 1959), 336–45.

10. F. M. Putintsev, *Politicheskaia rol' i taktika sekt* (Moscow: Gosudarstvennoe antireligioznoe izdatel'stvo, 1935), 23–36. GMIR, f. 2, op. 16, d. 187; GARF, f. 102 (DP/OO), op. 1898, d. 12, ch. 4, ll. 32, 53, 56; and GMIR, f. 14, op. 3, dd. 1668, 1258, 1676, 1870, 2117, 2124, 2130. Putintsev's book also includes a photograph of the questionnaire and excerpts from many responses, all from evangelicals.

11. GMIR, f. 14, op. 3, d. 1676, l. 2.

12. Bonch-Bruevich, *Izbrannye sochineniia*, 1:344, 169–70.

13. This list of the contents of *Besieda* is found in the papers of Bonch-Bruevich (GMIR, f. 2, op. 6, d. 200). There are quotations from Prokhanov in RGIA, f. 821, op. 133, d. 198, ll. 95–96. See also Klibanov, *Istoriia religioznogo sektantstva*, 233, 255.

14. See, for example, B. Pravdin, "Otnoshenie 'shtundizma' k sotsial'demokratii," *Razsviet* no. 2 (February 1904): 43–46; P. Raevskii, "Vstriechi i riechi. (Iz vpechatlienii i nabliudenii sotsial'demokrata)," *Razsviet*, no. 4 (April 1904): 110–11. On Kiev shtundists' participation in peaceful strikes, see also RGB, f. 369, k. 352, d. 23, l. 4.

15. For their correspondence on this matter, see GMIR, f. 2, op. 16, d. 62, ll. 1–26. Pavlov told Bonch-Bruevich that he was happy to send him Baptist documents but wanted them published separately from other kinds of articles so that the enemies of sectarians could not say that they preached socialist ideas (ll. 11–12).

16. Putintsev, *Politicheskaia rol'*, 27. A government official who met with Pavlov, who was then serving as presbyter of Odessa, and that congregation's missionary, Kh. I. Kravchenko, in 1909 did not think they were connected to antistate groups but reported that, nevertheless, they aspired to a "Christian-socialist state within a state" (RGIA, f. 821, op. 133, d. 342, l. 18).

17. D. Khilkov, *Revoliutsiia i sektanty* (N.p.: Tipografiia Partii Sotsialistov-revoliutsionerov, [1905]), 5–8.

18. *Bratskii listok* (March 1906): 5. Note that I. S. Prokhanov, the editor, praised the youth for this venture, but reminded them that their main focus should be on evangelization rather than political economy (6).

19. Lialina, "Liberal'no-burzhuaznoe techenie," 318–22. There is a typed copy of the alleged platform at the State Museum of the History of Religion, but it is neither dated nor signed (GMIR, koll. 1, op. 8, d. 3). Prokhanov does not mention this in his rather tendentious memoirs, written in the 1930s for an American audience, and the union is never mentioned in the journal *Bratskii listok*.

20. GMIR, koll. 1, op. 8, d. 32, folder 10, l. 7.

21. *Bratskii listok* (December 1906): 7.

22. Klibanov, *Istoriia religioznogo sektantstva*, 268–69; L. N. Mitrokhin, *Baptizm*, 2nd ed. (Moscow: Izdatel'stvo politicheskoi literatury, 1974), 7.

23. GARF, f. 102 (DP/OO), op. 1913, d. 85; on accusations, see RGIA, f. 796, op. 442, d. 2105, l. 115; d. 2127, l. 120b.–13; and f. 821, op. 133, d. 342, l. 130b.; on the Timoshenko case, see RGIA, f. 1284, op. 185 (1908), d. 83, l. 80; on Konovalov, see GMIR, koll. 1, op. 8, d. 311, l. 160b.

24. V. Popov, "Khristianskie kommuny Prokhanova," *Nauka i religiia*, no. 7 (1990): 48–49; I. S. Prokhanoff, *In the Cauldron of Russia* (New York: All-Russian Evangelical Christian Union, 1933), 87–91; V. V. Ivanov, "Tsarstvo bozhie," *Baptist*, no. 34 (18 August 1910): 265–67.

25. GMIR, koll. 1, op. 8, d. 69, ll. 34, 40 (Ivanov to Pavlov, 4 April 1900).

26. GARF, f. 102 (DP/OO), op. 1898, d. 12, ch. 4, ll. 59–60.

27. P. V. Ivanov-Klyshnikov, the son of V. V. Ivanov mentioned above, disclosed in the 1920s that Sermiaga [the word means a coarse, undyed cloth] was a pseudonym he used in his student days. Ivanov-Klyshnikov seems to have remained involved with the Socialist Revolutionaries right through 1917 (GMIR, koll. 1, op. 8, d. 32, folder 1, ll. 1–6). A copy is also found in RGIA, f. 821, op. 133, d. 177, l. 289.

28. See, for example, N. I. Makarevskii, *Sbornik obrashchenii na evangel'skii put' zhizni* (St. Petersburg: Tipografiia Andersona i Loitsianskago, n.d.), 8–9; *Otchet baptistskago missionerskago obshchestva za 1907–1908 god* (Odessa: Tipografiia aktsionernago

iuzhno-russkago obshchestva pechatnago diela, 1909), 10; Vasilii Skaldin, "Ot Neviezh-estva k istinie," *Slovo istiny*, no. 32 (April 1914): 361; Alexander Dobrinin, "Story of My Simple Life and Its Environment," *European Harvest Field*, no. 10 (1931): 14–15; "Pis'mo br. A. S. Makarenko iz g. Odessy," *Bratskii listok*, no. 6 (June 1910): 3.

29. See, for example, *Otchet Obshchago Sobraniia chlenov SPB Obshchiny Evangel'skikh Khristian, sostoiavshagosia 15-go avgusta 1908 goda* (St. Petersburg, 1908), 9, 22; A. Ivanov, *Otchet o sobranie* (Novgorod, 1910), 1–5; "Besiedy 'Baptista,'" *Baptist*, no. 40 (29 September 1910); GMIR, koll. 1, op. 8, d. 69, l. 429.

30. Zapros o presliedovaniiakh sektantov," *Utrenniaia zvezda*, no. 19 (10 May 1913): 1–2.

31. See, for example, N. Raevskii, "Vozmozhna-li reformatsiia v Rossii," *Slovo istiny*, no. 22 (January 1914): 260–61.

32. Richard Bauckham, "Millenarianism," in *Dictionary of Ethics, Theology, and Society*, ed. Paul Barry Clarke and Andrew Linzey (London: Routledge, 1996), 566.

33. V. Pavlov, "Kto moi bliznii (Okonchanie)," *Baptist*, no. 4 (April 1908): 3. See also N. I. Sapunkov, "[untitled]," *Baptist*, no. 2 (February 1908): 2.

34. V. Pavlov, "Pravda o baptistakh," *Baptist* (9 November 1911): 363.

35. Sotsial'nyi vopros," *Molodoi vinogradnik*, no. 1 (1911): 2; cited in Samuel John Nesdoly, "Evangelical Sectarianism in Russia: A Study of the Stundists, Baptists, Pashkovites, and Evangelical Christians, 1855–1917" (Ph.D. dissertation, Queen's University, 1971), 330.

36. Orlando Figes, *A People's Tragedy* (London: Jonathan Cape, 1996), 335, 358, 359.

37. Orlando Figes and Boris Kolonitskii, *Interpreting the Russian Revolution* (New Haven: Yale University Press, 1999), 30–32.

38. Blane, "Relations between the Russian Protestant Sects and the State," 130; Steeves, "Russian Baptist Union," 99.

39. S. M. Bessarab, "Ingulka, Khers. gub.," *Slovo istiny*, no. 15–16 (December 1917): 226.

40. GMIR, koll. 1, op. 8, d. 68, l. 5.

41. RGIA, f. 1278, op. 5, d. 1328, ll. 45, 28. Baptist and Evangelical Christian telegrams are found on ll. 19–68. Some of these telegrams were also sent to the Council of Workers' and Soldiers' Deputies, but its files were inaccessible in the St. Petersburg city archive during my research trips in 1995–96 and 1999.

42. Figes, *A People's Tragedy*, 368.

43. V. Pavlov, "Na Nivie Bozhiei. Moskva," *Slovo istiny*, no. 2–3 (June 1917): 46.

44. Vladimir G-n, "Na Nivie Bozh'ie (Kratkii obzor evangel'skago dvizheniia za 1917 god)," *Slovo istiny*, no. 3–4 (February 1918): 36.

45. K Momentu," *Slovo istiny*, no. 1 (May 1917): 2. Although she is overly enthusiastic about finding ideological division and bourgeois political motives among Baptist leaders, Lialina correctly points to the more politicized tradition of this Odessa group, tracing it through V. G. Pavlov's tenure as editor of *Baptist* in 1910–11 and the appearance of *Slovo istiny* in 1913–14. See Lialina, "Liberal'no-burzhuaznoe techenie," 327–28.

46. *Otchet 4-go Vserossiiskago S"iezda*, 50–53, 3.

47. GMIR, koll. 1, op. 8, d. 69, l. 198; for an Evangelical Christian who participated in the Revel workers' soviet, see GMIR, f. 13, op. 1, d. 196, l. 5; "Khristianstvo i politicheskiia partii (Posliednie otviety na anketu v No. 4 'Neotlozhnaia zadacha')," *Slovo istiny*, no. 13–14 (November 1917): 185.

48. Figes, *A People's Tragedy*, 347.

49. Figes, "The Russian Revolution of 1917 and Its Language in the Village," *Russian Review* 56 (July 1997): 339.

50. Boris I. Kolonitskii, "Antibourgeois Propaganda and Anti-'Burzhui' Consciousness in 1917," *Russian Review*, 53, no. 2 (April 1994): 193.

51. Figes, *A People's Tragedy*, 352.

52. K Momentu," *Slovo istiny*, no. 1 (May 1917): 2; *Otchet Baptistkago*, 90; Putintsev, *Politicheskaia rol'*, 158.

53. Dobrinin, "Story of My Simple Life," 17.

54. P.V.P., "Politicheskiia trebovaniia baptistov," *Slovo istiny*, no. 1 (May 1917): 2–3.

55. Piligrim, *Kto vy?* (Moscow: Slovo istiny, 1917), 8. On the term "comrade" in 1917, see Figes and Kolonitskii, *Interpreting the Russian Revolution*, 61.

56. See, for example, Prokhanoff, *In the Cauldron of Russia*, 173–74; A. Vodlinger, "Revoliutsiia dukha," *Slovo istiny*, no. 11 (October 1917): 146–47; "Novosti i Rossii," *Seiatel'* (August 1917): 5–6; V. V. Ivanov, "Propovied' Evangeliia na iugie," *Slovo istiny*, no.13–14 (November 1917): 198; Skromnyi, "Shtrikhi zhizni," *Slovo istiny*, no. 5–6 (March 1918): 61.

57. *Otchet 4-go Vserossiiskago S"iezda*, 47.

58. Dobrinin, "Story of My Simple Life," 17.

59. Figes, "The Russian Revolution of 1917," 328–29; Kolonitskii, "Antibourgeois Propaganda," 187.

60. Vladimir Martsinkovskii, *Zapiski veruiushchego* (St. Petersburg: Khristianskoe obshchestvo "Bibliia dlia vsekh," 1995), 23, 33. See also the anonymous leaflet announcing the religious revolution received by the Petrograd Soviet in GARF, f. 1235, op. 53, d. 68, l. 131.

61. Bernice Glatzer Rosenthal and Martha Bohachevsky-Chomiak, eds., *A Revolution of the Spirit* (New York: Fordham University Press, 1990): 1–37. They take their title from the writings of Andrei Bely.

62. Bernice Glatzer Rosenthal, "Political Implications of the Early Twentieth-Century Occult Revival," in *The Occult in Russian and Soviet Culture*, ed. Bernice Glatzer Rosenthal (Ithaca, N.Y.: Cornell University Press, 1997), 391–92.

63. Bergman, "The Image of Jesus," 238–39; see also Mark D. Steinberg, "Workers on the Cross: Religious Imagination in the Writings of Russian Workers, 1910–1924," *Russian Review* 53 (April 1994): 213–39.

64. *Otchet 5-go Vserossiiskago S"iezda Evangel'skikh Khristian (sostoiavshagosia v g. Moskve s 25 dekabria 1917g. po 1 ianvaria 1918g.)* (Petrograd: "Raduga," 1918), 2; GMIR, koll. 1, op. 8, d. 69, ll. 198–99, 228; RGIA, f. 1278, op. 5, d. 1328, ll. 28, 33, 38, 47, 67, 68; V. Pavlov, "Otdelenie Tserkvi ot Gosudarstva," *Slovo istiny*, no. 1 (May 1917): 10; Ivanov, "Propovied' Evangeliia na iugie," 198; Southern Baptist Historical Library and Archives, Adolf J. Klaupiks Papers, AR. 672, box 1, folder 28 (Pavlov, Vasily Gur'evich—Diary, 1906, 1910–12, 1914, 1917, 1919–20), page 1917-11 (July 2).

65. On the moral conception of socialism, see Nesdoly, "Evangelical Sectarianism in Russia," 241.

66. Ivanov, "Propovied' Evangeliia na iugie," 198. See also "Riech' I. S. Prokhanova na gosudarstvennom sovieshchanii v Moskvie, 14 avgusta 1917g.," *Slovo istiny*, no. 8 (August 1917): 106; P. Ch., "2-kh nediel'naia evangelizatsiia v g. Samarie," *Slovo istiny*, no. 2 (January 1918): 27.

67. P.V.P., "Politicheskiia trebovaniia baptistov," 24.

68. Figes, "The Russian Revolution of 1917," 335; and idem, *A People's Tragedy*, 357–59.

69. Kolonitskii, "Antibourgeois Propaganda," 188.

70. GMIR, koll. 1, op. 8, d. 68, folder 2, l. 50b.

71. Ivanov, "Propovied' Evangeliia na iugie," 198. An evangelical activist later recalled an extreme incident of politicization: "In 1917 I was visiting a Baptist Church in a certain city, which was the capital of the province. After I had preached a sermon the pastor took the pulpit. His sermon was nothing but a political speech" (N. I. Saloff-Astakoff, *Real Russia from 1905–1932* [New York, 1932], 94). The identity of the pastor is unclear.

72. *Otchet 4-go Vserossiiskago S"iezda*, 90.

73. For a similar blurring of these boundaries, see Phillips, *A Kingdom of God on Earth*, 2.

74. V. Finogenov, "Pis'mo s fronta," *Slovo istiny*, no. 15–16 (December 1917): 229; for similar views, see also 123, 147.

75. A. F., "Khristianstvo i politicheskiia partii (Otvet na anketu v No. 4 'Neotlozhnaia zadacha')," *Slovo istiny*, no. 11 (October 1917): 147. See also the Samara youth group's event in October where the theme was "Christ in personal and public life" (Drug, "Na Bozhiei nivie," *Slovo istiny*, no. 13–14 [November 1917]: 195).

76. I. A. Varganov, "Trapezond," *Slovo istiny*, no. 13–14 (November 1917): 196.

77. P.V.P., "Politicheskiia trebovaniia baptistov," 24.

78. GMPIR, f. 2, d. 17564. On List no. 3 were I. S. Prokhanov, V. A. Guliaev, I. F. Epifanov, and A. G. Iaitsov. I thank Dr. Aleksandr G. Kalmykov for this information.

79. *Khristiansko-demokraticheskaia partiia "Voskresenie." Raz"iasnenie tsielei i programma* (Kiev, 1917), 6.

80. Klibanov, *Istoriia religioznogo sektantstva*, 281. Klibanov cites *Utrenniaia zviezda*, no. 1 (1917): 7. I have not been able to locate this issue and so have used the platform of the Kiev branch of the party for my summary. It is identical to the quotations in Klibanov's rather tendentious summary, except for the absence of any mention of continuing the war.

81. William G. Rosenberg, *Liberals in the Russian Revolution* (Princeton, N.J.: Princeton University Press, 1974), 12–20, 99–106.

82. Figes, *A People's Tragedy*, 335.

83. "Chto to budet?" *Slovo istiny*, no. 2–3 (June 1917): 17–18; P. Nikolaev, "Khodiat slukhi . . . (K dannomu momentu)," *Slovo istiny*, no. 2–3 (June 1917): 18.

84. Arvid, "Sovremennye soiuzy, federatsii i vsevozmozhniia iniia soedineniia s khristianskoi tochki zrieniia," *Slovo istiny*, no. 4 (July 1917): 51.

85. Neotlozhnaia zadacha," *Slovo istiny*, no. 4 (July 1917): 63.

86. Putintsev, *Politicheskaia rol'*, 234–39; Southern Baptist Historical Library and Archives, Adolf J. Klaupiks Papers, AR. 672, box 1, folder 28 (Pavlov, Vasily Gur'evich—Diary, 1906, 1910–12, 1914, 1917, 1919–20), page 1917-17 (27 December 1917).

87. "Khristianstvo i politicheskiia partii (Posliednie otviety na anketu v No. 4 'Neotlozhnaia zadacha')," *Slovo istiny* no. 13–14 (November 1917): 184. *Slovo istiny* printed six complete answers from readers; the summary quoted from an additional six respondents' letters.

88. A. F., "Khristianstvo i politicheskiia partii," 147. See also P. Lopukhin, "Khristianstvo i politicheskiia partii (Otviety na anketu v No. 4 'neotlozhnaia zadacha')," *Slovo istiny*, no. 9–10 (September 1917): 123.

89. Lopukhin, "Khristianstvo i politicheskiia partii. (Otviety na anketu v No. 4 'Neotlozhnaia zadacha')," *Slovo istiny* no. 9–10 (September 1917): 123; on a similar theme, see 147, 107.

90. Vladimir G-n, "Khristianstvo i politicheskiia partii (Otviet na anketu v No. 4 'Neotlozhnaia zadacha')," *Slovo istiny,* no. 8 (August 1917): 108.

91. Against communism, see Savel'ev, "Khristianstvo i politicheskiia partii (Otviet na anketu v No. 4 'Neotlozhnaia zadacha')," *Slovo istiny,* no. 12 (November 1917): 166–67; see also 107, 122, 147, 185.

92. A. F., "Khristianstvo i politicheskiia partii," 147; *Slovo istiny,* no. 13–14 (November 1917): 184; Vladimir G-n, "Khristianstvo i politicheskiia partii," 108.

93. The Evangelical Christians struggled with the same issue. Their youth wing's congress in January 1918 held a debate on the matter, and a resolution passed declaring that Christianity was compatible with the responsibilities of citizenship but that the believer had to ensure that his religious commitment remained his driving motivation (*Otchet 5-go Vserossiiskago S"iezda Khristianskoi Molodezhi* [Petrograd: "Raduga," 1918], 30–31).

94. Reprinted in "Riech' I. S. Prokhanova na gosudarstvennom sovieshchanii v Moskvie," 108–9. See also Prokhanov's letter of support to Kerenskii shortly after the conference, in M. M. Persits, *Otdelenie tserkvi ot gosudarstva i shkoly ot tserkvi v SSSR (1917–1919 gg.)* (Moscow: Izdatel'stvo Akademii Nauk SSSR, 1958), 97.

95. "Na rasput'i," *Slovo istiny,* no. 5–6 (August 1917): 65–66.

96. They later endorsed Kerenskii's view that General Lavr Kornilov had attempted a putsch against the Provisional Government and called for the general and his supporters to be brought to trial ("Mezhdousobitsa," *Slovo istiny,* no. 7 [August 1917]: 89).

97. A. Regnildov, "Spasenie Rossii," *Slovo istiny,* no. 7 (August 1917): 90–91.

98. Vodlinger, "Revoliutsiia dukha," 146.

99. Bratoubiistvennyi koshmar," *Slovo istiny,* no. 12 (November 1917): 162; V. Pavlov, "Idealy narodov," *Slovo istiny,* no. 13–14 (November 1917): 179–80.

100. Figes, *A People's Tragedy,* 358–59.

101. "Baptist," "Otnoshenie vieruiushchago k politicheskim partiiam," *Slovo istiny,* no. 9–12 (May–June 1918): 84.

102. V. V. Ivanov, "Kak vragi Kresta Khristova (Vnimaniiu vsekh veruiushchikh)," *Slovo istiny,* no. 9–12 (May–June 1918): 94.

103. E. Gerasimenko, "Khar'kov," *Slovo istiny,* no. 15–16 (December 1917): 226.

104. "Pochtovyi iashchik," *Slovo istiny,* no. 9–10 (September 1917): 144; "Khristianstvo i politicheskiia partii," *Slovo istiny,* no. 13–14 (November 1917): 184; Vladimir G-n, "Na Nivie Bozhiei," 36. For this theme in poetry and stories, see A. Mendelieeva, "Skorbnye dni," *Slovo istiny,* no. 15–16 (December 1917): 208; N. K., "Zvier' (Iz Apokalipsisa)," *Slovo istiny,* no. 15–16 (December 1917): 208–9; A. Mendelieeva, "On griadet," *Slovo istiny,* no. 1 (January 1918): 3.

105. GMIR, koll. 1, op. 8, d. 69, folder of sermon drafts, ll. 1–360b.

106. Ivanov, "Kak vragi Kresta," 94. This view may have arisen from personal experience: in a letter to his son dated March 25, Ivanov had described the terror and "robbery" that came with the arrival of the Bolsheviks in the village where he was staying (GMIR, koll. 1, op. 8, d. 69, folder of letters to P. V. Ivanov-Klyshnikov, l. 257).

107. Lynne Viola, "The Peasant Nightmare: Visions of Apocalypse in the Soviet Countryside," *Journal of Modern History* 62 (December 1990): 750–51; Steinberg,

"Workers on the Cross," 227–33; Rosenthal and Bohachevsky-Chomiak, *A Revolution of the Spirit*, 5, 34.

108. Evmenii [*sic*] Gerasimenko, "Glavnye usloviia k sokhraneniiu dukhovnosti Tserkvi Bozhiei," *Slovo istiny*, no. 9–12 (May–June 1918): 94.

109. "Vozzvanie," *Slovo istiny*, no. 15–16 (December 1917): 229.

110. P. Ch., "2-kh nediel'naia evangelizatsiia v g. Samarie," 27.

111. *Otchet 5-go Vserossiiskago s"iezda*, 1.

112. "Arvid," "Sotsializm i khristianstvo," *Slovo istiny*, no. 1 (January 1918): 5–7.

113. "Arvid," "Sotsializm i khristianstvo," *Slovo istiny*, no. 7–8 (April 1918): 71.

114. "Arvid," "Sotsializm i khristianstvo," *Slovo istiny*, no. 9–12 (May–June 1918): 85.

8. REVOLUTION AND OPPORTUNITY

1. For example, Liudmila Alekseeva, *Istoriia inakomyslia v SSSR* (Benson, Vt.: Khronika, 1984), 171; Walter Kolarz, *Religion in the Soviet Union* (New York: St. Martin's, 1966), 287–300; A. A. Rudenko, "Evangel'skie khristiane-baptisty i perestroika v SSSR," in *Na puti k svobode sovesti*, ed. D. E. Furman and Mark (Smirnov) (Moscow: Progress, 1989), 345.

2. W. T. Whitley, ed., *Third Baptist World Congress* (London: Kingsgate, 1923), 87. Rushbrooke noted that his figures included the Evangelical Christians.

3. Julius F. Hecker, *Religion under the Soviets* (New York: Vanguard, 1927), 133, 151.

4. R. Khomiak, "10-ti letnii iubiliei," *Baptist Ukrainy*, no. 4 (1928): 54–57; on Khomiak and his wife working as a preaching team, see idem, "Iz zhizni nashikh obshchin na Ukraine," *Baptist Ukrainy*, no. 11 (1927): 50–51.

5. See, for example, Iv. Filadel'fiiskii, "Peskovskie torzhestva," *Baptist Ukrainy*, no. 9 (1927): 48–51; "Soobshcheniia s mest," *Khristianin*, no. 11 (1925): 61.

6. S. P. Fadiukhin, *Vospominaniia o perezhitom* (St. Petersburg: Bibliia dlia vsekh, 1993), 96; M. Grachev, "Den' radosti i torzhestva," *Khristianin*, no. 7 (1925): 56–57.

7. See, for example, Richard Stites, *Revolutionary Dreams* (New York: Oxford University Press, 1989), 121–22; Lewis H. Siegelbaum, *Soviet State and Society between Revolutions* (New York: Cambridge University Press, 1992), 163.

8. Siegelbaum, *Soviet State and Society*, 136.

9. William B. Husband, *"Godless Communists"* (DeKalb: Northern Illinois University Press, 2000), 38.

10. GMIR, f. 2, op. 16, d. 94, l. 2; Peter Brock, ed., *Testimonies of Conscience* (Toronto: Privately printed, 1997), 30.

11. The decree is reprinted in P. V. Gidulianov, *Otdelenie tserkvi ot gosudarstva*, ed. P. A. Krasikov (Moscow: Iuridicheskoe izdatel'stvo N.K.Iu. R.S.F.S.R., 1926), 615–17; Arto Luukkanen, *The Party of Unbelief* (Helsinki: Suomen Historiallinen Seura, 1994), chap. 2, esp. 54, 80, 83, 95; N. A. Krivova, *Vlast' i tserkov' v 1922–1925gg.* (Moscow: AIRO-XX, 1997), 13–14; Daniel Peris, *Storming the Heavens* (Ithaca, N.Y.: Cornell University Press, 1998), 19.

12. Luukkanen, *The Party of Unbelief*, 230.

13. Ibid., 91.

14. Ibid., 91–94, 101; Eberhard Müller, "Opportunismus oder Utopie?" *Jahrbücher für Geschichte Osteuropas* 35 (1987): 518–20, 525; Aleksandr Etkind, "Russkie sekty i sovetskii kommunizm," *Minuvshee*, no. 19 (1996): 293.

15. For example, this point was made at a meeting of the Agitation Department

of the Moscow party organization in May 1921 (RGASPI, f. 17, op. 60, d. 114, l. 1). See also Ia. Nikulikhin, "O sektantakh," *Sputnik kommunista*, no. 6 (30 March 1927): 27–32.

16. GMIR, koll. 1, op. 8, d. 34, l. 20b. In 1925 the Evangelical Christians published advice on how to get around these prohibitions ("Otdelam, obshchinam i gruppam evangel'skikh khristian v SSSR," *Khristianin*, no. 5 [1925]: 44–45; M. V. Shkarovskii, *Peterburgskaia eparkhiia v gody gonenii i utrat 1917–1945* [St. Petersburg: Liki Rossii, 1995], 36).

17. GARF, f. 393, op. 27, d. 1388, l. 308; op. 43a, d. 74, l. 7.

18. GARF, f. 353, op. 3, d. 780, l. 79; f. 130 op. 3, d. 214; f. 1235, op. 40, d. 69.

19. "Gonimaia," *Slovo istiny*, no. 2 (January 1918): 17–18. See also Skromnyi, "Shtrikhi zhizni," *Slovo istiny*, no. 2 (January 1918): 25–26. The term "Orthodox department" refers to the fact that the Holy Synod was the "Orthodox department" of the imperial state.

20. Timo, "Religiia bez Khrista," *Slovo istiny*, no. 13 (1918): 98–99.

21. Sviataia vata i kosti," *Slovo istiny*, no. 1 (1919): 2–3; GMIR, koll. 1, op. 8, d. 35, folder 3, l. 100b.

22. GARF, f. A353, op. 8, d. 8, l. 109; GMIR, f. 13, op. 1 d. 273, l. 9.

23. GARF, f. 130, op. 3, d. 209, l. 47.

24. Luukkanen, *The Party of Unbelief*, 76.

25. V. Popov, "Khristianskie kommuny Prokhanova," *Nauka i religiia*, no. 7 (1990): 49.

26. M. T., "Ne pora li?" *Slovo istiny*, no. 13 (1918): 98.

27. Southern Baptist Historical Library and Archives, Adolf J. Klaupiks Papers, AR. 672, box 1, folder 28 (Pavlov, Vasily Gur'evich—Diary, 1906, 1910–12, 1914, 1917, 1919–20), 2 June 1920; GMIR, koll. 1, op. 8, d. 35, folder 2, l. 8.

28. "Gonimaia," *Slovo istiny*, no. 2 (January 1918): 18.

29. Luukkanen, *The Party of Unbelief*, 62.

30. Siegelbaum, *Soviet State and Society*, 25; Orlando Figes, *A People's Tragedy* (London: Jonathan Cape, 1996), 733–45.

31. Jochen Hellbeck, "Writing the Self in the Time of Terror," in *Self and Story in Russian History*, ed. Laura Engelstein and Stephanie Sandler, 69–93 (Ithaca, N.Y.: Cornell University Press, 2000), 78; Igal Halfin, "From Darkness to Light," *Jahrbücher für Geschichte Osteuropas* 45, no. 2 (1997): 220, 235.

32. For example, RGIA, f. 831, op. 1, d. 62, l. 6; "Est' Bog ili net?" *Slovo istiny*, no. 2 (1919): 15; "Na Nive Bozh'ei," *Vestnik baptistov*, no. 1 (1919): 4; Vladimir Martsinkovskii, *Zapiski veruiushchego* (St. Petersburg: Khristianskoe obshchestvo "Biblia dlia vsekh," 1995), 23–30, 73–78, 93–101, 118.

33. John Shelton Curtiss, *The Russian Church and the Soviet State* (Boston: Little, Brown, 1953), 72–80, 87–89; Martsinkovskii, *Zapiski veruiushchego*, 47, 118.

34. P. Krasikov, "Religiia i kommunizm," *Revoliutsiia i tserkov'*, no. 3–5 (1919): 6–12. Despite the date on the cover, an introductory note from the editorial board explained that this issue was appearing only in May 1920 because the print shop had been closed for the entire winter because of a lack of fuel.

35. 7-i Vserossiiskii S"ezd Evangel'skikh Khristian v Moskve s 27 maia po 7 iiunia 1920," *Utrenniaia zvezda*, no. 2 (June 1920): 8. For similar examples of lively encounters with Communist opponents at meetings, see "Na Nive Bozhiei," *Istochnik iz kamnia*, no. 15–21 (1920): 14.

36. G. V. Grigor'ev, "Vselenskoe Khristianstvo ili vselenskii sotsializm? (Khristos i Antikhrist)," *Istochnik iz kamnia*, no. 15–24 (August–December 1920): 2.

37. "Baptist," "Vosem' dnei na s"ezde v Moskve," *Slovo istiny*, no. 5–6 (1921): 42.

38. Diane P. Koenker, "Urbanization and Deurbanization in the Russian Revolution and Civil War," in *Party, State, and Society in the Russian Civil War*, ed. Diane P. Koenker, William G. Rosenberg, and Ronald Grigor Suny (Bloomington: Indiana University Press, 1989), 81–104. Numbers in the Moscow and Petrograd congregations were greatly reduced (*Bratskii soiuz*, no. 1 [1920]: 10; "Iz zhizni Doma Evangeliia," *Istochnik iz kamnia*, no. 304 [1920]: 3).

39. *Drug*, no. 2 (February 1919): 15.

40. A. Sh., "Iz zhizni Novo-Pavlovskoi obshchiny," *Baptist Ukrainy*, no. 6 (1928): 50.

41. I. I., "Na Nive Bozh'ei," *Vestnik baptistov*, no. 1 (1919): 4; "Baptist," "Neskol'ko slov brat'iam propovednikam," *Slovo istiny*, no. 5–6 (1921): 46; *Drug*, no. 2 (February 1919): 15; GMIR, koll. 1, op. 8, d. 80, folder 3, ll. 21–22; folder 5, ll. 2–70b.

42. On competition leading to inflated numbers, see GMIR, koll. 1, op. 8, d. 45, l. 20b.

43. P. V. Ivanov-Klyshnikov, "Zadachi baptistov v SSSR v 1926 g.," *Baptist*, no. 1 (1926): 15; Timo, "Skol'ko baptistov v mire," *Baptist*, no. 5–6 (1926): 12; N. V. Odintsov, "Sostoianie dela Bozhiia v Rossii," *Baptist*, no. 1 (1927): 21.

44. GMIR, koll. 1, op. 8, d. 34, folder 3, l. 7.

45. The materials are found in the 2,189 pages of GMIR, koll. 1, op. 8, d. 61. Unfortunately, I was unable to get through more than a sample before the archive closed for an undetermined period. In 1926, Pavel Ivanov-Klyshnikov reported that the union had information on 3,028 congregations, with more coming in (Ivanov-Klyshnikov, "Zadachi," 14).

46. GMIR, koll. 1, op. 8, d. 341, l. 96; W. T. Whitley, ed., *Fourth Baptist World Congress* (Toronto: Stewart Printing Service, 1928), 76.

47. *Utrenniaia zvezda*, no. 6–8 (June–August 1922): 24.

48. *Zapisi zasedanii 10-go Vsesoiuznogo S"ezda Evangel'skikh Khristian* (Leningrad: Izdanie I. S. Prokhanova i Ia. I. Zhidkova, 1927), 15.

49. RGIA, f. 1278, op. 5, d. 605, ll. 10–21. This is probably a low figure, since many congregations were unregistered.

50. *Vestnik baptistov*, no. 1 (1919): 1–2.

51. GMIR, f. 2, op. 16, d. 87, l. 4; *Slovo istiny*, no. 1 (1919): 4; I. S. Prokhanoff, *In the Cauldron of Russia* (New York: All-Russian Evangelical Christian Union, 1933), 218.

52. *Istoriia evangel'skikh khristian-baptistov v SSSR* (Moscow: Izdanie Vsesoiuznogo Soveta Evangel'skikh Khristian-Baptistov, 1989), 140, 182–86, 190, 199–202; M. T., "O Vseukrainskom S"ezde Baptistov," *Vestnik baptistov*, no. 1 (1919): 3–4; GMIR, koll. 1, op. 8, d. 34, folders 3, 10. On Ukrainization, see Orest Subtelny, *Ukraine*, 3rd ed. (Toronto: University of Toronto Press, 2000), 387–90.

53. *Protokoly 9-go Vsesoiuznogo S"ezda Evangel'skikh Khristian v Petrograde v 1923 godu* (Petrograd: Izdanie VSEKh, 1923), 11; *Utrenniaia zvezda*, no. 1–2 (January–February 1922): 1.

54. Among many examples are GMIR, koll. 1, op. 8, folder 2, l. 50b.; "Blagovieshchensk na Amurie," *Slovo istiny*, no. 13–14 (November 1917): 196.

55. Tserkvam Bozhim! I vsem brat'em vo Khriste, razseiannym po nashei Rossii 'radovat'sia'!" *Istochnik iz kamnia*, no. 3–4 (1920): 7; *Bratskii soiuz*, no. 1 (March 1920): 2–3.

56. Among many examples, see "Edinstvo veruiushchikh v Petrograde" and "Raznyia izvestiia," *Bratskii soiuz,* no. 2 (May 1920): 3–4; V. I. Martynov, "Kavkazskii S"ezd Evangel'skikh Khristian Baptistov," *Slovo istiny,* no. 3 (1920): 23; "Raionnye s"ezdy," *Slovo istiny,* no. 1–2 (1921): 11.

57. "Ot Kollegii Soveta Vserossiiskogo Soiuza Baptistov" and "Priglashenie na obshchii Vserossiisskii S"ezd Baptistov i Evangel'skikh Khristian," *Slovo istiny,* no. 1–2 (1921): 6–8. Part of the problem was that official permission for a congress was withheld (GARF, f. A353, op. 5, d. 231, l. 28).

58. Plenum Soveta Soiuza Baptistov SSSR (Kratkii otchet)," *Baptist,* no. 1 (1926): 22. Prokhanov was not reelected at the next congress of the Baptist World Alliance in 1928.

59. On the tent mission, see N. I. Saloff-Astakhoff, *Interesting Facts of the Russian Revolution* (New York, 1931); on joint sectarian congresses in 1919, see "Na Nive Bozhiei," *Utrenniaia zvezda,* no. 1 (January 1920): 6–8.

60. Martsinkovskii, *Zapiski veruiushchego,* 178, 224.

61. Gregory L. Freeze, "Counter-reformation in Russian Orthodoxy," *Slavic Review* 54, no. 2 (summer 1995): 334–36. Although it is unclear how accurate they are, figures published in the antireligious press suggest that *Baptist* and *Khristianin* had far higher circulation rates than any of the other twelve religious magazines published in 1928 (I. Bodiakshin, "Dela nashikh vragov. [O religioznoi pechati za 1928 god]," *Antireligioznik,* no. 6 [1929]: 82–83). The figure given for *Khristianin* conforms with that reported in *Khristianin* itself ("K nashim podpischikam i chitateliam!" *Khristianin,* no. 10 [1928]: 65).

62. See, for example, I. A. Goliaev, "Vyezdnaia missionerskaia rabota v 1925 g.," *Baptist,* no. 1–2 (1926): 17–19; A. Bukreev, "Nasha poezdka po Sibiri," *Baptist Ukrainy,* no. 5 (1928): 51–53.

63. N. Varganov, "Ogon' zagorelsia," *Baptist Ukrainy,* no. 7 (July 1927): 52–53.

64. GMIR, koll. 1, op. 8, d. 35, folder 3, l. 50b.

65. "Plenum Soveta Soiuza Baptistov SSSR," *Baptist,* no. 1–2 (1926): 19–20; *26-oi Vsesoiuznyi S"ezd Baptistov SSSR* (Moscow: Izdanie Federativnogo Soiuza Baptistov SSSR v litse N. V. Odintsova, 1927), 33–45.

66. 7-i Vserossiiskii S"ezd Evangel'skikh Khristian v Moskve s 27 maia po 7 iiunia 1920g.," *Utrenniaia zvezda,* no. 2 (June 1920): 4; *Protokoly 9-go Vsesoiuznogo S"ezda,* 12. Prokhanoff, *In the Cauldron of Russia,* 152–53.

67. See, for example, the letters from the Evangelical Christian missionary Mariia Antonenko ("Iakutiia," *Khristianin,* no. 10 [1926]: 23–24).

68. 7-i Vserossiiskii S"ezd," 4; GMIR, koll. 1, op. 8, d. 35, folder 8, l. 20b.

69. See "Our Missionaries," *Friend of Russia,* no. 5 (May 1923): 68; and "Russian Missionary Society," *Friend of Russia,* no. 7–8 (July–August 1924): 117.

70. Prokhanoff, *In the Cauldron of Russia,* 208; GMIR, koll. 1, op. 8, d. 45, l. 6, d. 310, d. 364.

71. GARF, f. A353, op. 8, d. 8, ll. 145, 151, 157; *Istoriia evangel'skikh khristian-baptistov v SSSR,* 215, 222; T. S. Smirnova, "Torzhestvo otkrytiia Moskovskikh Bibleiskikh kursov Baptistov," *Baptist,* no. 12 (December 1927): 11–17.

72. *Utrenniaia zvezda,* no. 1–2 (January–February 1922): 10; *Istoriia evangel'skikh khristian-baptistov v SSSR,* 214–15.

73. "Mesiats Vserossiiskoi Evangelizatsii," *Slovo istiny,* no. 5–6 (1921): 49.

74. "O dvukhnedel'nike Vserossiiskoi Evangelizatsii," *Slovo istiny,* no. 5–6 (1921): 43.

75. GMIR, koll. 1, op. 8, d. 45, folder 9, ll. 1–3. See also A.V.K., "Iz otcheta o deiatel'nosti Leningradskoi obshchiny evangel'skikh khristian za 1924 god," *Khristianin,* no. 1 (1925): 50–51; I. Motorin, "Nedelia molitvy v Khar'kovskoi obshchine," *Khristianin,* no. 4 (1928): 49.

76. GMIR, koll. 1, op. 8, d. 34, folder 3, l. 14.

77. See, for example, *Khristianin,* no. 12 (December 1925): 60.

78. Timo, "Poeticheskoe i prakticheskoe," *Baptist,* no. 3–4 (1926): 29.

79. Soobshcheniia s mest," *Khristianin,* no. 12 (1925): 60–61.

80. Husband, *"Godless Communists,"* 91.

81. Georgii Vins, *Tropoiu vernosti,* 2nd ed. (St. Petersburg: Biblia dlia vsekh, 1997), 20.

82. *Utrenniaia zvezda,* no. 3–4–5 (1922): 14–16.

83. "Soobshcheniia Kollegii Soveta Soiuza Baptistov," *Slovo istiny,* no. 1–2 (1921): 8; S., "Regentskie Kursy v Sredne-Iuzhnom Ob"edinenii Baptistov," *Baptist Ukrainy,* no. 7 (1927): 56–57; one of many columns of musical advice is Ia. I. Viazovskii, "Zaniatiia s khorom," *Baptist,* no. 2 (1925): 23.

84. GMIR, koll. 1, op. 8, d. 311, ll. 110ob., 159, 164ob.; d. 84, folder 2, l. 35ob.; d. 45, l. 13.

85. GMIR, koll. 1, op. 8, d. 311.

86. "Izuchenie Biblii," *Gost',* no. 10 (October 1927): 188.

87. GMIR, koll. 1, op. 8, d. 311, ll. 56ob., 66, 106, 110. Iunyi voin, "Rabota Bakinskogo kruzhka v Zakavkaz'i," *Baptist,* no. 4–5 (1925): 35; Ia. P. Grishchenko, "Zhivaia rabota," and P. T. Leshkov, "Molodezh' v Sibiri," *Baptist,* no. 1 (1927): 31.

88. *Gost',* no. 1 (September 1925): 10.

89. Soobshcheniia s mest," *Khristianin,* no. 12 (1927): 62.

90. Iu. S. Grachev, *V Irodovoi bezdne,* Kniga I (Moscow: Blagovestnik, 1994), 21, 24, 32, 35–36, 45–46, 55–57.

91. See, for example, I. Shilov, "Iz zhizni Doma Evangeliia," *Istochnik iz kamnia,* no. 3–4 (1920): 3–4; A. K. Trapaki, "Pervyi Vsekrymskii prazdnik veruiushchei pevcheskoi molodezhi," *Baptist,* no. 4 (1927): 18–19.

92. I. Ia. Eliashevich, *Religiia v bor'be za rabochuiu molodezh'* (Leningrad: Priboi, 1928), 62. The text for a similar dialogue between a believer and a nonbeliever is found in the files of the journal *Baptist,* dated 1927 (GMIR, koll. 1, op. 8, d. 464, ll. 1–4).

93. Br. Luka, "Prazdnik molodezhi i Novyi molitvennyi zal v gor. Leningradie," *Gost',* no. 10 (October 1926): 138. Regarding concern about the surrounding culture of materialism and atheism, see I. Dovgaliuk, "Kruzhkam molodezhi pri obshchinakh baptistov i otdel'nym rabotnikam sredi baptistskoi molodezhi," *Baptist,* no. 4–5 (1925): 19–21.

94. A. Mazina, "Pervyi prazdnik sester obshchin Kievskogo Otdela V. S. E. Kh.," *Khristianin,* no. 4 (1926): 56.

95. GMIR, koll.. 1, op. 8, d. 369, ll. 120ob.–130ob.; "How God Is Working in Russia," *Friend of Russia* (May 1925): 72; "Revival among Women," *Friend of Russia* (December 1926): 141.

96. Mrs. R. D., "Many Israelites Seeking Salvation," *Friend of Russia,* (July–August 1925): 97.

97. *Zapisi zasedanii 10-go Vsesoiuznogo s"ezda*, 21; *Protokoly i materialy Pervogo S"iezda Volgo-Kamskogo Soiuza Baptistov* (Troitsk: Izdanie N. V. Odintsova, 1928), 29.

98. See E. I-skaia, "O zhenskoi rabote," *Utrenniaia zvezda*, no. 3–5 (1922): 11–12; I. Matorin, "O Evangel'skom sluzhenii sester (Zametki)," *Khristianin*, no. 6 (1924): 37–39.

99. I.S.P., "Po zhenskomu voprosu v oblasti Evangel'skogo dvizheniia v Rossii," *Utrenniaia zvezda*, no. 3–5 (1922): 11.

100. GMIR, koll. 1, op. 8, d. 369, l. 140b.

101. GMIR, koll. 1, op. 8, d. 369, l. 16.

102. E. B. Iagubiants-Tarasova, "Bibliia i zhenshchina," *Baptist*, no. 3–4 (1926): 15–17; I. A. Goliaev, "Po povodu stat'i 'Bibliia i zhenshchina,'" *Baptist*, no. 5–6 (1926): 19–20.

103. TsGA SPb, f. 1001, op. 7, d. 47, l. 194. It is unclear why only 85 out of the 227 attending voted on this issue. Note also that the good work of the women's group was specifically recognized at this meeting (l. 1930b.). The congregation was required to report new members to the Leningrad city government in the mid-1920s. The great majority of these were women (TsGA SPb, f. 1001, op. 7, d. 47, ll. 810b.–82, 87, 91, 94, 99, 1240b., 1760b).

104. GMIR, koll. 1, op. 8, d. 320, ll. 2050b., 199. The course "journal" shows that there were, in fact, women among the students in the fall of 1928 (GMIR, koll. 1, op. 8, d. 322, l. 80b.).

105. See K. Petrus, *Religious Communes in the USSR* (New York: Research Program on the USSR, 1953); William Edgerton, trans. and ed., *Memoirs of Peasant Tolstoyans in Soviet Russia* (Bloomington: Indiana University Press, 1993); and A. I. Klibanov, *Religioznoe sektantstvo i sovremennost'* (Moscow: Izdatel'stvo "Nauka," 1969), 238–40.

106. RGASPI, f. 17, op. 84, d. 799, l. 28; and *Istoriia evangel'skikh khristian-baptistov v SSSR*, 174; Dorothy L. Atkinson, *The End of the Russian Land Commune* (Stanford: Stanford University Press, 1983), 219–21.

107. RGB, f. 369, k. 35, d. 29, ll. 29–32; f. 369, k. 36, d. 2, ll. 1–7; f. 435, k. 96, d. 38, ll. 1–2; RGASPI, f. 17, op. 84, d. 799, l. 1.

108. GMIR, f. 13, op. 1, d. 196, ll. 1–7; RGASPI, f. 17, op. 84, d. 799, l. 27. Note that the term "commune" here denotes the *kommuna* rather than the traditional village commune, the *mir* (Siegelbaum, *Soviet State and Society*, 44).

109. RGAE, f. 4106, op. 14, d. 14, ll. 20, 77–78; RGASPI, f. 17, op. 84, d. 799, ll. 14–15.

110. I.S.P., "Pesnia pervo-khristian," *Utrenniaia zvezda*, no. 3–5 (1922): 4. See also *Khristianin*, no. 3 (1925): 37–38.

111. GMIR, f. 2, op. 16, d. 74, l. 1.

112. *Istoriia evangel'skikh khristian-baptistov v SSSR*, 176; RGASPI, f. 17, op. 84, d. 799, l. 15; RGAE, f. 4106, op. 14, d. 14, l. 78; A. Mariinskii, "Popovshchina i sektantstvo," *Novyi mir*, no. 11 (November 1928): 272; V. Ch., "Pishcheprodukt v rukakh sektantov," *Bezbozhnik*, no. 35 (26 August 1928): 6.

113. Brotherly Aid was registered by Mosfinotdel on 2 August 1922 (GMIR, koll. 1, op. 8, d. 338, l. 2; Z. V. Kalinicheva, *Sotsial'naia sushchnost' baptizma* [Leningrad: Izdatel'stvo "Nauka," 1972], 121).

114. GMIR, koll. 1, op. 8, d. 45, folder 5, l. 6.

115. GARF, f. 1235, op. 58, d. 34, l. 37; *Utrenniaia zvezda*, no. 1–2 (January–February 1922): 3–4.

116. A. Mariinskii, "Popovshchina i sektantstvo," *Novyi mir*, no. 11 (November 1928): 272; Pishcheprodukt v rukakh sektantov," *Bezbozhnik*, no. 35 (26 August 1928): 6; "'Brati'ia'—komersanty," *Vecherniaia Moskva*, 1 February 1927.

117. S. P. Fadiukin, *Vospominaniia o perezhitom* (St. Petersburg: Bibliia dlia vsekh, 1993), 83.

118. I. S. Prokhanov, "Novaia, ili Evangel'skaia zhizn'" and "Ko vsem riadovym chlenam i rukovoditeliam evangel'skikh obshchin i otdelov," *Khristianin*, no. 1 (1925): 4–21, 23–27; *Zapis' zasedanii 10-go Vsesoiuznogo S"ezda*, 22–23. Prokhanov had apparently also outlined many of these ideas in a 1919 booklet, "Evangel'skoe khristianstvo i sotsial'nyi vopros" (Tash-Otlu-Kei, "Ekspeditsiia po izyskaniiu zemel' dlia goroda sol'ntsa," *Khristianin*, no. 2 [1928]: 44).

119. Tash-Otlu-Kei, "Ekspeditsiia po izyskaniiu zemel'," 44–52; M. P. Shop-Mishich, "Vifaniia," *Khristianin*, no. 7 (1928): 26–34.

120. Husband, *"Godless Communists,"* 69; S. Frederick Starr, "Visionary Town Planning during the Cultural Revolution," in *Cultural Revolution in Russia*, ed. Sheila Fitzpatrick, 207–40 (Bloomington: Indiana University Press, 1978), 208–9.

121. Pomoshch' golodaiushchim," *Utrenniaia zvezda*, no. 6–8 (1922): 25; GMIR, koll. 1, op. 8, d. 34, folder 12, ll. 120b.–13.

122. GMIR, koll. 1, op. 8, d. 312, ll. 310b., 35, 144; d. 320, l. 22.

123. "Editorial Foreword," *Friend Of Russia*, no. 6 (June 1923): 81.

124. GARF, f. 130, op. 3, d. 214; f. 353, op. 8, d. 8, l. 10; f. 1235, op. 40, d. 69, ll. 162–63.

125. A. Mazina, "Pervyi prazdnik sester obshchin Kievskogo Otdela V.S.E.Kh.," *Khristianin*, no. 3 (1926): 57; "Soobshcheniia," *Khristianin*, no. 6 (1924): 46–47; "Bratskie raz"iasneniia," *Khristianin*, no. 2 (1926): 47–48.

126. *Friend of Russia*, no. 3 (March 1925): 40; "How God Is Working in Russia," *Friend of Russia*, no. 5 (May 1925): 72; "Messages from our Missionaries," *Friend of Russia*, no. 3–4 (March–April 1926): 28–29.

127. See, for example, Shkarovskii, *Peterburgskaia eparkhiia*, 36, 105–07; N. B. Lebina, *Povsednevskaia zhizn' sovetskogo goroda* (St. Petersburg: Letnii Sad, 1999), 129; Husband, *"Godless Communists,"* 77.

128. P. V. Pavlov, "Svoboda sovesti na mestakh i novye Pravitel'stvennye rasporiazheniia," *Slovo istiny*, no. 5–6 (1921): 44. See also P. V. Pavlov, "Svoboda sovesti na mestakh," *Slovo istiny*, no. 5–6 (1920): 41.

129. GARF, f. 353, op. 4, d. 372, l. 114; RGASPI, f. 17, op. 112, d. 565a, ll. 10, 14, 39, 46, 56.

9. A MIXED BLESSING

1. GMIR, koll. 1, op. 8, d. 6, folder 5, l. 59. For a similarly religiously worded judge's statement, allegedly quoted verbatim from the original, see Vladimir Martsinkovskii, *Zapiski veruiushchego* (St. Petersburg: Khristianskoe obshchestvo "Bibliia dlia vsekh," 1995), 88.

2. A correspondent to the War Resisters' International estimated that, by 1921, there had been more than thirty thousand applications (Peter Brock, *Studies in Peace History* [York: William Sessions, 1991], 90; another estimate suggested that the total number of applications was forty thousand (A. I. Klibanov, *Religioznoe sektantstvo i sovremennost'* [Moscow: Izdatel'stvo "Nauka," 1969], 203). The files of the organization

that supplied applicants with statements of sincerity suggest that the numbers were lower, although the central office, in theory, only dealt with those who wished to be freed of all forms of service, not merely to be assigned noncombatant duties. E. I. Getel' estimates that the central organization reviewed more than three thousand applications in 1919 ("Ob"edinennyi Sovet religioznykh obshchin i grupp kak odno is proiavlenii russkogo religioznogo patsifizma," in *Dolgii put' rossiiskogo patsifizma*, ed. T. A. Pavlova [Moscow: Institut Vseobshchei istorii RAN, 1997], 308). At a meeting at the Commissariat of Justice in April 1920, a representative of the organization stated that it had registered approximately eighty-two hundred applications so far (GARF, f. A353, op. 4, d. 412, l. 6ob.). Specific figures on Baptists are not available, but circumstantial evidence suggests that they formed a large percentage of applicants. See Peter Brock, ed., *Testimonies of Conscience* (Toronto: Privately printed, 1997), 2; and idem, *Soviet Conscientious Objectors, 1917–1939* (Toronto: Privately printed, 1999).

3. Mark von Hagen, *Soldiers in the Proletarian Dictatorship* (Ithaca, N.Y.: Cornell University Press, 1990), 28–30, 37, 46.

4. Peter Brock, *Twentieth-Century Pacifism* (New York: Van Nostrand Reinhold, 1970), 105.

5. "Dekret ob osvobozhdenii ot voinskoi povinnosti po religioznym ubezhdeniiam," *Revoliutsiia i tserkov'*, no. 1 (1919): 29.

6. A. B. Roginskii, ed., *Vospominaniia krest'ian-tolstovtsev* (Moscow: "Kniga," 1989), 465–70; Getel', "Ob"edinennyi Sovet," 262–65; Peter Brock and Nigel Young, *Pacifism in the Twentieth Century* (Syracuse: Syracuse University Press, 1999), 301–20.

7. RGASPI, f. 17, op. 60, d. 114, l. 1.

8. Arto Luukkanen, *The Party of Unbelief* (Helsinki: Suomen Historiallinen Seura, 1994), 80.

9. GARF, f. 130, op. 2, d. 166, l. 29. V. A. Alekseev, *Illiuzii i dogmy* (Moscow: Izdatel'stvo politicheskoi literatury, 1991), 69–71, 105–9; Alexei Zverev and Bruno Coppieters, "V. D. Bonch-Bruevich and the Doukhobors," *Canadian Ethnic Studies*, 27, no. 3 (1995): 73–85.

10. Klibanov, *Religioznoe sektantstvo*, 196; Luukkanen, *The Party of Unbelief*, 68.

11. Paul R. Dekar, *For the Healing of the Nations* (Macon, Ga.: Smyth and Helwys, 1993), 7; Walter Sawatsky, "Patsifisty-protestanty v Sovetskoi Rossii mezhdu dvumia mirovymi voinami," in Pavlova, *Dolgii put' rossiiskogo patsifizma*, 5–6; Robert G. Torbet, *A History of the Baptists* (Valley Forge: Judson, 1963), 453.

12. RGIA, f. 821, op. 133, d. 23, l. 113.

13. "Khristianstvo i voina. (Anketa)," *Slovo istiny*, no. 13–14 (November 1917): 197; G. Sergeev, "Khristianstvo i voennaia sluzhba (Otvet na anketu)," *Slovo istiny*, no. 7–8 (April 1918): 72–73; S. Khromov, "Khristianstvo i voennaia sluzhba (Otvet na anketu)," *Slovo istiny*, no. 9–12 (May–June 1918): 88–89; V. Mamontov, "Otnoshenie khristian k voine," *Slovo istiny*, no. 14 (1918): 102.

14. Orlando Figes, *Peasant Russia, Civil War* (Oxford: Clarendon, 1989), 309–12. See also Brock, *Studies in Peace History*, 81–82; and Paul D. Steeves, "Russian Baptists and the Military Question, 1918–1929," in *Challenge to Mars*, ed. Peter Brock and Thomas P. Socknat (Toronto: University of Toronto Press, 1999), 21–40.

15. "Otradnoe iavlenie," *Slovo istiny*, no. 1 (1919): 3.

16. Ob"edinennyi Sovet," *Vestnik baptistov*, no. 1 (1919): 2–3; "6-i Vserossiiskii S"ezd Evangel'skikh Khristian," *Utrenniaia zvezda*, no. 1 (January 1920): 3–4.

17. Klibanov, *Religioznoe sektantstvo*, 197.

18. GMIR, koll. 1, op. 8, d. 6, folder 3, ll. 4, 7.

19. Steeves, "Russian Baptists and the Military Question," 25.

20. GMIR, f. 3, op. 1, d. 2, ll. 12, 28. In February 1921, Baptists contributed 69 percent of the funds.

21. *26-oi Vsesoiuznyi S"ezd Baptistov S.S.S.R.* (Moscow: Izdanie Federativnogo Soiuza Baptistov SSSR v litse N. V. Odintsova, 1927), 103–4.

22. GMIR, koll. 1, op. 8, dd. 311, 312. Twelve applicants made no mention of their military situation, while the remainder had either served, were registered to serve, or were undergoing preconscription military training. Delegates to the 1923 Baptist national congress were asked whether they had suffered for their faith. Among the 204 surviving applications were 12 that mentioned arrest or imprisonment for refusing to fight, 7 of them before the revolution (GMIR, koll. 1, op. 8, d. 35, folder 11).

23. GARF, f. A353, op. 5, d. 250.

24. Klibanov, *Religioznoe sektantstvo*, 200.

25. Raionnye s"ezdy," *Slovo istiny*, no. 1–2 (1921): 11; "Na Nive Bozhiei," *Utrenniaia zvezda*, no. 1 (January 1920): 6; GMIR, koll. 1, op. 8, d. 34, folder 12, l. 40b.; folder 9, l. 10b.; V. I. Martynov, "Kavkazskii S"ezd Evangel'skikh Khristian Baptistov," *Slovo istiny*, no. 3 (1920): 23.

26. Voennaia sluzhba i raionnye s"ezdy," *Slovo istiny*, no. 2 (1920): 13.

27. GMIR, koll. 1, op. 8, d. 35, folder 1, ll. 90b., 12–120b.

28. "Na Nive Bozhiei," 6; "6-i Vserossiiskii S"ezd Evangel'skikh Khristian," *Utrenniaia zvezda*, no. 1 (January 1920): 4.

29. GARF, f. A353, op. 3, d. 780, l. 91.

30. OR RGB, f. 435, k. 65, d. 11, l. 2; GARF, f. 1235, op. 55, d. 2, l. 95.

31. GARF, f. A353, op. 4, d. 412, ll. 2, 4.

32. Von Hagen, *Soldiers*, 69–76; Figes, *Peasant Russia*, 311, 316–18.

33. Brian Bond, *War and Society in Europe, 1870–1970* (Bungay: Fontana Paperbacks, 1984), 32; Zverev and Coppieters, "V. D. Bonch-Bruevich," 73.

34. Quoted in Alekseev, *Illiuzii*, 70.

35. Alekseev, *Illiuzii*, 70, 105–14; Luukkanen, *The Party of Unbelief*, 92.

36. P. Krasikov, "Vedaiut li, chto tvoriat? (Vol'nye ili nevol'nye zashchitniki agentov Antanty)," *Revoliutsiia i tserkov'*, no. 9–12 (1920): 20–30.

37. GARF, f. A353, op. 5, d. 238, ll. 73–730b.

38. GMIR, koll. 1, op. 8, d. 312, ll. 10–100b.

39. Brock, *Testimonies of Conscience*, 23–24.

40. *Baptist Ukrainy* (December 1927): 58; OR RGB, f. 435, k. 65, d. 10; GARF, f. A353, op. 3, d. 749; f. A353, op. 3, d. 412, l. 73; f. A353, op. 3, d. 780.

41. GARF, f. A353, op. 3, d. 780, l. 90; "Tsirkuliar," *Slovo istiny*, no. 5–6 (1921): 48.

42. P. V. Gidulianov, *Otdelenie tserkvi ot gosudarstva*, 3rd ed. (Moscow: Iuridicheskoe izdatel'stvo N.K.Iu. R.S.F.S.R., 1926), 378–79.

43. "Zakon 4-go ianvaria 1919," *Revoliutsiia i tserkov'*, no. 9–12 (1920): 86–88. On the preparation of the decree, see GARF, f. A353, op. 4, d. 412, ll. 6–70b.

44. GARF, f. A353, op. 3, d. 780, l. 43; *Istochnik iz kamnia*, no. 3–4 (1920): 6; GARF, f. A353, op. 3, d. 780, l. 43. A representative of the United Council tried unsuccessfully to make this argument to an April 1920 meeting at the Commissariat of Justice (GARF, f. A353, op. 4, d. 412, ll. 6–70b.). Saying that politics did not matter was, perhaps, worse than saying that it did.

45. V. A. Shishkin, ed., *Petrograd na perelome epokh* (St. Petersburg: Izdatel'stvo "Dmitrii Bulanin," 2000), 272.

46. GMIR, f. 3, op. 1, d. 154, Ambartsumov folder, l. 2.

47. Sheila Fitzpatrick, "New Perspectives on the Civil War," in *Party, State, and Society in the Russian Civil War*, ed. Diane P. Koenker, William G. Rosenberg, and Ronald Grigor Suny, 3–23 (Bloomington: Indiana University Press, 1989), 5.

48. Sheila Fitzpatrick, "Ascribing Class," *Journal of Modern History* 65 (December 1993): 745.

49. GARF, f. 130, op. 2, d. 166, l. 29. Gidulianov, *Otdelenie tserkvi ot gosudarstva*, 391.

50. Gidulianov, *Otdelenie tserkvi ot gosudarstva*, 386. On the historical inaccuracy of this list, see Brock, *Studies in Peace History*, 82; Pavlova, *Dol'gii put'*, 132.

51. GARF, f. A353, op. 8, d. 8, l. 27.

52. Gidulianov, *Otdelenie tserkvi ot gosudarstva*, 379–80.

53. Elise Kimerling, "Civil Rights and Social Policy in Soviet Russia, 1918–1936," *Russian Review*, 41, no. 1 (January 1982): 25, 30.

54. Von Hagen, *Soldiers*, 35.

55. Luukkanen, *The Party of Unbelief*, 78.

56. OR RGB, f. 369, k. 35, d. 29, ll. 27–270b.

57. Daniel Peris, "The 1929 Congress of the Godless," *Soviet Studies*, 43, no. 4 (1991): 172; Luukkanen, *The Party of Unbelief*, 99. On the change in the assessment of enemies and how to combat them, see Anne E. Gorsuch, "NEP Be Damned! Young Militants in the 1920s and the Culture of Civil War," *Russian Review*, 56 (October 1997): 566. A secret police policy paper emphasized the need to break apart national sectarian organizations in April 1921 (GARF, f. 353, op. 4, d. 372, l. 1160b.).

58. N. A. Krivova, *Vlast' i tserkov' v 1922–1925 gg.* (Moscow: AIRO-XX, 1997), 13–19.

59. On the formation of the Antireligious Commission and its activities, see Luukkannen, *The Party of Unbelief*, 126–28; Edward E. Roslof, *Red Priests* (Bloomington: Indiana University Press, 2002), 86–87; S. Savel'ev, "Bog i komissary (k istorii komissii po provedeniiu otdeleniia tserkvi ot gosudarstva pri TsK VKP (b)—antireligioznoi komissii)," in *Religiia i demokratiia*, ed. A. R. Bessmertnyi and S. B. Filatov (Moscow: Izdatel'skaia gruppa "Progress" "Kul'tura," 1993), 164–75.

60. RGASPI, f. 17, op. 112, d. 443a, ll. 1–16, 30, 32; d. 565a, ll. 10, 14.

61. N. N. Pokrovskii and S. G. Petrov, eds., *Arkhivy Kremlia*, 2 vols. (Novosibirsk-Moscow: "Sibirskii Khronograf" and ROSSPEN, 1997–98), 2:361, 409.

62. Reprinted in Felix Corley, *Religion in the Soviet Union* (New York: New York University Press, 1996), 48–49.

63. GMIR, f. 2, op. 16, d. 184.

64. RGASPI, f. 17, op. 112, d. 443a, l. 35; GARF, f. A353, op. 8, d. 8, ll. 250b.–26.

65. GARF, f. A353, op. 7, d. 13, ll. 2–3.

66. Corley, *Religion*, 48; RGASPI, f. 17, op. 84, d. 570, l. 5.

67. W. T. Whitley, ed. *Third Baptist World Congress* (London: Kingsgate, 1923), xxx–xxxi.

68. *Izvestiia*, 12 August 1923; GMIR, koll. 1, op. 8, d. 45, folder 4, l. 12.

69. Although Tuchkov is not quite so specific about his methods, his account and that of the group of sectarians who complained to the government in early 1924 about this and other violations are remarkably in tune (Corley, *Religion*, 48; GARF, f. A353, op. 8, d. 8, l. 26; see also *Protokoly 9-go Vsesoiuznogo S"ezda Evangel'skikh Khristian* [Petrograd: Izdanie VSEKh, 1923]).

70. GMIR, koll. 1, op. 8, d. 68, folder 2, l. 6.

71. Corley, *Religion*, 49; GARF, f. A353, op. 8, d. 8, l. 260b.

72. GMIR, koll. 1, op. 8, d. 35, folder 8, l. 5.

73. GMIR, koll. 1, op. 8, d. 6, folder 5, ll. 109, 112–13; RGASPI, f. 17, op. 60, d. 535, l. 209.

74. GMIR, koll. 1, op. 8, d. 45, folder 5, ll. 1–10b. The statistics gathered from the delegates at the time of the congress suggest that only four delegates were formerly of the noble estate and 56 percent of the delegates had been of the peasant estate; 39 percent were formerly *meshchane* [urban middle- to lower class]. Among current reported occupations, 36 percent were farmers; 15 percent, workers; 7 percent, artisans; and 24 percent, office workers (GMIR koll. 1, op. 8, d. 35, folder 4, l. 1).

75. GMIR, koll. 1, op. 8, d. 68, folder 2, l. 6; folder 6, l. 3.

76. GMIR, koll. 1, op. 8, d. 6, folder 5, ll. 117–18, 130.

77. Iu. S. Grachev, *V Irodovoi bezdne* (Moscow: Blagovestnik, 1994), 55.

78. N. M., "Ne nashi puti," *Baptist Ukrainy*, no. 12 (December 1927): 58. Restrictions similar to those in the Russian Republic theoretically existed in the Ukrainian Republic, too. See also Sergei Petrovich Fadiukhin, *Vospominaniia o perezhitom* (St. Petersburg: Bibliia dlia vsekh, 1993), 90; and Martsinkovskii, *Zapiski veruiushchego*, 85–90.

79. Konstantin Vladimirovich Stvolygin, "Politika osvobozhdeniia grazhdan ot voinskoi povinnosti po religioznym ubezhdeniiam v sovetskom gosudarstve (1918–1939 gg.) (Candidate dissertation, Belorusskii gosudarstvennyi universitet, 1997), 70; M. Gaintsev and Krivokhatskii, "Tri mesiatsa s sektantami," *Antireligioznik*, no. 7 (1928): 60. It would appear that the largest group were Mennonites, followed by the Baptists.

80. Smolensk Archive, WKP 129, l. 1920b.

81. William Henry Chamberlin, *Soviet Russia* (Boston: Little, Brown, 1930), 320; Stvolygin, "Politika ozvobozhdeniia," 73. See also Maurice Hindus, *Red Bread* (New York: Jonathan Cape and Harrison Smith, 1931), 163.

82. Grachev, *V Irodovoi bezdne*, 56.

83. *Zapiski zasedanii 10-go Vsesoiuznogo s"ezda eEvangel'skikh khristian* (Leningrad: Izdanie I. S. Prokhanova i Ia. I. Zhidkova, 1927), esp. 18; *26-oi Vsesoiuznyi S"ezd Baptistov S.S.S.R.*, 13–15.

84. Grachev reports that the local leaders in Samara wished to leave the question up to each individual, but Ia. Ia. Vins, representing the Baptist Union, refused (*V Irodovoi bezdne*, 56). See also *Protokoly i materialy Pervogo S"iezda Volgo-Kamskogo Soiuza Baptistov* (Troitsk: Izdanie N. V. Odintsova, 1928); GMIR, koll. 1, op. 8, d. 34; GARF f. 393, op. 77, d. 74, l. 104; and Paul Steeves, "The Russian Baptist Union, 1917–1935" (Ph.D. dissertation, University of Kansas, 1976), 589–92.

85. Editors' note, following N. Ziubanov, "Trinadtsatyi S"ezd Sredne-Iuzhnogo Ob"edineniia Kh. B.," *Baptist Ukrainy*, no. 4 (1928): 49.

86. GMIR, koll. 1, op. 8, d. 625, l. 10b.

87. For example, GMIR, koll. 1, op. 8, d. 312, l. 22.

88. No evangelical journals were published in 1923. Only after they affirmed their support of military service were the Evangelical Christians permitted to resume publication of their journal, *Khristianin*, in January 1924, and the Baptists of *Baptist* in January 1925. On "tactical" censorship during the 1923 negotiations, see RGASPI, f. 17, op. 84, d. 605; f. 17, op. 60, d. 535; GARF, f. 5263, op. 1, d. 55, l. 249; and GMIR, koll. 1, op. 8, d. 45, folder 4, l. 5. On rejections of requests for con-

gresses, see GARF, f. 1235, op. 39, d. 86; f. 1235, op. 58, d. 34; and f. A353, op. 5, d. 231.

89. See Roslof, *Red Priests*, esp. 87.

90. Pokrovskii and Petrov, *Arkhivy Kremlia*, 1:419–30. On the similar attack on the Muslims, also in 1923, see Corley, *Religion*, 38–40.

10. PARALLEL LIVES?

1. An. Terskoi, *U sektantov* (Moscow: Molodaia Gvardiia, 1930), 14–15.

2. Richard Stites, *Revolutionary Dreams* (Oxford: Oxford University Press, 1989), 121. See also Ralph Talcott Fisher Jr., *Pattern for Soviet Youth* (New York: Columbia University Press, 1959), 143; and Lewis H. Siegelbaum, *Soviet State and Society between Revolutions* (New York: Cambridge University Press, 1992), 161–64.

3. See, for example, *Slovo Istiny*, no. 13 (1918): 98; *Utrenniaia zvezda*, no. 3–5 (1922): 4.

4. I. S. Prokhanov, "Novaia, ili evangel'skaia zhizn'," *Khristianin*, no. 1 (January 1925): 4–21; M. D. Timoshenko, "Khristianskii byt," in GMIR, koll. 1, op. 8, d. 84, folder 6, ll. 1–10; Tash-Otlu-Kei, "Ekspeditsiia po izyskaniiu zemel' dlia goroda sol'ntsa," *Khristianin*, no. 2 (1928): 44–52.

5. GMIR, koll. 1, op. 8, d. 452, ll. 1–10b. The "Christian Internationale" was repeatedly reported on and quoted in the Soviet press. See, for example, M. Shakhnovich, "Sektantstvo—nash klassovyi vrag," *Smena*, 16 December 1928, 4.

6. See, for example, Mikhail Timoshenko, "Soiuz Baptistov i ego deiatel'nost' (V poriadke obsuzhdeniia)," *Baptist*, no. 11–12 (1926): 20; TsGA Spb, f. 1001, op. 7, d. 47, l. 1930b.; I. S. Prokhanov, "Ko vsem riadovym chlenam i rukovoditeliam evangel'skikh obshchin i otdelov," *Khristianin*, no. 1 (1925): 27.

7. Daniel Peris, *Storming the Heavens* (Ithaca, N.Y.: Cornell University Press, 1998), 8.

8. RGAE, f. 4106, op. 14, d. 14, l. 1; f. 7446, op. 6, d. 10, l. 1; and RGASPI, f. 17, op. 84, d. 570, l. 2. See also A. I. Klibanov, *Religioznoe sektantstvo i sovremennost'* (Moscow: Izdatel'stvo "Nauka," 1969), 239.

9. *Kommunisty i sektanty* (Moscow, 1919), 3, 16.

10. P. V. Gidulianov, *Otdelenie Tserkvi ot Gosudarstva*, ed. P. A. Krasikov, 3rd ed. (Moscow: Iuridicheskoe izdatel'stvo NKIu RSFSR, 1926), 660.

11. Ibid., 553–57.

12. A. I. Klibanov, ed., *Kritika religioznogo sektantstva* (Moscow: Izdatel'stvo "Mysl'," 1974), 19.

13. See V. Dubovskoi, "Prosveshchanie. Sektanty. Predrassudki," and Vlad. Bonch-Bruevich, "Vozmozhnoe uchastie sektantov v khoziaistvennoi zhizni SSSR," *Pravda*, 15 May 1924, 6; Ia. Nikulikhin, "Ne delat' oshibki," *Pravda*, 21 May 1924, 6; Em. Iaroslavskii, "Nuzhny li privilegii sektantam?" *Pravda*, 23 May 1924, 4

14. Sheila Fitzpatrick, "The Soft Line on Culture and Its Enemies," in idem, *The Cultural Front* (Ithaca, N.Y.: Cornell University Press, 1992), 91–114; RGASPI, f. 52, op. 1, d. 40, l. 90.

15. William B. Husband, *"Godless Communists"* (DeKalb: Northern Illinois University Press, 2000), 69–70, 98–99.

16. Quoted in V. A. Shishkin, ed., *Petrograd na perelome epokh* (St. Petersburg: Izdatel'stvo "Dmitrii Bulanin," 2000), 267.

17. Peter Kenez, *The Birth of the Propaganda State* (New York: Cambridge University Press, 1985), 140–68.

18. Sheila Fitzpatrick, "The Problem of Identity in NEP Society," in *Russia in the Era of NEP*, ed. Sheila Fitzpatrick, Alexander Rabinowitch, and Richard Stites (Bloomington: Indiana University Press, 1991), 16–17, 24.

19. Elizabeth A. Wood, *The Baba and the Comrade* (Bloomington: Indiana University Press, 1997), 194.

20. Moshe Lewin, *The Making of the Soviet System* (New York: New Press, 1994): 216.

21. Klibanov, *Kritika religioznogo sektantstva*, 17; Resolution of the TsK RKP(b) of 8 February 1922.

22. See the early and influential statement of this view in A. Lukachevskii, *Sektantstvo prezhde i teper'* (Moscow: Izdanie zhurnala "Bezbozhnik u stanka," 1925), 35–36. Lukachevskii singled out the Baptists as the key problem.

23. RGASPI, f. 17, op. 60, d. 792, l. 110.

24. Daniel Peris, "The 1929 Congress of the Godless," *Soviet Studies* 43, no. 4 (1991): 712.

25. On the change in the assessment of enemies and how to combat them, see Anne E. Gorsuch, "NEP Be Damned! Young Militants in the 1920s and the Culture of Civil War," *Russian Review* 56 (October 1997): 566.

26. Peter Gooderham, "The Komsomol and Worker Youth: The Inculcation of 'Communist Values' in Leningrad during NEP," *Soviet Studies* 34, no. 4 (October 1982): 506–28; Igal Halfin, "From Darkness to Light: Student Communist Autobiography during NEP," *Jahrbücher für Geschichte Osteuropas* 45, no. 2 (1997): 219; Isabel A. Tirado, "The Revolution, Young Peasants, and the Komsomol's Antireligious Campaigns (1920–1928)," *Canadian-American Slavic Studies* 26, no. 1–3 (1992): 97.

27. OR RGB, f. 435, k. 65, d. 12, ll. 1–4; I. S. Prokhanoff, *In the Cauldron of Russia, 1869–1933* (New York: All-Russian Evangelical Christian Association, 1933), chap. 22.

28. TsGA, SPb f. 1001, op. 7, d. 10, ll. 6–7. Around the same time the Baptists' youth union complained that the authorities were preventing them from publishing their journal, *Drug molodezhi* [Friend of youth]: Southern Baptist Historical Library and Archives, Historical Papers of Mrs. I. V. Neprash on Religion in Russia, Publication no. 3475, circular of the Baptists' All-Russian Union of Youth Circles, April 1922. The Baptists apparently did not abandon all hope of resurrecting *Drug molodezhi*. A secret memo from the NKVD to the OGPU, dated 22 September 1927, expressed concern that this had been discussed at a meeting of the council of the Baptist Union the previous month (GARF, f. 393, op. 43a, d. 74, l. 22).

29. GMIR, koll. 1, op. 8, d. 84, folder 2, l. 38. The Central Committee's Antireligious Commission decided to release Timoshenko and Levindanto early: RGASPI, f. 17, op. 112, d. 775, 136. Four others were also exiled at the same time.

30. GMIR, koll. 1, op. 8, d. 35, folder 8, ll. 20b., 26–36.

31. All conference programs were approved by the NKVD, in consultation with the secret police (GARF, f. 393, op. 43s, d. 66, ll. 4, 7). *Slovo istiny* was forbidden from publishing a section for youth (GARF f. 353, op. 5, d. 238, l. 157).

32. Clipping in GMIR, koll. 1, op. 8, d. 339, l. 29.

33. "O konchine Vsevoloda Ivanovicha Prokhanova (Mladshego syna I. S. Prokhanova)," *Khristianin*, no. 3 (1927): 59–60.

34. See, for example, *Revoliutsiia i tserkov'*, no. 9–12 (1920): 96.

35. RGAE, f. 4106, op. 14, d. 14, ll. 65–76. These included the Evangelical Christians, Baptists, Adventists, Dukhobors, Molokans, Mennonites, Novyi Izrail, Trezvenniki, and Tolstoyans. The Evangelical Christians who had left Prokhanov's union in late 1923 also participated.

36. Klibanov, *Religioznoe sektantstvo i sovremennost'*, 243.

37. Iv. Tregubov, "Sotsial'no-revoliutsionnaia rol' sektantstva," and F. Putintsev, "Otvet gr. Tregubovu," *Bezbozhnik*, no. 49 (6 December 1925): 2–4; no. 50 (13 December 1925): 3–5; F. Putintsev, "Klassovaia sushchnost' sektantskikh teorii i praktiki (Otvet sektantu Goncharovu)," and Ia. Goncharov, "O sotsial'no-revoliutsionnoi roli sektantov," *Antireligioznik*, no. 1 (1926): 34–55, 83–88.

38. Putintsev, "Klassovaia sushchnost'," 54.

39. P. V. Ivanov-Klyshnikov, "Nashi obshchiny, kak estestvennye kollektivy (Opyt raskrytiia sotsial'no-ekonomicheskogo znacheniia obshchin veruiushchikh)," *Baptist*, no. 1 (January 1925): 13–14.

40. Klibanov, *Kritika religioznogo sektantstva*, 18 (emphasis added).

41. Gidulianov, *Otdelenie tserkvi ot gosudarstva*, 567–82. To be sure, the preamble did emphasize that the Commissariat rejected the notion that a commune could be religiously exclusive.

42. GMIR. f. 13, op. 1, d. 192.

43. GMIR, koll. 1, op. 8, d. 338, l. 2.

44. GMIR, f. 2, op. 16, d. 91, l. 8.

45. RGAE, f. 7446, op. 6, d. 10, ll. 30–33.

46. GMIR, koll. 1, op. 8, d. 342, l. 32; d. 339, l. 29; d. 341, l. 116; RGASPI f. 17, op. 60, d. 52, ll. 10, 59. Of course, it was a good strategy for apostates from either side to claim that they had mistaken one "faith" for the other.

47. GARF, f. 5407, op. 1, d. 13, l. 27.

48. OR RGB, f. 435, k. 65, d. 11, l. 1.

49. RGASPI, f. 17, op. 113, d. 353, l. 49 and d. 871, l. 11.

50. Reprinted in *Kommunisticheskaia partiia i Sovetskoe pravitel'stvo o religii i tserkvi* (Moscow: Gosudarstvennoe izdatel'stvo politicheskoi literatury, 1961), 68–69.

51. RGASPI, f.17, op. 112, d. 565a, l. 14 and d. 620, l. 16.

52. Peris, *Storming the Heavens*, 42–44.

53. RGASPI, f. 17, op. 112, d. 620, ll. 16–21. In the secret printed stenographic report of this meeting, of twenty-five paragraphs one each was devoted to the Orthodox Church, the Muslims, and the Jews, whereas the sects received eight paragraphs. See RGASPI, f. 17, op. 112, d. 780. For a similar report from Ukraine, see RGASPI, f. 17, op. 84, d. 748, l. 83.

54. RGASPI, f. 89, op. 4, d. 184, l. 2.

55. RGASPI, f. 17, op 60, d. 792, ll. 88, 90.

56. RGASPI, f. 17, op 60, d. 792, ll. 96, 99.

57. RGASPI, f. 17, op 60, d. 792, ll. 112–14.

58. Sektantstvo i antireligioznaia propaganda (tezisy, priniatye partiinym soveshchaniem po antireligioznoi propagande pri TsK VKP(b) 27–30 aprelia 1926 goda)," *Antireligioznik*, no. 8 (August 1926): 71–72.

59. RGASPI, f. 17, op. 60, d. 792, l. 87, 96.

60. RGASPI, f. 89, op. 4, d. 119, ll. 25–26; d. 123, ll. 52–66; f. 17, op. 113, d. 42, l. 5; d. 231, l. 3.

61. GARF, f. 5263, op. 1s, d. 5, l. 81.

62. GARF, f. 5263, op. 1s, d. 5, ll. 45–49, 93–102; in fact, the manner in which the circular was implemented led to a series of orders from the VTsIK that it be implemented more subtly lest the sectarians suspect something (ll. 83–88).

63. *Komsomol'skaia pravda*, 13 May 1928, 3.

64. Clipping from *Trud*, 14 August 1928, 5, in GMIR, koll. 1, op. 8, d. 342, l. 31. Among many other examples, see G. Sokolov, "Zashchitite komsomolku ot posiagatel'stv baptista!" *Krasnaia gazeta*, 27 February 1929; and M. Shakhnovich, "Bapsomol," *Smena*, 11 November 1928.

65. V. Chernevskii, "Baptistskie gnezda v Moskve," *Komsomol'skaia pravda*, 4 August 1928, 6.

66. TsGAMO, f. 699, op. 1, d. 1059, l. 14. I thank Diane Koenker for this reference.

67. See, for example, Al. Klibanov, *Klassovoe litso sovremennogo sektantstva* (Leningrad: Priboi, 1928), 52–68; B. Tikhomirov, *Baptizm i ego politicheskaia rol'* (Moscow: Gosudarstvennoe izdatel'stvo, 1929), 50–56; A. Iartsev, *Sekta evangel'skikh khristian*, 2nd ed. (Moscow: Izdatel'stvo aktsionernago o-vo "Bezbozhnik," 1928), 34–36.

68. I. Ia. Eliashevich, *Religiia v bor'be za rabochuiu molodezh* (Leningrad: Priboi, 1928), 19–48. There was also a large section devoted to the activities of the YMCA abroad, which should be seen as a discussion of the Baptists and Evangelical Christians, since the YMCA was incorrectly interpreted as being the source of their ideas, direction, and financing.

69. Klibanov, *Klassovoe litso*, 48–55.

70. A. Mariinskii, "Popovshchina i sektantstvo," *Novyi mir*, no. 11 (November 1928): 269.

71. Eliashevich, *Religiia*, 21–22.

72. N. Boldyrev, "Religiia, zhenshchina, iunoshestvo, byt i formy nashei raboty," *Antireligioznik*, no. 5 (1927): 63; see also Oleshuk, "Tserkovniki i sektanty za rabotoi," *Kommunistka*, no. 9 (September 1928): 39–43; Abramenko, "Na zabytom uchastke," *Kommunistka*, no. 5–6 (March 1929): 55. On the problems of drawing young women into the Komsomol (and keeping them there), see Anne E. Gorsuch, "'A Woman Is Not a Man': The Culture of Gender and Generation in Soviet Russia, 1921–1928," *Slavic Review*, 55, no. 3 (fall 1996): 636–60.

73. Ne oboroniat'sia, a nastupat'," *Derevenskii bezbozhnik*, no. 7 (September 1928): 1.

74. I. Eliashevich, "Muzyka, religiia i ateizm. (Opyt provedeniia antireligioznogo muzykal'nogo vechera)" *Antireligioznik*, no. 11 (1927): 56.

75. Eliashevich, *Religiia*, 72. See also Boldyrev, "Religiia, zhenshchina, iunoshestvo," 63.

76. F. Putintsev, *Sektantstvo i antireligioznaia propaganda* (Moscow: Izdatel'skoe aktsionernago o-vo "Bezbozhnik," 1928), 30. A 1926 Smolensk Province OGPU report stated that evangelical leaders were taught "not to attend any meetings of Soviet public life [*obshchestvennosti*]" (Smolensk Archive, WKP 129, l. 192).

77. Putintsev, *Sektantstvo i antireligioznaia propaganda*, 35. Eliashevich, *Religiia*, 21; Klibanov, *Klassovoe*, 40. See also Andr. Rostovtsev, *Nravstvennost' sektantskaia i proletarskaia* (N.p.: Priboi, 1931).

78. For example, Vinogradov, "Raskaianie Evangelista," *Privol'zhskaia pravda*, 12 December 1929; clipping in GMIR f. 2, op. 26, d. 100, l. 4.

79. Klibanov, *Klassovoe litso*, 62.

80. Ibid., 54; "Antireligioznaia rabota sredi molodezhi," *Antireligioznik*, no. 5 (1929): 77; Klibanov, *Kritika religioznogo sektantstva*, 167; N. S. Timasheff, *Religion in Soviet Russia* (New York: Sheed and Ward, 1942), 61–62, 91.

81. Fitzpatrick, "The Soft Line," 112–13; Lewin, *The Making of the Soviet System*, 216–18.

82. For example, Peris, "The 1929 Congress of the Godless"; "Vovlechenie v partiiu rabochikh s proizvodstva i zadachi massovoi raboty," *Kommunisticheskaia revoliutsiia*, no. 5 (March 1928): 6; "Ratsionalizatsiia dobrovol'noi obshchestvennosti stuchitsia k nam v dver'," *Kommunisticheskaia revoliutsiia*, no. 5 (March 1929): 94; B. Spektor, "O ratsionalizatsii raboty dobrovol'nykh obshchestv," *Kommunisticheskaia revoliutsiia*, no. 2 (January 1929): 85–86; and F. Oleshchuk, "Chem boleiut dobrovol'nye O-va?" *Antireligioznik*, no. 5 (1927): 7–14.

83. Glennys Young, "Trading Icons: Clergy, Laity, and Rural Cooperatives, 1921–28," *Canadian-American Slavic Studies* 26, no. 1–4 (1992): 332; and idem, *Power and the Sacred in Revolutionary Russia* (University Park: Pennsylvania State University Press, 1997).

84. Tirado, "The Revolution," 115.

85. Peris, "The 1929 Congress of the Godless," 724.

86. GARF, f. 5263, op. 1s, d. 7, l. 1. Circular of 24 January 1929, no.10400/s.

87. Gerd Shtrikker, ed., *Russkaia Pravoslavnaia Tserkov' v sovetskoe vremia. Kniga I* (Moscow: Izdatel'stvo "Propilei," 1995), 307–10.

88. Ibid., 311.

89. Arto Luukkanen, *The Religious Policy of the Stalinist State* (Helsinki: Suomen Historiallinen Seura, 1997), 38, 67.

90. GARF, f. 393, op. 81, d. 63, ll. 42–49.

91. GARF, f. 393 op. 81, d. 22; f. 5363, op. 1s, d. 5, ll. 30–36ob. On the official investigation into the closing of Bethany commune, see RGAE, f. 7446, op. 6, d. 10, ll. 14–41; GARF, f. 5263, op. 1s, d. 5, ll. 27–29ob. See also K. Petrus, *Religious Communes in the U.S.S.R.* (New York: Research Program on the U.S.S.R., 1953).

92. Grachev, *V Irodovoi bezdne*, chaps. 14–18.

93. Georgii Vins, *Tropoiu vernosti*, 2nd ed. (St. Petersburg: Bibliia dlia vsekh, 1997), 47.

94. GMIR, koll. 1, op. 8, d. 322, l. 120b.

95. *Istoriia evangel'skikh khristian-baptistov v SSSR* (Moscow: Izdanie Vsesoiuznogo Soveta Evangel'skikh Khristian-Baptistov, 1989), 222–23. Vins, *Tropoiu vernosti*, 184.

96. GMIR, f. 22, op. 1, d.? [not yet processed]; the first page of the letter is also found in GARF, f. 5407, op. 1, d. 37, l. 1.

97. Grachev, *V Irodovoi bezdne*, 75.

98. GARF, f. 5407, op. 1, d. 37, l. 5; Valentin Rozhitsyn, "Baptistskaia kontrrevoliutsiia," *Bezbozhnik*, no. 46 (10 November 1929); no. 47 (17 November 1929).

99. M. V. Popov, *Sektantstvo Ivanovskoi promyshlennoi oblasti prezhde i teper'* (Ivanovo-Voznesensk: Izdatel'stvo Ogiz, 1931), 6.

100. "More Sufferings of Christians in Russia," *Friend of Russia* (October 1924): 148.

AFTERWORD

1. Paul D. Steeves, "The Russian Baptist Union, 1917–1935" (Ph.D. dissertation, University of Kansas, 1976), 257; *26-oi Vsesoiuznyi s"ezd baptistov S.S.S.R.* (Moscow:

Izdanie Federativnogo Soiuza Baptistov SSSR, 1927), 65; *Istoriia evangel'skikh khristian-baptistov v SSSR* (Moscow: Izdanie Vsesoiuznogo Soveta Evangel'skikh Khristian-Baptistov, 1989), 221–27.

2. GARF, f. 5263, op. 1s, d. 5, ll. 31–32, 42–43.

3. Steeves, "The Russian Baptist Union," 258–92, 68–71; *Istoriia evangel'skikh khristian-baptistov v SSSR*, 23–24.

4. Felix Corley, *Religion in the Soviet Union* (New York: New York University Press, 1996), 185; Walter Sawatsky, *Soviet Evangelicals since World War II* (Kitchener, Ont.: Herald, 1981), 241–42, 410–11.

5. I. V. Podberezskii, *Byt' protestantom v Rossii* (Moscow: Izdatel'stvo "Blagovestnik," 1996).

6. E. P. Thompson, *The Making of the English Working Class* (New York: Vintage, 1966), 375.

SELECTED BIBLIOGRAPHY

ARCHIVAL SOURCES

Moscow

RGASPI, Rossiisskii gosudarstvennyi arkhiv sotsial'no-politicheskoi istorii
  fond 89, op. 4—Emelian Iaroslavskii
  fond 17, op. 60—Central Committee, Agitprop Department
  fond 17, op. 112 and 113—Central Committee, Secretariat and Organizational
  Bureaus
  fond 381—Editorial board of "Rassvet."
GARF, Gosudarstvennyi arkhiv Rossiiskoi federatsii
  fond 102—Department of Police, Ministry of Internal Affairs (Imperial
  Government)
  fond 130—Council of People's Commissars
  fond A353—People's Commissariat of Justice RSFSR
  fond 393—People's Commissariat of Internal Affairs RSFSR 1917–30
  fond 1235—All-Russian Central Executive Committee
  fond 5263—Commission on Issues of Cults
  fond 5407—All-Union League of the Militant Godless
RGAE, Rossiiskii gosudarstvennyi arkhiv ekonomiki
  fond 478—People's Commissariat of Agriculture
  fond 4106—All-Russian Union of Agricultural Cooperatives (Sel'skosoiuz)
  fond 7446—All-Russian Union of Agricultural Collectives (Kolkhoztsentr RSFSR)
OR RGB, Otdel rukopisei Rossiiskoi gosudarstvennoi biblioteki
  fond 369—V. D. Bonch-Bruevich
  fond 435—V. G. Chertkov
RGA KFD, Rossiiskii gosudarstvennyi arkhiv kino-foto dokumentov

St. Petersburg

GMIR, Gosudarstvennyi muzei istorii religii
  collection 1, op. 8—Materials on Baptists
  fond 2—V. D. Bonch-Bruevich
  fond 13—I. M. Tregubov
  fond 14—"Svobodnoe slovo" Publishing House
RGIA, Rossiiskii gosudarstvennyi istoricheskii arkhiv
  fond 796—Holy Synod
  fond 797—Over-Procurator of the Holy Synod

fond 821—Department of Spiritual Affairs, Ministry of Internal Affairs
fond 831—Patriarch Tikhon and the Holy Synod, 1918–24
fond 1284—Department of General Affairs, Ministry of Internal Affairs
fond 1278—State Duma
fond 1574—K. P. Pobedonostsev
TsGA g. SPb, Tsentral'nyi gosudarstvennyi arkhiv goroda Sankt-peterburga
fond 1001—Petrograd provincial administration

Nashville

Southern Baptist Historical Library and Archives
Adolf J. Klaupiks Papers
Historical Papers of Mrs. I. V. Neprash on Religion in Russia
Historical Papers of Waldemar Gutsche on Religion in Russia and Poland

Microfilmed Archive

Smolensk Archive
WKP 124, 127, 129, 142

NEWSPAPERS

Izvestiia
Komsomol'skaia pravda
Kolokol
Moskovskiya viedomosti
Novoe vremia
Peterburgskii listok
Pravda
Riech'
Russkoe slovo
Trud
Utrenniaia zvezda

JOURNALS

Ateist
Antireligioznik
Baptist
Baptist Ukrainy
Bezbozhnik
Blagoviestnik
Bratskii listok
Drug
Drug molodezhi
Friend of Russia
Golos khristianskoi molodezhi
Gost'
Istochnik iz kamnia
Khristianin

Selected Bibliography

Kommunisticheskaia revoliutsiia
Kommunistka
Missionerskoe obozrienie
Prikhodskii sviashchennik
Razsviet
Revoliutsiia i tserkov'
Slovo istiny
Slovo i zhizn'
Svobodnoe slovo
Tserkovniia viedomosti
Vestnik baptistov

PRIMARY SOURCES

Aleksii (Dorodnitsyn). *Iuzhno-russkii neobaptizm, izviestnyi pod imenem shtundy (Po ofitsial'nym dokumentam)*. Stavropol'-Kavkazskii: Tipo-litografiia T. M. Timofeeva, 1903.

——. *Materialy dlia istorii religiozno-ratsionalisticheskogo dvizheniia na iuge Rossii vo vtoroi polovine 19-go st.* Kazan': Tsentral'naia tipografiia, 1908.

——. *Vnutrenniaia organizatsiia obshchin iuzhno-russkikh neobaptistov (shtundistov—to zhe)*. Kazan': Tsentral'naia tipografiia, 1908.

Anderson, Vladimir. *Staroobriadchestvo i sektantstvo. Istoricheskii ocherk russkago religioznago raznomysliia*. St. Petersburg: Izdanie V. I. Gubinskago, 1908.

Arsen'ev, K. K. *Svoboda soviesti i vieroterpimost'. Sbornik statei*. St. Petersburg: "Obshchestvennaia Pol'za," 1905.

Balikhin, Fedor Prokhorovich. *Kratkaia avtobiografiia presvitera-propoviednika evangel'skikh khristian-baptistov Fedora Prokhorovicha Balikhina*. Rostov-on-Don: Tipografiia F. Pavlova, 1908.

Baptist World Alliance. Second Congress. Philadelphia, June 19–25, 1911. Record of Proceedings. Philadelphia, 1911.

Baptisty, ikh uchenie i zadachi. Rostov-on-Don: Izdanie russkikh baptistov, 1909.

Baptisty, kak naiboliee zlovrednaia sekta. Shamordino, 1912.

Baptisty kak naibolee zlovrednaia sekta. Moscow: Pod'bor'e Russkogo na Afone Sviato-Panteleimonova monastyria v g. Moskve, 1995.

Bobrishchev-Pushkin, A. *Sud i raskol'niki-sektanty*. St. Petersburg: Senatskaia tipografiia, 1902.

Bogoliubov, D. I. *Religiozno-obshchestvennyia techeniia v sovremennoi russkoi zhizni i nasha pravoslavno-khristianskaia missiia*. St. Petersburg: Tipografiia I. V. Leont'eva, 1909.

Bonch-Bruevich, Vladimir D. *Izbrannye sochineniia*. Vol. 1, *O religii, religioznom sektantstve i tserkvi*. Moscow: Izdatel'stvo Akademii Nauk SSSR, 1959.

——. *Krivoe zerkalo sektantstva*. Moscow: Zhizn' i Znanie, 1922.

——. "Presliedovanie baptistov v Rossii." *Viestnik Evropy* 45, no. 6 (June 1910): 160–83.

——, ed. *Materialy k istorii i izucheniiu russkago sektantstva i raskola. Vyp. 1*. St. Petersburg: Tipografiia B. M. Vol'fa, 1908.

——, ed. *Presliedovanie baptistov evangelicheskoi sekty. Materialy k istorii i izucheniiu russkago sektantstva. Vyp. 6*. Christchurch: Izdanie "Svobodnago slova," 1902.

Bondar', S. D. *Sovremennoe sostoianie russkogo baptizma.* St. Petersburg: M.V.D. Departament Dukhovnykh Diel, 1911.

Borozdin, A. K. *Russkoe religioznoe raznomyslie.* 2nd ed. St. Petersburg: Izdanie "Prometei," 1907.

Butkevich, T. I. *Obzor russkikh sekt i ikh tolkov.* Khar'kov: Tipografiia gubernskago pravleniia, 1910.

Byford, Chas. T. *Peasants and Prophets (Baptist Pioneers in Russia and South Eastern Europe).* 2nd ed. London: Kingsgate, 1912.

Chamberlin, William Henry. *Soviet Russia: A Living Record and a History.* Boston: Little, Brown, 1930.

"Chudesa po molitvan k Sviatiteliu Feodosiiu Uglitskomu." *Pribavlenie k Chernigovskim eparkhial'nym izvestiiam* 36, no. 3 (1 February 1896): 91–127.

Corley, Felix. *Religion in the Soviet Union: An Archival Reader.* New York: New York University Press, 1996.

Dobrinin, Alexander. "Story of My Simple Life and Its Environment." *European Harvest Field,* no. 10 (1931).

Dolotov, A. *Tserkov'i sektantstvo v Sibiri.* Novosibirsk: Sibkraiizdat, 1928.

Eliashevich, I. Ia. *Religiia v bor'be za rabochuiu molodezh.* Leningrad: Priboi, 1928.

Evangel'skii klich. Poslanie vysshemu tserkovnomu upravleniiu pravoslavnoi tserkvi i gruppe "Zhivoi Tserkvi." Ot svobodnoi narodnoi evangel'skoi tserkvi (Vserossiiskogo Soiuza Evangel'skikh Khristian). Petrograd, 1922.

Fadiukhin, S. P. *Vospominaniia o perezhitom.* St. Petersburg: Bibliia dlia vsekh, 1993.

Fetler, V. A. *Pokornieishee khodataistvo.* St. Petersburg, 1913.

Fetler, V. A., ed. *Statistika russkikh evangel'skikh khristian baptistov za 1910 god.* St. Petersburg: Tipografiia poleznoi literatury, 1911.

Fetler, William (Basil Malof). *The Marvellous Results of Work among Russian War Prisoners and the Greatest Missionary Challenge of the Christian Era.* 2nd ed. Chicago: Russian Missionary Society, n.d.

Gidulianov, P. V. *Otdelenie tserkvi ot gosudarstva: Sistematizirovannyi sbornik deistvuiushchego v SSSR zakonodatel'stva.* 3rd ed. Moscow: Iuridicheskoe izdatel'stvo N.K.Iu. R.S.F.S.R., 1926.

Grachev, Iu. S. *V irodovoi bezdne: Vospominaniia o perezhitom.* Kniga I. Moscow: Blagovestnik, 1994.

Griniakin, N. *Beregis' shtundy!* St. Petersburg: Tipografiia "Kolokol," 1912.

Gumilevskii, N. "Iz psikhologii baptizma." *Rukovodstvo dlia sel'skikh pastyrei* 52, no. 30–31 (24–31 July 1911): 293–310.

———. *Kratkaia istoriia i oblichenii novykh ratsionalisticheskikh sekt.* Kiev, 1910.

Hecker, Julius Friedrich. *Religion under the Soviets.* New York: Vanguard, 1927.

Hindus, Maurice. *Red Bread.* New York: Jonathan Cape and Harrison Smith, 1931.

Iartsev, A. *Sekta evangel'skikh khristian.* 2nd ed. Moscow: Izdatel'stvo aktsionernago o-vo "Bezbozhnik," 1928.

Iasevich-Borodaevskaia, V. *Bor'ba za vieru.* St. Petersburg: Gosudarstvennaia tipografiia, 1912.

Ignat'ev, R. S. "Pashkovtsy-baptisty v Peterburgie." *Istoricheskii viestnik* 116, no. 4 (April 1909): 184–92.

Institut Marksizma-leninizma pri TsK KPSS. *Vtoroi s"ezd RSDRP. Iul'–avgust 1903 goda. Protokoly.* Moscow: Gosudarstvennoe izdatel'stvo politicheskoi literatury, 1959.

Iskrinskii, M. *Kto takie sektanty.* Moscow: Izdatel'stvo "Bezbozhnik," 1930.

Iudin, P. L. "Baptisty Novouzenskie (K istorii Povolzhskago raskola)." *Russkii arkhiv* 51, no. 1 (1903): 87–92.

Ivanov, A. *Otchet o sobranie.* Novgorod, 1910.

Kal'nev, M. I. ed. *Istoriia sektantskikh molitvennykh piesnopienii.* Odessa, 1911.

———. *Russkie sektanty ikh uchenie, kul't, i sposoby propagandy.* Odessa: Tipografiia E. I. Fesenko, 1911.

Khilkov, D. *Revoliutsiia i sektanty.* N.p.: Tipografiia Partii Sotsialistov-revoliutsionerov, [1905].

Khristiansko-demokraticheskaia partiia "Voskresenie." Raz"iasnenie tsielei i programma. Kiev, 1917.

Klibanov, A. *Klassovoe litso sovremennogo sektantstva.* Leningrad: Priboi, 1928.

Kommunisticheskaia partiia i Sovetskoe pravitel'stvo o religii i tserkvi. Moscow: Gosudarstvennoe izdatel'stvo politicheskoi literatury, 1961.

Kommunisty i sektanty. Moscow, 1919.

Krasikov, Petr Anan'evich. *Izbrannye ateisticheskie proizvedeniia.* Moscow: Izdatel'stvo "Mysl'," 1970.

Kushnerov, Ivan Petrovich, Vasilii Ivanovich Dolgopolov, and Vasilii Nikolaevich Ivanov. *Kratkaia zapiska o vozniknovenii, razvitii i o nastoiashchem polozhenii evangel'skogo dvizheniia v Rossii i o nuzhdakh russkikh evangel'skikh khristian.* St. Petersburg, 1905.

Leskov, Nikolai. *Schism in High Society: Lord Radstock and His Followers.* Edited and translated by James Muckle. Nottingham: Bramcote, 1995.

Lukachevskii, A. T. *Sektantstvo prezhde i teper'.* Moscow: Izdanie zhurnala "Bezbozhnik u stanka," 1925.

Makarevskii, N. I. *Sbornik obrashchenii na evangel'skii put' zhizni.* St. Petersburg: Tipografiia Andersona i Loitsianskago, [1914].

Margaritov, Sergei. *Istoriia russkikh misticheskikh i ratsionalisticheskikh sekt.* 3rd ed. Simferopol': Tavricheskaia gubernskaia tipografiia, 1910.

Mariinskii, A. "Popovshchina i sektantstvo" *Novy mir* 12 (November 1928).

Martsinkovskii, Vladimir. *Zapiski veruiushchego.* St. Petersburg: Khristianskoe obshchestvo "Biblia dlia vsekh," 1995.

Mel'gunov, S. P. "Shtundisty ili baptisty? (Po povodu presliedovaniia sektantov po 29 st. Ust. o nak.)." *Russkaia mysl'* 24, no. 11 (November 1903): 159–66.

———. *Staroobriadcheskiia i sektantskiia obshchiny (Zakon 17 oktiabria 1906 g.).* Moscow: Tipografiia tovarishchestva I. D. Sytina, 1907.

———. *Svoboda viery v Rossii. Obshchedostupnyia stat'i.* Moscow: Tipografiia tovarishchestva I. D. Sytina, 1907.

———. *Tserkov' i gosudarstvo v Rossii. (K voprosu o svobode soviesti). Sbornik statei. I.* Moscow: Izdanie tovarishchestva I. D. Sytina, 1907.

———. *Tserkov' i gosudarstvo v Rossii. V perekhodnoe vremia. Vyp. vtoroi. Sbornik statei (1907–1908 gg.).* Moscow, 1909.

Miliukov, P. *Ocherki po istorii russkoi kul'tury. Chast' vtoraia: Tserkov' i shkola (viera, tvorchestvo, obrazovanie).* 4th ed. St. Petersburg: Izdanie redaktsii zhurnala "Mira Bozhii," 1905.

Mitin, M. ed. *Voinstvuiushchee bezbozhie v SSSR za 15 let, 1917–1932.* Moscow, 1932.

Morozov, I. *Sektantskie kolkhozy.* Moscow, 1931.

Nikulikhin, Ia. "O sektantakh." *Derevenskii kommunist,* no. 7 (1 April 1927).

———. "O sektantakh." *Sputnik kommunista,* no. 6 (30 March 1927): 27–32.

O molitvennom domie v S-Peterburgie. 1908.

Otchet baptistkago missionerskago obshchestva za 1907–1908 god. God pervyi. Odessa: Tipografiia aktsionernago iuzhno-russkago obshchestva pechatnago diela, 1909.

Otchet obshchago sobraniia chlenov SPB obshchiny evangel'skikh khristian, sostoiavshagosia 15-go avgusta 1908 goda. St. Petersburg, n.d.

Otchet 4-go Vserossiiskago S"iezda Evangel'skikh Khristian, sostoivshagosia v g. Petrograde s 18-go po 25-oe maia 1917g. Petrograd: "Raduga," 1917.

Otchet 5-go Vserossiisskago S"iezda Evangel'skikh Khristian (sostoiavshagosia v g. Moskve s 25 dekabria 1917g. po 1 ianvaria 1918g). Petrograd: "Raduga," 1918.

Pankratov, A. S. *Ishchushchie Boga.* Moscow, 1911.

Pervyi Vserossiiskii S"iezd Kruzhkov baptistskoi molodezhi, iunoshei i dievits, v Rostovie na Donu. 1909 goda. Rostov-on-Don: Tipografiia tovarishchestva Pavlova i Slavgorodskago, 1909.

Pestriakov, Sviashch. V. "Iz nabliudenii nad zhizn'iu sektantov-baptistov." *Rukovodstvo dlia sel'skikh pastyrei* 52, no. 37 (11 September 1911): 3–10.

Piligrim. *Kto vy?* Moscow: Slovo istiny, 1917.

"Polozhenie o missionerskom Sovete pri Sv. Sinode." *Pravoslavnyi blagovestnik,* no. 10 (1913): 293–95.

Popov, M. V. *Sektantstvo Ivanovskoi promyshlennoi oblasti prezhde i teper'.* Ivanov-Voznesensk: Izdatel'stvo Ogiz, 1931.

Pokrovskii, N. N., and S. G. Petrov, eds. *Arkhivy Kremlia. Politbiuro i tserkov' 1922–1925 gg.* 2 vols. Moscow: ROSSPEN, 1997–98.

Prilozheniia k stenograficheskim otchetam gosudarstvennoi dumy. Chetvertyi sozyv. Sessia vtoraia. 1913–1914 gg. Vyp. 5. St. Petersburg, 1914.

Proekt ustava Khar'kovskago Iunosheskago Kruzhka vieruiushchikh Evangel'skikh Khristian. Khar'kov: Tipografiia-Litografiia Kh. M. Arshavskoi, 1910.

Prokhanoff, I. S. *In the Cauldron of Russia, 1869–1933.* New York: All-Russian Evangelical Christian Union, 1933.

Prokhanov, Ivan Stepanovich. *Presliedovaniia evangel'skikh i srodnykh im khristian v Rossii vo vremia voiny.* Petrograd, 1915.

———. *Zapiska o pravovom polozhenii evangel'skikh khristian, a takzhe baptistov i srodnykh im khristian v Rossii.* St. Petersburg: Izdanie Vserossiiskogo Soiuza Evangel'skikh Khristian, 1913.

———, ed. *Respublika i svoboda sovesti. Kratkii spravochnik po ukazaniiam i rasporiazheniiam sovetskoi vlasti po religioznym voprosam v primenii evangel'skim khristianam i drugikh svobodovertsam.* Petrograd: Izdanie Vserossiiskogo Soiuza Evangel'skikh Khristian, 1921.

Protokoly i materialy Pervogo S"iezda Volgo-Kamskogo Soiuza Baptistov. Troitsk: Izdanie N. V. Odintsova, 1928.

Protokoly 9-go Vsesoiuznogo s"ezda evangel'skikh khristian v Petrograde v 1923 godu. Petrograd: Izdanie VSEKh, 1923.

Prugavin, A. S. *Raskol i sektantstvo v russkoi narodnoi zhizni.* Moscow: Tipografiia tovarishchestva I. D. Sytina, 1905.

Putintsev, F. M. *Politicheskaia rol' i taktika sekt.* Moscow: Gosudarstvennoi antireligioznoe izdatel'stvo, 1935.

———. *Politicheskaia rol' sektantstva.* Moscow, 1928.

———. "Sektantstvo i antireligioznaia propaganda." *Kommunisticheskoe prosveshchenie* 5, no. 6 (November–December 1926): 31–36.

————. *Sektantstvo i antireligioznaia propaganda.* Moscow: Izdatel'skoe aktsionernago o-vo "Bezbozhnik," 1928.

R., E. "Russkie ratsionalisty." *Viestnik Evropy,* no. 7 (1881): 279–96.

Roshchin, A. *Kto takie sektanty?* Moscow-Leningrad, 1930.

Rostovtsev, Andr. *Nravstvennost' sektantskaia i proletarskaia.* N.p.: Priboi, 1931.

Rozhdestvenskii, A. *Iuzhno-russkii shtundizm.* St. Petersburg: Tipografiia Departamenta Udielov, 1889.

Rushbrooke, J. H. *The Baptist Movement in the Continent of Europe.* 2nd ed. London: Carey, 1923.

————. *Some Chapters in European Baptist History.* London: Kingsgate, 1929.

Saloff-Astakhoff, N. I. *Interesting Facts of the Russian Revolution; or, In the Flame of Russia's Revolution with God and the Bible.* New York, 1931.

————. *Real Russia from 1905–1932.* New York, 1932.

————. *Real Russia from 1905 to 1932: And Communism in America.* New York, 1932.

S.-Peterburgskii Eparkhial'nyi Missionerskii Soviet. *Slovo zhizni dvukh byvshikh sektantov-baptistov.* St. Petersburg: Tipografiia Aleksandra-Nevskogo Obshchestva Trezvosti, 1911.

Sanktpeterburgkaia obshchina evangel'skikh khristian. *S"iezdu russkikh baptistov.* St. Petersburg, 1910.

Shchelchkov, G. *Voiunstvuiushchii shtundo-baptizm i pravoslavnaia missiia.* Mogilev, 1912.

Shchepkin, E., and Volzhanin. *Sektanty na Urale.* Sverdlovsk, 1928.

Shtrikker, Gerd, ed. *Russkaia pravoslavnaia tserkov' v sovetskoe vremia (1917–1991).* Materialy i dokumenty po istorii otnoshenii mezhdu gosudarstvom i Tserkov'iu. Kniga I. Moscow: Izdatel'stvo "Propilei," 1995.

Skvortsov, Dmitrii. *Pashkovtsy v tverskoi eparkhii.* Tver': Tipografiia gubernskago pravleniia, 1893.

Skvortsov, V. M. *Dieianiia 3-go Vserossiiskago Missionerskago S"iezda v Kazani, po voprosam vnutrennei missii i raskolosektantstva.* Kiev: Tipografiia I. I. Chokolova, 1898.

Sokolov, N. M. *Ob ideiakh i idealakh russkoi intelligentsii.* St. Petersburg: M. M. Stasiulevich, 1904.

Terletskii, V. N. *Ocherki, izsliedovaniia i stat'i po sektantstvu.* Vyp. I. 2nd ed. Poltava: Elektricheskaia tipografiia G. I. Markevicha, 1913.

Terskoi, An. *U sektantov.* Moscow: Molodaia gvardiia, 1930.

Tikhomirov, B. *Baptizm i ego politicheskaia rol'.* Moscow: Gosudarstvennoe izdatel'stvo, 1929.

Timasheff, N. S. *Religion in Soviet Russia.* New York: Sheed and Ward, 1942.

Timoshenko, M. D. *V narymskii krai. Vospominaniia i vpechatlieniia ssyl'nago.* Moscow: Slovo istiny, 1917.

Timoshenko, Mikhail. *Za ubiezhdenie (Iz vospominanii ssyl'nago).* Odessa, 1913.

Troitskii, Prot. I. "Osobennaia zlovrednost' shtundo-baptizma i niekotoryia miery prikhodskoi bor'by s etoi sektoi." *Rukovodstvo dlia sel'skikh pastyrei,* no. 17 (1912): 512–17.

Umanets, S. I. "Protestantskie missionery v Rossii (1876–1906 gg.)." *Istoricheskii viestnik,* 104 (June 1906): 902–8.

V., A. M. and A.S.A. *Obrashchenie na istinnyi put' i vospominaniia baptista G.I.M.* Omsk: Pravlenie Sibirskago Otdela Soiuza Baptistov, 1919.

Vasilevskii, G. *Baptizm i svoboda voli.* St. Petersburg, 1914.

"Vopros o malorusskom nariechii v otnoshenii k shtundizmu." *Kievskiia eparkhial'nyia viedomosti*, no. 4 (28 January 1881): 1–4.

Voronov, A. "Shtundizm." *Russkii viestnik* 170 (March 1884): 5–45.

Vostorgov, Protoierei I. *Vrazheskii dukhovnyi avangard "Nemetskaia viera." K voprosu o sushchnosti russkago sektantstva.* Moscow: "Russkaia Pechatnia," 1914.

Vsepoddanneishii otchet Ober-Prokurora Sviatieishago Sinoda po viedomstvu pravoslavnago ispoviedaniia za 1908–1909 gody. St. Petersburg: Sinodal'naia tipografiia, 1911.

Vsepoddannieishii Otchet Ober-Prokurora Sviatieishago Sinoda po viedomstvu pravoslavnago ispoviedaniia za 1910 god. St. Petersburg: Sinodal'naia tipografiia, 1913.

Vvedenskii, Aleksandr. *Bor'ba s sektantstvom.* Odessa: Tipografiia Eparkhial'nogo doma, 1914.

———. *Dieistvuiushchiia zakonopolozheniia kasatel'no staroobriadtsev i sektantov.* Odessa: Tipografiia Odesskikh Novostei, 1912.

———. "Gosudarstvo i tserkov' v otnoshenie k sektantam." *Golos tserkvi* 3, no. 1 (January 1914): 160–70.

Whitley, W. T., ed. *Fourth Baptist World Congress. Toronto, Canada, 23–29 June 1928.* Toronto: Stewart Printing Service, 1928.

———, ed. *Third Baptist World Congress. Stockholm, July 21–27, 1923.* Record of Proceedings. London: Kingsgate, 1923.

Zapis' zasedanii 10-go Vsesoiuznogo S"ezda Evangel'skikh Khristian v Leningrade s 30-go noiabria do 6-oe dekabria 1926g. v Dome Spaseniia po ul. Zheliabova, 25. Leningrad: Izdanie I. S. Prokhanov i Ia. I. Zhidkov, 1927.

Zapisi zasedanii 10-go Vsesoiuznogo S"ezda Evangel'skikh Khristian. Leningrad: Izdanie I. S. Prokhanova i Ia. I. Zhidkova, 1927.

12 Dekabria 1904 g. Na pamiat' o svobodie v religioznykh ubiezhdeniiakh. 15 maia 1905 g. Rostov-on-Don, 1905.

26-oi Vsesoiuznyi S"ezd Baptistov S.S.S.R. (Protokoly i materialy). Moscow: Izdanie Federativnogo Soiuza Baptistov SSSR v litse N. V. Odintsova, 1927.

SECONDARY SOURCES

Agadjanian, Alexander. "Revising Pandora's Gifts: Religious and National Identity in the Post-Soviet Societal Fabric." *Europe-Asia Studies* 53, no. 3 (2001): 473–88.

Alekseev, V. A. *Illiuzii i dogmy.* Moscow: Izdatel'stvo politicheskoi literatury, 1991.

Alekseeva, Liudmila. *Istoriia inakomyslia v SSSR. Noveishii period.* Benson, Vt.: Khronika, 1984.

Ascher, Abraham. *The Revolution of 1905: Russia in Disarray.* Stanford: Stanford University Press, 1988.

Atkinson, Dorothy L. *The End of the Russian Land Commune.* Stanford: Stanford University Press, 1983.

Badone, Ellen, ed. *Religious Orthodoxy and Popular Faith in European Society.* Princeton, N.J.: Princeton University Press, 1990.

Batalden, Stephen K., ed. *Seeking God: The Recovery of Religious Identity in Orthodox Russia, Ukraine, and Georgia.* DeKalb: Northern Illinois University Press, 1993.

Berger, Peter L. *The Sacred Canopy: Elements of a Sociological Theory of Religion.* New York: Doubleday, 1967.

Bergman, Jay. "The Image of Jesus in the Russian Revolutionary Movement: The Case of Russian Marxism." *International Review of Social History* 35 (1990): 220–48.

Bermeo, Nancy, and Philip Nord, eds. *Civil Society before Democracy: Lessons from Nineteenth-century Europe*. Lanham, Md.: Rowman and Littlefield, 2000.

Bessmertnyi, A. R., and S. B. Filatov, eds. *Religiia i demokratiia. Na puti k svobode sovesti II*. Moscow: Izdatel'skaia gruppa "Progress" "Kul'tura," 1993.

Blane, Andrew. "Protestant Sects in Late Imperial Russia." In *The Religious World of Russian Culture: Russia and Orthodoxy*. Vol. 2, *Essays in Honor of Georges Florovsky*, ed. Andrew Blane, 268–303. The Hague: Mouton, 1975.

———. "The Relations between the Russian Protestant Sects and the State, 1900–1921." Ph.D. dissertation, Duke University, 1964.

Bond, Brian. *War and Society in Europe, 1870–1970*. Bungay: Fontana Paperbacks, 1984.

Bonnell, Victoria E. *Roots of Rebellion: Workers' Politics and Organizations in St. Petersburg and Moscow, 1900–1914*. Berkeley: University of California Press, 1983.

Bossy, John. *Christianity in the West, 1400–1700*. Oxford: Oxford University Press, 1985.

Bowen, Kurt. *Evangelism and Apostasy: The Evolution and Impact of Evangelicals in Modern Mexico*. Montreal: McGill-Queen's University Press, 1996.

Brackney, William Henry. *The Baptists*. Denominations in America series, no. 2. New York: Greenwood, 1988.

Bradley, Joseph. "Russia's Parliament of Public Opinion: Association, Assembly, and the Autocracy, 1906–1914." In *Reform in Modern Russian History*, ed. Theodore Taranovski, 212–36. Cambridge: Woodrow Wilson Center Press and Cambridge University Press, 1995.

———. "Subjects into Citizens: Societies, Civil Society, and Autocracy in Tsarist Russia." *American Historical Review* 107, no. 4 (October 2002): 1094–1123.

Breyfogle, Nicholas B. "Heretics and Colonizers: Religious Dissent and Russian Colonization of Transcaucasia, 1830–1890." Ph.D. dissertation, University of Pennsylvania, 1998.

Brock, Peter. *Soviet Conscientious Objectors, 1917–1939: A Chapter in the History of Twentieth-century Pacifism*. Toronto: Privately printed, 1999.

———. *Studies in Peace History*. York: William Sessions, 1991.

———. *Twentieth-Century Pacifism*. New Perspectives in Political Science series. New York: Van Nostrand Reinhold, 1970.

———, ed. *Testimonies of Conscience Sent from the Soviet Union to the War Resisters' International, 1923–1929*. Toronto: Privately printed, 1997.

Brock, Peter, and Nigel Young. *Pacifism in the Twentieth Century*. Syracuse: Syracuse University Press, 1999.

Brooks, Jeffrey. *When Russia Learned to Read*. Princeton, N.J.: Princeton University Press, 1985.

Burds, Jeffrey. "A Culture of Denunciation: Peasant Labor Migration and Religious Anathematization in Rural Russia, 1860–1905." In *Accusatory Practices: Denunciation in Modern European History, 1789–1989*, ed. Sheila Fitzpatrick and Robert Gellately, 40–72. Chicago: University of Chicago Press, 1997.

———. *Peasant Dreams and Market Politics*. Pittsburgh: University of Pittsburgh Press, 1998.

Byrnes, Robert F. *Pobedonostsev: His Life and Thought*. Bloomington: Indiana University Press, 1968.

Calhoun, Craig, ed. *Habermas and the Public Sphere*. Cambridge, Mass.: MIT Press, 1992.

Camfield, G. P. "The Pavlovtsy of Khar'kov Province, 1886–1905: Harmless Sectarians or Dangerous Rebels?" *Slavonic and East European Review* 68, no. 4 (October 1990): 692–717.

Chase, William J. *Workers, Society, and the Soviet State: Labor and Life in Moscow, 1918–1929.* Urbana: University of Illinois Press, 1987.

Cherniavsky, Michael. *Tsar and People: Studies in Russian Myths.* New Haven: Yale University Press, 1961.

Chulos, Chris J. "Peasant Religion in Post-Emancipation Russia: Voronezh Province, 1880–1917." Ph.D. dissertation, University of Chicago, 1994.

Clarke, Paul Barry, and Andrew Linzey, eds. *Dictionary of Ethics, Theology, and Society.* London: Routledge, 1996.

Clay, Eugene. "The Theological Origins of the Christ-Faith [Khristovshchina]." *Russian History* 15 (1988): 21–41.

Clowes, Edith W., Samuel D. Kassow, and James L. West, eds. *Between Tsar and People: Educated Society and the Quest for Public Identity in Late Imperial Russia.* Princeton, N.J.: Princeton University Press, 1991.

Coleman, Heather J. "Definitions of Heresy: The Fourth Missionary Congress and the Problem of Cultural Power in Russia after 1905." *Jahrbücher für Geschichte Osteuropas* 52, no. 1 (2004): 70–91.

Comtet, S. M. "Stepnjak-Kravcinskij et la Russie sectaire, 1851–1895." *Cahiers du Monde Russe et Sovietique* 12, no. 4 (October–December 1971): 422–38.

Crisp, Olga, and Linda Edmondson. *Civil Rights in Imperial Russia.* Oxford: Clarendon, 1989.

Cunningham, James W. *A Vanquished Hope: The Movement for Church Renewal in Russia, 1905–1906.* Crestwood, N.Y.: St. Vladimir's Seminary Press, 1981.

Curtiss, John Sheldon. *Church and State in Russia: The Last Years of the Empire, 1900–1917.* New York: Columbia University Press, 1940.

———. *The Russian Church and the Soviet State.* Boston: Little, Brown, 1953.

Davis, Natalie Zemon. "From 'Popular Religion' to Religious Cultures." In *Reformation Europe: A Guide to Research,* ed. Steven Ozment, 307–36. St. Louis: Center for Reformation Research, 1982.

———. *Society and Culture in Early Modern France.* Stanford: Stanford University Press, 1975.

———. "Some Tasks and Themes in the Study of Popular Religion." In *The Pursuit of Holiness in Late Medieval and Renaissance Religion,* ed. Charles Trinkaus with Heiko A. Oberman, 321–41. Leiden: Brill, 1974.

Dekar, Paul R. *For the Healing of the Nations: Baptist Peacemakers.* Macon, Ga.: Smyth and Helwys, 1993.

Desan, Suzanne. *Reclaiming the Sacred: Lay Religion and Popular Politics in Revolutionary France.* Ithaca, N.Y.: Cornell University Press, 1988.

Dixon, Simon Mark. "Church, State, and Society in Late Imperial Russia: The Diocese of St. Petersburg, 1880–1914." Ph.D. dissertation, University of London, 1993.

Dorsey, Peter A. *Sacred Estrangement: The Rhetoric of Conversion in Modern American Autobiography.* University Park: Pennsylvania State University Press, 1993.

Dunn, Ethel, and Stephen P. Dunn. "Religion as an Instrument of Culture Change: The Problem of the Sects in the Soviet Union." *Slavic Review,* no. 3 (September 1964): 459–78.

Edgerton, William, trans. and ed. *Memoirs of Peasant Tolstoyans in Soviet Russia.* Bloomington: Indiana University Press, 1993.

Eidberg, Peder A. "Baptist Developments in the Nordic Countries during the Twentieth Century." *Baptist History and Heritage* (winter–spring 2001): 136–52.

✓ Engelstein, Laura. *Castration and the Heavenly Kingdom: A Russian Folktale.* Ithaca, N.Y.: Cornell University Press, 1999.

Engelstein, Laura, and Stephanie Sandler, eds. *Self and Story in Russian History.* Ithaca, N.Y.: Cornell University Press, 2000.

Etkind, Alexander. "Russkie sekty i sovetskii kommunizm: Proekt Vladimira Bonch-Bruevicha." *Minuvshee,* no. 19 (1996): 284–88.

———. "Whirling with the Other: Russian Populism and Religious Sects." *Russian Review* 62, no. 4 (October 2003): 565–88.

Fath, Sebastien. "Another Way of Being a Christian in France: A Century of Baptist Implantation." *Baptist History and Heritage* (winter–spring 2001): 153–73.

———. "L'Etat face aux enjeux 'autorité-pouvoir' chez les baptistes: l'exemple français, 19ème-20ème siècle." *Social Compass* 48, no. 1 (2001): 51–61.

Field, Daniel. *Rebels in the Name of the Tsar.* Boston: Unwin Hyman, 1989.

Figes, Orlando. *Peasant Russia, Civil War: The Volga Countryside in Revolution (1917–1921).* Oxford: Clarendon, 1989.

———. *A People's Tragedy: The Russian Revolution, 1891–1924.* London: Jonathan Cape, 1996.

———. "The Red Army and Mass Mobilization during the Russian Civil War, 1918–1920." *Past & Present* no. 129 (November 1990): 168–211.

———. "The Russian Revolution of 1917 and Its Language in the Village." *Russian Review* 56 (July 1997): 323–45.

Figes, Orlando, and Boris Kolonitskii. *Interpreting the Russian Revolution: The Language and Symbols of 1917.* New Haven: Yale University Press, 1999.

Fisher, Ralph Talcott, Jr. *Pattern for Soviet Youth: A Study of the Congresses of the Komsomol, 1918–1954.* Studies of the Russian Institute of Columbia University. New York: Columbia University Press, 1959.

Fitzpatrick, Sheila. "Ascribing Class: The Construction of Social Identity in Soviet Russia." *Journal of Modern History* 65 (December 1993): 745–70.

———. *The Cultural Front: Power and Culture in Revolutionary Russia.* Ithaca, N.Y.: Cornell University Press, 1992.

———. "Lives under Fire: Autobiographical Narratives and Their Challenges in Stalin's Russia." In *De Russie et d'ailleurs: Feux croisés sur l'histoire,* ed. Martine Godet. Paris: Institut d'études slaves, 1995.

———, ed. *Cultural Revolution in Russia, 1928–1931.* Bloomington: Indiana University Press, 1978.

Fitzpatrick, Sheila, Alexander Rabinowitch, and Richard Stites, eds. *Russia in the Era of NEP: Explorations in Soviet Society and Culture.* Bloomington: Indiana University Press, 1991.

Ford, Caroline. "Religion and Popular Culture in Modern Europe." *Journal of Modern History* 65 (March 1993): 152–75.

Frank, Stephen P. "Popular Justice, Community, and Culture among the Russian Peasantry, 1870–1900." *Russian Review* 46 (1987): 239–65.

Frank, Stephen P., and Mark D. Steinberg, eds. *Cultures in Flux: Lower-Class Values, Practices, and Resistance in Late Imperial Russia.* Princeton, N.J.: Princeton University Press, 1994.

Freeze, Gregory. "Counter-reformation in Russian Orthodoxy: Popular Response to Religious Innovation, 1922–1925." *Slavic Review* 54 (summer 1995): 305–39.

————. "Handmaiden of the State? The Church in Imperial Russia Reconsidered." *Journal of Ecclesiastical History* 36, no. 1 (January 1985): 78–103.

————. *The Parish Clergy in Nineteenth-Century Russia: Crisis, Reform, Counter-Reform.* Princeton, N.J.: Princeton University Press, 1983.

————. "The Soslovie (Estate) Paradigm and Russian Social History." *American Historical Review* 91, no. 1 (1986): 11–36.

————. "Subversive Piety: Religion and the Political Crisis in Late Imperial Russia." *Journal of Modern History* 68 (June 1996): 308–50.

Frierson, Cathy A. "Crime and Punishment in the Russian Village: Rural Concepts of Criminality at the End of the Nineteenth Century," *Slavic Review* 46, no. 1 (spring 1987): 55–69.

————. *Peasant Icons: Representations of Rural People in Late Nineteenth-Century Russia.* New York: Oxford University Press, 1993.

Furman, D. E., and Mark (Smirnov), eds. *Na puti k svobode sovesti.* Moscow: Progress, 1989.

Geraci, Robert P., and Michael Khodarkovsky. *Of Religion and Empire: Missions, Conversion, and Tolerance in Tsarist Russia.* Ithaca, N.Y.: Cornell University Press, 2001.

Gibson, Ralph. "Female Religious Orders in Nineteenth-Century France." In *Catholicism in Britain and France since 1789,* ed. Frank Tallett and Nicholas Atkin. London: Hambledon, 1996.

Gilbert, Alan D. *Religion and Society in Industrial England: Church, Chapel, and Social Change, 1740–1914.* London: Longman, 1976.

Gooderham, Peter. "The Komsomol and Worker Youth: The Inculcation of 'Communist Values' in Leningrad during NEP." *Soviet Studies* 34, no. 4 (October 1982): 506–28.

Gorsuch, Anne E. "NEP Be Damned! Young Militants in the 1920s and the Culture of Civil War." *Russian Review,* 56 (October 1997): 564–80.

————. "'A Woman Is Not a Man': The Culture of Gender and Generation in Soviet Russia, 1921–1928," *Slavic Review* 55, no. 3 (fall 1996).

Gutsche, Waldemar. *Religion und Evangelium in Sowjetrussland zwischen zwei Weltkriegen (1917–1944).* Kassel: J. G. Oncken Verlag, 1959.

Haimson, Leopold H. "The Problem of Social Identities in Early Twentieth Century Russia." *Slavic Review* 47, no. 1 (spring 1988): 1–21.

————. "The Problem of Social Stability in Urban Russia, 1905–1917." *Slavic Review* 23 (1964): 619–42; 24 (1965): 1–22.

Halfin, Igal. *From Darkness to Light: Class, Consciousness, and Salvation in Revolutionary Russia.* Pittsburgh: University of Pittsburgh Press, 2000.

————. "From Darkness to Light: Student Communist Autobiography during NEP." *Jahrbücher für Geschichte Osteuropas* 45, no. 2 (1997): 210–36.

Harding, Susan F. "Convicted by the Holy Spirit: The Rhetoric of Fundamental Baptist Conversion." *American Ethnologist* 4, no. 1 (February 1987): 167–81.

Heier, Edmund. *Religious Schism in the Russian Aristocracy, 1860–1900: Radstockism and Pashkovism.* The Hague: Martinus Nijhoff, 1970.

Hempton, David. *The Religion of the People: Methodism and Popular Religion c. 1750–1900.* London: Routledge, 1996.

Hellman, Ben. "Kogda vremia slavianofil'stvovalo. Russkie filosofy i pervaia mirovaia voina." In *Studia Russica Helsingiensia et Tartuensia. Problemy istorii russkoi literatury nachala XX veka*. Slavic Helsingiensia 6. Helsinki: Department of Slavonic Languages, University of Helsinki, 1989.

Herrlinger, Kimberly Page. "Class, Piety, and Politics: Workers, Orthodoxy, and the Problem of Religious Identity in Russia, 1881–1914." Ph.D. dissertation, University of California, Berkeley, 1996.

Holquist, Peter. "'Information Is the Alpha and Omega of Our Work': Bolshevik Surveillance in Its Pan-European Context." *Journal of Modern History* 69 (September 1997).

Hosking, Geoffrey A. *Russia: People and Empire*. Cambridge, Mass.: Harvard University Press, 1997.

———. *The Russian Constitutional Experiment: Government and Duma, 1907–1914*. Cambridge: Cambridge University Press, 1973.

———, ed. *Church, Nation, and State in Russia and Ukraine*. New York: St. Martin's, 1991.

Hrushevs'kyĭ, Mikhailo. *Z istoriï relihiĭnoï dumky na Ukraïni*. Winnipeg: Ukrainian Evangelical Alliance of North America, 1962.

Hughes, Robert P., and Irina Paperno, eds. *Christianity and the Eastern Slavs*. 3 vols. Vol. 2, *Russian Culture in Modern Times*. California Slavic Studies series, no. 17. Berkeley: University of California Press, 1994.

Hunt, Lynn, ed. *The New Cultural History*. Berkeley: University of California Press, 1989.

Husband, William B. *"Godless Communists": Atheism and Society in Soviet Russia, 1917–1932*. DeKalb: Northern Illinois University Press, 2000.

Iannaccone, Laurence R. "Why Strict Churches Are Strong." *American Journal of Sociology* 99, no. 5 (March 1994): 1181.

Istoriia evangel'skikh khristian-baptistov v SSSR. Moscow: Izdanie Vsesoiuznogo Soveta Evangel'skikh Khristian-Baptistov, 1989.

James, William. *The Varieties of Religious Experience*. New York: Image Books, 1978.

Juster, Susan. *Disorderly Women: Sexual Politics and Evangelicalism in Revolutionary New England*. Ithaca, N.Y.: Cornell University Press, 1994.

Kahle, Wilhelm. *Evangelische Christen in Rußland und der Sovetunion: Ivan Stepanovič Prochanov (1869–1935) und der Weg der Evangeliumschristen und Baptisten*. Wuppertal und Kassel: Oncken Verlag, 1978.

Kalinicheva, Zoia Vasil'evna. *Sotsial'naia sushchnost' baptizma*. Leningrad: Izdatel'stvo "Nauka," 1972.

Kenez, Peter. *The Birth of the Propaganda State: Soviet Methods of Mass Mobilization, 1917–1929*. New York: Cambridge University Press, 1985.

Kimerling, Elise. "Civil Rights and Social Policy in Soviet Russia, 1918–1936." *Russian Review* 41 (January 1982): 24–46.

Kizenko, Nadieszda. *A Prodigal Saint: Father John of Kronstadt and the Russian People*. University Park: Pennsylvania State University Press, 2000.

Klibanov, A. I. *Istoriia religioznogo sektantstva v Rossii (60-e gody XIX g.–1917 g.)*. Moscow: Izdatel'stvo "Nauka," 1965.

———. *Religioznoe sektantstvo i sovremennost' (sotsiologicheskie i istoricheskie ocherki)*. Moscow: Izdatel'stvo "Nauka," 1969.

———, ed. *Kritika religioznogo sektantstva (Opyt izucheniia religioznogo sektantstva v 20-kh–nachale 30-kh godov)*. Moscow: Izdatel'stvo "Mysl'," 1974.

Klippenstein, Lawrence. "Religion and Dissent in the Era of Reform: The Russian Stundobaptists, 1858–1884." M.A. thesis, University of Minnesota, 1971.

Koenker, Diane P., William G. Rosenberg, and Ronald Grigor Suny, eds. *Party, State, and Society in the Russian Civil War: Explorations in Social History.* Bloomington: Indiana University Press, 1989.

Kolarz, Walter. *Religion in the Soviet Union.* New York: St. Martin's, 1966.

Kolonitskii, Boris Ivanovich. "Antibourgeois Propaganda and Anti-'Burzhui' Consciousness in 1917." *Russian Review* 53, no. 2 (April 1994): 183–96.

———. "'Democracy' in the Political Consciousness of the February Revolution." *Slavic Review* 57, no. 1 (spring 1998): 95–106.

Krivova, N. A. *Vlast' i tserkov' v 1922–1925g.g.: Politbiuro i GPU v bor'be za tserkovnye tsennosti i politicheskoe podchinenie dukhovenstva.* Moscow: AIRO-XX, 1997.

Kurov, M. N. "Problema svobody sovesti v dorevoliutsionnoi Rossii." In *Voprosy Nauchnogo Ateizma. Vyp. 27. Svoboda sovesti v sotsialisticheskom obshchestve.* Moscow: "Mysl'," 1981.

Lancaster, Roger N. *Thanks to God and the Revolution: Popular Religion and Class Consciousness in the New Nicaragua.* New York: Columbia University Press, 1988.

Laqueur, Walter. *Russia and Germany: A Century of Conflict.* New Brunswick, N.J.: Transaction, 1990.

Lebina, N. B. *Povsednevskaia zhizn' sovetskogo goroda: normy i anomalii. 1920–1930 gody.* St. Petersburg: Letnii sad, 1999.

Levin, Alfred. "Toward the End of the Old Regime: The State, Church, and Duma." In *Religion and Modernization in the Soviet Union,* ed. Dennis J. Dunn, 23–59. Boulder, Colo.: Westview, 1977.

Lewin, Moshe. *The Making of the Soviet System: Essays in the Social History of Interwar Russia.* New York: New Press, 1994.

Lialina, G. S. *Baptizm: illiuzii i real'nost'.* Moscow: Izdatel'stvo politicheskoi literatury, 1977.

———. "Liberal'no-burzhuaznoe techenie v baptizme (1905–1917 gg.)." *Voprosy nauchnogo ateizma.* Vyp. 1. Moscow: Izdatel'stvo "Mysl'," 1966.

Lindenmeyer, Adele. *Poverty Is Not a Vice: Charity, Society, and the State in Imperial Russia.* Princeton, N.J.: Princeton University Press, 1996.

Lord, F. Townley. *Baptist World Fellowship: A Short History of the Baptist World Alliance.* Nashville: Broadman, 1955.

Lovegrove, Deryck W. *Established Church, Sectarian People: Itinerancy and the Transformation of English Dissent, 1780–1830.* Cambridge: Cambridge University Press, 1988.

Luukkanen, Arto. *The Party of Unbelief: The Religious Policy of the Bolshevik Party, 1917–1929.* Studia Historica 36. Helsinki: Suomen Historiallinen Seura, 1994.

———. *The Religious Policy of the Stalinist State: A Case Study—The Central Standing Commission on Religious Questions, 1928–1938.* Studia Historica 57. Helsinki: Suomen Historiallinen Seura, 1997.

Maevskii, Vl. A. *Vnutrenniaia missiia i ee osnovopolozhnik.* Buenos Aires, 1954.

Martin, David. *Tongues of Fire: The Explosion of Protestantism in Latin America.* Oxford: Basil Blackwell, 1990.

Maynes, Mary Jo. *Taking the Hard Road: Life Course in French and German Workers' Autobiographies in the Era of Industrialization.* Chapel Hill: University of North Carolina Press, 1995.

Maza, Sara. "Stories in History: Cultural Narratives in Recent Works in European History." *American Historical Review* 101 (December 1996): 1493–1515.

McCarthy, F. M. "The Kazan Missionary Congress." *Cahiers du monde russe et soviétique* 14, no. 3 (July–September 1973): 308–32.

McLeod, Hugh. *Secularisation in Western Europe, 1848–1914.* New York: St. Martin's, 2000.

———, ed. *European Religion in the Age of Great Cities, 1830–1930.* Christianity and Society in the Modern World series. London: Routledge, 1995.

McLoughlin, William G. *Soul Liberty: The Baptists' Struggle in New England, 1630–1833.* Hanover, N.H.: University Press of New England, 1991.

Misner, Paul. *Social Catholicism in Europe: From the Onset of Industrialization to the First World War.* New York: Crossroad, 1991.

Mitrokhin, L. N. *Baptizm.* 2nd ed. Moscow: Izdatel'stvo politicheskoi literatury, 1974.

Modern Encyclopedia of Religion in Russia and the Soviet Union. Edited by Paul D. Steeves. Vol. 3. Gulf Breeze, Fla.: Academic International Press, 1991.

Müller, Eberhard, "Opportunismus oder Utopie? V. D. Bonč-Bruevich und die russischen Sekten vor und nach der Revolution." *Jahrbücher für Geschichte Osteuropas* 35, no. 4 (1987): 509–33.

Nesdoly, Samuel John. "Evangelical Sectarianism in Russia: A Study of the Stundists, Baptists, Pashkovites, and Evangelical Christians, 1855–1917." Ph.D. dissertation, Queen's University, Kingston, 1971.

Nezhnyi, Aleksandr. *Kommisar d'iavola.* Moscow: Protestant, 1993.

Nichols, Robert L., and Theofanis George Stavrou, eds. *Russian Orthodoxy under the Old Regime.* Minneapolis: University of Minnesota Press, 1978.

Obelkevich, Jim, Lyndal Roper, and Raphael Samuel, eds. *Disciplines of Faith: Studies in Religion, Politics, and Patriarchy.* History Workshop series. London: Routledge and Kegan Paul, 1987.

Odintsov, M. I. *Gosudarstvo i tserkov' v Rossii.* Moscow: Rossiiskaia akademiia upravleniia, 1994.

———. *Gosudarstvo i tserkov' (Istoriia vzaimootnoshenii, 1917–1938 gg.).* Moscow: Znanie, 1991.

Pascal, Pierre. *The Religion of the Russian People.* Translated by Rowan Williams. London: Mowbrays, 1976.

Pavlova, T. A., ed. *Dolgii put' rossiiskogo patsifizma: Ideal mezhdunarodnoto i vnutrennego mira v religiozno-filosofskoi i obshchestvenno-politicheskoi mysli Rossii.* Moscow: Institut vseobshchei istorii RAN, 1997.

Peris, Daniel. "The 1929 Congress of the Godless." *Soviet Studies* 43, no. 4 (1991): 711–32.

———. *Storming the Heavens: The Soviet League of the Militant Godless.* Ithaca, N.Y.: Cornell University Press, 1998.

Persits, M. M. *Otdelenie tserkvi ot gosudarstva i shkoly ot tserkvi v SSSR.* Moscow: Izdatel'stvo Akademii Nauk SSSR, 1958.

Pestana, Carla Gardina. *Quakers and Baptists in Colonial Massachusetts.* Cambridge: Cambridge University Press, 1991.

Petrus, K. *Religious Communes in the USSR.* Mimeographed Series no. 44. New York: Research Program on the USSR, 1953.

Phillips, Paul T. *A Kingdom of God on Earth: Anglo-American Social Christianity, 1880–1940.* University Park: Pennsylvania State University Press, 1996.

Podberezskii, I.V. *Byt' protestantom v Rossii.* Moscow: Izdatel'stvo "Blagovestnik," 1996.

Polunov, A. Iu. *Pod vlast'iu ober-prokurora: Gosudarstvo i tserkov' v epokhu Aleksandra III.* Seriia "Pervaia monografiia." Moscow: "AIRO-XX," 1996.

Pospielovsky, Dimitry. *The Russian Church under the Soviet Regime, 1917–1982*. Crestwood, N.Y.: St. Vladimir's Seminary Press, 1984.

Popov, V. "Khristianskie kommuny Prokhanova." *Nauka i religiia*, no. 7 (1990): 48–49.

Popovskii, Mark. *Russkie muzhiki rasskazyvaiut . . . Posledovateli L. N. Tolstogo v Sovetskom Soiuze*. London: Overseas Publications Interchange, 1983.

Rambo, Lewis R. *Understanding Religious Conversion*. New Haven: Yale University Press, 1993.

Read, Christopher. *Religion, Revolution, and the Russian Intelligentsia, 1900–1912*. London: Macmillan, 1979.

Robson, Roy R. *Old Believers in Modern Russia*. DeKalb: Northern Illinois University Press, 1995.

Rogger, Hans. "Russia in 1914." *Journal of Contemporary History* 1, no. 4 (October 1966): 95–120.

———. *Russia in the Age of Modernization and Revolution, 1881–1917*. Longman History of Russia series. London: Longman, 1983.

Roginskii, A. B., ed. *Vospominaniia krest'ian-tolstovtsev 1910–1930-e gody*. Moscow: Kniga, 1989.

Rosenberg, William G. *Liberals in the Russian Revolution: The Constitutional Democratic Party, 1917–1921*. Princeton, N.J.: Princeton University Press, 1974.

Rosenthal, Bernice Glatzer, ed. *The Occult in Russian and Soviet Culture*. Ithaca, N.Y.: Cornell University Press, 1997.

Rosenthal, Bernice Glatzer, and Martha Bohachevsky-Chomiak, eds. *A Revolution of the Spirit: Crisis of Value in Russia, 1890–1924*. New York: Fordham University Press, 1990.

Roslof, Edward E. "The Heresy of 'Bolshevik' Christianity: Orthodox Rejection of Religious Reform during NEP." *Slavic Review* 55, no. 3 (fall 1996): 614–35.

———. *Red Priests: Renovationism, Russian Orthodoxy, and Revolution, 1905–1946*. Bloomington: Indiana University Press, 2002.

Rowe, Michael. *Russian Resurrection: Strength in Suffering—A History of Russia's Evangelical Church*. London: Marshall Pickering, 1994.

Sannikov, S. V. *Istoriia baptizma*. Vyp. 1. Odessa: OBS "Bogomyslie," 1996.

Sarychev, Vasilii Viktorovich. "Sotsial'no-ekonomicheskie i politicheskie aspekty rasprostraneniia baptizma v Rossii (Evropeiskaia chast', 1860-e–1917 gg.)." Candidate dissertation, Gor'kii State University, 1989.

Savinskii, S. N. *Istoriia Evangel'skikh Khristian-Baptistov Ukrainy, Rossii, Belorussii (1867–1917)*. St. Petersburg: Bibliia dlia vsekh, 1999.

Sawatsky, Walter. *Soviet Evangelicals since World War II*. Kitchener, Ont.: Herald Press, 1981.

Scott, James C. *Domination and the Arts of Resistance: Hidden Transcripts*. New Haven: Yale University Press, 1990.

Sheils, W. J., and Diana Wood, eds. *Voluntary Religion: Papers Read at the 1985 Summer Meeting and the 1986 Winter Meeting of the Ecclesiastical History Society*. Studies in Church History, no. 23. Oxford: Basil Blackwell, 1986.

Shevzov, Vera. "Popular Orthodoxy in Late Imperial Rural Russia." Ph.D. dissertation, Yale University, 1994.

Sheinman, M. M. *Khristianskii sotsializm*. Moscow: Izdatel'stvo "Nauka," 1969.

Shishkin, V. A., ed. *Petrograd na perelome epokh: Gorod i ego zhiteli v gody revoliutsii i grazhdanskoi voiny*. St. Petersburg: Izdatel'stvo "Dmitrii Bulanin," 2000.

Shkarovskii, M. V. *Peterburgskaia eparkhiia v gody gonenii i utrat 1917–1945.* St. Petersburg: Liki Rossii, 1995.

Shterin, Marat S., and James T. Richardson. "Local Laws Restricting Religion in Russia: Precursors of Russia's New National Law." *Journal of Church and State* 40, no. 2 (spring 1998): 319–41.

Siegelbaum, Lewis H. *Soviet State and Society between Revolutions, 1918–1929.* Cambridge Soviet Paperbacks series. New York: Cambridge University Press, 1992.

Siegelbaum, Lewis H., and Ronald Grigor Suny, eds. *Making Workers Soviet: Power, Class and Identity.* Ithaca, N.Y.: Cornell University Press, 1994.

Slocum, John Willard. "The Boundaries of National Identity: Religion, Language, and Nationality Politics in Late Imperial Russia." Ph.D. dissertation, University of Chicago, 1993.

Smirnov, N. A., ed. *Tserkov' v istorii Rossii (IX v.–1917) Kriticheskie ocherki.* Moscow: Izdatel'stvo "Nauka," 1967.

Smith, S. A. "Citizenship and the Russian Nation during World War I: A Comment." *Slavic Review* 69, no. 2 (summer 2000): 316–29.

Spohn, Willfried. "Religion and Working-Class Formation in Imperial Germany, 1871–1914." In *Society, Culture, and the State in Germany, 1870–1930,* ed. Geoff Eley, 163–87. Ann Arbor: University of Michigan Press, 1996.

Steeves, Paul D. "The Russian Baptist Union, 1917–1935: Evangelical Awakening in Russia." Ph.D. dissertation, University of Kansas, 1976.

———. "Russian Baptists and the Military Question, 1918–1929." In *Challenge to Mars: Essays on Pacifism from 1918 to 1945,* ed. Peter Brock and Thomas P. Socknat, 21–40. Toronto: University of Toronto Press, 1999.

Steinberg, Mark D. *Moral Communities: The Culture of Class Relations in the Russian Printing Industry, 1867–1907.* Berkeley: University of California Press, 1992.

———. "Workers on the Cross: Religious Imagination in the Writings of Russian Workers, 1910–1924." *Russian Review* 53 (April 1994): 213–39.

Stites, Richard. *Revolutionary Dreams: Utopian Vision and Experimental Life in the Russian Revolution.* New York: Oxford University Press, 1989.

Stvolygin, Konstantin Vladimirovich. "Politika osvobozhdeniia grazhdan ot voinskoi povinnosti po religioznym ubezhdeniiam v Sovetskom gosudarstve (1918–1939 gg.)." Candidate dissertation, Belarus State University, 1997.

Subtelny, Orest. *Ukraine: A History.* 3rd ed. Toronto: University of Toronto Press, 2000.

Thompson, E. P. *The Making of the English Working Class.* New York: Vintage, 1966.

Tirado, Isabel A. "The Revolution, Young Peasants, and the Komsomol's Antireligious Campaigns (1920–1928)." *Canadian-American Slavic Studies* 26, no. 1–3 (1992): 97–117.

Torbet, Robert G. *A History of the Baptists.* 3rd ed. Valley Forge: Judson, 1963.

Troeltsch, Ernst. *The Social Teaching of the Christian Churches.* Introduction by H. Richard Niebuhr. Translated by Olive Wyon. 2 vols. Chicago: University of Chicago Press, 1981.

Tsamutali, A. N., et al., eds. *Problemy sotsial'no-ekonomicheskoi i politicheskoi istorii Rossii XIX–XX vekov.* St. Petersburg: Izdatel'stvo "Aleteiia," 1999.

Turner, Bryan S. *Religion and Social Theory.* 2nd ed. London: Sage, 1991.

Van der Veer, Peter, ed. *Conversion to Modernities: The Globalization of Christianity.* New York: Routledge, 1996.

Vincent, David. *Bread, Knowledge, and Freedom: A Study of Nineteenth-Century Working Class Autobiography.* London: Europa, 1981.

Vins, Georgi. *Testament from Prison.* Edited by Michael Bourdeaux. Translated by Jane Ellis. Elgin, Ill.: David C. Cook, 1975.

———. *Tropoiu vernosti.* 2nd ed. St. Petersburg: Bibliia dlia vsekh, 1997.

Viola, Lynne. "The Peasant Nightmare: Visions of Apocalypse in the Soviet Countryside." *Journal of Modern History* 62 (December 1990).

Viswanathan, Gauri. *Outside the Fold: Conversion, Modernity, and Belief.* Princeton, N.J.: Princeton University Press, 1998.

Von Hagen, Mark. *Soldiers in the Proletarian Dictatorship: The Red Army and the Soviet Socialist State, 1917–1930.* Studies of the Harriman Institute. Ithaca, N.Y.: Cornell University Press, 1990.

Vylegzhanin, Iu. P. "O rabote sotsial-demokratov sredi religioznykh sektantov (1903–1904 gg.)." In *Nauchnye trudy po istorii KPSS.* Vyp. 123. *II s"ezd RSDRP i ego vsemirno-istoricheskoe znachenie.* Kiev: Vishcha shkola, 1983.

Wagner, William L. *New Move Forward in Europe: Growth Patterns of German Speaking Baptists in Europe.* South Pasadena, Calif.: William Carey Library, 1978.

Waldron, Peter. "Religious Reform after 1905: Old Believers and the Orthodox Church." *Oxford Slavonic Papers*, New Series 20 (1987): 110–39.

Wardin, Albert W., Jr. "Baptists (German) in Russia and USSR." In *Modern Encyclopedia of Religion in Russia and the Soviet Union*, ed. Paul D. Steeves, 3:192–200. Gulf Breeze, Fla.: Academic International Press, 1991. Pages. 192–200.

Evangelical Sectarianism in the Russian Empire and the USSR: A Bibliographic Guide. ATLA Bibliography Series, no. 36. Lanham, Md.: American Theological Library Association and Scarecrow Press, 1995.

Ware, Timothy. *The Orthodox Church.* Harmondsworth: Penguin, 1980.

Weeks, Theodore R. *Nation and State in Late Imperial Russia.* DeKalb: Northern Illinois University Press, 1996.

Wood, Elizabeth A. *The Baba and the Comrade: Gender and Politics in Revolutionary Russia.* Bloomington: Indiana University Press, 1997.

Worobec, Christine D. *Possessed: Women, Witches, and Demons in Imperial Russia.* DeKalb: Northern Illinois University Press, 2001.

Young, Glennys J. "Bonch-Bruevich, Vladimir Dmitrievich (1873–1955)." In *Modern Encyclopedia of Religion in Russia and the Soviet Union*, ed. Paul D. Steeves, 4:149–56. Gulf Breeze, Fla.: Academic International Press, 1991.

———. *Power and the Sacred in Revolutionary Russia: Religious Activists in the Village.* University Park: Pennsylvania State University Press, 1997.

———. "Trading Icons: Clergy, Laity, and Rural Cooperatives, 1921–28." *Canadian-American Slavic Studies* 26, no. 1–4 (1992): 315–34.

Zelnik, Reginald E. "Russian Bebels: An Introduction to the Memoirs of the Russian Workers Semen Kanatchikov and Matvei Fisher." *Russian Review* 35, no. 3 (July 1976): 249–89; no. 4 (October 1976): 417–47.

Zverev, Alexei, and Bruno Coppieters. "V. D. Bonch-Bruevich and the Doukhobors: On the Conscientious Objection Policies of the Bolsheviks." *Canadian Ethnic Studies* 27, no. 3 (1995): 73–85.

INDEX

Numbers in *italics* refer to illustrations.

HEATHER J. COLEMAN is Canada Research Chair in Imperial Russian History and an associate professor in the Department of History and Classics, University of Alberta, Canada.

THE
INNER
SIDE
OF THE
WIND

MILORAD
PAVIĆ

THE INNER SIDE OF THE WIND,

OR

THE NOVEL OF HERO AND LEANDER

TRANSLATED
FROM THE
SERBO-CROATIAN
BY CHRISTINA
PRIBIĆEVIĆ-ZORIĆ

ALFRED A. KNOPF
NEW YORK 1993

Originally published in Serbo-Croatian as
Унутрашња страна ветра или роман о Хери и Леандру
by Prosveta, Belgrade. Copyright © 1991 by Prosveta.

Library of Congress Cataloging-in-Publication Data
Pavić, Milorad.
[Unutrašnja strana vetra, ili, Roman o Heri i Leandru.
English]
The inner side of the wind, or The Novel of Hero and
Leander / Milorad Pavić ; translated from the Serbo-Croatian
by Christina Pribićević-Zorić.—1st American ed.
p.   cm.
ISBN 0-679-42085-1
I. Title.   II. Title: Inner side of the wind.   III. Title: Novel
of Hero and Leander.
PG1419.26.A78U5713   1993
891.8'235—dc20   92-24235   CIP

Manufactured in the United States of America
First American Edition

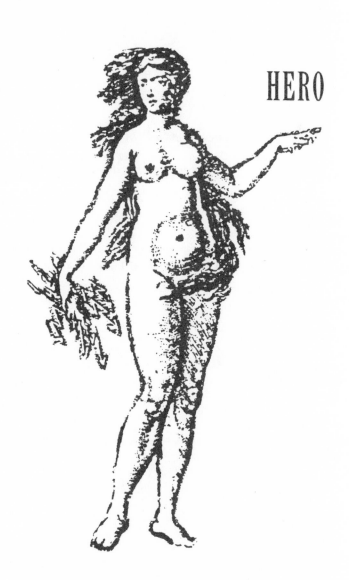

HERO

The inner side of the wind is the one

that remains dry when the wind

blows through the rain

—ONE OF THE CHEAP PROPHETS

1 /

"In the first part of her life, a woman gives birth, and in the second, she kills and buries either herself or those around her. The question is, when does this second part begin?"

Thinking these thoughts, chemistry student Heronea Bukur cracked the hard-boiled egg against her brow and ate it. That was all she had by way of provisions. Her hair was so long she used it in place of a shoehorn. She lived in the busiest part of Belgrade, in a rented room above the Golden Keg café, and kept her refrigerator full of love stories and cosmetics. She was young; she would crumple the banknotes in her hand like a hanky when she went shopping, and she dreamed of lying on the water somewhere on the coast and sleeping for half an hour in the afternoon. She remembered her father's hands, with their wrinkles that rippled like waves in the wind, and she knew how to keep silent in both major and minor keys. They called her Hero; she adored peppers, she sported an ever-spicy kiss and, under her white chemist's coat, a pair of mustachioed breasts. She was so fast she could bite off her own ear; she digested food before it left her mouth, and realized that every couple of centuries some women's names become men's, while the rest remain the same.

There was something, however, that she simply could not fit into her clear picture of the world: dreams. How, in such a simple life, with only one's two ears to run between, could something as inexplicable as dreams occur every night—something that lasted even after death?

"Dreams reincarnate themselves," thought Hero, "and often they are female dreams in male bodies and vice versa. . . . How many people one meets in dreams nowadays! As never before! I'm already overpopulated!"

Thus concluded Hero. Without a second thought, she bought a hard-covered register and, following all the rules of double-entry bookkeeping, began taking stock of her dreams. She was determined to clear the matter up. She wrote down everything that appeared in these dreams—porcelain, pears and buildings, unicorns and horses, hairpins and ships, wild donkeys and angels, glasses and the peridex tree where the alighting dove became a crow, kitchen chairs and chimeras that fertilized through the ear, automobiles and the aromatic bellow of the panther that irresistibly attracted other game from her dreams—entering them all one by one in the separate sections, giving each article a number, price, and date of entry in the book. Appearing especially often in her dreams was a serpent that dared not cross the shadow of a tree. In such instances, the serpent usually slithered up the tree and acted like a branch until a bird alit on it. Then the serpent would ask the bird a question. If it did not give the correct answer, the serpent would eat it. Hero did not know whether this merited one column or two. The other most frequently entered item in Hero's book of dreams was a tiny little boy. The boy's father ate nothing but meat, and his mother nothing but lentils. Because of the father, the child dared taste only meat; and because of the mother, only lentils; and so he came to Hero's dream to die of hunger.

"Obviously, we inside ourselves and others

within us run an enormous distance every day," Hero noted on the margins of her register. "We make this journey by some kind of internal movements that are quick and capable of covering an expanse we will never cover in life. This internal movement in dreams is more perfect than external movement, because immobility is infallible, it is the prime mover of everything and embraces even movement in its motionlessness. But," she thought on, "a dream can also be perceived as an animal."

Since she and her brother had been learning foreign languages ever since childhood, Hero took special care with the inventory of linguistic forms she and others used in her dreams. It was rather like a grammar book of dreams—the linguistics of dreaming, and a lexicon of words used while sleeping. This dictionary of Hero's was a lot like those "doggie dictionaries" that were the rage among young ladies in the late 1920s, in which they wrote expressions understood by their wolfhounds, poodles, or bull terriers. So too in Hero's dictionary a dream was treated like an animal that did not speak the same language as its master, but could learn the occasional word from Hero's language of reality, just as Hero herself slowly started to learn the grammar of this strange animal's language. She concluded that, in the language of dreams, all the nouns exist but the verbs do not have all the tenses they have in reality.

This particular morning, however, she did not care about dreams. March was stealing days from February, the grass stuffing in the armchairs exuded smells as if the grass were fresh, while with a red pencil she corrected and graded the postcards written to her in French by her pupils during winter recess. She earned her living by tutoring bad students, but now was not the season; two hearts beat in her canines, one in each tooth, she suffered from hunger like a fish, and her left thigh burned her right while she leafed through the newspaper. There it was written:

> *French teacher wanted twice a week*
> *to tutor children.*
> *Dobrachina St. 6/III.*

She wrapped her ears up in braids and found herself in No. 6 Dobrachina Street, third floor, courtyard entrance. Here the apartments each had one window in the sun and one in the wind, but in summer even the dogs inside were full of moths. She leaned the back of her head against the doorbell, took lip gloss out of her bag, rubbed her lower lip with the upended case of rouge, then her lower against her upper lip, and pressed the bell with her head. SIMONOVICH—she read on the nameplate, and entered. She was admitted by a ten-year-old boy; she knew immediately that he was to be her pupil and, following him in, she thought: "This one's got a high ass, it starts at the waist."

The Simonoviches seated her on a three-legged chair. First they needed to determine how much she would receive monthly for tutoring. A thousand dinars per child was inviting, and she agreed. She sat girded by her hair, counted her teeth with her tongue, and watched Mr. Simonovich's left eye blink every time he pronounced an "r." They waited a bit for night to fall, and then poured strong drinks into three slender glasses.

"To your hearty health!" said the host, blinking twice with his left eye as though counting the bones in his tongue. Hero had just started to feel that she was wasting her time when she noticed a strange supplicating smile on the lips of the woman. It quivered there like a frightened little animal.

"Their children must be as shallow as the palm of the hand for things to have come to this!" Hero decided. At that very moment, her hand grazed the glass. A few drops spilled on her dress. She looked at the spot, noticed that the stain was spreading, and quickly took her leave. Departing, she had the feeling that her nails were growing at vertiginous speed.

In Vasina Street she bought two big notebooks, and that same evening prepared them for her future pupils. As she had been taught when she was a child, she drew a red line down each page, dividing it in two. The right-hand column was for the *present* and *past tenses* of French verbs; the left-hand was for the *future tense,* the *conditional,* and the *participle,* which denotes action parallel to the main clause.

Outside, winter dampness was alternating with summer dampness, and houses were releasing last year's smells into the rooms, when Hero took the notebooks and went to give her first lesson in Dobrachina Street. The "devil bites" on the soles of her feet were hurting her as she entered the Simonovich apartment on the third floor.

"Tell me, but honestly, what day is it?" she asked her pupil, watching him the way a snake does a frog. He became flustered; she saw him steam with a strange sweat, and he again turned his backside to her.

He led her to a table surrounded by three green chairs; the lamp burned in the dark room by day and was turned off at night, because nobody sat here in the evenings. A moment later, they were sipping tea; she watched the boy crush a lump of sugar into the cup with his nails and then suck his finger, after which he started to write his first French verbs in the new notebook. Placed on the table in front of them was a third teacup, but it remained unused.

"Are you afraid of death?" he suddenly asked Hero.

"I don't know anything about death; all I know is that I will die at twelve-oh-five."

"What do you mean, at twelve-oh-five?"

"Just what I said. All the Bukurs in my family were sappers. They set the mines to explode at noon, a fact that was known where they worked—in the mine, on the railroad, or elsewhere—and so people took cover as soon as the noonday siren blew. If the mine didn't explode, then at twelve-oh-five one of the Bukurs would have to go and see what was wrong. And that was usually the end of them."

"But why should you die at twelve-oh-five when you're not a sapper?"

"Simple. The chemical institute where I study closes at noon. I leave the dangerous, forbidden experiments for after twelve, when everybody has gone, and then I light a real fire. Everybody tells me: 'You'll die like the rest of your people at twelve-oh-five. . . .' Now, please be so kind as to get on with your lesson, or else you'll never become your own man; for the rest of your life, you'll sneeze like your father and yawn like your mother."

While she was talking, Hero looked at that third, unused cup and the other notebook that lay on the table facing the third chair, and she was disappointed that the other child had not appeared as well; the family's ad and conversations had used the plural, and the remuneration was to be commensurate.

"These people rise three days before dawn," she thought, then assigned a new lesson and descended into the rain, walking on the "devil bites," which now hurt even more. Her arches were falling.

But they had not even had time to fall flat when something unexpected happened. The month was drawing to a close; it was a time when dogs fed on grass, and one morning, for the first time, she found on the table in Dobrachina Street her pay envelope. Instead of a thousand dinars, twice that amount was inside: she had been paid for two pupils, not one.

"What are these other thousand dinars doing here?" she asked the boy.

"They're for Kachunchitsa."

"Kachunchitsa?"

"We have a Kachunchitsa."

"I'll hit you so hard I'll knock your hair off! Who is Kachunchitsa?"

"My sister," replied the boy, with a smile so broad it chased his ears down his neck.

"But why doesn't this Kachunchitsa of yours appear for her lessons?"

"I wish I knew."

"How come you don't know?"

"I don't know. I've never seen Kachunchitsa."

"It's always afternoon to him," Hero said to herself, and then added, aloud: "Does this Kachunchitsa of yours exist or not?"

"My parents say she does. Mama gets very angry if anybody doubts it. I don't know. All I know is that every day they set the table for four, although Kachunchitsa's chair is always empty, they boil a fourth egg in the morning for Kachunchitsa's breakfast, and they say our dog, Kolya, is hers.... Last winter, they moved me out of my room, because, they said, a boy and a girl her age should no longer share the same room...."

The boy fell silent, and Hero saw him stare fixedly at the third, empty chair at the round table.

"Strange, isn't it?" he added, and Hero knew that his left eye would blink as soon as his tongue struck the sound "r."

"They're as crazy as the wind!" she decided, took her double pay, and left.

At the next lesson, however, waiting for her at

the glass doors was not the boy but his mother. To protect herself against the dampness, the woman had used her hair as a scarf while crossing the terrace; but, once inside, she unveiled a French such as Hero, with her paltry four years of study, simply could not match. The woman seated the guest at the round table and asked her to pay particular attention in her lessons to the things the children found difficult. While she spoke, she moved her ears in alternation like guards, and mentioned children in the plural again; her smile quivered even more, and she hooked the fingernails of one hand onto the table edge. Pain, in the form of a hair-part, was almost visible on her head. She was talking about French homework, but she looked as though she were talking about matters of life and death.

"My ears will wither with sorrow!" Hero thought, listening to her.

"Of course, we are generally satisfied with the children's progress," the woman mollified Hero, "but they've proved to have difficulties with the *present* and *past tenses.* The *future tense,* on the other hand, they know well. They do not require any extra work on that...."

Hero sat on her long hair and was quite unable to figure out why this woman, whose flawless French she was listening to, did not take the children in hand herself, but chose, rather, to raise them on white honey. Just then, from a sunny outer room into the darkness in which they were sitting came the boy. The mother retreated, and Hero lay into the culprit. She motioned with her chin for him to sit down, used her foot to disentangle his legs under the table, and grabbed the notebook of French conjugation, determined to test him on the *present* and *past tenses*. But, that same moment, she again felt her nails madly growing. She looked at them, saw that they really were growing, and could not remember a single form, a single letter from the right-hand column of the notebook, which she had wanted to test him on. She opened the notebook to refresh her memory and, reading the headings, instructed the boy to repeat the *present* and *past tenses* of French auxiliary verbs. The boy knew the answers perfectly, and Hero was amazed.

"Here you know everything, but at school you're blocked up like a half-milked cow. What have you been up to again? Your mother complains about you."

"It's not me she's complaining about, it's Kachunchitsa."

"Back to that again?"

"Kachunchitsa, Mama says, knows the *future tense* perfectly but is simply unable to learn the *pres-*

ent and *past*. It's inconceivable to me that she doesn't know that, because it's simple, easier than the other two. . . . But Mama says that's why you're here, to pull Kachunchitsa out of the tight spot she's in. . . ."

Hero gazed at the boy, pensively girded herself in her hair, and departed. The next time, she appeared with a two-color hairdo, as was the vogue, and gave the boy ten verses to translate from the lesson about Hero and Leander, which came next in the French textbook. The boy slowly read the French text, actually the French translation of an ancient Greek poem:

Tant que Héro tint son regard baissé vers la terre,
Léandre, de ses yeux fous d'amour, ne se lassa pas
De regarder le coup délicat de la jeune fille. . . .

Here in the textbook the boy came upon a picture and broke off his reading.

"What's that he's swimming in?" he asked.

"What a stupid question! What else would he be swimming in but the waves, the sea?"

"And is Leander coming toward you? Why, you are Hero!"

"I'm the Hero who bites the nails on her hands

and feet—which you, young man, are forbidden to do."

"And why did Leander set out toward you?"

"Because he fell in love with Hero. She gave him light while he swam."

"And you're not afraid of him? What if he swims to shore?"

"You wouldn't understand the answer," replied Hero, who sported a pair of well-molded breasts, a navel as deep as an ear, and rings on her toes.

"And what did they do to him in the end? Did he swim to shore?"

"Read and you'll find out. . . . He did not swim to shore. According to one story, Hero's brother lit the lamp on the boat, drew Leander out to sea with this other light, and then blew it out. He returned to shore, leaving Leander to drown in the dark far away from Hero."

"I like that! Your brother defended you!"

"You keep talking nonsense. My brother is in Prague, studying music; it's best to leave him alone. Go on reading, and pay attention, or you'll get up on the wrong side of the bed in the morning."

But in the morning, it was Hero who got up on the wrong side of the bed. The left side. She woke up with the impression that her tongue had forked like a snake's, though she could only feel its left prong—the right was unusable. She got up, dabbed on some "wild water," dusted the table with her hair, and started to study for her senior finals. The studying went well up to a point, and then faltered. So she decided to go through her students' homework. She noticed that she herself no longer knew the *present* and *past tenses*. In short, the forms on the right-hand side of the notebook gave her a headache. The left-hand side, however, was increasingly clear to her; indeed, never before had she had such a mastery of the *future tense* in her own and the French language. She was especially engrossed by the *future perfect* in French. She felt that some people nibble at time as far as they can get from the end nearest to the present, but that there are also those who, like the gypsy moth, flit in and gnaw at time in the middle, leaving behind a hole. These thoughts made her feel as though she had two kinds of hair on her head, and she decided to rest. . . .

On the shelf she found the dress with the stain from the drink that had been spilled that first day in Dobrachina Street, and she took it to the cleaner's.

"Frighten a man and an animal will respond!" she thought on the way. "So, if somebody startles you, be careful what part of you responds first and fastest to the danger and surprise: the voice, the hands, the mind, the eyes, the hair, the saliva that changes taste, or the sweat that changes smell.... And fix it in your mind, if it's not already too late. They are the forerunners, the advance guard, the first sign that something is threatening you...."

For, on the day when the drink had spilled, nothing in Hero had reacted—or almost nothing, if one considered the hand that had accidentally grazed the glass and on which the nails had begun to grow so terribly. That had been the only alarm signal, which she had not understood for half a year. Now, when it seemed too late, when she had already been caught off balance, Hero looked aghast at this hand grown into nails, which she had not heeded in time.

"Not up to it anymore?" a coed addressed her maliciously in front of the university building, and asked her the time. Hero discovered that she was unable to answer, although she knew what time it was. She wanted to walk on, down the two currents of wind that came from Kalemegdan, without replying, but suddenly she blurted out the answer, and it was in the *future tense:*

"It will soon be twelve-oh-five."

"Be careful you're not the one to catch it at twelve-oh-five; you look awfully absent-minded," the coed replied, leaving her openmouthed. Obviously, the malady suffered by Hero's French, this paralysis in the *present,* had spread to her native tongue as well.

"What's going to happen to my *present tense* now that I'm leaving it?" Hero wondered in horror. "Is it going to somebody else now? Is somebody else now taking over my memories and inheriting them?"

Indeed, Hero seemed to be using some other language, different from that of her contemporaries, although it was the same tongue. She felt as if she were on a ship standing still in the middle of the open sea; the "tritoothed" bird of her dreams was fighting the ship's sail with its own huge wings, cutting off the wind that could have moved it. She began wearing small clocks in place of buttons, but in vain. She failed her finals, because, from the way she described the sequence of procedures in the experiment that had been entrusted to her, one did not know what came first and what came later. Her nails grew wildly, she cut them wherever she went, even when paying visits, although people warned her that this brought them bad luck.

She no longer went to Dobrachina Street, because the boy knew the right-hand side of the notebook better than she did, and she caught herself testing him more and more about only the left-hand side, the side of the *future tense,* which was close and familiar to her. But the main reason she stopped the lessons in Dobrachina Street was different, and more important. She was afraid that one day she would see, not the boy at the round table in the dark room, but Kachunchitsa sitting there, flashing her ring in Hero's eye, smiling with half her mouth. She was afraid that she would not be surprised and that she would start giving her lessons as though nothing had happened. She was afraid that she would not be able to teach Kachunchitsa the *present tense* now that she herself no longer recognized it. And that was not all. The two of them, she feared and knew, would get along easily and well in the *future tense,* regarding their given but still-unaccomplished tasks, making wine out of Jewish cherries, which one is never supposed to drink. And the third chair, the boy's, the chair of the *present tense,* would remain forever empty to the two of them.

Wrapped up in these thoughts, she happened to see on the shelf her register of dreams. She wiped away the cobwebs and opened it, and immediately the veil lifted from her eyes. It was all obvious. Gazing at her register, she discovered that even in dreams you did not have the *present tense* of the dreamer, but, rather, something like its *participle,* in the form of action parallel to the tense in which the dreamer sleeps. The linguistics of dreams clearly bespoke the existence of the adverb in the dreamed tense, and showed that the road to the present leads through the future, and it does so through dreams. Because dreams have no past tense either. Everything is like something as yet unexperienced, like some strange tomorrow that has started ahead of time, like an advance loan taken on future life, the future that is realized after the dreamer (enclosed in the *future tense*) has avoided the inevitable *now*.

And so everything was suddenly very simple and comprehensible. Hero's language had all the traits and shortcomings of the grammar of dreams she so closely studied in her register. It did not have the *present tense*. Hero finally came to the conclusion that her malady of language came from the fact that she had actually been asleep the entire time and was simply unable to break out of her sleep into reality. She tried to wake up in every possible way, but to no avail. And, somewhat panic-stricken, she decided that there was only one possibility for her to break free. At 12:05, as soon as everyone left, she would blow up the chemical institute and awaken in her death if she was awake, or in her life, in her reality, if she was asleep.

"I'll have to do it," Hero whispered, hurrying along Chika Lyubina Street. And then she noticed that it was still early, that there was still half an hour until 12:05. She was passing the cleaner's to which she had taken her dress.

"I'll stop in and pay; I've got the time," she said, and did.

"Here, it's cleaned," said the man. "But I must warn you that it was not a stain. What you thought was a stain, here on the right side—that was really the only clean place on the dress. . . ."

"The man could be right," said Hero, stepping out into the street. "The devil with the right-hand side of the notebook! It'll always be dirtier than the left-hand side anyway!" And she did not go to the institute to blow it up at 12:05 but, rather, went straight to Dobrachina Street to give her lesson at the Simonoviches'.

Mrs. Simonovich led her triumphantly into Mr. Simonovich's smile as though into a church; they took Hero's repentant return as a victory, and in the presence of the entire family she seated the boy at the round table in the dark living room, where the third chair, for Kachunchitsa, always stood empty. And then, to the shock of the household, Hero drew a fourth chair to the round table, thinking: "Now I'll turn the joke around on you until your ears drop off!"

"Who's that for?" the boy's mother asked in

horror, and her smile began to quiver like a frightened hamster.

"That's for Leander," Hero calmly replied. "He has swum over, and from now on he will attend the lessons with me, with Kachunchitsa, and with your boy. I now boil an egg every morning for Leander as well."

At that moment, Hero felt that her bewitchment, dream, daydream, or whatever it was had burst around her like a soap bubble.

"Why are you looking at me like a half-milked cow?" she asked the boy. Then she laughed and departed, to head straight for her brother in Prague.

2 /

HERO'S DECISION to go to her brother in Prague and continue her studies there was not as sudden as we may think. She had long felt the need to change her way of life. Although she was beautiful, had a lovely swanlike neck, and carried the day in one eye and the night in the other, she was lonely. From her solitary life in Belgrade, full of dreams, meanderings, and marvels, with its fourth egg and third chair, she had long wanted to embark on ordinary, everyday family life, the kind she could have with her brother in Prague, because Hero's brother, Manasia Bukur, a student at the

Prague Conservatory, was the only family she had left in the world. Hero had not seen him for three years, which weighed heavily on her heart, because the last Bukur in their family had long ago finished up at 12:05 in some quarry somewhere. Tired of loneliness, she had kept in touch with her brother through letters, but the correspondence was unusual, to say the least.

It should be noted in this connection that Hero had secret literary ambitions. Since no publisher had accepted her manuscripts, she had decided to do some translating, and this paid off. Except, between the lines of the texts she translated—that is, in the novels of Anatole France, Pierre Loti, or Musil— she would insert one of her own short stories that nobody had wanted to publish, or at least a part of one of these stories, so that through her various translations she finally published in the novels of others an entire book of her own stories.

Whenever one of the novels Hero translated was published in installments in a newspaper, or as a book, she would mark her own insertion in the text with lipstick and send the whole thing as a letter to her brother in Prague. Interestingly enough, these insertions always contained a secret message that only brother and sister could understand.

Hero did not like poetry. She would say: "If poetry is given to writers as punishment, prose comes as a pardon."

As an example of Hero's correspondence with her brother, one might take the story she insinuated like a cuckoo egg into her translation of a novel by Anatole France or some other translated book:

The Story of Captain Peter de Vitkovich

That morning, in the autumn of 1909, at the sound of the bugle, the captain of the Austro-Hungarian army's engineer unit, the noble Mr. Peter de Vitkovich, woke up not in his bed but in somebody else's soul.

Admittedly, at first glance it was quite a spacious soul, poorly aired and quite low-vaulted—in short, a soul like any other, but obviously a stranger's. The lighting was somewhat brighter than in Captain de Vitkovich's own previous soul, but all the same he could not be sure that he would not unexpectedly hit upon the edge or the brink of this stranger's soul. Although the captain believed that the most important thing in life was to reach one's fiftieth year on time, he nonetheless felt uncomfortable. Naturally, he noticed the change immediately, although his escorts, two guards in military dress and with rifles, registered not a thing. One might also say that this change passed unnoticed by the military prosecutor, Lieutenant-Colonel Koch, and by the investigative judge, Major von Palanski, who during Captain de Vitkovich's hearing proceeded to get gasping fits whenever the examinee began to call events, people, or things connected with the trial by their real name.

Despite this inattentiveness on the part of the judicial and investigative bodies, or perhaps precisely because of it and them, the matter of Captain de Vitkovich became more complicated still. Apart from the fact that he had been sentenced to life imprisonment (for maintaining ties with the military representatives of a foreign power—i.e., the Kingdom of Serbia) and was to be taken quickly by train from Vienna to Petrovaradin, where he was to serve out his sentence, Captain Peter de Vitkovich now also had the additional inconvenience of a stranger's soul. There were at least two inconveniences. First, he rightly wondered where his own soul was and what had happened to it when, shackled in fine long chains, escorted by two guards, he had been traveling through that stranger's soul (now assigned to him) to Petrovaradin. In that stranger's soul (there could now be no doubt about it) he felt growingly worse. He was unable to find his coordinates, and was uncertain whether there existed military compasses for getting one's bearings while moving through another's soul.

Snapping out of these thoughts, Captain de Vit-kovich suddenly recognized on his own face, reflected in the glass of the compartment window, the weary eyes of his father, and that same moment he wondered what had happened to the owner of the soul that had now been assigned to his keeping. What was the person doing, who was he, where did he live, and where had he been banished to before his own soul was assigned to another? The worst thing, however, was that the captain could not know how that stranger's soul, at the bottom of which he was now traveling, together with his prison lice, would react to his habits and the intricate circumstances of his new, present life.

It was impossible to know, for instance, how it would react to his chronic toothache, or to his occasional practice of roasting and eating one of the prison mice.

Just then, the captain's thoughts were cut short by a high-pitched voice behind him in the train that began singing tristfully, as though the notes were passing through freshly washed hair. And as if in response to that voice, Mr. de Vitkovich's toothache got worse, and the stranger's soul allotted to his use quivered in its every chord. The captain thus immediately noticed that the stranger's soul was very musical, which certainly could not be said about his own. . . . At that point, the noble de Vitkovich decided to poke around this new soul a bit; to seek out the unknown spheres that it surely embraced and that, quite naturally, were completely alien to him. And so, sitting chained on the train bench, he proceeded on his rounds.

As he moved (blindly, the only way one can through another's soul), Captain de Vitkovich came upon a window. A plain, ordinary window ("So, souls too have windows," he thought as he gazed through it). There was nothing on the other side. Absolutely nothing. But the actual window in this soul had an entirely new meaning, such as no other window had ever had in the life of Captain de Vitkovich. Instead of simply representing a wooden cross with a lock or a handle in the middle, this window represented an explanation of the life and times of Mr. de Vitkovich, and of everyone else in the world as well. Gauss's disciple, the famous eighteenth-century physicist Atanas Stoikovich, knew even in the century before last that there were two eternities, not one, and Captain de Vitkovich was perfectly aware of this, because physics was part of the curriculum of military schools. These two eternities (which come from God) were now depicted by the vertical bar on the window, while mere time (which comes from the devil) was embodied in the horizontal bar on the window. The place where eternity and time cross was marked by the little window-handle or lock. And therein lay the secret, or the key of life; there, where time and eternity crossed, was the present moment in which alone there was life, because in that intercrossing time stops.

One could conclude, therefore, that the answer to the question "Where does time come from?" was: *"Time comes from death."* Because as long as there is death there will be time. Once death disappears, there will be no time either. So death weaves our time like a spider. If life is there where time stops still, arrested in the moment of the present, then death is in the sphere through which time flows. In other words, time flows through death and stops in life, at exactly the point where eternity and time cross on the window of the soul. . . .

Here Mr. de Vitkovich felt the chain chafe him, and he abandoned his search. Such thoughts and wanderings were not to torture him for long. After traveling three days, they arrived at Petrovaradin, beards crumpled and legs stiff. This place on the banks of the great river was the last the captain saw in his life. One of the guards told him something that might have been a consolation, a threat, or a moral, or all three together:

"Human life is a strange race: the goal is not at the end but in the middle of the track; you run, and you may have passed the goal a long time ago, but you don't know it—you never even noticed when, and you'll never find out when. And so you keep running."

The chains were removed from the prisoner; he was lowered down a ladder into an underground cell where it was eternally autumn, or, more precisely, eternally an autumnal night, because it had no contact with the light of day. Before the trap door was lowered above him, Captain de Vitkovich caught sight of an army cot with its icy iron bars, a Catholic crucifix on the wall (although the captain himself was Eastern Orthodox), and a large grating over an opening into a deep dark mine. Next to the opening was a table, and on it an unlit candle, writing paper, and a Smith-Corona typewriter. On the bed was a Bible in Czech translation (although Mr. de Vitkovich was a Serb).

When the trap door slammed shut on him, two disturbing thoughts came to Captain de Vitkovich's mind. First, could one (legally speaking) condemn a stranger's soul (in this case, admittedly, inhabited by the condemned man himself) to life imprisonment? In order to avoid any unpleasant legal oversight, should one draw the court investigators' attention to this intricate situation? And, second, was this new soul, which spread for kilometers and then on both sides of the world for miles around him, Eastern Orthodox like his own soul, was it Protestant, or was it even Catholic? This was an important question, because Captain Peter de Vitkovich wanted to be clear whether on Judgment Day the devils would take the measure of this stranger's— who knows whose?—soul, perhaps Moslem or some rabbi's, or that of his own little Orthodox soul, which had taken flight as soon as sentence had been passed on him.

And so Captain de Vitkovich decided to keep an eye on this stranger's soul within which he was imprisoned, inside his dungeon and Petrovaradin above it; to keep an eye on this new, strange soul through which the invisible Danube and his own, barely more visible life now flowed.

But he was not the only one watching. Another eye was being kept on him as well. Sitting on the iron bed, the captain of course knew that, although he was already condemned, further confessions and information were expected from him concerning the entire military case in which he was involved, and that the investigator, Major von Mölk, had left the candle and typewriter in the fervent hope that his prisoner would fill the ream of paper neatly stacked by the typewriter with further confessions. Every now and then, the investigator would lift the trap door of the cell and peer down at the tiny, frail body so profusely sown with shag like black wheat. And he wondered whether the years flitted across the prisoner's face faster than across his own. But he never dreamed that this body in which he took such an official interest could see only through another's, through a third soul, which thus seriously threatened his official perception of the whole affair, introducing unforeseeable difficulties in the entire matter of Captain de Vitkovich. Naturally, the guards had the strictest orders to notify the investigator of any change in the prisoner's conduct, and they kept a vigilant eye on their victim, while he, for his part, kept an eye on the stranger's soul at the bottom of which he lay.

Time passed quickly in this mutual observation until one sunny morning (Mr. de Vitkovich noticed that the stranger's soul knew it was a sunny morning up there outside, whereas he himself did not and could not know it). That morning, then, the captain irrefutably concluded that the stranger's soul in which he was currently sitting and breakfasting was considerably slower than his own, real soul. And then, one night (if night it was), Captain de Vitkovich was awoken by a cough. Somebody had coughed in the dense darkness of his cell. The stranger's soul had caught some kind of metaphysical cold and had coughed. But this would not have worried Captain de Vitkovich; he was worried about something else. It was easy to tell from the cough that this new soul was a female, not a male soul.

"Perhaps male and female souls go in pairs, like death," Mr. de Vitkovich thought, and then, for the first time, he sat down at the typewriter. He began to type, and the guards, who had been given strict orders, if such a thing were to occur, not to disturb him on any account, not even by observation, happily bent their avid ears.

"At last," Investigator von Mölk cried out; his nose gurgled like a stomach, and he hurried off to hear for himself. The tapping flowed rapidly, albeit with occasional lapses; Captain de Vitkovich would stop for a bit at a key, then sometimes would tap several keys at once and they would bunch together; but for the most part the matter progressed quite well for somebody who, like Mr. de Vitkovich, knew by heart all the proportions of his wife's body in thumbs.

So as not to disturb the prisoner, the guards had been instructed on no account to collect the written part of the report, confession, or whatever it was the captain typed every morning, but merely to keep him regularly supplied with fresh candles.

But then something unexpected happened that threatened to drown all the hopes of the investigator and his superiors. One of the guards (who was not very bright but knew that you do not blow out a candle in the cellar) defied the ban and peered through a little hole into the cell while Captain de Vitkovich sat on the very edge of that stranger's soul in which he was enclosed and typed on his type-writer. The guard was astonished by what he saw, or, to be more precise, by what he did not see, and immediately called in the investigator so that he could see too. Captain de Vitkovich was sitting in the pitch dark, typing. He did not light the candle at all and spent his days and nights in total darkness, touch-typing in the blackness.

"What's the point of a candle?" he thought, since he had in any event to grope his way through the dark in the stranger's soul that surrounded him.

Investigator von Mölk, however, was not entirely unhappy about this turn of affairs. He hoped that what the captain was typing in the dark might be useful to the investigation against the other suspects in this involved case. And he issued orders not to change Mr. de Vitkovich's prison routine. He knew the golden rule of failure in the military: swallow your tears and keep going. And so, every evening, Captain de Vitkovich lay down on his military cot, firmly grasped the armrest of the iron chair by the bed, and fell asleep through that stranger's soul; like all Serbs, he never forgave but he immediately forgot, and thus his sleep was unblighted.

But this routine was suddenly interrupted. The Serbo-Austrian conflict broke out, triggering off World War I, and the case of Captain Peter de Vitkovich was re-examined and his sentence changed. Early one evening, the captain was led to the ramparts before a firing squad. He watched them aim and heard them fire. He was executed. The very first volley of shots left him dead on the spot. A second round was unnecessary. An officer came up to him to make sure and then went away again. They loaded the captain onto a mule that reeked of sour sweat, took him to a tree beneath which three soldiers dug a hole, and lowered him into the earth. They buried him, stopping occasionally to wipe away sweat with their caps. The grave was finally closed, the waves of the Danube exploded, smashing against the rocks at the foot of the fortress, and the captain's tooth still ached slightly.

A pile of typewritten paper was found on the table in his cell. But on these pages, which immediately became the subject of extensive investigation by the most competent Austrian code-experts, were letters typed randomly in the dark; they meant absolutely nothing, and no secret keys could decipher them. These blindly written letters had no secret meaning, carried no hidden or unhidden message. Nothing could be wrung, for instance, from the following inscription:

JIJK, KOL, OHJZFE, WFZGDGEHS...

Hero inserted such a text into a book by Loti, or somebody else she was translating at the time, and when the book was published, she sent the first copy (marking her intruder-text with lipstick, as usual) to her brother in Prague. This, as has already been said, was a kind of secret correspondence between brother and sister. He found the marked spot immediately, scanned it, and stopped at the end, where Hero gave the line typed on the Smith-Corona typewriter, actually the note written by the unfortunate Captain de Vitkovich.

Manasia Bukur, Hero's brother, laughed and wrote back that what the noble Mr. de Vitkovich had recorded was a trivocal invention in F minor by Johann Sebastian Bach played on a typewriter instead of a piano. . . .

APART FROM this correspondence, also found, in the papers of one of Hero's girlfriends, was the following perfectly ordinary letter casting light on a voyage the Bukur siblings had made to Italy:

"Last year, my brother and I spent the winter and spring between the old and young Saint Nicholas in Italy," Hero wrote in the letter. "In order to support us, my brother played in the evenings in a tavern where two young girls undressed and dressed each other in full sight of the exuberant customers. On his evenings off, he would take me to concerts and the theater. We lived in Rome and breakfasted at an inn in the local ghetto. One morning, a theater ad in the paper caught my brother's eye and he showed it to me. It was an invitation from the Ibicus theater troupe to the premiere of Musaeus' *The Love and Death of Hero and Leander*.

" 'This is something about you,' my brother joked, and we went to get the tickets. The ad gave the street where the play was showing and quoted a few lines from the ancient Greek poet. The lines read: 'For as long as he has been on earth, man has been opting between two *no*s.' The theater had a strange name (The Boys' Theater), and my brother and I had never heard of it before. We hired a car and found the back street, narrow and full of steps, which rang out in particular ways, like piano keys. Our driver had never heard of a theater being there. But we had the address, and the driver told us that there were passages leading from this little street into a parallel, broader street, and he supposed the entrance might be there. And so we found the address, saw two posters on the wall announcing the play, and carefully read them. The first included an excerpt from the stage adaptation of Musaeus' story:

LEANDER: I've been dead for three days now. And you?

HERO: When we lose sight of and forget something, and then try to remember it, this forgotten something, this void which has spread at the expense of our memory, loses its real proportions; behind the curtains of our forgetfulness, it changes, grows, and gets larger. And when we finally remember the thing we have forgotten, we are disappointed to see that it wasn't worth all the effort we spent and put into remembering it. It is the same with our soul, which we lose sight of every minute and forget.

LEANDER: Except the soul can grow even after death. Like nails. But longer, much longer, as long as our death lasts. Beware, however. Your death can get younger; it can become much younger than you. It can go hundreds of years back into the past. Then again, my death can become much older than I am, it can last from now on into future centuries....

"The other ad for the play about Hero and Leander was stranger:

Manuscripts and Editions
of the Poetic Tale
of Hero and Leander
by Musaeus the Grammarian

(In honor of the Ibicus Theater Company's stage production)

BAROCCIANUS 50 SAEC. X.
E CUIUS FAMILIA:
  VOSSIANUS GR. Q. 59 CA. 1500.
  ESTENSIS III A 17 SAEC. XV.
  ESTENSIS III C 12 PARS ANTIQUA (U. 250–343) SAEC. XIV.
  HARLEIANUS 5659 SAEC. XV EX.
  PARISINUS GR. 2600 SAEC. XVI IN.
NEAPOLITANUS II D 4 SAEC. XIV.
E CUIUS FAMILIA:
  PALATINUS HEIDELBERGENSIS GR. 43 SAEC. XIV.
VATICANUS GR. 915 SAEC. XIII EX. UEL POTIUS SAEC. XIV IN.
  MARCIANUS GR. 522 SAEC. XV VATICANI GR. 915
    APOGRAPHON.
PRAEBENT TANTUM U. 1–245:
  PARISINUS GR. 2763 SAEC. XV EX.
  LEIDENSIS B.P.G. 74 C SAEC. XV.
  AMBROSIANUS S 31 SUP. SAEC. XV EX.
  PARISINUS GR. 2833 SAEC. XV EX.
  LAURENTIANUS LXX 35 SAEC. XV.
  RICCARDIANUS GR. 53 SAEC. XV.
  ESTENSIS III C 12 PARS RECENTIOR (U. 1–245) SAEC. XV.
CODICES DETERIORES:
  PRAGENSIS STRAHOVIENSIS 30 SAEC. XV.
  BAROCCIANUS 64 SAEC. XVI.
  AMBROSIANUS E 39 SUP. SAEC. XVI.
  GOTHANUS B 238 SAEC. XVII IN.
EDITIONES:
  EDITIO PRINCEPS ALDINA, VENETIIS EXCUSA CA. 1494.
  EDITIO FLORENTINA JOH. LASCARIDE AUCTORE CA. 1494.

"That is how we tracked down the Ibicus Theater Company, but The Boys' Theater, where it was being performed, was harder to trace. When we went down into a cellar, our driver said 'Amen' three times; we climbed up to an attic, but in vain. True, the building did have a serviceway for men, and another for children, and even a 'women's door' off a third, still wider, brighter street, and we squeezed through, but there was no theater there either. No one had ever heard of such a theater. We gave up then, but a few days later my brother showed me the papers where again they were advertising the stage production of Musaeus' poetic tale of Hero and Leander. But that was not all. The paper also had one Ileana Bongiorno reviewing the Ibicus Theater Company's production, stressing the brilliant performance given by the young Irene Plaar in the title role. This time, we went to a ticket office in the middle of Rome which sold tickets for various theaters, and we inquired about The Boys' Theater. They said they had no tickets for that play. The saleswoman called over an old gentleman with eyebrows bigger than a mustache, as though his nose were upside down, and he remembered. Where we had looked, there had indeed once been a theater; it wasn't called The Boys' Theater—he thought that was the name of a play, not the theater

—but long ago he had seen one of Pirandello's plays there; to be more precise, he had seen the pianist who had accompanied the production, and who while playing would fall silent one minute, as though reading a book that lay on the keys, and jump the next, as though he had burned his fingers, or lean back as though trying to reach for a shoe under the piano with his foot . . . or else, without leaving his hard seat, would lift himself up on his toes, raising high his elbows and knees. . . .

"As soon as we got rid of the old gentleman, my brother and I went to the newly given address and discovered that a 'pocket' theater truly did exist there. They let us in, but with surprise. We entered and froze. It was a real 'showboat' theater, but all that remained of it was the skeleton. Awful! The mice had been dining on it for at least twenty years. In a Roman attic. My brother asked when the theater was founded and was appalled: it was his contemporary.

"We ran out, horrified, but my brother calmed me down with the words: 'Look, things that in life seem incredible, mysterious, or fantastic conceal behind their deceptive exteriors the most ordinary of stories.'

" 'That means,' I said, 'beware of the most ordinary things and events, because behind these ordinary masks they conceal horror, disaster, and death.'

"And so it was. A few weeks later, we told the story to some Roman friends, and they said with a laugh that such cases do indeed exist. They had not actually heard of The Boys' Theater, but they remarked that the Ibicus Theater Company, which had advertised the premiere of the ancient Greek poet Musaeus, had actually made artful use of this announcement to earn a name for itself. Who would check whether they had actually performed it or not? And ads, sometimes even paid reviews of un-held performances, prove that they *did* perform, in Rome or in Paris, and with this fact and evidence in their hands they might get a real engagement somewhere else in the world, in some third city. And there they could actually perform their 'love and death.'

"My brother and I had a good laugh ourselves, not because of this unusual incident but because we had had a good time in Rome. Watching my brother, who never turned his back on me, as though I were his daily bread, and listening to him play so beautifully in the taverns at night, I thought how men are cursed: at the peak of their passion and pleasure, the sweet female fruits in their hands suddenly turn into two bags of sand. . . ."

3 /

B EFORE I DRAW the story of Hero to a close, let me tell you something about myself. My name is unimportant in this story, just as I myself play a very incidental role in it. Where I come from, when a child is born they make cheese, store it in a cold place, and when the person dies eat it for his peace of soul. My cheese is still waiting in some cellar. I hope that you who read these lines will not eat it. I never had any particular wants; I never, as they say, looked beyond what two calm eyes could see at a glance. I blink like a white duck when I eat, and I know that love is like a bird in a cage: if you don't feed it every day, it dies. And this story—or, better said, its end—is about love.

In those years, when I had not yet started to build the silence inside me, I spent my days weighing my hands to see which was the heavier. I learned the sad trade from which I earn my living to this day, but in parallel to that, and joyfully, I studied music, following the celebrated Czech master Otokar Shevchik from Kiev to Vienna, from Vienna to Prague. Trailing after him and with me, a horde of students of all colors and complexions gathered at the Prague Conservatory, so that his classroom reeked with sweat from three continents. Every other day, I went to the Conservatory, carrying a box under my arm, as though I were burying a child. I went into the long ground-floor chamber whose ceiling was so low the door scraped against it. In the cupboards, in the corners, on the walls, bare or wrapped in bags, lay and hung violins: with their bows stuck behind the strings, red, gleaming quarter violins, obviously worthless, full-sized violins striped like piglets, and dark unshining pieces of half-instruments, about which there was nothing to say at first glance. No matter how often I entered the room, each time they seemed to change place or be different. All this (especially at dusk, when the fish in the Vltava outside begin to bite) started to make a racket on its own and to call out to the floorboards, which raised the rugs and creaked. The bows began to rub against the sides of the instruments, the violins against one another, the strings began to give way and snap, the horsehairs to sow their whitish powder around the room, the polished bellies to swell to bursting point, and the pegs to turn by themselves.

One autumn evening, four of us found ourselves in this room, not separately at our lessons but together to practice. All of us were, of course, pupils. Shevchik gave us the notes for a quartet, I took my cello out of its box, another pupil brought his bassoon, the third sat down at the piano with the black keys and white semitones, and the last to appear was the most famous among us—the violinist. I had not seen him up close before, but I had heard about my compatriot from Belgrade, Manasia Bukur, and his beautiful sister, Heronea, who smiled with her lips and her breasts at the same time. It was in vogue in those days to wear cat-gold rings and to order death masks in advance, and Manasia was reputed to follow this fashion. They said that on holidays he would take Gypsy Communion—vinegar and horseradish—and then vanish for a few months, disregarding the warnings of Maestro Shevchik, who dispatched in his wake sealed letters wrapped in jute. His exams were anticipated with special interest and filled the Conservatory's auditorium, and one evening of Manasia's carousing was worth more than a month of ordinary evenings. When he entered, I noticed immediately that he really was wearing a cat-gold ring and that he had polished the nails on his left hand in four different colors. When he played, you could clearly see which finger was working.

We introduced ourselves and after rehearsal sat in a tavern drinking beer, with Manasia blowing the foam into other people's glasses.

One evening, he looked at me through lashes white with beer foam and asked: "You're not afraid of even numbers, are you?"

"No," I replied, surprised. "Why?"

"Because even numbers are the numbers of the dead. Flowers are given in uneven numbers only to the living; even numbers go to the grave. The uneven number is at the beginning, the even at the end...."

He wore buttons made of little silver spoons whose handles had been removed, and two little holes had been pierced at the bottom for the thread. He resolved trigonometry problems for his own amusement and relaxation.

"You know what?" he said to me on one of those evenings, rubbing his polished nails against his sideburns. "It's not in vain that they say: 'Keep all four eyes open!' I've been thinking, and I've come to the conclusion that this saying doesn't refer to some four-eyed monster, but to two people whose eyes have something in common. Just as one can look with one's left eye through the right, so maybe one can see with one's own eyes through somebody else's. One has only to find the common connection between them. All eyes—you've seen it a hundred times—have different depths and colors. And this depth can be measured quite precisely trigonometrically. I've done some research, and I'm convinced that eyes of the same depth and color have a common denominator. . . ."

He fell silent for a moment, and I noticed that his right eye blinked once for every two blinks of his left.

"The same is true of music," he went on. "Things that are removed from one another, such as four eyes or four instruments, should be brought into touch, employed on the same task. You should not play to the deaf or teach the mute to sing in church. You can't win a card game by playing only hearts and clubs. You have to take spades and diamonds into account as well, you have to play with all four suits, you have to open all four eyes."

He unpacked my cello and, to the astonishment

of those present, played my part of the quartet flaw-
lessly. By heart. When he came to the trill and
touched the string in rapid succession with his fore-
finger and middle finger, which were polished blue
and yellow, one saw the color green.

"If you don't understand, I'll explain it to you
by a simple illustration," Manasia resumed his lec-
ture. "You know, in Greece there is a peninsula so
narrow that buffaloes hitched to an ordinary anchor
can plow across and cut it off from the mainland.
That is Mount Athos, the center of Eastern Christianity's civilization. For a thousand years, the peninsula has been a settlement of monks; it is
autocephalous and borders on the Greek state; it has
its own customs zone and its government of three
minister monks and the *protos*—the prime minister.
Each of them holds a quarter of the seal with which
approval is stamped for entry to Mount Athos.
These, they say, are three male and one female part
of the seal. Only if each of the four monks gives his
quarter of the seal can it be composed: the parts are
wrapped in red thread and thus are entry visas
stamped for Mount Athos. . . . It is the same with
your music. It has to be passed through all four
seasons of the year, it is not the same in summer as
in autumn. If you want to enter its essence, you
must learn all four parts of the quartet we are play-

ing, you must know how to use all four instruments, even if you play only one in the quartet."

"Isn't music the same as mathematics?" I asked Manasia Bukur in response. "If it applies to one instrument, it applies to all!"

It was then that I noticed how something like an eleventh fingernail was appearing under the skin on the tip of his nose; as if it were an index finger, he pointed this nose-nail straight at me. "One must also take into account the origin of the numbers that constitute mathematics. If you look at it that way, then you'll also have to take into account the origin of the elements that constitute music. Take, for instance, this instrument, the one I play. The violin. Do you know what it's made of?"

And I was then edified.

"First of all, there is the wood. The body of the violin is made out of juniper wood that has been aged longer than the man who felled the tree has lived. The back and ribs are made of maple wood. The scroll is carved out of the soft, sweet wood of the cherry tree, and the ebony fingerboard is glued onto the neck of the violin. Every violin has a 'soul,' its hostess, a little stick that supports its belly and is made of fir. The range from the lowest to the highest tone depends on that little support. The violin, then, has a female soul. The bow is made of rose birch grown in the wind, and the resin comes from conifers.

"In addition to these parts of vegetable origin, the violin has others of animal origin. The bow strings are made of horse-tail hair, and in olden times (before the birth of the violin) it was best to use the tail of the unicorn. The two thicker strings are made of twined animal gut, and the mute is made of bone in the form of a miniature rider for a tiny mare. The wedge placed at the head of the bow to hold the hank of hair is also made of bone, and sometimes (in the case of Paganini, they say) the bone was human. The end peg on which the tail-piece is hooked like a slingshot is made of deer bone, and the glue with which the parts of the in-strument are stuck together is also of animal origin. Amati, they say, used glue made from the boiled meat of the chimera, because it gives birth in the air, and so its glue is lighter. A bit of mother-of-pearl from a seashell is encrusted on each side of the bow handle. The mother-of-pearl is always slightly colder than the wood, making it easier for the fin-gers to hold their proper place, because the ring finger always rests on this nacre button.

"Finally, there are parts that belong to the min-erals of the earth. Two thinner strings are made of metal, their ridge is sometimes made of stone, and the screw at the end of the frog for tightening the bow hair is made of silver. Along with all this, there is the strong, soft flame on which the wood is bent and the glue and varnish are made. The varnish is a separate story. It is always different, and every violin-maker mixes his own while protecting the slow and fast secrets he has inherited from his spiritual father. These fast and slow secrets in the violin varnish ensure the instrument's success—if the secrets are about the future. If they are about the past, the varnish is no good. . . .

"The essence," said Manasia, finishing his story, "is to be able to tell just from listening which wood rustles in the night—the juniper or the maple. The instrument in your hands does not break the connection with its origin, with the material and technique used to make it, even when it is played; indeed, it is only through this connection that the music acquires its warranty. The fingers do not really play on the violin but, rather, through it establish contact with the basic elements of water, air, fire, and earth, and with their secrets, which in every instrument are joined differently."

I T H A S B E E N a long time since I heard that story. The winds, as they say, have washed and lashed my bones long and hard since then, and I never had the desire to learn the other three parts of our quartet. Manasia's story seemed too complicated to me, and I did not believe it, just as I do not believe that those who don't sneeze on Passion Sunday will not live long. But even if you are not superstitious yourself and aren't afraid when a black cat crosses your path, you never know whether the black cat isn't superstitious. . . .

And so I played my cello in the quartet, tapping out the time with my foot, and thus caught musical laws in the mathematical net, without paying heed to the origin of the numbers making up the three-quarter or any other rhythm. Everything, of course, turned out well: I performed my part at the recital, passed the test the way one winds and snaps shut a watch, and abandoned music forever, following my left hand instead of the right.

Only occasionally, during great heat waves, when the polish melts and oozes down one's shoes, when the body feels only the button of its sweaty clothes, did music seem to return to my life. I myself returned to music only once.

In 1934, our Maestro Shevchik died, and that year his pupils staged commemorative concerts across Europe. I was in mid-journey—I could see neither ahead nor behind, I was afraid of dawn, I preferred taverns that served breakfast to those that served dinner. And insomnia had taken hold of me. I caught flies by closing books and among the pages found many of my victims crushed and dried. Still, I left for Prague as soon as I received news of the death, attended to my usual business, and went to the first concert that was scheduled. One of Shevchik's pupils, whose name I forget, was playing.

It was a violin concert. The maestro had straight hair that was completely black, like the horsehairs of his bow. The first movement was sedate, with the sedateness whereby a man can rest watching a book fall off the table, because he experiences the fall of each of its pages separately. The second movement was sweeping and slow, as when the leaves of the chestnut tree join their shadows forever. The cadenza was frenzied; the artist, unaccompanied, then removed his mask, and I thought: "If this one cries in July, you'll still hear him in August." Lastly, there was the breakneck closing movement of somebody who can sleep in three speeds, somebody whose dreams have tremendous tractive power one moment, and great, vulnerable speed the next. . . . Before me was not Orpheus, who with his music forces the beast, rock, ore, tree, fire, and resin, the howling wind in the seashell and the bowels of animals to listen to him. This one was even more powerful—he made them all respond, made them speak in his instrument themselves, as if on an altar, where it was not just they with their wombs and bones being sacrificed to the music, but the hand doing the sacrificing as well.... And I remembered Manasia Bukur and his story.

But, I confess, I never would have recognized Manasia Bukur himself under the black wig of the artist I was listening to. He recognized me among all those people who had come to hear him. After the concert, they sought me out and took me to him. He was performing under another name and another's hair, but what I found beneath the wig barely resembled his once-beautiful face. One eye had slipped under his hair, the other did not know where the former was, but these eyes still blinked as they used to: the left twice to every one blink of the right.

"I can't stand on my feet long anymore. Let's sit down somewhere and have a beer," I said to him.

"You can't stand up anymore? I can't lie down anymore, my friend," he retorted. "It's awful how much lying around we've already done in life! An eternity! I can't do it anymore, I've had enough. I don't lie down at all anymore...."

We went down the street, strewn with straw that evening so that the traffic would not disturb the audience in the auditorium, and sat down as in olden times to order a beer.

"I need you," he said as soon as he took his seat; I saw that his nails were no longer polished.

"Why, you know that I don't play anymore."

"I know. That's exactly why. I need your present vocation, not your past one."

I was surprised and shaken by these words. He told me what was troubling him only after I promised him the services of my trade. And, listening to him, I learned of the story I had long since known better than he. But there was something in that story that did astonish me. I discovered that for years now he had been searching for the sections of an entirely new kind of quartet. This new quartet and his efforts to find it had led him into madness and completely divorced him from music. Because music was not what this was about, although the quartet was clearly discernible. Sitting on my left leg, I listened to his confession, which could be called:

The Story of Brother and Sister

You know that I had a sister, Heronea; you remember she was beautiful—one eye was the day, the other the night, and she knew that there was more beauty than love in the world. She was born in 1910, and after a few weeks, one morning that nobody, not even she, remembered, Hero began to die, and continued to die imperceptibly for decades until that recent last day when her dying finally ceased. Perhaps this dying actually started much earlier, before Hero was ever born, and it may have lasted for centuries before her birth, until it came to an end in a way that shall be discussed later. As for me, one evening that nobody noticed, which I myself could not distinguish from my other evenings, I began quite imperceptibly to love. Not a woman, or my mother, or brother, or sister—indeed, at the time I was only a few years old. I began to love generally somehow, in the form of having a readiness for it, but with determination, like a ship setting out for the open sea whence there is no return. And thereafter, into my love, onto my ship, embarked and disembarked all the fellow travelers of my fate, sharing with me for a while the same wash of the waves, ebb of the tide, sun, and winds. Among those who embarked on my ship was my sister, Heronea, but she had a special place on this vessel. Not on the captain's bridge, no, not there, but in the most beautiful of chairs. And this most beautiful of chairs on my ship seemed to suit her better than anyone else.

Indeed, perhaps this chair became the most beautiful of seats on the deck only when Heronea took her place on it. When that happened, she was barely fifteen, and she no longer ate in the presence of others. I myself have never once seen her eat lunch or dinner since then. In the family it was whispered that she did not eat the same things as others. She crossed herself in church quickly, as though catching flies, and it was said that she ate just as quickly. She was still a thin-legged child with an old, an ancient soul inside her, a soul that was getting accustomed to her body by force, as if to a new, immature god who himself did not yet understand the language of the prayers being addressed to him, a god who had yet to learn how to talk. . . . I always had the impression that all the women around me could be divided into cooks, chambermaids, or nurses, and I had good reason to learn while still a child that my sister, Heronea, belonged in the latter category. With her tyrannical, awkward, and panicky care for the dying, who provoked in her a thousand irresistible kinds of clumsiness, she (in her futile attempts to help them) made the last hours of most of our pets miserable. . . . When they died in her arms, exhausted as much by her panic-stricken efforts to keep them alive as by death, she would turn away from them mutely, saying: "I feel like some kind of Wednesday. I'm always late, I always arrive after Tuesday."

Heronea studied chemistry in Belgrade, and when she came here to Prague in her fish-skin hat to continue her studies, we rented an apartment in one of those narrow, deep streets in the old quarter of town. An apartment with an attic that was reachable by a wooden ladder lowered from the ceiling into the room by means of a chain and winch. At the time, I was a young man and, as they say, like a mountain stream—shallow and transparent. I no longer spent the energy I drew from the music with which I still fed myself daily. I got heavy in the soul, accumulating unnecessary spiritual fat, just like a man who gains weight from not using the energy he has acquired from food. On the balcony Hero put a pot with aloe that "the devil had licked," so that the edges of its thorny leaves were white. She had brought this aloe from Belgrade, and she placed a mirror in front of it in her room so she could see the plant when she combed her hair. One day, she noticed that a young lieutenant who lived on the same floor in the building across the street was combing his hair and shaving in her mirror. His window was so close to our balcony that the lieutenant could see himself in Hero's mirror without leaving his room, and so he would shave using her mirror and his saber. Surprisingly, the lieutenant was very deft at shaving with his officer's saber, using its gold tassel to lather his face. A burning match could be tossed from there to here, and that is how the lieutenant and I began lighting each other's pipe in the evenings, laughing.

"Careful, never light a second candle or a third pipe on the same flame," our new acquaintance told us cheerfully.

Between the lieutenant, whose name was Jan Kobala, and my sister there developed something I can only describe as sniffing. But time never stands on just one leg. Matters went further. Each evening, he turned the light on just when Hero turned hers off. I sat on the balcony and smoked my pipe, every so often raising my hat and driving the smoke into it. And I watched how, on the other side of the street, Jan Kobala removed his boots, tossing one in one corner of the room and the other in another, how he drank holding the bottle with only his teeth, how with his saber he sliced the drumstick off the roast chicken on the table. Next he lay down on the bed, gnawed at the drumstick, and tossed away the bone, aiming it straight into the boot in the corner of the room. Then he took off his shirt, and that same moment the door slowly opened, the moonlight entered the room, and through the moonlight entered my sister, Hero. She stared fixedly at the lieutenant as though blind, approached him, and bent over him; he began unbuttoning her blouse with his tongue. Then Hero cast a glance at the balcony where I was sitting and smoking, spat at the candle, and, lashing the moonlight with her hair, stepped around his bed with him in it and slowly, like snow drifting to the ground, never once drawing back, began to descend on her prey. . . .

With my hat and hair full of smoke, I sometimes got up and went to the Conservatory to practice, or to a tavern sticky with beer, or to watch the Jews bury books, but something inside me was seething, and I felt that my beard was growing faster through my warts than around them, I felt I would have to change. Indeed, I was beginning to change, and I kept working at it.

One afternoon, my sister appeared with eyes like overripe fruits and hands forgotten in her muff. Lieutenant Jan Kobala was no longer opening the door. He was receiving some other love in his room. Hero said nothing; I sat as usual, smoking and waiting. The time came for her to turn the light off in her room and for him to turn it on in his. I watched from the balcony as he removed his boots, threw down his belt, drank from the bottle holding it with only his teeth, sliced off the drumstick with his saber, and ate in bed. And chills ran down my spine, the hairs on my back untangled, my shirt rustled. I put out my pipe with my thumb, leaving the smell of flesh on the embers. I got up quietly, descended into the street, crossed it, and went up to Kobala's apartment. I opened the door; the moonlight entered the room, and through the moonlight so did I. I stared at him fixedly as though blind, approached him, and bent over him; he began unbuttoning my trousers with his tongue. Then I cast a glance at our balcony, where Hero was sitting, spat at the candle, and lay down with Kobala. Because it was me he was now expecting every night instead of Hero.

One day, Hero got up early and braided her hair in a way that made her feel it was spring. She had different ways of combing her hair: when she braided a ribbon in her hair, she felt as though it were summer; when she combed her hair into a whip, she had the feeling it was spring. That day, she combed her hair into a braid at the nape of her neck and left the house early. I never saw her again. I was informed that Hero had committed suicide. At 12:05 the same day, she died in an explosion she had set off herself in the laboratory. And so I never had the chance to ask her why she had crossed that line, whether it was because of Jan or because of me. They would not let me see her even on the bier.

Since then, I have carried my pocketwatch fixed at the hour of her death; it always shows 12:05 and every day it passes through that moment of its own frightful accuracy. And the terrible question of whose act, the lieutenant's or mine, which of these two infidelities had pushed her into death, became for me a question of life or death.

Naturally, I immediately broke off my relationship with Jan Kobala. He vanished without a trace, and ever since I have been wandering, tripping over my own shadow. I changed my name and my hair and started playing at gypsy weddings, taking Communion the way I used to, with vinegar and horseradish, and the only thing that soothes me is resolving trigonometry problems. The adage about the four eyes comes to my mind, and I am trying to understand it again. I have calculated the depth of Hero's clear eyes countless times, and I know this magic number by heart and repeat it at night. I have started observing the eye depth of the people I meet, in the hope that a miracle may occur, that eyes of the same color and depth may appear, from which I might perhaps get the answer to my question, which I will never get from my sister. And one more thing. I have realized that, just as there are male and female instruments, and the only good quartet is one in which they are mixed, so every face has one male and one female eye. Look in the mirror and you'll find it easy to tell which of your two eyes is male and which is female. Hero's left eye was male, and it led her to her death. Her female, right eye tried to keep her alive. This too must be taken into account. . . . But let us get to the point!

I was in Cracow, playing there, when a gentleman by the name of Dr. Alfred Wiezhbitsky caught my eye. He used to drop in at our father's house and had known Hero and me as children. He invited me to play at his home, and I had the chance to do some observation and concluded that with him one had to be careful. The doctor's eyes were the same depth and color as my late sister's. In one eye the day, in the other the night. Perhaps one might expect from him the answer to the question asked of her, and an assessment of my conduct with Jan Kobala. For a long time, I followed Wiezhbitsky, a cordial, nice fellow, as mute as a book and buttoned up to his ears, but nothing came of it. He carried the nails of one hand under the nails of the other and politely kept his silence. However, now I am going back to Poland, where I have a concert scheduled at the home of one of the doctor's relatives. If I use this opportunity to learn something from Wiezhbitsky, I will be in need of your services, and so I would like you to come along on the trip —which could actually be pleasant for you, were you not traveling with me.

That is how Manasia Bukur finished his story. Although he paid me immediately for the future services he expected of my trade, we did not leave for Poland until 1937. My friend was almost in a good mood. He had a strange presentiment; he wore my hat on top of his own, as in our student days, and in Warsaw he introduced me to Dr. Alfred Wiezhbitsky. We sat down in the doctor's office and drank Polish vodka, and the doctor smoked a pipe without having the faintest idea of the true purpose of our visit. Indeed, who could have guessed that we were nurturing the insane hope that with his help, with the help of somebody's eyes similar to those of Hero, we would open all four eyes for my friend Manasia Bukur? All this, of course, could have been dismissed as the whimsicalness of my friend, whereas the real aim, the real purpose of our trip and stay in Poland, as I thought and hoped, was the concert arranged on the estate of the doctor's relative. An objection could be made, however, to this latter assumption. That objection was me. If the concert was the purpose of the trip, then why the devil was I necessary in the whole affair?

Our host spoke so little that his lips stuck together from the silence and would crack like ripe poppies whenever he uttered a word. We rode in his car through the dusk, and I tried to fall asleep. Wiezhbitsky stopped the car; we got out, and he wanted to show us something. It was already getting dark, but what he was showing us, blowing the silvery smoke from his pipe in that direction, was clearly visible. In front of us was a climatic dividing line. A straight line passed through the field as far as the eye could see, marking the border between the snow and the dry earth under the grass. For a moment, we stood on that dryness as if in a room, and then stepped out into the blizzard. And we immediately saw the castle. A lantern burned on either side of its gate, showing the falling snow, black on this side and white on that side of the light.

We soon found ourselves in a sitting room with doorknobs in the shape of human hands. I walked over to the piano, on which Manasia had placed his violin, and noticed a book on the piano lid. That same moment, shaking hands first with a doorknob and then with us, our hostess entered.

Her dress rustled, brushing against her stockings, and that noise disturbed me. Her hair was pulled back tight, leaving her ears and neck to her face. That evening, she taught me that in winter one salts the plate before putting food on it, because twice salted keeps us twice as warm. The double doors opened behind us, and in the side hall we saw a table set for four. The two three-branched candelabra on the table gave more light than one would have expected, and I noticed that the outside windows were ajar, so that one had the double reflection of the candelabra—instead of six, there were twelve flames burning out there, behind the glass in the snowy night. In that light, the curves of our chairs gleamed as though they had been waxed.

Our hostess took the first bite, said *"Bon appétit,"* and then looked at Dr. Wiezhbitsky; I thought I saw him secretly signal her to keep quiet.

"Ah, my good angel, have you completely abandoned me?" she addressed me unexpectedly in French. I looked at her in astonishment, because until that moment and those words our relationship had not gone an inch beyond the formal interchange of two people with nothing in common. To this, Dr. Wiezhbitsky, staring at his spoon, added an even more incredible sentence in French, addressed to Manasia Bukur: "I waited for you, because I knew that your consideration would not last long, and your remorse even less so!"

For a second, I thought Dr. Wiezhbitsky's eyes really did look like Hero's—one carried the day, the other the night—and I realized that our hosts were ceasing to communicate with us in the usual way, and that here, in this (to us) foreign land, they were suddenly removing their masks and putting their cards on the table. Manasia was as pale as if he had been smeared with bow resin, and he wrung his hands. My shallow sense of the future saved me. I laid eyes on the spoon. It was a silver spoon, and I used it. We had soup cooked in a clay dish shaped like a lute that could rock over an open flame, so that the sediment would be left at the bottom of the asymmetrical vessel instead of spread through the liquid. Then a piping-hot, almost dry sauce was served, rather tart, seasoned with salt from a deer horn. For a moment, we felt bilious and hot-headed, and a flame flashed in Dr. Wiezhbitsky's eyes. I clearly saw that his right eye was female and his left male. We had moved on to the forks when he said, again in French, as though resuming an interrupted conversation, and looking straight at Manasia: "I think, my love, that was an under-handed, bad way to behave!" And his lips cracked like a roast chestnut.

I grabbed the fork, clenched it in my hand, and knew that it had happened. The answer to my friend Manasia Bukur's question to his sister, Hero, had been given here, at the dining table of Dr. Wiezhbitsky and his lady friend. As if Hero had used Dr. Wiezhbitsky's lips, for want of any other possibility.

Manasia jumped at these words like a madman, and as we watched him in amazement, he raced out of the room.... A minute later, we heard the front door. At first, I wanted to run after and stop him, because I knew what he intended to do. But something prevented me from doing that. Not our kind hosts, of course, who comforted me, claiming that Manasia would return as soon as he got tired of walking in the blizzard. What had stopped me was my conviction that, if there was a way to save Manasia, it was for me to unravel the secret of this room with these people, where everything had occurred so inexplicably, where the fatal words had been uttered, and where from the outset the dinner conversation had been such that I could barely believe my own ears. And so I stayed, concealing my trepidation and looking at Manasia's violin on the piano.

Along with the rusty-colored wine, another, resin-scented wine was served, in a small silver-

netted jug. I was told it was with this wine that the
former had been colored five years before.

"You know," Dr. Wiezhbitsky said to me, "they
say that fish are better if they come from rivers that
flow from south to north rather than the other way
round. An uncorked bottle of red wine was sewn
into the fish we are now eating, and the wine evap-
orated into the meat on the fire. . . ."

Wiezhbitsky spoke Polish this time, and there
was nothing unusual in what he said, but I noticed
that they were both looking at me somehow
strangely again, twirling the stems of their glasses
in their hands. And I, as though in a dream, thanks
perhaps to the slower breathing in this andante part
of the meal, noticed that I had already been eating
for an hour without having a clue as to what they
were feeding me. I had never tasted any of the
dishes before. Now it was salmon, cut and cleaned
from the dorsal side, rolled back and baked "eye to
eye," the meat facing the rose-birch fire. Next we
were served venison, from deer caught in the moonlight and left overnight in the frost, cold and black,
its meaty parts tied with the intestines and its bones
tipped with a thick coil of horsehair, so the meat
could be easily lifted to the mouth without slipping
from one's fingers. With it went a sauce of sour
cherries, full of mixed aromas. We felt melancholic;

our silver forks slowly penetrated the meat until they reached the bones, and our knives encountered the tines of the forks in the meat, slowly feeling them out. . . . I sat, I ate, and I waited. Everything that happened thereafter seemed to me to be terribly slow and long, although, truth be told, no more than a few minutes passed before the secret was revealed.

On the table was a mixture of plants, the juices of the earth, the fruits of the sea, minerals, silver, fire, and meat. One of the most beautiful things was a pastry filled with shellfish and roasted on dry horseradish instead of on wood. It was as if the invisible maestro feeding us had spoken through that shell, and I thought how all his life he had been cooking one and the same everlasting meal, which, if he ever successfully finished it, he would never recommence, because that is not and cannot be done. . . . And I wished to see him.

"Who is that fourth person in this room?" I asked my hosts.

"At last!" Wiezhbitsky cried out with relief and gave a sign. In the candlelight there appeared a little man in a shirt buttoned up to his neck, underneath a huge white cap. Looking out from under it were two gray eyes accustomed to fire and water, and the hands, strewn with boiled hairs, were lined with blue veins like some kind of letters. He bowed to us with a smile which was cut short by a wrinkle on his face. It was as though he were bowing instead of Manasia Bukur, whose violin lay mutely on the piano.

"You never told us," said Dr. Wiezhbitsky to the cook, "how you succeed in your art."

"There's no secret to it," replied the little man. "The art of cooking lies in the dexterity of the fingers. One has to practice at least three hours a day in order to keep the fingers nimble. Like a musician . . ."

Indeed, the little man's hands that day held the same materials as Manasia's instrument case over there. Silver and ores, animal guts and bones, wood, seashells, minerals, and horsehair all were stretched tight in his hands, as they were over there. Now, when the music had long since left me, he set in motion the same things by a different means, giving me one more chance, one more time not to become completely estranged from music. This was not a meal, this was a hymn to the earth, to its mountains and plains, its rivers, its seas, its wind, its fire, its plants, and its wild game, and to the skill of the human hand that is capable of killing and of nourishing life with death.

Served in the dead of winter, beside the coffee and cakes carried rapidly into the small Chinese sitting room with its polish, mother-of-pearl, and ivory, was watermelon that had been whitewashed and stuffed into a wooden box packed with wheat so that it would keep until November. It smelled of the juniper boards, and suddenly, as though this were the smell of the instrument, I felt I could play the second part of the long-forgotten quartet, my friend Manasia Bukur's violin part. But it was too late. The remaining two parts of my quartet stood forever out of reach, who could tell where, and I knew that the four parts of the seal—the three male and one female part—would never be wound in red thread to stamp my own visa to Mount Athos. So it was with me.... But in the case of Bukur, nothing had yet been explained, and that was what I was waiting for.

My persistence then reached its climax and turned into immense fatigue, as though all my life I had been counting the clouds in the sky and the bones in my mouth. With my last ounce of strength, I joined in the conversation that had resumed as soon as we reached for the ice-cream spoon.

"I advise you to come and spend the night in my room," my hostess said to me, again in French, playing with her silver spoon.

I froze in surprise. Dr. Wiezhbitsky sat chuckling quietly into his beard, and I finally turned over my own spoon and quickly retorted in French: "What? On Good Friday?"

And my hosts burst out laughing. Indeed, everything was finally clear. During dinner they had not really been talking to us but, rather, playing a game they knew and we didn't: they had been reading the inscriptions on their silver cutlery. I now did this myself, remembering where the inscriptions on the silver handles of our forks and knives came from.

They were dialogue from Jan Potocki's book; a good part of his *Manuscript Found in Saragossa* had been engraved into some one hundred pieces of a luxurious set of silver cutlery. Among the sentences taken from Potocki and engraved on the forks, spoons, and silver napkin rings was, of course, the sentence Manasia and I understood as the magic answer to his question. The answer he so eagerly awaited from his sister Hero: "I think, my love, that was an underhanded, bad way to behave!"

I IMMEDIATELY took my leave, knowing that somewhere Bukur was dying with that sentence on his lips and that I could save him only if I revealed to him the truth about the silver cutlery. I arrived in Warsaw very late, during a terrible storm. But even more terrible was that I arrived at our inn too late to do anything for his life. Manasia Bukur was lying in bed; the candle in his hand had already burned halfway down, and the servant gave me his short letter:

"I am dying of my own free will and happy, because I have received the answer to the question of my life. I now know, she did it because of me, not because of Jan Kobala. 'My love,' she said to me and you heard it, 'I think that was an underhanded, bad way to behave!' Hero had chosen Jan to torture me, just as I had chosen him to torture her, and not because of him. Neither she nor I could have cared less about Kobala! Hero died thinking touching was possible after all!

"P.S. Thank you for the job you'll do. I kiss your soft fingers."

I put the letter on the floor next to the bed, and over it the heavy box containing the bags and tools of my sad trade. I bent over the bier and touched his face. I put his left eye back in place (in his case it was male), smoothed the wrinkles out around the other, female eye, which when he was alive had blinked twice as much and was older and more tired than the former. I arranged his features to look as nice as they used to. And then I coated him with a gray mixture and cast his death mask. . . .

Unfortunately, there is nothing mysterious in the world. The world is not full of secrets; it is full of buzzing ears. The whole story can fit into the crack of a whip! Except that people in my business, for instance, come to know a bit more than other mortals.

Waiting for the mixture to set, I thought about Hero and my unfortunate friend. It must be said that I had long known that Hero had not committed suicide at all but, rather, had been murdered. She had been murdered in a fit of jealousy, or some other kind of fit, by Lieutenant Jan Kobala. And then comes the part of the story that had been so carefully concealed from Hero's brother, because it could truly have hurt him. Jan kept Hero's severed head in his apartment for three days before turning himself in to the military authorities, who kept the case far from the public eye.

According to the crazed lieutenant, it was not until the evening of the third day that Hero's head cried out in a terrible, deep, masculine voice.

THE
INNER
SIDE
OF THE
WIND

MILORAD PAVIĆ

THE INNER SIDE OF THE WIND,

OR

THE NOVEL OF HERO AND LEANDER

TRANSLATED
FROM THE
SERBO-CROATIAN
BY CHRISTINA
PRIBIĆEVIĆ-ZORIĆ

ALFRED A. KNOPF
NEW YORK 1993

THIS IS A BORZOI BOOK
PUBLISHED BY ALFRED A. KNOPF, INC.

Copyright © 1993 by Alfred A. Knopf, Inc.

Originally published in Serbo-Croatian as
Унутрашња страна ветра или роман о Хери и Леандру
by Prosveta, Belgrade. Copyright © 1991 by Prosveta.

Library of Congress Cataloging-in-Publication Data
Pavić, Milorad.
[Unutrašnja strana vetra, ili, Roman o Heri i Leandru.
English]
The inner side of the wind, or The Novel of Hero and
Leander / Milorad Pavić ; translated from the Serbo-Croatian
by Christina Pribićević-Zorić.—1st American ed.
p. cm.
ISBN 0-679-42085-1
I. Title.   II. Title: Inner side of the wind.   III. Title: Novel
of Hero and Leander.
PG1419.26.A78U5713   1993
891.8'235—dc20   92-24235   CIP

Manufactured in the United States of America
First American Edition

LEANDER

He was half of something. A strong, beautiful, talented half of something that was, perhaps, even stronger, greater and more beautiful than he. He was, then, the magical half of something magnificent and unfathomable. She was a complete whole. A small, disoriented, not very strong or harmonious whole, but a whole all the same.

1 /

"ALL FUTURES have one great virtue: they never look the way you imagine them," said the father to Leander.

At the time, Leander was not yet a full-grown man, he was still illiterate, but he was already handsome; he was not yet called Leander, but his mother had already twined his hair like Dutch lace so that he would not have to comb it on his journey. Seeing him off, his father said: "He has a long, fine neck, like a swan's; God forbid that he should die from the saber."

And Leander was to remember those words all of his life.

From generation to generation, everybody in Leander's Chihorich family, with the exception of his father, had been a mason, a blacksmith, and a beekeeper. The Chihoriches had descended to the Danube at the foot of Belgrade from Herzegovina, from a region where church chanting was learned before the alphabet, and where the water drained off the roof into two seas: on one side of the roof the rain poured to the west, into the Neretva River and the Adriatic Sea, and on the other it poured to the east, down the Drina into the Sava River and down the Danube into the Black Sea. The only renegade of the family was Leander's father, who refused even to hear of house-building.

"When I venture out in Vienna or Buda, among those buildings you put up so remorselessly wherever you can, I get lost immediately, and it is only when I emerge by the Danube, where pike is at its stupidest in February, that I know where and who I am."

The Chihoriches, however, never knew where or who the father of the family was, or what it was they lived on. The only thing he told them was that they lived on water and death, because one always lives on death. And, indeed, Leander's father would come home late, wet from the Danube or the Sava; they were easy to distinguish, because every river has its own stench. And, wet as he was, around midnight he would sneeze ten times, as though counting.

Leander, who as a boy had also carried the names Radacha and Milko, had been taught since childhood to follow the example of his grandfathers and uncles and to continue the family trade of masonry. He was adroit at building and at chiseling marble; he could be helpful in burying icons, and he had an innate gift for decorating a hive with pictures or catching a swarm of bees effortlessly and swiftly. When, in the scorching heat of the summer fast, someone had to go the distance of twenty shot-ranges to get fish from the river there in Herzegovina, they would send Leander, and he alone would manage to catch the fish, stuff it with nettles, and bring it back before it began to smell. Later, on one of his voyages, he saw (and would forever remember) how, in memory of the despot Djurdje Brankovich, bread kneaded with water from the Danube and blessed at Smederevo, in the Church of Our Lady, was carried hand to hand by wagoners all the way to Mount Avala. It went so quickly that the bread was still hot when it arrived from the Danube upon the despot's dining table, where it was broken and passed around with salt extracted from under Zrnovo.

"We are all builders," Grandfather Chihorich was wont to say to Leander at dinner, "but we have been given unusual marble to build with: hours, days, and years, with sleep and wine as the mortar. We are all builders of time, we drive shadows away and catch water in our navels; out of hours everybody builds his house, out of time everybody builds his beehive and collects his honey, we carry time in bellows to our fire. Like gold coins mixed with copper in a pouch, like white sheep and black, so our white marbles and black are mixed for building. And woe unto him whose copper devours the gold in his pouch, or whose nights swallow up the days. He shall build unseasonably and unreasonably...."

Leander, who listened to all this and always thought not of the morrow but of the day after, noticed with surprise that his father took and ate one spoonful of horsebeans to every three of his own. In their family the total number of spoonfuls per person was set in advance, and none of them ever exceeded the amount he or she had been allotted for the meal; but Leander ate the same amount as the others in a third of the time. Bit by bit, he noticed even among animals those that ate faster and those slower, those that moved faster and those slower, and gradually he began to distinguish two different rhythms of life in the world around him, two uneven pulses of blood, or juices in plants, two kinds of beings compressed within the frameworks of the same days and nights, which last equally long for everyone, and thus stint some and plentifully reward others. And, involuntarily, he began to feel intolerant toward people, animals, and plants that were not driven by a pulse kindred to his own. He listened to the birds and picked out those that had his own rhythm of singing. One morning, waiting for the jug while his father drank water from it and counting the gulps, he realized that the time had come for him to leave his father's house. He realized suddenly that his father had already invested so much love and knowledge in him and in his brothers that it would be enough to warm and feed him for the rest of his life, and that there was no longer any point in amassing a portion of love that was obviously relegated to a time in the future when not even Leander himself (the object and consumer of this love) would be among the living, and paternal love would be carried by the wind, futilely over-reaching its target.

Leander's departure came to pass as follows. He knew how to play the santir, and people, pleased with his playing on holidays, would often toss copper coins into the instrument. Living on the docks of the Sava at the time were four old merchants, renowned for their playing of the santir. One of them happened to fall ill on a trip, and the group needed a fourth to play. One morning, the very same morning on which Father Chihorich had decided to teach his son how to write and had just shown him his first character, the letter Θ, with which the word Theotokos (Mother of God) begins, they received a visit. Leander had not even dug in with his pen properly when the eldest of the merchants entered the Chihorich house, took Leander's santir down from the wall, and weighed it in his hand. Its weight, which came from the coins inside it, was recommendation enough for the young player. The merchant asked Chihorich senior to lend him his son as their fourth santir-player long enough for them to make one trip to Constantinople. Leander accepted without thinking twice, and that is how his writing lessons were interrupted at the very start, and never got beyond his first letter. But the old merchant who had sought him out fell ill himself at the same time, and so they had to take along a friend of Leander's, a fellow from the Herzegovinian border named Diomides Subota, to fill out the number of santir-players.

The merchants set out on their trip from Belgrade along the old Constantinople road, via Salonika to the city of Constantine. They saw the Hellespont, passed through Sestos and Abydos, and returned two years later, but on the journey one of the two remaining santir-playing merchants met his death in a strange way. He ordered his camel to kneel so that he might tend to his own needs unseen behind it; while he was peeing, the camel lay down on top of him and killed him. The next year, when they were getting ready to go to Constantinople again, they found a replacement for him, but on the day of departure the fourth merchant, the last of the old santir-players, failed to show up in the caravan. The young men who had assembled as usual to replace the merchants on the santir exchanged surprised glances when they realized that not one of the older players was among them; they threw down their instruments as if by agreement and continued their journey as merchants instead of musicians.

The dangerous trip and lucrative trade between two worlds, West and East, Europe and Asia, at a time when Turkish might was moving against Vienna, paid off, and on that journey Leander realized that, as with his father's love, so with music, he had had his fill for a lifetime, and that whatever he might add to it would merely spill over and vanish into the void. And so, entertained by the trading, he never went back to the santir, did not take it into his hands, did not even feel the need to listen to music in this world which devoured its days all around him. He became enamored of his new trade, of traveling, of camels with their slow, syncopated gait, which actually concealed an incredible ability to swallow up space, a swiftness and efficiency, and he tried to imitate them, disguising his innate pulse, his inner time, his swiftness, with soft, gentle, long-drawn-out movements. Speed cloaked in laziness—that was his goal. Knowing that this was the best way to protect himself, he always concealed how low his candle had burned and kept silent about what he had seen ahead of time, behind the wind's back. So it was that, by watching the camels and practicing for years, he managed to conceal completely his unusual power, treating his virtue as though it were a vice, realizing that swiftness such as his was a dangerous weapon that people distrusted. And this protected him against trouble. For the times were hard and the roads full of blood-stained robes. From the tradesmen Leander heard his fill of terrible tales about the saber-wielding Turks, hunters of speed, beheaders, who intercepted caravans and played havoc with the merchants and tradesmen. They told him that a sabreur always keeps the hand with which he masturbates behind his back, like a treasure, so as not to overtire it, that he does nothing with it, and slays only with the other hand. In vain did Leander think that the devil cannot kill, that only God takes life away; he was afraid; his eyes leaped all over his cheeks and face in fear at the very thought of the sabreur.

That fear inside him was reinforced by a soothsayer.

The soothsayer lived in a battered water tank, and when he could not sleep at night he would get up and sharpen knives, or wash his feet in his socks, and his loneliness would quickly spoil like cheese. People told Leander: "If you give him a coin, he'll shave you, if you give him two, he'll tell you your fortune while he shaves you. But take care, he is a better fortune-teller than he is a barber."

Leander sat down on a rock in front of the tank and held out two coins. The prophet smiled, and one could see that his smile was the only thing on him that did not age. He told Leander to open wide, spat suddenly into his mouth, and then opened wide his own. When Leander responded by spitting back into the prophet's mouth, the latter spat at each of Leander's cheeks, spread the saliva, and began to shave him.

"Will the Turks strike tomorrow or the day after?" asked Leander half-jokingly.

"I've no idea." The soothsayer's voice floated around them in large blocks.

"Well, what kind of a prophet are you, then?"

"You know, there are two kinds of soothsayers —expensive and cheap. But don't think that the former are good and the latter bad. That's not the point. The former deal with fast secrets, and the latter with slow, and hence the difference between them. I, for instance, am a cheap soothsayer, because I don't see tomorrow's day or next year any more than you do. I see very far into the future; I can prophesy two to three hundred years in advance how the wolf will be called, and which empire will fall. And who needs to know what will happen in two or three hundred years? Nobody, not even I. I don't give a hoot about it. But there are also other, expensive soothsayers—in Dubrovnik, for instance —who prophesy what will happen tomorrow, or in a year, and everybody needs that the way a bald man needs a hat, and you don't ask how much such a thing costs, you give with an open hand and an open cask, as you would for piglet wings. But you shouldn't think that these two kinds of prophets and prophecies have nothing to do with each other, or that they are mutually contradictory. It's really one and the same prophecy; it can be compared to the wind, which has its outer and inner sides, the inner side being the one that remains dry when the wind blows through the rain. So, one soothsayer sees only the outer side of the wind, and the other sees only the inner side. Neither sees both. That's why you have to go to at least two of them in order to compose the whole picture, to sew the right side of your wind to the lining....

"And now let me tell you what you can get from me. A man is like a ship's compass: he spins in a circle on his axis and sees all four sides of the world as he turns, but above and below him he sees and is shown nothing. And this is precisely where the two things that he cares and wants to know about are: the love underneath him and the death overhead.

"There are various kinds of love. Some can be pierced only with a fork; others are eaten with one's hands, like oysters; some have to be cut with a knife so as not to choke on them; and there are those that are so soupy only a spoon can help. Or they are picked like the apple plucked by Adam.

"As for death, it is the only thing under the heavenly skies that, like a snake, can climb up and down the tree of our origin. Death can lie in ambush waiting for you for centuries before you are born, and it can also come back for you, can come to meet you from the most distant future. Somebody you don't know and will never see can sic his death on you like a hunting dog on a partridge and send it to catch you from an immeasurable distance....

"But let's put that aside. You have a fine neck. That kind of neck attracts a woman's hand and a soldier's saber. Indeed, I see a soldier in boots; he's shaving with a gold-tasseled saber, and it is with the saber that he will slay you. Because, look, I see your head clearly too. It's on a plate like the head of Saint John the Baptist. And a woman is the cause.... But, don't worry, it will not be soon. A great deal of time will pass, a great many pregnant years before then. Meanwhile, guard your neck, my swan, against women and against the saber. And wash...."

So the shave and the prophecy were finished. As he left, the first snow of the year fell behind Leander, and the powerful voice of the prophet rang out. Snow can stick to such a voice the way it can to a rug, thought Leander. And he shivered from the cold above and the chill inside him.

The prophecy disturbed Leander. Fear of the sabreurs seemed to him more justified than ever. His heart moved from his left side to his right, the fear made his dreams contagious; if Leander dreamed that a crow had pecked him in the tooth because he had laughed at it in his dream, all the people he touched that day would dream that a crow was pecking them in the teeth.

But at this time, when he was most afraid of the sabreur, Leander did not meet him. Before the sabreur, he met a girl. While they were wintering in Ohrid, he felt that he had exaggerated his fear and had lost his innate rhythm, that he was regressing instead of progressing in his secret virtue. One evening he heard the jangle of the santir. Instead of being indifferent as before, he caught himself listening. And that seemed to him like a step backward. It was a woman playing, not a man, and that difference, although he could not have known what caused it to start with, did not escape Leander. Listening, he noticed one other thing. In the passages of the music where the fingers were supposed to cross on the strings, the santir would die out and resume several seconds later, as though there had been a pause for breath. Leander realized what it was, and the next day, when he saw the girl who had been playing, the first thing he said to her was: "I heard you playing. You're missing a finger on your left hand, your fourth finger. But you learned to play before you lost it. Right?"

"That's right," replied the girl. "Three years ago, to ward off curses, they slipped me a metal santir with red-hot strings. Ever since, I have been playing like this, to remind myself, but you don't have to listen. . . ."

Leander immediately thought that his own way of life might help the girl to forget her misfortune. He tried to explain to her how one should live quickly without paying heed; night after night, they strolled by the lake and he tried to teach her his unusual, hidden virtue. It transpired that Despina —that was the girl's name—was a good learner, and soon the days of her misfortune with the hot-stringed santir were forgotten. She discarded the instrument forever, just as Leander was leaving the merchants, fed up with their doings and full of fear and the money he had earned. Despina gradually acquired his rhythm in eating, she successfully imitated his speech and walk, she practiced using her eyes with the same dizzying speed that he used his, and at moments she had the impression that in every one of her days she lived two. But in the course of these lessons and lakeside strolls, fleeing from inquisitive eyes and hiding their common speed like a secret, they slowly grew closer. She would sometimes flash her ring in his eyes, and, looking at her, he would wonder whether she, like some of the sinful women in the frescoes, had two spiral sow's tails on her breasts instead of nipples. At the time, Leander knew little about women or himself. He knew that wine had to be treated like women: one way in the summer and another in the winter; he also knew that strong wines were decanted in summer and weak wines in winter. That is all Leander knew about women from family talk, but the girl with the missing finger attracted him. Waiting for him somewhere at the time was his *fabula rasa,* his "empty story," crying out for Leander finally to move into it.

The Drin River flows through Lake Ohrid, cutting it in half. One evening, Despina and Leander tossed a fishing net into the boat and pushed off across the lake and down the river, which at dawn deposited them on the other bank. That night, in the boat on that double water, sheltered by the net, they lay down together for the first time.

But it transpired that Leander had known hours in advance everything that was going to happen, and, just when his expectations were fulfilled, he was so much faster than his companion that they did not even manage to touch. His rhythm was, after all, entirely different from hers, and for the first time he confronted the terrible fate that lay at the bottom of his secret virtue. They were unable to harmonize even later, and Leander, as though he were spawning roe in the lake and through it the river, spent the following nights filling the net beneath him instead of the woman.

On the last evening, Despina bought two candles at the Monastery of Saint Naum. One she gave to Leander, and the other she kept in its little jar. As usual, they set off for the river through the lake, and Leander tried once more. For the last time. When even this failed, because he spilled himself before touching the girl, Despina let him deflower her with the candle. Later, sometime before dawn, she took the oar and pushed the boat up onto the big beach in front of Our Lady of Zahum, the monastery of the Serbian despots, accessible only by water. There she lit the other, her own candle, held it out to Leander, kissed him, and left him in the monastery, while she rowed herself down the Drin.

Distraught and exhausted, they parted forever, convinced that touching was impossible for them. When Leander put ashore with the candle in his hand, the morning service was almost over. Even before he entered the church, he noticed that in the monastery burial rites were being performed for an icon. It was very old, from Pelagonia, and before they placed the icon in the grave and poured wine over it, Leander managed to see the holy painting. It depicted the Virgin Mother nursing her infant, and a man holding an adz—actually it was Saint John the Baptist—standing beside them. The infant's sandal had fallen off his little foot, and the man beside the woman had taken the strap to slip it over the child's heel; the child, feeling the sudden touch, bit his mother's breast, and she, realizing what had happened, glanced at the man putting on the sandal.

Thus the circle closed and an unbroken line flowed between the man, his hand, the heel of the child's foot, the woman's breast, and her gaze, which returned to the man. That line, which Leander took in at a glance before the icon was buried under the earth, looked like the only letter he had ever learned, like the letter theta, Θ, and seeing it, he thought: "So, touching is possible after all!"

Then he entered the monastery and became a monk.

H O W E V E R, Leander was not allowed to become one right away. First of all, because he was still beardless. And when he said where he came from and that his people belonged to neither Eastern nor Western Christianity, but were of their fathers' faith, that of the Bogomils or the Patarenes of yore, he was obliged to spend several years atoning as a novice before being admitted into the brotherhood. During that time he installed himself in the book-filled wooden belfry. He slept on the coiled bell ropes, which jerked beneath him and woke him when the winds rocked the bells at night, and he listened to the drunken lake as with terrible force it hurled pebbles at the monastery doors. But there was no fear in Leander anymore. After what had happened to him with Despina, the stories of sabreurs and the nightmares looked to him like child's play.

"Never full, as though sired by a starving father," the monks would say of him, while he, in a leeward spot near the monastery, nicely arranged the small icon graveyard and planted it with flowers, enclosed it with rocks, and made a gate for it. Late at night, he would light the small candle in the window to block out the darkness, and he would sharpen the quills of the scribe monks and make their ink, out of berries and gunpowder. Then he would spit at the candle and, in the blackness, dream of the day when he would be admitted into the monastery and when he too would learn to write and to read the books lining the walls of the belfry, until he finally dropped off into a sleep that was so hard and fast that by midnight service he was fully rested.

In 1689, he was admitted into the monastic order, and when, at the end of the rites, the prior said to him, "From this day forward, my son, the name Irinei shall thee cover!," Leander heard the bells begin to ring. First they rang at Saint Naum behind the lake, then in their own church, Our Lady of Zahum, and farther northward, in Ohrid, at Saint Sofia, then at Perivlepta, and at Saint Clement, and so on until the ringing had circled the lake and merged on the other side with the ringing at Saint Naum, where it had originated. Just then, into the monastery burst Leander's friend Diomides Subota, all dusty and exhausted, and he announced that Skoplje had been burned down, that the commander of the Austrian troops, General Piccolomini, had died in Prizren, that the plague had swept the Christian army, and that Turkish punitive squads were advancing unremittingly to the north along the Vardar Valley and from Sofia, setting fire and saber to everything in front of them, from villages to monasteries. Diomides Subota and the other merchants had lost all their wares and money, and he had only his beard and shirt when he came to beg Leander for help.

"They'll destroy everything, everything!" he kept saying, twisting his fingers and continually grabbing hold of his ears and pressing them closed with crossed hands, to block out the ringing. While they talked, the other monks were already packing valuables into bags, bolting the doors, pushing out the boats, and sailing miles away from the cove; up on the road above the lake, one could hear and see people leaving their homes and, as they fled north, driving their cattle, having removed the animals' copper bells or blocked them with grass. Just then, a heavy, oily wind full of smoke and malodors descended upon the lake, and Leander realized that the peasants had set fire to whatever they could not take with them. . . .

And so Irinei Zahumski spent not even a day in the monastery as a monk, and once again his writing lessons were put off for better times. He stuck several hooks on his cassock, placed his gold coins close to his chest, toured the icon cemetery, and in front of the grave of the icon from Pelagonia cut off a lock of his own hair and wrapped the cross up in it, the way he had seen women do in his childhood, leaving the cut plaits on their husbands' burial mounds. Then he gave Diomides two gold coins to tie up and hide in his beard, and they set off on their journey.

The very first days of their flight, he saw that there were at least two kinds of people, even among the fugitives. One kind hurried night and day without sleep or respite and kept getting ahead of them, hoping to reap what they had sown in between two camps and two fires. Later they saw these people on the road, exhausted, giving one oke of wax for two of wine, unable to continue the journey. The other kind traveled more quietly, but when they came to rest, they would be frantic, inquire about news from the battlefield, wander around the refugee camps, or sit by the fire and listen to the blind men playing the gusle. Their flight progressed slowly, and soon they were all overtaken by the few who had done as Leander did. He had had trouble persuading Diomides Subota to flee his way. Measuring by Byzantine time, they divided the day in half, and also the night; at midday and at midnight they rested, and they took care to go neither too quickly, so as not to catch up with the Austrian army, which plundered as it fled, nor too slowly, so as not to be overtaken by the Tatar advance guard of the sultan's army. Behind them came the fear of the stragglers, and that fear drove their own ahead of them. Behind all this came the plague and hunger, and behind the plague came the Turks, setting fires, ravaging, and letting the sword feed on everything within reach. Sometimes in this dreadful mayhem, Leander and Diomides Subota would encounter a man standing rigid by the refugee-crammed road; he had planted a seed in a handful of earth and vowed to keep standing there until it blossomed.

"They'll destroy everything, everything! If not one group, then the other," Diomides Subota kept saying, standing on one leg while he warmed the other with his hands. And then, one evening, Leander cut short Diomides' moaning.

"Now, let me tell you something, Diomides. I think it's crazy for us to set fire to everything we leave behind; after all, the enemy won't be able to destroy and burn everything. It's not as though he can dry out the earth the way the frost dries out fish. On the contrary, the more we leave behind and the longer it takes for the enemy to destroy, the more hope we have that at least something of us will remain after we're gone. That's why we shouldn't burn and destroy. We should build, even now. Indeed, we are all builders. We have been given unusual marble to build with: hours, days, and years, with sleep and wine as the mortar. Woe unto him whose copper devours the gold in his pouch, or whose nights swallow up the days. . . ."

As he spoke, Leander was himself surprised by what he was saying; he wondered at his voice, which reached the ear from inside, from the throat, before it reached Diomides, and above all at the sudden decision, which seemed to have been there already, inside him, without his realizing it until this very minute. It was as though all this time he had been walking the road in the dark and had felt the road underfoot, but did not know and would never learn when it was that in the darkness and night he and the road had crossed the invisible bridge beneath. What was obvious was that he was on the other bank; that he had simply made a decision and announced that decision to his companion:

"The time has come for us to build something with our marble, Diomides, the time has come for us to return to the building trade of our ancestors. And henceforward that is just what we shall do. From this day on, we shall build. We shall flee, and build fleeing. If you like, you may join me; if not, then go with your two gold coins in your beard, let them be yours for the trip. Henceforth, at every third stop I shall build. Anything. Whatever I know how."

Diomides Subota was horrified by such an awful proposal. He begged his friend not to err now, when even the sinless were paying with their lives: "You'll be caught by someone who has long since discarded the scabbard and is roaming the world with a bare saber, looking for a neck like yours. The roads are full of such men now. Let's flee while there's still time."

But Leander was no longer afraid of men. He was afraid of women. This strange self-confidence of Leander's, inexplicably bolstered by the gold coins of which he had so many and Diomides so few, broke Diomides Subota. Against his will he consented, remembering how on the wagon trips Leander had coped well between two empires and three faiths, among the languages that blow through there like the winds.

In the morning, Irinei Zahumski, as Leander was now called, paid with pure gold to hire a camel, sat Diomides on it, and gave him ten ducats. He sent Diomides three days' walk ahead of him toward the Ibar Valley to extract the stone, bake the tiles, and prepare the foundation for building. Leander followed on foot, as usual. On the third day, he fell asleep while walking and dreamed of waves, of the water, and a torch in the distant high seas toward which he had to swim, and when he awoke he saw that the waves from his dream were his footsteps, because he was walking in his sleep. And the sabreur was in front of him.

He was straddling the road, enormous, on a horse, its hooves painted red with female brazil-wood. His head was bare, and instead of a pigtail on top of it he sported a set of luxurious red mustaches, neatly combed into a part. When the refugees came nearer, because they all kept coming toward him as though in a trance, Leander among them, the sabreur suddenly slapped himself on the back of the head, with his other hand deftly caught the artificial crystal eye that popped out of his head, and at the same time dashed into the midst of the fugitives watching this spectacle in astonishment, and slashed away with his drawn saber. Then, when he came to Leander, he suddenly stopped. He poked the tip of his saber underneath Leander's curly, sweaty beard and carefully—without hurting him, but resolutely—began to lift his victim's chin until the back of Leander's head caught sight of his ass. At first he seemed to be looking for the gold coins tied up and concealed in the beard, but soon it was obvious that it was Leander's neck the sabreur was staring at. And then he lowered the saber and said to Leander: "Don't be afraid to die; to die means no longer being somebody's son. Only then and thus does this happen. It isn't possible earlier. But I won't cut off your head. Your neck is as though made for Issiah. I give it as a present to Issiah. Let it bring joy to Issiah. You'll be found by Issiah. Maybe you are already being looked for by Issiah. Let him have you!"

And the sabreur trotted off cheerfully, collecting his bloody booty.

When it was all over, Leander, like the others, continued the journey, only he was so tired that he went on sleeping while he walked, and soon he no longer knew where that terrible name Issiah ringing in his ears had come from, and whether he had dreamed of the sabreur or actually met him. On the appointed day, he duly arrived at the scheduled venue and there found Diomides Subota, who had not defected. Near the Zicha Monastery in Gradats, above the mineral waters, Subota had chosen a place, baked the tiles, and dug a foundation as agreed, and was hospitably waiting for Leander with the prepared mash and pile of rocks and the wooden beams bought for a song from peasants abandoning their homes; these peasants were astonished by the crazy camel-driver who paid for things that were for the pyre and the scrap heap. The friends dined together and slept through the night; in the morning, Leander gave Diomides another ten ducats and their next assignation. All of Subota's praying and pleading was to no avail. They parted with tears in their eyes, and Diomides rode off on his camel, fleeing farther north, while Leander remained beneath the blood-soaked snow that fell out of season that year, three days' walk from the Turks and the plague, in no-man's-land between two fronts, between two quarreling empires, between two faiths neither of which was his.

Here he cast off his mantle and, alone in the field, while the river of refugees rolled down the Ibar Valley, and the Serbian monasteries of Milesheva, Racha, Ravanitsa, and Dechani burned, he began building the small Church of the Presentation on soil that for years had been made barren by all the blood, counting the bricks and hours on which his life depended. Along with his own mantle he cast off the seeming placidity and false languor learned from the camels, and, uninhibited by considerations about his surroundings, he set to work with a vengeance, letting loose into the world his inner lightning-time. For the first time since that terrible Ohrid night, he felt like a man again, and at an advantage over others. He grabbed hold of the adz and began squaring off and breaking the rock and building with the speed he had desired and imagined as a boy when watching his grandfather's slow, laborious movements in chiseling stelae all over Bosnia. Now he was a builder again, and he had a mouth full of salty sweat and dust, and ears full of damp hair, and under that damp hair a burning-hot skull, and the rocks and tiles cracked under his hand and under his acrid spit as though it were poisonous, and in his exertion the hot male seed seared his thigh and ate into his clothing. At midday, he stopped work, ate a bit of the mash, and lay down on the riverbank. He would attach the hooks to strands of his long hair and lower his head onto the rock by the river, and then his hair into the water. Thus he slept and fished, exhausted and hungry, in the hope that the fish would enter his dream and spoil it. Then he would get up, build until midnight, and lie down again until he was awoken by the barn owl, a bird that no one had ever seen and which knew when the hearer of its voice would die.

On the third day, when the little Church of the Presentation of the Virgin Mary in the Temple was covered, Irinei Zahumski slipped back into his mantle, consecrated the church, locked it, and continued his flight northward. For three days he fled, and during those three days of fleeing he rested up for the next building. By the Morava River, near Svilajnats, at the appointed place, he found Diomides with the new foundations laid, the mash prepared, the building material collected, but standing next to a dead camel. They ate the camel, hired a horse, and embraced. Only then, as they parted, did Leander, taking a long look at his friend, decide to tell him the worst.

"Now you won't flee north like the others anymore," he told him. "You'll turn east, and the next place where you'll prepare the material and foundations will be closer to the Turkish front line than before. If you are afraid, feel free to leave me—I won't hold it against you—but if you want to stay with me, you must do as I say. And ask for no explanations, because we haven't the time."

Then Diomides Subota decided for the first time to have his own say. "I know," he began, "that he who holds the cup is he who says the Lord's Prayer. But you are not on the right road. Language is now rising against language, and we want to build in these warrish times, which are not for building. Peace is to be won, but nobody has ever won a single war. Small nations like ours have to be able to rule with a scepter hanging overhead, no matter whose scepter it may be. Wisdom and patriotism in peacetime are more important than patriotism in wartime, but just yesterday, before everything burst into flames and your blood mixed with your tears, you didn't know what you'd start with your hatred and love. . . ."

"Look," replied Leander, "a tree is growing out of that window. It isn't waiting for peace in order to grow. And it isn't the builder but the master of the edifice who picks the site, the season, the good weather or the bad. And our job is to build. For whoever promised you peace and happiness, an armful of wheat, or that a better life would follow you on the road as the tail follows a donkey?"

Diomides was in despair, but his continued questions and pleas were in vain. He agreed to all of Leander's conditions, and they parted a third time, not knowing whether they would meet again.

Leander remained in no-man's-land, on a hillock gnawed to the bone, its flesh worn away by winds that had left only its skeleton. He built yet another church dedicated to the Virgin Mary, waiting for the frost to dry out the fish Diomides had left him. He rested at midday and at midnight, and all he feared was losing count of the hours. This time there was no barn owl to rouse him, and he slept, waiting for the noonday sun to awaken him. This time, however, it was not the sun that woke him, but somebody's fingers under his throat, somebody's breath smelling of parsley wine. Leander opened his eyes. Standing next to his edifice was an unsaddled horse with red hooves, and lying in the snow beside it was a huge bitch, whom somebody called by name. The name of the bitch was Pussy. That is how the anonymous voice summoned her, and she trotted over to Leander. Peering down at Leander were the bitch, which seemed drunk because it too reeked of parsley wine, and an enormous gray head that looked soapy and unrinsed. And Leander immediately realized that crouching over him was Issiah.

"I heard of you long ago," the sabreur told him. "I'll tell you what I'm looking for and why I have chosen you. I'm not a headsman in vain, for the fun of it or for gain. I fight neither for the Turks nor for the Germans. I have my own objective. You must have heard the story of the severed head. You separate someone from life like that, stuff his head into a feed bag, take it to the first tavern, place it on the table, comb it to look nice, and drink. You drink for three days and you wait. You wait and keep waiting, and on the third day the head on your table screams. That's how long it needs to realize it is dead. Some need even longer. Much longer. But not every head or every saber can do that. You have to be adroit, like me, in order to pick a good neck with a high Adam's apple like yours, which was made for the saber. You must have been told that already, and I'm sure sabreurs besiege you; indeed, it's a wonder you're still alive, it truly amazes me. Fear not: I'm not a butcher, I'm quick, I can fuck a bird in mid-flight, I can slice a bee with a saber. Were I otherwise, grass would have grown on me long ago, not hair. Now then, say something, so that later I can recognize your voice."

But that same instant Leander lost his voice in horror. And that saved his life. Pointing, he indicated to Issiah that he could not talk. Issiah jumped up as though scalded, brandished his saber, and sliced off Leander's ear, but Leander was unable to scream. The scream stayed inside him for some other time. He was petrified. The sabreur then spat, tossed a silver coin into the snow, and rode off. He said in departing: "That's for your ear. And because henceforward they will call you One-Ear. . . . Now you are marked, and I will easily recognize you if you get your voice back."

People are divided into various clans according to what they wish to forget. Leander stood immobile next to his edifice, not recognizing it anymore. He realized that he had long been traveling and roaming but that all this time his soul had been standing still. He took from his satchel a crust of dry bread that, back at the monastery on the lake, he had dunked in vinegar and then dried. Now he wet it again with snow, and it yielded a handful of good vinegar, with which he washed. He looked around. Waters flowed under the ice, and he listened to their voices. He walked over to a spot, broke the ice, and uttered a few words. The voice of the water repeated them precisely, one by one, like an echo. Leander smiled. He uttered a word in Greek, the word Theotokos, and the water repeated the word in Greek. "If I knew Latin," thought Leander, "I could teach the water Latin." The water was like a parrot. It was able to learn. "The inner side of the water," Leander thought. Just then, overhead, flew a fugue bird, which has a terrible smell that kills other birds in flight, downing them from the sky. This made Leander snap out of his spell or nightmare; he looked at his edifice as though he had just woken up, completely regained his speech, and continued to build as if nothing had happened. He completed the new church and consecrated it like the one before; it was to be remembered in the region as "Milko's monastery."

Then Leander fled onward to the Danube. Somewhere near Smederevo, he found his friend, exhausted and lost in the crush of refugees pushing to cross the water. They ate the horse; Leander hired a boat for Diomides Subota and sent him across the river to Austrian territory with a dozen ducats and instructions to lay the foundations for a new church at the foot of Slankamen in Srem. He himself stayed by the Danube. While the crowd jostled across and floundered in the raging river that springs from Paradise, Leander, off to one side, on the shore near Grotska, began to build his third church. He built it in Rainovats, out of stone, to celebrate the Birth of the Virgin Mary; the higher the wall rose, the harder it was for him, alone and increasingly tired, to reach it with the stone. Sometimes he would cast a glance at the opposite bank of the Danube, where the refugee boats lay on the shore like cast-off shoes. The work progressed more and more slowly; with his last ounce of strength, Leander placed the final stones at the top of the church, far behind schedule. Here he realized that it was not just people and beasts who were of two types that did not live with the same rhythm. His own two hands did not live or react with the same speed. Finishing the church, he noticed that his right hand lagged behind his left. It was as though even inside him there were two kinds of time, venous and arterial time, which did not mix together. At one such moment the stone crushed the ring finger of his left hand. The church was finished, but Leander no longer had either the strength or the time to climb down from under the roof, which was where he was when the Turks reached the Danube. He saw from his hiding place how the cavalry raced to the river. They had been riding without a break, he knew, for more than sixty hours, and now, as they reached the frontier of the enemy empire, many slept, holding on to the manes with their teeth, and they had tied the horses' genitals with the hair of their tails to keep the animals under them from falling asleep on the way as well. He saw how, racing up to the shore, they woke up, how they let the horses drink, and how, exhausted, they peed from the saddle into the water. And he imagined how they would slay him with those pee-stained hands. He saw other soldiers ride into the church and gaze at the spattered blood from Leander's wound, thinking that somebody had already beat them to the slaughter and plunder, and he saw how they set fire to the building. He waited until the fire was blazing so fiercely that the Turkish horsemen had to move slightly away from the heat and the smoke, and then he darted suddenly past the sabers and out the door and tumbled straight into the Danube. He swam with his finger in his mouth so that the river would not draw his blood; the soldiers fired at him and shot at the waves, and under the water he sweated from the strain, pain, and fear. When he had crossed to the other side, it was night, but his road was illuminated. On the other side of the Danube, his church in Rainovats was aflame, and piece by piece the raging-hot burning stones hurtled down the slope into the waves, lighting up the entire shore and fizzling out in the river.

On the new shore, he lay in the mud and reeds and slept. He dreamed he was wearing an earring on the ear he did not have, and that he wove a little basket out of the reeds' shadows and in it caught an ignited bird. He woke up in the shadow of a cloud in a Christian empire, missing a finger and an ear, hungry, but no longer having to hide and flee as before.

"Of course," he thought as he got up from the mud, "a pipe chewed through German words looks completely different from a pipe chewed through Turkish words."

A day's walk away, he heard the bell of the clock tower in Slankamen, but when he reached the town, Diomides was nowhere to be seen. He finally found him chained up in the dungeon. The Jesuits would not let Diomides build a church according to Eastern Christian law, and he was not allowed to dig the foundations or buy and collect the materials until he received special approval from Vienna. In the meantime, he was detained as a suspicious character, and Leander barely got him out by paying a ransom for him. The job undone, the two of them at last stood safe but miserable, for the first time lost amid the throngs of refugees from the south who, swept up by the migration, washed the Danube's shores all the way to Buda. Seeing this, Leander went to the Jesuits and asked for permission to build any kind of church according to any kind of rites, because the main thing to him was to build; nothing else was so important. He was told that he could contribute the money for building the church immediately, of course, but that, since he was a monk of Eastern Christianity, he first had to renounce his original faith and could build only after being admitted into the new, only true Catholic, papal faith, as they put it, and that would take time.

Upon hearing this, Leander decreed for the first time that they should wait. Winter was afoot; stars as big as walnuts shone unblinkingly out of the blue night; the two armies waited in their winter quarters for the spring and summer; Leander's ear and finger were healing and hurt him in two voices, like the playing of a double flute. They had not even rested properly when July came, the time when wines need to be protected against thunder and lightning. The armies were speedily preparing to resume the fighting, while One-Ear and his friend pitched their little tent in Slankamen's field, bought watermelons and poured brandy into them to make them tasty, caught their fill of fish, and waited. And when the Turkish and Tatar hordes had crossed the Danube, captured Belgrade in an unprecedented attack, and moved on to Srem, Leander waited to see who would flee Slankamen first, the Jesuits or he. And so the monks from the Ravanitsa Monastery crossed the Danube in boats, fleeing northward, carrying the body of the Serbian Prince Lazar Hrebelyanovich, saint among tsars, and behind them went the monks of Shishatovats with the relics of the despot Stevan Stilyanovich, but the monk Irinei Zahumski and his friend continued to wait. Then the monks from Krushedol, with the relics of the last Brankoviches, set out along the Danube for Buda and Vienna, and those from Hopovo, with the relics of the holy warrior Theodore Tiron, but Leander and Diomides still sat in the Slankamen field and waited. And then the Jesuits left the deserted town of Slankamen, and Diomides was finally free to make his preparations. Again the edge they had in the face of the Turkish army dissolved, and again they had just three or four days to build, and so in the end they began to build in Slankamen's field a little church named after the Blessed Mary. When its bell too rang out, and when everything was done, Leander embraced his friend and bade him farewell. He told him regretfully that they had reached the point where they must part. Henceforward, Leander would build alone. Irinei Zahumski wanted to build the next edifice in his birthplace, and that meant that he had to ford the Danube again, pass through the Austrian army, penetrate the front ranks of the Turkish fighting force, and again enter its rear lines. When Diomides asked his friend whether it wasn't crazy to go back whence they had barely escaped with their heads on their necks, in lieu of an answer Leander drew him a single letter in the Danubian sand.

After they parted, Diomides went to Buda, and there he built a beautiful house which still stands today. Meanwhile, Leander once more swam the Danube and entered the Turkish rear lines unnoticed. He returned to Bosnia, where, in Drenovitsa, he planned to build a shrine to the Virgin Nursing the Infant. But just then, following its terrible defeat on August 19, 1691, at Slankamen, where the mighty Mehmed-Pasha Chuprilich himself fell, the Turkish army rebounded off the Danube like a great wave and headed back southward. Now it drove everything ahead of it in the opposite direction, slaying and burning in furious retreat. And so Leander found himself once again among the sabreurs, once again in his constant situation of fleeing and building, building and fleeing.

There is a kind of "aquascript" to rivers. Every water has its own writing: rivers inscribe certain letters and leave messages visible only to birds from great heights. Leander inscribed something similar on his journey. The churches he built and left in his wake all had one unusual trait. They were connected by an orbital path and were easiest to find if one followed a certain line that actually constituted the endlessly magnified Greek letter Θ (theta), the first letter of the Holy Virgin's name. The same letter that Leander had learned during his first and only writing lesson in his earliest childhood and had recognized on the icon from Pelagonia. And so he left an inscription in the earth between Zicha, Morava, Smederevo, Slankamen, and Drenovitsa, writing across the vast expanse of his native land the only letter he had learned in the only way he had been given to write—with the mason's adz.

2 /

WHEN HE HAD HAD his fill of roving and building, of toting a mouth full of sweat, of being afraid of the sabreurs between the two wrangling armies, of drinking tea for the deaf in taverns where swearwords are part of every menu, his hair moth-eaten, himself illiterate, one-eared, and fingerless, Leander went back to his father in Belgrade, which was reportedly again held by the Austrian garrison. He returned to the city in the rainy season of the year, constantly treading on snails, which cracked under his feet as though made of glass and kept getting in his way. He returned to

Belgrade thinking how really he hardly knew his own father at all.

He found his father alive and alone, talking as he walked to who knows which of his long-dead peers. His pleasure at the sight of his son was somehow distant: "You age like wine or a Bukhara carpet: you improve with the years. But take care not to become too old for school."

At night, his father would lie down in the boatman's net and, in his thoughts and memories, correct each and every word uttered in the conversations of his youth. He wanted to go over his entire life once more, through all the decades, every question, every answer, to correct whatever was necessary, and to see how this corrected life would turn out.

In the morning, he would go to the hospital-ship anchored off the shore of the Sava to devote himself to his secret work. He was literate; he even always put a little cross in place of the letter "a"; but he was unable to teach reading and writing to Leander. He took his son to the Ruzhitsa Church, where they would teach him how to chant, saying: "You can salute only with the cap you have." And Leander, alias Irinei Zahumski, demonstrated that he knew how to chant in church better than anybody, but his father was not surprised, just as he was not really interested in what his son had been doing all those years he had been absent from town. In short, father and son knew nothing about each other.

As time passed, Leander noticed that his father had no fixed name; rather, passersby, both known and unknown, addressed him by the first name that came into their heads, and he answered to all these names equally. It seemed to Leander that his father was buried in and had virtually disappeared under the unusual appellations people gave him, maliciously sometimes. His father pointed out these passersby, cautioning him: "There are those who pull their shirts out through the sleeve all their lives; beware of their kind." He taught him how to tie nautical knots, and would say from under the net of red loops, mending it:

"Look at those knots and knotlets; they are done so that the rope holds its own tail tight and doesn't let it come loose. No matter how hard you pull, it won't give way, because it is forced into exertion by nobody other than itself. And so it is with people. Their paths are so tied into knots that they sustain one another in seeming peace and form an impenetrable military border, whereas actually, as on a net when it's drawn out of the water, they're constantly strained to breaking point. Because each of them does what it must do, not what it would like to do.

"For instance, you yourself, son, are not softly kneaded. You've got strong blood; it could lift rocks. But that is not enough. You and your generation are not destined for empire, but for subjection and hard labor. And for you it makes no difference whom you toil for, the Turk or the German. You won't even be able to sing because you want to, but because somebody rules your mind like a little organ and puffs it up to sing. . . ."

Not believing in such a fate, and surprised that his father did not care what had happened to him during all those years before his return to Belgrade, Leander began to revert to his masonry. For the moment, in his own, pleasant way. He went increasingly often to watch how the new town was growing. It sprang up as though from water, as though Leander himself had built it with his mind and painted it with his eyes.

He usually sat on top of the hill in the fortress and rested his eyes upon the wing of a bird, which would plunge down headlong, and he would let the bird carry his gaze around the town springing up along the river like the stone teeth of the earth, renewing itself from within. Thus, if he was flying on a bird, nothing could be left to chance or pass

unnoticed; with time, through the network of these
flights, he was bound to cover and observe the entire
ancient city, its every nook and cranny; Leander,
blinking as though he were swallowing, drank in
every detail that his bird-borne gaze would touch in
that descent. Carried on plumed wings, he observed
the Neboisha Tower, which was mirrored in two
rivers at once, the Sava and the Danube, and
through its facing windows he could see a patch of
the sky from the other side of the water, which it
hid from view. His gaze flew past Belgrade's bell
towers, which could be heard in two empires, and
when the bird, carried off by a sudden current of
air, would streak through the newly built triumphal
arch of Charles VI, the conqueror of Belgrade, and
soar up, frightened by the narrow strait it had penetrated, he ascended too; racing on wings to the
Ruzhitsa Church, he touched the drummer who
beat his drum at the city gate, whose face was invisible but whose every button could be counted when
they all flashed in the sunlight. Carried by the bird,
Leander's gaze again plunged down headlong, with
a slight shudder, to the Sava's meadows at the foot
of the fortress, where by the stone steps cows had
broken into the small enclosed field of leeks next to
thatched huts and grazed, so that the next day their
milk would smell of onion. And again there would

be in his eyes a bit of blue Sava water, several rows of fine new homes, with brass apples at the doorways to hold on to while cleaning one's shoes on the sickle beneath them. Then he would suddenly be carried off to the Panchevo side, where one could see the spot where the grass was bitter, skirted by the cattle. Here one could feel how the wind carried the water of the Danube back to the group of soldiers marching in formation, their bayonets so agleam that they looked wet. The town above them, which the Austrians and Serbs were fortifying at an accelerated pace, was full of clocks that called out to one another above the governor's residence, which had as many windows as the year has days. The shops were new and full, the churches had crosses of three kinds and three faiths, the nicely enclosed gardens attracted nightingales from both banks of the Sava, and carriages passed by the gardens, entering a downpour that enveloped only two or three streets. Again in his eyes there was a bit of cloud, of reed, and of the mist that drifts along the Sava and flows into the deeper, swifter mist of the Danube. On the other side, slanting rays of sunlight could be seen in the woods, and in them Leander felt the hot and cold scents of the smoking thickets. The town was back in his gaze. He could see the masons finishing the Ragusan church: the carpenter swung and struck with his adz, but the blow was heard only in the ricochet of the adz, so that the bird could fly between the sound and its source in the blade. Then Leander saw how the wind angered the bird, carrying it off course, and how down below the bell swayed but the sound was not heard until later, as though it had broken away from its metal stem. He saw how the sound quivered, crossing the river with the bird, and how it came upon the Austrian cavalry horses, which pricked up their ears in the pasture on the other side of the Sava. And then he could follow the ringing, and how on its journey it spread, like the shadow of a cloud, toward Zemun and a group of shepherds, and how they, upon hearing it, turned their small heads toward Belgrade, which had already plunged back into silence on its side of the water. And then the bird in sharp flight would sew onto the sky, like a lining, this world in which Leander lay caught, as if in a net. Because it sufficed to open a single gate for the Turkish horsemen and beheaders to storm into Belgrade and in no time at all turn this treasure above the rivers, which defied them on the edge of their world, into dust and smoke. Leander did not know—he could not even dream—that, there on the ramparts of Belgrade, he was the last systematically to observe this town, which was to disappear without a trace, and forever, just a few years later.

In October of that same year, Leander's father took him to see the Russians arriving in town. Leander had expected horsemen with spears thrust into their boots, but instead of an army he beheld a three-horse sleigh, and out of it stepped a lone man in a huge fur coat. The stranger had two sprigs of sweet basil stuck in his nostrils; he stepped down from the sleigh and walked straight into the metropolitan's office. Behind him the other arrival carried in the chest and the icon. That was all.

"That's your teacher," his father told him. "He will teach you how to write. They asked to have everyone who can sing in church sent to him. Don't worry, there are others who are illiterate and warstalled like you. And they're not much younger than the teacher. But remember, the literate look at the book, the learned look at the wise, and the wise look at the sky or a skirt—which the illiterate can do too . . ."

And so Leander started to learn reading, arithmetic, and a bit of Latin as well. During this time, before their very eyes, Maxim Terentyevich Suvorov, as the Russian teacher was called, lost his hair. His brow wrinkled like a stocking from some inner unyielding effort, and his skin became so thin that the blue of his eyes showed through the closed lids. In class one could quite clearly discern a red tongue moving behind his cheeks, and during recess one could see how, somewhere under the ears, that tongue shivered from the Ukrainian winds that raged in the Russian's mouth.

"All of us here are between the hammer and the anvil, and we are kneading pepper-bread," he was wont to tell his students in incomprehensible half-Serbian, which was said to be the language of his tsar. It was only when he taught them Latin that the foreigner was for a moment relieved of his fear; eagerly he instructed them in the art of good memory, mnemonics, developed through the examples of Demosthenes' and Cicero's speeches, and taught from a big notebook on which they stealthily read the inscription *Ad Herennium*. In order to remember a text well, according to the Russian teacher, you had to recall to memory the façade of a building you often passed and were therefore familiar with. Then you had to imagine that you were opening in succession every window and door of that building, and into each aperture, loophole, or skylight you had to declaim one of Cicero's long sentences. Thus, by the time you had finished touring the building in your mind's eye and declaiming a part of the speech through each window or gate, the address would be remembered and could be repeated without great difficulty. In this way, students at Belgrade's Serbian-Latin school learned by heart the whole of Cicero's speech *In Catilinam,* and then the Russian brought them the Latin translation of a lovely Greek story for them to learn as well. The story was in verse; it had been composed by one Musaeus the Grammarian, perhaps a Christian, more than a thousand years earlier, and it was called *The Love and Death of Hero and Leander.* This poetic tale was composed in Greek, and the Latin translation had been printed in Venice in 1494, the Russian explained. It was from this Leander in Musaeus' poetic tale that Radacha Chihorich, the descendant of the famous stonemasons, now already earless and advanced in years, finally got his new, sixth name. This is how:

The Russian did not remember the names of his students. He found it especially difficult to pronounce the name of his oldest pupil, Radacha Chihorich. He once asked what obstacle had stood between the two lovers Hero and Leander (who, following the light of the burning torch, swam every night through the stormy waves of the sea to Hero's tower). And the oldest pupil, whose name the teacher was unable to pronounce, gave an unexpected answer. Radacha, on his journeys as a merchant in Constantinople, had been to the Hellespont and passed through Sestos, and there he and his santir-playing compatriots had been taught to sing the Greek song about Hero and Leander, and instead of a coin for a tip, somebody had tossed into his instrument a tiny cameo bearing the image of Hero. He knew that Europe was separated from Asia not only by water but also by wind—that is, by time. And so he said that perhaps it had not been water and the waves of the sea that had separated Hero from Leander but something else, which they had to master in order to reach each other. He was thinking of the girl he had been unable to reach in that boat on Lake Ohrid.

"What else could it have been, other than water, one of the four elements making up the world?" the Russian asked in astonishment, to which his oldest pupil calmly replied: "Perhaps it was the waves of time, not of the sea that separated Hero from Leander. Perhaps Leander swam through time, not through water."

This reply elicited tumultuous laughter from the class, and Radacha Chihorich was left with the name Leander ever after. That is what the Russian called him too. The pupil was not angered by it; he learned the poetic tale of Hero and Leander by heart, and instead of Cicero's speeches, through the windows of the patriarchal palace, where they were already installing lovely tabernacles for writing, with small windows at the back, he recited at night the odd verse from his favorite poem. In both Greek and Latin.

At the time, the students had started, with particular pleasure, to tour and examine the metropolitan's palace being built in Belgrade, which embraced more than forty rooms.

In this edifice, for days and weeks, every morning on their way to school and every evening touring it in their thoughts before going to sleep, Leander and his classmates spoke a sentence from their lessons into the keyholes, church offices, studies, dining halls, and choirs. Touring the library, which had two separate locks, one for locking from without and the other from within, or the bedchambers of the metropolitan, facing west, and of his courtiers and guests, facing east (so that the younger might awaken before their elders), the boys recited the sentences: "Where are we in the world? In what city do we live? Assembled among us here are the elders, who are thinking about everybody's downfall, about the ruination of this city. . . ." And so, slowly and imperceptibly, the speech etched itself into his memory. "... *Quid enim mali aut sceleri fingi aut cogitari potest, quod non ille conceperit?* They squandered their patrimony, plunged their property into debt, lost their money long ago, and more recently their faith as well, but for all that they have retained the same passion they had when they lived in affluence...."

The building was not yet finished, and the palace was being occupied wing by wing. Scalelike in the far recesses of the rooms, the high rounded arches of the connecting halls held lustrous furnishings: fireplaces, floral-painted porcelain stoves, fabrics in velvet and brocade, china made of Carlsbad, Viennese, and English porcelain, silver cutlery from Leipzig, glassware made of Czech crystal and stained cut glass, candlesticks and mirrors from Venice, musical clocks, and chests full of men's silk socks. "Go, then, and deliver me from this fear: if it is real, so that it may not torment me, if it is false, so that I may finally stop being afraid," the pupils recited the Latin phrases like prayers, winding up their lessons just when it looked as though their teacher, the Russian, would crumble inside like those monasteries they had seen around Belgrade, abandoned and overgrown with trees. When this actually happened, and the Russian teacher went back to Srem, Leander continued his education in an Austrian military-engineering school for junior officers.

And just as he was about to finish that school, it was said in town that two new towers were due to be built at the Sava gate to replace the old ones, destroyed in 1690. The building of one of them, the northern one, had been entrusted to an experienced builder, Sandal Krasimirich, and he had already laid the foundations. Things did not go quite so easily with the other, southern, tower. Sandal's colleagues, who were building in Belgrade at the time, all refused to work on it, because it had to be built on marshland.

"Before getting to the water, you must dig the well," they said. And so work on it simply never got off the ground. When the work was already long overdue, a great piece of news was learned one morning, to everybody's surprise.

That dawn, Leander had been awoken by an intoxicating smell which pervaded the house from outside. It was his father urinating; his urine always smelled strongly of musk deer, a garden of lilies or sandalwood. And this heady smell would wake up the household and the children in the neighborhood.

"Chihorich is having an attack of wisdom

again," they would say then. Indeed, in these late years of his life, Leander's father was wise only when he peed.

That morning, the father emitted the smell of sandalwood in liquid form and scolded his son: "Young a gallant, old a beggar! As though he hadn't been nursed through the third night, God forbid! Who knows where he went off to and where! He left one without attaining the other. . . ."

And so Leander knew that his father knew. And that meant that the whole town knew. Indeed, Leander had agreed to build the southern tower. This meant that he appeared as a rival to the famous Sandal Krasimirich, for whom birds hunted fish in the Sava and Danube, driving them into the nets, and whose name the horses snorted in three languages, so powerful was he.

Sandal Krasimirich was considerably older than Leander; in age he could have been his father. And in position Leander could have been his servant. Krasimirich had entered Belgrade with the Austrian army in 1717 under a leather helmet that was tied to his beard so that he had to snip it off when it was time to remove his war gear. Having done so, and being finally left bare-headed, he discovered he was completely gray. During the war, he had been attached to the Austrian army's engineer corps, which had built bridges on boats, and in town, following the blueprints of the Swiss mercenary Nicolas Doxat, he joined in rebuilding the destroyed ramparts and towers. He had no other training for this except what he had acquired in the campaigns, but he retained the confidence of the military even in peacetime, and was entrusted with building several small powder-plants and warehouses in the city. Although these projects took place during autumns when the rains filled the food dishes faster than the workers could empty them, Sandal completed the job. His craft started coming into demand in a town that was growing after the war, and he and his helpers moved farther and farther away from home as the letter "r" moved away from the end of the names of the months.

"Don't expect me home in months without a bone in their name," Krasimirich would tell his wife, and, truly, when the letter "r" disappeared from the name of the month, Sandal and his helpers left their families, not to be seen until the first heavy rains, when, in the month of September, the magic letter of their repose would again enter the tail of the year.

Sandal Krasimirich began building his tower the way he had learned and with people who were used to him. He stuck a gold coin in the bread, lowered it into the water of the Danube, and started. The funds had been provided because the authorities in town knew him, and they unstintingly gave him buckets of salt and copper cauldrons of wine. But Leander had to start by strewing the marsh with rocks and sand; he built, in other words, "upon tears of milk," and that they did not count. The paymasters, who knew Sandal Krasimirich, shied away from the young man, who had lost his own path, and was now joining that of others, who had not sown blood during the war, and to whom the land had not returned blood, and he undertook to do what Sandal Krasimirich considered unfeasible. And so, from the very beginning, Leander built, so to speak, in his own way and sway.

When the first floors of the two towers sprang up, it was immediately evident that Sandal's was the one people were gathering around. Their chins greasy from breakfast, perked awake by coffee, his peers and Austrian craftsmen came to marvel at the new edifice draped in scaffolding.

"Our eyes have not yet had their fill of beauty, nor our hearts been stirred as they can, and look what Sandal has done! It's a miracle," they said, fingering the stone that was as rosy as the underbelly of a bread loaf. They grabbed the backs of their necks, measuring the height to which the future tower would climb, and praised the architect.

During this time, Leander had dragged a boat to his marsh in the middle of the building, and there in the boat, where it was more or less dry, he ate, he slept, but mostly he kept an eye on his drawings, figures, and rulers, which, laid out on his arm, he carried with him even to the scaffolding that had been installed on the inside of the edifice, so that one could not follow the work on the outside. At night, he would light the lamp at the tip of the boat, and by its illumination build the tower from within, as though he were sailing somewhere through the dark—not along the rivers, whose roar could be heard, but upward, toward the invisible clouds, which also roared when torn by the wind or by the horns of the young moon. He felt as though he had been stowed in the womb of a ship and anchored for a lifetime in a port he had never even seen, as though the only way out was through a single porthole, straight into death. Now, suddenly, this ship in unknown waters started to move and set sail for the equally invisible but stormy open sea.

He had to sail unerringly through the night, watching only the dreams of others in his own. It was with such feelings, calculating by candlelight, that Leander wrested his tower from the dark. In the course of his calculations, he concluded that only geometric bodies had the same value both in heaven and on earth, however they may be denoted. This was not true of numbers. Their significance was variable, and Leander realized that in building he also had to take into account the origin of the numbers, not merely their momentary value. Because, like money, numbers are rated differently under different conditions, he decided, and their value is not constant. Once, though, he did seem to waver and almost abandoned the entire art of counting taught him by the Russian with the blue eyes that changed color in his sleep. At one moment, it seemed to him that Sandal Krasimirich had used numbers more purposefully than he, and that the Swiss school where his rival had been educated held the advantage over his own, Byzantine school. Indeed, one morning, some workers came running from the shores of the Sava and reported to Sandal Krasimirich that his tower had risen above the ramparts and was already reflected in the water! In no time, the news had spread all over town. A big festivity was planned, and Leander, feeling bested and behindhand, secretly instructed a muleteer to go and see whether his own, southern tower was visible in the Sava as well. The muleteer replied indifferently that of course Leander's southern tower was visible, and had been for a long time, so there was no reason to go down to the river. At about this same time, Leander noticed that his need for supervisors and workers was growing, and that his peers and schoolmates, whom he had hired, were thinning out and disappearing from the building site one by one.

Among Sandal's friends, who had come to Belgrade when and in the same way as he, there was one by the name of Shishman Gak. He was versed in both construction and the stars, but he no longer built. He believed that the deed should reflect the power of the doer, and that, if this proportion was absent, it was pointless even to start work. Thus he held the night in his mouth and occupied a spacious house that abutted an Austrian gunpowder depot; the place was abandoned and dangerous, for, although a fire inside it could not spread to the powder magazine, the reverse was inevitable. Undisturbed, Gak arranged in it his books, instruments, binoculars, and leather globes and (so it was thought) spent his time in idleness, looking for gold rain and female stars.

"Even the bird falls, why not the man," it was said of him. And evil tongues added that he was not really capable of transporting his enormous knowledge from place to place. In the process of moving, it melted like ice, and in each new place, outside his powder magazine, he would be left helpless and empty, and his skill and art would become brittle and unreliable, his memory for names and figures would fail him, and he could no longer be counted on because he behaved like a transplanted tree. One day, at dusk, when there was no one left at the construction site, this man, whose gaze aged noticeably in conversation, and whose hair always had flies in it, unexpectedly dropped in and toured Leander's tower. He licked the stone, tested the mortar under his fingers, tossed a tuft of grass into the lye, and then smelled it, placed three fingers in a corner, and measured something in the air. Finally, he addressed Leander:

"An ear instead of a pillow, and all that work, all that knowledge," he said. "I don't know where and when you learned so much, but be careful! Nobody knows where the morning will end: in the ditch or in the attic. It's good that you hung the scaffolding on the inside. It is with an uneasy eye that these people around us would watch you build faster and better than Sandal. That should be concealed for as long as possible...."

Thus spoke Gak, who was known to have sown his days into the night. Departing, he turned around once more and said: "Do you want some advice? Friendly advice? Here it is: when you finish the tower, don't ever build anything again. You'll be the happier for it. Anyway, you've already shown all there is to show. Don't build anymore!"

And so he left, and Leander went on with his work. Increasingly lonely, he would sometimes look for company, and it was to be found in abundance on the other side of the Sava gate. The first time he appeared, which was during the celebration of Sandal's tower rising above the ramparts, they received him nicely. He washed his hands behind his back as usual, and joined the crowd. Some of Leander's peers, who had worked with him before but had now gone over to Sandal Krasimirich, took him around and showed and explained to him enthusiastically the masonic feats at the top of the tower, where the rectangular part of the wall was being rounded. Among those singing the praise of Sandal's tower was Gak himself, but, like the others, he did not mention Leander's tower, nor was Leander's name pronounced, as though everyone had forgotten it.

There were strange folk about, who laughed when they were surprised, folk who held their tears in their noses and simply hawked when they felt bad. There were women Leander recognized (although they did not recognize him) because he had slept with them, sometimes hurriedly, somewhere in a hay cart, returning from the field at dusk, and he would pay the owner to climb down and leave the cartload to the newly forged couple for half an hour, until they reached the city gate. The women soon forgot him, knowing at first glance that he was the kind who was heavy as a bell if he entered them but who thought: Happiness is a job you love and a woman who loves. Women do not like that sort. And so they went to Sandal Krasimirich and his builders and found what they needed there. Of Leander, who spawned his roe and milt in the hay instead of in them, they would say: "His father, when he catches a big sturgeon, fucks it all night long, and doesn't fry and eat it until the next day. This one can't do even that."

Among the other curious people who enlarged the number of those admiring the progress made on Sandal's tower, Leander that evening noticed a figure behind the fire, shouldering a net of red knots. Sporting high rubber boots, it mingled with the crowd for a while and then, unbeknown to Leander, moved off into the dark.

"He's gone to bury his dead in the boats," some observed aloud, and thus, after so many decades, Leander finally learned what his father actually did, and how and on what he himself had been nurtured. On dead bread.

As though he had not heard a word, Leander asked: "How will you make the transition to the round part of the dome? With the help of a squinch or a pendentive?"

"With the help of a squinch," replied some. "With the help of a pendentive," thought others. They all turned toward Sandal, but he was busy with another conversation and merely smiled disdainfully, as though the question had been unseemly.

In the evening, when he returned to his tower, Leander stuck a candle in the bread, lay down in the boat, coiled his pigtail like a snake under his head, and gazed at the big rectangular cake of darkness that stood by the window on the inside of the building. He lay there and waited for something to happen. Something had to happen and to change, he sensed and hoped. It was the dead of night everywhere, even in his ears; nothing could be heard from the darkness, which was deaf and smelled of the earth, of a mouth after wine. A cockchafer had flitted into his jerkin, and it buzzed and simply would not come out. "On a night like this," thought Leander, "even dogs don't bite, just fleas, as though you had a shirt full of stars blinking all over you. And anything you didn't see has flown away. . . ."

Then he got up, put out the candle, and groped in the dark for the walls of the tower. It was there, cold and real; it existed as much as he himself existed. And in the morning, something really did happen, just as a bell buried underground suddenly begins to hum in a storm.

The guest was careful not to trip over anything, not to get confused by the knobs, to sit down quickly and smartly, so that everything would look as natural and ordinary as possible, as though it had happened many times before and did not rank as anything extraordinary or strange at all. Sandal Krasimirich took hold of his mustache with his teeth, as they say, and paid a personal call on Leander, not at his building site but at his father's little fisherman's hut on the shore. They sat on barrels, their hands cupping their knees, and the conversation began over the toes of their shoes. In mid-word, Sandal withdrew from his sleeve a roll of papers and drawings, held the sleeve with his fingers the way one does when putting on a coat, with the sleeve wiped the dust off the papers, and offered them to Leander with the words: "Here are my calculations and my blueprints. I don't think everything there is quite as it should be, but you'll check that easily enough. No well is without mud. Do me this favor. It would be awkward in front of everyone if your tower were to be finished before mine. . . ."

After these words, the visitor turned around at the door and added nonchalantly: "By the way, please draw for me the squinch that will support the round part of the dome. I'm in a big hurry and haven't got the time."

That is how Leander discovered that Sandal had not succeeded in transferring the support of the tower from the rectangular to the round part.

"Well, well, the meadow has teeth," he thought, and calculated everything that was needed, but he could not make corrections on what had already been done, because the mistakes had been built into the very foundations, which were unable to support the kind of tower that had been envisaged. In the morning, Leander went to Sandal and brought him the papers and corrections, thinking how people said that dogs never entered the dwelling of Sandal Krasimirich, because they sensed how fiercely he could hate. Leander told him frankly that he had to finish the tower immediately, for the top would not hold out. Sandal received all this unusually calmly, collected his papers, thanked Leander, and apolo-

gized for having to leave so quickly, but his students
were waiting for him. Leander saw that, in a ware-
house next to Sandal's edifice, building courses had
been temporarily arranged upon orders from the
metropolitan's palace, and among Sandal's students
Leander recognized some who had studied and
learned with him how to transfer the rectangular
part of a tower to the squinch and move from the
squinch to the rounded top.

And so Sandal's tower, as indeed Leander had
predicted, had to be completed before it reached the
height prescribed for observation towers, but Sandal's friends, the clergy in town, the soldiers in the
prince's court, and others in the taverns, speaking
over glasses into which they steered their tobacco
smoke, said that the architect had finished his job
ahead of schedule. It was concluded that Sandal had
overtaken that "short-winded" mason on the other
side of the Sava gate, and that Leander was running
late with his building.

Sandal's northern tower was ceremoniously covered with lead; an archer was assigned to make sure
that no crow flew overhead before it was consecrated, an ox was roasted, the scarecrow was im-
mured in the new edifice, and a cock was placed on
top of the tower. And then, in the morning, Sandal's
tower cast a shadow on Leander's southern tower,

and henceforward Leander built in that shadow. With festivities that could be heard even on the other side of the Danube and the Sava, the new building was opened to the public, but Leander was still spending the nights in his boat at the bottom of the southern tower, which had not even reached the point where it was supposed to become a round wall. Near the end of the job, he was already without assistants, without money, as alone as a nail in dough, and every morning the soldiers would warn him not to create a mess around the edifice, because he would be slapped with a fine for dirtying the street. Friends steered clear of drafts in the tower, and he worked with a handful of builders who, so as not to be reduced to eating straw, sneaked over from the Turkish side to earn the odd penny, and at the end of the week returned home by night in boats, wrapping the oars in their shirts, their words costly and their lives cheap.

Having gone mute from loneliness and the altitude, Leander chewed his tongue like a bitter fruit in his mouth; he spoke with his hands and his stone, and at moments it seemed to him that a word without something hard and heavy to support it, a word that would not be the name of something that could carry it up to the sturdy pedestal or transport it from place to place, looks like a bird without feet, which has no place to alight and builds its nest and hatches its chicks on water.

One night, he lay down in the boat and felt how his pulse was throbbing against the wood, how his hair was hurting him, the heat singeing the tips of his ears, and the frost permeating his bones from inside; he realized that all his life he had carried inside him a terrible winter, the way a mirror carries its silence with it everywhere. The nights had passed by somewhere, on the other side of the tower, and the snow had piled up, when his father came and brought news. He sat down, brewing herbs and maize tea for his son, and, invisible somewhere in the corner of the tower, conversed with an unknown and, to the patient, equally invisible collocutor.

"The first sip and the first morsel should be thrown to the devil," Leander's father sighed in the dark on the other side of the flame, "but how can they be thrown by someone who steals his own cap and goes begging for bread? I remember I hadn't even cut my permanent teeth and I already had sack in hand, begging and stuffing the bag. From here to the Land of No Return, on to the Back of Beyond, and home again. I would bring back a hundred morsels of bread and turn them out on the table. Heels, crusts, slabs, pieces, scraps, tidbits, lumps, orts, crumbs, yesterday's rye in pilaf that's turned, the day before yesterday's crêpes, beggar's polenta, buckwheat cake, and berry wheat-cake; pie's castaways and curdled 'God's cheeks,' oat bread and soldiers' wheat-bread tooth-breakers, Jewish matzos, and monastic one-monthers made with grass so as not to turn hard; breads made of fishmeal flour and oat toast; cornbread without cheese and cornbread without crackling; underdone twin rolls, fallen-flat pussy puffs, and moldy turnovers, oat rings that are hung on the horns of cattle for All Souls' Day, Grandma's sighs, soldier's bread from the last war, droopy Saint Day cakes, stale popovers, 'merry man's' bread, whose very name must not be mentioned, or the one that is called 'Papa-bought-me-a-pretzel-but-I-goofed-and-ate-it-without-bread'; melba toast and French toast, hardtacks and the cakes you send to Constantinople to buy back a life, leavened bread and wafers, spitballs, crumble and breadstuff, oatcakes, millet bread, rye bread, eucharistic wafers, and barley bread, all mushy and mealy, crustless fillings and fillingless pies, curdled cornmeal, flat snots and a handful of runts, all gut-gnawers and ass-ticklers—literally everything that ever heard the words, 'Take that away!'—came from all over the world onto your table to tell you how that world was yesterday what you will be tomorrow. You must fashion every morsel differently, and when you make off with the big workman's bread on the stove and put it under your head at night, you'll be rich for three days! It crackles under your ears, it warms and yawns when you break it, and you, full, covered, sleep on it, hiccup in your sleep, and dream of wine. Liters of wine. Barrels of wine, caravans of wine. And not a teardrop of wine anywhere! . . .

"That's how it is with us poor. But, as if that weren't bad enough, now even those above us are stumbling. Cranes recently poisoned the city wells with their shadows, and lots of people perished. Two men even carried Krasimirich on a rug in between the horses to the metropolitan's palace, to the herbal healing room. He is worn out too; they say that long work on the tower has squeezed him dry, building has drawn the sweat out of him, and that is not good: a man without sweat is like a person without a shadow. How unfortunate for someone who's as good as gold down to his nails. His hair should be replanted, that's how good he is. And he carried his age so well, like a pregnant woman who manages to carry her child pridefully. It's a shame, he could have lived twice that long, to the benefit of the people and the town, but, there you are, attention is not paid where it is due. But I hope he will recover, God willing. And so, I hope, will my son here, who drank too much unsettled water, and became weak...."

And then this stream of saltless words would abruptly run dry, old man Chihorich, Leander's father, would go out in front of the tower, and suddenly out of the darkness would waft the marvelous sprawling scent of sandalwood, and completely different words would issue forth:

"You think that you die just like that. You lie down and die. But it's not that simple. Everything behind and ahead of us lasts much longer than we suspect. For instance, do you know the difference between the heart and the soul? When we cast our inner eye on our heart, we see it as it is at that very moment. When we look into our soul, we see it as it was many thousands of years ago, not as it is now, because that's how long it takes for our gaze to reach the soul and observe it; in other words, that's how much time it takes for the light of the soul to reach our inner eye and shine upon it. Sometimes that's how we see a long-vanished soul. If that's how it is with the soul, you can imagine how it is with death. Human death lasts exactly as many years as human life, and maybe even much longer, because death is a complex affair, a job and an effort that's harder and longer than human life. . . . Your death can live twice as long as you. . . ."

But then, at the crucial point, the old man's flow was suddenly cut short when that second flow underneath him ran dry, and from Leander's father again issued forth pure gibberish.

And Leander did indeed recover. Suddenly, in the middle of the night, his nose opened up, and for the first time in many long weeks he inhaled and was surprised by the smells of his own body, alien and strong as though he were about to die. He felt that all this time through him had passed a myriad of dreams, which he did not remember, just as the banks of the Sava showed that during the preceding nights vast waters had thundered past, although nobody counted the waves in the dark. With the first butterflies Leander went out into the tilting meadow, and it seemed to him that the water on the river was high, higher than the banks, and that only a miracle was holding him on his hillock. And so, his ears drunk and his eyes sober, he continued work on the tower.

As though in a dream, he finished building, opened the windows near the top of the edifice, and installed the shutters and gates in the apertures near the bottom; suddenly he noticed that into each of

these apertures he was inadvertently reciting, as he
had once done as a student, a verse from the poetic
tale of Hero and Leander:

Leander, his eyes crazed with love,
Kept staring at the young girl's delicate neck. . . .

But this time Leander was not doing it to memorize
the text. This Greek text he had learned by heart
long ago. He recited the verse about Hero and
Leander for the last time and forgot it forever after,
leaving it in the windows and doors of the building
he had built the way one buries a secret in a pit:

Κὰδδ' Ἡρὼ τέθνηκε σὺν ὀλλυμένῳ
παρακοίτῃ
ἀλλήλων δ' ἀπόναντο καὶ ἐν πυμάτῳ
περ ὀλέθρῳ.

"This world does not belong to us anyway,"
thought the mason, "but to our fathers and their
peers, and they feel and act like its sole owners. I
and my peers were and remain the wretched little
servants of those who descended into this town lean-
ing on their sabers and who swam over with foreign
armies. From our fathers' generation we acquired

not only the position of little servants, but also a
burned out, half-destroyed world, a hungry childhood, and those who gave it to us turned it into a
virtue, to which we are still slaves. And we ourselves, we are here to toss the odd word into the
windows and doors we pass. . . ."

When the tower was completed, and when the
cock was placed atop it, Leander climbed up to it
with a glass of wine in his hand and the desire to
consecrate the edifice and observe the city from high
above. But in the abyss below him there was no city
at all. The top of the southern tower had pierced
the clouds, and from it one could see nothing on the
ground. Up there high silences reigned like an overflowing pond, broken only occasionally by barking
or the clang of an ax from the depths down
below. . . .

From the ground, in turn, one could not see its
top or the cock that was supposed to show citizens
the time and the winds. Leander climbed down
confused and frightened. The crowd that had assembled at the foot of the tower stared up at the
infinite heights where the tower hid in the stillness
of the sky. Then the crowd dispersed, grumbling
that nobody could know what he had made up
there in the clouds. Only Shishman Gak walked up

to him, shook his hand, and mumbled: "Splendid, peerless; now you don't have to build anything anymore. Leave that to others. . . ."

But Leander's travails did not end there. With springtime, when the clear skies struck, when the eyes sent the sight far off, both towers appeared simultaneously to the inhabitants of the city, glistening in the sun on one side and somehow dark and stumbling down the other. And it transpired that the cocks crowning them did not show the same time. The cock on Sandal's small tower kept spinning and jumped every minute, showing a new wind, sensitive to any, even the slightest, breeze and change. The cock on Leander's big tower showed some other time of its own, conditions of its own, obviously linked to the broad expanse of its view and to the rowdy winds that did not blow down on the ground.

"You can't see anything properly from that height," some said.

"It is not good to strain one's sight either; what do we need two cocks for?" others sometimes wondered, and there were suggestions that Leander's southern tower should be shortened and leveled with Sandal Krasimirich's northern tower, so that it too might serve the daily needs of the city. And when the towers were engraved on a copper plate from which maps bearing the image of the town of Belgrade could be printed, the engraver, one of that Russian's students, made Leander's tower somewhat smaller, and that of Sandal (who had commissioned him to do the job) just slightly bigger than they actually were, so both fit onto the same sheet of copper. Indeed, this sheet of copper brought Leander once more, for the last time, before one of the sabreurs who had been chasing him all his life. Only this time it was the sabreur of sabreurs.

3 /

L EANDER consecrated his tower on the day of Saint John the Forerunner, who baptized Christ, and the icon depicting the Baptist's severed head on a plate was carried in a circle around the tower. Two weeks later, Leander embarked on his last journey, remembering that same icon. Under the pretext of going back into trade, he went to Dubrovnik to hear the prophecy of his other sooth-sayer. The inner side of the wind, the one that re-mains dry when the wind blows through the rain, had to be observed as well. Judging from a letter sent by Leander to a person unknown to us, travel-ing with him on this voyage, as in times of yore, was Diomides Subota. Leander's letter read as follows:

"One afternoon last year, around the time when the cheese is put in oil, Diomides Subota and I set out to see that Benjamin Cohen who knows how to whistle dreams. It is said that in summer he milks the cows in the pasture into a cowbell, and in winter he secretly shows some kind of picture that makes people faint. We found him sitting by the window, looking through his smile as though through a loop-hole. We asked him to show us the picture and he agreed, but we each had to give him a gold coin. And he would not let us both in at once, pleading lack of space. Diomides went in first and pinched him in passing, as he had done in his youth and ours, when Cohen had done plays on a cart that was drawn around the marketplace. He had not been inside long, not even as long as between two crows of the cock, when he burst out, green in the face, and there on the street vomited fish with olives in red wine from Kolochep. I did not allow myself to be afraid, and went in. Inside it was like being on a ship, and the lamp under the ceiling swung as though on waves. On the table I saw a clock that is wound by means of a gun barrel, a writing box, and a piece of paper on which Cohen was penning something, and I etched that too into my mind as best I could; perhaps you will find it helpful when you read my letter:

" 'In matters of the greatest import,' Cohen wrote, 'the memory of the wolfhound, not of man, is taken into account, because it is deeper, longer-lasting, and more accurate. And it has no need to interpret, as does human memory, but, rather, is a kind of home in time.'

" 'Why are you so expensive?' I asked him.

" 'Because my field of vision encompasses rapid secrets, which are realized almost immediately,' he replied, laughing.

" 'What is my rapid secret?'

" 'Just as everybody is somebody's child,' replied Cohen, 'so everybody is inevitably somebody's death. Just as somebody's life is repeated by being embodied in you, so in you shall be reincarnated and embodied somebody's death. That means that this inherited life and this inherited stranger's death will in you wed like a second father and mother. . . . But better see for yourself.'

"And then Cohen rolled out on the floor a paper as large as a small sail, covered with drawings and full of tiny human figures shown to be doing something in groups and in the hundreds, each one busy with a different job. On the edge of the map, some kind of instructions about laughing had been penned in red ink. The first sentence read: 'Man smiles for the first time forty days before birth, and for the last time forty days after death. . . .' The rest was illegible. When I moved a bit closer and inspected these vermin, depicted on pieces of paper that Cohen had pasted together and composed into a sheet as big as a map, I noticed that they were soldiers and spies in innumerable groups, swarming in from all sides and killing the condemned. Each of the condemned was depicted at the moment of his death, and there were as many of these deaths as there were flowers in the meadow; they were diverse, and each looked from his own death into that of someone else. They choked on their death rattles, shrieking like camels, but the scream could not be heard on the map and it turned inward, into the condemned men, ripping their insides like a knife. . . . Examining the paper, I asked my host what had frightened Diomides so much. And he replied: 'Choose the way he did and you'll see.'

" 'Choose what?'

" 'Choose which side you will look from. See, here, along the lower edge of the picture, soldiers are lined up in formation, all of them looking at you as their officer and waiting for your orders. Choose one of them, whichever you want, to be your guide and guard, and watch carefully what happens.'

"I picked a small drummer, because words came out of his eyes and those words could be seen and read as though his gaze were inscribing them in the air: 'Just as there are migrations of souls, so there are migrations of deaths.' As soon as I read this, I noticed that the drummer, although he had his eye on me, was pointing with his little stick at something askew above the line of soldiers. My eyes traversed the map in the direction indicated by the little stick and stopped at a soldier who had just received an order inscribed on a scroll of paper. Then I saw that, at the next crossroad, he handed over the scrolled order to a cavalryman. Accompanying this scene was a note that the horseman's saddle was full of Turkish hair. Then I saw the horse carry the messenger through the huge mob in the picture to a town overlooking rivers where a battle was being waged between the Turks and the Christians. Here the man dismounted and proceeded on foot to a tower on which was written 'Maherus.' The man entered the building, but left the scroll outside on the ground. Written on the scroll were the words 'You will die by fire!' And beneath these words was the date: April 22, 1739.

" 'There, you chose your own death,' Cohen told me, 'you'll die by fire like that man who entered the tower. Had you looked not at the drummer but at one of the other soldiers lined up at the bottom of the map, that other soldier would have taken you a different way, would have received a different order and delivered it to some third person, and so you would have gone in a completely different direction and ended in a different manner, as written in that different verdict. But this is your death, and you need no better. Anyway, it's no use talking with one's ears. God himself speaks mouth to mouth with his chosen one and avoids the ears as unreliable. . . .'

" 'And that day,' I interrupted him, 'is that the day of my death?'

" 'Yes, it is,' he told me.

" 'And has Diomides Subota seen his own date as well?'

" 'He has seen it,' he said.

" 'And what is his?'

" 'His is quite near. . . .'

"I went out into the light and at the door hit Cohen as hard as I could. He merely picked his cap up off the ground, looked at me with that shallow eye, and said: 'You should thank me. And let me tell you something else. Henceforward we are brothers, because our deaths are sisters.'

"There you have it, that was all.

"However, in June of this year, as you know,

Diomides was in Tsrevlyar Bakich's boat, and at Novi the wind seized them and turned them over. After he drowned, I kept counting my days, and finally I pulled myself together. Once again I sought out Cohen, and asked him to revoke or shift what we had seen as our common death in front of that tower on the map. One could read in his beard what he was about to say.

" 'That is not in my power,' he said; 'that date cannot be moved. All I can do is give myself a present on my birthday. I will give one of my three souls two extra days of life. I will take them from my other two souls, which will live that much less. . . .'

"And he took the map and on it marked, instead of that day, a new date: April 24, 1739.

" 'And what about me?' I asked.

" 'You have not three souls but one, and so you cannot divide death into three parts.' "

After the death of his friend Diomides Subota, after Dubrovnik and the new prophecy that had been given him, Leander turned back for home. As he traveled, he whispered like a prayer: "I thank Thee, Lord, Thou hast given time to grow. Into infinity. Thou hast given it space to grow and to die. Because death exists, but there is no birth. Time is not born, but it shall die...."

Somewhere on the Danube, within reach of Belgrade, Leander was captured. The Turkish soldier who approached him looked gently under his hair for his ear and said: "It must be him. A navel instead of an ear. Take him to Ded-Aga Ochuz. He's been looking for him for a long time."

"When I think: How long I've existed; when I think: Never more!" Ded-Aga Ochuz whispered into his beard, hurrying by the shortest route to Belgrade, which in that year of 1739 lay heavy with the Austrian army at the confluence of the two Danubes (the Sava had been called the "western Danube" in these parts since the days of the Argonauts). It was known among his units that the commander had sworn to enter the town before any other Turkish detachment, and to break into the Ruzhitsa Church, which was dedicated to the Virgin Mary. That is why the detachment hastened to cover as much of its journey from East to West as possible before the sun struck the eyes and forced the horses to trot sideways, which slowed down the march more every day.

"It matters which path you take to arrive at your destination," thought the commander, and selected for his unit a special approach, chosen in quite an unexpected manner. In 1709, Ded-Aga Ochuz, the celebrated sabreur and beheader, had fought against Russia on the Prut and there had seen how the Russian generals had brought, along with their staff, their own ballet troupes, choirs, and theater companies to entertain them during the war. Ever since, he had had singers and tambourine-players in his own army, and it was now their job to compose, out of the names of the places they had to pass through en route to Belgrade, a song that would tell each soldier who sang it how far the march had come. The singers caught enemy Christian spies and guides, and on the basis of their statements composed for each section of the trip a new verse of the song, made up out of the names of the places through which the troops advanced:

> *Kozla, Brlog, Yasikova,*
> *Plavna, Rechka, Slatina,*
> *Kamenitsa, Sip, Korbova,*
> *Buchye, Zlot, and Zlatina . . .*

When Ded-Aga's army had marched through to the end of the song and was within reach of Belgrade, an incident brought it to a halt.

In the village of Bolech, at daybreak, the detachment encountered a group of boys carrying on their heads copper pans with pies and bread straight from the oven. In the narrow passage somebody's horse trod upon a child, he dropped his load, the pie spilled onto the cobblestones, and glistening in the sun, jangling like a tambourine, was the empty pan, its bottom decorated with unusual markings deeply etched into the copper. The boy kneeled down and gathered the pie into the pan, and Ded-Aga Ochuz pulled to a halt for a second. He was riding an expensive black steed that had been trained to rack, one that had grown up fettered in a special way and that threw out both left legs one minute, and both right legs the next, without jogging in its gait. Such horses moved forward and backward with equal ease, and so Ded-Aga Ochuz did not turn the animal around, but forced it back two paces to come abreast of the boy.

"Eat!" he ordered the soldiers, and they instantly went for the boy's pie pan.

"Open wide!" he then ordered the boy, ripped an expensive button off his own sleeve, and, with a hand unaccustomed to missing, tossed the button into the boy's mouth.

"That's for the pie and the pan," said Ded-Aga Ochuz, and rode off, taking the empty dish with him.

In the evening, the copper pan was brought into

Ded-Aga Ochuz's tent (pitched above the stream of acidic water). Seating themselves around the dish were the Aga, his retinue, and a dervish from Aleppo, who was known still to dream in his native Persian. It befell him to interpret the markings on the dish. The dervish carefully examined the copper as though looking for a hole and said:

"Here, on the outside of the pan, a map has been drawn of the universe, heaven and earth, a map of all visible and invisible space, and it consists of four towns, or four worlds, called Yabarut, Molk, Malakut, and Alam al Mital.

"It should be known," the dervish added, "that what are called fields of vision are not evenly divided between the four cities. They say that the field for cock fights is cut into four parts by crossed lines to depict the four worlds, which are also drawn on this pan. As you know, it makes a great deal of difference which part of the universe, or the map of it traced in the sand of the fighting ring, the cock dies or wins in. Because places of strong visibility and good results, places of lasting memory, are distributed in this field of contest in such a way that death and defeat in the eastern and western parts of the circle are worth more than victory and life in the southern or northern parts, which, in turn, are located in the space of poor visibility, where deaths and victories leave no permanent impression or major trace, and pass by almost in vain. In other words," said the dervish from Aleppo, finishing his explanation, "it makes a great deal of difference from which part of the pan any given soldier ate his part of the pie this morning. Because only he who can do the same thing in at least three different worlds is powerful. The others have time behind their ears...."

With Ded-Aga Ochuz, whose beard looked like the tail of his horse, one never knew when he would move effortlessly backward instead of forward. And so now, instead of replying to the dervish's story, he took the pan, weighed it in his hand, and suddenly flipped it over, asking the dervish to interpret the other markings too, those etched on the inside of the dish. Since it transpired that the dervish was unable to read these other markings, because they were not his kind and had not been etched by an Islamic master, a burning candle was affixed to the bottom of the dish, and Leander was summoned to Ded-Aga Ochuz.

When he was led into the tent, Leander looked at Ded-Aga Ochuz and at the gold-tasseled saber he carried. And the Aga looked at the graying man whose face had been furrowed by smiles and tears the way the path of the stars furrows the sky. Judg-

ing by his severed ear, this was one of the masons
who had built the Sava ramparts of the fortress that
Ded-Aga wanted to conquer.

"This one's old," Ded-Aga Ochuz thought to
himself. "He must know everything. Where every
church is in Belgrade and when the birds pee..."
Aloud, he asked Leander the following: "What do
you see in the pan?"

"My face," Leander replied.

"You have lost face if you're here," replied Ded-
Aga Ochuz. "Take a closer look. This was once an
engraved copper plate made to print maps with, and
later a pan was forged out of it. Can you read what
is inscribed on it?"

"Griechisch Weissenburg."

"What does that mean?"

"Belgrade."

"Greek Belgrade?"

"No. That's how the Austrians denote that we
Serbs in Belgrade are not of their faith."

"Nor of ours."

"We know."

"And you have none of your own if you're of
the Greek faith. But that's unimportant to us. We
want you to tell us what is painted on the pan and
when it was engraved. We need a detailed report
about Belgrade. As detailed as possible. About the

ramparts, buildings, builders, gates, entrances, about the wealth, inhabitants, churches, about everything. We've got the whole night, but how much life we've got left, that we don't know. And it's hard to divide the bread fairly if you don't know how much of it is left. So talk at your leisure. From marking to marking. And you would do better to have a few more than a few less. Just think: How long you've existed, and then think: Never more! And think how your neck is just made for the saber. . . ."

Sitting on a saddle, slowly turning the pan, Leander looked into the bottom, taking care not to let the flame of the candle lick his mustache or eyebrows, and he read from the copper as if from a book. His artery beat through his brow and struck back like a clock, so that the hairs quivered like butterflies on Leander's desiccated face. This clock, which had begun to tick inside Leander so suddenly that it surprised even him, could be expected to measure some time of its own and count off the exact hour before stopping. . . .

Throughout Leander's story, Ded-Aga Ochuz sat still, stroked his beard as though he were holding a fleet little animal in his paw, and carefully sniffed strand after strand of its hair, his eyes glowing with each new smell he discovered. The talk around army campfires was that at moments those

eyes lost their sight, and that sometimes, upon dis-
mounting, Ded-Aga Ochuz did not see the ground
from which he had mounted. Be that as it may, now
he listened, pretending not to pay much attention to
the story, and he seemed to be sniffing like a hunting dog, in an attempt to rediscover some long-lost
place where he had once been but no longer knew
how to find. Only this place, this lair, was not somewhere outside, beyond the tent; it was somewhere
inside his own self, hidden and grown in time.
Waiting for the familiar, long-sought smell to
awaken his memory and lead him where it should,
Ded-Aga Ochuz listened. He lay in wait for the
moment when both places of accommodation would
appear: a suitable place in Leander's story and pan
to attack the city, and an appropriate place in Ded-
Aga Ochuz himself whence to launch the attack.
To those in the tent that evening, the sultan's all-
out war campaign, along with the report Leander
submitted, seemed like a less important part of that
other, inner campaign which at one uncertain moment would merge with the former into a single,
irrepressible operation and fulfill the Aga's previously given pledge. At least, that is what those in
the tent thought. But Ded-Aga Ochuz, smelling his
beard, thought something quite different. He remembered how, in those dusty days during the

march, early one evening, he saw a scene whose meaning he was not sure he immediately understood. From his position in the saddle, he first noticed only the dog that had crossed his path. Then he understood: the dog was trying to catch a firefly. And then he did not see them anymore. He even wondered: had anyone else in the column noticed them other than himself? And he decided: "I, too, am chasing a firefly. It is already inside me, but I keep chasing it. So it is not enough to swallow it. The light still has to be conquered, even when you have swallowed it. . . ."

When Leander's report was finished, Ded-Aga Ochuz, who was at the far end of his beard, seemed to have completed his inspection. It was all clear to him. . . .

The next day, when the Turkish troops entered Belgrade, Ded-Aga Ochuz was among the first to storm the Sava gate, hurrying to reach the Ruzhitsa Church ahead of all the others.

"Everyone tows his own death with him to the occasion," he thought, and, afraid that someone else would best him, hurled his lance from his galloping horse into the lock; like a key, it penetrated straight into the temple, creaking open Ruzhitsa's doors. And as troops on all sides laid a fire around the church and ramparts and set it aflame, Ded-Aga

Ochuz rode into the church and, from the saddle, scraped with his saber the eyes on the miraculous icon of the Virgin Mary and licked the medicinal paint right off the blade, cutting his tongue; he was waiting for a miracle to restore his sight.

During this time, Leander stood in front of the church and waited where he had been left. One could tell from his hair that he was going to die. But he was the only one in town who was still. The others were all in a terrible commotion and fired up, slashing each other. But the artery above Leander's eye continued to beat its inexorable time, and, like butterflies spreading their wings before taking flight, his eyebrows counted off the minutes. Then, suddenly, he realized that his time had run out. His brows stopped, and Leander came to and, instead of waiting in the open space in front of the church for Ded-Aga Ochuz to cut him down as soon as he rode out of the temple, he took off in a headlong dash through the narrow streets of Belgrade. The thudding sound of the sabreurs could be heard behind him, and Leander had no time to turn around and see whether it was Ded-Aga Ochuz chasing him or somebody else. Along with the sound of the thudding hooves, Leander also caught wind of a terrible stench, and it made him realize that he would be beheaded by an ordinary shitpants, who in battle had already shat in his saddle from fear. And this stench grew stronger, which meant that the man was gaining upon him. At the steps leading down to the Sava, Leander stopped for a moment, as though hesitating between two fates, and then, at the last moment, he plunged down the stairs, trampling the shadow of the houses that was toothed like a saw in the noonday sun. The thudding hooves stopped in front of the steps, and Leander thus escaped the horseback rider and his saber, and flew straight into his tower. It was as quiet as a freshly washed soul. It looked alien to him; he felt strange somehow, as though his mustache were touching his eyelashes and obstructing his vision. He was finally hidden. It was April 22, 1739, and Leander knew it. But he did not know that, at that very same moment, both towers at Belgrade's Sava gate had already been mined. They say that, a second before the explosion, the cocks atop the towers showed the same wind and the same hour. For the first time and the last, the same wind and the same hour. It was 12:05 when the towers blew up in a terrible explosion, carrying away the fire in which Leander's body disappeared.